LEADERSHIP

Theory, Application, & Skill Development 4e

Robert N. Lussier, Ph.D.
Springfield College

Christopher F. Achua, D.B.A.
University of Virginia's College at Wise

SOUTH-WESTERN
CENGAGE Learning

Australia • Brazil • Japan • Korea • Mexico • Singapore • Spain • United Kingdom • United States

***Leadership*, Fourth Edition**

Robert N. Lussier, Christopher F. Achua

VP/Editorial Director: Jack W. Calhoun

Editor-in-Chief: Melissa S. Acuña

Executive Editor/Acquisitions Editor: Joe Sabatino

Developmental Editor: Leslie Kauffman, LEAP Publishing Services

Editorial Assistant: Ruth Belanger

Executive Marketing Manager: Kimberly Kanakes

Sr Marketing Coordinator: Sarah Rose

Sr Marketing Communications Manager: Jim Overly

Marketing Manager: Clint Kernen

Director, Content and Media Production: Barbara Fuller-Jacobsen

Content Project Manager: Emily Nesheim

Media Editor: Danny Bolan

Sr Manufacturing Coordinator: Doug Wilke

Production Service: Integra

Sr Art Director: Tippy McIntosh

Internal Design: Patti Hudepohl

Cover Design: Tippy McIntosh

Cover Image: David Madison, Photographer's Choice/Getty

Text Permissions Manager: Roberta Broyer

Photo Permissions Manager: Mandy Groszko

Library of Congress Control Number: 2008939476

ISBN-13: 978-0-324-59655-7
ISBN-10: 0-324-59655-3

South-Western Cengage Learning
5191 Natorp Boulevard
Mason, OH 45040
USA

Cengage Learning products are represented in Canada by Nelson Education, Ltd.

For your course and learning solutions, visit **www.cengage.com**

Purchase any of our products at your local college store or at our preferred online store **www.ichapters.com**

Printed in the United States of America
2 3 4 5 6 7 12 11 10

To my wife Marie and our six children:
Jesse, Justin, Danielle, Nicole, Brian, and Renee

Robert N. Lussier

To all the Achua brothers and sisters, my mother Theresia
Sirri, and last but not least, my wife Pauline and our children:
Justin, Brooke, Jordan, Cullen, Gregory, and Zora

Christopher F. Achua

BRIEF CONTENTS

Preface xiii

Acknowledgments xxiii

About the Authors xxvi

part one **Individuals as Leaders** 1

1 Who Is a Leader? 2
2 Leadership Traits and Ethics 30
3 Leadership Behavior and Motivation 68
4 Influencing: Power, Politics, Networking, and Negotiation 108
5 Contingency Leadership Theories 150

part two **Team Leadership** 187

6 Communication, Coaching, and Conflict Skills 188
7 Leader–Follower Relations 238
8 Team Leadership and Self-Managed Teams 278

part three **Organizational Leadership** 327

9 Charismatic and Transformational Leadership 328
10 Leadership of Culture, Ethics, and Diversity 368
11 Strategic Leadership and Change Management 416
12 Crisis Leadership and the Learning Organization 450

Appendix: Leadership and Spirituality in the Workplace 481

Glossary 487

Endnotes 492

Index 515

Preface xiii

Acknowledgments xxiii

About the Authors xxvi

part one **Individuals as Leaders 1**

1 WHO IS A LEADER? 2

Leadership Is Everyone's Business 3

Why Leadership Is Important 4 / Defining Leadership 5 / *Self-Assessment 1: Leadership Potential 5* / Are Leaders Born or Made? 9

Leadership Managerial Roles 9

Interpersonal Roles 10 / Informational Roles 11 / Decisional Roles 11

Levels of Analysis of Leadership Theory 13

Individual Level of Analysis 13 / Group Level of Analysis 14 / Organizational Level of Analysis 14 / Interrelationships among the Levels of Analysis 15

Leadership Theory Paradigms 15

The Trait Theory Paradigm 16 / The Behavioral Leadership Theory Paradigm 16 / The Contingency Leadership Theory Paradigm 17 / The Integrative Leadership Theory Paradigm 17 / From the Management to the Leadership Theory Paradigm 17

Objectives of the Book 18

Leadership Theory 18 / Application of Leadership Theory 20 / Leadership Skill Development 20 / Flexibility 21

Organization of the Book 21

Chapter Summary 22
Key Terms 23
Review Questions 23
Communication Skills 24
Case: Steve Jobs—Apple 24
Video Case: Leadership at P.F. Chang's 26
Skill-Development Exercise 1: Getting to Know You by Name 26
Self-Assessment 2: Names 27
Skill-Development Exercise 2: Identifying Leadership Traits and Behaviors 28

2 LEADERSHIP TRAITS AND ETHICS 30

Personality Traits and Leadership 32

Self-Assessment 1: Personality Profile 32 / Personality and Traits 33 / The Big Five Model of Personality 33 / Personality Profiles 35

Traits of Effective Leaders 37

Dominance 37 / High Energy 38 / Self-Confidence 38 / Locus of Control 38 / Stability 38 / Integrity 39 / Intelligence 39 / Flexibility 40 / Sensitivity to Others 41

The Personality Profile of Effective Leaders 42

Achievement Motivation Theory 42 / *Self-Assessment 2: Motive Profile 44* / Leader Motive Profile Theory 44 / *Self-Assessment 3: Motive Profile with Socialized Power 45* / *Self-Assessment 4: Leadership Interest 46*

Leadership Attitudes 47

Theory X and Theory Y 48 / *Self-Assessment 5: Theory X and Theory Y Attitudes 48* / The Pygmalion Effect 49 / Self-Concept 50 / How Attitudes Develop Leadership Styles 52

Ethical Leadership 52

Self-Assessment 6: How Ethical Is Your Behavior? 52 / Does Ethical Behavior Pay? 54 / How Personality Traits and Attitudes, Moral Development, and the Situation Affect Ethical Behavior 54 / How People Justify Unethical Behavior 56 / Simple Guides to Ethical Behavior 58 / Stakeholder Approach to Ethics 58 / Being an Ethical Leader 59

Chapter Summary 60
Key Terms 61
Review Questions 62
Communication Skills 62
Case: The Bill & Melinda Gates Foundation 62
Video Case: "P.F." Chang's Serves Its Workers Well 64
Skill-Development Exercise 1: Improving Attitudes and Personality Traits 64
Skill-Development Exercise 2: Personality Perceptions 66
Skill-Development Exercise 3: Ethics and Whistleblowing 67

3 LEADERSHIP BEHAVIOR AND MOTIVATION 68

Leadership Behavior and Styles 70

Leadership Behavior 70 / Leadership Styles and the University of Iowa Research 70

University of Michigan and Ohio State University Studies 71

Self-Assessment 1: Your Leadership Style 71 / University of Michigan: Job-Centered and Employee-Centered Behavior 72 / Ohio State University: Initiating Structure and Consideration Behavior 73 / Differences Between Leadership Models—and Their Contributions 75

The Leadership Grid 75

Leadership Grid Theory 75 / Leadership Grid and High-High Leader Research and Contributions 77 / *Self-Assessment 2: Your Personality Traits and Leadership Styles 78*

Leadership and Major Motivation Theories 79

Motivation and Leadership 79 / The Motivation Process 79 / An Overview of Three Major Classifications of Motivation Theories 80

Content Motivation Theories 80

Hierarchy of Needs Theory 81 / Two-Factor Theory 82 / *Self-Assessment 3: Job Motivators and Maintenance Factors 83* / Acquired Needs Theory 85 / The Need to Balance Professional and Personal Needs 87

Process Motivation Theories 87

Equity Theory 87 / Expectancy Theory 88 / Goal-Setting Theory 90

Reinforcement Theory 92

Types of Reinforcement 93 / Schedules of Reinforcement 94 / You Get What You Reinforce 95 / Motivating with Reinforcement 96 / Giving Praise 97

Putting the Motivation Theories Together Within the Motivation Process 99

Chapter Summary 100
Key Terms 102
Review Questions 102
Communication Skills 102
Case: Art Friedman—Friedmans Appliance 102
Video Case: Motivation at Washburn Guitars 104
Skill-Development Exercise 1: Writing Objectives 104
Behavior Model Skills Training 1: Session 1 105
Behavior Model Video 1: Giving Praise 105
Skill-Development Exercise 2: Giving Praise 105

4 INFLUENCING: POWER, POLITICS, NETWORKING, AND NEGOTIATION 108

Power 110

Sources of Power 110 / Types of Power and Influencing Tactics, and Ways to Increase Your Power 111 / *Self-Assessment 1: Influencing Tactics, Power, and Personality Traits 119* / Acquiring and Losing Power 119

Organizational Politics 120

Self-Assessment 2: Use of Political Behavior 120 / The Nature of Organizational Politics 121 / Political Behavior 122 / Guidelines for Developing Political Skills 124

Networking 127

Self-Assessment 3: Networking 127 / Perform a Self-Assessment and Set Goals 128 / Create Your One-Minute Self-Sell 129 / Develop Your Network 130 / Conduct Networking Interviews 131 / Maintain Your Network 132

Negotiation 133

Self-Assessment 4: Negotiating 133 / Negotiating 134 / The Negotiation Process 135

Ethics and Influencing 140

Chapter Summary 141
Key Terms 142
Review Questions 142
Communication Skills 142
Case: Ron Johnson—Department of Accounting 143
Video Case: Employee Networks at Whirlpool Corporation 145
Skill-Development Exercise 1: Influencing Tactics 145
Skill-Development Exercise 2: Influencing, Power, and Politics 146
Skill-Development Exercise 3: Networking Skills 147
Skill-Development Exercise 4: Car Dealer Negotiation 148

5 CONTINGENCY LEADERSHIP THEORIES 150

Contingency Leadership Theories and Models 152

Leadership Theories versus Leadership Models 152 / Contingency Theory and Model Variables 152 / Global Contingency Leadership 153

Contingency Leadership Theory and Model 154

Leadership Style and the LPC 155 / *Self-Assessment 1: Leadership Style Your Fiedler LPC 155* / Situational Favorableness 156 / Determining the Appropriate Leadership Style 156 / Research 158

Leadership Continuum Theory and Model 159
Path-Goal Leadership Theory and Model 161

Situational Factors 162 / Leadership Styles 163 / Research 164

Normative Leadership Theory and Models 165

Leadership Participation Styles 166 / Model Questions to Determine the Appropriate Leadership Style 167 / Selecting the Time-Driven or Development-Driven Model for the Situation 169 / Determining the Appropriate Leadership Style 170 / Research 170

Putting the Behavioral and Contingency Leadership Theories Together 171

Prescriptive and Descriptive Models 173

Leadership Substitutes Theory 173

Substitutes and Neutralizers 173 / Leadership Style 174 / Changing the Situation 174 / Research 174 / *Self-Assessment 2: Your Personality and Contingency Leadership Theories 175*

Chapter Summary 175
Key Terms 177
Review Questions 177
Communication Skills 177
Case: Rick Parr—Archer Daniels Midland (ADM) Company 178
Video Case: Leadership at McDonald's 179
Self-Assessment 3: Determining Your Preferred Normative Leadership Style 180
Skill-Development Exercise 1: Identifying Normative Leadership Styles 183
Skill-Development Exercise 2: Using the Normative Leadership Models 183
Self-Assessment 4: Your Leadership Continuum and Path-Goal Leadership Styles 185

part two Team Leadership 187

6 COMMUNICATION, COACHING, AND CONFLICT SKILLS 188

Communication 189

Communication and Leadership 190 / Sending Messages and Giving Instructions 190 / Receiving Messages 193 / *Self-Assessment 1: Listening Skills 193*

Feedback 197

The Importance of Feedback 197 / Common Approaches to Getting Feedback on Messages—and Why They Don't Work 198 / How to Get Feedback on Messages 199 / 360-Degree Multirater Feedback 200

Coaching 201

Coaching and Leadership 201 / How to Give Coaching Feedback 201 / What Is Criticism and Why Doesn't It Work? 205 / The Coaching Model for Employees Who Are Performing Below Standard 207 / Mentoring 209

Managing Conflict 210

The Psychological Contract 210 / Conflict and Leadership 210 / Conflict Management Styles 210

Collaborating Conflict Management Style Models 215

Initiating Conflict Resolution 215 / Responding to Conflict Resolution 217 / Mediating Conflict Resolution 217 / *Self-Assessment 2: Your Personality Traits and Communication, Feedback, Coaching, and Conflict Management Style 218*

Chapter Summary 220
Key Terms 221
Review Questions 221
Communication Skills 221
Case: Lawrence Weinbach—from Unisys Corporation to Yankee Hill Capital Management 222
Video Case: Communication at Navistar International 224
Skill-Development Exercise 1: Giving Instructions 224
Behavior Model Skills Training 1 226
Self-Assessment 3: Determining Your Preferred Communication Style 226
The Situational Communications Model 229
Behavior Model Video 6.1: Situational Communications 232
Skill-Development Exercise 2: Situational Communications 232
Behavior Model Skills Training 2 233
The Coaching Model 233
Behavior Model Video 6.2: Coaching 232
Skill-Development Exercise 3: Coaching 233
Behavior Model Skills Training 3 235
The Initiating Conflict Resolution Model 235
Behavior Model Video 6.3: Initiating Conflict Resolution 235
Skill-Development Exercise 4: Initiating Conflict Resolution 235
Behavior Model Video 6.4: Mediating Conflict Resolution 237

7 LEADER–FOLLOWER RELATIONS 238

Evolution of the Dyadic Theory 240

Vertical Dyadic Linkage (VDL) Theory 241 / *Self-Assessment 1: Dyadic Relationship with Your Manager 241* / Leader–Member Exchange (LMX) Theory 243 / Team Building 244 / Systems and Networks 245

Leader–Member Exchange Theory 247

The Influence of LMX on Follower Behavior 247 / *Self-Assessment 2: In-Group and Out-Group 249* / The Three-Stage Process for Developing Positive LMX Relations 249 / Factors that Determine LMX Quality 250 / Effective Leader–Follower Feedback 251 / Limitations of LMX Theory Application 252 / *Self-Assessment 3: Your LMX Relationship with Your Manager 253* / Bias in LMX: Employee Career Implications 254

Followership 254

The Effective Follower, and Follower Types 255 / *Self-Assessment 4: Effective Followership 257* / Guidelines to Becoming an Effective Follower 258 / Determinants of Follower Influence 261 / Dual Role of Being a Leader and a Follower 263

Delegation 264

Delegating 264 / Delegation Decisions 265 / *Self-Assessment 5: Followership and Personality 266* / Delegating with the Use of a Model 267

Chapter Summary 269
Key Terms 270
Review Questions 271
Communication Skills 271
Case: W. L. Gore & Associates 271
Video Case: Delegation at Boyne USA Resorts 274
Skill-Development Exercise 1: Improving Dyadic Relationships—Followership 274
Behavior Model Skills Training 275

The Delegation Model 275
Behavior Model Video 7.1: Delegating 275
Skill-Development Exercise 2: Delegating 275

8 TEAM LEADERSHIP AND SELF-MANAGED TEAMS 278

The Use of Teams in Organizations 280

Groups Versus Teams: What Is the Difference? 281 / Advantages and Disadvantages of Teamwork 282 / *Self-Assessment 1: Assessing Teamwork in Your Group 284* / Characteristics of Effective Teams 285 / *Self-Assessment 2: Assessing the Climate for Creativity 292*

Types of Teams 293

Functional Team 293 / Cross-Functional Team 294 / Virtual Team 296 / Self-Managed Team (SMT) 296

Decision Making in Teams 297

Leader-Centered Decision-Making Model 297 / Team-Centered Decision-Making Model 298 / *Self-Assessment 3: Personality Traits and Teams 299* / Normative Leadership Model 300

Leadership Skills for Effective Team Meetings 300

Planning Meetings 300 / Conducting Meetings 302 / Handling Problem Members 303

Self-Managed Teams 305

The Nature of Self-Managed Teams 306 / The Benefits of Self-Managed Teams 308 / Guidelines for Improving Self-Managed Team Effectiveness 309 / The Changing Role of Leadership in Self-Managed Teams 312 / The Challenges of Implementing Self-Managed Teams 313

Chapter Summary 314
Key Terms 317
Review Questions 317
Communication Skills 317
Case: Frederick W. Smith—FedEx 318
Video Case: The NEADS Team: People and Dogs 320
Behavior Model Skills Training 320
Leadership Decision-Making Model: Deciding Which Leadership Decision-Making Style to Use (Part I) 320
Behavior Model Video 8.1 and Video Exercise: Deciding Which Leadership Decision-Making Style to Use (Part II) 323
Skill-Development Exercise 1: Deciding Which Leadership Decision-Making Style to Use (Parts III & IV) 323
Skill-Development Exercise 2: Individual Versus Group Decision Making 325

part three **Organizational Leadership 327**

9 CHARISMATIC AND TRANSFORMATIONAL LEADERSHIP 328

Personal Meaning 330

Factors That Influence Personal Meaning 331

Charisma 334

Weber's Conceptualization of Charisma 334 / Differentiating Between Charismatic and Noncharismatic Leaders 335

Charismatic Leadership 337

Locus of Charismatic Leadership 337 / The Effects of Charismatic Leadership 338 / Qualities of Charismatic Leaders 341 / How One Acquires Charismatic Qualities 344 / Charisma: A Double-Edged Sword 345

Transformational Leadership 347

The Effects of Transformational Leadership 348 / Charismatic versus Transformational Leadership 349 / Transformational Leader Behaviors and Attributes 350 / Transformational versus Transactional Leadership 352 / *Self-Assessment 1: Are You More of a Transactional or Transformational Leader? 352* / The Transformation Process 354

Stewardship and Servant Leadership 356

The Nature of Stewardship and Servant Leadership 357 / Framework for Stewardship 357 / Framework for Servant Leadership 358 / *Self-Assessment 2: Personality and Charismatic and Transformational Leadership 360*

Chapter Summary 360
Key Terms 363
Review Questions 363
Communication Skills 364
Case: Anne Mulcahy and Ursula Burns: Xerox's Dynamic Duo 364
Video Case: Timbuk2: Former CEO Sets a Course 366
Skill-Development Exercise 1: Is the President of the United States a Charismatic Leader? 366

10 LEADERSHIP OF CULTURE, ETHICS, AND DIVERSITY 368

Culture Creation and Sustainability 370

The Power of Culture 371 / Low- and High-Performance Cultures 373 / Characteristics of Low-Performance Cultures 373 / Characteristics of High-Performance Cultures 375 / The Role of Leadership in Culture Creation and Sustainability 378 / Cultural Value Types 382

Values-Based Leadership 387

Self-Assessment 1: Personal Values 387 / The Leader's Role in Advocating Ethical Behavior 388 / National Culture Identities—Hofstede's Value Dimensions 391 / Implications for Leadership Practice 392

Changing Demographics and Diversity 394

Current State of Workforce Diversity 394 / The Impact of Globalization on Diversity 395 / Reasons for Embracing Diversity 396 / Obstacles to Achieving Diversity 398 / Creating a Culture That Supports Diversity 400 / Diversity Awareness Training and Leadership Education 403 / *Self-Assessment 2: Personality, Culture, Values, and Diversity 406*

Chapter Summary 407
Key Terms 409
Review Questions 409
Communication Skills 410
Case: Robert Stevens Continues Lockheed Martin's Diversity Initiatives 410
Video Case: Diversity at PepsiCo 412
Skill-Development Exercise 1: Identifying and Improving Organizational Culture 413
Skill-Development Exercise 2: Diversity Training 413
Skill-Development Exercise 3: Developing an Effective Multicultural Team 414

11 STRATEGIC LEADERSHIP AND CHANGE MANAGEMENT 416

Strategic Leadership 418

Strategic Leadership Failures 419 / Strategic Management 420 / The Strategic Management Process 421

Implementing Change 431

The Need for Change 432 / The Role of Leadership in Implementing Change 434 / The Change Management Process 435 / Why People Resist Change 438 / Strategies for Minimizing Resistance to Change 441 / *Self-Assessment 1: Personality, Leadership, and Change 442*

Chapter Summary 443
Key Terms 444
Review Questions 445
Communication Skills 445
Case: Mark Parker: A Seasoned Veteran Takes the Helm at Nike 445
Video Case: Original Penguin Spreads Its Wings 447
Skill-Development Exercise 1: Strategic Planning 447
Skill-Development Exercise 2: Planning a Change Using the Force-Field Model 448
Skill-Development Exercise 3: Managing Change at your college 449

12 CRISIS LEADERSHIP AND THE LEARNING ORGANIZATION 450

Crisis Leadership 452

The Impact of Environmental Factors 453 / Crisis Management Plan 453 / Effective Crisis Communication 460

The Learning Organization and Knowledge Management 463

What Is a Learning Organization? 464 / *Self-Assessment 1: Learning Organizations 465* / The Traditional versus the Learning Organization Culture 466 / The Role of Leaders in Creating a Learning Organization 469 / *Self-Assessment 2: Personality and Crisis and the Learning Organization 473*

Chapter Summary 473
Key Terms 475
Review Questions 475
Communication Skills 475
Case: CEO A. G. Lafley's Transformation of P&G 476
Video Case: Managing in Turbulent Times at Second City Theater 478
Skill-Development Exercise 1: Handling a Crisis 478
Skill-Development Exercise 2: The Learning Organization 479

Appendix: Leadership and Spirituality in the Workplace 481

Glossary 487

Endnotes 492

Index 515

Target Market

This book is intended for leadership courses offered at the undergraduate and graduate levels in schools of business, public administration, health care, education, psychology, and sociology. No prior coursework in business or management is required. The textbook can also be used in management development courses that emphasize the leadership function, and can supplement management or organizational behavior courses that emphasize leadership, especially with an applications/skill development focus.

Goals and Overview of Competitive Advantages

In his book *Power Tools,* John Nirenberg asks: "Why are so many well-intended students learning so much and yet able to apply so little in their personal and professional lives?" Is it surprising that students cannot apply what they read and cannot develop skills, when most textbooks continue to focus on theoretical concepts? Textbooks need to take the next step, and develop students' ability to apply what they read and to build skills using the concepts. I (Lussier) started writing management textbooks in 1988—prior to the calls by the Association to Advance Collegiate Schools of Business (AACSB) and the Secretary's Commission on Achieving Necessary Skills (SCANS) for skill development and outcomes assessment—to help professors teach their students how to apply concepts and develop management skills. Pfeffer and Sutton concluded that the most important insight from their research is that knowledge that is actually implemented is much more likely to be acquired from learning by doing, than from learning by reading, listening, or thinking.[1] We designed this book to give students the opportunity to learn by doing.

The overarching goal of this book is reflected in its subtitle: theory, application, skill development. We developed the total package to teach leadership theory and concepts, to improve ability to apply the theory through critical thinking, and to develop leadership skills. Following are our related goals in writing this book:

- To be the only traditional leadership textbook to incorporate the three-pronged approach. We make a clear distinction between coverage of theory concepts, their application, and the development of skills based on the concepts. The Test Bank includes questions under each of the three approaches.
- To make this the most "how-to" leadership book on the market. We offer behavior models with step-by-step guidelines for handling various leadership functions (such as how to set objectives, give praise and instructions, coach followers, resolve conflicts, and negotiate).
- To offer the best coverage of traditional leadership theories, by presenting the theories and research findings without getting bogged down in too much detail.
- To create a variety of high-quality application material, using the concepts to develop critical-thinking skills.

- To create a variety of high-quality skill-development exercises, which build leadership skills that can be used in students' personal and professional life.
- To offer behavior-modeling leadership skills training.
- To make available a video package, including 7 Behavior Model Videos and 12 Video Cases.
- To suggest self-assessment materials that are well integrated and illustrate the important concepts discussed in the text. Students begin by determining their personality profile in Chapter 2, and then assess how their personality affects their leadership potential in the remaining chapters.
- To provide a flexible teaching package, so that professors can design the course to best meet the leadership needs of their students. The total package includes more material than can be covered in one course. Supplemental material is included, thus only one book is needed—making it a low-cost alternative for the student.

Flexibility Example

The textbook, with 12 chapters, allows time for other materials to be used in the leadership course. The textbook includes all the traditional topics in enough detail, however, to use only the textbook for the course. It offers so much application and skill-development material that it cannot all be covered in class during one semester. Instructors have the flexibility to select only the content and features that best meet their needs.

Specific Competitive Advantage—Pedagogical Features

Three-Pronged Approach

We created course materials that truly develop students into leaders. As the title of this book implies, we provide a balanced, three-pronged approach to the curriculum:

- A clear understanding of the traditional theories and concepts of leadership, as well as of the most recently developed leadership philosophies
- Application of leadership concepts through critical thinking
- Development of leadership skills

The three-pronged approach is clear in the textbook and is carried throughout the Instructor's Manual and Test Bank.

Theory

Leadership Theories, Research and References, and Writing Style: This book has been written to provide the best coverage of the traditional leadership theories, presenting the theories and research findings clearly without being bogged down in too much detail. The book is heavily referenced with classic and current citations. Unlike the textbooks of some competitors, this book does not use in-text citations, to avoid distracting the reader and adding unnecessary length to the text chapters.

Readers can refer to the notes at the end of the book for complete citations of all sources. Thus, the book includes all the traditional leadership topics, yet we believe it is written in a livelier, more conversational manner than those of our competitors.

The following features are provided to support the first step in the three-pronged approach—theory.

Learning Outcomes: Each chapter begins with Learning Outcomes. At the end of the chapter, the Learning Outcomes are integrated into the chapter summary.

Key Terms: A list of key terms appears at the beginning and end of each chapter. Clear definitions are given in the text for approximately 15 of the most important concepts from the chapter (with the key term in bold and the definition in italic).

Chapter Summary: The summary lists the Learning Outcomes from the beginning of the chapter and gives the answers. For each chapter, the last Learning Outcome requires students to define the key terms of the chapter by writing the correct key term in the blank provided for each definition.

Review Questions: These questions require recall of information generally not covered in the Learning Outcomes.

Product Support Web Site: The product support Web site, **www.cengage.com/management/lussier**, has information for both professors and students. Students can take interactive quizzes, written by Kenneth Zula of Keystone College, and quiz themselves on key terms.

Test Bank (Assessment of Understanding of Theory/Concepts) and Instructor's Manual: The Test Bank includes traditional assessment of student knowledge. It also includes the Learning Outcomes and Review Questions for each chapter. The Instructor's Manual includes the answers to all Review Questions.

Application

The second prong of our textbook is to have students apply the leadership theories and concepts so that they can develop critical-thinking skills. Students develop their application skills through the following features.

Opening Case Application: At the beginning of each chapter, information about an actual manager and organization is presented. The case is followed by four to eight questions to get students involved. Throughout the chapter, the answers to the questions are given to illustrate how the manager/organization actually uses the text concepts to create opportunities and solve problems through decision making. A distinctive head (Opening Case **APPLICATION**) appears when the opening case is applied in the text.

1. What Big Five personality traits does Lorraine Monroe possess?

To a large extent, Lorraine Monroe was a successful founder and leader because of her strong personality in the Big Five. She has a strong need for surgency, is conscientious, and is open to new experience as she does consulting to bring about better educational leadership to help public school children. Lorraine was not afraid to step on toes and be disagreeable at Frederick Douglass Academy as she took strong control over the school and enforced discipline conducive to learning, while maintaining overall emotional stability.

Work Application 1

Recall a present or past job. Were you both a leader and a follower? Explain.

Work Applications: Open-ended questions, called Work Applications, require students to explain how the text concepts apply to their own work experience; there are over 100 of these scattered throughout the text. Student experience can be present, past, summer, full-time, or part-time employment. The questions help the students to bridge the gap between theory and the real world. The Work Applications are also included in the Test Bank, to assess students' ability to apply the concepts.

Applying the Concept: Every chapter contains a series of two to six Applying the Concept boxes that require students to determine the leadership concept being illustrated in a specific, short example. All the recommended answers appear in the Instructor's Manual with a brief explanation. In addition, the Test Bank has similar questions, clearly labeled, to assess students' ability to apply the concepts.

Applying the **Concept 1**

Big Five Personality Dimensions

Identify each of these seven traits/behaviors by its personality dimension. Write the appropriate letter in the blank before each item.

a. surgency
b. agreeableness
c. adjustment
d. conscientiousness
e. openness to experience

____ 1. The manager is influencing the follower to do the job the way the leader wants it done.

____ 2. The sales representative submitted the monthly expense report on time as usual.

____ 3. The leader is saying a warm, friendly good morning to followers as they arrive at work.

____ 4. The leader is seeking ideas from followers on how to speed up the flow of work.

____ 5. As a follower is yelling a complaint, the leader calmly explains what went wrong.

____ 6. The leader is being very quiet when meeting some unexpected visitors in the work unit.

____ 7. The leader is giving in to a follower to avoid a conflict.

Communication Skills: New to this edition are more than 80 critical-thinking questions (an average of 7 per chapter) that can be used for class discussion and/or written assignments to develop communication skills.

Cases: Following the Review Questions and Communication Skills, students are presented with another actual manager and organization. The students learn how the manager/organization applies the leadership concepts from that chapter. Each Case is followed by questions for the student to answer. Chapters 2 through 11 also include cumulative case questions. Cumulative questions relate case material from prior chapters. Thus, students continually review and integrate concepts from previous chapters. Answers to the Case questions are included in the Instructor's Manual.

Video Cases: All chapters include one Video Case. Seeing actual leaders tackling real management problems and opportunities enhances student application of the concepts. The 12 Video Cases have supporting print material for both instructors and students, including a brief description and critical-thinking questions. Answers to the Video Case questions are included in the Instructor's Manual.

VIDEO CASE

Motivation at Washburn Guitars

Founded in the late 1800s in Chicago, Washburn Guitars boasts a rich tradition of fine instrument making. Today the company sells more than 50,000 guitars annually, totaling about $40 million in revenue. Washburn Guitars produces a variety of acoustic and electric guitars. Washburn craftsmen also enjoy making custom guitars. In recent years, custom shop production has grown dramatically from 20 to 300 guitars per month. Having a motivated workforce is essential because guitar making is labor intensive and requires attention to detail. Quality materials combined with quality craftsmanship are necessary to produce quality guitars. Washburn Guitars' workforce is motivated because they love music and care about the instruments.

1. What motivates most employees at Washburn Guitars?
2. What kinds of guitars do employees most like to produce?
3. What is the connection between quality guitars and workforce motivation?

Test Bank (Assessment of Application Ability) and Instructor's Manual: The Test Bank includes Work Applications and Applying the Concept questions. The Instructor's Manual contains detailed answers for all of the application features.

Skill Development

The difference between learning about leadership and learning to be a leader is the acquisition of skills, our third prong. This text focuses on skill development so students can use the leadership theories and concepts they learn to improve their personal and professional life.

Self-Assessments: Scattered throughout the text are 37 Self-Assessments. Students complete these exercises to gain personal knowledge. All information for completing and scoring the assessments is contained within the text. Students determine their personality profile in Chapter 2, and then assess how their personality affects their leadership in the remaining chapters. Self-knowledge leads students to an understanding of how they can and will operate as leaders in the real world. Although Self-Assessments do not develop a specific skill, they serve as a foundation for skill development.

SELF-ASSESSMENT 2

Personality and Charismatic and Transformational Leadership

Charismatic leaders have charisma based on personality and other personal traits that cut across all of the Big Five personality types. Review the ten qualities of charismatic leaders in Exhibit 9.3 on page 341. Which traits do you have?

____

____

If you have a high surgency Big Five personality style and a high need for power, you need to focus on using socialized, rather than personalized, charismatic leadership.

Transformational leaders tend to be charismatic as well. In Self-Assessment 1 on pages 352-353 you determined if you were more transformational or transactional. How does your personality affect your transformational and transactional leadership styles?

____

____

Ethical Dilemma: There are 24 Ethical Dilemma boxed items. The boxes present issues of ethics for class discussion, with many presenting actual situations faced by real companies. Each dilemma contains two to four questions for class discussion.

Ethical **Dilemma 2**

Executive Compensation

Executive compensation is a complex and controversial subject. Executive management skill has a direct impact on the success of the firm. Top executives should be paid multimillion dollar compensation packages; after all, if it weren't for some effective CEOs, companies would not be making the millions of dollars of profits they make each year. They deserve a peace of the pie they helped create.[65]

However, top executives have been criticized for being overpaid. In 2006, total direct compensation (including salary, bonus, and the value of restricted stock) for CEOs of 350 major companies was $6.05 million (not including generous pensions, deferred compensation, and other perks).[66] Investors have been complaining about executive pay and trying to cut it back, without much success.[67]

1. Do executives deserve to make 200 times as much as the average worker?
2. Is it ethical for managers to take large pay increases while laying off employees?
3. Are companies being socially responsible when paying executives premium compensation?

Case Role-Play Exercise: Following each Case are instructions to prepare students to conduct an in-class role-play, based on a situation presented in the Case. Through role-playing, students develop their skills at handling leadership situations. For example, students are asked to conduct a motivational speech and to develop a vision and a mission statement for an organization.

Step-by-Step Behavior Models: In addition to traditional theories of leadership, the text includes behavior models: how-to steps for handling day-to-day leadership functions, such as how to set objectives, give praise, coach, resolve conflicts, delegate, and negotiate.

Behavior Model Videos: There are seven Behavior Model Videos that reinforce the development of skills. The videos demonstrate leaders successfully handling common leadership functions, using the step-by-step behavior models discussed earlier in the Theory section. Students learn from watching the videos and/or using them in conjunction with the Skill-Development Exercises. Material in the text integrates the videos into the chapters. Ideas for using all videos are detailed in the Instructor's Manual.

Behavior Model Video 7.1

Delegating

Objective

To observe a manager delegating a task to an employee.

Video *(4½ minutes)* Overview

You will watch a production manager, Steve, delegate the completion of a production output form to Dale.

Skill-Development Exercises: There are between one and four Skill-Development Exercises at the end of each chapter. We use the term *skill-development exercise* only in referring to an exercise that will develop a skill that can be used in the students' personal or professional life at work. Full support of 30 activities can be found in the Instructor's Manual, including detailed information, timing, answers, and so on. There are three primary types of exercises:

Individual Focus. Students make individual decisions about exercise questions before or during class. Students can share their answers in class discussions, or the instructor may elect to go over recommended answers.

Group/Team Focus. Students discuss the material presented and may select group answers and report to the class.

Role-Play Focus. Students are presented with a model and given the opportunity to use the model to apply their knowledge of leadership theories through role-playing exercises.

Behavior Model Skills Training: Six of the Skill-Development Exercises may be used as part of behavior modeling by using the step-by-step models in the text and the Behavior Model Videos. Meta-analysis research has concluded that behavior modeling skills training is effective at developing leadership skills. For example, students read the conflict resolution model in the text, watch the video in class, and then complete a Skill-Development Exercise (role-play) to resolve a conflict, using the model and feedback from others.

Behavior Model Skills Training

In this behavior model skills training session, you will perform three activities:

1. Read the section, "Delegation," in this chapter (to learn how to use Model 7.1, page 268).
2. Watch Behavior Model Video 7.1, "Delegating."
3. Complete Skill-Development Exercise 2 (to develop your delegating skills).

For further practice, use the delegation model in your personal and professional life.

Test Bank (Assessment of Skill Development) and Instructor's Manual. The Test Bank includes skill-development questions. The Instructor's Manual contains detailed answers for all of the skills featured in the text, including timing, information, answers, logistics, and so on. It also explains how to test on the specific Skill-Development Exercises, and provides information that can be shared with students to help them prepare for exams.

Ancillary Support

Instructor's Manual with Test Bank (0-324-78300-0)

(Prepared by Robert N. Lussier, Christopher F. Achua, and David McCalman, University of Central Arkansas)

The Instructor's Manual and Test Bank are organized to complement the three-pronged approach of the text—theory, application, and skill development.

The Instructor's Manual contains the following for each chapter of the book: a detailed outline for lecture enhancement, Review Question answers, Applying the Concept answers, Case and Video Case question answers, instructions on use of videos, and Skill-Development Exercise ideas (including setup and timing). The Instructor's Manual also contains an introduction that discusses possible approaches to the course, and provides an overview of possible uses for various features and how to test and grade them. It explains the use of permanent groups to develop team leadership skills, and provides guidance in the development of a course outline/syllabus.

The Test Bank offers over 800 true/false, multiple choice, and fill-in-the-blank questions from which to choose. In addition, the authors provide distinct questions to test each of the three components of the text—theory, application, and skill development.

ExamView® (0-324-78526-7)

All questions from the printed Test Bank are available in ExamView®, an easy-to-use test-creation program, on the Instructor's Resource CD.

PowerPoint™ (0-324-78525-9)

(Prepared by Rhonda S. Palladi, Georgia State University)

PowerPoint™ slides are available on the Instructor's Resource CD and the product support Web site for a more flexible and professional presentation in the classroom.

Behavior Model Videos (0-324-78535-6)

To reinforce the development of skills for students, seven Behavior Model Videos are provided. The videos teach students, step-by-step, how to handle common leadership functions such as giving praise, communicating, coaching, resolving conflict, delegating, and decision making. Students learn from watching the videos and/or using them in conjunction with the Skill-Development Exercises. Material in the text integrates the videos into the chapters. Ideas for using all videos are detailed in the Instructor's Manual.

Video Cases (0-324-78535-6)

Accompanying and integrated within the text are 12 Video Cases. These videos show real businesses dealing with issues that are discussed in the text. These Video Cases add variety in the classroom presentation and stimulate students to learn about organizations, teams, and leadership.

Instructor's Resource CD-ROM (0-324-78538-0)

Get quick access to the Instructor's Manual with Test Bank, ExamView®, and PowerPoint™ slides from your desktop via one CD-ROM.

Product Support Web Site

The dedicated *Leadership* Web site, **www.cengage.com/management/lussier**, offers broad online support. Log on for downloadable ancillaries and more.

Summary of Key Innovations

Our goal is to make both students and instructors successful in the classroom by providing learning features that not only teach about leadership but also help students become leaders. Here are the special ways in which this is done:

- Three-pronged approach (theory, application, skill development) in the textbook, and corresponding assessment of the three areas in the Test Bank
- Unique skill-development materials that build leadership skills for use in students' personal and professional life
- Unique application material to develop critical-thinking skills
- Unsurpassed video package, with 12 Video Cases and 7 Behavior Model Videos
- Flexibility—use any or all of the features that work for you!

Changes to the Fourth Edition

The fourth edition has been thoroughly revised:

- Although we have maintained the *individual, team, organizational* parts framework, we have added a new chapter. In the third edition, crisis management was part of Chapter 11 and knowledge management or the learning organization was part of Chapter 10. We have brought these two topics together to make up Chapter 12.

- The number of references has increased from 1,100 to more than 1,400, and over 80 percent are new references.
- New to this edition are approximately 85 communication skills critical-thinking questions for class discussion and/or written assignments.
- The skill development exercises now indicate which AACSB learning standard(s) is developed through the exercise.
- Over half of the chapter opening and end-of-chapter cases are new, and the remaining cases have been updated.
- Twelve new Video Cases have been added.
- All chapters have new and updated Test Bank questions and PowerPoint slides.

Chapter 1

The "Why Leadership Is Important" subsection has been revised. Two new key terms—"management to the leadership theory paradigm" and "evidence-based management (EBM)"—have been added. Discussions on "Evidence-Based Management (EBM)" and "AACSB Learning Standards" have been added to the "Leadership Theory" subsection. The "Application of Leadership Theory" and "Leadership Skill Development" subsections have been revised.

Chapter 2

The "Personality Profiles" subsection has been rewritten and now includes current research relating the Big Five to "Job Performance" and "The Big Five Correlates with Leadership." The prior heading "Derailed Leadership Traits" is now discussed in the "Personality Profiles" subsection.

Chapter 3

A new Applying the Concept has been added.

Chapter 4

The introductions to the "Power" and "Networking" sections have been rewritten. The introduction and first part of the "Organizational Politics" section has been reordered and rewritten.

Chapter 5

A new opening case features PepsiCo's CEO, Indra Nooyi, and the end-of-chapter case now features ADM, with information on its new CEO, Patricia Woertz.

Chapter 6

The introduction to the "Communication" section has been revised.

Chapter 7

The "Leader–Member Exchange Theory" section has undergone a significant rewrite. The section entitled "Strategies for Developing Positive Leader–Member Relations" has been updated and changed to "The Three-Stage Process for Developing Positive LMX Relations." The section entitled "Factors that Determine LMX Quality" has been updated to provide a more in-depth discussion on "Follower Attributes," "Leader-Follower Perceptions of Each Other," and "Situational Factors." The "Effective Leader–Follower Feedback" subsection has been moved from the

"Followership" section to the "Leader–Member Exchange Theory" section and is now titled "Effective Leader-Follower Feedback." Exhibit 7.3 has been modified.

Chapter 8

This chapter has been reorganized and shortened. The "Advantages and Disadvantages of Teamwork" subsection has been reorganized into bulleted points so that they stand out. A subsection on the "Virtual Team" has been added. To eliminate redundancy and repetition, the "Decision Making in Teams" section has been heavily revised. The "Team versus Individual Decision Making" subsection has been cut. The "Leader-Centered versus Group-Centered Approaches" subsection is now two separate subsections: "Leader-Centered Decision-Making Model" and "Team-Centered Decision-Making Model." The subsection titled "Factors That Influence Self-Managed Team Effectiveness" has been replaced with a much shorter and pointed discussion on the "Characteristics of Effective Self-Managed Teams."

Chapter 9

The "Behavioral Components of Charisma" subsection has been heavily edited and updated and retitled to "Differences Between Charismatic and Noncharismatic Leaders." The "Locus of Charismatic Leadership" subsection has been moved to the "Charismatic Leadership" section. Learning Outcome 3 (formerly LO 4—Describe the four behavioral components of charisma) has been rephrased for clarity and focus on the purpose of the discussion. A new subsection, "The Effects of Transformational Leadership," has been added to the "Transformational Leadership" section.

Chapter 10

Chapter 10 was previously titled "Leadership of Culture and Diversity, and the Learning Organization." The chapter has been reorganized to focus on three key topics: Organizational Culture, Values-Based Leadership, and Diversity. The discussion on learning organizations has been moved to Chapter 12. A new introductory section, "Culture Creation and Sustainability," has been added. The section on "Weak and Strong Cultures" has been merged with the section on "Low- and High-Performance Cultures." A new subsection, "The Impact of Globalization on Diversity," has been added. The section titled "Leadership Initiatives for Achieving Full Diversity" has been significantly reorganized to focus on three separate topics—"Obstacles to Achieving Diversity," "Creating a Culture That Supports Diversity," and "Diversity Awareness Training and Leadership Education."

Chapter 11

This chapter now combines strategic leadership and change management. A new subsection, "The Role of Leadership in Implementing Change," has been added. The "Guidelines for Overcoming Resistance to Change" section has been renamed "Strategies for Minimizing Resistance to Change." The subsections in this section have also been renamed from "People-Oriented Actions" and "Task-Oriented Actions" to "People-Centered Recommendations for Minimizing Change" and "Task-Centered Recommendations for Minimizing Change."

Chapter 12

Chapter 12 is new. In the third edition, "Crisis Leadership" was part of Chapter 11, and the "Learning Organization and Knowledge Management" was part of Chapter 10. We have brought these two topics together to make up Chapter 12.

I'm deeply honored that Judi Neal, Executive Director, Association for Spirit at Work (**http://www.spiritatwork.org**), wrote the Appendix, "Leadership and Spirituality in the Workplace." I also want to thank my mentor and coauthor of many publications, Joel Corman, for his advice and encouragement during and after my graduate education at Suffolk University.

I hope everyone who uses this text enjoys teaching from these materials as I do.

Robert N. Lussier, *Springfield College*

As it has been with the last three editions of this book, working with Bob Lussier is always a learning and growth experience that I value very much. He is a good friend and a mentor. To my students, friends, and colleagues who have encouraged and supported me morally, I say thanks. And, finally, I give recognition and thanks to the leadership of my school, the University of Virginia's College at Wise, for their support of scholarship of this kind.

Christopher F. Achua, *The University of Virginia's College at Wise*

Finally, we both would like to acknowledge the superb assistance we received from our editorial team. The guidance, support, and professionalism of Joe Sabatino (executive editor), Clint Kernen (marketing manager), Emily Nesheim (content project manager), Tippy McIntosh (senior art director), Danny Bolan (media editor), and Ruth Belanger (editorial assistant) were invaluable to the completion of this project. Special thanks to Leslie Kauffman (developmental editor) for all her help in updating and upgrading this new fourth edition. We sincerely acknowledge the reviewers and survey respondents of this and past editions who provided feedback that greatly improved the quality of this book in many areas.

Reviewers

Chris Adalikwu, *Concordia College—Selma, Alabama*
Kathy Bohley, *University of Indianapolis*
John Bonosoro, *Webster University*
Brian W. Bridgeforth, *Herzing College*
Carl R. Broadhurst, *Campbell University*
Jon Burch, *Trevecca Nazarene University*
Debi Cartwright, *Truman State University*
Don Cassiday, *North Park University*
Ken Chapman, *Webster University*
Felipe Chia, *Harrisburg Area Community College*
Valerie Collins, *Sheridan College*
George W. Crawford, *Clayton College & State University*
Joseph Daly, *Appalachian State University*
Frederick T. Dehner, *Rivier College*
Melinda Drake, *Limestone College*
Rex Dumdum, *Marywood University*
Ray Eldridge, *Freed-Hardeman University*
Debi Carter-Ford, *Wilmington College*
Gerald A. Garrity, *Anna Maria College*

Thomas Garsombke, *Northland College*
Ronald Gayhart, *Lakeshore Tech College*
Michele Geiger, *College of Mount St. Joseph*
James Gelatt, *University of Maryland University College*
Don R. Gibson, *Houston Baptist University*
Eunice M. Glover, *Clayton College & State University*
Garry Grau, *Northeast State Community College*
Ray Grubbs, *Millsaps College*
Deborah Hanson, *University of Great Falls*
Mary Ann Hazen, *University of Detroit Mercy*
Linda Hefferin, *Elgin Community College*
Marilyn M. Helms, *Dalton State College*
Mary Hogue, *Kent State University, Stark Campus*
Stewart Husted, *Virginia Military Institute*
Gale A. Jaeger, *Marywood University*
Lori Happel-Jarratt, *The College of St. Scholastica*
David Jones, *North Carolina State University*
Thomas O. Jones, Jr., *Greensboro College*
Paul N. Keaton, *University of Wisconsin–La Crosse*
Gary Kleemann, *Arizona State University East*
Bill Leban, *DeVry University*
Chet Legenza, *DeVry University*
Sondra Lucht, *Mountain State University*
James Maddox, *Friends University*
Kathleen B. Magee, *Anna Maria College*
Charles Mambula, *Suffolk University*
Gary May, *Clayton College & State University*
David McCalman, *University of Central Arkansas*
Lee E. Meadows, *Walsh College*
Ken Miller, *Mountain State University*
Steve Morreale, *Worcester State College*
Jamie Myrtle, *MidAmerica Nazarene University*
Rhonda S. Palladi, *Georgia State University*
Patricia Parker, *Maryville University*
Jeff Pepper, *Chippewa Valley Tech College*
Nicholas Peppes, *St. Louis Community College*
Melinda Phillabaum, *Indiana University*
Laura Poppo, *Virginia Tech*
William Price, *North County Community College*
Gordon Rands, *Western Illinois University*
Kira K. Reed, *Syracuse University*
Marlys Rizzi, *Simpson College*
Mary Sacavage, *Alvernia College Schuylkill Center*
Khaled Sartawi, *Fort Valley State University*
Christopher Sieverdes, *Clemson University*
H. D. Sinopoli, *Waynesburg College*
Thomas G. Smith, *Fort Valley State University*
Emeric Solymossy, *Western Illinois University—Quad Cities*

Martha C. Spears, *Winthrop University*
Shane Spiller, *Morehead State University*
Bill Tracey, *Central Connecticut State University*
Robin Turner, *Rowan-Cabarrus Community College*
John Waltman, *Eastern Michigan University*
Fred A. Ware, Jr., *Valdosta State University*
Kerr F. Watson, *Mount Olive College*
Kristopher Weatherly, *Campbellsville University*
Amy Wojciechowski, *West Shore Community College*
Mike Woodson, *Northeast Iowa Community College*
Benjamin R. Wygal, *Southern Adventist University*
Kimberly S. Young, *St. Bonaventure University*
Kenneth J. Zula, *Keystone College*
Joseph E. Zuro, *Troy State University*

Robert N. Lussier

Robert N. Lussier is a professor of management at Springfield College and has taught management for more than 25 years. He has developed innovative and widely copied methods for applying concepts and developing skills that can be used in one's personal and professional life. He was the director of Israel Programs and taught there. Other international experiences include Namibia and South Africa.

Dr. Lussier is a prolific writer, with over 300 publications to his credit. His articles have been published in the *Academy of Entrepreneurship Journal, Business Horizons, Entrepreneurship Theory and Practice, Journal of Business Strategies, Journal of Management Education, Journal of Small Business Management, Journal of Small Business Strategy, SAM® Advanced Management Journal,* and others. His other textbooks include *Management Fundamentals: Concepts, Applications, Skill Development* 4e (South-Western/Cengage); *Human Relations in Organizations: Applications and Skill Building* 7e (Irwin/McGraw-Hill); *Business, Society and Government Essentials: An Applied Ethics Approach* (Waveland); *Sport Management Principles and Applications: A Skills Approach* 2e (Human Kinetics); and others.

When not writing, Dr. Lussier consults to a wide array of commercial and nonprofit organizations. In fact, some of the material in the book was developed for such clients as Baystate Medical Center, Coca-Cola, Friendly's Ice Cream, the Institute of Financial Education, Mead, Monsanto, Smith & Wesson, the Social Security Administration, the Visiting Nurses Associations of America, and the YMCA.

Dr. Lussier holds a bachelor of science in business administration from Salem State College, two master's degrees in business and education from Suffolk University, and a doctorate in management from the University of New Haven.

Christopher F. Achua

Christopher F. Achua is a Full Professor in the Department of Business and Economics at the University of Virginia's College at Wise. During the past 17 years, Dr. Achua's teaching has centered on three disciplines: strategic management, marketing, and organizational leadership. Dr. Achua's interest in engaging students in real-life learning opportunities led him to create and direct programs such as the Center for Entrepreneurship, Leadership, and Service (a program funded by the Appalachian Regional Commission) and the Small Business Institute (an SBA program) at his university. These programs focused on developing students' leadership and entrepreneurial skills through applied theory in real-world situations.

Dr. Achua has actively presented scholarly papers at regional and national conferences. His papers have been published in many refereed proceedings, the *Small Business Institute Journal,* and the *Journal of Small Business Strategy.* He has also consulted for a variety of public and not-for-profit organizations. When not involved in academic pursuits, he lends his expertise to community development programs and initiatives. He has served on several boards of organizations in the local community, and was chair of the Mountain Empire Regional Business Incubator Board of Directors.

Dr. Achua received his undergraduate degree in business administration and accounting from the University of Sioux Falls, South Dakota; his MBA from the University of South Dakota; and his doctorate from the United States International University (now Alliant International University) in San Diego, California.

Individuals as Leaders

part one

chapter 1
Who Is a Leader? 2

chapter 2
Leadership Traits and Ethics 30

chapter 3
Leadership Behavior and Motivation 68

chapter 4
Influencing: Power, Politics, Networking, and Negotiation 108

chapter 5
Contingency Leadership Theories 150

1
Who Is a Leader?

Chapter Outline

Leadership Is Everyone's Business
Why Leadership Is Important
Defining Leadership
Are Leaders Born or Made?

Leadership Managerial Roles
Interpersonal Roles
Informational Roles
Decisional Roles

Levels of Analysis of Leadership Theory
Individual Level of Analysis
Group Level of Analysis
Organizational Level of Analysis
Interrelationships among the Levels of Analysis

Leadership Theory Paradigms
The Trait Theory Paradigm
The Behavioral Leadership Theory Paradigm
The Contingency Leadership Theory Paradigm
The Integrative Leadership Theory Paradigm
From the Management to the Leadership Theory Paradigm

Objectives of the Book
Leadership Theory
Application of Leadership Theory
Leadership Skill Development
Flexibility

Organization of the Book

Learning Outcomes

After studying this chapter, you should be able to:

1. Briefly describe the five key elements of leadership. p. 5
2. List the ten managerial roles based on their three categories. p. 9
3. Explain the interrelationships among the levels of leadership analysis. p. 15
4. Describe the major similarity and difference between the trait and behavioral leadership theories. p. 16
5. Discuss the interrelationships between trait and behavioral leadership theories and contingency theories. p. 17
6. Define the following **key terms** (in order of appearance in the chapter):

leadership
influencing
managerial role categories
interpersonal leadership roles
informational leadership roles
decisional leadership roles
levels of analysis of leadership theory
leadership theory
leadership theory classifications
leadership paradigm
leadership trait theories
behavioral leadership theories
contingency leadership theories
integrative leadership theories
management to the leadership theory paradigm
evidence-based management (EBM)

Opening Case APPLICATION

We begin each chapter by introducing an exceptional leader and company, followed by some questions for you to answer, and we answer the questions throughout the chapter. We selected General Electric (GE) for the first chapter because it was ranked number 1 in the world for leaders by *Fortune Magazine,*[1] and its CEO Jeffrey Immelt has been named one of the best CEOs in the world by *Barron's,* ranked in the top 10 of *Fortune's* Most Powerful Businesspeople in the World, and named man of the year by the *Financial Times. Fortune Magazine, Financial Times, Forbes,* and *Business Week* consistently rank GE among the most admired companies in the United States and in the world. Over the past five years, GE has grown its earnings an average of ten percent annually.[2]

GE is Imagination at Work; it has a history of bringing innovation to market. GE is a diversified technology, media, and financial services company focused on solving some of the world's toughest problems. More than half of the company is located outside the United States. It serves customers in more than 100 countries and employs more than 300,000 people worldwide.[3] You are either a customer of GE or have indirectly been exposed to its products and services without realizing it. GE is a conglomerate with multiple lines of business under the following six business units:

- GE Commercial Finance
- GE Healthcare
- GE Industrial
- GE Infrastructure
- GE Money
- NBC Universal

If you are interested in working for a company that is seeking people with leadership skills, or one that will develop your leadership skills, GE is a company to consider. Like most major organizations, GE's Web site provides information regarding career opportunities.

Opening Case Questions:

1. Why is GE so successful?
2. Does GE use our definition of leadership ("the influencing process of leaders and followers to achieve organizational objectives through change")?
3. Can leadership skills be developed, and can you develop your leadership skills through this course?
4. What leadership managerial roles does CEO Jeff Immelt perform at GE?

Can you answer any of these questions? You'll find answers to these questions about General Electric and its leadership throughout the chapter.

To learn more about General Electric, visit the company's Web site at **http://www.ge.com**.

The focus of this chapter is on helping you understand what leadership is and what this book is all about. We begin by defining leadership and the ten roles that leaders perform. Then we explain the three levels of leadership analysis, which provides the framework for the book. After explaining the four major leadership paradigms that have developed over the years, we end this chapter by stating the objectives of the book and presenting its organization.

Leadership Is Everyone's Business

In this section, we begin with a discussion of the importance of leadership, followed by our definition of leadership that is used throughout this book. We end by answering the question: Are leaders born or made?

Why Leadership Is Important

Here are just a few reasons why leadership is so important.

- The success of individual careers and the fate of organizations are determined by the effectiveness of leaders behavior.[4] Leadership is considered crucial for success, and some researchers have argued that it is the most critical ingredient.[5] Domino's Pizza chain CEO David Brandon states that the success of each store is based on the leadership provided by the manager.[6] Organizations are recruiting job candidates with leadership potential and skills for all types of careers.
- Chief Executive Officers (CEOs) understand that they can't run companies on their own; the secret is to foster a leadership mentality throughout the organization.[7] Winning the war for talent will be a predominant business challenge for this century; it's about recruiting and retaining talent and creating leadership opportunities.[8]
- Well-publicized corporate failures (Enron and WorldCom) have brought home the critical role that leadership plays in the success or failure of almost every aspect of the profit and not-for-profit environment. CEOs who don't perform get fired, as CEO tenure is shrinking. The following CEOs were recently replaced for poor performance—Gary Forsee of Sprint Nextel, Angelo Mozilo of Countrywide Financial,[9] Charles Prince of Citigroup,[10] and Stan O'Neal of Merrill Lynch.[11]

As the examples illustrate, leadership is important,[12] and there is a great need for better leaders.[13] If you want to be successful, you must develop your leadership skills.[14] To this end, the focus of this book is to help you develop your leadership skills, so that you can become a successful leader in your personal and professional life.

Opening Case APPLICATION

1. Why is GE so successful?

CEO Jeff Immelt says that you either get out ahead of new trends or you get stomped by them. GE is so successful because for more than 100 years it has been a world leader in getting ahead of trends. In fact, Immelt understands the importance of environmental issues and global warming. He sees green in the future, so GE is developing technology to be a world leader in clean energy. He is one of the leading advocates of government-mandated caps on carbon emissions because he knows caps are coming, and GE is going to be in front of the issue.[15]

Sustainability requires leadership development. GE is known as the company that develops leaders. It is commonly stated that more executives from GE have developed leadership skills and then gone on to become CEOs of other major firms than from any other company, with hundreds more who have gone on to hold senior corporate positions.

Ethical **Dilemma 1**

Is Leadership Really Important?

Scott Adams is the creator of the cartoon character Dilbert. Adams makes fun of managers, in part because he distrusts top-level managers, saying that leadership is really a crock. Leadership is about manipulating people to get them to do something they don't want to do, and there may not be anything in it for them. CEOs basically run the same

continued

(Ethical Dilemma 1 continued)

scam as fortune-tellers, who make up a bunch of guesses and when by chance one is correct, they hope you forget the other errors. First, CEOs blame their predecessors for anything that is bad, then they shuffle everything around, start a new strategic program, and wait. When things go well, despite the CEO, the CEO takes the credit and moves on to the next job. Adams says we may be hung up on leadership as part of our DNA. It seems we have always sought to put somebody above everybody else.[16]

1. Do you agree with Scott Adams that leadership is a crock?
2. Do we really need to have someone in the leadership role?

Learning Outcome 1 *Briefly describe the five key elements of leadership.*

Defining Leadership

The topic of leadership has generated excitement and interest since ancient times. When people think about leadership, images come to mind of powerful dynamic individuals who command victorious armies, shape the events of nations, develop religions, or direct corporate empires. How did certain leaders build such great armies, countries, religions, and companies? Why do certain leaders have dedicated followers while others do not? Why were Gandhi, Mother Theresa, Martin Luther King, and Nelson Mandela such influencial leaders? How did Adolf Hitler rise to a position of great power? In this book, you will learn the major leadership theories and research findings regarding leadership effectiveness.

There is no universal definition of leadership because leadership is complex, and because leadership is studied in different ways that require different definitions. As in leadership research studies, we will use a single definition that meets our purpose in writing this book. Before you read our definition of leadership, complete Self-Assessment 1 to get a better idea of your leadership potential. In the following section, we will discuss each question as it relates to the elements of our leadership definition and to your leadership potential.

SELF-ASSESSMENT 1

Leadership Potential

As with all of the self-assessment exercises in this book, there are no right or wrong answers, so don't try to pick what you think is the right answer. Be honest in answering the questions, so that you can better understand yourself and your behavior as it relates to leadership.

For each pair of statements distribute 5 points, based on how characteristic each statement is of you. If the first statement is totally like you and the second is not like you at all, give 5 points to the first and 0 to the second. If it is the opposite, use 0 and 5. If the statement is usually like you, then the distribution can be 4 and 1, or 1 and 4. If both statements tend to be like you, the distribution should be 3 and 2, or 2 and 3. Again, the combined score for each pair of statements must equal 5.

Here are the scoring distributions for each pair of statements:

0–5 or 5–0	One of the statements is totally like you, the other not like you at all.
1–4 or 4–1	One statement is usually like you, the other not.
2–3 or 3–2	Both statements are like you, although one is slightly more like you.

continued

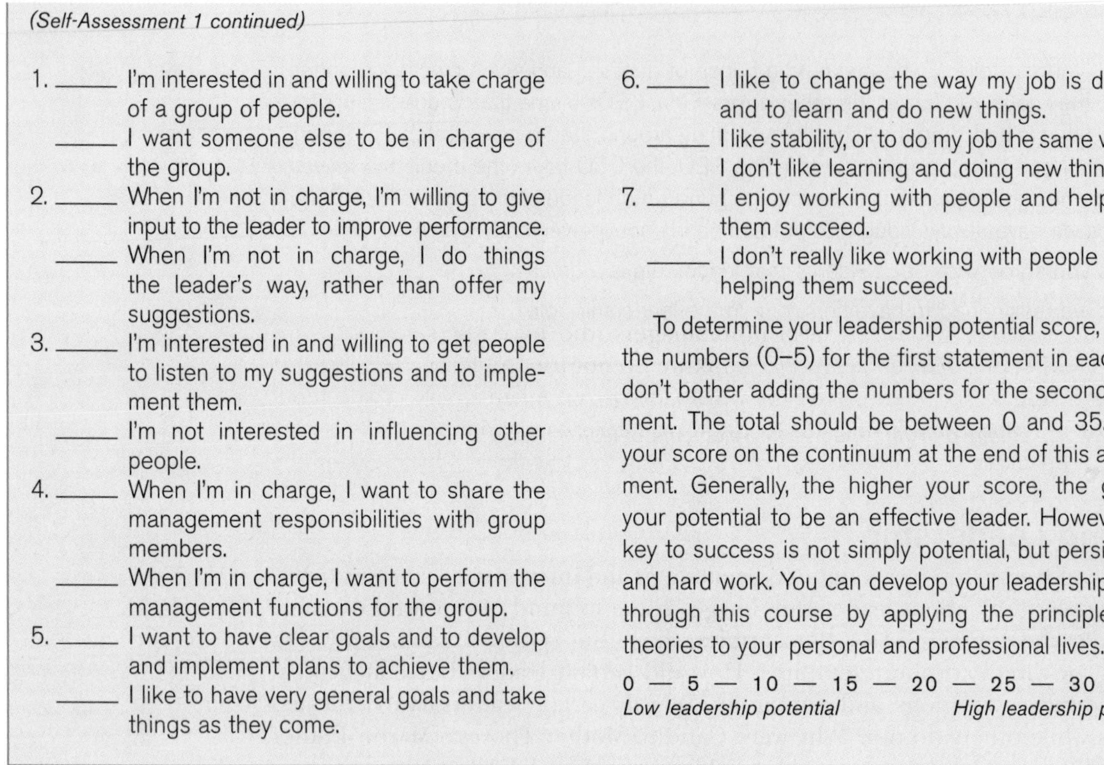

(Self-Assessment 1 continued)

1. _____ I'm interested in and willing to take charge of a group of people.
   _____ I want someone else to be in charge of the group.
2. _____ When I'm not in charge, I'm willing to give input to the leader to improve performance.
   _____ When I'm not in charge, I do things the leader's way, rather than offer my suggestions.
3. _____ I'm interested in and willing to get people to listen to my suggestions and to implement them.
   _____ I'm not interested in influencing other people.
4. _____ When I'm in charge, I want to share the management responsibilities with group members.
   _____ When I'm in charge, I want to perform the management functions for the group.
5. _____ I want to have clear goals and to develop and implement plans to achieve them.
   _____ I like to have very general goals and take things as they come.
6. _____ I like to change the way my job is done and to learn and do new things.
   _____ I like stability, or to do my job the same way; I don't like learning and doing new things.
7. _____ I enjoy working with people and helping them succeed.
   _____ I don't really like working with people and helping them succeed.

To determine your leadership potential score, add up the numbers (0–5) for the first statement in each pair; don't bother adding the numbers for the second statement. The total should be between 0 and 35. Place your score on the continuum at the end of this assessment. Generally, the higher your score, the greater your potential to be an effective leader. However, the key to success is not simply potential, but persistence and hard work. You can develop your leadership ability through this course by applying the principles and theories to your personal and professional lives.

0 — 5 — 10 — 15 — 20 — 25 — 30 — 35

Low leadership potential *High leadership potential*

Leadership *is the influencing process of leaders and followers to achieve organizational objectives through change.* Let's discuss the five key elements of our definition; see Exhibit 1.1 for a list.

EXHIBIT 1.1 Leadership Definition Key Elements

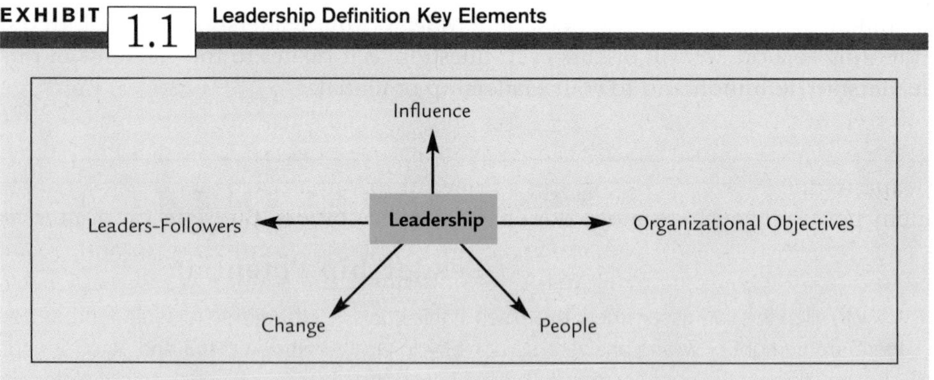

Leaders–Followers

Question 1 of Self-Assessment 1 is meant to get you thinking about whether you want to be a leader or a follower. If you are not interested and not willing to be in charge, you are better suited to be a follower. However, as you will learn in this section, good followers also perform leadership roles when needed. And followers influence leaders. Thus, in our definition of leadership, the influencing process is *between* leaders and followers, not just a leader influencing followers; it's a two-way street. Knowing how to lead and developing leadership skills will make you a better leader and follower.[17] So whether you want to be a leader or a follower, you will benefit from this book.

Throughout this book, leadership is referred to in the context of formal organizational settings in business corporations (GE, IBM), government agencies (Department of Motor Vehicles, the Police Department), and nonprofit organizations (Red Cross, Springfield College). Organizations have two major classifications of employees: managers, who have subordinates and formal authority to tell them what to do; and employees, who do not. All managers perform four major functions: planning, organizing, leading, and controlling. Leadership is thus a part of the manager's job. However, there are managers—you may know some—who are not effective leaders. There are also nonmanagers who have great influence on managers and peers. Therefore, in this book we do not use the terms *manager* and *leader* interchangeably. When we use the word *manager,* we mean a person who has a formal title and authority. When we use the term *leader,* we mean a person who may be either a manager or a nonmanager. A leader always has the ability to influence others; a manager may not. Thus, a leader is not necessarily a person who holds some formal position such as manager.

A *follower* is a person who is being influenced by a leader.[18] A follower can be a manager or a nonmanager. Good followers are not "yes people" who simply follow the leader without giving input that influences the leader. In short, effective leaders influence followers, and their followers influence them.[19] The qualities needed for effective leadership are the same as those needed to be an effective follower. Throughout this book, we use the term *behavior* when referring to the activities of people or the things they do and say as they are influenced. You will learn more about followership in Chapter 7.

Work Application 1

Recall a present or past job. Were you both a leader and a follower? Explain.

As implied in question 2 of Self-Assessment 1, good followers give input and influence leaders. If you want to be an effective follower, you need to share your ideas.[20] Also, as a leader you need to listen to others and implement their ideas to be effective.[21] According to GE CEO Jeff Immelt, GE is not run like a big company; it is run like a big partnership, where every leader can make a contribution not just to their job, but to the entire company.[22]

Influence

Influencing *is the process of a leader communicating ideas, gaining acceptance of them, and motivating followers to support and implement the ideas through change.* Influence is the essence of leadership.[23] Question 3 of Self-Assessment 1 asked if you were interested in and willing to influence others, as a leader or follower. When you have a management position, you have more power to influence others. But, effective followers also influence others. Your ability to influence others (to get what you want) can be developed.[24] Influencing includes power, politics, and negotiating; you will learn more about these concepts in Chapter 4.

Work Application 2

Briefly explain the influencing relationship between the leader and followers where you work(ed).

Influencing is also about the relationship between leaders and followers.[25] Managers may coerce subordinates to influence their behavior, but leaders do not. Leaders gain the commitment and enthusiasm of followers who are willing to be influenced.[26] Most of the leadership research is concerned with the relationship between leaders and followers.[27] Effective managers know when to lead and when to follow. Thus, leaders and followers often change roles throughout the influencing process.[28] Question 4 of Self-Assessment 1 asked if you want to share management responsibility as a leader.

Organizational Objectives

Effective leaders influence followers to think not only of their own interests but also of the interest of the organization through a shared vision.[29] Leadership occurs

Work Application 3

State one or more objectives from an organization where you work(ed).

when followers are influenced to do what is ethical and beneficial for the organization and themselves. Taking advantage of followers for personal gain is not part of leadership. Members of the organization need to work together toward an outcome that the leader and followers both want, a desired future or shared purpose that motivates them toward this more preferable outcome.[30] Leaders need to provide direction, but the group should set its goals.[31] As implied in question 5 of Self-Assessment 1, effective leaders set clear goals. You will learn how to set objectives in Chapter 3.

Change

Influencing and setting objectives is about change. Organizations need to continually change, in adapting to the rapidly changing global environment.[32] GE is the only company listed in the Dow Jones Industrial Index today that was also included in the original index in 1896. The other companies may have become too comfortable with doing business the same old way, perhaps causing these former business stars to fade. Effective leaders realize the need for continual change to improve performance.[33]

Work Application 4

Are the managers where you work(ed) effective at influencing their employees to bring about change? Explain.

Statements like these are not in a successful leader's vocabulary: *We've always done it this way; We've never done it that way before; It can't be done; No one else has done it;* and *It's not in the budget.* Leadership involves influencing followers to bring about change toward a desired future for the organization.[34]

As implied in question 6 of Self-Assessment 1 and the information in this section, to be an effective leader and follower you must be open to change.[35] The people who advance in organizations are those who are willing to take a risk and try new things.[36] When was the last time you did something new and different? You will learn more about leading change in Chapter 11.

People

Work Application 5

Do managers where you work(ed) treat their employees as valuable assets? Explain.

Although the term *people* is not specifically mentioned in our definition of leadership, after reading about the other elements, you should realize that leadership is about leading people. As implied in question 7 of Self-Assessment 1, to be effective at almost every job today, you must be able to get along with people. Effective leaders and followers enjoy working with people and helping them succeed.[37] People skills are more valuable than computer skills.[38] You will learn how to develop your people skills throughout this book.

Research, experience, and common sense all point to a direct relationship between a company's financial success and its commitment to leadership practices that treat people as assets.[39] There is little evidence that being a mean, tough manager is associated with leadership success. It is the collective efforts of all people contributing that make things happen.[40]

Opening Case APPLICATION

2. Does GE use our definition of leadership ("the influencing process of leaders and followers to achieve organizational objectives through change")?

Jeff Immelt is clearly the leader at GE. However, as he stated, GE is run like a big partnership where every leader can make a contribution to the job and the entire company. He doesn't make decisions and set obectives alone. Immelt has an executive team, and much of what GE does comes from these followers who influence Immelt. As stated in the opening case and under question 1, GE is always changing to stay ahead of the trends. So yes, GE does use our definition of leadership. You are learning the definition of leadership as used by hundreds of successful companies and nonprofit organizations.

Are Leaders Born or Made?

You may think this is a trick question, because most researchers say the answer is both. Effective leaders are not simply born or made, they are born with some leadership ability and develop it. So natural leadership ability offers advantages. You will learn more about leadership traits in Chapter 2. However, everyone has potential to lead,[41] and leadership skills can be developed.[42] If leadership skills could not be developed, or leaders were not made, major corporations would not spend millions of dollars on leadership training each year.[43] The Center for Creative Leadership (**http://www.ccl.org**) is one of the world's most respected nonprofit organizations that develops leaders in all sectors of the global economy. Clearly, it would not be in business if its global client organizations did not believe it can develop leadership skills.

Some researchers go so far as to say that experts are definitely made, not born,[44] and that everyone has equal potential to lead.[45] Legendary football coach Vince Lombardi once said, "Contrary to the opinion of many people, leaders are not born, leaders are made, and they are made by effort and hard work." Whatever your leadership ability is now (which is based on your natural ability and development), you can invest in developing your leadership skills, or you can allow them to remain as they are now. You may never become the CEO of an organization, but you can improve your leadership knowledge, ability, and skill through this course. As Vince Lombardi would put it, you can develop your leadership skills through this course if you put in the effort and work hard at it. We'll talk more about this in the last section of this chapter.

Work Application 6

Do you believe that you are a born leader? Do you believe that you can develop your leadership skills to improve job performance?

Opening Case APPLICATION

3. Can leadership skills be developed, and can you develop your leadership skills through this course?

For 50 years companies have been trying to emulate GE's legendary Crotonville training facility (John F. Welch Leadership Center) where thousands of its employees have honed their leadership skills. With increased globalization, GE has taken Crotonville on the road to hot spots around the world including Shanghai, Munich, and Bangalore. Staying ahead of the trends, GE employees from anywhere in the world can also tap online leadership workshops through the company intranet.[46] So the answer is yes, GE is clearly developing leadership skills, and that is why other organizations are hiring GE managers to become their leaders. You can develop your leadership skills through this course if you put in the effort and work hard at it.

Learning Outcome 2 *List the ten managerial roles based on their three categories.*

Leadership Managerial Roles

In this section, we discuss what leaders do on the job—leadership managerial roles.[47] Henry Mintzberg identified ten managerial roles that leaders perform to accomplish organizational objectives.[48] The roles represent the dominant classes of behavioral activities that managers or their followers perform. Mintzberg defined a *role* as a set of expectations of how a person will behave to perform a job. He grouped these roles into three categories. *The* **managerial role categories** *are interpersonal, informational, and decisional.* Mintzberg's management role theory has been supported by research studies. Exhibit 1.2 on the next page shows the ten managerial roles, based on the three categories.

EXHIBIT 1.2 Managerial Roles

Interpersonal Roles	Informational Roles	Decisional Roles
Figurehead	Monitor	Entrepreneur
Leader	Disseminator	Disturbance-handler
Liaison	Spokesperson	Resource-allocator
		Negotiator

Interpersonal Roles

The **interpersonal leadership roles** *include figurehead, leader, and liaison.*

Figurehead Role

Leaders perform the *figurehead role* when they represent the organization or department in legal, social, ceremonial, and symbolic activities. Top-level managers are usually viewed as figureheads for their organization.[49] However, leaders throughout the organization perform the following behavior, as well as other related activities:

- Signing official documents (expense authorization, checks, vouchers, contracts, and so on)
- Entertaining clients or customers as official representatives and receiving/escorting official visitors
- Informally talking to people and attending outside meetings as an organizational representative
- Presiding at meetings and ceremonial events (awards ceremonies, retirement dinners, and so on)

Leader Role

According to Mintzberg, the *leader role* is that of performing the *management functions* to effectively operate the managers' organization unit. Therefore, the leader role pervades all managerial behavior. In other words, the leader role influences how the leader performs other roles.[50] You will learn more about the leadership role throughout this book. Here are some of the many leader behaviors that can be performed by managers or followers:

- Hiring and training
- Giving instructions and coaching
- Evaluating performance

Work Application 7

Give one job example of the specific behavior you or some other leader displayed when performing the figurehead, leader, and liaison roles. For each of the three roles, be sure to identify the leader as you or another, the role by its name, and the specific behavior.

Liaison Role

Leaders perform the *liaison role* when they interact with people outside their organizational unit. Liaison behavior includes networking to develop relationships and gain information and favors.[51] Organizational politics is an important part of the liaison role, and you will learn more about how to gain and use power, how to conduct politics, and how to network in Chapter 4. Here are a few of the liaison role behaviors:

- Serving on committees with members from outside the organizational unit
- Attending professional/trade association meetings
- Calling and meeting with people to keep in touch

Informational Roles

The **informational leadership roles** *include monitor, disseminator, and spokesperson.* You will learn more about informational roles in Chapter 6.

Monitor Role

Leaders perform the *monitor role* when they gather information. Most of the information is analyzed to discover problems and opportunities, and to understand events outside the organizational unit.[52] Some of the information is passed on to other people in the organizational unit (disseminator role), or to people outside the unit (spokesperson role). Information is gathered by behavior, including:

- Reading memos, reports, professional/trade publications, newspapers, and so forth
- Talking to others, attending meetings inside and outside the organization, and so forth
- Observing (visiting a competitor's store to compare products, prices, and business processes)

Disseminator Role

Leaders perform the *disseminator role* when they send information to others in the organizational unit. Managers have access to information that is not available to employees. Some of the information that comes from higher levels of management must be passed on to employees, either in its original form or paraphrased. Using information translated into skills that advance the organization is now often being referred to as *knowledge management*.[53] Information is passed on in one or both of the following forms:

- Orally through voice mail, one-on-one discussions, and group meetings. You will learn how to conduct meetings in Chapter 8
- Written through e-mail and snail mail (U.S. mail)

Spokesperson Role

Leaders perform the *spokesperson role* when they provide information to people outside the organizational unit. People must report information to their boss (board of directors, owner, managers) and people outside the organizational unit (other departments, customers, suppliers). Leaders lobby and serve as public relations representatives for their organizational unit. Here are some examples of when the spokesperson role is performed:

- Meeting with the boss to discuss performance and with the budget officer to discuss the unit budget
- Answering letters
- Reporting information to the government (the IRS, OSHA)

Work Application 8

Give one job example of the specific behavior you or some other leader conducted when performing the monitor, disseminator, and spokesperson roles. For each of the three roles, be sure to identify the leader as you or another, the role by its name, and the specific behavior.

Decisional Roles

The **decisional leadership roles** *include entrepreneur, disturbance-handler, resource-allocator, and negotiator.*

Entrepreneur Role

Leaders perform the *entrepreneur role* when they innovate and initiate improvements.[54] Leaders often get ideas for improvements through the monitor role. Here are some examples of entrepreneur behavior:

- Developing new or improved products and services
- Developing new ways to process products and services
- Purchasing new equipment

Disturbance-Handler Role

Leaders perform the *disturbance-handler role* when they take corrective action during crisis or conflict situations. You will learn more about how to handle conflicts in Chapter 6. Unlike the planned action of the entrepreneur role to take advantage of an opportunity, the disturbance is a reaction to an unexpected event that creates a problem.[55] Leaders typically give this role priority over all other roles. Here are some examples of emergencies leaders may have to resolve:

- A union strike
- The breakdown of important machines/equipment
- Needed material arriving late
- A tight schedule to meet

Resource-Allocator Role

Leaders perform the *resource-allocator role* when they schedule, request authorization, and perform budgeting activities. Deciding who gets the organization's limited resources is an important task of managers.[56] Here are some examples of resource allocation:

- Deciding what is done now, done later, and not done (time management; priorities)
- Determining who gets overtime or a merit raise (budgeting)
- Scheduling when employees will use material and equipment

Negotiator Role

Work Application 9

Give one job example of the specific behavior you or some other leader performed when fulfilling the entrepreneur, disturbance-handler, resource-allocator, and negotiator roles. For each of the four roles, be sure to identify the leader as you or another, the role by its name, and the specific behavior.

Leaders perform the *negotiator role* when they represent their organizational unit during routine and nonroutine transactions that do not include set boundaries (such as only one price and term of a sale/purchase for a product/service, or pay of an employee). When there are no set prices or pay conditions, leaders can try to negotiate a good deal to get the resources they need. You will be involved in employment negotiations,[57] and you will learn how to negotiate in Chapter 4. Here are some examples of negotiations:

- Pay and benefits package for a new professional employee or manager
- Labor union contract
- Contract with a customer (sale) or supplier (purchase)

Although managers are responsible for all ten roles, which roles are most important—and which roles the manager performs and which are performed by other leaders—will vary based on the manager's job. The relative emphasis placed on these roles will vary as a function of organizational technology, the day-to-day problems faced by leaders, and the task environment of their organizations.[58] After answering Work Applications 7 through 9, you should realize that you and others perform the leadership roles regardless of management title.

Opening Case APPLICATION

4. What leadership managerial roles does CEO Jeff Immelt perform at GE?

Like all managers who are good leaders, Jeff Immelt plays all ten roles, and he delegates these roles to his followers. Immelt's interpersonal roles include signing documents, entertaining customers, running and attending meetings; leadership development and evaluation of followers; and serving on committees and boards. His informational roles include extensive communications. Immelt's decisional roles include developing new products and processes to keep ahead of the competition, dealing with crises, deciding which business units to give resources to and which to drain, as well as which to buy and to sell.

Applying the **Concept 1**

Leadership Managerial Roles

Identify each of the following 15 behaviors by its leadership role. Write the appropriate letter in the blank before each item.

Interpersonal roles	**Informational roles**	**Decisional roles**
a. figurehead	d. monitor	g. entrepreneur
b. leader	e. disseminator	h. disturbance-handler
c. liaison	f. spokesperson	i. resource-allocator
		j. negotiator

_____ 1. The leader is talking with two employees who were verbally fighting and refuse to work together.

_____ 2. The leader is holding a meeting with his followers to discuss a new company policy.

_____ 3. The production leader is talking to a maintenance person about fixing a machine.

_____ 4. The leader is conducting a job interview.

_____ 5. The sales leader is signing an expense reimbursement form for a sales representative.

_____ 6. The leader is holding a press conference with a local newspaper reporter.

_____ 7. The leader is assigning followers to various accounts and giving them the files.

_____ 8. A follower is asking the leader for a raise.

_____ 9. The leader is presenting organizational pins to employees for 5 years of service during a special meeting of all organizational unit members.

_____ 10. The leader is reading the daily e-mail.

_____ 11. The leader and his manager, who must authorize the funding of the project, are discussing having new customized software developed for the leader's department.

_____ 12. The leader is disciplining a follower for being late again.

_____ 13. The leader is visiting another organizational unit to watch how it processes work orders.

_____ 14. The leader of a stock brokerage branch is trying to get the telephones turned back on so brokers can use the phone.

_____ 15. The leader is having new customized software developed for the organizational unit.

Levels of Analysis of Leadership Theory

One useful way to classify leadership theory and research is by the levels of analysis. *The three* **levels of analysis of leadership theory** *are individual, group, and organizational.* Most leadership theories are formulated in terms of processes at only one of these three levels.[59] You will briefly learn about each level in this section, and the details of each in Parts One through Three of this book.

Individual Level of Analysis

The individual level of analysis of leadership theory focuses on the individual leader and the relationship with individual followers. The individual level can also be called the *dyadic process*. As discussed in our definition of leadership, dyadic theories view leadership as a reciprocal influencing process between the leader and the follower. There is an implicit assumption that leadership effectiveness cannot be understood without examining how a leader and follower influence each other over time. Recall that influencing is also about the relationships between leaders and followers. As a leader and as a follower, you will influence other individuals and they will influence your behavior at work. You will also have multiple dyadic relationships at work.[60] In Part One, "Individuals as Leaders" (Chapters 1 through 5), the focus is on the individual level of analysis.

Group Level of Analysis

The second level of analysis of leadership theory focuses on the relationship between the leader and the collective group of followers.[61] This level is also called *group process.* Group process theories focus on how a leader contributes to group effectiveness.[62] Extensive research on small groups has identified important determinants of group effectiveness, which you will learn about in Part Two, "Team Leadership" (Chapters 6 through 8). An important part of group process is meetings. In Chapter 8, you will learn how to conduct productive meetings.

Organizational Level of Analysis

The third level of analysis of leadership theory focuses on the organization. This level is also called *organizational process.* Individuals and teams contribute to organizational success.[63] Organizational performance in the long run depends on effectively adapting to the environment and acquiring the necessary resources to survive, and on whether the organization uses an effective transformation process to produce its products and services.[64]

Much of the current research at the organizational level focuses on how top-level managers can influence organizational performance. Successful leaders, like Jeff Immelt of GE, have had a positive impact on organizational performance. You will learn more about determinants of organizational performance in Part Three, "Organizational Leadership" (Chapters 9 through 12).

Ethical **Dilemma 2**

Executive Compensation

Executive compensation is a complex and controversial subject. Executive management skill has a direct impact on the success of the firm. Top executives should be paid multimillion dollar compensation packages; after all, if it weren't for some effective CEOs, companies would not be making the millions of dollars of profits they make each year. They deserve a peace of the pie they helped create.[65]

However, top executives have been criticized for being overpaid. In 2006, total direct compensation (including salary, bonus, and the value of restricted stock) for CEOs of 350 major companies was $6.05 million (not including generous pensions, deferred compensation, and other perks).[66] Investors have been complaining about executive pay and trying to cut it back, without much success.[67]

1. Do executives deserve to make 200 times as much as the average worker?
2. Is it ethical for managers to take large pay increases while laying off employees?
3. Are companies being socially responsible when paying executives premium compensation?

Learning Outcome 3 — *Explain the interrelationships among the levels of leadership analysis.*

Interrelationships among the Levels of Analysis

Exhibit 1.3 illustrates the interrelationships among the levels of analysis of leadership theory. Note that the individual is placed at the bottom of the triangle because group and organizational performance are based on individual performance. It has been said that an organization is the sum of all of its individual transactions. Depending on the size of the group and organization you work for, your individual performance may influence the performance of the group and organization positively or negatively. If individual performance is low throughout the organization, the triangle will fall because it will not have a firm foundation, or performance will be low.

EXHIBIT 1.3 Interrelationships among the Levels of Analysis of Leadership Theory

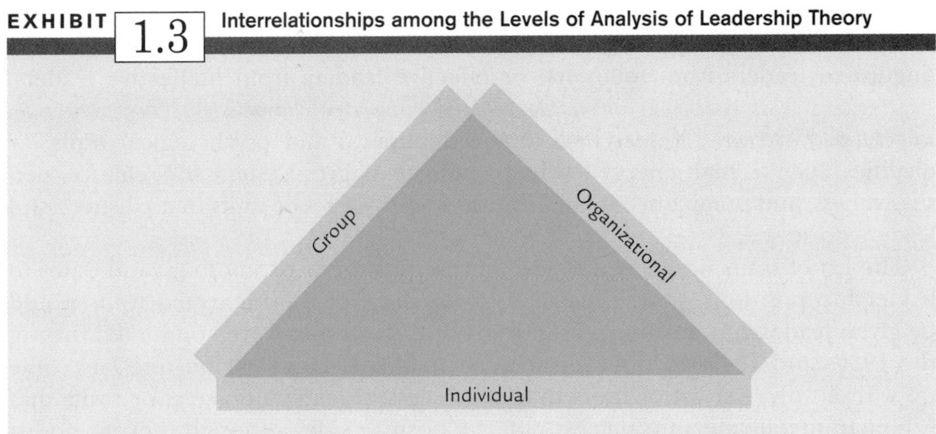

The group-level approach provides a better understanding of leadership effectiveness than the individual, but groups function in a larger social system; and group effectiveness cannot be understood if the focus of research is limited to a group's internal process level of analysis. Thus, the group part of the triangle supports the organizational side. If the groups are not effective, the triangle will fall or organizational performance will be low.

Both group and organizational performance also affect the performance of the individual. If both the group members and the group are highly motivated and productive (or not productive), chances are the individual will be productive (or not) as well. Success tends to be contagious. Working for a winning organization, like Apple, tends to motivate individuals to perform at their best to stay on top. However, an organization and its performance are more than the simple sum of its individuals and groups.

Leadership Theory Paradigms

The first thing we need to do is define the important concepts of this section. *A* **leadership theory** *is an explanation of some aspect of leadership; theories have practical value because they are used to better understand, predict, and control successful leadership.* So, the main purpose of a theory is to inform practice.[68] It has been said that there is nothing as practical as a good theory.[69] There are four major classifications of leadership theory,[70] also called *research approaches,* used to explain leadership.

Leadership theory classifications *include trait, behavioral, contingency, and integrative.* In this section, we discuss each classification and indicate where it is covered in more detail later in this book.

A **leadership paradigm** *is a shared mindset that represents a fundamental way of thinking about, perceiving, studying, researching, and understanding leadership.* The leadership paradigm has changed in the 60 years during which it has been studied. The four major classifications of leadership theory all represent a change in leadership paradigm. You will also learn about the change in paradigm from management to leadership in this section.

Learning Outcome 4 *Describe the major similarity and difference between the trait and behavioral leadership theories.*

The Trait Theory Paradigm

Early leadership studies were based on the assumption that leaders are born, not made. Researchers wanted to identify a set of characteristics or traits that distinguished leaders from followers, or effective leaders from ineffective leaders. **Leadership trait theories** *attempt to explain distinctive characteristics accounting for leadership effectiveness.* Researchers analyzed physical and psychological traits, or qualities, such as high energy level, appearance, aggressiveness, self-reliance, persuasiveness, and dominance in an effort to identify a set of traits that all successful leaders possessed.

The list of traits was to be used as a prerequisite for promoting candidates to leadership positions. Only candidates possessing all the identified traits would be given leadership positions. Hundreds of trait studies were conducted during the 1930s and 1940s to discover a list of qualities. However, no one has come up with a universal list of traits that all successful leaders possess, or traits that will guarantee leadership success. On the positive side, although there is no list of traits that guarantees leadership success, traits that are related to leadership success have been identified. You will learn more about trait theory in the next chapter.

The Behavioral Leadership Theory Paradigm

Work Application 10

Give examples of traits and behaviors that helped make your past or present manager a successful leader.

By the 1950s, most of the leadership research had changed its paradigm, going from trait theory to focusing on what the leader actually did on the job (behavior). In the continuing quest to find the one best leadership style in all situations, researchers attempted to identify differences in the behavior of effective leaders versus ineffective leaders. Another subcategory of behavioral leadership focuses on the nature of management work.[71] Thus, **behavioral leadership theories** *attempt to explain distinctive styles used by effective leaders, or to define the nature of their work.* Mintzberg's ten managerial roles are an example of behavioral leadership theory. Behavioral research focuses on finding ways to classify behavior that will facilitate our understanding of leadership. Hundreds of studies examined the relationship between leadership behavior and measures of leadership effectiveness. However, there was no agreement on one best leadership style for all management situations. On the positive side, Mintzberg's leadership theory is widely used to train leaders. And other researchers did identify two generic dimensions of leader behavior: task- and people-oriented leadership, which have importance in accounting for leadership effectiveness.[72] You will learn about some of the most popular behavioral leadership theories in Chapter 3 and about applications in Chapter 4.

Learning Outcome 5 *Discuss the interrelationships between trait and behavioral leadership theories and contingency theories.*

The Contingency Leadership Theory Paradigm

Both the trait and behavioral leadership theories were attempts to find the one best leadership style in all situations; thus they are called *universal theories.* In the 1960s, it became apparent that there is no one best leadership style in all situations; the right answer often depends on the situation.[73] Thus, the leadership paradigm shifted to contingency theory. **Contingency leadership theories** *attempt to explain the appropriate leadership style based on the leader, followers, and situation.* In other words, which traits and/or behaviors will result in leadership success given the situational variables? The contingency theory paradigm emphasizes the importance of situational factors, including the nature of the work performed, the external environment, and the characteristics of followers. One aspect of this research is to discover the extent to which managerial work is the same or different across different types of organizations, levels of management, and cultures. Some cultures prefer autocratic leaders while others prefer participative leaders.[74] You will learn about the major contingency leadership theories in Chapter 5.

The Integrative Leadership Theory Paradigm

In the mid-to-late 1970s, the paradigm began to shift to the integrative, to tie the theories together, or neo-charismatic theory.[75] As the name implies, **integrative leadership theories** *attempt to combine the trait, behavioral, and contingency theories to explain successful, influencing leader–follower relationships.* Researchers try to explain why the followers of some leaders are willing to work so hard and make personal sacrifices to achieve the group and organizational objectives, or how effective leaders influence the behavior of their followers. Theories identify behaviors and traits that facilitate the leader's effectiveness, and explore why the same behavior by the leader may have a different effect on followers, depending on the situation. The integrative leadership theory paradigm is emphasized in our definition of leadership and thus influences this entire book, especially Chapters 6 through 12.

From the Management to the Leadership Theory Paradigm

There are differences between managers and leaders.[76] Managers focus on doing things right, and leaders focus on doing the right thing. Managers are concerned with stablility and the best way to get the job done, and leaders place greater concern on innovation and change. In the first section, we talked about some of the differences between a manager (formal position of authority) and a leader (has the ability to influence others), because the overarching paradigm has shifted from management to leadership. Successful managers use a truly participative form of leadership as they share the responsibility of management with employees, or as leadership responsiblities are transitioned from managers to team members.[77]

The old command-and-control model of management just doesn't work in today's global economy.[78] The old-style autocratic managers are not climbing today's corporate ladder.[79] Today, managers must be able to lead through motivating others and creating favorable conditions for success, as well as manage. Leaders and followers have a good working relationship because people are the most important asset. They set objectives together and influence each other to bring about change to continually improve the organization.[80] So, going from the **management to the leadership theory paradigm** *is a shift from the older autocratic management style to the newer participative leadership style of management.*

Work Application **11**

Does your present or past manager focus more on management or leadership? Explain, using examples.

Although we have made a comparison between managers and leaders, you should realize that successful leaders are also good at managing, and successful managers are good leaders. There is overlap between the two paradigms—a successful organization needs both managers and leaders. The focus is on how to integrate management and leadership, or on developing leadership skills of managers and employees, which we do in this book. To simplistically stereotype people as either managers or leaders does little to advance our understanding of leadership.[81] Also, because the term *manager* is an occupational title, to foster an inaccurate, negative stereotype of managers is certainly not our intent.

Applying the **Concept 2**

Leadership Theories

Identify each research approach by its leadership theory paradigm. Write the appropriate letter in the blank before each item.

a. trait
b. behavioral
c. contingency
d. integrative
e. management to leadership

____ 16. The researcher is investigating the specific company, work environment, and followers to determine which leadership style is most appropriate.

____ 17. The organization's human resources director is training its managers to be more effective in their interpersonal relationships with their followers so that managers can better influence their followers to work to accomplish the organization's vision.

____ 18. The researcher is observing managers to determine how much time they spend giving employees praise for doing a good job and criticism for poor performance.

____ 19. The researcher is attempting to understand how leaders who are charismatic influence followers to achieve high levels of performance.

____ 20. The researcher is attempting to determine if there is a relationship between how a manager dresses and leadership effectiveness.

Objectives of the Book

The overarching objectives of this book are reflected in its subtitle: *Theory, Application, and Skill Development.* We call it a three-pronged approach, with these objectives:

- To teach you the theory and concepts of leadership
- To develop your ability to apply leadership theory through critical thinking
- To develop your leadership skills in your personal and professional life

This book offers some unique features relating to each of the three objectives (see Exhibit 1.4). So that you can get the most from this book, we encourage you to turn back to the preface and read our goals in writing this book, and the descriptions of the features.

Leadership Theory

Throughout this book, you will learn about several leadership theories and the concepts on which they are based. You will learn about the relationship between leadership and organizational success, as well as the difficulties and challenges

EXHIBIT 1.4 The Three-Pronged Approach: Features of the Book

Theory	Application	Skill Development
Research	Opening cases	Self-assessment exercises
References	Work applications	Ethical dilemmas
Learning outcomes	Applying the concepts	Case role-playing exercises
Key terms	Communication skills	Step-by-step behavior models
Summary	Cases	Behavior model videos
Review questions	Video cases	Skill-development exercises
		Behavior modeling training

leaders face. Your knowledge of leadership theory may be part of your grade; you may be tested. As shown in Exhibit 1.4, this book offers six features to help you learn the leadership theory. The theories and concepts you will learn are based on research (EBM) and are considered important (AACSB), as discussed below.

Evidence-Based Management

Research-based knowledge is relevant and useful to practice,[82] and evidence-based management translates theory° into practice.[83] **Evidence-based management (EBM)** *means that decisions and organizational practices are based on the best available scientific evidence.*[84] The theories and concepts you will learn are based on scientific research (not opinions, outdated research, or myths). If you look at the references at the end of this book, you will see that a majority of the journal articles are published by the premier professional association, the Academy of Management (AoM), and what it publishes is immediately relevant to practicing leaders.[85] However, unlike the AoM journals, we write the theory and concepts at a level that is easy for students to read and understand.[86]

Published research influences what people do in organizations;[87] however, many organizations do not practice EBM.[88] As suggested by the AoM president, our objective is to move you away from making decisions based on personal preference and unsystematic experience toward EBM.[89] If you go to the next level and apply EBM, you can make better decisions and develop your leadership skills in both your personal and professional life.

AACSB Learning Standards

It is important to develop managerial leadership competencies.[90] So how do we know what leadership competencies are important to your career success? For the answer, we turned to the Association to Advance Collegiate Schools of Business (AACSB), which gives accreditation to business schools. AACSB accreditation is highly sought after, and even the business schools that aren't accredited tend to strive to meet its standards.[91] Below is a list of competencies based on AACSB learning standards that are related to this course.[92]

- Leadership—Students develop the capacity to lead in organizational situations. This is the focus of the entire course.
- Reflective Thinking and Self-Management—Students develop reflective thinking through identifying personal strengths and developmental needs as a first step in leading others. Self-assessment is the first step.[93] Each chapter has self-assessment exercises to help you better understand yourself and how to improve your competencies.

- Analytic Skills—Students learn to set goals, adjust, and resolve problems and make decisions as they respond to internal and external stakeholder needs by applying knowledge in new and unfamiliar circumstances. You will learn to write objectives in Chapter 3, and you will learn about using participation in decision making in Chapter 8. Essentially, all of the application and skill material in every chapter develops analytical skills.
- Communication Abilities—Students learn to effectively listen, share ideas, negotiate, and facilitate the flow of information to improve performance. You will develop communication competency in Chapter 6 and negotiation skills in Chapter 4.
- Global and Multicultural Trends, Diversity, and Ethics—Students are challenged to recognize the impact of global trends on an organization to value diversity, and to conduct business in an ethical manner. You will develop these competencies in Chapters 2 and 10. In addition, each chapter has an average of two Ethical Dilemmas to help you develop your competencies in being ethical based on a given situation.
- Teamwork—Students enhance group and individual dynamics in organizations to create a healthy team environment by combining talents and resources for collaboration and information sharing. You will develop team competency in Chapter 8, as well as through the skill-development exercises in most chapters.
- Strategic Management—Students learn how to develop creative strategies to guide organizations, achieve goals, minimize risks, and gain a competitive advantage. Strategic management is the ability to adapt and innovate to solve problems, to cope with unforeseen events, and to manage in unpredictable environments. Chapters 11 and 12 focus on strategic leadership, crises, and change, but you will develop these competencies throughout all the chapters.

All of the skill-development exercises state which AACSB learning standard skills are developed through completing the exercise.

Application of Leadership Theory

We can't think of theory and practice as separate.[94] Reading and lectures are not enough to lead; you need to apply the theory.[95] The question has been asked: Why are well-intended students learning so much, yet able to apply so little to their personal and professional lives? Clearly, there is a gap between theory and practice of EBM.[96] Many frame this gap as a knowledge transfer problem.[97] Knowing is not enough. We need synergies between research and practice,[98] to link theory and practice,[99] and we must apply what we learn.[100] Building on John Dewey's notion of learning-by-doing, students need to be given the opportunity to properly apply what they learn.[101] To this end, this book offers you six features (see Exhibit 1.4, the Application column) to practice applying the concepts and theory. The ability to apply leadership theory may be part of your grade.

Leadership Skill Development

To be successful, knowledge must be translated into skills.[102] The third and highest-level book objective is to develop leadership skills that can be used in your personal and professional life as a leader and as a follower. Organizations recruit people with leadership skills that can be applied on the job.[103] Thus, there is a call for courses that enable students to learn skills that have direct application in the workplace[104] and for students to these practice skills.[105] AACSB standards include developing leadership skills.[106] Developing leadership skills is referred to as "action learning."[107] Students learn best from their own experiences by using the classroom's social system and their personal and professional experiences to develop leadership skills through a variety of interactive approaches.[108] To this end, this book offers you seven features (see Exhibit 1.4, the Skill Development column) to help you develop your leadership skills. Skill development may be part of your grade. We discuss behavior modeling in more detail here.

Models versus Exhibits

All of the behavioral "models" in this book provide specific, step-by-step instructions, and they are labeled as models. They are "prescriptive models." When we offer general advice without a specific instruction, we label the guidelines "exhibits." However, the purpose of both models and exhibits is to help you improve your performance.

Behavior Modeling Leadership Skills Training

Behavior modeling is the only multiple leadership skills training that has been empirically validated by rigorous procedures.[109] In some of the chapters, the features listed in Exhibit 1.4 are combined in behavior modeling skills training. For these exercises you may do a self-assessment. In any case, follow this procedure: (1) read the step-by-step models, (2) watch a behavior modeling video, and (3) practice the skill (which may include role-playing) through a skill-development exercise. The last step in this training is using the skill in your personal and/or professional life for further development of the leadership skill.

Practice

A major concern in organizational leadership training is the transfer of knowledge to on-the-job application.[110] So AACSB is calling for better leadership skill practices;[111] we need practice-based learning.[112] AACSB consultant Milton Blood challenges you. Only you can create actionable knowledge. Are you willing to make changes?[113] As with just about everything in life, you cannot become skilled by simply reading or trying something once. Recall that Vince Lombardi said that leaders are made by effort and hard work. If you want to develop your leadership skill, you need to learn the leadership concepts, apply the concepts, and do the preparation and skill-development exercises. But most important, to be successful, you need to be disciplined to practice using your leadership skills in your personal and professional life, and you have to keep repeating them.[114] Think of leadership development like a sport. If you don't practice, you will not be good at it.

Flexibility

This book has so many features that they most likely cannot all be covered in class during a one-semester course. Your instructor will select the features to be covered during class that best meet the course objectives and the amount of class time available. You may do some or all of the features not covered in class on your own, or do some exercises with the assistance of others outside of class.

Organization of the Book

This book is organized by level of leadership analysis and leadership theory paradigm. See Exhibit 1.5 on the next page for an illustration of the organization of this book.

Go to the Internet (www.cengage.com/management/lussier)
where you will find a broad array of resources to help maximize your learning.

- **Review the vocabulary**
- **Try a quiz**
- **Find related links**

EXHIBIT 1.5 Organization of the Book, Including Level of Analysis and Leadership Paradigm

PART ONE. INDIVIDUALS AS LEADERS (individual-level analysis of leadership theory—Trait, Behavioral, and Contingency Leadership Theories)

1. Who Is a Leader?
2. Leadership Traits and Ethics
3. Leadership Behavior and Motivation
4. Influencing: Power, Politics, Networking, and Negotiation
5. Contingency Leadership Theories

PART TWO. TEAM LEADERSHIP (group-level analysis of leadership theory—Integrative Leadership Theory Applications)

6. Communication, Coaching, and Conflict Skills
7. Leader–Follower Relations
8. Team Leadership and Self-Managed Teams

PART THREE. ORGANIZATIONAL LEADERSHIP (organizational-level analysis—Integrative Leadership Theory Applications)

9. Charismatic and Transformational Leadership
10. Leadership of Culture, Ethics, and Diversity
11. Strategic Leadership and Change Management
12. Crises Leadership and the Learning Organization

Chapter Summary

The chapter summary is organized to answer the six learning outcomes for Chapter 1.

1. **Briefly describe the five key elements of leadership.**

   Leader–Follower—leaders influence the behavior of followers, and vice versa. *Influencing*—the relationship between leaders and followers, who change roles. *Organizational objectives*—outcomes that leaders and followers want to accomplish. *Change*—needed to achieve objectives. *People*—leadership is about leading people.

2. **List the ten managerial roles based on their three categories.**

   Leaders perform the interpersonal role when they act as figurehead, leader, and liaison. Leaders perform the informational role when they act as monitor, disseminator, and spokesperson. Leaders perform the decisional role when they act as entrepreneur, disturbance-handler, resource-allocator, and negotiator.

3. **Explain the interrelationships among the levels of leadership analysis.**

   The three levels of leadership analysis are individual, group, and organizational. The individual performance affects the group and organizational performance. The group performance affects the organizational performance. And both the group and organization affect the performance of the individual.

4. **Describe the major similarity and difference between the trait and behavioral leadership theories.**

   The similarity between the trait and behavioral leadership theories is that they are both universal theories, or they are seeking one best leadership style for all situations. The difference is the approach to determining leadership effectiveness. Trait theory attempts to explain personal characteristics of effective leaders, whereas behavioral theory attempts to explain what leaders actually do on the job.

5. **Discuss the interrelationships between trait and behavioral leadership theories and contingency theories.**

   The contingency theory is interrelated with the trait and behavioral leadership theories because it uses these two theories as the foundation for determining which leadership style is most appropriate—based on the leader, followers, and situation.

6. **Define the following key terms (in order of appearance in the chapter).**

Select one or more methods: (1) fill in the missing key terms from memory; (2) match the key terms from the following list with their definitions below; (3) copy the key terms in order from the list at the beginning of the chapter.

__________ is the influencing process of leaders and followers to achieve organizational objectives through change.

__________ is the process of a leader communicating ideas, gaining acceptance of them, and motivating followers to support and implement the ideas through change.

__________ are interpersonal, informational, and decisional.

__________ include figurehead, leader, and liaison.

__________ include monitor, disseminator, and spokesperson.

__________ include entrepreneur, disturbance-handler, resource-allocator, and negotiator.

__________ are individual, group, and organizational.

__________ is an explanation of some aspect of leadership; theories have practical value because they are used to better understand, predict, and control successful leadership.

__________ include trait, behavioral, contingency, and integrative.

__________ is a shared mindset that represents a fundamental way of thinking about, perceiving, studying, researching, and understanding leadership.

__________ attempt to explain distinctive characteristics accounting for leadership effectiveness.

__________ attempt to explain distinctive styles used by effective leaders, or to define the nature of their work.

__________ attempt to explain the appropriate leadership style based on the leader, followers, and situation.

__________ attempt to combine the trait, behavioral, and contingency theories to explain successful, influencing leader–follower relationships.

__________ is a shift from the older autocratic management style to the newer participative leadership style of management.

__________ means that decisions and organizational practices are based on the best available scientific evidence.

Key Terms

behavioral leadership theories, 16

contingency leadership theories, 17

decisional leadership roles, 11

evidence-based management (EBM), 19

influencing, 7

informational leadership roles, 11

integrative leadership theories, 17

interpersonal leadership roles, 10

leadership, 6

leadership paradigm, 16

leadership theory, 15

leadership theory classifications, 16

leadership trait theories, 16

levels of analysis of leadership theory, 13

management to the leadership theory paradigm, 17

managerial role categories, 9

Review Questions

1. Why is leadership important?
2. What are the five key elements in our leadership definition? How do the elements interrelate to form this definition?
3. Are leaders born or made, and can leadership skills be developed?
4. List and define the interpersonal managerial leadership roles.
5. List and define the informational managerial leadership roles.
6. List and define the decisional managerial leadership roles.
7. List and define the levels of analysis of leadership theory.
8. List and define the leadership theory paradigms.
9. How can the shift in paradigm from management to leadership possibly help—and hurt—the management profession?
10. What are the three-pronged approach objectives to this book?

Communication Skills

The following critical-thinking questions can be used for class discussion and/or as written assignments to develop communication skills. Be sure to give complete explanations for all questions.

1. Should leadership be the manager's job, or should leadership be a shared process?
2. Are you interested in sharing leadership, or do you prefer to be a follower?
3. Some people say the hard skills (finance, quantitative analysis) are more important for managers than soft skills (developing relationships, leadership), and some say the opposite is true. What is your view?
4. Should leadership courses focus on teaching students about leadership or on teaching students to be leaders?
5. Can college students really develop their leadership skills through a college course? Why or why not?
6. Is leadership ability universal, or is a good leader in one environment also effective in another? For example, can a leader in one industry (e.g., a hospital) be successful in another industry (e.g., a bank)?

CASE

Steve Jobs—Apple

Fortune ranked Apple #1 on its list of America's and the World's Most Admired Companies,[115] and Steve Jobs was ranked #1 on its Most Powerful Businesspeople in the World.[116] But he didn't start at the top. Together with Apple Computer co-founder Steve Wozniak, 21-year-old Steven Paul Jobs developed and built the personal computer (PC) in 1976 in Jobs's family garage. The Apple II kicked off the PC era in 1977, and in 1984 the Macintosh altered the direction of the computer industry. Jobs is also credited with desktop publishing, laser printers, and for pioneering personal computer networks.

Jobs went on to create Pixar technology and a new business model for creating computer-animated feature films. More recent innovations under Jobs's leadership include the iPod, iTunes, iMovie, Apple TV, games, QuickTime Player (and other software), Apple Stores, and iPhone. He is ranked #1 for his leadership and power in influencing five industries: computers, Hollywood, music, retailing, and wireless phones. So far, no one has had more influence over a broader range of businesses than Jobs.[117]

Apple hasn't left its PC computer roots. When most people think of Apple today, the "i"products may come to mind; however, the hottest line is actually its Macintosh business because it has the status as the company's largest revenue source. Mac sales have grown at triple the rate of the rest of the PC industry. Apple is growing faster because it improves its hardware and software more often than anyone else.[118]

Apple and Jobs have had some problems along the way in their 30+ year history. In the late 1970s and early 1980s, IBM saw the success of the Apple PC and developed its own PC for business that was not compatible with the Apple operating system. IBM PCs were soon outselling Apple. Jobs decided that to compete he needed to bring in professional management to grow the company. Jobs hired John Sculley to replace him as CEO. Apple ran into problems, and Sculley and Jobs did not agree on how to run the company. The Apple board of directors choose Sculley over Jobs as CEO. Jobs lost control over the company he had started.

As chairman of the board, Jobs had no real power or meaningful work to do. So Jobs left Apple in 1985 to start NeXT (a computer platform development company specializing in the higher education and business markets). In 1986, Steve Jobs started what became Pixar Animated Studios and became its CEO. Jobs contracted with Disney to produce a number of computer-animated feature films, which Disney would co-finance and distribute. Films included *Toy Story, A Bug's Life, Monsters, Inc., Finding Nemo, The Incredibles,* and *Cars.* In 1997, Apple acquired NeXT to use its technology in its Apple computers and Jobs returned to Apple. Apple was still not doing well so the board appointed Jobs to his earlier position as CEO. In 2006, Jobs sold Pixar to Disney and remains on its board as its largest shareholder.

Back as CEO of Apple, Jobs led the company from the brink of bankruptcy through the most dramatic corporate turnaround in the history of Silicon Valley.[119] Jobs changed its culture back to a more entrepreneurial atmosphere. Jobs is a visionary, and Apple's success is born of continual and artful innovation in every aspect of its business. According to Jobs, Apple's success comes from simply trying to make great products that we want for ourselves, and then hope that customers love them as much as we do. Through self-assessment, Jobs realized his strength was in developing new products. The future of Apple depends on frequent product introductions and transitions. Therefore, Jobs places his focus and time on overseeing design teams who develop new products; the design teams have input into what is designed and how.

Jobs is also among the most controversial figures in the business. People who have worked for Jobs over the years have mixed reactions to his leadership style. Some call him temperamental, aggressive, tough, intimidating, and very demanding. He has been known to verbally attack people who make mistakes and are not meeting goals and expectations. Yet, employees who perform up to expectation are well rewarded. He is outspoken and not afraid to anger employees and customers. Even many who feared him also had great respect for him as he did inspire loyalty, enthusiasm, and high levels of performance through continuous innovation. Even people who left Apple say it's often brutal and Jobs hogs the credit, but they've never done better work.[120]

Bill Gates, co-founder of Microsoft, calls Jobs a visionary with intuitive taste. Steve makes decisions based on a sense of people and products. He does things differently, and it's magical. Jobs's ability to always come around and figure out where that next bet should be has been phenomenal. Gates and Jobs worked together in the early days of the development of the PC.[121] *Fortune* states that Jobs "sets a dazzling new standard for innovation and mass appeal driven by an obsessive CEO who wants his products to be practically perfect in every way."[122]

In summary, at age 21 Steve Jobs co-founded Apple and built the first PC business; at age 25 Jobs was running Apple with a net worth of $25 million; at age 26 he made the cover of *Time* magazine; and at age 30 he was thrown out of the company he started. He went on to start two other companies and ended up back at Apple to save it from bankruptcy and then lifted it, and himself, to be ranked as the best in the world. Like all successful leaders, Steve Jobs wants to bring about change, takes innovative risk, is not afraid to fail, and is not always successful; but he comes back. At age 53 Jobs is listed as "co-founder" on 103 separate Apple patents and his net worth exceeds $5 billion (Disney stock value $4.6 billion and Apple stock value $628 million).[123] Steve Jobs loves his work because he discovered what he was good at and what he enjoys doing—the secret to career fulfillment.

GO TO THE INTERNET: To learn more about Steve Jobs and Apple, visit its Web site **(http://www.apple.com)**.

Support your answers to the following questions with specific information from the case and text or with information you get from the Web or another source.

1. Explain how each of the five elements of our definition of leadership applies to Steve Jobs leading Apple (see Exhibit 1.1 on page 6).
2. Identify leadership roles played by Jobs as CEO of Apple. Which role was the most important?
3. Which level of analysis is the primary focus of this case?
4. Explain how each of the leadership theory classifications applies to this case, and which one is most relevant.
5. When Steve Jobs leaves Apple again, will Apple's performance deteriorate and go back into a crisis of near bankruptcy? Why or why not?

CASE EXERCISE AND ROLE-PLAY

Preparation: Assume that you were a powerful board member of Apple in the 1980s. You were involved in helping Jobs select the new CEO, John Sculley, and that you have worked with Jobs on the board for five years. The board has disagreed with Jobs's recommendation to replace Sculley as CEO, so Sculley stays in power and Jobs is out of power. You have to tell Jobs the bad news, which you know he will not want to hear.

Your instructor may elect to let you break into small groups to share ideas and develop a plan for your meeting with Jobs. If you develop a group plan, select one leader to present the meeting with Jobs.

Role-Play: One person (representing him- or herself or their group) conducts the meeting with Steve Jobs (to notify him that Sculley stays as CEO and he is removed from power) before the entire class. Or, multiple role-plays may take place in small groups of 5 to 6; however, role-players can't conduct the meeting in front of the team that developed the meeting plan. They must present to a group that did not develop the plan for the meeting. The people role-playing Jobs should put themselves in his place. How would you feel about being thrown out of the company you co-founded and led?

VIDEO CASE

Leadership at P.F. Chang's

Rick Federico is chairman and CEO of P.F. Chang's, which owns and operates a chain of Asian restaurants across the country. During the time he has been head of the company, Federico has taken on the huge tasks of taking the company public and launching Pei Wei, the firm's chain of diners. In addition, he has developed management teams and laid out clear expectations for his employees. He has earned the respect of his managers, his workers, his customers, and even his competitors.

Rick Federico knows the restaurant industry. He began his career as a dishwasher for a steak house and worked his way up the management chain. So he understands everyone's job, from busboy to chef to manager. Federico expects results from every team, manager, and worker. But he expects no less from himself. He believes his greatest tasks as a leader involve remaining focused on his customers, his workers, and the food they serve. As P.F. Chang's grows Federico wants to be sure that the quality of service, atmosphere, and food are always at their highest.

1. Describe some of Rick Federico's personal leadership traits.
2. Choose three of the leadership managerial roles and explain how Rick Federico might use them as head of P.F. Chang's.

Skill-Development Exercise 1

Getting to Know You by Name

Preparing for Skill-Development Exercise 1

Complete Self-Assessment 2 on page 27, and read the accompanying information before class.

Objectives

1. To get acquainted with some of your classmates
2. To get to know your instructor

   The primary AACSB learning standard skill developed through this exercise is communication ability.

   To develop your skill at remembering and calling people by their name

In this chapter you learned about the importance of leader–follower relationships. An important part of leadership relations is making people feel important. It has been said that the sweetest sound people can hear is their own name. Have you ever had a person whom you don't know (or hardly know) call you by name? Have you ever had a person whom you believe should be able to call you by name not be able to—or call you by the wrong name? How did these two situations make you feel? Being able to call people by name will improve your leadership effectiveness.

Tips for Remembering People's Names

- The first thing you need to do is make a conscious effort to improve your skill at calling people by name. If you say you are no good at remembering names, you won't be. If you say "I can be good at it," and work at it, you can.
- When you are introduced to a person, consciously greet them by name. For example, say, "Hi, Juan, glad to meet you." Then, during your conversation, say the name a few more times until it sticks with you. Use the person's name when you ask and answer questions.
- When you meet a person whom you will see again, without being introduced by someone else, introduce yourself by name—and get the other person to say their name. Then, as before, call them by name during your conversation. For example, if you get to class early and want to talk, introduce yourself to someone rather than just talking without learning the person's name. If someone you don't know just starts talking to you, introduce yourself.
- When you are in a small group being introduced to people, don't just say hi and ignore the names. Depending on the number of people, you can say hello and repeat each name as you look at the person. If you don't remember a name, ask. Just say, "I'm sorry, I didn't get your name." You may also want to mentally repeat the person's name several times. As you talk to the people in the group, use their names. If you forget a name, listen for others to say it as the discussion continues.
- If you have been introduced to a person and forget their name the next time you meet them, you have

two choices. You can apologetically ask them their name. Or, before talking to the person, you can ask someone else for the person's name, then greet them by name. Again, use the person's name during the conversation.

- Use association to help you remember. For example, if you meet John Higby you could picture him hugging a bee. If the person's name is Ted, picture him with the body of a teddy bear. If you know the person likes something, say tennis, picture them with a tennis ball on their head. Think of other people you know who have the same name and make an association.
- Ask for a business card, or ask for the person's telephone number so you can write it down; this will help you remember the name. In business, it's a good idea to carry a pen and some small pieces of paper, such as your own business cards or a few 3 × 5 cards for taking notes.
- Write down the person's name and some information about them after you meet them. Sales representatives use this technique very effectively to recall personal information they may forget. If you are on a committee with people you don't know and don't see very often, use the membership list of names (or write them yourself). Then write an association for each person, so that you can identify all members (this may be done during the meeting without drawing attention). Your notes might include personal characteristics (tall, thin, dark hair) or something about their work (marketing, engineer). Then, before the next meeting, review the list of names and characteristics so you can make the association and greet each person by name.

Doing Skill-Development Exercise 1 in Class

Procedure 1 *(5–8 minutes)* Break into groups of five or six, preferably with people you do not know. In the group, have each member give his or her name and two or three significant things about himself or herself. After all the members have finished, ask each other questions to get to know each other better.

Procedure 2 *(2–4 minutes)* Can anyone in the group call the others by name? If so, he or she should do so. If not, have each member repeat his or her name. Follow with each member calling all members by name. Be sure that each person has a turn to call everyone by name.

Procedure 3 *(5–8 minutes)* Select a person to play the spokesperson role for your group. Remember, this is a leadership course. The spokesperson writes down questions in the following two areas:

- *Course:* Is there anything more that you want to know about the course, such as any expectations or concerns that you have?
- *Instructor:* Make a list of questions for the instructor in order to get to know him or her better.

Procedure 4 *(10–20 minutes)* Each spokesperson asks the instructor one question at a time, until all questions are asked. If time permits, people who are not the spokesperson may ask questions.

Conclusion

The instructor may make concluding remarks.

Apply It *(2–4 minutes)* What did I learn from this experience? How will I use this knowledge in the future? Specifically state which tip for remembering names you will use in the future. Identify precisely when you will practice this skill e.g., on "*x*" day/date when I go to class—or to work, or to a party—I will introduce myself to someone I don't know.

____

____

____

Sharing

In the group, or to the entire class, volunteers may give their answers to the "Apply It" questions.

SELF-ASSESSMENT 2

Names

On the line before each statement, write Y for yes, or N for no.

_____ 1. I enjoy meeting new people.
_____ 2. I'm good at remembering people's names.
_____ 3. When I meet new people, I learn their names and call them by name.
_____ 4. I'm interested in and willing to improve my ability to remember and use names.

If you answered yes to questions 1–3, you have developed some skill in this area. Your answer to question 4 indicates whether you intend to further develop your skill. The choice is yours.

Skill-Development Exercise 2

Identifying Leadership Traits and Behaviors

Objective

To gain a better understanding of leadership traits and behavior

The primary AACSB learning standard skill developed through this exercise is analytic skills.

Preparing for Skill-Development Exercise 2

Read and understand the trait and behavioral leadership theories. On the following lines, list specific traits and behaviors that you believe effective leaders have or should have. Your answers may or may not be based on your observation of successful leaders.

Traits: ______________________________

____

Behaviors: ______________________________

____

Doing Skill-Development Exercise 2 in Class

Option 1 *(5–15 minutes)* Students give their answers to the instructor, who writes them on the board under the heading of *Traits* or *Behaviors*. During or after the answers are listed, the class may discuss them.

Option 2 *(10–20 minutes)* Break into groups of five or six, and select a leader to perform the spokesperson role (remember, this is a leadership class). The spokesperson records the answers of the group, then writes them on the board (5–10 minutes). The instructor leads a class discussion (5–10 minutes).

2 Leadership Traits and Ethics

Chapter Outline

Personality Traits and Leadership

Personality and Traits

The Big Five Model of Personality

Personality Profiles

Traits of Effective Leaders

Dominance

High Energy

Self-Confidence

Locus of Control

Stability

Integrity

Intelligence

Flexibility

Sensitivity to Others

The Personality Profile of Effective Leaders

Achievement Motivation Theory

Leader Motive Profile Theory

Leadership Attitudes

Theory X and Theory Y

The Pygmalion Effect

Self-Concept

How Attitudes Develop Leadership Styles

Ethical Leadership

Does Ethical Behavior Pay?

How Personality Traits and Attitudes, Moral Development, and the Situation Affect Ethical Behavior

How People Justify Unethical Behavior

Simple Guides to Ethical Behavior

Stakeholder Approach to Ethics

Being an Ethical Leader

Learning Outcomes

After studying this chapter, you should be able to:

1. List the benefits of classifying personality traits. p. 33
2. Describe the Big Five personality dimensions. p. 33
3. Explain the universality of traits of effective leaders. p. 37
4. Discuss why the trait of dominance is so important for managers to have. p. 37
5. State how the Achievement Motivation Theory and the Leader Motive Profile are related and different. p. 42
6. Identify similarities and differences among Theory X and Theory Y, the Pygmalion effect, and self-concept. p. 48
7. Describe how attitudes are used to develop four leadership styles. p. 52
8. Compare the three levels of moral development. p. 54
9. Explain the stakeholder approach to ethics. p. 58
10. Define the following **key terms** (in order of appearance in the chapter):

traits
personality
Big Five Model of Personality
surgency personality dimension
agreeableness personality dimension
adjustment personality dimension
conscientiousness personality dimension
openness-to-experience personality dimension
personality profiles
self-awareness
social awareness
self-management
relationship management
Achievement Motivation Theory
Leader Motive Profile Theory
Leader Motive Profile (LMP)
attitudes
Theory X and Theory Y

Pygmalion effect
self-concept
ethics
moral justification
displacement of responsibility
diffusion of responsibility
advantageous comparison
disregard or distortion of consequences
attribution of blame
euphemistic labeling
stakeholder approach to ethics

Opening Case APPLICATION

In this opening case we feature a highly successful African-American woman who founded a nonprofit organization to develop leadership skills in public schools.

Lorraine Monroe was the principal of Harlem's Frederick Douglass Academy from 1991 to 1997. When Monroe started the new high school, the goal was to create a special college preparatory high school. The prior school was well known for its violence, its poor attendance, and its persistently low level of academic achievement. Within five years, student test scores ranked among New York City's best, and 96 percent of the school's graduates went on to college. How did she turn an inner-city school around? Through great leadership. Monroe restored order and discipline primarily through her "Twelve Non-Negotiable Rules," which are based on respect for oneself, for one's associates, and for property.

In order to develop school administrators' leadership skills, she founded the School Leadership Academy at the Center for Educational Innovation in 1997. She went on to found the Lorraine Monroe Leadership Institute (LMLI) in July 2001. She is its director and continues to consult to develop leaders. The Mission of LMLI is to develop and support public school leaders who view solid education as a necessity for transforming children's lives and who are committed to leading consistently high-achieving schools where all students, beginning with kindergarten, are prepared to enter and graduate from college. The Lorraine Monroe Leadership Institute impacts over 17,000 students in the United States.

The work of Dr. Monroe and the Frederick Douglass Academy has been featured on ***60 Minutes***, *Tony Brown's Journal*, and *The McCreary Report*; in *Ebony Magazine*, *The New York Times*, *Reader's Digest*, *Parade Magazine*, *Fast Company Magazine*; and in her book *Nothing's Impossible: Leadership Lessons from Inside and Outside the Classroom.*[1]

Opening Case Questions:

1. What Big Five personality traits does Lorraine Monroe possess?
2. Which traits of effective leaders does Lorraine Monroe possess?
3. Does Lorraine Monroe have the personality profile of an effective leader? And what does she say in response to businesspeople who continually ask her, "What makes a good leader"?
4. How did "attitude" help change the performance of Frederick Douglass Academy?
5. How did Lorraine Monroe's self-concept affect her leadership?
6. What role did ethics play in changing the performance of Frederick Douglass Academy?

Can you answer any of these questions? You'll find answers to these questions and learn more about LMLI and its leadership throughout the chapter.

To learn more about Lorraine Monroe and LMLI, visit LMLI's Web site at **http://www.lorrainemonroe.com**.

Lorraine Monroe is a strong, entrepreneurial leader. The focus of this chapter is on leadership traits, which includes ethics. We begin by learning about personality traits of leaders and the personality profile of effective leaders. Next we learn how attitudes affect leadership. We end with a discussion of ethics in leadership.

Personality Traits and Leadership

Recall that trait theory of leadership was the foundation for the field of leadership studies and that trait theory seeks to identify the characteristics effective leaders possess. Trait researchers examined personality, physical abilities, and social- and work-related characteristics. Trait theory is still being studied today as empirical research on leadership has come full circle by re-visiting the original belief that traits play a role in predicting leadership qualities and identifying potential leaders.[2] Substantial progress in the development of personality theory and traits has been made since the early 1990s.[3] In this section, we discuss traits and personality, the Big Five Model of Personality, reasons why executives fail, and the traits of effective leaders.

Before you learn about personality traits, complete Self-Assessment 1 to determine your personality profile. Throughout this chapter, you will gain a better understanding of your personality traits, which help explain why people do the things they do (behavior).

SELF-ASSESSMENT 1

Personality Profile

There are no right or wrong answers, so be honest and you will really increase your self-awareness. We suggest doing this exercise in pencil or making a copy before you write on it. We will explain why later.

Using the scale below, rate each of the 25 statements according to how accurately it describes you. Place a number from 1 to 7 on the line before each statement.

Like me		Somewhat like me			Not like me	
7	6	5	4	3	2	1

__6__ 1. I step forward and take charge in leaderless situations.

__4__ 2. I am concerned about getting along well with others.

__4__ 3. I have good self-control; I don't get emotional, angry, or yell.

__7__ 4. I'm dependable; when I say I will do something, it's done well and on time.

__6__ 5. I try to do things differently to improve my performance.

__5__ 6. I enjoy competing and winning; losing bothers me.

__2__ 7. I enjoy having lots of friends and going to parties.

__6__ 8. I perform well under pressure.

__7__ 9. I work hard to be successful.

__6__ 10. I go to new places and enjoy traveling.

__6__ 11. I am outgoing and willing to confront people when in conflict.

__4__ 12. I try to see things from other people's points of view.

__6__ 13. I am an optimistic person who sees the positive side of situations (the cup is half full).

__6__ 14. I am a well-organized person.

__5__ 15. When I go to a new restaurant, I order foods I haven't tried.

__3__ 16. I want to climb the corporate ladder to as high a level of management as I can.

__3__ 17. I want other people to like me and to view me as very friendly.

__5__ 18. I give people lots of praise and encouragement; I don't put people down and criticize.

__3__ 19. I conform by following the rules of an organization.

__6__ 20. I volunteer to be the first to learn and do new tasks at work.

__5__ 21. I try to influence other people to get my way.

__3__ 22. I enjoy working with others more than working alone.

__6__ 23. I view myself as being relaxed and secure, rather than nervous and insecure.

__7__ 24. I am considered to be credible because I do a good job and come through for people.

__6__ 25. When people suggest doing things differently, I support them and help bring it about; I don't make statements like these: it won't work, we never did it before, no one else ever did it, or we can't do it.

continued

(Self-Assessment 1 continued)

To determine your personality profile: (1) In the blanks, place the number from 1 to 7 that represents your score for each statement. (2) Add up each column—your total should be a number from 5 to 35. (3) On the number scale, circle the number that is closest to your total score. Each column in the chart represents a specific personality dimension.

Surgency			Agreeableness			Adjustment			Conscientiousness			Openness to Experience		
		35			35			35			35			35
		30			30			30			30			30
6	1.	25	4	2.	25	4	3.	25	7	4.	25	6	5.	25
5	6.	20	2	7.	20	6	8.	20	7	9.	20	6	10.	20
6	11.	15	4	12.	15	6	13.	15	6	14.	15	5	15.	15
3	16.	10	3	17.	10	5	18.	10	3	19.	10	6	20.	10
5	21.	5	3	22.	5	6	23.	5	7	24.	5	6	25.	5
25	Total	Scale	16	Total	Scale	27	Total	Scale	30	Total	Scale	29	Total	Scale

The higher the total number, the stronger is the personality dimension that describes your personality. What is your strongest dimension? Your weakest dimension? Continue reading the chapter for specifics about your personality in each of the five dimensions.

You may visit **http://ipip.ori.org** to complete a 50- or 100-item Big Five Personality Assessment.

Learning Outcome 1 *List the benefits of classifying personality traits.*

Personality and Traits

Why are some people outgoing and others shy, loud and quiet, warm and cold, aggressive and passive? This list of behaviors is made up of individual traits. **Traits** *are distinguishing personal characteristics.* **Personality** *is a combination of traits that classifies an individual's behavior.* Personality also influences the decisions we make.[4] Understanding people's personalities is important because personality affects behavior as well as perceptions and attitudes.[5] Knowing personalities helps you to explain and predict others' behavior and job performance.[6] For a simple example, if you know a person is very shy, you can better understand why he or she is quiet when meeting new people. You can also predict that the person will be quiet when going places and meeting new people. You can also better understand why the person would not seek a job as a salesperson; and if he or she did, you could predict that the person might not be very successful.

Personality is developed based on genetics and environmental factors. The genes you received before you were born influence your personality traits. Your family, friends, school, and work also influence your personality.

Learning Outcome 2 *Describe the Big Five personality dimensions.*

The Big Five Model of Personality

There are many personality classification methods. However, the Big Five Model of Personality traits is the most widely accepted way to classify personalities because of its strong research support and its reliability across age, sex, race, and language groups.[7]

The purpose of the Big Five is to reliably categorize, into one of five dimensions, most if not all of the traits you would use to describe someone else. Thus, each dimension includes multiple traits. *The* **Big Five Model of Personality** *categorizes traits into the dimensions of surgency, agreeableness, adjustment, conscientiousness, and openness to experience.* The dimensions are listed in Exhibit 2.1 and described below. As noted in the descriptions, however, some researchers have slightly different names for the five dimensions.

EXHIBIT 2.1 Big Five Dimensions of Traits

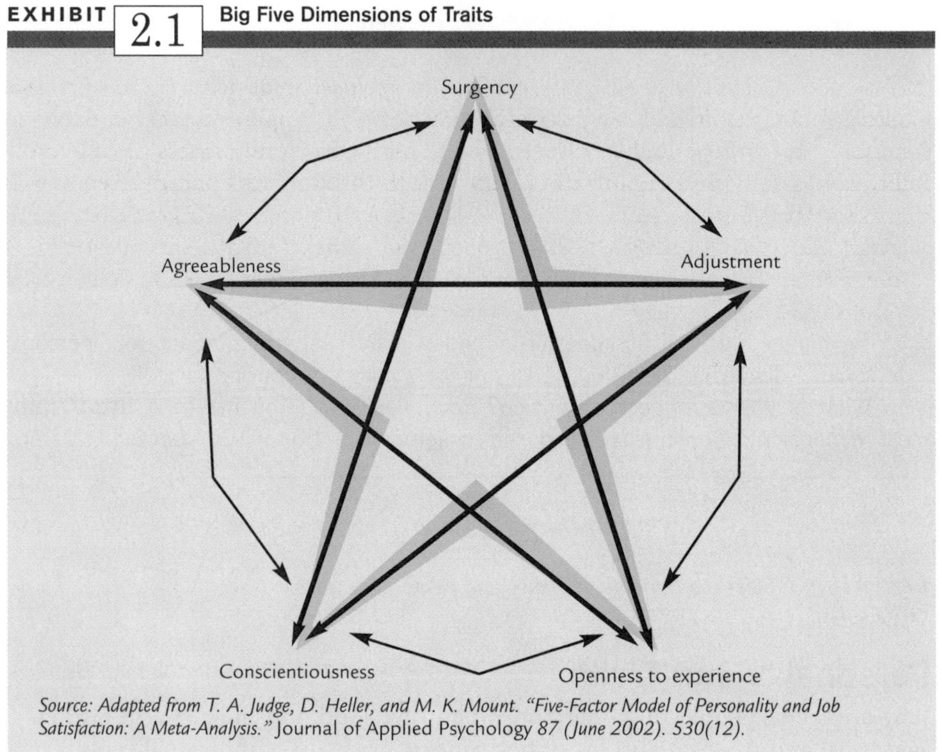

Source: Adapted from T. A. Judge, D. Heller, and M. K. Mount. "Five-Factor Model of Personality and Job Satisfaction: A Meta-Analysis." Journal of Applied Psychology *87 (June 2002). 530(12).*

Surgency

The **surgency personality dimension** *includes leadership and extraversion traits.* (1) People strong in surgency—more commonly called *dominance*—personality traits want to be in charge. Their dominant behavior ranges from interest in getting ahead and leading through competing and influencing. People weak in surgency want to be followers, and don't want to compete or influence. (2) Extraversion is on a continuum between extravert and introvert. Extraverts are outgoing, like to meet new people, and are assertive and willing to confront others, whereas introverts are shy. Review Self-Assessment 1 statements 1, 6, 11, 16, and 21 on page 32 for examples of surgency traits. How strong is your desire to be a leader?

Agreeableness

Unlike surgency behavior to get ahead of others, the **agreeableness personality dimension** *includes traits related to getting along with people.* Agreeable personality behavior is strong when a person is called warm and caring, easygoing and compliant, compassionate and gentle, friendly, and sociable; it is weak when a person is called cold, difficult, uncompassionate, unfriendly, and unsociable. Strongly agreeable personality types are sociable, spend most of their time with people, and have lots of friends. Review Self-Assessment 1 statements 2, 7, 12, 17, and 22 for examples of agreeableness traits. How important is having good relationships to you?

Adjustment

The **adjustment personality dimension** *includes traits related to emotional stability.* Adjustment is on a continuum between being emotionally stable and unstable. *Stable* refers to self-control, being calm—good under pressure, relaxed, secure, and positive—praising others; *unstable* (also called neuroticism) is out of control—poor under pressure, nervous, insecure, negative, and hostile—criticizing others. Review Self-Assessment 1 statements 3, 8, 13, 18, and 23 for examples of adjustment traits. How emotionally stable are you?

Conscientiousness

The **conscientiousness personality dimension** *includes traits related to achievement.* Conscientiousness is also on a continuum between responsible/dependable to irresponsible/undependable. Other traits of high conscientiousness include credibility, conformity, and organization. People with this trait are characterized as willing to work hard and put in extra time and effort to accomplish goals to achieve success—also called organization citizenship behavior. Review Self-Assessment 1 statements 4, 9, 14, 19, and 24 for examples of conscientiousness. How strong is your desire to be successful?

Openness to Experience

The **openness-to-experience personality dimension** *includes traits related to being willing to change and try new things.* They are imaginative, nonconforming, unconventional, and autonomous, while those with a weak openness dimension avoid change and new things. Review Self-Assessment 1 statements 5, 10, 15, 20, and 25 for examples of openness-to-experience traits. How willing are you to change and try new things?

Personality Profiles

Personality profiles *identify individual stronger and weaker traits.* Students completing Self-Assessment 1 tend to have a range of scores for the five dimensions. Review your personality profile. Do you have higher scores (stronger traits) on some dimensions and lower scores (weaker traits) on others?

Work Application 1

Select a present or past manager, and describe his or her personality profile using each of the Big Five dimensions. After rating each dimension as strong, moderate, or weak, give an example of traits and typical behavior of the manager for each dimension. Which dimensions are strongest and weakest?

Job Performance

Many organizations (including the National Football League) give personality tests to ensure a proper match between the worker and the job.[8] Personality profiles are also used to categorize people as a means of predicting job success, and high conscientiousness is a good predictor of job performance,[9] whereas people who are unstable tend to have poor job performance.[10] Change in behavior allows more effective work.[11] People who are high in openness to experience tend to lead innovation to improve organizational performance.[12]

The Big Five Correlates with Leadership

Researchers conducted a major meta-analysis combining 73 prior studies to correlate the Big Five personality dimensions with leadership. The highest correlation with leadership was surgency (.31), followed by concensiousness (.28) and openness to experience (.24). Agreeableness was weakly correlated (.08), and adjustment was negatively correlated with leadership (–.24).[13] In other words, people high in surgency are perceived as leaderlike—they work hard, and they bring about change. They are not too concerned about being well-liked and trying to please everyone, and they are stable or not overly emotional. How does your Big Five personality correlate with leadership? If it is not a perfect match, don't be too concerned because there are always exceptions to the norm. For example, Steve Jobs (Chapter 1 case) sometimes gets emotional and yells at employees.

Applying the **Concept 1**

Big Five Personality Dimensions

Identify each of these seven traits/behaviors by its personality dimension. Write the appropriate letter in the blank before each item.

a. surgency
b. agreeableness
c. adjustment
d. conscientiousness
e. openness to experience

____ 1. The manager is influencing the follower to do the job the way the leader wants it done.

____ 2. The sales representative submitted the monthly expense report on time as usual.

____ 3. The leader is saying a warm, friendly good morning to followers as they arrive at work.

____ 4. The leader is seeking ideas from followers on how to speed up the flow of work.

____ 5. As a follower is yelling a complaint, the leader calmly explains what went wrong.

____ 6. The leader is being very quiet when meeting some unexpected visitors in the work unit.

____ 7. The leader is giving in to a follower to avoid a conflict.

Opening Case APPLICATION

1. What Big Five personality traits does Lorraine Monroe possess?

To a large extent, Lorraine Monroe was a successful founder and leader because of her strong personality in the Big Five. She has a strong need for surgency, is conscientious, and is open to new experience as she does consulting to bring about better educational leadership to help public school children. Lorraine was not afraid to step on toes and be disagreeable at Frederick Douglass Academy as she took strong control over the school and enforced discipline conducive to learning, while maintaining overall emotional stability.

Derailed Leadership Traits

Work Application 2

Select a present or past manager, and state whether he or she has any of the six traits of derailment. Give specific examples of weaknesses.

Before we go on to the next section and discuss the traits of effective leaders, let's identify traits that led to leadership failure. A study was conducted that compared 21 derailed executives with 20 executives who had successfully climbed the corporate ladder to the top. The derailed executives had prior success and were expected to go far, but they were passed over for promotion again, were fired, or were forced to retire early. See Exhibit 2.2 for a list of the six major reasons for derailment.[14] Overall, the problem of derailed managers is poor human relations skills.[15] Destructive narcissistic (adjustment trait) managers cause significant damage to an organization.[16] Greed and resistance to change also contribute to failed leadership.[17]

You'll learn about the more specific personality profile of successful leaders in the "Leader Motive Profile Theory" section of this chapter. But first, let's identify specific traits of effective leaders in more detail.

EXHIBIT 2.2 **Why Executives Are Derailed**

- They used a bullying style viewed as intimidating, insensitive, and abrasive.
- They were viewed as being cold, aloof, and arrogant.
- They betrayed personal trust.
- They were self-centered and viewed as overly ambitious and thinking of the next job.
- They had specific performance problems with the business.
- They overmanaged and were unable to delegate or build a team.

Learning Outcome 3 *Explain the universality of traits of effective leaders.*

Traits of Effective Leaders

Researchers who were not concerned with personality or a system of categorizing traits wanted to identify a list of traits that effective leaders have. There appear to be some traits that consistently differentiate leaders from others, so trait theory does have some claim to universality. For the theory to be truly universal, all leaders would have to have all the same traits. However, again you should realize that there is no one list of traits accepted by all researchers, and that not all effective leaders have all these traits. In this section, you will learn which traits have strong research support. So if you are not strong on every one, it doesn't mean that you can't be a successful leader. Furthermore, you can develop these traits with some effort.

See Exhibit 2.3 for a list of the nine traits. In the following paragraphs, we will categorize each trait using the Big Five.

EXHIBIT 2.3 **Traits of Effective Leaders**

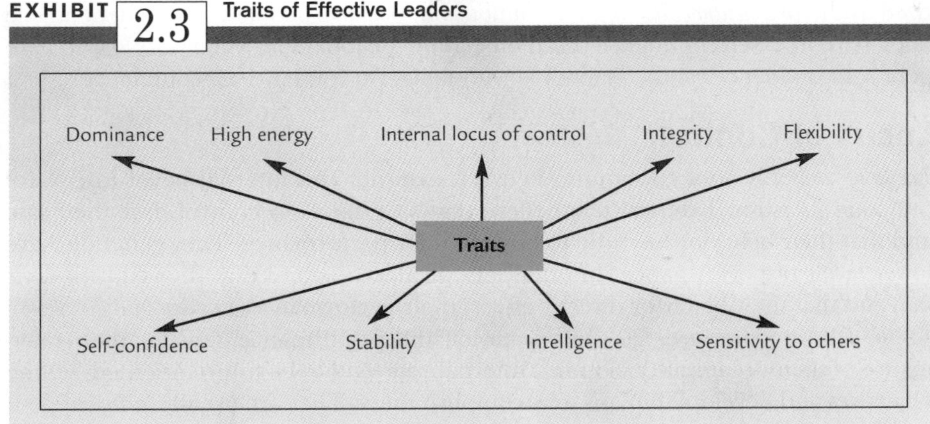

Learning Outcome 4 *Discuss why the trait of dominance is so important for managers to have.*

Dominance

Dominance is one of the two major traits of the *surgency* Big Five, and it is correlated with leadership.[18] Successful leaders want to be managers and to take charge. However, they are not overly bossy, nor do they use a bullying style. If a person does not want to be a leader, chances are he or she will not be an effective manager. Thus, the dominance trait affects all the other traits related to effective leaders. For example, if you push people into management positions, there is a high probability that they will lack self-confidence and not have much energy for the job. Due to the pressure of the job they don't want, they may also not be stable in the position or sensitive to others, and the trait of intelligence may be questioned. To reach full leadership potential, you've got to want to be a leader, work to develop your skills, and enjoy it. Do you want to be a leader?

High Energy

Leaders have high energy with a positive drive to work hard to achieve goals.[19] They focus on the positive and have stamina and tolerate stress well.[20] Their optimism shapes their decisions to lead.[21] Leaders have enthusiasm and don't give up as they project a positive attitude.[22] They deal with but don't accept setbacks. However, they are not viewed as pushy and obnoxious. They have a high tolerance for frustration as they strive to overcome obstacles through persistence.[23] Leaders take initiative to bring about improvements rather than ask permission; they don't have to be told what to do. High energy is best categorized as the *conscientiousness* dimension of the Big Five. Do you have a high energy level?

Self-Confidence

Self-confidence, on a continuum from strong to weak, indicates whether you are self-assured in your judgments, decision making, ideas, and capabilities. Leaders display self-assurance about their abilities and foster confidence among followers. As leaders gain their followers' respect, they also influence them.[24] Self-confidence influences individual goals, efforts, and task persistence. Leaders refuse to give in to self-doubt.[25] Self-confidence is positively related to effectiveness and is a predictor of success.[26] Leaders are, however, realistically self-confident; they are not viewed as arrogant "know it alls" who alienate people, and they are emotionally stable.[27] Self-confidence is best categorized as the *conscientiousness* Big Five dimension, because people who are dependable often have high self-confidence based on getting the job done, while people who have poor self-confidence can be emotionally unstable. Do you have self-confidence?

Locus of Control

Locus of control is on a continuum between external and internal belief in control over one's destiny. Externalizers believe that they have no control over their fate and that their behavior has little to do with their performance. They generally have lower levels of performance. Internalizers (leaders) believe that they control their fate and that their behavior directly affects their performance. Leaders take responsibility for who they are, for their behavior and performance, and for the performance of their organizational unit.[28] Internalizers tend to be future oriented, setting objectives and developing plans to accomplish them. They are usually self-confident and learn from their mistakes, rather than blaming others or just bad luck.[29] The Big Five category is the *openness-to-experience* dimension. Externalizers (followers) are generally reluctant to change. Are you more of an internalizer or an externalizer?

Work Application **3**

Select a present or past manager. For that person, decide which of the following traits is or was strongest and weakest: dominance, high energy, self-confidence, internal locus of control, and stability. Explain your answers.

Stability

Stability, the *adjustment* Big Five dimension, is associated with managerial effectiveness and advancement.[30] Being too emotional can cause problems.[31] Stable leaders are emotionally in control of themselves.[32] They don't let their anger have negative outcomes.[33] Unfortunately, there were and are some unstable leaders—such as Adolph Hitler—who misused power. Handling our emotions is a juggling act. Emotions help engage us in our work, but we also need to figure out what's going on with our feelings and then limit the impact.[34] It has also been shown that effective leaders have a good understanding of their own strengths and weaknesses, and they are oriented toward self-improvement rather than being defensive. This relates to effective leaders knowing when to lead and when to follow; they compensate for weaknesses by letting others with the strength lead in those areas. If you are an internalizer, you will tend to believe this; and if you are conscientious, you will work to improve yourself and advance.

Integrity

Integrity refers to behavior that is honest and ethical, making a person trustworthy. Integrity is the opposite of seeking self-interest at the expense of others; it's about being honest—no lying, cheating, or stealing.[35] Integrity is essential to running a successful business.[36] Therefore, we need to foster leadership integrity,[37] as our integrity affects our behavior.[38] Ethics will be discussed later in this chapter. To be viewed as trustworthy, leaders need to be honest, support their followers, and keep confidences. If followers find out their leader has been dishonest or in some way manipulated them for personal gain, the leader will lose the followers' trust. Honesty and trust are so important at CompUSA that any employee caught telling a lie is fired immediately; according to the CEO, "We all trust each other."[39] Integrity is categorized as the Big Five dimension of *conscientiousness,* but people who are dishonest can be emotionally unstable. Integrity tests are being used to successfully predict whether someone will steal, be absent, or otherwise take advantage of employers through dishonesty.[40] Do you have integrity?

Ethical **Dilemma 1**

Downsizing and Part-Time Workers

As firms struggle to compete in the global economy, many have downsized. *Downsizing* is the process of cutting resources to increase productivity. The primary area of cutting is human resources, which has led to layoffs. Another method of keeping costs down is using part-time employees who do not receive benefits (e.g., health care) rather than full-time employees who receive benefits.

Wal-Mart is known for having a heavy ratio of part- to full-time employees to keep costs down. Wal-Mart is expanding its sales of grocery items, competing directly with supermarket chains. One of the reasons Wal-Mart has lower prices is because it uses mostly part-time workers at or close to minimum wage and without benefits. Most supermarket chain employees are unionized and get higher wages and more benefits, and they want better pay and benefits. But supermarket chains state that they can't afford to pay more; they must compete with Wal-Mart.

1. Do you view Wal-Mart as a company with integrity?
2. Is downsizing ethical and socially responsible?
3. Is using part-time employees, rather than full-time, ethical and socially responsible?

Intelligence

Intelligence refers to cognitive ability to think critically, to solve problems, and to make decisions. It is also referred to as general mental ability. Intelligence is the best predictor of job performance.[41] The manager's job calls for a high degree of intelligence,[42] and leaders generally have above-average intelligence.[43] Neuroscientists are finding that business leaders may think differently.[44] Contemporary research suggests going beyond conventional intelligence quotient (IQ) measures to multiple intelligence. Simply, multiple intelligence means that people are better at some things than others. Intelligence has been categorized with the Big Five *openness-to-experience* dimension. Being in college implies that you most likely have above-average intelligence. This is one reason why most college graduates get better jobs and are paid more than those who do not go to (or finish) college.

Emotional Intelligence

An offshoot of IQ is EQ (emotional quotient—EQ or emotional intelligence—EI). EI is the ability to work well with people, and EI is essential to healthy relationships.[45] EI increases job performance,[46] as EQ can outweigh IQ when it comes to personal achievement.[47] EI has been touted as a silver-bullet.[48] Jeff Taylor, founder of Monster.com, and Matt Goldman, cofounder of Blue Man Group, recommend developing your people skills, or your EI. Procter & Gamble hires for EI.[49] Many organizations, including Intel, Sun Microsystems, Netscape, Advanced Micro Devices, and Lucent Technologies, have their employees attend EQ training programs to build better relationships. There are four components of EQ:[50]

- **Self-awareness** *relates to being conscious of your emotions and how they affect your personal and professional life.* Self-awareness is the cornerstone of all insight.[51] Use your self-awareness (the exercises in this book help) to accurately assess your strengths and limitations, which leads to higher self-confidence.
- **Social awareness** *relates to the ability to understand others.* Steve Case, cofounder of America Online, recommends developing your empathy skills. Empathy is the ability to put yourself in other people's situations, sense their emotions, and understand things from their perspective.[52] Social awareness also includes the ability to develop networks and play organizational politics, which we discuss in Chapter 4.
- **Self-management** *relates to the ability to control disruptive emotions.* Successful leaders don't let negative emotions (worry, anxiety, fear, anger) interfere with getting things done.[53] Characteristics of self-management include self-motivation, integrity, conscientiousness, adaptability, and optimism. Optimism can be learned, so think and be positive.[54]
- **Relationship management** *relates to the ability to work well with others,* which is dependent on the other three EI components. Successful leaders build effective relationships by communicating, responding to emotions, handling conflict, and influencing others. Most of this book focuses on developing relationship management skills.

These four components of EI explain the way we manage emotions. Note that these components are included in the AACSB learning standards. EI is related to the Big Five personality dimension of *adjustment* and to some extent *agreeableness.* How high is your EI?

Flexibility

Flexibility refers to the ability to adjust to different situations. Recall that leaders who set objectives and possess the ability to influence others bring about change. Leaders need to stay ahead of the immense number of changes in the world, and the pace of change will continue to increase. Without flexibility, you will not be successful.[55] Thus, effective leaders are flexible and adapt to the situation. A general manager of the Hewlett-Packard Medical Products Group said that change is painful and someone may have to be the bad guy. You need to charge ahead, accepting that not everyone will follow. Flexibility is categorized with the Big Five *openness-to-experience* dimension. Are you flexible?

Sensitivity to Others

Sensitivity to others refers to understanding group members as individuals, what their positions on issues are, and how best to communicate with and influence them. To be sensitive to others requires EI. Lack of sensitivity is part of the reason for executive derailment. You need to have and convey an interest in other people. Sensitivity means not focusing on putting yourself first and remembering that the more you help others, the more you get in return. Sensitivity is critical when playing the negotiator leadership role. If you are concerned only about yourself and don't understand what the other party wants, you probably will not be very successful. You will learn how to negotiate in Chapter 4. Sensitivity to others is categorized as the Big Five dimension of *agreeableness*. Are you sensitive to others?

Work Application 4

Select a present or past manager. For that person, decide which of the following traits is or was strongest and weakest: integrity, intelligence, flexibility, and sensitivity to others. Explain your answers.

Applying the **Concept 2**

Personality Traits of Effective Leaders

Identify each of the following eight behaviors by its trait. The leader may be behaving effectively, or the behavior may be the opposite of the effective trait behavior. Write the appropriate letter in the blank before each item.

a. dominance	d. internal locus of control	g. intelligence
b. high energy	e. stability	h. flexibility
c. self-confidence	f. integrity	i. sensitivity to others

____ 8. The leader is engaged in getting the production line working.

____ 9. The leader is acting very nervous while she is disciplining an employee.

____ 10. The leader tells a follower that he can have Tuesday off next week. But the next day, the leader tells the follower that he has changed his mind.

____ 11. The leader very attentively listens to the follower complain, then paraphrases the complaint back to the follower.

____ 12. The leader in situation 8 above is still working to solve the problem; it's her fifth attempt.

____ 13. The leader is telling her manager that her unit's poor performance is not her fault; she says that the employees are lazy and there's nothing she can do to improve performance.

____ 14. The leader is telling his manager that his department is right on schedule to meet the deadline, hoping that he can catch up before the boss finds out.

____ 15. The leader assigns a task to one follower, giving him very specific instructions. Then the leader gives another assignment to a different follower, telling her to complete the task any way she wants to.

Opening Case APPLICATION

2. What traits of effective leaders does Lorraine Monroe possess?

She has dominance, high energy, and self-confidence, and she founded and led two leadership institutes and was a high school principal. Monroe is an internalizer (locus of control); she believed she could turn a poorly performing high school into a top performer. The key to Monroe's leadership success in high school was her stability and integrity, and the teachers trusted and followed her to success. She is intelligent, holding a doctorate degree, but she also has emotional intelligence to motivate others to achieve her vision. Monroe is flexible, as shown in her doctrine where she suggests breaking the rules to meet your mission. Her sensitivity to students and faculty was critical to the successful turnaround of Frederick Douglass Academy.

The Personality Profile of Effective Leaders

Effective leaders have specific personality traits.[56] McClelland's trait theories of Achievement Motivation Theory and Leader Motive Profile Theory have strong research support and a great deal of relevance to the practice of leadership. Achievement Motivation Theory identifies three major traits, which McClelland calls *needs*. Leader Motive Profile Theory identifies the personality profile of effective leaders. You will learn about both of these theories in this section.

Learning Outcome 5 *State how the Achievement Motivation Theory and the Leader Motive Profile are related and different.*

Achievement Motivation Theory

Achievement Motivation Theory *attempts to explain and predict behavior and performance based on a person's need for achievement, power, and affiliation.* The late David McClelland originally developed Achievement Motivation Theory in the 1940s.[57] He believed that we have needs and that our needs motivate us to satisfy them. Our behavior is thus motivated by our needs. However, McClelland says this is an unconscious process. He further states that needs are based on personality and are developed as we interact with the environment. All people possess the need for achievement, power, and affiliation, but to varying degrees. One of the three needs tends to be dominant in each one of us and motivates our behavior.

The Need for Achievement (n Ach)

The *need for achievement* is the unconscious concern for excellence in accomplishments through individual efforts. People with strong n Ach tend to have an internal locus of control, self-confidence, and high energy traits. High n Ach is categorized as the Big Five dimension of *conscientiousness.* People with high n Ach tend to be characterized as wanting to take personal responsibility for solving problems. They are goal oriented and set moderate, realistic, attainable goals. They seek challenge, excellence, and individuality; take calculated, moderate risk; desire concrete feedback on their performance; and work hard. People with high n Ach think about ways to do a better job, how to accomplish something unusual or important, and career progression. They perform well in nonroutine, challenging, and competitive situations, while people low in n Ach do not.

McClelland's research showed that only about 10 percent of the U.S. population has a "strong" dominant need for achievement. There is evidence of a correlation between high achievement need and high performance in the general population. People with high n Ach tend to enjoy entrepreneurial-type positions.

The Need for Power (n Pow)

The *need for power* is the unconscious concern for influencing others and seeking positions of authority. People with strong n Pow have the dominance trait and tend to be self-confident with high energy. High n Pow is categorized as the Big Five dimension of *surgency.* People with a high need for power tend to be characterized as wanting to control the situation, wanting influence or control over others, enjoying competition in which they can win (they don't like to lose), being willing to confront others, and seeking positions of authority and status. People with high n Pow tend to be ambitious and have a lower need for affiliation. They are more concerned about getting their own way (influencing others) than about what others think of them. They are attuned to power and politics as essential for successful leadership.

The Need for Affiliation (n Aff)

The *need for affiliation* is the unconscious concern for developing, maintaining, and restoring close personal relationships. People with strong n Aff have the trait of sensitivity to others. High n Aff is categorized as the Big Five dimension of *agreeableness*. People with high n Aff tend to be characterized as seeking close relationships with others, wanting to be liked by others, enjoying lots of social activities, and seeking to belong; so they join groups and organizations. People with high n Aff think about friends and relationships. They tend to enjoy developing, helping, and teaching others. They seek jobs as teachers, in human resource management, and in other helping professions. People with high n Aff are more concerned about what others think of them than about getting their own way (influencing others). n Aff is negatively related to leadership.[58] Those with a high n Aff tend to have a low n Pow; they tend to avoid management because they like to be one of the group rather than its leader.

Applying the **Concept 3**

Achievement Motivation Theory

Identify each of the five behaviors below by its need, writing the appropriate letter in the blank before each item. The person may be behaving based on a strong need, or the behavior may be the opposite, indicating a weak need. Also state how the behavior meets the need and predict the performance.

a. achievement b. power c. affiliation

____ 16. The person is refusing to be the spokesperson for the group.

____ 17. The person is going to talk to a fellow employee, with whom she had a disagreement earlier in the day, to peacefully resolve the conflict.

____ 18. The person is working hard to meet a difficult deadline.

____ 19. An accounting major has volunteered to calculate the financial analysis for the group's case and to make the presentation to the class.

____ 20. The fellow employee in situation 17 above has made up his mind that he will not be the first one to make a move to resolve the conflict with the other person; but when the other party comes to him, he will be receptive.

Your Motive Profile

Note that McClelland does not have a classification for the *adjustment* and *openness-to-experience* Big Five personality dimensions; they are not needs. A person can have a high or low need for achievement, power, and affiliation and be either well adjusted or not, and either open or closed to new experiences. So these two dimensions of personality are ignored in determining the Achievement Motivation Theory personality profile. Complete Self-Assessment 2 to determine your motive profile now.

SELF-ASSESSMENT 2

Motive Profile

Return to Self-Assessment 1 on page 32 and place the scores from your Big Five personality profile in the following blanks, next to their corresponding needs. On the number scale, circle your total score for each need.

Need for Achievement (conscientiousness)	**Need for Power** (surgency)	**Need for Affiliation** (agreeableness)
35	35	35
30	30	30
25	25	25
20	20	20
15	15	15
10	10	10
5	5	5
Total Score 30	Total Score 25	Total Score 15

There is no right or wrong score for this profile. To interpret your score, check to see if there is much difference between the three need scores. If all three are about the same, one need is not stronger than the others are. If scores vary, one need is higher than the others and is called the stronger or dominant need, and the lower score is the weaker need. You can also have other combinations, such as two stronger and one weaker, or vice versa. Do you have stronger and weaker needs?

Work Application 5

Explain how your need for achievement, power, and/or affiliation has affected your behavior and performance, or that of someone you work with or have worked with. Give an example of the behavior and performance, and list your predicted motive need.

Knowing a motive profile is useful, because it can explain and predict behavior and performance. For example, if you know people have a high need for affiliation, you can understand why they tend to have friends and get along well with people. You can predict that if they are assigned a job as a mentor, they will enjoy the tasks and display helpful, supportive behavior toward the mentoree and will do a good job. Complete Work Application 5, then read on to determine if you have the motive profile of an effective leader.

Leader Motive Profile Theory

Leader Motive Profile Theory *attempts to explain and predict leadership success based on a person's need for achievement, power, and affiliation.* McClelland found that effective leaders consistently have the same motive profile, and that Leader Motive Profile has been found to be a reliable predictor of leader effectiveness.[59] Let's first define the profile of effective leaders and then discuss why it results in success. *The* **Leader Motive Profile (LMP)** *includes a high need for power, which is socialized; that is, greater than the need for affiliation and with a moderate need for achievement.* The achievement score is usually somewhere between the power and affiliation score, and the reason is described below.

Power

Power is essential to leaders because it is a means of influencing followers. Without power, there is no leadership. To be successful, leaders need to want to be in charge and enjoy the leadership role. You will need power to influence your followers, peers, and higher-level managers. You will learn more about how to gain power and be successful in organizational politics in Chapter 4.

Socialized Power

McClelland further identified power as neither good nor bad. It can be used for personal gain at the expense of others (personalized power), or it can be used to help oneself and others (socialized power).[60] Social power is discussed later, with ethics. Effective leaders use socialized power, which includes the traits of sensitivity to others and stability, and is the Big Five *adjustment* dimension. Thus a person with a low need for affiliation can have a high sensitivity to others. McClelland's research supports the reasons for executive derailment, because these negative traits are personalized power. Socialized power is not included in the motive profile, so complete Self-Assessment 3 to determine your motive profile with socialized power.

Achievement

To be effective, leaders generally need to have a moderate need for achievement. They have high energy, self-confidence, and openness-to-experience traits, and they are *conscientious* (Big Five dimension). The reason for a moderate rather than a high need for achievement, which would include a lower need for power, is the danger of personalized power. People with a high need for achievement tend to seek individual achievement, and when they are not interested in being a leader, there is the chance for personalized power and derailment.

Affiliation

Effective leaders have a lower need for affiliation than power, so that relationships don't get in the way of influencing followers. If the achievement score is lower than that for affiliation, the probability of the following problems occurring may be increased. Leaders with high n Aff tend to have a lower need for power and are thus

SELF-ASSESSMENT 3

Motive Profile with Socialized Power

Return to Self-Assessment 1 on page 32 and place the scores from Self-Assessment 2 (your motive profile) in the following blanks. On the number scale, circle your total score.

Need for Achievement (conscientiousness)	**Need for Power** (surgency)	**Socialized Power** (adjustment)	**Need for Affiliation** (agreeableness)
35	35	35	35
30	30	30	30
25	25	25	25
20	20	20	20
15	15	15	15
10	10	10	10
5	5	5	5
Total Score ______	Total Score ______	Total Score ______	Total Score ______

Again, there is no right or wrong score. The adjustment score will give you an idea if your power is more social or personal. Also realize that the questions in Self-Assessment 1 (3, 8, 13, 18, and 23) are not totally focused on social power. Thus, if you believe you have higher sensitivity to others, your score on McClelland's LMP could be higher.

reluctant to play the bad-guy role, such as disciplining and influencing followers to do things they would rather not do—like change. They have been found to show favoritism behavior toward their friends. However, recall that effective leaders do have concern for followers—socialized power.

Work Application 6

Make an intelligent guess about your present or past manager's motive profile. Is it an LMP? Explain.

The Leader Motive Profile is included in the definition of leadership. Our definition of leadership includes the five key elements of leadership (see Exhibit 1.1 on page 6) in the LMP. Our definition of leadership includes *influencing* and *leaders–followers* (power) and getting along with *people* (social power). It also includes *organizational objectives* (which achievers set and accomplish well) and *change* (which achievers are open to).

Opening Case APPLICATION

3. Does Lorraine Monroe have the personality profile of an effective leader? And what does she say in response to businesspeople who continually ask her, "What makes a good leader?"

Lorraine Monroe has an LMP. Her need for power is illustrated through being a school principal and founding two leadership institutes to train leaders. Monroe has a socialized need for power since she shows concern for students, teachers, and administrators. Her need for achievement leads to continued success. She also has a lower need for affiliation as she set standards for discipline in school, and she consistently observed teachers (although they complained at first), improving their performance.

Businesspeople continually ask Monroe, "What makes a good leader?" Part of her answer is that the leader is the person who keeps a vision in front of people and reminds them of their mission. Leaders need to give employees a sense of purpose beyond a paycheck, the feeling that they can make a difference, and something to be proud of. Leaders have high expectations and demand continuous measurable improvement through creativity. Employees have latent productivity; it is the leader's job to bring it out. Leaders demonstrate their ability. They walk around and watch people do their work and talk to them about improving as they give praise. Leaders treat people well, listen to what they have to say, do nice things for them, and get them together to talk so they feel connected.

Do you have an LMP? Complete Self-Assessment 4 now.

SELF-ASSESSMENT 4

Leadership Interest

Select the option that best describes your interest in leadership now.

_____ 1. I am, or want to become, a manager and leader.

_____ 2. I am, or want to become, a leader without being a manager.

_____ 3. I am not interested in being a leader; I want to be a follower.

If you want to be a leader, recall that research has shown that you can develop your leadership skills.

If you selected option 1, do you have an LMP? If you answered yes, it does not guarantee that you will climb the corporate ladder. However, having an LMP does increase your chances, because it is a predictor of leadership success. On the other hand, an LMP is not enough; you need leadership skills to be successful. If your Self-Assessment 3 score doesn't indicate that you have an LMP, go back to Self-Assessment 1 on page 32 and review questions 1, 6, 11, 16, and 21. Did you score them accurately? The most important question is 16. If you believe you have an LMP, be aware that your profile could be different using McClelland's LMP questionnaire. Also recall that not all successful leaders have an LMP; you can still be successful.

continued

(Self-Assessment 4 continued)

Developing your leadership skills, through effort, will increase your chances of leadership success.

If you selected option 2, don't be concerned about your LMP. Focus on developing your leadership skills. However, your personality profile can help you to better understand your strengths and weaknesses to identify areas to improve upon. This also holds true for people who selected option 1.

If you selected option 3, that's fine. Most people in the general population probably would select this option. Many professionals who have great jobs and incomes are followers, and they have no interest in becoming managers. However, recall that research has shown that leaders and followers need the same skills, that organizations are looking for employees with leadership skills, and that organizations conduct skills training with employees at all levels. To increase your chances of having a successful and satisfying career, you may want to develop your leadership skills. You may someday change your mind about becoming a leader and manager.

Your need for power and LMP can change over time, along with your interest in leadership and management and your skill level, regardless of which option you selected.

Before we go on to discuss leadership attitudes, let's review what we've covered so far in Exhibit 2.4 by putting together the Big Five Model of Personality, the nine traits of effective leaders, and Achievement Motivation Theory and LMP.

EXHIBIT 2.4 Combined Traits and Needs

The Big Five Model of Personality	Nine Traits of Effective Leaders	Achievement Motivation Theory and LMP
Surgency	Dominance	Need for power
Agreeableness	Sensitivity to others	Need for affliation
Adjustment	Stability	Socialized power (LMP)
Conscientiousness	High energy Self-confidence Integrity	Need for achievement
Openness to experience	Internal locus of control Intelligence Flexibility	No separate need; included within other needs

Leadership Attitudes

Attitudes *are positive or negative feelings about people, things, and issues.* We all have favorable or positive attitudes, and unfavorable or negative attitudes about life, work, school, leadership, and everything else. Job attitudes and performance are perhaps the two most central sets of constructs in individual-level organizational analysis research.[61] Employees with positive attitudinal states are more willing to work hard,[62] and attitudes help to explain and predict job performance.[63] W. Marriott, Jr., president of Marriott Corporation, stated that the company's success depends more upon employee attitudes than any other single factor. Legendary football coach Lou Holtz says that attitude is the most important thing in this world and that we each choose the attitude we have. So, being a positive or negative person is your choice. Successful leaders have positive, optimistic attitudes. Do you?

In this section, we'll discuss how leadership attitudes relate to Theory X and Theory Y, and how the Pygmalion effect influences followers' behavior and performance. Then we will discuss self-concept and how it affects the leader's behavior and performance. Lastly, we will consider how the leader's attitudes about followers, and about his or her self-concept, affect the leadership style of the leader.

Learning Outcome 6 *Identify similarities and differences among Theory X and Theory Y, the Pygmalion effect, and self-concept.*

Theory X and Theory Y

Today, **Theory X and Theory Y** *attempt to explain and predict leadership behavior and performance based on the leader's attitude about followers.* Before you read about Theory X and Y, complete Self-Assessment 5.

SELF-ASSESSMENT 5

Theory X and Theory Y Attitudes

For each pair of statements distribute 5 points, based on how characteristic each statement is of your attitude or belief system. If the first statement totally reflects your attitude and the second does not, give 5 points to the first and 0 to the second. If it's the opposite, use 0 and 5. If the statement is usually your attitude, then distribution can be 4 and 1, or 1 and 4. If both statements reflect your attitude, the distribution should be 3 and 2, or 2 and 3. Again, the combined score for each pair of statements must equal 5.

Here are the scoring distributions for each pair of statements:

0–5 or 5–0 One of the statements is totally like you, the other not like you at all.

1–4 or 4–1 One statement is usually like you, the other not.

2–3 or 3–2 Both statements are like you, although one is slightly more like you.

_____ 1. People enjoy working.

_____ People do not like to work.

_____ 2. Employees don't have to be closely supervised to do their job well.

_____ Employees will not do a good job unless you closely supervise them.

_____ 3. Employees will do a task well for you if you ask them to.

_____ If you want something done right, you need to do it yourself.

_____ 4. Employees want to be involved in making decisions.

_____ Employees want the managers to make the decisions.

_____ 5. Employees will do their best work if you allow them to do the job their own way.

_____ Employees will do their best work if they are taught how to do it the one best way.

_____ 6. Managers should let employees have full access to information that is not confidential.

_____ Managers should give employees only the information they need to know to do their job.

_____ 7. If the manager is not around, the employees will work just as hard.

_____ If the manager is not around, the employees will take it easier than when being watched.

_____ 8. Managers should share the management responsibilities with group members.

_____ Managers should perform the management functions for the group.

To determine your attitude or belief system about people at work, add up the numbers (0–5) for the first statement in each pair; don't bother adding the numbers for the second statements. The total should be between 0 and 40. Place your score on the continuum below.

Theory X 0—5—10—15—20—25—30—35—40 *Theory Y*

Generally, the higher your score, the greater are your Theory Y beliefs, and the lower the score, the greater your Theory X beliefs.

Douglas McGregor classified attitudes or belief systems, which he called assumptions, as *Theory X* and *Theory Y*.[64] People with Theory X attitudes hold that employees dislike work and must be closely supervised in order to do their work. Theory Y attitudes hold that employees like to work and do not need to be closely supervised in order to do their work. In each of the eight pairs of statements in Self-Assessment 5, the first lines are Theory Y attitudes and the second lines are Theory X attitudes.

Managers with Theory X attitudes tend to have a negative, pessimistic view of employees and display more coercive, autocratic leadership styles using external means of controls, such as threats and punishment. Managers with Theory Y attitudes tend to have a positive, optimistic view of employees and display more participative leadership styles using internal motivation and rewards. In 1966 when McGregor published his Theory X and Theory Y, most managers had Theory X attitudes, and he was calling for a change to Theory Y attitudes. More recently, the paradigm shift from management to leadership also reflects this change in attitudes, as more managers use participative leadership styles.[65]

A study of over 12,000 managers explored the relationship between managerial achievement and attitudes toward subordinates.[66] The managers with Theory Y attitudes were better at accomplishing organizational objectives and better at tapping the potential of subordinates. The managers with strong Theory X attitudes were far more likely to be in the low-achieving group. If you scored higher in Theory X for Self-Assessment 5, it does not mean that you cannot be an effective leader. As with personality traits, you can change your attitudes, with effort. You don't have to be an autocratic leader.

The Pygmalion Effect

The **Pygmalion effect** *proposes that leaders' attitudes toward and expectations of followers, and their treatment of them, explain and predict followers' behavior and performance.* Research by J. Sterling Livingston popularized this theory, and others have supported it as discussed here.[67] We have already talked about attitudes and how they affect behavior (how to treat others) and performance, so let's add expectations. In business, expectations are stated as objectives and standards. Effective leaders train ordinary employes to do a great job.[68]

In a study of welding students, the foreman who was training the group was given the names of students who were quite intelligent and would do well. Actually, the students were selected at random. The only difference was the foreman's expectations. The so-called intelligent students did significantly outperform the other group members. Why this happened is what this theory is all about: The teacher's expectations influenced the behavior and performance of the students.[69]

Lou Holtz advises setting a higher standard; the worst disservice you can do as a coach, teacher, parent, or leader is to say to your followers, "I don't think you are capable of doing very much—so I'm going to lower the standard," or just to do it without saying anything. Holtz says there are two kinds of leaders: those who are optimists and lift others up, and those who pull everybody down. If you are in a leadership role, don't worry about being popular; worry about raising the self-image and productivity of your followers.

Work Application 7

Give an example of when a person (parent, friend, teacher, coach, manager) really expected you either to perform well or to fail, and treated you like you would, which resulted in your success or failure.

Opening Case APPLICATION

4. How did "attitude" help change the performance of Frederick Douglass Academy?

A major factor in Lorraine Monroe's turning Harlem's Frederick Douglass Academy from a poor performer into a high performer, with 96 percent of inner-city graduates going on to college, was through her Theory Y attitude and use of the Pygmalion effect. Monroe encouraged her faculty to be creative and try new things. Unlike the trend of most educators, she set higher standards and treated students and teachers like capable winners—which they became.

Self-Concept

So far, we have discussed the leaders' attitudes about followers. Now we will examine leaders' attitudes about themselves. **Self-concept** *refers to the positive or negative attitudes people have about themselves.* If you have a positive view of yourself as being a capable person, you will tend to have the positive self-confidence trait.[70] A related concept, *self-efficacy,* is the belief in your own capability to perform in a specific situation. Self-efficacy is based on self-concept and is closely related to the self-confidence trait, because if you believe you can be successful, you will often have self-confidence.

There is a lot of truth in the saying, "if you think you can, you can; if you think you can't, you can't." Recall times when you had positive self-efficacy and were successful or negative self-efficacy and failed. Think of sports: sinking a basket, getting a goal or a hit. Think of school: passing a test or getting a good grade on an assignment. Think of work: completing a task, meeting a deadline, making a sale, or solving a problem. Successful leaders have positive attitudes with strong self-concepts, are optimistic, and believe they can make a positive difference.[71] If you don't believe you can be a successful leader, you probably won't be.

Opening Case APPLICATION

5. How did Lorraine Monroe's self-concept affect her leadership?

Lorraine Monroe grew up in Harlem and went to its public schools. Her parents did not go to college, but they did teach her to never doubt that she could do whatever she applied herself to accomplish. If she did not believe she could successfully turn the academy around, things would not have changed. Monroe began her leadership training in school. For example, she served as class president in high school. As stated in her doctrine, "Becoming a leader is an act of self-invention. Imagine yourself as a leader: Act as if you are a leader until you actually become one."

Developing a More Positive Attitude and Self-Concept

Your behavior and performance will be consistent with the way you see yourself.[72] Think and act like a winner, and you may become one. Following are some ideas to help you change your attitudes and develop a more positive self-concept:

1. *Consciously try to have and maintain a positive, optimistic attitude.* If you don't have a positive attitude, it may be caused by your unconscious thoughts and behavior. Only with conscious effort can you improve your self-concept.
2. *Realize that there are few, if any, benefits to negative, pessimistic attitudes about others and yourself.* Do holding a grudge, worrying, and being afraid of failure help you to succeed?
3. *Cultivate optimistic thoughts.* Scientific evidence suggests that your thoughts affect every cell in your body. Every time you think positive thoughts, your body, mind, and spirit respond. You will likely feel more motivated and energetic. Use positive self-talk—I will do a good job; it will be done on time; and so on. Also use mental imagery—picture yourself achieving your goal.
4. *If you catch yourself complaining or being negative in any way, stop and change to a positive attitude.* With time, you will catch yourself less often as you become more positive about yourself.

5. *Avoid negative people, especially any that make you feel negative about yourself.* Associate with people who have a positive self-concept, and use their positive behavior.
6. *Set and achieve goals.* Set short-term goals (daily, weekly, monthly) that you can achieve. Achieving specific goals will improve your self-concept, helping you to view yourself as successful.
7. *Focus on your success; don't dwell on failure.* If you achieve five of six goals, dwell on the five and forget the one you missed. We are all going to make mistakes and experience failure. Winston Churchill defined success as the ability to go from failure to failure without losing your enthusiasm. The difference between effective leaders and less-effective leaders is that the successful ones learn from their mistakes. They bounce back from disappointment and don't let it affect them negatively in the future. Lou Holtz says happiness is nothing more than a poor memory for the bad things that happen to you.
8. *Accept compliments.* When someone compliments you, say thank you; it builds self-concept. Don't say things like it was nothing, or anyone could have done it, because you lose the opportunity for a buildup.
9. *Don't belittle accomplishments or compare yourself to others.* If you meet a goal and say it was easy anyway, you are being negative. If you compare yourself to someone else and say they are better, you are being negative. No matter how good you are, there is almost always someone better. So focus on being the best that you can be, rather than putting yourself down for not being the best.
10. *Think for yourself.* Develop your own attitudes based on others' input; don't simply copy others' attitudes.
11. *Be a positive role model.* If the leader has a positive attitude, the followers usually do too. We can choose to be optimistic or pessimistic—and we usually find what we are looking for. If you look for the positive, you are likely to be happier and get more out of life; why look for the negative and be unhappy? Even when the worst in life happens to you, you have the choice of being positive or negative. Christopher Reeve was a successful film star, best known as Superman, until he fell off a horse and was paralyzed. Rather than being bitter and negative toward life, and sitting at home feeling sorry for himself, Reeve started a foundation (The Christopher Reeve Foundation) to raise money to develop a cure for spinal cord injuries. Reeve raised millions of dollars by getting out and asking for donations. He also starred in a TV movie and was a director. During an interview, he said, "I'm actually busier now than I was before the accident. I find work more fulfilling than ever." When asked how he maintained a positive attitude that kept him going, he said, "I believe you have two choices in life. One is to look forward and the other is to look backwards. To look backwards gets you nowhere. Backwards thinking leads to a place of negativity. That's not where I want to dwell."[73] Hopefully, your disappointments in life will not be so dramatic. But we all have disappointments in life, and we have the choice of going on with a positive or negative attitude. Here's one final tip.
12. *When things go wrong and you're feeling down, do something to help someone who is worse off than you.* You will realize that you don't have it so bad, and you will realize that the more you give, the more you get. Volunteering at a hospital, soup kitchen, or becoming a Big Brother or Sister can help change your attitude. This is also a great cure for loneliness.

Learning Outcome 7 *Describe how attitudes are used to develop four leadership styles.*

How Attitudes Develop Leadership Styles

We now put together the leader's attitudes toward others, using Theory X and Theory Y, and the leader's attitude toward self, using self-concept, to illustrate how these two sets of attitudes develop into four leadership styles. Combining attitudes with the Leader Motive Profile (LMP), an effective leader tends to have Theory Y attitudes with a positive self-concept. See Exhibit 2.5 to understand how attitudes toward self and others affect leadership styles.

Work Application 8

Recall a present or past manager. Using Exhibit 2.5, which combinations of attitudes best describe your manager's leadership style? Give examples of the manager's behavior that illustrate his or her attitudes.

EXHIBIT 2.5 Leadership Styles Based on Attitudes

	Theory Y Attitudes	Theory X Attitudes
Positive self-concept	The leader typically gives and accepts positive feedback, expects others to succeed, and lets others do the job their way.	The leader typically is bossy, pushy, and impatient; does much criticizing with little praising; and is very autocratic.
Negative self-concept	The leader typically is afraid to make decisions, is unassertive, and is self-blaming when things go wrong.	The leader typically blames others when things go wrong, is pessimistic about resolving personal or organizational problems, and promotes a feeling of hopelessness among followers.

Ethical Leadership

Before we discuss ethical behavior, complete Self-Assessment 6 to find out how ethical your behavior is.

SELF-ASSESSMENT 6

How Ethical Is Your Behavior?

For this exercise, you will be using the same set of statements twice. The first time you answer them, focus on your own behavior and the frequency with which you use it for each question. On the line before the question number, place the number 1–4 that represents how often you "did do" the behavior in the past, if you "do the behavior now," or if you "would do" the behavior if you had the chance.

These numbers will allow you to determine your level of ethics. You can be honest without fear of having to tell others your score in class. *Sharing ethics scores is not part of the exercise.*

Frequently			Never
1	2	3	4

The second time you use the same statements, focus on other people in an organization that you work/worked for. Place an "O" on the line after the number if you observed someone doing this behavior. Also place an "R" on the line if you reported (whistle-blowing) this behavior within the organization or externally.

O—observed R—reported

continued

(Self-Assessment 6 continued)

1–4 O–R

College

4 1. R Cheating on homework assignments.

4 2. R Cheating on exams.

4 3. R Passing in papers that were completed by someone else, as your own work.

Workplace

4 4. O Lying to others to get what you want or stay out of trouble.

4 5. O Coming to work late, leaving work early, taking long breaks/lunches and getting paid for it.

4 6. R Socializing, goofing off, or doing personal work rather than doing the work that should be done and getting paid for it.

3 7. O Calling in sick to get a day off, when not sick.

4 8. R Using the organization's phone, computer, Internet, copier, mail, car, and so on for personal use.

4 9. O Taking home company tools/equipment for personal use without permission and then returning them/it.

4 10. O Taking home organizational supplies or merchandise and keeping it.

4 11. R Giving company supplies or merchandise to friends or allowing them to take them without saying anything.

4 12. O Putting in for reimbursement for meals and travel or other expenses that weren't actually eaten or taken.

4 13. O Taking spouse/friends out to eat or on business trips and charging it to the organizational expense account.

4 14. O Accepting gifts from customers/suppliers in exchange for giving them business.

4 15. O Cheating on your taxes.

4 16. R Misleading customers to make a sale, such as short delivery dates.

4 17. ___ Misleading competitors to get information to use to compete against them, such as saying/pretending to be a customer/supplier.

4 18. ___ Manipulating data to make you look good, or others bad.

4 19. O Selling more of the product than the customer needs, to get the commission.

4 20. O Spreading false rumors about coworkers or competitors to make yourself look better for advancement or to make more sales.

4 21. R Lying for your boss when asked/told to do so.

4 22. R Deleting information that makes you look bad or changing information to look better than actual results—false information.

4 23. R Being pressured, or pressuring others, to sign off on documents with false information.

4 24. O Being pressured, or pressuring others, to sign off on documents you haven't read, knowing they may contain information or decisions that might be considered inappropriate.

4 25. ___ If you were to give this assessment to a person you work with and with whom you do not get along very well, would she agree with your answers? Use a scale of yes 4—1 on the line before the number 25 and skip O or R.

Other Unethical Behavior:

Add other unethical behaviors you observed. Identify if you reported the behavior by using R.

26. ___

27. ___

28. ___

Note: This self-assessment is not meant to be a precise measure of your ethical behavior. It is designed to get you thinking about ethics and your behavior and that of others from an ethical perspective. There is no right or wrong score; however, each of these actions is considered unethical behavior in most organizations. Another ethical issue of this exercise is your honesty when rating the frequencies of your behavior. How honest were you?

Scoring: To determine your ethics score, add the numbers 1–4. Your total will be between 25 and 100. Place the number here 99 and on the continuum below that represents your score. The higher your score, the more ethical is your behavior, and vice versa for lower scores.

25—30—40—50—60—70—80—90—100

Unethical *Ethical*

It has been said that a culture of lying is infecting American business. A recent survey found that over two-thirds (71 percent) of Americans rated corporations low for operating in a fair and honest manner.[74] Ethics is so important that some large organizations have ethics officers who are responsible for developing and implementing ethics codes. **Ethics** *are the standards of right and wrong that influence behavior.* Right behavior is considered ethical, and wrong behavior is considered unethical. Business ethics, and ethics codes, guide and constrain everyday business conduct.[75]

Government laws and regulations are designed to help keep business honest. After the unethical and illegal business practices of WorldCom, Enron, and Arthur Andersen, Congress passed the Sarbanes-Oxley Act of 2002 to help ensure that complaints about financial irregularities would surface and be swiftly acted upon, without retaliation against the person who exposed the unethical behavior ("whistleblower"). However, the government can't make people be ethical.

In this section, you will learn that ethical behavior does pay; how personality traits and attitudes, moral development, and the situation affect ethical behavior; how people justify unethical behavior; some simple guides to ethical behavior, and about being an ethical leader.

Does Ethical Behavior Pay?

Generally, the answer is yes. Research studies have reported a positive relationship between ethical behavior and leadership effectiveness.[76] It pays to be ethical.[77] From the societal level of analysis, the public has a negative image of big business. Enron's unethical behavior cost many organizations and people a great deal of money directly, but it also hurt everyone in the stock market, and the general economy. From the organizational level, Enron is no longer the company it was, and its auditor Arthur Andersen lost many of its clients and had to sell most of its business due to unethical behavior. From the individual level, you may say that people like former Enron executives made millions for their unethical behavior. However, some went to prison, and they may never hold high-level positions again. With all the negative media coverage, unethical leaders' lives will never be the same. Unethical employees have helped ruin organizations and the lives of countless stakeholders.[78] Employee deviant behavior (theft, abuse of privileges, lack of regard for cost control or quality) costs businesses more than $20 billion annually, and is the cause of 30 percent of business failures.[79] CEOs need to be honest and lead with integrity.[80] Values and ethics are essential to running a successful business.[81] Thus, corporate recruiters are seeking ethical job candidates.[82]

Learning Outcome 8 *Compare the three levels of moral development.*

How Personality Traits and Attitudes, Moral Development, and the Situation Affect Ethical Behavior

Personality Traits and Attitudes

Our ethical behavior is related to our individual needs and personality traits.[83] Leaders with surgency (dominance) personality traits have two choices: to use power for personal benefit or to use socialized power. To gain power and to be conscientious with high achievement, some people will use unethical behavior; also, irresponsible people often do not perform to standard by cutting corners and other behavior which may be considered unethical. An agreeableness personality sensitive to others can lead to following the crowd in either ethical or unethical behavior; having a high self-concept tends to lead to doing what the person believes is right and not following the crowd's unethical behavior. Emotionally unstable people and those with external locus of control (they do not take personal responsibility for their behavior—it is not their fault) are more likely to use unethical behavior. Being ethical is part of integrity. People open to new experiences are often ethical. People with positive attitudes about ethics tend to be more ethical than those with negative or weak attitudes about ethics. But personality alone is not a good predictor of unethical behavior.[84]

Moral Development

A second factor affecting ethical behavior is *moral development,* which refers to understanding right from wrong and choosing to do the right thing.[85] Our ability to make ethical choices is related to our level of moral development.[86] There are three levels of personal moral development, as discussed in Exhibit 2.6.

EXHIBIT 2.6 Levels of Moral Development

3. Postconventional

Behavior is motivated by universal principles of right and wrong, regardless of the expectations of the leader or group. One seeks to balance the concerns for self with those of others and the common good. He or she will follow ethical principles even if they violate the law at the risk of social rejection, economic loss, and physical punishment (Martin Luther King, Jr., broke what he considered unjust laws and spent time in jail seeking universal dignity and justice).

"I don't lie to customers because it is wrong."

The common leadership style is visionary and committed to serving others and a higher cause while empowering followers to reach this level.

2. Conventional

Living up to expectations of acceptable behavior defined by others motivates behavior to fulfill duties and obligations. It is common for followers to copy the behavior of the leaders and group. If the group (can be society/organization/department) accepts lying, cheating, stealing, and so on, when dealing with customers/suppliers/government/competitors, so will the individual. On the other hand, if these behaviors are not accepted, the individual will not do them either. Peer pressure is used to enforce group norms.

"I lie to customers because the other sales reps do it too."

It is common for lower-level managers to use a similar leadership style of the higher-level managers.

1. Preconventional

Self-interest motivates behavior to meet one's own needs to gain rewards while following rules and being obedient to authority to avoid punishment.

"I lie to customers to sell more products and get higher commission checks."

The common leadership style is autocratic toward others while using one's position for personal advantage.

Source: Adapted from Lawrence Kohlberg, "Moral Stages and Moralization: The Cognitive-Development Approach." In Thomas Likona (ed.), Moral Development and Behavior: Theory, Research, and Social Issues *(Austin, TX: Holt, Rinehart and Winston, 1976), 31–53.*

At the first level, preconventional, you choose right and wrong behavior based on your self-interest and the consequences (reward and punishment). People at this level often end up using unethical behavior not only because it was to their advantage, but also because they had created their own rationale for what was acceptable.[87] Therefore, there is a need for codes of ethics in order to standardize ethical behavior. With ethical reasoning at the second level, conventional, you

Work Application 9

Give an organizational example of behavior at each of the three levels of moral development.

seek to maintain expected standards and live up to the expectations of others. One does what the others do. Around 60 percent of workers admit to stealing pens and pencils from their office supply rooms,[88] at an estimated cost to businesses of $52 billion a year.[89] Does this mean it is ethical? At the third level, postconventional, you make an effort to define moral principles regardless of leader or group ethics. Although most of us have the ability to reach the third level of moral development, postconventional, only about 20 percent of people reach this level.

Most people behave at the second level, conventional, while some have not advanced beyond the first level, preconventional. How do you handle peer pressure? What level of moral development are you on? What can you do to further develop your ethical behavior? We will discuss how to be an ethical leader.

The Situation

Our third factor affecting ethical behavior is the situation. People consider the situational forces in determining ethical conduct.[90] Highly competitive and unsupervised situations increase the odds of unethical behavior. Unethical behavior occurs more often when there is no formal ethics policy or code of ethics, and when unethical behavior is not punished, and it is especially prevalent when it is rewarded. People are also less likely to report unethical behavior (blow the whistle) when they perceive the violation as not being serious and when the offenders are their friends.[91]

To tie the three factors affecting ethical behavior together, we need to realize that personality traits and attitudes and moral development interact with the situation to determine if a person will use ethical or unethical behavior.[92] In this chapter we use the individual level of analysis, meaning: Am I ethical, and how can I improve my ethical behavior? At the organizational level, many firms offer training programs and develop codes of ethics to help employees behave ethically. The organizational level of analysis is examined in Part Three of this book; therefore, ethics and whistleblowing will be further discussed in Chapter 10.

6. What role did ethics play in changing the performance of Frederick Douglass Academy?

As discussed thus far, Lorraine Monroe possesses the traits and attitudes of effective leaders; therefore, we can assume that she uses ethical behavior. Monroe is on the postconventional level of moral development. During her consulting, ethics is an important issue. As a school principal, in her "Twelve Non-Negotiable Rules," Monroe made it clear what ethical behavior was and rewarded it, and what unethical behavior was and punished it. Ethics played a role in transforming Frederick Douglass Academy.

How People Justify Unethical Behavior

Most people understand right and wrong behavior and have a conscience. So why do good people do bad things? When most people use unethical behavior, it is not due to some type of character flaw or being born a bad person. Few people see themselves as unethical. We all want to view ourselves in a positive manner. Therefore, when we do use unethical behavior, we often justify the behavior to protect our self-concept so that we don't have a guilty conscience or feel remorse. We *rationalize* with statements like "everybody does it" and "I deserve it."[93] Let's discuss several thinking processes used to justify unethical behavior.

Moral justification *is the process of reinterpreting immoral behavior in terms of a higher purpose.* The terrorists of 9/11 killed innocent people, as do suicide bombers; yet they believe their killing is for the good and that they will go to heaven for their actions. People state that they have conducted unethical behavior (lie about a competitor to hurt its reputation, fix prices, steal confidential information, and so on) for the good of the organization or employees.

People at the postconventional level of moral development may seek higher purpose (Martin Luther King, Jr.), as well as those at lower levels. However, people at the preconventional and conventional levels of moral development more commonly use the following justifications:

- **Displacement of responsibility** *is the process of blaming one's unethical behavior on others.* "I was only following orders; my boss told me to inflate the figures."
- **Diffusion of responsibility** *is the process of the group using the unethical behavior with no one person being held responsible.* "We all take bribes/kickbacks; it's the way we do business," or "We all take merchandise home (steal)." As related to conventional morality, peer pressure is used to enforce group norms.[94]
- **Advantageous comparison** *is the process of comparing oneself to others who are worse.* "I call in sick when I'm not sick only a few times a year; Tom and Ellen do it all the time." "We pollute less than our competitors do."
- **Disregard or distortion of consequences** *is the process of minimizing the harm caused by the unethical behavior.* "If I inflate the figures, no one will be hurt and I will not get caught. And if I do, I'll just get a slap on the wrist anyway." Was this the case at Enron?
- **Attribution of blame** *is the process of claiming the unethical behavior was caused by someone else's behavior.* "It's my coworker's fault that I repeatedly hit him and put him in the hospital. He called me/did xxx, so I had to hit him."
- **Euphemistic labeling** *is the process of using "cosmetic" words to make the behavior sound acceptable. Terrorist group* sounds bad but *freedom fighter* sounds justifiable. *Misleading* or *covering up* sounds better than *lying to others.*

Which justification processes have you used? How can you improve your ethical behavior by not using justification?

Work Application 10

Give at least two organizational examples of unethical behavior and the process of justification.

Ethical **Dilemma 2**

Sex and Violence

Over the years, various social activist groups, including the Parents Television Council, the National Viewers and Listeners Association, and the National Coalition Against Censorship, have taken a stance for and against censorship of sex and violence on TV and in the movies. People call for more censorship to protect children from seeing sex and violence (many children watch as many as five hours of TV per day), while others don't want censorship, stating it violates free speech laws.

Advocates for less regulation state that TV shows like *CSI: Crime Scene Investigation* are shown late at night while children should not be watching. However, advocates of regulation state the fact than many daytime soap operas are sexual and that cable stations show reruns of major network shows in the daytime and early evening when children are watching. For example, many of the former *Seinfeld* shows were based on sexual themes, and the show was not aired until 9:00, but now it is shown on cable stations at all hours. *Sex and the City* is aired in California at 7:00.

1. Does the media (TV, movies, and music) influence societal values?
2. Does the media, with sex and violence, reflect current religious and societal values?

continued

(Ethical Dilemma 2 continued)

3. The Federal Communications Commission (FCC) has the power to regulate television. Should the FCC regulate the media, and if yes, how far should it go? Should it require toning down the sex and violence, or take shows like ***Sex and the City*** off the air?
4. Is it ethical and socially responsible to show sex and violence against women, and to portray women as sex objects?
5. Which of the six justifications of unethical behavior does the media use to defend sex and violence?

Simple Guides to Ethical Behavior

Every day in your personal and professional life, you face situations in which you can make ethical or unethical choices. As discussed, you make these choices based on your personality traits and attitudes, level of moral development, and the situation. Never misrepresent yourself.

Following are some guides that can help you make the right decisions.

Golden Rule

Following the golden rule will help you to use ethical behavior. The golden rule is:

"Do unto others as you want them to do unto you." Or, put other ways, "Don't do anything to other people that you would not want them to do to you." "Lead others as you want to be led."

Four-Way Test

Rotary International developed the four-way test of the things we think and do to guide business transactions. The four questions are (1) Is it the truth? (2) Is it fair to all concerned? (3) Will it build goodwill and better friendship? (4) Will it be beneficial to all concerned? When making your decision, if you can answer yes to these four questions, it is probably ethical.

Learning Outcome 9 *Explain the stakeholder approach to ethics.*

Stakeholder Approach to Ethics

Under the **stakeholder approach to ethics,** *one creates a win-win situation for relevant parties affected by the decision.* A win-win situation meets the needs of the organization and employees as well as those of other stakeholders, so that everyone benefits from the decision. The effective leader uses the moral exercise of power—socialized power, rather than personalized. Stakeholders include everyone affected by the decision, which may include followers, governments, customers, suppliers, society, stockholders, and so on. The higher up in management you go, the more stakeholders you have to deal with. You can ask yourself one simple question to help you determine if your decision is ethical from a stakeholder approach:

"Am I proud to tell relevant stakeholders my decision?"

If you are proud to tell relevant stakeholders your decision, it is probably ethical. If you are not proud to tell others your decision, or you keep justifying it, the decision may not be ethical. Justifying by saying everybody else does it is usually a cop-out. Everybody does *not* do it, and even if many others do it, that doesn't make it right. If you are not sure whether a decision is ethical, talk to your manager, higher-level managers, ethics committee members, and other people with high ethical standards. If you are reluctant to talk to others for advice on an ethical decision because you think you may not like their answers, the decision may not be ethical.

Being an Ethical Leader

Now let's focus on how to be an ethical leader, not necessarily an ethical manager. Most people are followers when it comes to ethics, and to some degree, silence means you are a follower despite your own personal conduct.[95] So you have to lead by example from the postconventional level, be one of the 20 percent by doing the right thing even when no one is looking, and you should blow the whistle when appropriate.

Ethical leadership requires *courage*—the ability to do the right thing at the risk of rejection and loss. Courage is difficult in an organization that focuses on getting along and fitting in without rocking the boat in order to get approval, promotions, and raises. It is difficult to say no when most others are saying yes, to go against the status quo and offer new alternatives to the group. Courage doesn't mean that you don't have doubt or fear rejection, ridicule, and loss; it means you do the right thing in spite of fear. You need to take risks to make change by speaking your mind and fighting for what you believe is right. Courage also requires taking responsibility for mistakes and failures, rather than trying to cover them up or blaming others when you do take risks.

You need to remember that moral values are important and that business is not just about making money; it's about meeting the needs of all stakeholders. It's not okay to lie. Any lie has hidden costs, not only in teamwork and productivity, but also in your own self-respect. One lie often leads to a trail of lies as you try to cover up the first lie. Once you start to lie, it's easy to continue on to bigger lies.[96] It is okay to blow the whistle.

People tend to make rapid judgments about ethical dilemmas. So slow down your decisions that affect various stakeholders. Seek out mentors who can advise you on ethical dilemmas. If you are a manager, make sure you lead by ethical example and enforce ethical standards. If you are not in power and observe unethical behavior and want to blow the whistle, go to someone higher in the organization who is committed to ethical behavior. If there are no higher-level managers who care about ethics, maybe you should search for another job.

Here are a few ways you can find courage to do the right thing:

- *Focus on a higher purpose,* such as helping or looking out for the well-being of customers and employees. FBI staff attorney Colleen Rowley, in Minneapolis, blew the whistle by sending a letter calling attention to the FBI shortcoming that may have contributed to the September 11, 2001, terrorist tragedy.
- *Draw strength from others.* People with courage often get it from the support of friends at work and/or a supporting family.
- *Take risks without fear of failure.* Accept the fact that we all fail at times and that failure leads to success. Thomas Edison had something like a thousand failures before he got the electric light to work. Learn from failure and don't repeat the same mistakes, but focus on the positive successes. Recall that happiness is nothing more than a poor memory for failure. Keep taking reasonable risks.
- *Use your frustration and anger for good.* When you observe unethical or ineffective wrong behavior, use your emotions to have the courage to take action to stop it and prevent it from happening again. When Warren Buffett took over Salomon Brothers it was full of scandals for unethical behavior. Buffett called a meeting with employees saying the unethical behavior had to stop. He was the compliance officer; he gave his home phone number and told employees to call him if anyone observed any unethical behavior.

Work Application **11**

Give examples of times when you or others you know had the courage to do what was right.

Go to the Internet (www.cengage.com/management/lussier)
where you will find a broad array of resources to help maximize your learning.

- **Review the vocabulary**
- **Try a quiz**
- **Find related links**

Chapter Summary

The chapter summary is organized to answer the ten learning outcomes for Chapter 2.

1. **List the benefits of classifying personality traits.**

   Classifying personality traits helps to explain and predict behavior and job performance.

2. **Describe the Big Five personality dimensions.**

   The *surgency* personality dimension includes leadership and extraversion traits. The *agreeableness* personality dimension includes traits related to getting along with people. The *adjustment* personality dimension includes traits related to emotional stability. The *conscientiousness* personality dimension includes traits related to achievement. The *openness-to-experience* personality dimension includes traits related to being willing to change and try new things.

3. **Explain the universality of traits of effective leaders.**

   Traits are universal in the sense that there are certain traits that most effective leaders have. However, traits are not universal in the sense that there is no one list of traits that is clearly accepted by all researchers, and not all effective leaders have all the traits.

4. **Discuss why the trait of dominance is so important for managers to have.**

   Because the dominance trait is based on the desire to be a leader, this trait affects the other traits in a positive or negative way based on that desire.

5. **State how the Achievement Motivation Theory and the Leader Motive Profile are related and different.**

   Achievement Motivation and Leader Motive Profile theories are related because both are based on the need for achievement, power, and affiliation. They are different because the Achievement Motivation Theory is a general motive profile for explaining and predicting behavior and performance, while the LMP is the one profile that specifically explains and predicts leadership success.

6. **Identify similarities and differences among Theory X and Theory Y, the Pygmalion effect, and self-concept.**

   The concept of Theory X and Theory Y is similar to the Pygmalion effect, because both theories focus on the leader's attitude about the followers. The Pygmalion effect extends Theory X and Theory Y attitudes by including the leader's expectations and how he or she treats the followers, using this information to explain and predict followers' behavior and performance. In contrast, Theory X and Theory Y focus on the leader's behavior and performance. Both approaches are different from self-concept because they examine the leader's attitudes about others, whereas self-concept relates to the leader's attitude about him- or herself. Self-concept is also different because it focuses on how the leader's attitude about him- or herself affects his or her behavior and performance.

7. **Describe how attitudes are used to develop four leadership styles.**

   The leader's attitude about others includes Theory Y (positive) and Theory X (negative) attitudes. The leader's attitude about him- or herself includes a positive self-concept or a negative self-concept. Combinations of these variables are used to identify four leadership styles: Theory Y positive self-concept, Theory Y negative self-concept, Theory X positive self-concept, and Theory X negative self-concept.

8. **Compare the three levels of moral development.**

   At the lowest level of moral development, preconventional, behavior is motivated by self-interest, seeking rewards, and avoiding punishment. At the second level, conventional, behavior is motivated by meeting the group's expectations to fit in by copying others' behavior. At the highest level, postconventional, behavior is motivated to do the right thing, at the risk of alienating the group. The higher the level of moral development, the more ethical is the behavior.

9. **Explain the stakeholder approach to ethics.**

   Under the stakeholder approach to ethics, the leader (or follower) creates a win-win situation for relevant parties affected by the decision. If you are proud to tell relevant stakeholders your decision, it is probably ethical. If you are not proud to tell others your decision, or you keep justifying it, the decision may not be ethical.

10. **Define the following key terms (in order of appearance in the chapter).**

    Select one or more methods: (1) fill in the missing key terms from memory; (2) match the key terms from the following list with their definitions below; (3) copy the key terms in order from the list at the beginning of the chapter.

__________ are distinguishing personal characteristics.

__________ is a combination of traits that classifies an individual's behavior.

__________ categorizes traits into the dimensions of surgency, agreeableness, adjustment, conscientiousness, and openness to experience.

__________ includes leadership and extraversion traits.

__________ includes traits related to getting along with people.

__________ includes traits related to emotional stability.

__________ includes traits related to achievement.

__________ includes traits related to being willing to change and try new things.

__________ identify individual stronger and weaker traits.

__________ relates to being conscious of your emotions and how they affect your personal and professional life.

__________ relates to the ability to understand others.

__________ relates to the ability to control disruptive emotions.

__________ relates to the ability to work well with others.

__________ attempts to explain and predict behavior and performance based on a person's need for achievement, power, and affiliation.

__________ attempts to explain and predict leadership success based on a person's need for achievement, power, and affiliation.

__________ includes a high need for power, which is socialized, that is, greater than the need for affiliation and with a moderate need for achievement.

__________ are positive or negative feelings about people, things, and issues.

__________ attempt to explain and predict leadership behavior and performance based on the leader's attitude about followers.

__________ proposes that leaders' attitudes toward and expectations of followers, and their treatment of them, explain and predict followers' behavior and performance.

__________ refers to the positive or negative attitudes people have about themselves.

__________ are the standards of right and wrong that influence behavior.

__________ is the process of reinterpreting immoral behavior in terms of a higher purpose.

__________ is the process of blaming one's unethical behavior on others.

__________ is the process of the group using the unethical behavior with no one person being held responsible.

__________ is the process of comparing oneself to others who are worse.

__________ is the process of minimizing the harm caused by the unethical behavior.

__________ is the process of claiming the unethical behavior was caused by someone else's behavior.

__________ is the process of using "cosmetic" words to make the behavior sound acceptable.

__________ creates a win-win situation for relevant parties affected by the decision.

Key Terms

Achievement Motivation Theory, 42

adjustment personality dimension, 35

advantageous comparison, 57

agreeableness personality dimension, 34

attitudes, 47

attribution of blame, 57

Big Five Model of Personality, 34

conscientiousness personality dimension, 35

diffusion of responsibility, 57

displacement of responsibility, 57

disregard or distortion of consequences, 57

ethics, 54

euphemistic labeling, 57

Leader Motive Profile (LMP), 44

Leader Motive Profile Theory, 44

moral justification, 56

openness-to-experience personality dimension, 35

personality, 33

personality profiles, 35

Pygmalion effect, 49

relationship management, 40

self-awareness, 40

self-concept, 50
self-management, 40
social awareness, 40
stakeholder approach to ethics, 58
surgency personality dimension, 34
Theory X and Theory Y, 48
traits, 33

Review Questions

1. What are the Big Five dimensions of traits?
2. What is the primary use of personality profiles?
3. What are some of the traits that describe the high-energy trait?
4. Is locus of control important to leaders? Why?
5. What does intelligence have to do with leadership?
6. Does sensitivity to others mean that the leader does what the followers want to do?
7. Does McClelland believe that power is good or bad? Why?
8. Should a leader have a dominant need for achievement to be successful? Why or why not?
9. How do attitudes develop leadership styles?
10. Which personality traits are more closely related to ethical and unethical behavior?
11. Do people change their level of moral development based on the situation?
12. Why do people justify their unethical behavior?

Communication Skills

The following critical-thinking questions can be used for class discussion and/or as written assignments to develop communication skills. Be sure to give complete explanations for all questions.

1. Would you predict that a person with a strong agreeableness personality dimension would be a successful computer programmer? Why or why not?
2. McGregor published Theory X and Theory Y over 30 years ago. Do we still have Theory X managers? Why?
3. In text examples related to the Pygmalion effect, Lou Holtz calls for setting a higher standard. Have the standards in school, society, and work increased or decreased over the last five years?
4. Do you believe that if you use ethical behavior it will pay off in the long run?
5. Can ethics be taught and learned?
6. Which justification do you think is used most often?
7. As related to the simple guide to ethical behavior, how do you want to be led?

CASE

The Bill & Melinda Gates Foundation

William (Bill) H. Gates, III, was born in 1955 and began programming mainframe computers at age 13. While attending Harvard University, Gates developed a version of the programming language BASIC for the first microcomputer—the MITS Altair. In 1975, Gates and his childhood friend Paul Allen founded Microsoft as a partnership, and it was incorporated in 1981. He invented the software industry, masterminded the rise of the PC, and has hung in there as a force on the Internet. Bill Gates is consistently ranked as one of the richest men in the world, and was ranked by *Fortune* as the seventh most powerful businessperson in the world. He retired from Microsoft in 2008 to devote most of his time to the Bill & Melinda Gates Foundation.[97]

Bill Gates can be abrasive and is known as a demanding boss who encourages creativity and recognizes employee achievements. Several of his early employees are now millionaires. Employees are expected to be well-informed, logical, vocal, and thick-skinned. Teams must present their ideas at "Bill" meetings. During the meetings, Gates often interrupts presentations to question facts and assumptions. He shouts criticisms and challenges team members. Team members are expected to stand up to Gates, giving good logical answers to his questions.

Melinda French grew up in Dallas in a hard-working, middle-class family. Unlike Bill, she graduated from college, earning a BA (double major in computer science and economics) and an MBA from Duke University. She went to work for Microsoft in 1987; at age 22 she was the youngest recruit and the only woman among ten MBAs. For nine years she was a hotshot who climbed the corporate ladder to become general manager of information products, managing 300 employees. Along the way, Bill asked her out (in the parking lot), which led to their wedding on January 1, 1994. Melinda stopped working at Microsoft after having the first of their three children (Jennifer, Rory, and Phoebe), but she continued to serve on corporate boards, including that of Duke University. Melinda's foremost concern is that the kids lead lives as normal as possible. But she remains Bill's greatest business advisor. He continues to consult her on decisions at Microsoft, and Melinda is credited for helping Bill make better decisions. Now that their youngest child is in school, Melinda is more active in leadership outside the home, and she was ranked as number 1 of the Women to Watch, by *The Wall Street Journal*.[98]

Malinda Gates is a total systems thinker who constantly sets and achieves goals. She is known as a strong team builder, who strives for collaboration in decision making. Melinda is loving and charming; she wins people over by being persuasive. She is compassionate and not afraid to get involved as she travels the world to help solve its problems. She held AIDS babies with dirty pants and comforted patients when she visited Mother Teresa's Home for the Dying in India. She has more influence than Bill when it comes to investing their assets in philanthropic projects.[99]

Before Bill and Melinda were even married, they talked about giving away 95 percent of their wealth during their lifetime. That is why they co-founded and co-chair their foundation. They agreed to focus on a few areas of giving, choosing where to place their money by asking two questions: Which problems affect the most people? and Which problems have been neglected in the past? They give where they can effect the greatest change. They have pumped billions into easing the suffering of those plagued by some of the world's deadliest diseases (AIDS, malaria, and tuberculosis) and revitalized failing public high schools in the United States with their financial support.[100]

Guided by the belief that every life has equal value, the Bill & Melinda Gates Foundation works to reduce inequities and improve lives around the world. It has three Grantmaking Areas: Global Development Program, Global Health Program, and United States Program. So far, it has commitment grants of $16.5 billion. The foundation has an asset trust endowment of $37.3 billion, making it the world's largest foundation with more than 500 employees.[101] Personal friend Warren Buffett has also teamed up with the Gateses and will contribute billions more. The Gates Foundation has already given away more than any other foundation. But they don't use a go-it-alone approach. They seek partners in their grants to create the best approach to solving world problems. Bill and Melinda will very likely give away more than $100 billion in their lifetime.[102] Bill and Melinda are truly world leaders.

GO TO THE INTERNET: To learn more about Bill and Melinda Gates and their foundation, visit their Web site **(http://www.gatesfoundation.org)**.

Support your answers to the following questions with specific information from the case and text or with other information you get from the Web or other sources.

1. What do you think Bill and Melinda Gates's personality traits are for each of the Big Five dimensions? Compare the two.
2. Which of the nine traits of effective leaders would you say has had the greatest impact on Bill and Melinda Gates's success? Compare the two.
3. Which motivation would McClelland say was the major need driving Bill and Melinda Gates to continue to work so hard despite being worth many billions of dollars?
4. Do Bill and Melinda Gates have an LMP? Compare the two.
5. What type of self-concept do Bill and Melinda Gates have, and how does it affect their success?
6. Is Bill Gates ethical in business at Microsoft? Which level of moral development is he on?

CUMULATIVE CASE QUESTION

7. Which leadership managerial role(s) played by Bill and Melinda Gates have an important part in the success of their foundation (Chapter 1)?

CASE EXERCISE AND ROLE-PLAY

Preparation: Think of a business that you would like to start some day and answer these questions that will help you develop your plan. (1) What would be your company's name? (2) What would be its mission (purpose or reason for being)? (3) What would your major products and/or services be? (4) Who would be your major competitors? (5) What would be your competitive advantage? (What makes you different from your competitors? Why would anyone buy your product or service rather than the competition's?) Your instructor may elect to let you break into groups to develop a group business idea. If you do a group business, select one leader with a thick skin who can handle a "Bill" meeting to present the proposal to the entire class. An alternative is to have a student(s) who has an actual business idea/project/proposal of any type present it for feedback.

Role-Play "Bill" Meeting: One person (representing oneself or a group) may give the business proposal idea to the entire class; or break into groups of five or six and, one at a time, deliver proposals. The members of the class that listen play the role of Bill Gates during the "Bill" meeting, or they challenge presenters and offer suggestions for improvement.

VIDEO CASE

"P.F." Chang's Serves Its Workers Well

Founded in 1993, P.F. Chang's owns and operates over 120 full-service, casual dining Asian bistros and contemporary Chinese diners across the country. P.F. Chang's strives to create an exceptional dining experience for every customer—and that includes a friendly, knowledgeable staff. By treating employees with respect, restaurant managers find that they can expect more from their staffs—and get it. Unlike many hourly restaurant employees, those at P.F. Chang's have the authority to make decisions that benefit customers. Giving employees the freedom to make decisions has had a huge impact on their attitudes and performance. Managers at P.F. Chang's receive extensive training on how to create and nurture a positive attitude among their employees, and all workers receive an employee handbook, which clearly spells out exactly what is expected of them.

1. In what ways does P.F. Chang's create organizational commitment among its workers?
2. How might a manager at P.F. Chang's use the Big Five personality factors to assess whether a candidate for a position on the wait staff would be suitable?

Skill-Development Exercise 1

Improving Attitudes and Personality Traits

Preparing for Skill-Development Exercise 1

You should have read and now understand attitudes and personality traits. Effective leaders know themselves and work to maximize their strengths and minimize their weaknesses. As the name of this exercise implies, you can improve your attitudes and personality traits through this exercise by following these steps.

1. **Identify strengths and weaknesses.** Review the six self-assessment exercises in this chapter. List your three major strengths and areas that can be improved:

Strengths: 1. ______

2. ______

3. ______

Areas to Improve: 1. ______

2. ______

3. ______

We don't always see ourselves as others do. Research has shown that many people are not accurate in describing their own personalities, and that others can describe them more objectively. Before going on with this exercise, you may want to ask someone you know well to complete your personality profile (see Self-Assessment 1 on page 32), rate your attitude as positive or negative, and list your strengths and areas for improvement.

2. **Develop a plan for improving.** Start with your Number One area to improve on. Write down specific things that you can do to improve. List specific times, dates, and places that you will implement your plans. You may want to review the 12 tips for developing a more positive attitude and self-concept for ideas. Use additional paper if you need more space.

____

____

____

____

3. **Work on other areas for improvement.** After you see improvement in your first area, develop a new plan for your second area, and proceed through the steps again.

Optional: If you have a negative attitude toward yourself or others—or you would like to improve your behavior with others (family, coworkers), things, or issues (disliking school or work)—try following the internationally known motivational speaker and trainer Zig Ziglar's system.[129] Thousands of people have used this system successfully. This system can also be used for changing personality traits as well.

Here are the steps to follow, with an example plan for a person who has a negative self-concept and also wants to be more sensitive to others. Use this example as a guide for developing your own plan.

1. *Self-concept.* Write down everything you like about yourself. List all your strengths. Then go on and list all your weaknesses. Get a good friend to help you.
2. *Make a clean new list, and using positive affirmations, write all your strengths.* Example: "I am sensitive to others' needs."
3. *On another sheet of paper, again using positive affirmations, list all your weaknesses.* For example, don't write "I need to lose weight." Write, "I am a slim (whatever you realistically can weigh in 30 days) pounds." Don't write, "I have to stop criticizing myself." Write, "I positively praise myself often, every day." Write "I have good communications skills," not "I am a weak communicator." The following list gives example affirmations for improving sensitivity to others. Note the repetition; you can use a thesaurus to help.

   I am sensitive to others.

   My behavior with others conveys my warmth for them.

   I convey my concern for others.

   My behavior conveys kindness toward others.

   My behavior helps others build their self-esteem.

   People find me easy to talk to.

   I give others my full attention.

   I patiently listen to others talk.

   I answer others slowly and in a polite manner.

   I answer questions and make comments with useful information.

   My comments to others help them feel good about themselves.

   I compliment others regularly.

4. *Practice.* Every morning and night for at least the next 30 days, look at yourself in the mirror and read your list of positive affirmations. Be sure to look at yourself between each affirmation as you read. Or, record the list on a tape recorder and listen to it while looking at yourself in the mirror. If you are really motivated, you can repeat this step at other times of the day. Start with your areas for improvement. If it takes five minutes or more, don't bother with the list of your strengths. Or stop at five minutes; this exercise is effective in short sessions. Although miracles won't happen overnight, you may become more aware of your behavior in the first week. In the second or third week, you may become aware of yourself using new behavior successfully. You may still see some negatives, but the number will decrease in time as the positive increases.

   Psychological research has shown that if a person hears something believable repeated for 30 days, he or she will tend to believe it. Ziglar says that you cannot consistently perform in a manner that is inconsistent with the way you see yourself. So, as you listen to your positive affirmations, you will believe them, and you will behave in a manner that is consistent with your belief. Put simply, your behavior will change with your thoughts without a lot of hard work. For example, if you listen to the affirmation, "I am an honest person" (not, "I have to stop lying"), in time—without having to work at it—you will tell the truth. At first you may feel uncomfortable reading or listening to positive affirmations that you don't really believe you have. But keep looking at yourself in the mirror and reading or listening, and with time you will feel comfortable and believe it and live it.

   Are you thinking you don't need to improve, or that this method will not work? Yes, this system often does work. Zig Ziglar has trained thousands of satisfied people. One of this book's authors tried the system himself, and within two or three weeks, he could see improvement in his behavior. The question isn't will the system work for you, but rather will you work the system to improve?

5. *When you slip, and we all do, don't get down on yourself.* In the sensitivity-to-others example, if you are rude to someone and catch yourself, apologize and change to a positive tone. Effective leaders admit when they are wrong and apologize. If you have a hard time admitting you are wrong and saying you are sorry,

at least be obviously nice so that the other person realizes you are saying you are sorry indirectly. Then forget about it and keep trying. Focus on your successes, not your slips. Don't let ten good discussions be ruined by one insensitive comment. If you were a baseball player and got nine out of ten hits, you'd be the best in the world.

6. *Set another goal.* After 30 days, select a new topic, such as developing a positive attitude toward work, school, or trying a specific leadership style that you want to develop. You can also include more than one area to work on.

Doing Skill-Development Exercise 1 in Class

Objective

To develop your skill at improving your attitudes and personality traits. As a leader, you can also use this skill to help your followers improve.

The primary AACSB learning standard skills developed through this exercise are reflective thinking and self-management and analytic skills.

Preparation

You should have identified at least one area for improvement and developed a plan to improve.

Procedure 1 *(1–2 minutes)* Break into groups of two or preferably three; be sure the others in your group are people you feel comfortable sharing with.

Procedure 2 *(4–6 minutes)* Have one of the group members volunteer to go first. The first volunteer states the attitude or personality trait they want to work on and describes the plan. The other group members give feedback on how to improve the plan. Try to give other plan ideas that can be helpful and/or provide some specific help. You can also make an agreement to ask each other how you are progressing at set class intervals. Don't change roles until you're asked to do so.

Procedure 3 *(4–6 minutes)* A second group member volunteers to go next. Follow the same procedure as above.

Procedure 4 *(4–6 minutes)* The third group member goes last. Follow the same procedure as above.

Conclusion

The instructor may lead a class discussion and/or make concluding remarks.

Apply It *(2–4 minutes)* What did I learn from this exercise? Will I really try to improve my attitude and personality by implementing my plan?

____

____

____

Sharing

In the group, or to the entire class, volunteers may give their answers to the "Apply It" questions.

Skill-Development Exercise 2

Personality Perceptions

Preparing for Skill-Development Exercise 2

Read the section on "Personality Traits and Leadership," and complete Self-Assessment 1 on page 32. From that exercise, rank yourself below from the highest score (1) to lowest (5) for each of the Big Five traits. Do not tell anyone your ranking until asked to do so.

_____ surgency _____ agreeableness
_____ adjustment _____ conscientiousness
_____ openness to experience

Doing Skill-Development Exercise 2 in Class

Objective

To develop your skill at perceiving personality traits of other people. With this skill, you can better understand and predict people's behavior, which is helpful to leaders in influencing followers.

The primary AACSB learning standard skill developed through this exercise is analytic skills.

Procedure 1 *(2–4 minutes)* Break into groups of three. This group should be with people you know the best in the class. You may need some groups of two. If you don't know people in the class, and you did Skill-Development Exercise 1 in Chapter 1, "Getting to Know You by Name," get in a group with those people.

Procedure 2 *(4–6 minutes)* Each person in the group writes down their perception of each of the other two group members. Simply rank which trait you believe to be the highest and lowest (put the Big Five dimension name on the line) for each person. Write a short reason for your perception, including some behavior you observed that leads you to your perception.

Name ______________ Highest personality score ___________ Lowest score ___________
Reason for ranking ______________________

____

Name ______________ Highest personality score ___________ Lowest score ___________
Reason for ranking ______________________

____

Procedure 3 *(4–6 minutes)* One of the group members volunteers to go first to hear the other group members' perceptions.

1. One person tells the volunteer which Big Five dimension he or she selected as the person's highest and lowest score, and why these dimensions were selected. Do not discuss this information yet.
2. The other person also tells the volunteer the same information.
3. The volunteer gives the two others his or her actual highest and lowest scores. The three group members discuss the accuracy of the perceptions.

Procedure 4 *(4–6 minutes)* A second group member volunteers to go next to receive perceptions. Follow the same procedure as above.

Procedure 5 *(4–6 minutes)* The third group member goes last. Follow the same procedure as above.

Conclusion
The instructor may lead a class discussion and/or make concluding remarks.

Apply It *(2–4 minutes)* What did I learn from this exercise? How will I use this knowledge in the future?

____

____

____

Sharing
In the group, or to the entire class, volunteers may give their answers to the "Apply It" questions.

Skill-Development Exercise 3

Ethics and Whistleblowing

Preparing for Skill-Development Exercise 3

Now that you have completed Self-Assessment 6 on pages 52-53 regarding ethical behavior, answer the discussion questions based on that assessment.

Discussion Questions

1. For the "College" section, items 1–3, who is harmed and who benefits from these unethical behaviors?
2. For the "Workplace" section, items 4–24, select the three items (circle their numbers) you consider the most seriously unethical behavior. Who is harmed and who benefits by these unethical behaviors?
3. If you observed unethical behavior but didn't report it, why didn't you report the behavior? If you did blow the whistle, why did you report the unethical behavior? What was the result?
4. As a manager, it is your responsibility to uphold ethical behavior. If you know employees are using any of these unethical behaviors, will you take action to enforce compliance with ethical standards?

Doing Skill-Development Exercise 3 in Class

Objective

To better understand ethics and whistleblowing, and decide what you will do about unethical behavior.

The primary AACSB learning standard skills developed through this exercise are reflective thinking and self-management and analytic skills.

Preparation
You should have completed the preparation for this exercise.

Experience
You will share your answers to the preparation questions, but are not requested to share your ethics score.

Procedure 1 *(5–10 minutes)* The instructor writes the numbers 1–24 on the board. For each statement, students first raise their hands if they have observed this behavior, then if they have reported the behavior. The instructor writes the numbers on the board. (Note: Procedure 1 and Procedure 2A can be combined.)

Procedure 2 *(10–20 minutes)*
Option A: As the instructor takes a count of the students who have observed and reported unethical behavior, he or she leads a discussion on the statements.

Option B: Break into groups of four to six, and share your answers to the four discussion questions at the end of the preparation part of this exercise. The groups may be asked to report the general consensus of the group to the entire class. If so, select a spokesperson before the discussion begins.

Option C: The instructor leads a class discussion on the four discussion questions at the end of the preparation part of this exercise.

Conclusion
The instructor may make concluding remarks.

Apply It (2–4 minutes) What did I learn from this exercise? How will I use this knowledge in the future to be ethical? When will I use a simple guide to ethics?

____

____

____

Sharing
Volunteers may give their answers to the "Apply It" questions.

3 Leadership Behavior and Motivation

Chapter Outline

Leadership Behavior and Styles
Leadership Behavior
Leadership Styles and the University of Iowa Research

University of Michigan and Ohio State University Studies
University of Michigan: Job-Centered and Employee-Centered Behavior
Ohio State University: Initiating Structure and Consideration Behavior
Differences Between Leadership Models—and Their Contributions

The Leadership Grid
Leadership Grid Theory
Leadership Grid and High-High Leader Research and Contributions

Leadership and Major Motivation Theories
Motivation and Leadership
The Motivation Process
An Overview of Three Major Classifications of Motivation Theories

Content Motivation Theories
Hierarchy of Needs Theory
Two-Factor Theory
Acquired Needs Theory
The Need to Balance Professional and Personal Needs

Process Motivation Theories
Equity Theory
Expectancy Theory
Goal-Setting Theory

Reinforcement Theory
Types of Reinforcement
Schedules of Reinforcement
You Get What You Reinforce
Motivating with Reinforcement
Giving Praise

Putting the Motivation Theories Together Within the Motivation Process

Learning Outcomes

After studying this chapter, you should be able to:

1. List the University of Iowa leadership styles. p. 70
2. Describe similarities and differences between the University of Michigan and Ohio State University leadership models. p. 72
3. Discuss similarities and differences between the Ohio State University Leadership Model and the Leadership Grid. p. 75
4. Discuss similarities and differences among the three content motivation theories. p. 80
5. Discuss the major similarities and differences among the three process motivation theories. p. 87
6. Explain the four types of reinforcement. p. 93
7. State the major differences among content, process, and reinforcement theories. p. 99
8. Define the following **key terms** (in order of appearance in the chapter):

- leadership style
- University of Michigan Leadership Model
- Ohio State University Leadership Model
- Leadership Grid
- motivation
- motivation process
- content motivation theories
- hierarchy of needs theory
- two-factor theory
- acquired needs theory
- process motivation theories
- equity theory
- expectancy theory
- goal-setting theory
- writing objectives model
- reinforcement theory
- giving praise model

Opening Case APPLICATION

Market America is a product brokerage and Internet marketing company that specializes in One-to-One Marketing. With more than three million customers and over 160,000 distributors worldwide (with international operations in the United States, Canada, Taiwan, Hong Kong, and Australia), Market America has generated more than $2.4 billion in accumulated retail sales. It markets a wide variety of high-quality products and services (including anti-aging, health, nutrition, personal care, and many other types of products).

J. R. Ridinger founded Market America in April of 1992 using the business model to sell directly to consumers through distributor business owners. Market America places the dream of starting your own distributor business to achieve financial independence and freedom of time within the reach of anyone. It offers the benefits of franchising (a proven business plan, management and marketing tools, and training) without the risk and high cost (franchise fees, monthly royalties, territorial restrictions) of a traditional franchise. There are minimal startup expenses, and people often start part time (8 to 12 hours per week). Existing businesses can also become partners—distributors. Market America will build, or improve, a Web site and take a distributor into the world of e-commerce. Through its revolutionary One-to-One Marketing concept, Market America combines the Internet with the power of people to ensure the most efficient and friendliest customer experience. Thus, Market America is fast becoming the World Wide Web's ultimate online destination.[1]

Opening Case Questions:

1. Which Ohio State University and Leadership Grid leadership style is emphasized at Market America?
2. What does Market America do to motivate its distributors, and how does it affect performance?
3. (a–c). How does Market America meet its distributors' content motivation needs?
4. (a–c). How does Market America meet its distributors' process motivation needs?
5. How does Market America use reinforcement theory to motivate its distributors?

Can you answer any of these questions? You'll find answers to these questions and learn more about Market America and its leadership throughout the chapter.

To learn more about Market America, visit the company's Web site at **http://www.marketamerica.com**.

Let's begin this chapter by discussing the importance of leadership behavior and motivation. The success of individual careers and organizations is based on how effectively leaders behave.[2] Recall that our definition of leadership stressed the importance of influencing others to achieve organizational objectives through change. Employee performance is based on behavior,[3] and to succeed, employees need to be motivated.[4] High levels of performance occur when leaders establish motivational environments that inspire followers to achieve objectives. According to John Deere CEO, Bob Lane, to be successful you have to set clear goals and motivate employees to achieve them.[5] Managerial behavior influences organizational outcomes,[6] and the leader's style impacts the relationship with followers and affects their motivation to achieve organizational objectives.[7] Thus, the objectives you set, your leadership style, and your ability to motivate yourself and others will affect your career success and the organization's performance. So how can you, as a leader, set good objectives and motivate followers to go beyond mediocrity? That is what this chapter is all about. We will discuss four behavioral leadership models and seven motivation theories.

Leadership Behavior and Styles

Leadership Behavior

By the late 1940s, most of the leadership research had shifted from the trait theory paradigm (Chapter 2) to the behavioral theory paradigm, which focuses on what the leader says and does. In the continuing quest to find the one best leadership style in all situations, researchers attempted to identify the differences in the behavior of effective leaders versus ineffective leaders. Although the behavioral leadership theory made major contributions to leadership research, which we will discuss more fully later, it never achieved its goal of finding one best style. Unfortunately, no leadership behaviors were found to be consistently associated with leadership effectiveness.[8] The leadership behavior theory paradigm lasted nearly 30 years. Today research continues to seek a better understanding of behavior.[9] And more importantly, to predict behavior.[10]

Leadership Behavior Is Based on Traits

Although the behavioral theorists focus on behavior, it's important to realize that leaders' behavior is based on their traits and skills.[11] The manager's leadership personality traits and attitudes directly affect his or her behavior and relationship with employees.[12] Recall that the Pygmalion effect is based on traits, attitude expectations, and the manager's treatment (behavior) of employees, which in turn determines the followers' behavior and performance.

Leading by example is important to managers. In fact, as Albert Einstein said, "Setting an example is not the main means of influencing another; it is the only means." Leading by example takes place as followers observe the leader's behavior and copy it. And the leader's behavior is based on his or her traits. Thus, traits and behavior go hand-in-hand, or trait leadership theory influences behavioral leadership theory. However, behavior is easier to learn and change than traits.

Learning Outcome 1 *List the University of Iowa leadership styles.*

Leadership Styles and the University of Iowa Research

Leadership style *is the combination of traits, skills, and behaviors leaders use as they interact with followers.* Although a leadership style is based on traits and skills, the important component is the behavior, because it is a relatively consistent pattern of behavior that characterizes a leader. A precursor to the behavior approach recognized autocratic and democratic leadership styles.

Work Application 1

Recall a present or past manager. Which of the University of Iowa leadership styles does or did your manager use most often? Describe the behavior of your manager.

University of Iowa Leadership Styles

In the 1930s, before behavioral theory became popular, Kurt Lewin and associates conducted studies at the University of Iowa that concentrated on the leadership style of the manager.[13] Their studies identified two basic leadership styles:

- *Autocratic leadership style.* The autocratic leader makes the decisions, tells employees what to do, and closely supervises workers.
- *Democratic leadership style.* The democratic leader encourages participation in decisions, works with employees to determine what to do, and does not closely supervise employees.

The autocratic and democratic leadership styles are often placed at opposite ends of a continuum, as shown in Exhibit 3.1; thus a leader's style usually falls somewhere between the two styles.

EXHIBIT 3.1 University of Iowa Leadership Styles

Autocratic---------------------------------Democratic

Source: Adapted from K. Lewin, R. Lippett, and R. K. White. 1939. "Patterns of Aggressive Behavior in Experimentally Created Social Climates." Journal of Social Psychology *10:271–301.*

The Iowa studies contributed to the behavioral movement and led to an era of behavioral rather than trait research. With the shift in paradigm from management to leadership, the leadership style of effective managers is no longer autocratic, but more democratic.

University of Michigan and Ohio State University Studies

Leadership research was conducted at Ohio State and the University of Michigan at about the same time during the mid-1940s to mid-1950s. These studies were not based on prior autocratic and democratic leadership styles, but rather sought to determine the behavior of effective leaders. Although these two studies used the term *leadership behavior* rather than *leadership styles,* the behaviors identified are actually more commonly called leadership styles today. In this section we discuss leadership styles identified by these two universities. Before reading about these studies, complete Self-Assessment 1 to determine your leadership style.

SELF-ASSESSMENT 1

Your Leadership Style

For each of the following statements, select one of the following:

1– "I **would not** tend to do this."

0– "I **would** tend to do this."

as a manager of a work unit. There are no right or wrong answers, so don't try to select correctly.

0 ____ 1. I (would or would not) let my employees know that they should not be doing things during work hours that are not directly related to getting their jobs done.

0 ____ 2. I (would or would not) spend time talking to my employees to get to know them personally during work hours.

0 ____ 3. I (would or would not) have a clearly written agenda of things to accomplish during department meetings.

0 ____ 4. I (would or would not) allow employees to come in late or leave early to take care of personal issues.

0 ____ 5. I (would or would not) set clear goals so employees know what needs to be done.

1 ____ 6. I (would or would not) get involved with employee conflicts to help resolve them.

1 ____ 7. I (would or would not) spend much of my time directing employees to ensure that they meet department goals.

0 ____ 8. I (would or would not) encourage employees to solve problems related to their work without having to get my permission to do so.

0 ____ 9. I (would or would not) make sure that employees do their work according to the standard method to be sure it is done correctly.

continued

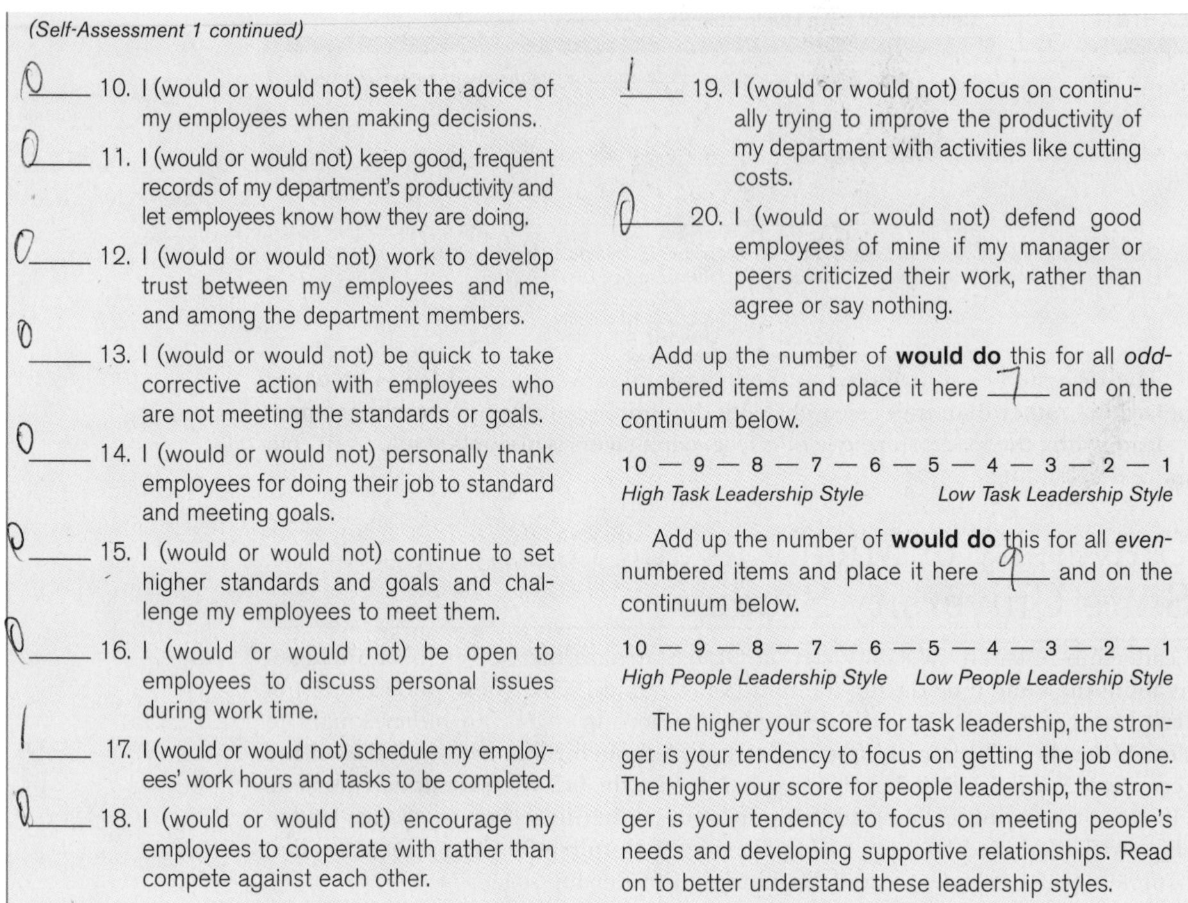

(Self-Assessment 1 continued)

____ 10. I (would or would not) seek the advice of my employees when making decisions.

____ 11. I (would or would not) keep good, frequent records of my department's productivity and let employees know how they are doing.

____ 12. I (would or would not) work to develop trust between my employees and me, and among the department members.

____ 13. I (would or would not) be quick to take corrective action with employees who are not meeting the standards or goals.

____ 14. I (would or would not) personally thank employees for doing their job to standard and meeting goals.

____ 15. I (would or would not) continue to set higher standards and goals and challenge my employees to meet them.

____ 16. I (would or would not) be open to employees to discuss personal issues during work time.

____ 17. I (would or would not) schedule my employees' work hours and tasks to be completed.

____ 18. I (would or would not) encourage my employees to cooperate with rather than compete against each other.

____ 19. I (would or would not) focus on continually trying to improve the productivity of my department with activities like cutting costs.

____ 20. I (would or would not) defend good employees of mine if my manager or peers criticized their work, rather than agree or say nothing.

Add up the number of **would do** this for all *odd*-numbered items and place it here ____ and on the continuum below.

10 — 9 — 8 — 7 — 6 — 5 — 4 — 3 — 2 — 1

High Task Leadership Style *Low Task Leadership Style*

Add up the number of **would do** this for all *even*-numbered items and place it here ____ and on the continuum below.

10 — 9 — 8 — 7 — 6 — 5 — 4 — 3 — 2 — 1

High People Leadership Style *Low People Leadership Style*

The higher your score for task leadership, the stronger is your tendency to focus on getting the job done. The higher your score for people leadership, the stronger is your tendency to focus on meeting people's needs and developing supportive relationships. Read on to better understand these leadership styles.

Learning Outcome 2 *Describe similarities and differences between the University of Michigan and Ohio State University leadership models.*

University of Michigan: Job-Centered and Employee-Centered Behavior

The University of Michigan's Survey Research Center, under the principal direction of Rensis Likert, conducted studies to determine leadership effectiveness. Researchers created a questionnaire called the "Survey of Organizations" and conducted interviews to gather data on leadership styles. Their goals were to (1) classify the leaders as effective and ineffective by comparing the behavior of leaders from high-producing units and low-producing units; and (2) determine reasons for effective leadership.[14] The researchers identified two styles of leadership behavior, which they called *job-centered* and *employee-centered.* The University of Michigan model stated that a leader is either more job-centered or more employee-centered. *The* **University of Michigan Leadership Model** *thus identifies two leadership styles: job-centered and employee-centered.* See Exhibit 3.2 for the University of Michigan Leadership Model: a one-dimensional continuum between two leadership styles.

Job-Centered Leadership Style

The job-centered style has scales measuring two job-oriented behaviors of goal emphasis and work facilitation. Job-centered behavior refers to the extent to which the leader takes charge to get the job done. The leader closely directs subordinates

EXHIBIT 3.2 The University of Michigan Leadership Model: Two Leadership Styles, One Dimension

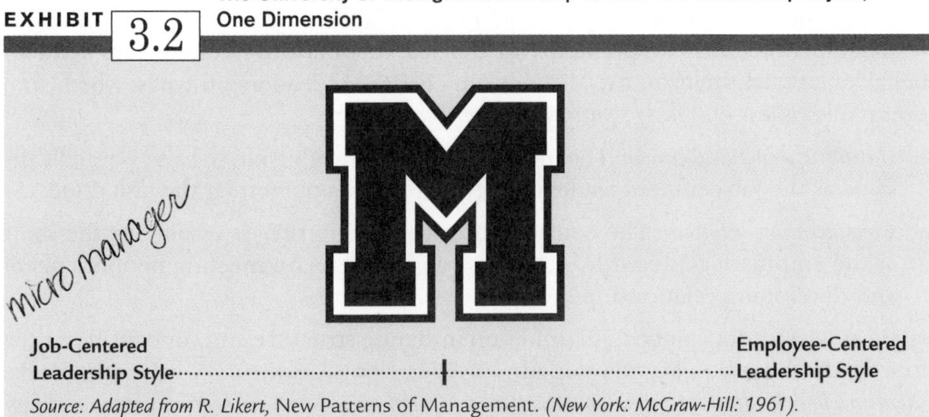

Source: Adapted from R. Likert, New Patterns of Management. *(New York: McGraw-Hill: 1961).*

with clear roles and goals, while the manager tells them what to do and how to do it as they work toward goal achievement. Review the odd-numbered items in Self-Assessment 1 for examples of job- (task-) oriented leadership behavior.

Employee-Centered Leadership Style

The employee-centered style has scales measuring two employee-oriented behaviors of supportive leadership and interaction facilitation. Employee-centered behavior refers to the extent to which the leader focuses on meeting the human needs of employees while developing relationships. The leader is sensitive to subordinates and communicates to develop trust, support, and respect while looking out for their welfare. Review the even-numbered items in Self-Assessment 1 for examples of employee- (people-) oriented leadership behavior.

Based on Self-Assessment 1, is your leadership style more job- (task-) or employee- (people-) centered?

Applying the **Concept 1**

University of Michigan Leadership Styles

Identify each of these five behaviors by its leadership style. Write the appropriate letter in the blank before each item.

a. job-centered b. employee-centered

____ 1. The manager is influencing the follower to do the job the way the leader wants it done.

____ 2. The manager just calculated the monthly sales report and is sending it to all the sales representatives so they know if they met their quota.

____ 3. The leader is saying a warm, friendly good morning to followers as they arrive at work.

____ 4. The manager is in his or her office developing plans for the department.

____ 5. The leader is seeking ideas from followers on a decision he or she has to make.

Ohio State University: Initiating Structure and Consideration Behavior

The Personnel Research Board of Ohio State University, under the principal direction of Ralph Stogdill, began a study to determine effective leadership styles. In the attempt to measure leadership styles, these researchers developed an instrument known as the *Leader Behavior Description Questionnaire (LBDQ)*. The LBDQ had 150 examples of definitive leader behaviors, which were narrowed down from 1,800 leadership functions. Respondents to the questionnaire perceived their leader's behavior toward them on two distinct dimensions or leadership types, which they eventually called *initiating structure* and *consideration*:[15]

- *Initiating structure behavior.* The initiating structure leadership style is essentially the same as the job-centered leadership style; it focuses on getting the task done.
- *Consideration behavior.* The consideration leadership style is essentially the same as the employee-centered leadership style; it focuses on meeting people's needs and developing relationships.

Because a leader can be high or low on initiating structure and/or consideration, four leadership styles are developed. *The* **Ohio State University Leadership Model** *identifies four leadership styles: low structure and high consideration, high structure and high consideration, low structure and low consideration, and high structure and low consideration.* Exhibit 3.3 illustrates the four leadership styles and their two dimensions.

EXHIBIT 3.3 The Ohio State University Leadership Model: Four Leadership Styles, Two Dimensions

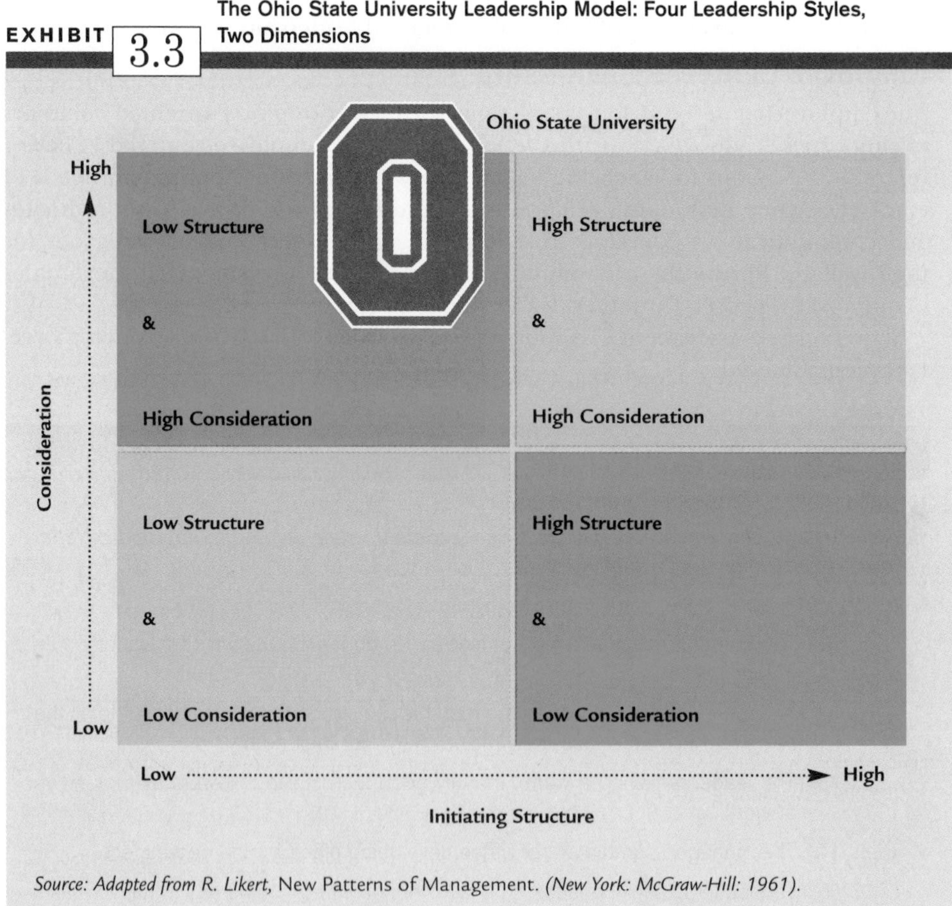

Source: Adapted from R. Likert, New Patterns of Management. *(New York: McGraw-Hill: 1961).*

Work Application 2

Recall a present or past manager. Which of the four Ohio State leadership styles does or did your manager use most often? Describe the behavior of your manager.

Leaders with high structure and low consideration behavior use one-way communications, and decisions are made by the managers, whereas leaders with high consideration and low structure use two-way communications and tend to share decision making. To determine your two-dimensional leadership style from Self-Assessment 1, put your two separate ("task" and "people") scores together and determine which of the four styles in Exhibit 3.3 is the closest match.

Differences Between Leadership Models—and Their Contributions

The Ohio State and University of Michigan leadership models are different in that the University of Michigan places the two leadership behaviors at opposite ends of the same continuum, making it one-dimensional. The Ohio State University model considers the two behaviors independent of one another, making it two-dimensional; thus this model has four leadership styles.

The two leadership behaviors on which the models of both universities are based have strong research support. Leadership behaviors were developed, and repeatedly tested, using statistical factor analysis to narrow the dimensions down to structure/job-centered and consideration/employee-centered. The LBDQ and modified versions have been used in hundreds of past studies by many different researchers.[16]

Research efforts to determine the one best leadership style have been weak and inconsistent for most criteria of leadership effectiveness. In other words, there is no one best leadership style in all situations; this is the first contribution, because it has helped lead researchers to the next paradigm—that of contingency leadership theory. Thus, the contribution of the behavioral leadership paradigm was to identify two generic dimensions of leadership behavior that continue to have importance in accounting for leader effectiveness today.

Although there is no one best leadership style in all situations, there has been a consistent finding that employees are more satisfied with a leader who is high in consideration. Prior to the two university leadership studies, many organizations had focused on getting the job done with little, if any, concern for meeting employee needs. So, along with other behavioral theory research, there was a shift to place more emphasis on the human side of the organization to increase productivity; this is a second contribution. The saying that a happy worker is a productive worker comes from this period of research, and this relationship is still be studied today.[17]

Another important research finding was that most leadership functions can be carried out by someone besides the designated leader of a group. Thus, due to behavioral leadership research, more organizations began training managers to use participative leadership styles. In fact, Rensis Likert proposed three types of leadership behavior: job-centered behavior, employee-centered behavior, and participative leadership. Thus, as a third contribution of these leadership models, Likert can be credited as being the first to identify the participative leadership style that is commonly used today.[18]

The Leadership Grid

In this section we discuss the Leadership Grid theory, including research and contributions of the high-concern-for-people and high-concern-for-production (team leader) leadership styles.

Learning Outcome 3 *Discuss similarities and differences between the Ohio State University Leadership Model and the Leadership Grid.*

Leadership Grid Theory

Behavior leadership theory did not end in the mid-1950s with the University of Michigan and Ohio State University studies. Robert Blake and Jane Mouton, from the University of Texas, developed the Managerial Grid® and published it in 1964, updated it in 1978 and 1985, and in 1991 it became the Leadership Grid® with Anne Adams McCanse replacing Mouton, who died in 1987.[19] Blake and Mouton published numerous articles and around 40 books describing their theories.[20] Behavioral leadership is still being researched today. The Leadership Grid was applied to project management by different researchers.[21]

The Leadership Grid builds on the Ohio State and Michigan studies; it is based on the same two leadership dimensions, which Blake and Mouton called *concern for production* and *concern for people.*[22] The concern for both people and production is measured through a questionnaire on a scale from 1 to 9. Therefore, the grid has 81 possible combinations of concern for production and people. However, *the* **Leadership Grid** *identifies five leadership styles: 1,1 impoverished; 9,1 authority compliance; 1,9 country club; 5,5 middle of the road; and 9,9 team leader.* See Exhibit 3.4 for an adaptation of the Leadership Grid.

EXHIBIT 3.4 Blake, Mouton, and McCanse Leadership Grid

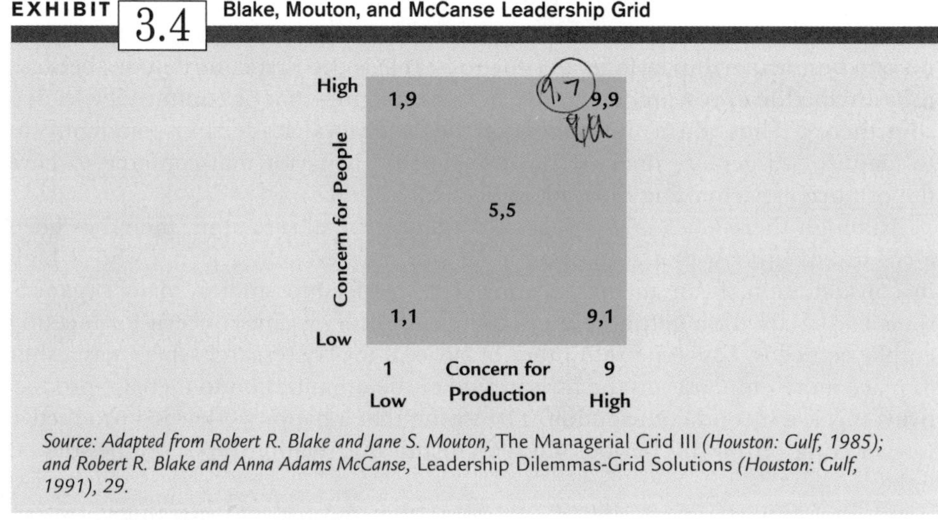

Source: Adapted from Robert R. Blake and Jane S. Mouton, The Managerial Grid III *(Houston: Gulf, 1985); and Robert R. Blake and Anna Adams McCanse,* Leadership Dilemmas-Grid Solutions *(Houston: Gulf, 1991), 29.*

Following are descriptions of leadership styles in the Leadership Grid:

- The *impoverished leader* (1,1) has low concern for both production and people. The leader does the minimum required to remain employed in the position.
- The *authority-compliance leader* (9,1) has a high concern for production and a low concern for people. The leader focuses on getting the job done while people are treated like machines.
- The *country-club leader* (1,9) has a high concern for people and a low concern for production. The leader strives to maintain a friendly atmosphere without regard for production.
- The *middle-of-the-road leader* (5,5) has balanced, medium concern for both production and people. The leader strives to maintain satisfactory performance and morale.
- The *team leader* (9,9) has a high concern for both production and people. This leader strives for maximum performance and employee satisfaction. According to Blake, Mouton, and McCanse, the team leadership style is generally the most appropriate for use in all situations.

To estimate your Leadership Grid leadership style, using Self-Assessment 1, use your task score as your concern for production and your people score, and plot them on the Leadership Grid in Exhibit 3.4. Then select the closest of the five leadership styles.

Work Application 3

Recall a present or past manager. Which of the five Leadership Grid styles does or did your manager use most often? Describe the behavior of your manager.

Opening Case APPLICATION

1. Which Ohio State University and Leadership Grid leadership style is emphasized at Market America?

Market America emphasizes the Ohio State University high structure and high consideration style, which is called the team leader's high concern for people and high concern for production (9,9) leadership style. Distributors make money by bringing in new distributors and selling more products, so they have a high concern for sales. But at the same time, distributors must develop good relationships with the distributors who sell for them, so they have a high concern for people as well because their success is based in part on their distributors' success. Distributors are commonly recruited, and some sales also take place, in distributors' homes through presentations, which is a social setting.

Applying the **Concept 2**

The Leadership Grid

Identify the five statements by their leader's style. Write the appropriate letter in the blank before each item.

a. 1,1 (impoverished)
b. 1,9 (country club)
c. 9,1 (authority compliance)
d. 5,5 (middle of the road)
e. 9,9 (team)

____ 6. The group has very high morale; members enjoy their work. Productivity in the department is one of the lowest in the company. The manager is one of the best liked in the company.

____ 7. The group has adequate morale; the employees are satisfied with their manager. They have an average productivity level compared to the other departments in the company.

____ 8. The group has one of the lowest levels of morale in the company; most employees do not like the manager. It is one of the top performers compared to other departments.

____ 9. The group is one of the lowest producers in the company; employees don't seem to care about doing a good job. It has a low level of morale, because the employees generally don't like the manager.

____ 10. The group is one of the top performers; the manager challenges employees to continue to meet and exceed goals. Employees have high morale because they like the manager.

Leadership Grid and High-High Leader Research and Contributions

The *high-high leader* has concern for both production and people; this is the team leadership style. However, authors of the Leadership Grid were not the only ones to conduct research to determine if the high-high style was the most effective leadership style in all situations. Blake and Mouton did conduct an extensive empirical research study that measured profitability before and after a 10-year period. In the study, one company subsidiary used an extensive Grid Organizational Development program designed to teach managers how to be 9,9 team leaders (experimental group), while another subsidiary did not use the program (control group). The subsidiary using the team leadership style increased its profits four times more than the control subsidiary. Thus, the researchers claimed that team leadership usually results in improved performance, low absenteeism and turnover, and high employee satisfaction.[23] Blake and Mouton support the high-high leader style as a universal theory.

However, another researcher disagreed with these findings, calling high-high leadership a myth.[24] A more objective meta-analysis (a study combining the results of many prior studies) found that although task and relationship behavior tends to correlate positively with subordinate performance, the correlation is usually weak.[25] In conclusion, although there is some support for the universal theory, the high-high leadership style is not accepted as the one best style in all situations.

Critics suggested that different leadership styles are more effective in different situations.[26] Thus, a contribution of behavioral research is that it led to the shift in paradigm to contingency leadership theory. As you will learn in Chapter 5, contingency leadership theory is based on the behavioral theory of production and people leadership styles. Situational leadership models don't agree with using the same leadership style in all situations, but rather prescribe using the existing behavioral leadership style that best meets the situation.

A second contribution of behavioral leadership theory was the recognition that organizations need both production and people leadership. A generic set of production-oriented and people-oriented leadership functions must be performed to ensure effective organizational performance.

A third related contribution of behavioral leadership theory supports coleadership. The manager does not have to perform both production and people functions. Thus, strong production-oriented leaders can be successful if they have coleaders to provide the people-oriented functions for them, and vice versa. So, if you tend to be more production- or people-oriented, seek coleaders to complement your weaker area.

Before we go on to motivation, let's tie personality traits from Chapter 2 together with what we've covered so far. Complete Self-Assessment 2 now.

SELF-ASSESSMENT 2

Your Personality Traits and Leadership Styles

We stated in the first section that *traits affect leadership behavior.* How does this relate to you? For the University of Michigan Leadership Model, generally, if you had a high personality score for the Big Five surgency dimension in Self-Assessment 1 in Chapter 2 (dominance trait, high need for power), you most likely have a high score for the task (job-centered) leadership style. If you had a high score for agreeableness (sensitivity to others trait, high need for affiliation), you most likely have a high score for the people (employee-centered) leadership style. My U of M leadership style is primarily ______________________________

______________________________.

For the Ohio State University Leadership Model, you need to score your personality for surgency and agreeableness as high or low. Then you combine them, and these personality scores should generally provide the same two-dimensional behaviors corresponding to one of the four leadership styles. My OSU leadership style is primarily ______________________________

______________________________.

For the Leadership Grid, you need to score your personality for surgency and agreeableness on a scale of 1 to 9. Then you combine them on the grid, and these personality scores should generally provide about the same score as Self-Assessment 1. My Leadership Grid style is primarily ______________________________

______________________________.

If you scored a Leader Motive Profile, your score for tasks should generally be higher than your score for people, because you have a greater need for power than affiliation. However, your leadership style on the Ohio State model could be high structure and high consideration, because this implies socialized power. You could also have a 9,9 team leader score on the Leadership Grid. My LMP is primarily ______________________________

______________________________.

Leadership and Major Motivation Theories

In this section we discuss motivation and leadership, the motivation process (which explains how motivation affects behavior), and three classifications of motivation theories (content, process, and reinforcement). We also briefly describe the need to balance professional and personal needs.

Motivation and Leadership

Motivation *is anything that affects behavior in pursuing a certain outcome.* Motivation is a quest for personal gain.[27] So why do we often do the things we do? Because we tend to seek to satisfy our self-interest.[28] The pursuit of happiness and satisfaction is fundamental to motivation.[29] Although there are exceptions, there is support for the belief that making employees happier and healthier increases their effort, contributions, and productivity,[30] and that satisification leads to good organizational citizenship behavior—going above and beyond the call of duty.[31] Satisfied employees can have a postive impact on customers' satisfaction with firm performance.[32] Satisfied employees stay on the job longer.[33] Joie de Vivre Hospitality CEO, Chip Conley, says that keeping staff happy is a top priority because satisfied workers stay in their jobs longer, and they treat customers better.[34] Employees can be motivated to make a positive difference.[35] As a leader, your job is to motivate your followers to work hard.[36]

So, if you want to motivate someone, answer their often-unasked question, "What's in it for me?" If you give people what they want, they will in turn give you what you want—creating win-win situations. Unfortunately, it's complex (easier said than done), but you will learn how in the rest of this chapter. The first step is to understand the motivation process.[37]

The Motivation Process

Through the **motivation process,** *people go from need to motive to behavior to consequence to satisfaction or dissatisfaction.* For example, you are thirsty (need) and have a drive (motive) to get a drink. You get a drink (behavior) that quenches (consequence and satisfaction) your thirst. However, if you could not get a drink, or a drink of what you really wanted, you would be dissatisfied. Satisfaction is usually short-lived. Getting that drink satisfied you, but sooner or later you will need another drink. For this reason, the motivation process has a feedback loop. Giving rewards as consequences for meeting organizational objectives leads to satisfaction and increased performance.[38] See Exhibit 3.5 for an illustration of the motivation process.

EXHIBIT 3.5 The Motivation Process

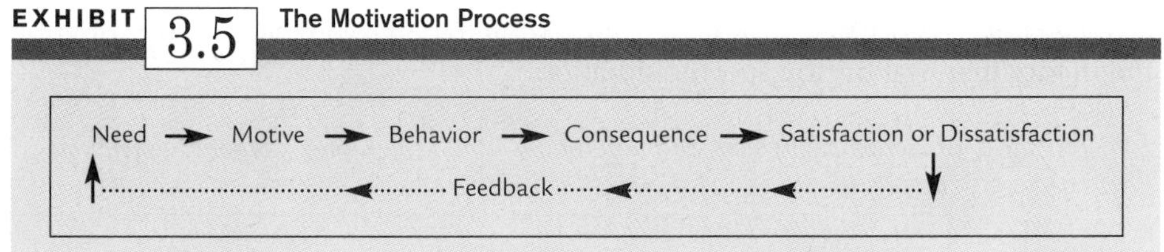

Some need or want motivates all behavior. However, needs and motives are complex: We don't always know what our needs are, or why we do the things we do. Have you ever done something and not known why you did it? Understanding needs will help you to better understand motivation and behavior.[39] You will gain a better understanding of why people do the things they do.

Like traits, motives cannot be observed; but you can observe behavior and infer what the person's motive is (attribution theory). However, it is not easy to know why people behave the way they do, because people do the same things for different reasons. Also, people often attempt to satisfy several needs at once.

Herb Kelleher, founder and chairman of Southwest Airlines, said that superior performance is not achieved through ordinary employee efforts; it takes good citizenship behavior.[40] Herb Kelleher focused on making work fun to motivate Southwest employees to be organizational citizens, and set many airline industry records, despite the fact that employees were paid less than at traditional airlines. David Neeleman, founder of JetBlue Airways, is described as someone who can inspire employees to organizational citizenship through the sheer force of his personality and the example of his dedication.

Opening Case APPLICATION

2. What does Market America do to motivate its distributors, and how does it affect performance?

Market America's primary motivator is self-motivation by making distributors their own boss, which is not successful with people who are not interested in entrepreneurship. Its team approach—with more experienced distributors helping newer distributors, and regular meetings—is key to motivating distributors to succeed. Market America has been successful at finding people who want to be their own boss, and its performance continues to improve. It has consistent sales growth. In 2004, it achieved its goals of having more six-figure earners than any other competitor company in America. The distributor approach motivates utilizing self-interest while helping others to create a win-win situation. The more sales distributors make, the more money they make. However, by helping other distributors succeed, they also make more money; and without helping customers by selling products they want to buy, Market America and its distributors would not have any sales.

An Overview of Three Major Classifications of Motivation Theories

There is no single, universally accepted theory of how to motivate people, or how to classify the theories. We will discuss motivation theories and how you can use them to motivate yourself and others. In the following sections, you will learn about content motivation theories, process motivation theories, and reinforcement theory. See Exhibit 3.6 for this classification, which is commonly used, with a listing of major motivation theories you will learn.

After studying all of the theories separately, we can put them back together using the unifying motivation process to see the relationship between the theories. You can select one theory to use, or take from several to make your own theory, or apply the theory that best fits the specific situation.

Learning Outcome 4 *Discuss similarities and differences among the three content motivation theories.*

Content Motivation Theories

Before we present the content motivation theories, let's discuss content motivation theories in general. **Content motivation theories** *focus on explaining and predicting behavior based on people's needs.* The primary reason people do what they do is to meet their needs or wants—to be satisfied.[41] Thus, it is important to understand needs (content motivation) theory.[42] People want job satisfaction, and they will leave one

EXHIBIT 3.6 Major Motivation Theories

CLASSIFICATION OF MOTIVATION THEORIES	SPECIFIC MOTIVATION THEORY
1. *Content motivation theories* focus on explaining and predicting behavior based on employee need motivation.	A. *Hierarchy of needs theory* proposes that employees are motivated through five levels of need—physiological, safety, social, esteem, and self-actualization. B. *Two-factor theory* proposes that employees are motivated by motivators (higher-level needs) rather than maintenance (lower-level needs) factors. C. *Acquired needs theory* proposes that employees are motivated by their need for achievement, power, and affiliation.
2. *Process motivation theories* focus on understanding how employees choose behaviors to fulfill their needs.	A. *Equity theory* proposes that employees will be motivated when their perceived inputs equal outputs. B. *Expectancy theory* proposes that employees are motivated when they believe they can accomplish the task, they will be rewarded, and the rewards for doing so are worth the effort. C. *Goal-setting theory* proposes that achievable but difficult goals motivate employees.
3. *Reinforcement theory* proposes that behavior can be explained, predicted, and controlled through the consequences for behavior.	Types of Reinforcement • Positive • Avoidance • Extinction • Punishment

organization for another to meet this need.[43] The key to successful leadership is to meet the needs of employees while achieving organizational objectives.[44]

Hierarchy of Needs Theory

In the 1940s, Abraham Maslow developed his hierarchy of needs theory,[45] which is based on four major assumptions: (1) Only unmet needs motivate. (2) People's needs are arranged in order of importance (hierarchy) going from basic to complex needs. (3) People will not be motivated to satisfy a higher-level need unless the lower-level need(s) has been at least minimally satisfied. (4) Maslow assumed that people have five classifications of needs, which are presented here in hierarchical order from low to high level of need.

Hierarchy of Needs

The **hierarchy of needs theory** *proposes that people are motivated through five levels of needs—physiological, safety, belongingness, esteem, and self-actualization:*

1. *Physiological needs:* These are people's primary or basic needs: air, food, shelter, sex, and relief from or avoidance of pain.
2. *Safety needs:* Once the physiological needs are met, the individual is concerned with safety and security.
3. *Belongingness needs:* After establishing safety, people look for love, friendship, acceptance, and affection. Belongingness is also called *social needs.*

4. *Esteem needs:* After the social needs are met, the individual focuses on ego, status, self-respect, recognition for accomplishments, and a feeling of self-confidence and prestige.
5. *Self-actualization needs:* The highest level of need is to develop one's full potential. To do so, one seeks growth, achievement, and advancement.

Maslow's hierarchy of needs is commonly taught in psychology and business courses,[46] because it offers a very rich theory of human motivation and its determinants at the individual level.[47] However, Maslow's work was criticized because it did not take into consideration that people can be at different levels of needs based on different aspects of their lives. Nor did he mention that people can revert back to lower-level needs. Today, Maslow's followers and others realize that needs are not on a simple five-step hierarchy. Maslow's assumptions have recently been updated to reflect this insight, and many organizations today are using a variety of the management methods he proposed 30 years ago. Maslow has also been credited with influencing many management authors, including Douglas McGregor, Rensis Likert, and Peter Drucker.

Motivating Employees with Hierarchy of Needs Theory

The major recommendation to leaders is to meet employees' lower-level needs so that they will not dominate the employees' motivational process. You should get to know and understand people's needs and meet them as a means of increasing performance. It is important to build self-esteem.[48] See Exhibit 3.7 for a list of ways in which managers attempt to meet these five needs.

Work Application 4

On what level of the hierarchy of needs are you at this time for a specific aspect of your life (professional or personal)? Be sure to specify the level by name, and explain why you are at that level.

Opening Case **APPLICATION**

3-a. How does Market America meet its distributors' content motivation needs?

Market America allows people to climb the *hierarchy of needs* as distributors: earn money (*physiological*), with minimum risk (*safety*), through customer contact and meetings (*social*), through the job itself with unlimited growth potential (*esteem*), and be the boss, which allows control over their job and time (*self-actualization*).

Two-Factor Theory

In the 1960s, Frederick Herzberg published his two-factor theory.[49] Herzberg combined lower-level needs into one classification he called *hygiene* or *maintenance*; and higher-level needs into one classification he called *motivators*. ***The* two-factor theory** *proposes that people are motivated by motivators rather than maintenance factors.* Before you learn about two-factor theory, complete Self-Assessment 3.

Maintenance—Extrinsic Factors

Maintenance factors are also called *extrinsic motivators* because motivation comes from outside the person and the job itself. Extrinsic motivators include pay, job security, and title; working conditions; fringe benefits; and relationships. These factors are related to meeting lower-level needs. Review Self-Assessment 3, the even-numbered questions, for a list of extrinsic job factors.

Motivators—Intrinsic Factors

Motivators are called *intrinsic motivators* because motivation comes from within the person through the work itself. Intrinsic motivators include achievement, recognition, challenge, and advancement. These factors are related to meeting higher-level needs, and are better at motivating than extrinsic factors.[50] Doing something we want to do and doing it well can be its own reward. Review Self-Assessment 3, the odd-numbered questions, for a list of intrinsic job factors.

EXHIBIT 3.7 How Organizations Motivate with Hierarchy of Needs Theory

Self-Actualization Needs
Organizations meet these needs by the development of employees' skills, the chance to be creative, achievement and promotions, and the ability to have complete control over their jobs.

Esteem Needs
Organizations meet these needs through titles, the satisfaction of completing the job itself, merit pay raises, recognition, challenging tasks, participation in decision making, and change for advancement.

Social Needs
Organizations meet these needs through the opportunity to interact with others, to be accepted, to have friends. Activities include parties, picnics, trips, and sports teams.

Safety Needs
Organizations meet these needs through safe working conditions, salary increases to meet inflation, job security, and fringe benefits (medical insurance/sick pay/pensions) that protect the physiological needs.

Physiological Needs
Organizations meet these needs through adequate salary, breaks, and working conditions.

SELF-ASSESSMENT 3

Job Motivators and Maintenance Factors

Here are 12 job factors that contribute to job satisfaction. Rate each according to how important it is to you by placing a number from 1 to 5 on the line before each factor.

Very important		Somewhat important		Not important
5	4	3	2	1

____ 1. An interesting job I enjoy doing

____ 2. A boss who treats everyone the same regardless of the circumstances

____ 3. Getting praise and other recognition and appreciation for the work that I do

____ 4. A job that is routine without much change from day-to-day

____ 5. The opportunity for advancement

____ 6. A nice title regardless of pay

____ 7. Job responsibility that gives me freedom to do things my way

____ 8. Good working conditions (safe environment, cafeteria, etc.)

____ 9. The opportunity to learn new things

____ 10. An emphasis on following the rules, regulations, procedures, and policies

____ 11. A job I can do well and succeed at

____ 12. Job security; a career with one company

continued

(Self-Assessment 3 continued)

For each factor, write the number from 1 to 5 that represents your answer. Total each column (should be between 6 and 30 points).

Motivating factors	Maintenance factors
1. 4	2. 2
3. 4	4. 2
5. 4	6. 1
7. 3	8. 4
9. 5	10. 4
11. 5	12. 2
Totals ____	15

Did you select motivators or maintenance factors as being more important to you? The closer to 30 (6) each score is, the more (less) important it is to you. Continue reading to understand the difference between motivators and maintenance factors.

Herzberg's Two-Factor Motivation Model

Herzberg and associates, based on research, disagreed with the traditional view that satisfaction and dissatisfaction were at opposite ends of one continuum (a one-dimensional model). There are two continuums: not dissatisfied with the environment (maintenance) to dissatisfied, and satisfied with the job itself (motivators) to not satisfied (a two-dimensional model). See Exhibit 3.8 for Herzberg's motivation model. Employees are on a continuum from dissatisfied to not dissatisfied with their environment. Herzberg contends that providing maintenance factors will keep employees from being dissatisfied, but it will not make them satisfied or motivate them. For example, Herzberg believes that if employees are dissatisfied with their pay and they get a raise, they will no longer be dissatisfied. However, before long people get accustomed to the new standard of living and will become dissatisfied again. Employees will need another raise to not be dissatisfied again. The vicious cycle goes on. So, Herzberg says you have to focus on motivators—the job itself.

EXHIBIT 3.8 Two-Factor Motivation Theory

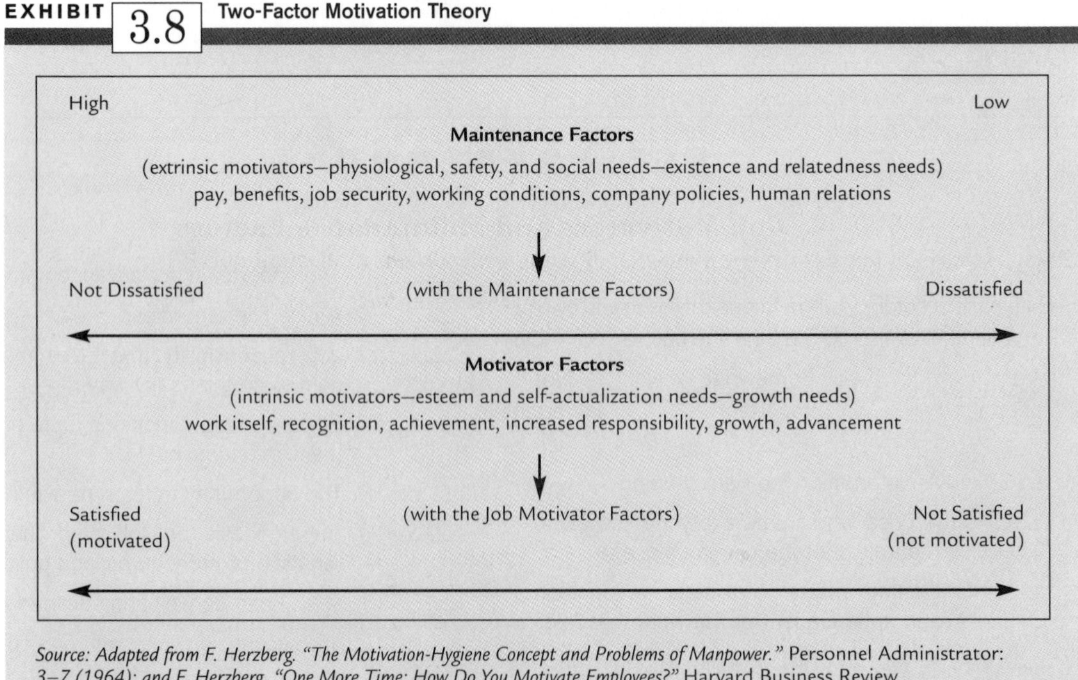

Source: Adapted from F. Herzberg. "The Motivation-Hygiene Concept and Problems of Manpower." Personnel Administrator: *3–7 (1964); and F. Herzberg. "One More Time: How Do You Motivate Employees?"* Harvard Business Review *(January–February 1967):53.*

Money as a Motivator

The current view of money as a motivator is that money matters more to some people than others, and that it may motivate some employees. However, money does not necessarily motivate employees to work harder. Have you ever gotten a raise? Were you more motivated and more productive? Money also is limited in its ability to motivate. For example, many commissioned workers get to a comfortable point and don't push to make extra money; and some employees get to the point where they don't want overtime work, even though they are paid two or three times their normal wage for overtime.

Research supports the statements that money alone just doesn't buy much happiness,[51] and what you have is never enough.[52] When we get the promotion or pay raise or buy that new item (house, car, vacation, clothes, toy), we are happy for awhile, but it's not long before we want something new.[53] Money can buy things, but there are lots of rich and famous people who are unhappy and make poor choices as a result.

But money is important.[54] As Jack Welch says, you can't just reward employees with trophies; you need to reward them in the wallet too. Employees often leave one organization for another to make more money. High compensation (pay and benefits) based on performance is a practice of successful organizations.[55]

Motivating Employees with Two-Factor Theory

Under the old management paradigm, money (and other extrinsic motivators) was considered the best motivator. Under the new leadership paradigm, pay is important, but it is not the best motivator; intrinsic motivators are. Herzberg's theory has been criticized for having limited research support. However, current research does support that giving more responsibility increases motivation and performance.[56] Herzberg fits the new paradigm: He says that managers must first ensure that the employees' level of pay and other maintenance factors are adequate. Once employees are not dissatisfied with their pay (and other maintenance factors), they can be motivated through their jobs. Herzberg also developed *job enrichment,* the process of building motivators into the job itself by making it more interesting and challenging. Job enrichment has been used successfully to motivate employees to higher levels of performance at many organizations, including AT&T, GM, IBM, Maytag, Monsanto, Motorola, Polaroid, and the Traveler's Life Insurance Company. Current research does support the use of job design to motivate employees.[57]

Work Application 5

Recall a present or past job; are you or were you dissatisfied or not dissatisfied with the maintenance factors? Are or were you satisfied or not satisfied with the motivators? Be sure to identify and explain your satisfaction with the specific maintenance and motivator factors.

Opening Case APPLICATION

3-b. How does Market America meet its distributors' content motivation needs?

Market America allows people to operate their own business. Related to *two-factor theory,* the focus is on *motivators* so that distributors can grow and meet their high-level needs of esteem and self-actualization. So the focus is on motivators not *maintenance* factors, although they are also met through the distributor model.

Acquired Needs Theory

Acquired needs theory *proposes that people are motivated by their need for achievement, power, and affiliation.* This is essentially the same definition given for achievement motivation theory in Chapter 2. It is now called *acquired needs theory* because David McClelland was not the first to study these needs, and because other management writers call McClelland's theory *acquired needs theory.* A general needs theory was developed by Henry Murray,[58] then adapted by John Atkinson[59] and David

McClelland.[60] You have already learned about McClelland's work, so we will be brief here. It's important to realize how closely linked traits, behavior, and motivation are. Acquired need is also widely classified as both a trait and a motivation, since McClelland and others believe that needs are based on personality traits. McClelland's affiliation need is essentially the same as Maslow's belongingness need; and power and achievement are related to esteem, self-actualization, and growth. McClelland's motivation theory does not include lower-level needs for safety and physiological needs.

Work Application 6

Explain how your need for achievement, power, and/or affiliation has affected your behavior, or that of someone you work with or have worked with. What were the consequences of the behavior, and was the need satisfied?

Acquired needs theory says that all people have the need for achievement, power, and affiliation, but to varying degrees. There is some support, although there are exceptions, stating that men tend to be more achievement oriented and women tend to be more relationship oriented.[61] Here are some ideas for motivating employees based on their dominant needs:

- *Motivating employees with a high n Ach.* Give them nonroutine, challenging tasks with clear, attainable objectives. Give them fast and frequent feedback on their performance. Continually give them increased responsibility for doing new things. Keep out of their way.
- *Motivating employees with a high n Pow.* Let them plan and control their jobs as much as possible. Try to include them in decision making, especially when they are affected by the decision. They tend to perform best alone rather than as team members. Try to assign them to a whole task rather than just part of a task.
- *Motivating employees with a high n Aff.* Be sure to let them work as part of a team. They derive satisfaction from the people they work with rather than the task itself. Give them lots of praise and recognition. Delegate responsibility for orienting and training new employees to them. They make great buddies and mentors.

Opening Case APPLICATION

3-c. How does Market America meet its distributors' content motivation needs?

Market America does help distributors meet all three *acquired needs.* It provides support so that they can *achieve* their goal of successfully running their own business, they have the *power* to be in control, and they can develop an *affiliation* with customers and other distributors.

Before we discuss the need to balance professional and personal needs, see Exhibit 3.9 for a comparison of the three content theories of motivation.

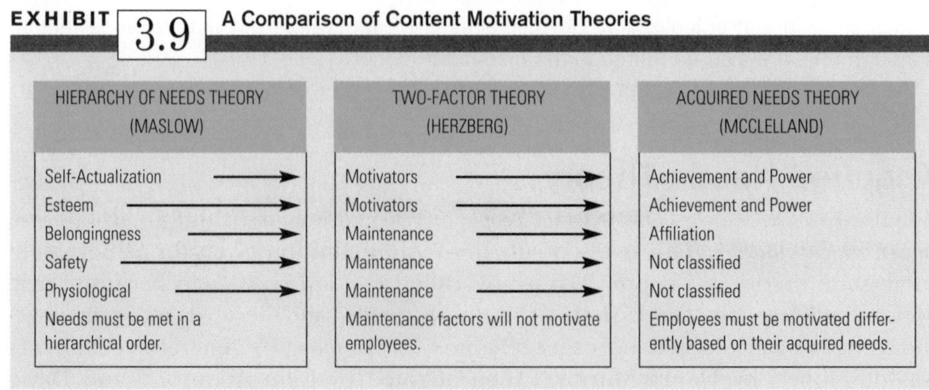

EXHIBIT 3.9 A Comparison of Content Motivation Theories

HIERARCHY OF NEEDS THEORY (MASLOW)	TWO-FACTOR THEORY (HERZBERG)	ACQUIRED NEEDS THEORY (MCCLELLAND)
Self-Actualization →	Motivators →	Achievement and Power
Esteem →	Motivators →	Achievement and Power
Belongingness →	Maintenance →	Affiliation
Safety →	Maintenance →	Not classified
Physiological →	Maintenance →	Not classified
Needs must be met in a hierarchical order.	Maintenance factors will not motivate employees.	Employees must be motivated differently based on their acquired needs.

The Need to Balance Professional and Personal Needs

You need a healthy balance between your life and your work.[62] The need to balance is currently a hot topic[63] because of the ascent of matrixed organizations working around the clock due to a global marketplace—and with the reengineered, downsizing, right-sizing world that focuses on how to get more done with fewer people.[64] Successful leaders use socialized power and strive to meet the needs of people and the organization to create a win-win situation for all stakeholders.[65] Two major things organizations are doing to help employees meet their personal needs are providing on-site day care centers—or giving employees information to help them find good day care—and offering flextime. Some leaders are also telling employees to go home and "get a life" before it is too late. Jack Welch says work–life balance is a personal decision, so choose what you want to do, be good at it, and live with the consequences.

Learning Outcome 5 *Discuss the major similarities and differences among the three process motivation theories.*

Process Motivation Theories

Process motivation theories *focus on understanding how people choose behavior to fulfill their needs.* Process motivation theories are more complex than content motivation theories. Content motivation theories simply focus on identifying and understanding people's needs. Process motivation theories go a step further by attempting to understand why people have different needs, why their needs change, how and why people choose to try to satisfy needs in different ways, the mental processes people go through as they understand situations, and how they evaluate their need satisfaction. In this section you will learn about three process motivation theories: equity theory, expectancy theory, and goal-setting theory.

Equity Theory

People want to be treated fairly.[66] If employees perceive organizational decisions and managerial actions to be unfair or unjust, they are likely to experience feelings of anger, outrage, and resentment.[67] Employees have to believe they are being treated fairly if they are to work together effectively.[68] Equity theory is primarily J. Stacy Adams's motivation theory, in which people are said to be motivated to seek social equity in the rewards they receive (output) for their performance (input).[69] **Equity theory** *proposes that people are motivated when their perceived inputs equal outputs.*

Rewarding People Equitably

Through the equity theory process, people compare their inputs (effort, experience, seniority, status, intelligence, and so forth) and outputs (praise, recognition, pay, benefits, promotions, increased status, supervisor's approval, and so forth) to that of relevant others. A relevant other could be a coworker or group of employees from the same or different organizations, or even from a hypothetical situation. Notice that our definition says *perceived* and not *actual* inputs to outputs. Others may perceive that equity actually exists, and that the person complaining about inequity is wrong.

Equitable distribution of pay is crucial to organizations.[70] Unfortunately, many employees tend to inflate their own efforts or performance when comparing themselves to others. Employees also tend to overestimate what others earn. Employees may be very satisfied and motivated until they find out that a relevant other is earning more for the same job, or earning the same for doing less work. A comparison with relevant others leads to one of three conclusions: The employee is underrewarded, overrewarded, or equitably rewarded. When inequity is perceived, employees attempt to reduce it by reducing input or increasing output.

Motivating with Equity Theory

Research supporting equity theory is mixed, because people who believe they are overrewarded usually don't change their behavior. Instead, they often rationalize that they deserve the outputs. A recent study used equity theory, and the results did support it.[71] One view of equity is that it is like Herzberg's maintenance factors. When employees are not dissatisfied, they are not actively motivated; but maintenance factors do demotivate when employees are dissatisfied. According to equity theory, when employees believe they are equitably rewarded they are not actively motivated. However, when employees believe they are underrewarded, they are demotivated.

Work Application 7

Give an example of how equity theory has affected your motivation, or that of someone else you work with or have worked with. Be sure to specify if you were underrewarded, overrewarded, or equitably rewarded.

Using equity theory in practice can be difficult, because you don't always know who the employee's reference group is, nor their view of inputs and outcomes. However, this theory does offer some useful general recommendations:

1. Managers should be aware that equity is based on perception, which may not be correct. It is possible for the manager to create equity or inequity. Some managers have favorite subordinates who get special treatment; others don't. So don't play favorites; treat employees equally but in unique ways.
2. Rewards should be equitable. When employees perceive that they are not treated fairly, morale and performance problems occur. Employees producing at the same level should be given equal rewards. Those producing less should get less.
3. High performance should be rewarded, but employees must understand the inputs needed to attain certain outputs. When incentive pay is used, there should be clear standards specifying the exact requirements to achieve the incentive. A manager should be able to objectively tell others why one person got a higher merit raise than another did.

Opening Case APPLICATION

4-a. How does Market America meet its distributors' process motivation needs?

Market America's distributor business model treats all distributors with *equity*. Distributors have unlimited potential since the more time and effort (*inputs*) they put into their business, the more potential rewards (*outputs*) are available. However, not everyone is cut out for sales and some people who start as independent distributors do not bring in other distributors under them, while others drop their distributorship entirely.

Expectancy Theory

Expectancy theory is based on Victor Vroom's formula: motivation = expectancy × instrumentality × valence.[72] **Expectancy theory** *proposes that people are motivated when they believe they can accomplish the task, they will get the reward, and the rewards for doing the task are worth the effort.* The theory is based on the following assumptions: Both internal (needs) and external (environment) factors affect behavior; behavior is the individual's decision; people have different needs, desires, and goals; and people make behavior decisions based on their perception of the outcome. Expectancy theory continues to be popular in the motivation literature today.[73]

Three Variables

All three variable conditions must be met in Vroom's formula for motivation to take place:

- *Expectancy* refers to the person's perception of his or her ability (probability) to accomplish an objective. Generally, the higher one's expectancy, the better the chance for motivation. When employees do not believe that they can accomplish objectives, they will not be motivated to try.
- *Instrumentality* refers to belief that the performance will result in getting the reward. Generally, the higher one's instrumentality, the greater the chance for motivation. If employees are certain to get the reward, they probably will be motivated.[74] When not sure, employees may not be motivated. For example, Dan believes he would be a good manager and wants to get promoted. However, Dan has an external locus of control and believes that working hard will not result in a promotion anyway. Therefore, he will not be motivated to work for the promotion.
- *Valence* refers to the value a person places on the outcome or reward. Generally, the higher the value (importance) of the outcome or reward, the better the chance of motivation.[75] For example, the supervisor, Jean, wants an employee, Sim, to work harder. Jean talks to Sim and tells him that working hard will result in a promotion. If Sim wants a promotion, he will probably be motivated. However, if a promotion is not of importance to Sim, it will not motivate him.

Motivating with Expectancy Theory

One study found that expectancy theory can accurately predict a person's work effort, satisfaction level, and performance—but only if the correct values are plugged into the formula. A meta-analysis (a study using the data of 77 other prior studies) had inconsistent findings with some positive correlations. A more recent study found that expectancy theory can be used to determine if leaders can be trained to use ethical considerations in decision making.[76]

Therefore, this theory works in certain contexts but not in others. Expectancy theory also works best with employees who have an internal locus of control, because if they believe they control their destiny, their efforts will result in success. The following conditions should be implemented to make the theory result in motivation:

1. Clearly define objectives and the performance necessary to achieve them.
2. Tie performance to rewards. High performance should be rewarded. When one employee works harder to produce more than other employees and is not rewarded, he or she may slow down productivity.
3. Be sure rewards are of value to the employee. Managers should get to know employees as individuals. Develop good human relations as a people developer.
4. Make sure your employees believe you will do what you say you will do. For example, employees must believe you will give them a merit raise if they do work hard. So that employees will believe you, follow through and show them you do what you say you'll do.
5. Use the Pygmalion effect (Chapter 2) to increase expectations. Your high expectation can result in follower self-fulfilling prophecy. As the level of expectation increases, so will performance.

Work
Application 8

Give an example of how expectancy theory has affected your motivation, or that of someone else you work with or have worked with. Be sure to specify the expectancy and valence.

Opening Case APPLICATION

4-b. How does Market America meet its distributors' process motivation needs?

Market America focuses on attracting people who have the *expectancy* that they can be successful at running their own business, and it provides the business model to help them succeed. The *valence* does vary, but most distributors are seeking their own business, to achieve financial independence, and to gain freedom of time.

Goal-Setting Theory

The research conducted by E. A. Locke and others has revealed that setting objectives has a positive effect on motivation and performance.[77] High-achievement, motivated individuals consistently engage in goal setting.[78] **Goal-setting theory** *proposes that specific, difficult goals motivate people.* Our behavior has a purpose, which is usually to fulfill a need. Goals give us a sense of purpose as to why we are working to accomplish a given task.[79]

Writing Objectives

To help you to write effective objectives that meet the criteria you will learn next, use the model. The parts of the **writing objectives model** *are (1) To + (2) action verb + (3) singular, specific, and measurable result to be achieved + (4) target date.* The model is shown in Model 3.1, which is adapted from Max E. Douglas's model.

Criteria for Objectives

For an objective to be effective, it should include the four criteria listed in steps 3 and 4 of the writing objectives model:

1. *Singular result.* To avoid confusion, each objective should contain only one end result. When multiple objectives are listed together, one may be met but the other(s) may not.
2. *Specific.* The objective should state the exact level of performance expected.[80]
3. *Measurable.* The saying, "what gets measured gets done," is true. If people are to achieve objectives, they must be able to observe and measure their progress regularly to monitor progress and to determine if the objective has been met.[81]
4. *Target date.* A specific date should be set for accomplishing the objective. When people have a deadline, they usually try harder to get the task done on time.[82] If people are simply told to do it when they can, they don't tend to get around to it until they have to. It is also more effective to set a specific date, such as October 29, rather than a set time, such as in two weeks, because you can forget when the time began and should end. Some objectives are ongoing and do not require a stated date. The target date is indefinite until it is changed, such as the Domino's objective in Model 3.1.

Work Application 9

1. Using the writing objectives model, write one or more objectives for an organization you work for or have worked for that meet the criteria for objectives.
2. Give an example of how a goal(s) affected your motivation and performance, or those of someone else you work with or have worked with.

In addition to the four criteria from the model, there are three other criteria that do not always fit within the model:

1. *Difficult but achievable.* A number of studies show that individuals perform better with moderately difficult objectives rather than (1) easy objectives, (2) objectives that are too difficult, or (3) simply told "do your best."[83] Be realistic about what you can achieve. Don't over-promise or try to do too much. GE's Jack Welch incorporated "stretch goals" in the early 1990s that led to dramatic improvements in productivity, efficiency, and profitability. Welch got everyone to focus on doing things quicker, better, and cheaper.

MODEL 3.1 Writing Effective Objectives Model

Four parts of the model with examples

(1) To +	(2) action verb +	(3) singular, specific, and measurable result +	(4) target date
Dominos			
To	deliver	pizza within 30 minutes	starting December 2007[84]
Toyota			
To	sell	10.4 million vehicles worldwide	by year-end 2009[85]
Nissan			
To	launch	electric vehicles in the United States and Japan	in 2010[86]
BMW			
To	increase	sales worldwide by more than 40 percent	by 2020[87]

2. *Participatively set.* People that participate in setting their objectives generally outperform those that are assigned objectives.
3. *Commitment.* For objectives to be met, employees must accept them. If employees are not committed to striving for the objective, even if they meet the other criteria, they may not meet the objective.[88] Using participation helps get employees to accept objectives.

Microsoft has a long tradition of having individuals set goals as part of its high performance-based culture. All employees are trained to set "SMART" (Specific, Measurable, Achievable, Results-based, and Time-specific) written goals. Managers are trained to assist in the goal-setting process, including how to provide relevant performance feedback during the review process.

Ethical **Dilemma 1**

Academic Standards

Lou Holtz, former successful Notre Dame football coach, said that the power of goal setting is an incredible motivator for high performance; to be successful we need to set a higher goal. Have colleges followed his advice? Have academic standards dropped, maintained, or increased over the years?

The academic credit-hour system was set many years ago to establish some formal standardization across colleges throughout the country so that academics and employers had the same expectations of the workload that a college student carried to earn a degree. This also allowed students to transfer credit from one university to another, assuming the same standards were met.

The credit-hour system was set at students doing two hours of preparation for each hour of in-class time. So, a student taking five classes should spend 15 hours in class

continued

(Ethical Dilemma 1 continued)

and 30 hours preparing for class, or a total of 40+ hours per week—which is a full-time schedule.

1. How many hours outside of class, on average, do you and other students use to prepare for class each week?
2. Are college professors throughout the country assigning students two hours of preparation for every hour in class today? If not, why have they dropped the standard?
3. Are students who are putting in part-time hours (20–30 hours) during college being well prepared for a career after graduation (40–60 hours)?
4. Is it ethical and socially responsible for professors to drop standards and for colleges to award degrees for doing less work today than 5, 10, or 20 years ago?

Using Goal Setting to Motivate Employees

Goal setting might be the most effective management tool available. Organizational behavior scholars rated goal-setting theory as number one in importance among 73 management theories.[89] Need we say anything more about it besides to follow the guidelines above?

Applying the **Concept 3**

Objectives

For each objective, state which "must" criteria is not met.

a. singular result
b. specific
c. measurable
d. target date

____ 11. To triple the sales of Lexus cars in Europe

____ 12. To sell 2 percent more mufflers and 7 percent more tires in 2010

____ 13. To increase revenue in 2011

____ 14. To be perceived as the best restaurant in the Springfield area by the end of 2011

____ 15. To write objectives within two weeks

Opening Case APPLICATION

4-c. How does Market America meet its distributors' process motivation needs?

Market America relies heavily on *goal-setting* theory. Two of its goals are to establish itself as a leader in the Direct Sales Industry and to become a Fortune 500 Company. Goal Setting is the second step in the five basic steps for success at Market America. Attitude and Knowledge, Retailing, Prospecting and Recruiting, and Follow-Up and Duplication are the other four. Distributors are taught to set business and personal long-term goals and to break them down for the next year by month, week, and day. Goals are to be read twice a day for motivation.

Reinforcement Theory

B. F. Skinner, reinforcement motivation theorist, contends that to motivate employees it is really not necessary to identify and understand needs (content motivation theories), nor to understand how employees choose behaviors to fulfill them (process motivation theories). All the manager needs to do is understand the relationship between behaviors and their consequences, and then arrange contingencies that reinforce desirable behaviors and discourage undesirable behaviors. **Reinforcement theory** *proposes that through the consequences for behavior, people will be motivated to behave in predetermined ways.* Reinforcement theory uses behavior modification (apply reinforcement theory to get employees to do what you want them to do) and operant conditioning (types and schedules of reinforcement). Skinner states that behavior is learned through experiences of positive and negative consequences. The three components of Skinner's framework are shown with an example in Exhibit 3.10.[90]

EXHIBIT 3.10 Components of Reinforcement Theory

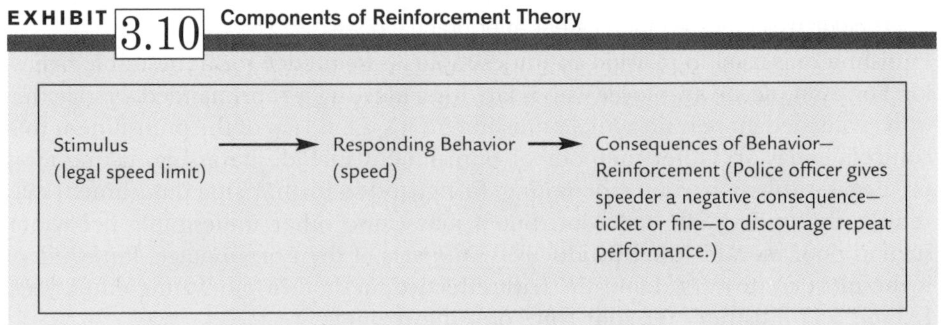

A recent meta-analysis of empirical research over the past 20 years found that reinforcement theory increased performance by 17 percent.[91] Thus, reinforcement theory can be a consistent predictor of job behavior. As illustrated in the example in Exhibit 3.10, behavior is a function of its consequences. Employees learn what is, and is not, desired behavior as a result of the consequences for specific behavior. In this section, we discuss the two important concepts used to modify behavior (the types of reinforcement and the schedules of reinforcement), that you get what you reinforce, how to motivate using reinforcement, and how to give praise.

Learning Outcome 6 *Explain the four types of reinforcement.*

Types of Reinforcement

The four types of reinforcement are positive, avoidance, extinction, and punishment.

Positive Reinforcement

A method of encouraging continued behavior is to offer attractive consequences (rewards) for desirable performance.[92] For example, an employee is on time for a meeting and is rewarded by the manager thanking him or her. The praise is used to reinforce punctuality. Other reinforcements are pay, promotions, time off, increased status, and so forth. Positive reinforcement results in positive results, and it is the best motivator for increasing productivity.[93] Giving praise is a positive reinforcement, and you will learn how to give praise at the end of this section.

Avoidance Reinforcement

Avoidance is also called *negative reinforcement.* As with positive reinforcement, you are encouraging continued desirable behavior. The employee avoids the negative consequence. For example, an employee is punctual for a meeting to avoid the negative reinforcement, such as a reprimand. *Rules* are designed to get employees to avoid certain behavior. However, rules in and of themselves are not a punishment. Punishment is given only if the rule is broken.

Extinction

Rather than encourage desirable behavior, extinction (and punishment) attempts to reduce or eliminate undesirable behavior by withholding reinforcement when the behavior occurs. For example, an employee who is late for a meeting is not rewarded with praise. Or the manager may withhold a reward of value, such as a pay raise, until the employee performs to set standards.

From another perspective, managers who do not reward good performance can cause its extinction.[94] In other words, if you ignore good employee performance, good performance may stop because employees think, "Why should I do a good job if I'm not rewarded in some way?"

Punishment

Punishment is used to provide an undesirable consequence for undesirable behavior. For example, an employee who is late for a meeting is reprimanded. Notice that with avoidance there is no actual punishment; it's the threat of the punishment that controls behavior. Other methods of punishment include harassing, taking away privileges, probation, fining, demoting, firing, and so forth. Using punishment may reduce the undesirable behavior; but it may cause other undesirable behaviors, such as poor morale, lower productivity, and acts of theft or sabotage. Punishment is the most controversial and the least effective method in motivating employees. Exhibit 3.11 illustrates the four types of reinforcement.

Schedules of Reinforcement

The second reinforcement consideration in controlling behavior is determining when to reinforce performance. The two major classifications are continuous and intermittent.

Work Application **10**

Give one or more examples of the types of reinforcement, and the schedules used, on a present or past job.

Continuous Reinforcement

With a continuous method, each and every desired behavior is reinforced. Examples of this method would be a machine with an automatic counter that lets the employee know (at any given moment) exactly how many units have been produced, a piece rate reward of $1 for each unit produced, or a manager who comments on every customer report.

Intermittent Reinforcement

With intermittent reinforcement, the reward is given based on the passage of time or output. When the reward is based on the passage of time, it is called an *interval*

EXHIBIT 3.11 Types of Reinforcement

As a manager, you have an assistant who makes many errors when completing correspondence. Your objective, which you discussed with the assistant, is to decrease the error rate by 50 percent by Friday, June 4, 2010. Based on the assistant's performance at that time, you have four types of reinforcement that you can use with her when you next review her work.

EMPLOYEE BEHAVIOR	TYPE OF REINFORCEMENT	MANAGER ACTION (CONSEQUENCE)	EMPLOYEE BEHAVIOR MODIFICATION (FUTURE)
Improved performance →	Positive →	Praise improvements →	Repeat quality work*
Improved performance →	Avoidance →	Do not give any reprimand →	Repeat quality work
Performance not improved →	Extinction →	Withhold praise/raise →	Do not repeat poor work
Performance not improved →	Punishment →	Discipline action, such as a written warning →	Do not repeat poor work

*Assuming the employee improved performance, positive reinforcement is the best motivator.

schedule. When it is based on output, it is called a *ratio* schedule. When electing to use intermittent reinforcement, you have four alternatives:

1. *Fixed interval schedule.* Giving a salary paycheck every week, breaks and meals at the same time every day.
2. *Variable interval schedule.* Giving praise only now and then, a surprise inspection, or a pop quiz.
3. *Fixed ratio schedule.* Giving a piece rate or bonus after producing a standard rate.
4. *Variable ratio schedule.* Giving praise for excellent work, or a lottery for employees who have not been absent for a set amount of time.

Ratios are generally better motivators than intervals. The variable ratio tends to be the most powerful schedule for sustaining behavior.

Ethical **Dilemma 2**

Airlines

An airline often charges higher fares for one-way tickets than round-trip tickets, and for direct flight tickets to its hub than for flight connections from its hub to another destination. So some travelers buy round-trip tickets and only go one way, and some end their travel at the hub instead of taking the connection (a "hidden city" itinerary), to save money. The airlines call this breach of contract: they have *punished* travel agencies for tickets that aren't properly used, they sometimes demand higher fares from travelers caught, and they have seized some travelers' frequent-flier miles, saying they were fraudulently obtained.

1. Not using the full travel of a ticket breaks airline rules but not the law, so it's not illegal, unless travelers lie about what they are doing. But is it ethical and socially responsible behavior of travelers?
2. Is it ethical and socially responsible for airlines to charge more for less travel?
3. Is it ethical and socially responsible to punish people who break the ticket rules?
4. Is reinforcement theory effective (does it motivate you and others) in today's global economy?
5. Is reinforcement theory ethical and socially responsible, or is it manipulative?

You Get What You Reinforce

You get what you reinforce, not necessarily what you reward. Recall that there are four types of reinforcement, and reward is only one of them; it doesn't always motivate the desired behavior. One of the important things you should learn in this course is that people will do what they are reinforced for doing. People seek information concerning what activities are reinforced, and then seek to do (or at least pretend to do) those things, often to the exclusion of activities not reinforced. The extent to which this occurs, of course, depends on the attractiveness of the rewards offered and the penalties for the behavior.[95]

For example, if a professor gives a class a reading list of several sources, but tells students (or they realize without being told) that they will not discuss them in class or be tested on them, how many students will read them? Or, if the professor says, "A, B, and C from this chapter are important and I'll test you on them, but X, Y, and Z will not be on the test," will students spend equal time studying both groups of material?

In the business setting, if the manager repeatedly says quality is important, but the standard of evaluation includes only quantity and meeting scheduled shipments, how many employees will ship poor-quality products to meet the scheduled shipment? How many will miss the scheduled shipment, take a reprimand for missing the scheduled shipment, and get a poor performance review in order to do a quality job? An incomplete standard measuring only quantitative output that is highly visible and easy to measure is a common problem.

The Folly of Rewarding A, While Hoping for B

Reward systems are often fouled up when the types of behavior being rewarded are those that the manager is trying to discourage, while the desired behavior is not being rewarded at all. This problem is called the folly of rewarding A, while hoping for B.[96] Exhibit 3.12 presents a couple of examples.

EXHIBIT 3.12 Common Management Reward Follies

MANAGERS HOPE FOR:	BUT MANAGERS FREQUENTLY REWARD:
Long-term growth and environmental social responsibility	Quarterly earnings
Innovative thinking and risk-taking	Proven methods and not making mistakes
Teamwork and collaboration	The best competitive individual performers
Employee involvement and empowerment	Tight control over operations and resources
High achievement	Another year's effort
Candor such as telling of bad news early	Reporting good news, whether it is true or not, and agreeing with the boss, whether the boss is right or wrong

Source: Adapted from S. Kerr. "On the Folly of Rewarding A, While Hoping for B." Academy of Management Executive *9 (February 1995): 32–40.*

Motivating with Reinforcement

Several organizations, including 3M, Frito-Lay, and B. F. Goodrich, have used reinforcement to increase productivity; Michigan Bell had a 50 percent improvement in attendance and above-standard productivity and efficiency level; and Emery Air Freight went from 30 percent of employees meeting the standard to 90 percent after using reinforcement. Emery estimated that its reinforcement program resulted in a $650,000 yearly savings.

Generally, positive reinforcement is the best motivator. Continuous reinforcement is better at sustaining desired behavior; however, it is not always possible or practical. Here are some general guidelines for using positive reinforcement:

1. Make sure employees know exactly what is expected of them. Set clear objectives.[97]
2. Select appropriate rewards.[98] A reward to one person could be considered a punishment by another. Know your employees' needs.
3. Select the appropriate reinforcement schedule.
4. Do not reward mediocre or poor performance.[99]

5. Look for the positive and give praise, rather than focus on the negative and criticize. Listen to people and make them feel good about themselves (Pygmalion effect).[100]
6. Never go a day without giving sincere praise.
7. Do things for your employees, instead of to them, and you will see productivity increase.

As a manager, try the positive first.[101] Positive reinforcement is a true motivator because it creates a win-win situation by meeting the needs of the employee as well as the manager and organization. From the employee's perspective, avoidance and punishment create a lose-win situation. The organization or manager wins by forcing employees to do something they really don't want to do.

Giving Praise

Pay can increase performance. But it is not the only, nor necessarily the best, reinforcer for performance. Empirical research studies have found that feedback and social reinforcers (praise) may have as strong an impact on performance as pay. Praise actually works by boosting levels of dopamine in the brain, a chemical linked to joy.[102] In the 1940s, a survey revealed that what employees want most from a job is full appreciation for work done. Similar studies have been performed over the years with little change in results.

Although research has shown praise to be an effective motivator, and giving praise costs nothing and takes only a minute, few employees are getting a pat on the back these days. When was the last time your manager thanked you or gave you some praise for a job well done? When was the last time your manager complained about your work? If you are a manager, when was the last time you praised or criticized your employees? What is the ratio of praise to criticism? On the other hand, the most praised generation is now coming to work,[103] and unearned praise is condescending and destructive; incentives can become entitlements, so be sure to only praise good performance.[104]

Giving praise develops a positive self-concept in employees and leads to better performance—the Pygmalion effect and self-fulfilling prophecy. Praise is a motivator (not maintenance) because it meets employees' needs for esteem and self-actualization, growth, and achievement. Giving praise creates a win-win situation. It is probably the most powerful, simplest, least costly, and yet most underused motivational technique there is.

Ken Blanchard and Spencer Johnson popularized giving praise back in the 1980s through their best-selling book, *The One-Minute Manager*.[105] They developed a technique that involves giving one-minute feedback of praise. Model 3.2, Giving Praise, is an adaptation. *The steps in the* **giving praise model** *are (1) Tell the employee exactly what was done correctly. (2) Tell the employee why the behavior is important. (3) Stop for a moment of silence. (4) Encourage repeat performance.* Blanchard calls it one-minute praise because it should not take more than one minute to give the praise. It is not necessary for the employee to say anything. The four steps are described below and illustrated in Model 3.2.

MODEL 3.2 Giving Praise

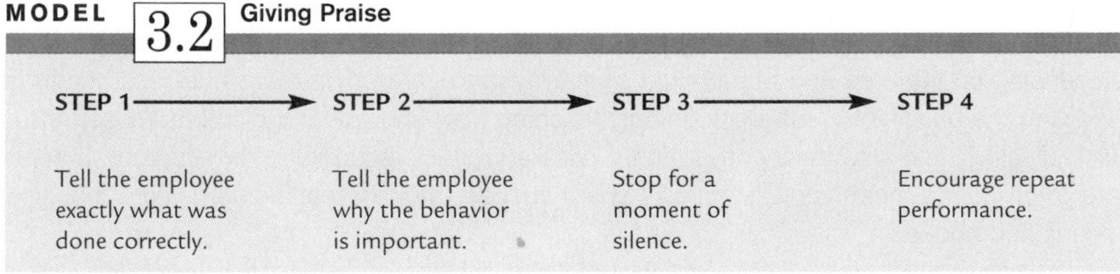
STEP 1
STEP 2
STEP 3
STEP 4
Tell the employee exactly what was done correctly.
Tell the employee why the behavior is important.
Stop for a moment of silence.
Encourage repeat performance.

Step 1. Tell the employee exactly what was done correctly. When giving praise, look the person in the eye. Eye contact shows sincerity and concern. It is important to be very specific and descriptive. General statements, like "you're a good worker," are not as effective. On the other hand, don't talk for too long or the praise loses its effectiveness.

Step 2. Tell the employee why the behavior is important. Briefly state how the organization and/or person benefits from the action. It is also helpful to tell the employee how you feel about the behavior. Be specific and descriptive.

Step 3. Stop for a moment of silence. Being silent is tough for many managers. The rationale for the silence is to give the employee the chance to "feel" the impact of the praise. It's like "the pause that refreshes." When you are thirsty and take the first sip or gulp of a refreshing drink, it's not until you stop, and maybe say, "Ah," that you feel your thirst quenched.

Step 4. Encourage repeat performance. This is the reinforcement that motivates the employee to continue the desired behavior. Blanchard recommends touching the employee. Touching has a powerful impact. However, he recommends it only if both parties feel comfortable. Others say don't touch employees; it could lead to a sexual harassment charge.

As you can see, giving praise is easy, and it doesn't cost a penny. Managers trained to give praise say it works wonders. It's a much better motivator than giving a raise or other monetary reward. One manager stated that an employee was taking his time stacking cans on a display. He gave the employee praise for stacking the cans so straight. The employee was so pleased with the praise that the display went up with about a 100 percent increase in productivity. Note that the manager looked for the positive, and used positive reinforcement rather than punishment. The manager could have given a reprimand comment such as, "Quit goofing off and get the display up faster." That statement would not have motivated the employee to increase productivity. All it would have done was hurt human relations, and could have ended in an argument. The cans were straight. The employee was not praised for the slow work pace. However, if the praise had not worked, the manager should have used another reinforcement method.[106]

In this global environment, it is not always possible to give praise in person, so when you don't see people face-to-face, use written communication, including e-mail, instead. Disney CEO, Bob Iger, writes personal, handwritten notes on Disney stationery to praise employees, even those he has never met. He says that writing a simple note goes a long way with people.[107]

Opening Case APPLICATION

5. How does Market America use reinforcement theory to motivate its distributors?

Market America uses *positive reinforcement* with a *continuous reinforcement schedule* as each and every sale results in compensation. It has a standardized meetings system throughout areas. However, the frequency of meetings is based on a *variable ratio schedule* depending on the area and the amount of activity in the area. There are business briefings, showing the business to others, trainings, teaching new and existing distributors, seminars, district rallies, and a national convention. *Praise* and other recognition for accomplishments are given during meetings. Distributors share success stories, testimonials, voice mail tips, videos and books.

Applying the **Concept 4**

Motivation Theories

Identify each supervisor's statement of how to motivate employees by the theory behind the statement. Write the appropriate letter in the blank before each item.

a. hierarchy of needs
b. two-factor
c. acquired needs
d. equity
e. goal setting
f. expectancy
g. reinforcement

____ 16. I motivate employees by making their jobs interesting and challenging.

____ 17. I make sure I treat everyone fairly to motivate them.

____ 18. I know Kate likes people, so I give her jobs in which she works with other employees.

____ 19. Carl would often yell in the halls because he knew it bothered me. So I decided to ignore his yelling, and he stopped.

____ 20. I got to know all of my employees' values. Now I can offer rewards that will motivate them when they achieve attainable task performance.

____ 21. Our company now offers good working conditions, salaries, and benefits, so we are working at developing the third need for socialization.

____ 22. When my employees do a good job, I thank them by using a four-step model.

____ 23. I used to try to improve working conditions to motivate employees. But I stopped and now focus on giving employees more responsibility so they can grow and develop new skills.

____ 24. I tell employees exactly what I want them to do, with a tough deadline that they can achieve.

____ 25. I now realize that I tend to be an autocratic manager because it helps fill my needs. I will work at giving some of my employees more autonomy on how they do their jobs.

Learning Outcome 7 *State the major differences among content, process, and reinforcement theories.*

Putting the Motivation Theories Together Within the Motivation Process

Goal-setting theory gurus Edwin Locke and Gary Latham recently stated that there is an urgent need to tie motivational theories and processes together into an overall model, insofar as it is possible.[108] Others have attempted to do so.[109] That is exactly what we do in this last section of the chapter.

Motivation is important because it helps to explain why employees behave the way they do. At this point you may be wondering: How do these theories fit together? Is one the best? Should I try to pick the correct theory for a given situation? The groups of theories are complementary; each group of theories refers to a different stage in the motivation process. Each group of theories answers a different question. Content motivation theories answer the question: What needs do employees have that should be met on the job? Process motivation theories answer the question: How do employees choose behavior to fulfill their needs? Reinforcement theory answers the question: What can managers do to get employees to behave in ways that meet the organizational objectives?

EXHIBIT 3.13 The Motivation Process with the Motivation Theories

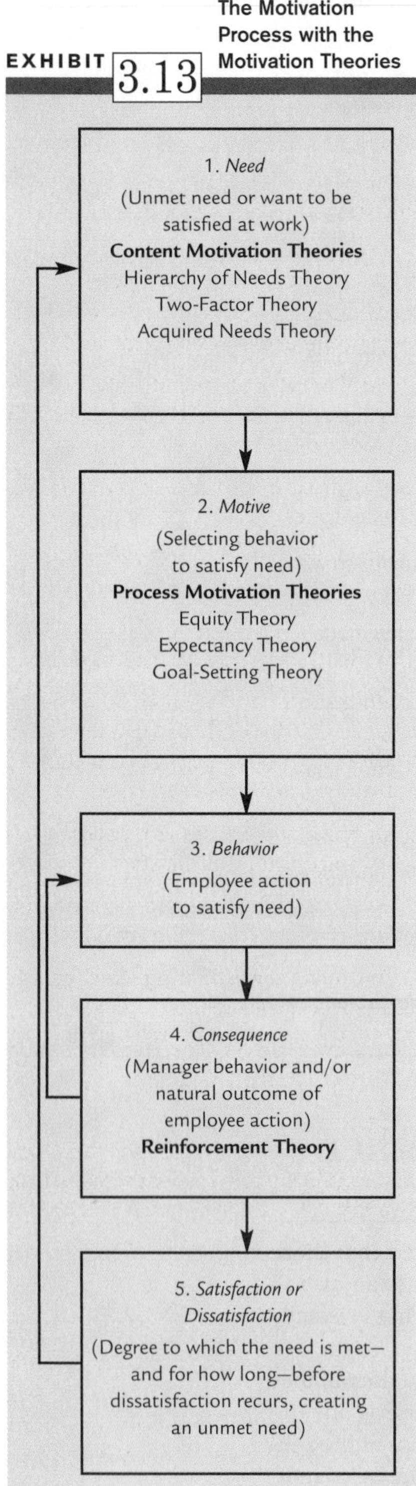

In this chapter you learned that the motivation process went from need to motive to behavior to consequence to satisfaction or dissatisfaction. Now let's make the motivation process a little more complex by incorporating the motivation theories, or answers to the preceding questions, into the process. See Exhibit 3.13 for an illustration. Note that step 4 loops back to step 3 because, according to reinforcement theory, behavior is learned through consequences. Step 4 does not loop back to steps 1 or 2 because reinforcement theory is not concerned about needs, motives, or satisfaction; it focuses on getting employees to behave in predetermined ways, through consequences provided by managers. Also note that step 5 loops back to step 1 because meeting needs is ongoing; meeting our needs is a never-ending process. Finally, be aware that according to two-factor theory, step 5 (satisfaction or dissatisfaction) is not on one continuum but on two separate continuums (satisfied to not satisfied, or dissatisfied to not dissatisfied), based on the level of need being met (motivator or maintenance).

Go to the Internet (www.cengage.com/management/lussier)
where you will find a broad array of resources to help maximize your learning.

- Review the vocabulary
- Try a quiz
- Find related links

Chapter Summary

The chapter summary is organized to answer the eight learning outcomes for Chapter 3.

1. **List the University of Iowa leadership styles.**

   The University of Iowa leadership styles are autocratic and democratic.

2. **Describe similarities and differences between the University of Michigan and Ohio State University leadership models.**

   The University of Michigan and Ohio State University leadership models are similar because they are both based on the same two distinct leadership behaviors, although the models use different names for the two behaviors. The models are different because the University of Michigan model identifies two leadership styles based on either job- or employee-centered behavior. The Ohio State University model states that a leader uses high or low structure and consideration, resulting in four leadership style combinations of these two behaviors.

3. **Discuss similarities and differences between the Ohio State University Leadership Model and the Leadership Grid.**

   Both theories are based on the same two leadership behaviors, but use different names for the two dimensions. The theories are different because the Leadership Grid identifies five leadership styles, with one being middle of the road, while the Ohio State model identifies four leadership styles. The Leadership Grid also gives each combination of the two-dimensional behaviors one leadership style name. Authors of the Leadership Grid were strong supporters of the high-high team leadership style as the best.

4. **Discuss similarities and differences among the three content motivation theories.**

Similarities among the content motivation theories include their focus on identifying and understanding employee needs. The theories identify similar needs, but are different in the way they classify the needs. Hierarchy of needs theory includes physiological, safety, belongingness, esteem, and self-actualization needs. Two-factor theory includes motivators and maintenance factors. Acquired needs theory includes achievement, power, and affiliation needs and includes no lower-level needs, as the other two theories do.

5. **Discuss the major similarities and differences among the three process motivation theories.**

The similarity among the three process motivation theories includes their focus on understanding how employees choose behaviors to fulfill their needs. However, they are very different in their perceptions of how employees are motivated. Equity theory proposes that employees are motivated when their perceived inputs equal outputs. Expectancy theory proposes that employees are motivated when they believe they can accomplish the task and the rewards for doing so are worth the effort. Goal-setting theory proposes that achievable, difficult goals motivate employees.

6. **Explain the four types of reinforcement.**

(1) Positive reinforcement provides the employee with a reward consequence for performing the desired behavior. (2) Avoidance reinforcement encourages employees to perform the desired behavior in order to avoid a negative consequence. (3) Extinction reinforcement withholds a positive consequence to get the employee to stop performing undesirable behavior. (4) Punishment reinforcement gives the employee a negative consequence to get the employee to stop performing undesirable behavior.

7. **State the major differences among content, process, and reinforcement theories.**

Content motivation theories focus on identifying and understanding employees' needs. Process motivation goes a step farther to understand how employees choose behavior to fulfill their needs. Reinforcement theory is not as concerned about employee needs; it focuses on getting employees to do what managers want them to do through the consequences provided by managers for their behavior. The use of rewards is the means of motivating employees.

8. **Define the following key terms (in order of appearance in the chapter).**

Select one or more methods: (1) fill in the missing key terms from memory; (2) match the key terms from the following list with their definitions below; (3) copy the key terms in order from the list at the beginning of the chapter.

__________ is the combination of traits, skills, and behaviors leaders use as they interact with followers.

__________ identifies two leadership styles: job-centered and employee-centered.

__________ identifies four leadership styles: low structure and high consideration, high structure and high consideration, low structure and low consideration, and high structure and low consideration.

__________ identifies five leadership styles: 1,1 impoverished; 9,1 authority-compliance; 1,9 country club; 5,5 middle of the road; and 9,9 team leader.

__________ is anything that affects behavior in pursuing a certain outcome.

__________ is when people go from need to motive to behavior to consequence to satisfaction or dissatisfaction.

__________ focus on explaining and predicting behavior based on people's needs.

__________ proposes that people are motivated through five levels of needs—physiological, safety, belongingness, esteem, and self-actualization.

__________ proposes that people are motivated by motivators rather than maintenance factors.

__________ proposes that people are motivated by their need for achievement, power, and affiliation.

__________ focus on understanding how people choose behavior to fulfill their needs.

__________ proposes that people are motivated when their perceived inputs equal outputs.

__________ proposes that people are motivated when they believe they can accomplish the task, they will get the reward, and the rewards for doing the task are worth the effort.

__________ proposes that specific, difficult goals motivate people.

__________ includes (1) To + (2) action verb + (3) singular, specific, and measurable result to be achieved + (4) target date.

__________ proposes that through the consequences for behavior, people will be motivated to behave in predetermined ways.

__________ includes four steps—(1) Tell the employee exactly what was done correctly. (2) Tell the employee why the behavior is important. (3) Stop for a moment of silence. (4) Encourage repeat performance.

Key Terms

acquired needs theory, 85
content motivation theories, 80
equity theory, 87
expectancy theory, 88
giving praise model, 97
goal-setting theory, 90
hierarchy of needs theory, 81
Leadership Grid, 76
leadership style, 70
motivation, 79
motivation process, 79
Ohio State University Leadership Model, 74
process motivation theories, 87
reinforcement theory, 93
two-factor theory, 82
University of Michigan Leadership Model, 72
writing objectives model, 90

Review Questions

1. Why was there a shift from the trait to the behavioral theory paradigm?
2. How is leadership behavior based on traits?
3. What are the University of Iowa leadership styles?
4. What are the University of Michigan leadership styles?
5. What are the Ohio State University leadership styles?
6. What are three important contributions of the University of Michigan and Ohio State University studies?
7. What are the Leadership Grid leadership styles?
8. What are the three important contributions of the Leadership Grid and high-high research?
9. What is motivation, and why is it important to know how to motivate employees?
10. What are the content motivation theories?
11. What are the process motivation theories?
12. What are the types and schedules of reinforcement theory?

Communication Skills

The following critical-thinking questions can be used for class discussion and/or as written assignments to develop communication skills. Be sure to give complete explanations for all questions.

1. Which leadership model do you prefer?
2. Do you agree with the University of Michigan model (with two leadership styles) or with the Ohio State model (with four leadership styles)?
3. Do you agree with the Leadership Grid's claim that the one best leadership style is the team leader (9,9)?
4. Which of the three content motivation theories do you prefer? Why?
5. Which of the three process motivation theories do you prefer? Why?
6. What is your motivation theory? What major methods, techniques, and so on, do you plan to use on the job as a manager to increase motivation and performance?
7. Reinforcement theory is unethical because it is used to manipulate employees. Do you agree with this statement? Explain your answer.
8. Which type and schedule of reinforcement do you plan to use most often as a leader?
9. Do you really get what you reinforce? Explain.

CASE

Art Friedman—Friedmans Appliance

Art Friedman started his business in 1970 as Friedmans Appliance, selling all types of major appliances. In 1976, Friedman changed the company name to Friedmans Microwave Ovens to match his new strategy of focusing only on microwave ovens, which was the new thing back then. His goal was to be the absolute best place to buy a microwave oven and its accessories. His third strategic move was to franchise his microwave business, using Art Friedman's motivational technique of making everyone a boss. Friedmans also went online. For more than 30 years, Friedmans has been accomplishing its goal by providing superior service, good prices, unconditional satisfaction guarantees, and cooking classes to educate customers on how to get the most from their microwave. Friedmans also offers installation and repair services. Friedmans has sold more than two million microwaves. Today, Art Friedman is retired, but his franchised name is still going strong, primarily in California. Some of the indepedently owned stores that bear the Friedmans name continue to sell only microwaves, others also sell other types of appliances, and some also offer full kitchen renovations.[110]

The original Friedmans store employed 15 people in Oakland, California. Friedman believed that his employees were not motivated, so he implemented the following changes to motivate his employees, and these techniques are still being used today. The following conversation took place between Bob Lussier and founder Art Friedman.

Bob: What is the reason for your success in business?

Art: My business technique.

Bob: What is it? How did you implement it?

Art: I called my 15 employees together and told them, "From now on I want you to feel as though the company is ours, not mine. We are all bosses. From now on you decide what you're worth and tell the accountant to put it in your pay envelope. You decide which days and hours you work and when to take time off. We will have an open petty cash system that will allow anyone to go into the box and borrow money when they need it."

Bob: You're kidding, right?

Art: No, it's true. I really do these things.

Bob: Did anyone ask for a raise?

Art: Yes, several people did. Charlie asked for and received a $100-a-week raise.

Bob: Did he and the others increase their productivity to earn their raises?

Art: Yes, they all did.

Bob: How could you run an appliance store with employees coming and going as they pleased?

Art: The employees made up schedules that were satisfactory to everyone. We had no problems of under- or overstaffing.

Bob: Did anyone steal from the petty cash box?

Art: No.

Bob: Would this technique work in any business?

Art: It did work, it still works, and it will always work!

GO TO THE INTERNET: To learn more about Art Friedman and Friedmans, visit their Web site **(http://www.friedmansappliance.com)**.

Support your answers to the following questions with specific information from the case and text or with other information you get from the Web or other sources.

1. Which University—Iowa, Michigan, and Ohio State—leadership styles does Art Friedman use?
2. Which specific motivation level, factor, and need (from the content motivation theories) applies to Friedmans Appliance?
3. Do equity and expectancy theory apply to this case? Explain.
4. Which type of reinforcement does Friedman use?
5. Do you know of any organizations that use any of Friedman's or other unusual techniques? If yes, what is the organization's name? What does it do?
6. Could Friedman's techniques work in all organizations? Explain your answer.
7. In a position of authority, would you use Friedman's techniques? Which ones?

CUMULATIVE CASE QUESTIONS

8. Which of the Big Five personality dimensions is best illustrated in this case by Art Friedman (Chapter 2)?
9. Does Friedman have a Theory X or Theory Y attitude (Chapter 2)?

CASE EXERCISE AND ROLE-PLAY

Preparation: From case question 7, which of Friedman's motivational techniques would you use to motivate franchisees? Which techniques of your own or from other organizations would you use? Justify your choice of motivation techniques.

In-Class Groups: Break into groups of 4 to 6 members and develop a list of motivational techniques group members would use, with justification. Select a spokesperson to record the techniques with justification and present them to the class.

Role-Play: One person (representing him- or herself or a group) may give the speech to the entire class, stating which new motivational techniques will be used and explaining each technique.

VIDEO CASE

Motivation at Washburn Guitars

Founded in the late 1800s in Chicago, Washburn Guitars boasts a rich tradition of fine instrument making. Today the company sells more than 50,000 guitars annually, totaling about $40 million in revenue. Washburn Guitars produces a variety of acoustic and electric guitars. Washburn craftsmen also enjoy making custom guitars. In recent years, custom shop production has grown dramatically from 20 to 300 guitars per month. Having a motivated workforce is essential because guitar making is labor intensive and requires attention to detail. Quality materials combined with quality craftsmanship are necessary to produce quality guitars. Washburn Guitars' workforce is motivated because they love music and care about the instruments.

1. What motivates most employees at Washburn Guitars?
2. What kinds of guitars do employees most like to produce?
3. What is the connection between quality guitars and workforce motivation?

Skill-Development Exercise 1

Writing Objectives

Preparing for Skill-Development Exercise 1
For this exercise, you will first work at improving objectives that do not meet the criteria for objectives. Then you will write nine objectives for yourself.

Part 1. For each objective below, identify the missing criteria and rewrite the objective so that it meets all essential criteria. When writing objectives, use the model:

To + action verb + singular, specific, and measurable result + target date

1. To improve our company image by year-end 2010.
   Criteria missing: ______
   Improved objective: ______
2. To increase the number of customers by 10 percent.
   Criteria missing: ______
   Improved objective: ______
3. To increase profits during 2010.
   Criteria missing: ______
   Improved objective: ______
4. To sell 5 percent more hot dogs and soda at the baseball game on Sunday, June 13, 2010.
   Criteria missing: ______
   Improved objective: ______

Part 2. Write three educational, personal, and career objectives you want to accomplish. Your objectives can be as short term as something you want to accomplish today, or as long term as 20 years from now. Be sure your objectives meet the criteria for effective objectives.

Educational objectives:

1. ______
2. ______
3. ______

Personal objectives:

1. ______
2. ______
3. ______

Career objectives:

1. ______
2. ______
3. ______

Doing Skill-Development Exercise 1 in Class

Objective

To develop your skill at writing objectives.

The primary AACSB learning standard skill developed through this exercise is analytic skills—students learn to set goals.

Preparation

You should have corrected and have written objectives during the preparation before class.

Experience

You will get feedback on how well you corrected the four objectives and share your written objectives with others.

Options *(8–20 minutes)*

A. The instructor goes over suggested corrections for the four objectives in part 1 of the preparation, and then calls on class members to share their written objectives with the class in part 2.

B. The instructor goes over suggested corrections for the four objectives in part 1 of the preparation, and then the class breaks into groups of four to six to share their written objectives.

C. Break into groups of four to six and go over the corrections for the four objectives in part 1. Tell the instructor when your group is done, but go on to part 2, sharing your written objectives, until all groups are finished with the four corrections. The instructor goes over the corrections and may allow more time for sharing objectives. Give each other feedback for improving your written objectives during part 2.

Conclusion

The instructor may lead a class discussion and/or make concluding remarks.

Apply It *(2–4 minutes)* What did I learn from this experience? How will I use the knowledge in the future?

Sharing

In the group, or to the entire class, volunteers may give their answers to the "Apply It" questions.

Behavior Model Skills Training 1

Session 1

This training for leadership behavior modeling skills has four parts, as follows:

1. First, read how to use the model.
2. Then, view the behavior model video that illustrates how to give praise, following the four steps in the model.
3. Develop the skill in class by doing Skill-Development Exercise 2.
4. Further develop this skill by using the model in your personal and professional life.

Giving Praise Model

Review Model 3.2, "Giving Praise," in the text.

Behavior Model Video 1

Giving Praise

Objective

To assist you in giving praise that motivates others to high levels of performance.

Video (4½ minutes) Overview

You will watch a bank branch manager give praise to an employee for two different jobs well done.

Skill-Development Exercise 2

Giving Praise

Preparing for Skill-Development Exercise 2

Think of a job situation in which you did something well-deserving of praise and recognition. For example, you may have saved the company some money, you may have turned a dissatisfied customer into a happy one, and so forth. If you have never worked or done something well, interview someone who has. Put yourself in a management position and write out the praise you would give to an employee for doing what you did. Briefly describe the situation:

Step 1. Tell the employee exactly what was done correctly.

Step 2. Tell the employee why the behavior is important.

Step 3. Stop for a moment of silence. (Count to five silently to yourself.)

Step 4. Encourage repeat performance.

Doing Skill-Development Exercise 2 in Class

Objective

To develop your skill at giving praise.

The primary AACSB learning standard skill developed through this exercise is leadership—motivating others.

Preparation

You will need your prepared praise.

Experience

You will give and receive praise.

Procedure *(10–15 minutes)* Break into groups of four to six. One at a time, give the praise you prepared.

1. Explain the situation.
2. Select a group member to receive the praise.
3. Give the praise. (Talk; don't read it off the paper.) Try to select the position you would use if you were actually giving the praise on the job (both standing, both sitting, etc.).
4. Integration. The group gives the praise-giver feedback on how he or she did:

Step 1. Was the praise very specific and descriptive? Did the giver look the employee in the eye?

Step 2. Was the importance of the behavior clearly stated?

Step 3. Did the giver stop for a moment of silence?

Step 4. Did the giver encourage repeat performance? Did the giver of praise touch the receiver (optional)?

Step 5. Did the praise take less than one minute? Was the praise sincere?

Conclusion

The instructor may lead a class discussion and/or make concluding remarks.

Apply It *(2–4 minutes)* What did I learn from this experience? How will I use this knowledge in the future? When will I practice?

Sharing

In the group, or to the entire class, volunteers may give their answers to the "Apply It" questions.

Influencing: Power, Politics, Networking, and Negotiation

Chapter Outline

Power

Sources of Power

Types of Power and Influencing Tactics, and Ways to Increase Your Power

Acquiring and Losing Power

Organizational Politics

The Nature of Organizational Politics

Political Behavior

Guidelines for Developing Political Skills

Networking

Perform a Self-Assessment and Set Goals

Create Your One-Minute Self-Sell

Develop Your Network

Conduct Networking Interviews

Maintain Your Network

Negotiation

Negotiating

The Negotiation Process

Ethics and Influencing

Learning Outcomes

After studying this chapter, you should be able to:

1. Explain the differences between position power and personal power. p. 110
2. Discuss the differences among legitimate, reward, coercive, and referent power. p. 111
3. Discuss how power and politics are related. p. 121
4. Describe how money and politics have a similar use. p. 122
5. List and explain the steps in the networking process. p. 128
6. List the steps in the negotiation process. p. 135
7. Explain the relationships among negotiation and conflict, influencing tactics, power, and politics. p. 135
8. Define the following **key terms** (in order of appearance in the chapter):

power	connection power
legitimate power	politics
reward power	networking
coercive power	reciprocity
referent power	one-minute self-sell
expert power	negotiating
information power	

Opening Case APPLICATION

Mark Cuban is known as the billionaire entrepreneur (net worth $2.8 billion) currently focusing on the sports and entertainment industries. Cuban's holdings include five companies. Cuban paid $280 million for 75 percent ownership of the NBA Dallas Mavericks basketball team, taking revenues from $40 million to $140 million. He is also part owner of the following: HDNet and HDNet Movies, which have more than 6.8 million subscribers; 2929 Productions, which released George Clooney's *Good Night, and Good Luck;* Magnolia Pictures, which distributed independent films like *Crazy Love;* and Landmark Theatres, one of the largest and most innovative art-house theater chains with 57 theaters in 24 markets. Cuban is in partnership with Todd Wagner for all five organizations. All five companies are privately held, so profitability is not available, and they have no plans to take the companies public.

But Mark Cuban didn't start at the top. Truth be told, Mark Cuban was the last guy anyone would have expected to become a billionaire. Here is Cuban's entrepreneurial story. His family's last name, Cuban, was shortened from Chabenisky when his grandparents, Russian Jews, arrived at Ellis Island. Cuban grew up in Mt. Lebanon, Pennsylvania, a suburb of Pittsburgh, in a working-class family. Cuban's first step into the business world occurred at age 12, when he sold garbage bags door-to-door. Soon after, he was selling stamps, coins, and baseball cards, which paid for his business degree at Indiana University. While attending IU, Cuban bought a Bloomington bar and named it Motley's, raising the money by selling shares to his friends.

After college, he moved to Dallas, Texas, and went into computer sales. Cuban and Martin Woodall founded MicroSolutions, and they sold the company for $6 million; Cuban netted approximately $2 million after taxes on the deal. Cuban moved to Los Angeles for awhile where he day-traded and took acting lessons. Todd Wagner proposed starting AudioNet, which later became Broadcast.com, and Cuban leapt at the chance. Broadcast.com's initial public offering (IPO) stock price was $18, but it climbed to $62 at the end of the first day; Cuban was suddenly $85 million richer. They sold Broadcast.com to Yahoo!, and Cuban became worth more than $1 billion in Yahoo! stock. With this fortune, he entered the sports and entertainment industries with his partner Todd Wagner. Today, Mark Cuban presides over his business empire almost entirely by e-mail from his home office.[1]

Opening Case Questions:

1. What sources and types of power does Mark Cuban have, and why has he had problems with power?
2. Why are organizational politics important to Mark Cuban's enterprises?
3. How has Mark Cuban used networking?
4. What types of negotiations has and does Mark Cuban engage in?
5. Is Mark Cuban ethical in influencing others?

Can you answer any of these questions? You'll find answers to these questions and learn more about Mark Cuban's businesses and leadership style throughout the chapter.

Besides excellent work, what does it take to get ahead in an organization? To climb the corporate ladder, you will have to influence people—to gain power, play organizational politics, network, and negotiate to get what you want. These related concepts are the topics of this chapter. Recall from our definition of leadership (Chapter 1) that leadership is the "*influencing*" process of leaders and followers to achieve organizational objectives through change. Leaders and followers influence each other, because we are all potential leaders.[2] Influencing is so important that it is called the essence of leadership. Influence has a direct effect on organizational performance and your career success.[3] In essence, this chapter is a continuation of Chapter 3; it focuses on leadership behavior by explaining how leaders influence others at the individual level of analysis. Let's begin with power.

Power

If you want to understand why organizations do the things they do, or why they perform the way they do, you must consider the powerful top executives.[4] Power is about achieving influence over others.[5] However, **power** *is the leader's potential influence over followers.* Because power is the *potential* to influence, you do not actually have to use power to influence others.[6] Often it is the perception of power, rather than the actual use of power, that influences others. Power is based on certain qualities or capabilities, but power itself is transactional and flows out of relationships, real or perceived.[7] In this section we discuss sources of power, types of power, influencing tactics, ways to increase your power, and how power is acquired and lost.

Learning Outcome 1 *Explain the differences between position power and personal power.*

Sources of Power

There are two sources of power: position power and personal power.

Position Power

Position power is derived from top management, and it is delegated down the chain of command. Thus, a person who is in a management position has more potential power to influence than an employee who is not a manager. Power is used to get people to do something they otherwise would not have done. Some people view power as the ability to make people do what they want them to do or the ability to do something to people or for people. These definitions may be true, but they tend to give power a manipulative, negative connotation, as does the old saying by Lord Acton, "Power corrupts. Absolute power corrupts absolutely."

Within an organization, power should be viewed in a positive sense. Without power, managers could not achieve organizational objectives.[8] Leadership and power go hand in hand. Leadership is the art of persuading others to want to do what you want them to do.[9] Employees are not influenced without a reason, and the reason is often the power a manager has over them. Managers rely on position power to get the job done.[10]

Personal Power

Personal power is derived from the followers based on the leader's behavior. Charismatic leaders have personal power. Again, followers do have some power over leaders. Followers must consent to the governing influence of managers for the organization to be successful.[11] Unions are often the result of follower dissatisfaction with management behavior and the desire to balance power. Followers can restrict performance, sabotage operations, initiate grievances, hold demonstrations, make complaints to higher managers, and hurt the leader's reputation. Power can be gained or lost—we will discuss how later.

The two sources of power are relatively independent, yet they have some overlap. For example, a manager can have only position power or both position and personal power, but a nonmanager can have only personal power. The trend is for managers to give more power (empowerment) to employees.[12] Today's effective leaders are relying less on position power and more on personal power to influence others,[13] and they are open to being influenced by followers with personal power.[14] Therefore, as a manager, it is best to have both position power and personal power.

Learning Outcome 2 *Discuss the differences among legitimate, reward, coercive, and referent power.*

Types of Power and Influencing Tactics, and Ways to Increase Your Power

Seven types of power are illustrated, along with their source of power and influencing tactics, in Exhibit 4.1. In the late 1950s, French and Raven distinguished five types of power (reward, coercive, legitimate, expert, and referent),[15] and they are still being used in research. Connection (politics) and information power have been added to update the important types of power. We will discuss these seven types of power, and explore ways to increase each type with *influencing tactics.* You can acquire power, and you do not have to take power away from others to increase your power. Generally, power is given to those who get results and have good human relations skills.[16]

Legitimate Power

Legitimate power ***is based on the user's position power, given by the organization.*** It is also called the *legitimization influencing tactic.* Managers assign work, coaches decide who plays, and teachers award grades. These three positions have formal authority from the organization. Without this legitimate authority, they could not influence followers in the same way.[17] Employees tend to feel that they ought to do what their manager says within the scope of the job.

Appropriate Use of Legitimate Power Employees agree to comply with management authority in return for the benefits of membership. The use of legitimate power is appropriate when asking people to do something that is within the scope of their job. Most day-to-day manager–employee interactions are based on legitimate power.

When using legitimate power, it is also helpful to use the *consultation influencing tactic.* With consultation, you seek others' input about achieving an objective and are open to developing a plan together to achieve the objective. This process is also known as *participative management* and *empowering employees.* We will talk more about participative management throughout the book.

Legitimate Use of Rational Persuasion. As a manager meeting objectives through your employees, or in dealing with higher-level managers and people over whom you have no authority, it is often helpful to use the *rational persuasion influencing tactic.* Rational persuasion includes logical arguments with factual evidence to persuade others to implement your recommended action.[18]

When you use rational persuasion, you need to develop a persuasive case based on the other party's needs. What seems logical and reasonable to you may not be to others. With multiple parties, a different logical argument may be made to meet

EXHIBIT 4.1 Sources and Types of Power with Influencing Tactics

Source: Position Power ⟶ ⟵ Personal Power

Types	Legitimate	Reward	Coercive	Connection	Information	Expert	Referent
Tactics	Legitimization Consultation Rational persuasion Ingratiation	Exchange	Pressure	Coalitions	Rational persuasion Inspirational appeal	Rational persuasion	Personal appeal Inspirational appeal

individual needs. Logical arguments generally work well with people whose behavior is more influenced by thinking than emotions. It works well when the leader and follower share the same shared interest and objectives.[19]

When trying to persuade others to do something for you, it is helpful to ask when they are in a good mood. To get people in a good mood, the *ingratiation influencing tactic* may be used by being friendly and praising others before you ask them for what you want.[20] The initial compliment must be sincere (use the giving praise model in Chapter 3), and it helps determine if the other party is in a good mood or not. If not, it is generally a good idea to wait to ask no matter how rational your request.

Using Rational Persuasion When you develop a rational persuasion, follow these guidelines:

1. Explain the reason why the objective needs to be met. Managers cannot simply give orders, since employees want to know the rationale for decisions. Even if you disagree with higher-level managers' decisions, as a manager it is your job to give employees the rationale for their decisions.
2. Explain how the other party will benefit by meeting the objective. Try to think of the other party's often-unasked question—what's in it for me? Sell the benefits to others, rather than focusing on how you and the organization benefit by achieving the objective.
3. Provide evidence that the objective can be met. Remember the importance of expectancy motivation theory (Chapter 3). When possible, demonstrate how to do a task—seeing is believing. Give examples of how others have met the objective. Offer a detailed step-by-step plan. Be supportive and encouraging, showing your confidence in the followers to meet the objective.
4. Explain how potential problems and concerns will be handled. Know the potential problems and concerns and deal with them in the rational persuasion. If others bring up problems that you have not anticipated, which is likely, be sure to address them. Do not ignore people's concerns or make simple statements like, "That will not happen, we don't have to worry about that." Get the followers' input on how to resolve any possible problems as they come up.[21] This will help gain their commitment.
5. If there are competing plans to meet the objective, explain why your proposal is better than the competing ones. Do your homework. You need to be well-versed about the competition.[22] To simply say "my idea is better than theirs" won't cut it. Be sure to state how your plan is superior to the others and the weaknesses and problems with the other plans.

Increasing Legitimate Power To increase your legitimate power, follow these guidelines:

1. To have legitimate power, you need management experience, which could also be a part of your job—for example, being in charge of a team project with your peers. Work at gaining people's perception that you do have power. Remember that people's perception that you have power gives you power.[23]
2. Exercise your authority regularly. Follow up to make sure that policies, procedures, and rules are implemented and that your objectives are achieved.
3. Follow the guidelines for using rational persuasion, especially if your authority is questioned.
4. Back up your authority with *rewards* and *punishment,* our next two types of power, which are primarily based on having legitimate power.

Reward Power

Reward power *is based on the user's ability to influence others with something of value to them.* Reward power affects performance expectations and achievement. In a management position, use positive reinforcements to influence behavior, with incentives such as praise, recognition (with pins, badges, hats, or jackets), special assignments or desirable activities, pay raises, bonuses, and promotions. Many organizations, including Kentucky Fried Chicken (KFC), have employee-of-the-month awards. Tupperware holds rallies for its salespeople, and almost everyone gets something—ranging from pins to lucrative prizes for top performers. A leader's power is strong or weak based on his or her ability to punish and reward followers. The more power, the more favorable the situation for the leader.

An important part of reward power is having control over resources, such as allocating expense and budget funds. This is especially true for scarce resources. Upper- and middle-level managers usually have more discretion in giving rewards (including scarce resources) than do lower-level managers.

Appropriate Use of Reward Power When employees do a good job, they should be rewarded, as discussed with reinforcement motivation theory (Chapter 3). Catching people doing things right and rewarding them is a great motivator to continue the behavior. When dealing with higher-level managers and people over whom you have no authority, you can use the *exchange influencing tactic* by offering some type of reward for helping you meet your objective. The incentive for exchange can be anything of value, such as scarce resources, information, advice or assistance on another task, or career and political support. Exchange is common in reciprocity (you do something for me and I'll do something for you—or you owe me one, for a later reward), which we will discuss with organizational politics. For example, when Professor Jones is recruiting a student aide, he tells candidates that if they are selected and do a good job, he will recommend them for an MBA fellowship at Suffolk University, where he has connection power. As a result he gets good, qualified help, at minimum wages, while helping both his student aide and his alma mater.

Increasing Reward Power To increase your reward power, follow these guidelines:

1. Gain and maintain control over evaluating your employees' performance and determining their raises, promotions, and other rewards.
2. Find out what others value, and try to reward people in that way. Using praise can help increase your power. Employees who feel they are appreciated rather than used will give the manager more power.[24]
3. Let people know you control rewards, and state your criteria for giving rewards. However, don't promise more than you can deliver. Reward as promised, and don't use rewards to manipulate or for personal benefit.

Coercive Power

The use of **coercive power** *involves punishment and withholding of rewards to influence compliance.* It is also called the *pressure influencing tactic.* From fear of reprimands, probation, suspension, or dismissal, employees often do as their manager requests. The fear of lost valued outcomes or rewards—such as receiving poor performance evaluations, losing raises and benefits, being assigned to less-desirable jobs, and hurting a relationship—causes employees to do as requested. Other examples of coercive power include verbal abuse, humiliation, and ostracism. Group members also use coercive power (peer pressure) to enforce group norms.

Work Application 1

Select a present or past manager who has or had coercive power. Give a specific example of how he or she uses or used reward and punishment to achieve an objective. Overall, how effective is (or was) this manager at using rewards and punishment?

Appropriate Use of Coercive Power Coercive power is appropriate to use in maintaining discipline and enforcing rules. When employees are not willing to do as requested, coercive power may be the only way to gain compliance. In fact, without it, employees may not take you seriously and ignore your requests. Coercion is effective when applied to a small percentage of followers under conditions considered legitimate by most of them. When leaders use coercion on a large scale against followers, it undermines their authority and creates a hostile opposition that may seek to restrict their power or to remove them from office. Employees tend to resent managers' use of coercive power. There has been a general decline in use of coercion by all types of leaders.[25] Managers that bully employees are being fired.[26] So keep your use of coercive power to a minimum by using it only as a last resort.

Increasing Coercive Power To increase your coercive power, follow these guidelines:

1. Gain authority to use punishment and withhold rewards. However, make sure employees know the rules and penalties, give prior warnings, understand the situation, remain calm and helpful, encourage improvement, use legitimate punishments (withhold rewards) that fit the infraction, and administer punishment in private.
2. Don't make rash threats; do not use coercion to manipulate others or to gain personal benefits.
3. Be persistent. If you request that followers do something and you don't follow up to make sure it is done, followers will take advantage of the situation and ignore your request. Set specific deadlines for task completion and frequently check progress. Put the deadline and progress checks on your calendar to make sure you persistently follow up.

When former President Okuda replaced about one-third of Toyota's highest-ranking managers, he was using coercive punishment for poor performers. When managers were promoted to replace them, they were rewarded for doing a good job.

Ethical Dilemma 1

Following Orders

The armed forces are hierarchical by rank, based on power. Officers tend to give orders to troops using legitimate power. When orders are followed, reward power is common. When orders are not followed, coercive power is commonly used to get the troops to implement the order. The conditioning of the military is to respect the power of authority and to follow orders, usually without questioning authority.

1. Is it ethical and socially responsible to teach people to follow orders without questioning authority in the military or any other organization?
2. What would you do if your boss asked you to follow orders that you thought might be unethical? (Some options include: just do it; don't say anything but don't do it; question the motives; look closely at what you are asked to do; go to your boss's boss to make sure it's okay to do it; tell the boss you will not do it; ask the boss to do it him- or herself; blow the whistle to an outside source like the government or media; and so on.)
3. Is following orders a good justification for unethical practices?

Referent Power

Referent power *is based on the user's personal relationships with others.* It is also called the *personal appeals influencing tactic* based on loyalty and friendship. Power stems primarily from friendship, or the employee's attractiveness to the person using power. The personal feelings of "liking" or the desire to be liked by the leaders also gives referent power. Today's successful leaders are relying more on relationships than position power to get the job done.[27]

Leaders can also use the *inspirational appeals influencing tactic.* The leader appeals to the follower's values, ideals, and aspirations, or increases self-confidence by displaying his or her feelings to appeal to the follower's emotions and enthusiasm.[28] So rational persuasion uses logic, whereas inspirational persuasion appeals to emotions and enthusiasm. Thus, inspirational appeals generally work well with people whose behavior is more influenced by emotions than logical thinking. Great sports coaches, such as Vince Lombardi, are well respected for their inspirational appeals to get the team to win the game. Have you heard the "win one for the Gipper" saying from Notre Dame?

To be inspirational, you need to understand the values, hopes, fears, and goals of followers. You need to be positive and optimistic and create a vision of how things will be when the objective is achieved. Use nonverbal communication to bring emotions to the verbal message, such as raising and lowering voice tone and pausing to intensify key points, showing moist eyes or a few tears, and maintaining eye contact. Facial expressions, body movement, and gestures like pounding a table effectively reinforce verbal messages. You can also include the ingratiation influencing tactic within your inspirational appeal.

Appropriate Use of Referent Power The use of referent power is particularly appropriate for people with weak, or no, position power, such as with peers. Referent power is needed in self-managed teams because leadership should be shared.

Increasing Referent Power To increase your referent power, follow these guidelines:

1. Develop your people skills, which are covered in all chapters. Remember that you don't have to be a manager to have referent power. The better you get along with more people (good working relationships), the more referent power you will have.
2. Work at your relationship with your manager and peers. Your relationship with your manager will have a direct effect on your job satisfaction. Gain your manager's confidence in order to get more power. Remember that the success of your manager and peers depends to some extent on you and your performance.

Expert Power

Expert power *is based on the user's skill and knowledge.* Being an expert makes other people dependent on you. Employees with expert power have personal power and are often promoted to management positions. People often respect an expert, and the fewer people who possess an expertise, the more power the individual has.[29] For example, because so few people have the ability to become the CEO of a large corporation, they have the power to command multimillion-dollar contracts,[30] and superstars at all levels are capable of negotiating distinctive employment conditions.[31] The more people come to you for advice, the greater is your expert power. In the changing global economy, expert power is becoming more important. It's wise to be sure that your expertise does not become unimportant or obsolete.

Experts commonly use the *rational persuasion influencing tactic* because people believe they know what they are saying and that it is correct.

Appropriate Use of Expert Power Managers, particularly at lower levels, are often—but not always—experts within their departments. New managers frequently depend on employees who have expertise in how the organization runs and know how to get things done politically. Thus, followers can have considerable influence over the leader. Expert power is essential to employees who are working with people from other departments and organizations. Because such employees have no direct position power to use, being seen as an expert gives them credibility and power.

Increasing Expert Power To increase your expert power, follow these guidelines:

1. To become an expert, take all the training and educational programs your organization provides.
2. Attend meetings of your trade or professional associations, and read their publications (magazines and journals) to keep up with current trends in your field. Write articles to be published. Become an officer in the organization.
3. Keep up with the latest technology. Volunteer to be the first to learn something new.
4. Project a positive self-concept (Chapter 2), and let people know about your expertise by developing a reputation for having expertise. You have no expert power unless others perceive that you have an expertise and come to you for advice. You may want to display diplomas, licenses, publications, and awards.

Information Power

Work Application 2

Select a past or present job. Who did (or do) you usually go to for expertise and information? Give examples of when you went to someone for expertise and when you went to someone for information.

Information power *is based on the user's data desired by others.* Information power involves access to vital information and control over its distribution to others. Managers often have access to information that is not available to peers and subordinates. Thus, they have the opportunity to distort information to influence others to meet their objective. Distortion of information includes selective editing to promote only your position, giving a biased interpretation of data and even presenting false information. Managers also rely on employees for information, so followers sometimes have the opportunity to distort information that influences management decisions. Distortion of information is an ethical issue. Some administrative assistants have more information and are more helpful in answering questions than the managers they work for.

Appropriate Use of Information Power An important part of the manager's job is to convey information. Employees often come to managers for information on what to do and how to do it. Leaders use information power when making *rational persuasion* and often with *inspirational appeals.*[32] Personal computers give organizational members information power, since information flows freely through informal channels.

Increasing Information Power To increase your information power, follow these guidelines:

1. Have information flow through you. For example, if customer leads come in to the company and all sales representatives have direct access to them, the sales manager has weak information power. However, if all sales leads go directly to the manager, who then assigns the leads to sales representatives, the manager

has strong information power. Having control of information makes it easier to cover up failures and mistakes, and to let others know of your accomplishments, which can also increase expertise.

2. Know what is going on in the organization. Provide service and information to other departments. Serve on committees because it gives you both information and a chance to increase connection power.
3. Develop a network of information sources, and gather information from them.[33] You will learn how to network later in this chapter.

Connection Power

Connection power *is based on the user's relationships with influential people.* Connection power is also a form of politics, the topic of our next major section, but first we discuss how power is acquired and lost. You rely on the use of contacts or friends who can influence the person you are dealing with. The right connections can give power, or at least the perception of having power. If people know you are friendly with people in power, they are more apt to do as you request. For example, if the owner's son has no position power but wants something done, he may gain compliance by making a comment about speaking to his father or mother about the lack of cooperation.

Sometimes it is difficult to influence others all alone. With a *coalition influencing tactic* you use influential people to help persuade others to meet your objective.[34] There is power and safety in numbers. The more people you can get on your side, the more influence you can have on others. Superiors, peers, subordinates, and outsiders can help you influence others. You can tell others who support your idea, have the supporters with you when you make a request, have supporters follow up, or ask a higher authority to get what you need done for you. Coalitions are also a political strategy—a tactic that will be discussed again later in this chapter.

Work Application 3

1. Think of a present or past manager. Which type of power does (or did) the manager use most often? Explain.
2. Which one or two suggestions for increasing your power base are the most relevant to you? Explain.

Appropriate Use of Connection Power When you are looking for a job or promotions, connections can help. There is a lot of truth in the statement, "It's not what you know, it's who you know."[35] Connection power can also help you to get resources you need and increase business.

Increasing Connection Power To increase connection power, follow these guidelines:

1. Expand your network of contacts with important managers who have power.
2. Join the "in-crowd" and the "right" associations and clubs. Participating in sports like golf may help you meet influential people.
3. Follow the guidelines for using the coalition influencing tactic. When you want something, identify the people who can help you attain it, make coalitions, and win them over to your side.
4. Get people to know your name. Get all the publicity you can. Have your accomplishments known by the people in power; send them notices without sounding like a bragger.

Work Application 4

Give three different influencing tactics you or someone else used to achieve an objective in an organization you have worked for.

Now that you have read about nine influencing tactics within seven types of power, see Exhibit 4.1 on page 111 for a review, and test your ability to apply them in Applying the Concept 1 and Applying the Concept 2 on the next page. Then, complete Self-Assessment 1 on page 119 to better understand how your personality traits relate to how you use power and influencing tactics to get what you want.

Applying the Concept 1

Influencing Tactics

Select the most appropriate individual tactic for each situation. Write the appropriate letter in the blank before each item.

a. rational persuasion
b. inspirational appeals
c. consultation
d. ingratiation
e. personal appeals
f. exchange
g. coalition
h. legitimization
i. pressure

____ 1. You are in sales and want some information about a new product that has not yet been produced, nor has it been announced inside or outside the company. You know a person in the production department who has been working on the new product, so you decide to contact that person.

____ 2. Two of your five crew workers did not come in to work today. You have a large order that should be shipped out at the end of the day. It will be tough for the small crew to meet the deadline.

____ 3. Although the crew members in situation 2 have agreed to push to meet the deadline, you would like to give them some help. You have an employee whose job is to perform routine maintenance and cleaning. He is not one of your five crew workers. However, you realize that he could be of some help filling in for the two missing workers. You decide to talk to this nonunion employee about working with the crew for two hours today.

____ 4. The nonunion employee in situation 3 is resisting helping the other workers. He is basically asking, "What's in it for me?"

____ 5. You have an employee who is very moody at times. You want this employee, who has a big ego, to complete an assignment before the established due date.

____ 6. You believe you deserve a pay raise, so you decide to talk to your manager about it.

____ 7. You serve on a committee, and next week the committee members will elect officers. Nominations and elections will be done at the same time. You are interested in being the president, but don't want to nominate yourself and lose.

____ 8. You have an employee who regularly passes in assignments late. The assignment you are giving the person now is very important; it must be done on time.

____ 9. You have an idea about how to increase performance of your department. You are not too sure if it will work, or if the employees will like the idea.

____ 10. The production person from situation 1 has given you the information you were looking for. She calls a week later to ask you for some information.

Applying the Concept 2

Using Power

Identify the relevant type of power to use in each situation. Write the appropriate letter in the blank before each item.

a. coercive
b. connection
c. reward or legitimate
d. referent
e. information or expert

____ 11. One of your best workers needs little direction from you. However, recently her performance has slumped. You're quite sure that a personal problem is affecting her work.

continued

(Applying the Concept 2 continued)

____ 12. You want a new personal computer to help you do a better job. PCs are allocated by a committee, which is very political in nature.

____ 13. One of your best workers wants a promotion. He has talked to you about getting ahead and has asked you to help prepare him for when the opportunity comes.

____ 14. One of your worst employees has ignored one of your directives again.

____ 15. An employee who needs some direction and encouragement from you to maintain production is not working to standard today. As occasionally happens, she claims that she does not feel well but cannot afford to take time off. You have to get an important customer order shipped today.

SELF-ASSESSMENT 1

Influencing Tactics, Power, and Personality Traits

Review the nine influencing tactics. Which ones do you tend to use most often to help you get what you want? Also review your personality profile self-assessment exercises in Chapter 2.

Surgency/High Need for Power

If you have n Pow, you are apt to try to influence others, and you enjoy it. You tend to hate to lose, and when you don't get what you want, it bothers you. Thus, you are more likely to use harder methods of influence and power, such as pressure, exchange, coalitions, and legitimization, than other personality types. You probably also like to use rational persuasion and don't understand why people don't think or see things the way you do. Be careful; use socialized rather than personalized power to influence others.

Agreeableness/High Need for Affiliation

If you have a high n Aff, you are apt to be less concerned about influencing others and gaining power than about getting along with them. Thus, you are more likely to use softer methods of influence, such as personal and inspirational appeals and ingratiation, as well as rational appeals. You may tend not to seek power, and even avoid it.

Conscientiousness/High Need for Achievement

If you have a high n Ach, you tend to be between the other two approaches to influencing others. You tend to have clear goals and work hard to get what you want, which often requires influencing others to help you. So, you don't want power for its own sake, only to get what you want. But you like to play by the rules and may tend to use rational persuasion frequently.

Based on the preceding information, briefly describe how your personality affects the ways you attempt to influence others.

____

____

____

Acquiring and Losing Power

Power can change over time. Personal power is more easily gained and lost than position power. Having strong power can lead to temptation to act in ways that misuse power and may eventually lead to failure.[36] Several baseball players, including Barry Bonds and Roger Clemens, lost some power and respect due to investigations into their use of steroids.

Social exchange theory explains how power is gained and lost as reciprocal influence processes occur over time between leaders and followers in small groups. Social interaction is an exchange of benefits or favors. Friendship is a social exchange, and some people place a higher value on the friendships they have at work than on the work itself. Group members especially watch managers, because they each have expectations of the leader. If the leader meets follower expectations, power is acquired and maintained. If not, the leader loses status and expert power with followers, and they may undermine the leader's legitimate authority as well.

Opening Case APPLICATION

1. What sources and types of power does Mark Cuban have, and why has he had problems with power?

Mark Cuban is used to getting his own way, and he wants to be famous and influential as he attempts to reorder the landscape of professional sports and entertainment. He has position power as an owner of five businesses. Because of his great success, many people as followers look up to him. As a business owner, Cuban has legitimate power, and he rewards his employees for doing a good job. He has used coercive power (he fired the Mavericks' coach), he has some referent power, and he is viewed as an expert in business. He also has information power and has connections with some influential people.

On the dark side, Cuban's behavior has cost him money and respect. Cuban is not your typical pro sports team owner who watches the games from the owner's box. He sits next to the Mavericks team bench and yells at the plays. He is also known to go out on the court during games and listen in on team huddles. Cuban has stormed into the locker room and cursed out the players when they lost. He has berated the referees and even gone after them on the court, which has led to fines and problems with the NBA. Some players and other owners view Cuban as being out of control and question when he will grow up.

Cuban admits that his behavior has worked against him in multiple situations. He'd like to own more pro sports teams, but has stated that other professional sports leagues might not consider him for ownership because of his NBA behavior. He has also alienated key strategic partners while trying to get HDNet off the ground. Three of the largest cable operators—Comcast, Cox, and Cablevision—have refused to carry the channel or its sister network, HDNet Movies, although ultimately HDNet reached an agreement with Comcast in September 2008.

Organizational Politics

Management has a political dimension.[37] Just as the nine influencing tactics (see Exhibit 4.1 on page 111) are used within the seven types of power, these tactics are also used in organizational politics. For example, to develop a successful rational persuasion, you need to base it within organizational politics. In this section, we discuss the nature of organizational politics, political behavior, and guidelines for developing political skills. But first, determine your own use of political behavior by completing Self-Assessment 2.

SELF-ASSESSMENT 2

Use of Political Behavior

Select the response that best describes your actual or planned use of the following behavior on the job. Place a number from 1 to 5 on the line before each statement.

1 — 2 — 3 — 4 — 5
Rarely *Occasionally* *Usually*

_____ 1. I use my personal contacts to get a job and promotions.

_____ 2. I try to find out what is going on in all the organizational departments.

_____ 3. I dress the same way as the people in power and take on the same interests

continued

(Self-Assessment 2 continued)

(watch or play sports, join the same clubs, and so forth).

_____ 4. I purposely seek contacts and network with higher-level managers.

_____ 5. If upper management offered me a raise and promotion requiring me to move to a new location, I'd say yes even if I did not want to move.

_____ 6. I get along with everyone, even those considered to be difficult to get along with.

_____ 7. I try to make people feel important by complimenting them.

_____ 8. I do favors for others and use their favors in return, and I thank people and send them thank-you notes.

_____ 9. I work at developing a good working relationship with my manager.

_____ 10. I ask my manager and other people for their advice.

_____ 11. When a person opposes me, I still work to maintain a positive working relationship with that person.

_____ 12. I'm courteous, pleasant, and positive with others.

_____ 13. When my manager makes a mistake, I never publicly point out the error.

_____ 14. I am more cooperative (I compromise) than competitive (I seek to get my own way).

_____ 15. I tell the truth.

_____ 16. I avoid saying negative things about my manager and others behind their backs.

_____ 17. I work at getting people to know me by name and face by continually introducing myself.

_____ 18. I ask some satisfied customers and people who know my work to let my manager know how good a job I'm doing.

_____ 19. I try to win contests and get prizes, pins, and other awards.

_____ 20. I send notices of my accomplishments to higher-level managers and company newsletters.

To determine your overall political behavior, add the 20 numbers you selected as your answers. The number will range from 20 to 100. The higher your score, the more political behavior you use. Place your score here _____ and on the continuum below.

20 — 30 — 40 — 50 — 60 — 70 — 80 — 90 — 100
Nonpolitical *Political*

To determine your use of political behavior in four areas, add the numbers for the following questions and divide by the number of questions to get the average score in each area.

A. *Learning the organizational culture and power players*
Questions 1–5 total: __9__ divided by 5 = __1.8__

B. *Developing good working relationships, especially with your boss*
Questions 6–12 total: __25__ divided by 7 = __5__

C. *Being a loyal, honest team player*
Questions 13–16 total: _____ divided by 4 = __3.2__

D. *Gaining recognition*
Questions 17–20 total: _____ divided by 4 = __1.4__

The higher the average score of items A–D, the more you use this type of political behavior. Do you tend to use them all equally, or do you use some more than others?

Learning Outcome 3 *Discuss how power and politics are related.*

The Nature of Organizational Politics

There is a relationship between power and organizational politics.[38] Managers use their existing position power and politics to increase their power. **Politics** *is the process of gaining and using power.* Politics is a reality of organizational life because politics affects behavior and decisions.[39] The amount and importance of politics vary from organization to organization. However, larger organizations tend to be more political; and the higher the level of management, the more important politics becomes.

Learning Outcome 4 *Describe how money and politics have a similar use.*

Politics Is a Medium of Exchange

Like power, politics often has a negative connotation due to people who abuse political power. Organizational politics is not about stabbing people in the back.[40] A positive way to view politics is to realize that it is simply a medium of exchange. Like money, politics in and of itself is inherently neither good nor bad. Politics is simply a system of getting what we want. In our economy, money is the medium of exchange (tangible currency); in an organization, politics is the medium of exchange (political behavior). Favors are the currency by which productivity is purchased and goodwill is gained.[41] You cannot really do a job well without political skills. Politically effective leaders marshal resources to accomplish personal and professional goals through the power and influence of their relationships.[42] So political skill is not about taking advantage of others, it's about building relationships to help you meet your objectives.[43] Leaders in organizations use political behavior, our next topic.

Political Behavior

How well you play politics directly affects your success.[44] Networking, reciprocity, and coalitions are common organizational political behaviors.

Networking

Networking is a critical facet of political skills.[45] **Networking** *is the process of developing relationships for the purpose of socializing and politicking.* The activities managers engage in and the time spent on each area have been studied. The activities have been categorized into four areas: traditional management, communication, human resource management, and networking. Of these four activities, networking has the highest relative contribution to successful management advancement. Successful managers spend around twice as much time networking as average managers, so reach out to establish an ongoing network of contacts.[46] Because networking is so important to career success, we are going to discuss it as our next major section, after we finish our other political skills discussions.

Reciprocity

Using **reciprocity** *involves creating obligations and developing alliances, and using them to accomplish objectives.* Notice that the exchange influencing tactic is used with reciprocity. When people do something for you, you incur an obligation that they may expect to be repaid. When you do something for people, you create a debt that you may be able to collect at a later date when you need a favor. Isn't part of relationships doing things for each other? Thus, ongoing reciprocal relationships are needed to meet your objectives,[47] and reciprocity builds trust in relationships.[48]

Here is a tip to increase your chances of getting help from others. When asking for help, use the word "favor," because the mere mention of the word "favor" can persuade people to help you. People have a modal, rote response to a favor request, which is, "Yeah, sure, what is it?"[49] So always start with the phrase, "Will you please do me a favor?"

Coalitions

Using coalitions as an influencing tactic is political behavior. Each party helps the others get what they want.[50] Reciprocity and networking are commonly used to achieve ongoing objectives, whereas coalitions are developed for achieving a specific objective. A political tactic when developing coalitions is to use co-optation.

Co-optation is the process of getting a person whose support you need to join your coalition rather than compete. During the 2008 Democratic presidential bid, people suggested ending the campaign by having Obama take Clinton as his vice presidential candidate to face McCain in the presidential elections.

The reality of organizational life is that most important decisions are made by coalitions outside of the formal meeting in which the decision is made. For example, let's say you are on a team and the captain is selected by a nomination and vote of the team members. If you want to be captain, you can politic by asking close teammates who they will vote for to try to get their votes; and if they are supportive, you can ask them to promote you for captain to others. If the majority of the team says they will vote for you, you have basically won the election before the coach even starts the meeting, nominating, and voting by building a coalition. If you don't get any support from your close teammates and others, you can drop the effort to build a coalition, knowing that you will lose. This same coalition-building process is used to influence all types of decisions.

Work Application 5

Give a job example of how networking, reciprocity, or a coalition was used to achieve an organizational objective.

We have not discussed how to increase your political skills with each type of political behavior, because all three may be used at the same time. As you will see, the upcoming guidelines can be used with any of the three political behaviors. Before considering how to develop political skills, review Exhibit 4.2 for a list of political behaviors and guidelines.

Opening Case APPLICATION

2. Why are organizational politics important to Mark Cuban's enterprises?

Mark Cuban has clearly used politics to gain and use power in creating his business empire. Being the owner of multiple businesses, organizational politics is not as important as using political skills outside the organization. The NBA is an organization of multiple team owners, so politics is important for making changes in the league. Because of Cuban's behavior, the NBA owners voted to pass rules of conduct that were really meant for Cuban. The NBA commissioner said the more stringent rules were called for to prevent individual owners from overshadowing the games. Cuban was so upset that he walked out of the meeting before the vote. So Cuban can improve on his organizational politics skills.

EXHIBIT 4.2 Political Behavior and Guidelines for Developing Political Skills

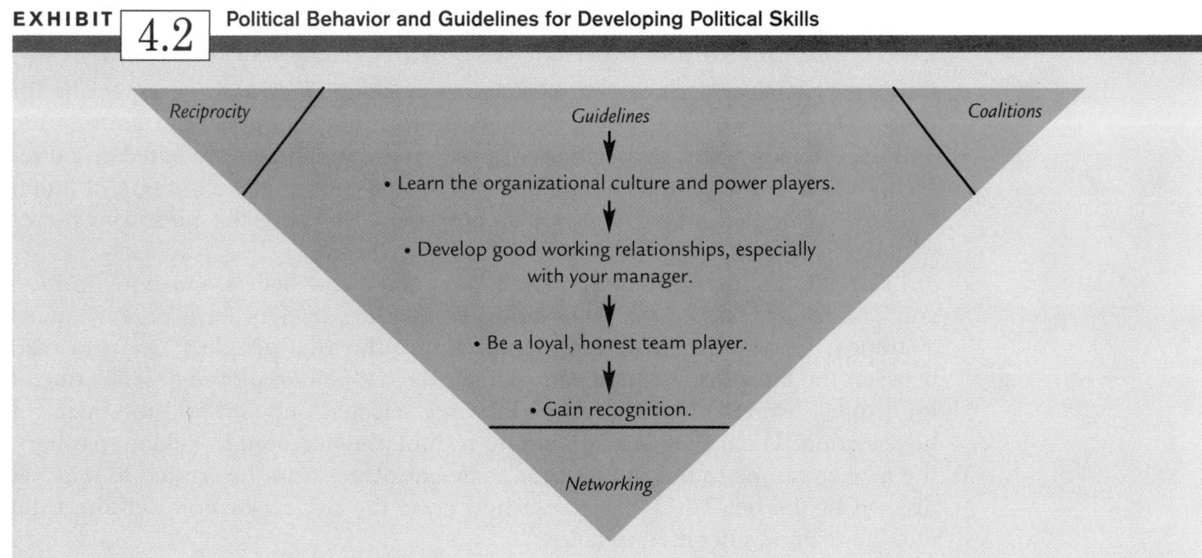

Ethical **Dilemma 2**

Dick Grasso, NYSE

Dick Grasso, the former New York Stock Exchange (NYSE) chief, is known to be a powerful man who uses politics to get what he wants. Grasso used coercive power to stop firms from taking trading away from the NYSE by moving it in-house electronically, thereby holding back the computer age. He was investigated for playing an inappropriate role in setting his own compensation. When Grasso left the NYSE, his retirement and severance package was $197.2 million, and he received $139.5 million.

Here is an example of how Grasso used his power and politics. Michael LaBranche agreed to merge his company with a smaller rival to create the largest specialist firm working on the NYSE. Grasso needed to okay the merger deal. Grasso "strongly" recommended that his longtime friend Robert Murphy, CEO of the smaller company in the merger (who served on the NYSE board and voted to approve his payout of $139.5 million), be named chief executive of the new LaBranche & Company main operating unit after the merger. Murphy had to stay at the top of a specialist firm to continue serving on the NYSE board, where Grasso wanted to, and did, keep him.[51]

1. How did Dick Grasso use the political behaviors of (a) networking, (b) reciprocity, and (c) coalitions while running the NYSE?
2. Was Dick Grasso's use of power and politics ethical and socially responsible?

Guidelines for Developing Political Skills

If you want to climb the corporate ladder, or at least avoid getting thrown off it, you should develop your political skills. Researchers have stated that women and minorities tend to be deficient in political skills and will have many more opportunities for advancement if they expand and exercise their political skills.[52] Carly Fiorina stated that she lost her job as CEO of HP due to politics.[53] Successfully implementing the behavior guidelines presented here can result in increased political skills. However, if you don't agree with a particular political behavior, don't use it. You do not have to use all of the political behaviors to be successful. Learn what it takes in the organization where you work as you follow the guidelines.

Learn the Organizational Culture and Power Players

Develop your connection power through politicking. It is natural, especially for young people, to take a purely rational approach to a job without considering politics. But many business decisions are not very rational; they are based on power and politics.[54] For example, a common reason for choosing the location of a new business facility is simply because it's convenient to where the person in power wants to live.

Learn the cultural (Chapter 10) shared values and beliefs and how business and politics operate where you work. Outstanding leaders have organizational awareness—reading the informal networks of influential people.[55] Learn to read between the lines. For example, a manager asked a new employee to select one of two project teams to work on. The employee selected one and told the manager his selection. The manager asked him to rethink the decision. In talking to others, the new employee found out that the manager of the team he wanted to join was disliked by the new CEO. No matter how good the project or how well the team did, the team was doomed to fail.

In all organizations, there are some powerful key players. Your manager is a key player to you. Don't just find out who the managers are; gain an understanding of what makes each of them tick. By understanding them, you can tailor the presentation of your ideas and style to fit each person's needs. For example, some managers want to see detailed financial numbers and statistics, while others don't. Some managers expect you to continually follow up with them, while others will think you are bugging them.

Review Self-Assessment 2, questions 1 through 5, on pages 120–121; you can use these tactics to increase your political skills. Network with power players. Try to do favors for power players. When developing coalitions, get key players on your side. When selecting a mentor, try to get one who is good at organizational politics. Your mentor can help you learn how to play politics. Also try to observe people who are good at politics, and copy their behavior.

Develop Good Working Relationships, Especially with Your Manager

The ability to work well with others is critical to your career success, and it's an important foundation of politics.[56] The more people like and respect you, the more power you will gain. Good human relations give you personal power and a basis for using the influencing tactic of personal appeal. You've already learned about relationships with higher-level managers and with peers who have influence and power, so let's focus on the relationship with your boss. The number one indicator of job satisfaction today is the relationship you have with your boss.[57]

If you want to get ahead, you need to have a good working relationship with your manager. Your boss usually gives you formal performance appraisals, which are the primary bases for raises and promotions. Fair or not, many evaluations are influenced by the manager's relationship with the employee. If your manager likes you, you have a better chance of getting a good review, raises, and promotions.[58]

Supervisors also give higher ratings to employees who share their goals (goal congruence) and priorities than they give to those who don't. Thus, get to know what your manager expects from you, and do it. Beat or at least meet deadlines, and don't miss them. Impress your boss by doing more than you are asked to do. If you don't agree with your boss's way of doing things, ask if you can do it your way, but don't go against your boss.

It's common to put off telling the manager bad news. But if you are having a problem on the job, don't put off letting your manager know about it. Most managers, and peers, like to be asked for advice. If you are behind schedule to meet an important deadline and your manager finds out about it from others, it is embarrassing, especially if your manager finds out from his or her manager. Also avoid showing up your manager in public, such as during a meeting. If you do, don't be surprised if the next time you open your mouth at a meeting, your manager embarrasses you.

If you cannot get along with your manager and are in conflict, avoid going to his or her manager to resolve the conflict. There are two dangers in going over the manager's head. First, chances are your manager has a good working relationship with his or her manager, who will side with your manager. Even if the higher-level manager agrees with you, you will most likely hurt your relationship with your manager. He or she may consciously or unconsciously take some form of retaliation, such as giving you a lower performance review, which can hurt you in the long run.[59]

Review Self-Assessment 2, questions 6 through 12, on pages 120–121; you can use these tactics to increase your political skills. Include your manager in your network, try to do favors for your manager, and include your manager in your coalitions.

Use the ingratiation tactic with everyone. When was the last time you gave anyone, including your manager, a compliment? When was the last time you sent a thank-you or congratulations note?

Be a Loyal, Honest Team Player

Ethical behavior is important in organizational politics.[60] The Indian leader Mohandas K. Gandhi called business without morality and politics without principle a sin. Some backstabbing gossips may get short-term benefits from such behavior, but in the long run they are generally unsuccessful because others gun them down in return. In any organization, you must earn others' respect, confidence, and trust.[61] Once you are caught in a lie, it's difficult to regain trust. There are very few, if any, jobs in which organizational objectives can be achieved without the support of a group or team of individuals. Even lone-wolf salespeople are subject to the systems effect, and they need the help of production to make the product, transportation to deliver it, and service to maintain it. The trend is toward teamwork, so if you're not a team player, work at it.[62]

Review Self-Assessment 2, questions 13 through 16, on pages 120–121; you can use these tactics to increase your political skills. Be a loyal, honest team player in your network, in your reciprocity, and with your coalition members.

Gain Recognition

Doing a great job does not help you to get ahead in an organization if no one knows about it, or doesn't know who you are. Recognition and knowing the power players go hand in hand; you want the power players to know who you are and what you can do. You want people higher in the organization to know your expertise and the contributions you are making to the organization.

Review Self-Assessment 2, questions 17 through 20, on pages 120–121; you can use these tactics to increase your political skills. Let people in your network and coalitions, and people you reciprocate with, know of your accomplishments. You can also serve on committees and try to become an officer, which gives you name recognition. A committee job many people tend to avoid is that of secretary. But when the meeting minutes are sent to higher management and throughout the organization with your name on it as secretary, you increase your name recognition.

Work Application 6

Which one or two suggestions for developing political skills are the most relevant to you? Explain.

Applying the **Concept 3**

Political Behavior

Identify the behavior in each situation as effective or ineffective political behavior. Write the appropriate letter in the blank before each item.

a. effective b. ineffective

____ 16. Julio is taking golf lessons so he can join the Saturday golf group, which includes some higher-level managers.

____ 17. Paul tells his manager's manager about mistakes his manager makes.

____ 18. Sally avoids spending time socializing, so that she can be more productive on the job.

____ 19. John sent a very positive performance report to three higher-level managers to whom he does not report. They did not request copies.

____ 20. Carlos has to drop off a daily report by noon. He delivers the report at around 10:00 A.M. on Tuesday and Thursday, so that he can run into some higher-level managers who meet at that time near the office where the report goes. On the other days, Carlos drops the report off at around noon on his way to lunch.

Networking

Power, politics, and networking have the same thing in common: influencing and helping one another.[63] People advance in their careers through contacts and connections.[64] In fact, the best way to advance in your career is by networking to learn about new opportunities.[65] More people find jobs through networking than all the other methods combined. But networking is also used for other reasons, including developing a business,[66] job satisfaction, enhanced performance, salary, power, and promotions.[67] Steve Case used networking to help him advance in his career to become cofounder of America Online (AOL), and Case used networking to advance AOL and to merge it with Time Warner. Case recommends that you develop your networking skills.

When you need any type of help, do you have a network of people readily available? Do you know how to develop a network to assist you? Networking sounds easy, and we tend to think it should come naturally. However, the reality is that networking is a learned skill that just about everyone struggles with at sometime or another. Women are, generally, not as skilled at networking as men, but they are getting better.[68] You can develop your networking skills through this section. Start by assessing your networking skills now in Self-Assessment 3.

SELF-ASSESSMENT 3

Networking

Identify each of the 16 statements according to how accurately it describes your behavior. Place a number from 1–5 on the line before each statement.

5 — 4 — 3 — 2 — 1

Describes me *Does not describe me*

_____ 1. When I start something (a new project, a career move, a major purchase), I seek help from people I know and seek new contacts for help.

_____ 2. I view networking as a way to create win-win situations.

_____ 3. I like to meet new people; I can easily strike up a conversation with people I don't know.

_____ 4. I can quickly state two or three of my most important accomplishments.

_____ 5. When I contact business people who can help me (such as with career information), I have goals for the communication.

_____ 6. When I contact business people who can help me, I have a planned short opening statement.

_____ 7. When I contact business people who can help me, I praise their accomplishments.

_____ 8. When I contact people who can help me, I have a set of questions to ask.

_____ 9. I know contact information for at least 100 people who can potentially help me.

_____ 10. I have a file/database with contact information of people who can help me in my career, and I keep it updated and continue to add new names.

_____ 11. During communications with people who can help me, I ask them for names of others I can contact for more information.

_____ 12. When seeking help from others, I ask them how I might help them.

_____ 13. When people help me, I thank them at the time and for big favors with a follow-up thanks.

_____ 14. I keep in touch with people who have helped or can potentially help me in my career at least once a year, and I update them on my career progress.

_____ 15. I have regular communications with people in my industry who work for different organizations, such as members of trade/professional organizations.

continued

(Self-Assessment 3 continued)

_____ 16. I attend trade/professional/career types of meetings to maintain relationships and to make new contacts.

Add up your score and place it here _____ and on the continuum below.

80 — 70 — 60 — 50 — 40 — 30 — 16
Effective Networking *Ineffective Networking*

If you are a full-time student, you may not score high on networking effectiveness, but that's okay as you can develop networking skills by following the steps and guidelines in this chapter.

Networking is not about asking everyone you know for a job (or whatever you need assistance with, such as feedback on your resume and career preparation, or information on hiring patterns and growth potential in your field; information about your current organization and its culture and power players; support and recognition from a colleague, or a mentor). How would you react if someone directly said, "I sell cars, and I have a good deal for you. Can you give me a job?" Networking is about building relationships through effective communications.[69] Power, politics, and networking have the same thing in common: building relationships to help you meet your objectives.[70] Although the same networking process applies to broad career development, we focus more on the job search. Whenever you start something—a new project, a career move, a car or house purchase—use your networks.

This section provides a how-to network process that will enhance your career development.[71] The process is summarized in Exhibit 4.3.

EXHIBIT 4.3 The Networking Process

1. Perform a self-assessment and set goals.
2. Create your one-minute self-sell.
3. Develop your network.
4. Conduct networking interviews.
5. Maintain your network.

Learning Outcome 5 *List and explain the steps in the networking process.*

Perform a Self-Assessment and Set Goals

The task of self-assessment can help to clarify your skills, competencies, and knowledge. Self-assessment can also give you insight into your transferable skills and the criteria that are important to you in a new job. Listing the major criteria that are most important to you in the new job and prioritizing these can help to clarify your ideal next position. Factors to consider are: industry, company size and growth, location, travel and commuting requirements, compensation package/benefits, job requirements, and promotion potential. Other factors to assess are the style of management, culture, and work style of the organization. Critical to career satisfaction are the ability to use your talents, grow in your field, and do what you do best in your job. Although many tools exist to assess skills and preferences, a simple list with priorities can suffice to clarify your talents and the characteristics of an ideal new career or job.

Accomplishments

After completing a self-assessment, you are ready to translate your talents into accomplishments. The results you achieved in your jobs and/or college are the best evidence of your skills. Your future employer knows that your past behavior predicts your future behavior and that if you achieved results in the past, you will likely produce similar results again. Accomplishments are what set you apart and provide evidence of your skills and abilities. To be an effective networker, you must articulate what you have accomplished in your past in a way that is clear, concise, and compelling. Write down your accomplishments (at least two or three) and include them in your resume. Whether you are looking for a job or not, you should always have an updated resume handy.

Tie Your Accomplishments to the Job Interview

You want to be sure to state your accomplishments that are based on your skill during the job interview. Many interviews begin with a broad question such as, "tell me about yourself." Oftentimes candidates do not reveal anything compelling. The second step after listing key results you have achieved is to elaborate on a problem that was solved or an opportunity taken and how you achieved it using your skills. These simple result statements should be transferred from your resume as critical results achieved. Thus, if you are asked a broad general question, such as "tell me about yourself," you have accomplishment statements as your answer.

Set Networking Goals

After your self-assessment focusing on your accomplishments, you need to clearly state your goal. For example: to get a mentor; to determine the expertise, skills, and requirements needed for XYZ position; to get feedback on my resume and job and/or career preparation for a career move into XYZ; or to attain a job as XYZ.

Work Application 7

Write a networking goal.

Create Your One-Minute Self-Sell

You need a networking plan,[72] so based on your goal, your next step is to create a one-minute sell to help you accomplish your goal, but keep it short.[73] *The* **one-minute self-sell** *is an opening statement used in networking that quickly summarizes your history and career plan and asks a question.* To take 60 seconds or less, your message must be concise, but it also needs to be clear and compelling. It gives the listener a sense of your background, identifies your career field and a key result you've achieved, plus provides the direction of your next job. It tells the listener what you plan to do next and why. It also stimulates conversation by asking your network for help in the area of support, coaching, contacts, or knowledge of the industry.

Part 1. History: Start with a career summary, the highlights of your career to date. Include your most recent career or school history and a description of the type of work/internship or courses you have taken. Also include the industry and type of organization.

Part 2. Plans: Next, state the target career you are seeking, the industry you prefer, and a specific function or role. You can also mention names of organizations you are targeting as well as let the acquaintance know why you are looking for work.

Part 3. Question: Last, ask a question to encourage two-way communication. The question will vary depending on the person and your goal or the reason you are using the one-minute self-sell, for example:

- In what areas might there be opportunities for a person with my experience?
- In what other fields can I use these skills or this degree?
- In what other positions in your organization could my skills be used?
- How does my targeted future career sound to you? Is it a match with my education and skills?
- Do you know of any job openings in my field?

Write and Practice Your One-Minute Self-Sell

Work Application **8**

Write a one-minute self-sell to achieve your networking goal from Work Application 7.

Write out your one-minute self-sell. Be sure to clearly separate your history, plans, and question, and customize your question based on the contact with whom you are talking. For example, *Hello, my name is Will Smith. I am a junior at Springfield College majoring in marketing, and I have completed an internship in the marketing department at the Big Y supermarket. I am seeking a job in sales in the food industry. Can you give me some ideas on the types of sales positions available in the food industry?* Practice delivering it with family and friends and get feedback to improve it. The more opportunities you find to use this brief introduction, the easier it becomes.

Develop Your Network

Networking is important, so how do individuals generate networks?[74] Begin with who you know. Everyone can create a written network list of about 200 people consisting of professional and personal contacts. You may already have a network on an online social-networking site, such as Facebook or MySpace, and you most likely have an e-mail account with an address book.[75] Address books and rolodexes are written network lists, but you need to continually develop and expand them.[76] An e-mail account is a good place to store your network list and information on each person because you can easily contact one or more people.[77] More and more, online networking is leading to employment. One word of caution regarding social-networking and other Web sites: Be careful with what is online.[78] If a potentially helpful person or employer looks you up online, and finds unflattering pictures of you (under the influence of drugs or alcohol, not fully dressed, doing embarrassing things, and so forth), it may cost you a contact or potential job.

Professional contacts include colleagues (past and present), professional organizations, alumni associations, vendors, suppliers, managers, mentors, and many other professional acquaintances. On a personal level, your network includes family, neighbors, friends, religious groups,[79] and other personal service providers (doctor, dentist, insurance agent, stock broker, accountant, hairstylist, politician). Compose a list of your network using the above categories, and continually update and add to your list with referrals from others.[80] You will discover that your network grows exponentially and can get you closer to the decision makers in a hiring position. In today's job market, it is critical to engage in a "passive job hunt" using your network and having your resume ready.

Now expand your list to people you don't know. Where should you go to develop your network? Anywhere people gather. Talk to everyone because you never know who's connected to whom.[81] To be more specific, get more involved with professional associations. Many have special student memberships, and some even have college chapters. If you really want to develop your career reputation, become a leader in your associations and not just a member. Volunteer to be on committees and boards, to give presentations, and so on. Other opportunities to network with people you don't know include the Chamber of Commerce, college alumni clubs/ reunions, civic organizations (Rotary, Lions, Kiwanis, Elks, Moose, and so on), courses of any type, trade shows and career fairs, community groups, charities and religious groups (Goodwill, American Cancer Society, your local church), and social clubs (exercise, boating, golf, tennis, and so on).

Another important point is to work at developing your ability to remember people by name. If you want to impress people you have never met or hardly know, call them by their name. Ask others who they are, then go up and call them by name and introduce yourself with your one-minute self-sell. When you are introduced to people, call them by name during the conversation two or three times. If you think the person can help you, don't stop with casual conversation; make an appointment at a later time for a phone conversation, personal meeting, coffee, or lunch. Get their business cards to add to your network list, and give your business card and/or resume when appropriate.

Conduct Networking Interviews

Based on your goal, use your network list of people to set up a networking interview to meet your goal. It may take many interviews to meet a goal, such as to get a job. An informational interview is a phone call or preferably a meeting that you initiate to meet a goal, such as to gain information from a contact with hands-on experience in your field of interest. You are the interviewer (in contrast to a job interview) and need to be prepared with specific questions to ask the contact regarding your targeted career or industry based on your self-assessment and goal. Keep your agenda short, focusing on what is most important.[82] Ask for a 20-minute meeting, and, as a result, many people will talk to you.

These meetings can be most helpful when you have accessed someone who is in an organization you'd like to join, or has a contact in an industry you are targeting. A face-to-face meeting of 20 minutes can have many benefits. Your contact will remember you after a personal meeting, and the likelihood of getting a job lead increases. Keeping the person posted on your job search progress as well as a thank-you note after the meeting also solidifies the relationship. The interviewing steps are:

Step 1. **Establish Rapport:** Provide a brief introduction and thank the contact for his or her time. Clearly state the purpose of the meeting; be clear that you are not asking for a job. Don't start selling yourself; project an interest in the other person. Do some research and impress the person by stating an accomplishment, such as, "I enjoyed your presentation at the CLMA meeting on...."

Step 2. **Deliver Your One-Minute Self-Sell:** Even if the person has already heard it, say it again. This enables you to quickly summarize your background and career direction.

Step 3. **Ask Prepared Questions:** As stated above, do your homework before the meeting and compose a series of questions to ask during the interview.[83] Your questions should vary depending on your goal, the contact, and how he or she may help you with your job search. Sample questions include the following:

- What do you think of my qualifications for this field?
- With your knowledge of the industry, what career opportunities do you see in the future?

- What advice do you have for me as I begin/advance in my career?
- If you were exploring this field, who else would you talk with?

During the interview, if the interviewee mentions anything that could hinder your search, ask how such obstacles could be overcome.

Step 4. Get Additional Contacts for Your Network: As mentioned previously, always ask who else you should speak with. Most people can give you three names, so if you are only offered one, ask for others. Add the new contacts to your network list. When contacting new people, be sure to use your network person's name. Be sure not to linger beyond the time you have been offered, unless invited to stay. Leave a business card and/or resume so the person can contact you in case something comes up.

Step 5. Ask Your Contacts How You Might Help Them: Offer a copy of a recent journal article or any additional information that came up in your conversation. Remember, it's all about building relationships, and making yourself a resource for other people.[84]

Step 6. Follow Up with a Thank-You Note and Status Report: By sending a thank-you note, along with another business card/resume, and following up with your progress, you are continuing the networking relationship and maintaining a contact for the future.

Be sure to assess the effectiveness of your networking meetings using the five steps as your criteria. Did you establish rapport and were you clear about the intent of the meeting? Did you deliver your one-minute self-sell, including a question? Did you follow with additional prepared questions? Did you get additional names to contact? And finally, did you send a follow-up thank-you note? It is always helpful to create a log of calls, meetings, and contacts in order to maintain your network as it expands.

Maintain Your Network

It is important to keep your network informed of your career progress. Get a mentor in your current or new role who can help you to focus on results that matter to your employer and guide your assimilation process.[85] If an individual was helpful in finding your new job, be sure to let him or her know the outcome. Saying thank you to those who helped in your transition will encourage the business relationship; providing this information will increase the likelihood of getting help in the future. It is also a good idea to notify everyone in your network that you are in a new position and provide contact information. Networking doesn't stop once you've made a career change. Make a personal commitment to continue networking in order to be in charge of your career development. Go to trade shows and conventions, make business friends, and continue to update, correct, and add to your network list. Always thank others for their time.

Networking is also about helping others, especially your network. As you have been helped, you should help others. You will be amazed at how helping others comes back to you. Jack Gherty, retired president and CEO of Land O' Lakes, said that he got ahead by helping other people win. Try to contact everyone on your network list at least once a year (calls, e-mail, and cards are good), and find out what you can do for them. Send congratulations on recent achievements.

After you have read this section on networking, you have at least two choices. One is to do nothing with it. The other choice is to begin developing your networking skills. Schedule the time to sit down and do one or all of the steps in the networking process: do a self-assessment and set a goal(s), create your one-minute self-sell to meet your goal, develop your network to meet the goal, set up and conduct network interviews, and maintain your network. What's it going to be? Skill-Development Exercise 3 can help get you started.

Opening Case APPLICATION

3. How has Mark Cuban used networking?

Mark Cuban first started networking by selling garbage bags door-to-door and then by selling stamps and baseball cards before the Internet was available. As the owner of Motley's, between bartending and spinning records, he schmoozed customers. In fact, people came to see him; and when he wasn't there, business wasn't as good. When Cuban was selling computers, he was constantly socializing and trading business cards. To be successful in the entertainment business, you have to network with the right people to get productions from HDNet and HDNet Movies, 2929 Productions, and Magnolia Pictures viewed. Cuban has more networking to do since HDNet and HDNet Movies can only be seen by about half of all cable subscribers. 2929 Productions still has to distribute its movies through big studios. Magnolia's *Bubble* flopped. Landmark Theatres is small with only 235 screens, compared to AMC Theatres with more than 5,000 screens. Only time will tell if Cuban can be as successful in sports and entertainment as he was in computers.

Negotiation

In this section, we focus on getting what you want by influencing others through negotiation. Influence tactics, power, and politics can all be used during the negotiation process.[86] Negotiation is used in managing conflict.[87] **Negotiating** *is a process in which two or more parties are in conflict and attempt to come to an agreement.* Are negotiation skills really important? Here are some answers. Whether you realize it or not, and whether you like it or not, we are all negotiators because we attempt to get what we want everyday. Negotiating is a core competency in life—particularly in the business world. Your negotiating ability directly affects your income, relationships, and station in life.[88] Wal-Mart keeps its everyday low prices lower than the competition because it is such a good negotiator. Before we get into the details of negotiating, complete Self-Assessment 4.

SELF-ASSESSMENT 4

Negotiating

Identify each of the 16 statements according to how accurately it describes your behavior. Place a number from 1–5 on the line before each statement.

5 — 4 — 3 — 2 — 1

Describes me *Does not describe me*

_____ 1. Before I negotiate, if possible, I find out about the person I will negotiate with to determine what they want and will be willing to give up.

_____ 2. Before I negotiate, I set objectives.

_____ 3. When planning my negotiating presentation, I focus on how the other party will benefit.

_____ 4. Before I negotiate, I have a target price I want to pay, a lowest price I will pay, and an opening offer.

_____ 5. Before I negotiate, I think through options and tradeoffs in case I don't get my target price.

continued

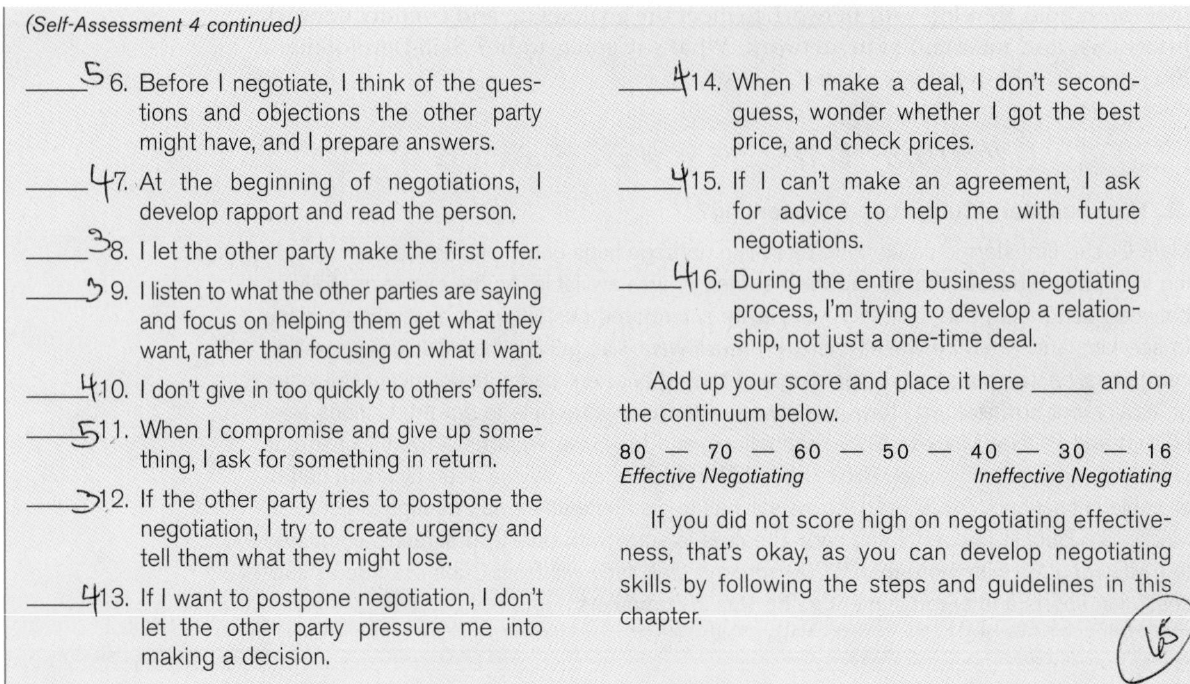

(Self-Assessment 4 continued)

_____ 6. Before I negotiate, I think of the questions and objections the other party might have, and I prepare answers.

_____ 7. At the beginning of negotiations, I develop rapport and read the person.

_____ 8. I let the other party make the first offer.

_____ 9. I listen to what the other parties are saying and focus on helping them get what they want, rather than focusing on what I want.

_____ 10. I don't give in too quickly to others' offers.

_____ 11. When I compromise and give up something, I ask for something in return.

_____ 12. If the other party tries to postpone the negotiation, I try to create urgency and tell them what they might lose.

_____ 13. If I want to postpone negotiation, I don't let the other party pressure me into making a decision.

_____ 14. When I make a deal, I don't second-guess, wonder whether I got the best price, and check prices.

_____ 15. If I can't make an agreement, I ask for advice to help me with future negotiations.

_____ 16. During the entire business negotiating process, I'm trying to develop a relationship, not just a one-time deal.

Add up your score and place it here _____ and on the continuum below.

80 — 70 — 60 — 50 — 40 — 30 — 16
Effective Negotiating *Ineffective Negotiating*

If you did not score high on negotiating effectiveness, that's okay, as you can develop negotiating skills by following the steps and guidelines in this chapter.

Negotiating

At certain times, negotiations are appropriate, such as when conducting management–union collective bargaining, buying and selling goods and services, accepting a new job compensation offer, or getting a raise—all situations without a fixed price or deal. If there's a set, take-it-or-leave-it deal, there is no negotiation. For example, in almost all U.S. retail stores, you must buy the product for the price listed; you don't negotiate price. Some car dealers have also stopped negotiating in favor of a set sticker price.

All Parties Should Believe They Got a Good Deal

Negotiation is often a zero-sum game in which one party's gain is the other party's loss. For example, every dollar less that you pay for a car is your gain and the seller's loss. Therefore, you don't have a true collaboration (win-win situation). Like power and politics, negotiating is not about taking advantage of others, it's about building relationships and helping each other get what we want.[89] To get what you want, you have to sell your ideas and convince the other party to give you what you want. However, negotiation should be viewed by all parties as an opportunity for everyone to win some, rather than as a win-lose situation. In other words, all parties should believe they got a good deal.[90] If union employees believe they lost and management won, employees may experience job dissatisfaction, resulting in lower performance in the long run. If customers believe they got a bad deal, they may not give repeat business.

Negotiation Skills Can Be Developed

Not everyone is born a great negotiator. In fact, most people don't have a clue about how to get what they want, other than making demands and digging in their heels. Taking the time to learn how to negotiate before entering a deal is the best way to arrive at a successful conclusion.[91] Following the steps in the negotiation process can help you develop your negotiation skills.

Learning Outcomes 6 and 7

List the steps in the negotiation process.

Explain the relationships among negotiation and conflict, influencing tactics, power, and politics.

The Negotiation Process

The negotiation process has three, and possibly four, steps: plan, negotiations, possibly a postponement, and an agreement or no agreement.[92] These steps are summarized in Model 4.1 and discussed in this section. Like the other models in this book, Model 4.1 is meant to give you step-by-step guidelines. However, in making it apply to varying types of negotiation, you may have to make slight adjustments.

Plan

The key to any negotiation is preparation,[93] so develop a plan.[94] Know what's negotiable and what's not.[95] Be clear about what it is you are negotiating over. Is it price, options, delivery time, sales quantity, or all four? Ask yourself, "Why am I doing this?"[96] Planning has four steps.

Step 1. Research the other party(ies). As discussed, know the key power players. Put yourself in the other party's shoes. Try to find out what the other parties want, and what they will and will not be willing to give up, before you negotiate.[97] Find out their personality traits and negotiation style by networking with people who have negotiated with the other party before.[98] The more you know about the other party, the better your chances of getting an agreement. If possible, establish a personal relationship before the negotiation. If you have experience working with the other party (for

MODEL 4.1 The Negotiation Process

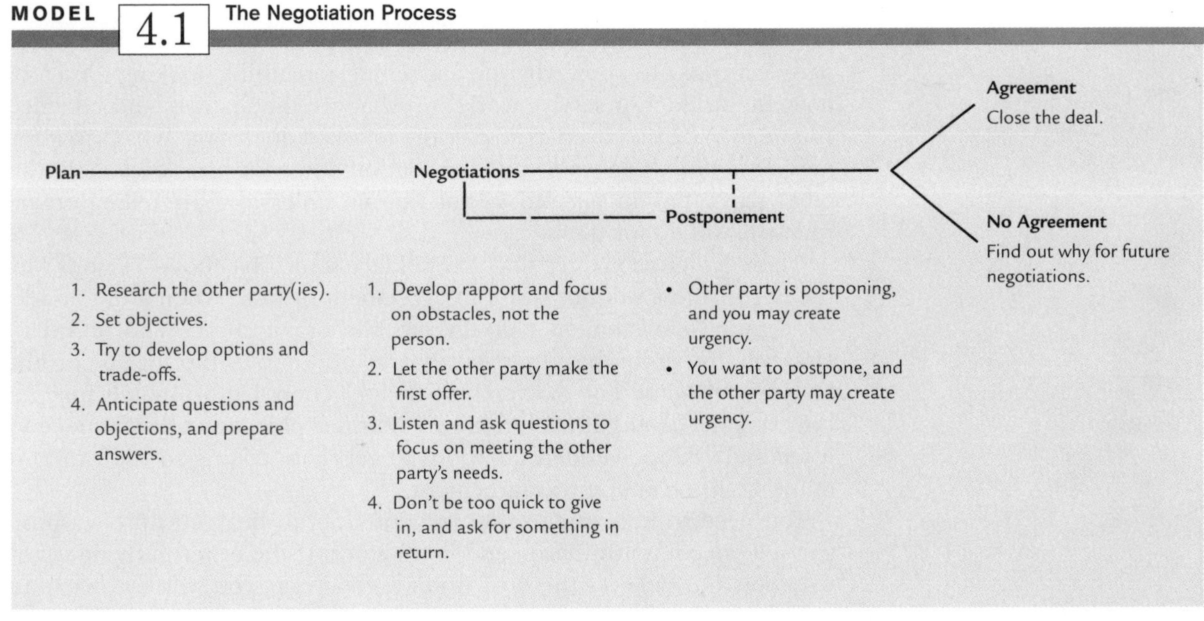

Plan
Negotiations
Postponement
Agreement
Close the deal.
No Agreement
Find out why for future negotiations.
1. Research the other party(ies).
2. Set objectives.
3. Try to develop options and trade-offs.
4. Anticipate questions and objections, and prepare answers.
1. Develop rapport and focus on obstacles, not the person.
2. Let the other party make the first offer.
3. Listen and ask questions to focus on meeting the other party's needs.
4. Don't be too quick to give in, and ask for something in return.
• Other party is postponing, and you may create urgency.
• You want to postpone, and the other party may create urgency.

example, your manager or a potential customer), what worked and did not work in the past? How can you use that experience in your negotiations (in getting a raise or making a sale)?

Step 2. Set objectives. Based on your research, what can you expect—your objective?[99] You have to identify the one thing you must come away with. Set a lower limit, a target objective, and an opening objective. In many negotiations the objective will be a price, but it could be working conditions, longer vacation, job security, and so on. Follow steps a, b, and c: (a) Set a specific lower limit and be willing to walk away; do not come to an agreement unless you get it. You need to be willing to walk away from a bad deal.[100] (b) Set a target objective of what you believe is a fair deal. (c) Set an opening objective offer that is higher than you expect; you might get it. Remember that the other party is probably also setting three objectives. So don't view their opening offer as final.[101] The key to successful negotiations is for all parties to get between their minimum and target objective. This creates a win-win situation.

Step 3. Try to develop options and trade-offs. In purchasing something as well as in looking for a job, if you have multiple sellers and job offers, you are in a stronger power position to get your target price. It is common practice to quote other offers and to ask if the other party can beat them.

Have a sincere concern for the other party in getting a good deal.[102] Try to invent options so that both parties get what they want. In other words, instead of fighting over the pie, think of ways to expand the pie.

If you have to give up something, or cannot get exactly what you want, be prepared to ask for something else in return. If you cannot get the higher raise you want, maybe you can get more days off, more in your retirement account, a nicer office, an assistant, and so on. When an airline was having financial difficulty, it asked employees to take a pay cut. Rather than simply accept a cut, they asked for a trade-off and got company stock. Based on your research, what trade-offs do you expect from the other party?

Step 4. Anticipate questions and objections, and prepare answers. The other party may want to know why you are selling something, looking for a job, how the product or service works, or what are the features and benefits. You need to be prepared to answer the unasked question, "What's in it for me?" Don't focus on what you want, but on how your deal will benefit the other party. Talk in *you* and *we* not *I* terms, unless you are telling others what you will do for them.

There is a good chance that you will face some objection—reasons why the negotiations will not result in agreement or sale. When a union asks for a raise, management typically says the organization can't afford it. However, the union has done its research and quotes the specific profits for a set period of time to overcome the objection. Unfortunately for you, not everyone comes out and tells you their real objections. So you need to listen and ask open-ended questions to get them talking so you can find out what is preventing the agreement.[103]

You need to fully understand your product or deal, and project positive self-esteem, enthusiasm, and confidence. If the other party does not trust you and believes the deal is not a good one, you will not reach an agreement. To use our examples, during the selection process, you must convince the manager that you can do the job or that your product will benefit the customer. When you are in sales, you should have some closing-the-sale statements prepared, such as, "Will you take the white one or the blue one?"

Negotiations

After you have planned, you are now ready to negotiate the deal. Face-to-face negotiations are generally preferred because you can see the other person's nonverbal behavior and better understand objections. However, telephone and written negotiations work too. Again, know the other party's preference. Handling negotiations also has four steps.

Step 1. **Develop rapport and focus on obstacles, not the person.** Smile and call the other party by name as you greet them. A smile tells people you like them, are interested in them, and enjoy them. Open with some small talk, like the weather, to get to know them.[104] Deciding on how much time to wait until you get down to business depends on the other party's style. Some people like to get right down to business; others, like the Japanese, want to get to know you first. However, you want the other party to make the first offer, so don't wait too long or you may lose your chance.

"Focus on the obstacle, not the person" means never to attack the other's personality or put others down with negative statements like, "You are being unfair to ask for such a price cut." If you do so, the other party will become defensive, you may end up arguing, and it will be harder to reach an agreement. So even if the other person starts it, refuse to fight on a name-calling level. Make statements like, "You think my price is too high?" Not saying negative things about others includes your competitors; just state your competitive advantage in a positive way.[105] People look for four things: inclusion, control, safety, and respect. Most people, if they perceive that you are trying to push them into something, threaten them in some way, or belittle them, will not trust you and make an agreement.

Step 2. **Let the other party make the first offer.** This gives you the advantage, because if the other party offers you more than your target objective, you can close the agreement. For example, if you are expecting to be paid $35,000 a year (your target objective) and the other party offers you $40,000, are you going to reject it? On the other hand, if you are offered $30,000 you can realize that it may be low and work at increasing the compensation. Ask questions like, "What is the salary range?" or "What do you expect to pay for a such a fine product?"

Try to avoid negotiating simply on price. When others pressure you to make the first offer with a common question like, "Give us your best price, and we'll tell you whether we'll take it," try asking them a question such as, "What do you expect to pay?" or "What is a reasonable price?" When this does not work, say something like, "Our usual (or list) price is *xxx*. However, if you make me a proposal, I'll see what I can do for you."

If things go well during steps 1 and 2, you may skip to closing the agreement. If you are not ready to agree, proceed to the next step or two.

Step 3. Listen and ask questions to focus on meeting the other party's needs. Create an opportunity for the other party to disclose reservations and objections. When you speak you give out information, but when you ask questions and listen, you receive information that will help you to overcome the other party's objections.[106] If you go on and on about the features you have to offer, without finding out what features the other party is really interested in, you may be killing the deal. Ask questions such as, "Is the price out of the ballpark?" or "Is it fast enough for you?" or "Is any feature you wanted missing?" If the objection is a "want" criteria, such as two years of work experience and you have only one, play up the features you know they want and that you do have, and you may reach an agreement. If the objection is something you cannot meet, at least you found out and don't waste time chasing a deal that will not happen. However, be sure the objection is really a "must" criteria: What if the employer gets no applicants with two years' experience and you apply? You may get the job offer.

Step 4. Don't be too quick to give in, and ask for something in return. Those who ask for more get more. Don't give up.[107] If your competitive advantage is service, and during negotiation you quickly give in for a lower price, you lose all the value in a minute. You want to satisfy the other party without giving up too much during the negotiation. Remember not to go below your minimum objective. If it is realistic, be prepared to walk away.[108] When you are not getting what you want, having other planned options can help give you bargaining power. If you do walk away, you may be called back; and if not, you may be able to come back for the same low price—but not always. If other parties know you are desperate, or just weak and will accept a low agreement, they will likely take advantage of you. Have you ever seen a sign on a product saying, "must sell—need cash"? What type of price do you think that seller gets? You also need to avoid being intimidated by comments such as this said in a loud voice: "Are you kidding me, that's too much." Many people will quickly drop the price, but you don't have to let it happen.

However, when you are dealing with a complex deal, such as a management–union contract negotiation with trade-offs, be willing to be the first to make a concession. The other party tends to feel obligated, and then you can come back with a counter trade-off that is larger than the one you gave up.

Avoid giving unilateral concessions. Recall your planned trade-offs. If the other party asks for a lower price, ask for a concession such as a large-volume sale to get it, or a longer delivery time, a less popular color, and so on. You need to send the message that you don't just give things away.

Postponement

Take your time.[109] When there doesn't seem to be any progress, it may be wise to postpone the negotiations.

The Other Party Is Postponing, and You May Create Urgency The other party says, "I'll get back to you." When you are not getting what you want, you may try to create urgency. For example, "This product is on sale, and the sale ends today." However, honesty is the best policy. The primary reason people will negotiate with you is that they trust and respect you.[110] Establishing a relationship of trust is the necessary first step in closing a deal. If you do have other options, you can use them to create urgency, such as saying, "I have another job offer pending; when will you let me know if you want to offer me the job?"

But what if urgency does not apply—or does not work—and the other party says, "I'll think about it?" You might say, "That's a good idea." Then at least review the major features the other party liked about your proposed deal and ask if it meets their needs. The other party may decide to come to an agreement or sale. If not, and they don't tell you when they will get back to you, ask, for example, "When can I expect to hear if I got the job?" Try to pin the other party down for a specific time; tell the person that if you don't hear from them by then, you will call them. If you are really interested, follow up with a letter (mail, e-mail, or fax) of thanks for their time, and again highlight the features you think they liked. If you forgot to include any specific points during the negotiation, add them in the letter.

One thing to remember when the other party becomes resistant to making the agreement is that the hard sell will not work. Take off the pressure. Ask something like, "Where do you want to go from here?" (to a client). If you press for an answer, it may be no agreement; however, if you wait you may have a better chance. To your manager, you might say, "Why don't we think about it and discuss it some more later?" (then pick an advantageous time to meet with your manager).

You also need to learn to read between the lines, especially when working with people from different cultures. Some people will not come right out and tell you there is no deal. For example, it is common for the Japanese to say something like, "It will be difficult to do business." Americans tend to think this means they can keep trying to close the deal; however, the Japanese businessperson actually means stop trying, but will not say so directly because it is impolite.

You Want to Postpone, and the Other Party May Create Urgency Don't be hurried by others, and don't hurry yourself.[111] If you are not satisfied with the deal, or want to shop around, tell the other party you want to think about it. You may also need to check with your manager or someone else, which simply may be for advice, before you can finalize the deal. If the other party is creating urgency, be sure it really is urgent. In many cases, you can get the same deal at a later date; don't be pressured into making a deal you are not satisfied with or may regret later. If you do want to postpone, give the other party a specific time that you will get back to them, and do so with more prepared negotiations or simply to tell them you cannot make an agreement.

Agreement

Once the agreement has been made, restate it and/or put it in writing when appropriate. It is common to follow up an agreement with a letter of thanks, restating the agreement to ensure the other parties have not changed their mind about what they agreed to. Also, after the deal is made, stop selling it. Change the subject to a personal one and/or leave, depending on the other person's preferred negotiations. If they want a personal relationship, stick around; if not, leave.

No Agreement

Rejection, refusal, and failure happen to us all, even the superstars. The difference between the also-rans and the superstars lies in how they respond to the failure. The successful people keep trying, learn from their mistakes, and continue to work hard; failures usually don't persevere. When you cannot come to an agreement, analyze the situation and try to determine where you went wrong so that you can improve in the future. You may also ask the other party for advice, such as, "I realize I did not get the job; thanks for your time. Can you offer me any suggestions for improving my resume and interview skills, or other ideas to help me to get a job in this field?"

Opening Case APPLICATION

4. What types of negotiations has and does Mark Cuban engage in?

A large part of Mark Cuban's job is negotiating. He had to negotiate to buy the Dallas Mavericks and to get HDNet and HDNet Movies on DirecTV. Cuban must continue to negotiate with cable companies Cox and Cablevision who refuse to air HDNet and HDNet Movies to be seen coast-to-coast. Some believe that Cuban is asking way too much money for his network to be viewed on cable. Cuban still needs to negotiate to distribute his 2929 Productions and Magnolia Pictures through big studios. But the Mavericks are winning more games, and fans are now coming to the games; and they adore Mark Cuban, who has bought the first $2,000 worth of drinks after winning games. Revenue for the Mavericks has gone from $40 million to $140 million under Cuban.

Ethics and Influencing

Recall that *influencing* is the process of affecting others' attitudes and behavior in order to achieve an objective, which is usually to get what you want. Power, politics, networking, and negotiating are all forms of influencing. When influencing, recall that it pays to be ethical[112] (Chapter 2). Power is neither good nor bad; it's what you do with it. Power is unethical (personalized power) when used to promote your self-interest at the expense of others. It is ethical when it is used to help meet organizational objectives and those of its members, as well as to get what you want (socialized power).

When playing organizational politics, it can be tempting to be unethical, but don't. Even if others are using unethical behavior, don't stoop to their level. Talking negatively about people behind their back or stabbing them in the back is usually destructive in the long run.[113] Confront others if you believe they are playing unethical politics and try to resolve the issues. If you cannot, or if the behavior does not directly affect you, going to higher-level managers to inform them of the unethical behavior may be a necessary option.

Recall that networking is about building relationships. Thus, being open and honest during networking is the best policy.[114] You should also try to give to your network, as well as take, and be open to helping others who want to include you in their network. In general, truly successful people take the time to help others. If you haven't learned it already, you will be surprised at how helping others comes back to you.

Ethics of telling the truth, or not lying to the other party or being lied to, is an issue you will face in negotiation. There is a difference between not giving information that is not asked for and lying to the other party. To be a successful negotiator, people have to trust you to do business with you.[115] In most positions, repeat customers are critical to long-term success. Lying to one customer and losing that person's business can cost you greatly in the long term. Also, the person who caught you lying may tell others, and you can lose more business. Doing the right things, even if you don't want to do them, is one of the keys to being truly happy.[116]

So when you are influencing others, try to use the stakeholders' approach to ethics by creating a win-win situation for relevant parties affected by the decision.

5. Is Mark Cuban ethical in influencing others?

As discussed, Mark Cuban's behavior has not always been appropriate, and thus has gotten him into some trouble in sports and entertainment. Cuban is aware of this shortcoming, and only time will tell if he will earn the respect he believes he deserves as he strives to be famous and influential.

Go to the Internet (www.cengage.com/management/lussier) *where you will find a broad array of resources to help maximize your learning.*

- **Review the vocabulary**
- **Try a quiz**
- **Find related links**

Chapter Summary

The chapter summary is organized to answer the eight learning outcomes for Chapter 4.

1. **Explain the differences between position power and personal power.**

   Position power is derived from top management and is delegated down the chain of command. Thus, people at the top of the organization have more power than those at the bottom of the organization. Personal power is derived from the followers based on the leader's behavior. All managers have position power, but they may or may not have personal power. Nonmanagers do not have position power, but they may have personal power.

2. **Discuss the differences among legitimate, reward, coercive, and referent power.**

   Legitimate, reward, and coercive power are all related. A leader with position power usually has the power to reward and punish (coercive). However, a person with referent power may or may not have position power to reward and punish, and the leader influences followers based on relationships.

3. **Discuss how power and politics are related.**

   Power is the ability to influence others' behavior. Politics is the process of gaining and using power. Therefore, political skills are a part of power.

4. **Describe how money and politics have a similar use.**

   Money and politics have a similar use, because they are mediums of exchange. In our economy, money is the medium of exchange. In an organization, politics is the medium of exchange.

5. **List and explain the steps in the networking process.**

   The first step in the networking process is to perform a self-assessment to determine accomplishments and to set goals. Second, create a one-minute self-sell that quickly summarizes history and career plans and asks a question. Third, develop a written network list. Fourth, conduct networking interviews to meet your goals. Finally, maintain your network for meeting future goals.

6. **List the steps in the negotiation process.**

   The first step in the negotiation process is to plan for the negotiation. The second step is to conduct the actual negotiation, which can be postponed, and results in an agreement or no agreement.

7. **Explain the relationships among negotiation and conflict, influencing tactics, power, and politics.**

   Negotiations take place when there is a conflict; and influencing tactics, power, and politics can be used during the negotiation process.

8. **Define the following key terms (in order of appearance in the chapter).**

   Select one or more methods: (1) fill in the missing key terms from memory; (2) match the key terms from the following list with their definitions below; (3) copy the key terms in order from the list at the beginning of the chapter.

__________ is the leader's potential influence over followers.

__________ is based on the user's position power, given by the organization.

__________ is based on the user's ability to influence others with something of value to them.

__________ involves punishment and withholding of rewards to influence compliance.

__________ is based on the user's personal relationships with others.

__________ is based on the user's skill and knowledge.

__________ is based on the user's data desired by others.

__________ is based on the user's relationships with influential people.

__________ is the process of gaining and using power.

__________ is the process of developing relationships for the purpose of socializing and politicking.

__________ involves creating obligations and developing alliances, and using them to accomplish objectives.

__________ is an opening statement used in networking that quickly summarizes your history and career plan and asks a question.

__________ is a process in which two or more parties are in conflict and attempt to come to an agreement.

Key Terms

coercive power, 113
connection power, 117
expert power, 115
information power, 116
legitimate power, 111
negotiating, 133
networking, 122
one-minute self-sell, 129
politics, 121
power, 110
reciprocity, 122
referent power, 115
reward power, 113

Review Questions

1. What are the seven types of power?
2. What are the nine influencing tactics?
3. What is ingratiation influencing?
4. What is the difference between inspirational appeal and personal appeal influencing?
5. What are the three political behaviors and four guidelines for developing political skills?
6. How many interview questions should you bring to a networking interview?
7. Which step of "conduct networking interviews" involves getting additional contacts for your network?
8. What type of situation (win/lose) is the goal of negotiation?
9. What are the steps in negotiations?
10. What are the steps in planning a negotiation?

Communication Skills

The following critical-thinking questions can be used for class discussion and/or as written assignments to develop communication skills. Be sure to give complete explanations for all questions.

1. Is power good or bad for organizations?
2. Which influencing tactics do you tend to use most and least? How will you change and develop the ability to influence using influencing tactics?
3. How would you rate your political skills, and which political behavior do you use most often? How will you change and develop your political skills?
4. How would you rate your relationship with your current or past boss? What will you do differently in the future to improve your relationship with your boss?
5. Can management stop the use of power and politics in their organizations?
6. Should people be judged based on their social skills?
7. How would you rate your networking skills? What will you do differently in the future to improve your networking skills?
8. Do people really need a written networking list?

9. How would you rate your negotiation skills? What will you do differently in the future to improve your negotiation skills?

10. Do you believe that most managers use influencing (power, politics, networking, and negotiating) for the good of the organization, or for their own personal benefit? What can be done to help managers be more ethical in influencing others?

CASE

Ron Johnson—Department of Accounting

Ron Johnson is a tenured professor of leadership at a small teaching college in the Midwest.[117] The Department of Accounting (DA) has nine faculty members; it is one of ten departments in the School of Arts and Sciences (SAS). The accounting department chair is Jean Williams, who is in her first year as chair. Six faculty members, including Ron, have been in the department longer than Jean. Jean likes to have policies in place, so that faculty members have guides for their behavior. On the college-wide level, however, there is no policy about the job of graduate assistant. Jean has asked the dean of the SAS about the policy. After a discussion with the vice president for academic affairs, the dean told Jean that there is no policy. The vice president and dean suggested letting the individual departments develop their own policy regarding what graduate assistants can and cannot do in their position. So, Jean has made developing a policy for graduate assistants an agenda item for the department meeting.

During the DA meeting, Jean asks for members' views on what graduate assistants should and should not be allowed to do. She is hoping that the department can come to a consensus on a policy. It turns out that Ron Johnson is the only faculty member using graduate assistants to grade exams. All but one of the other faculty members speaks out against having graduate assistants grade exams. Other faculty members believe it is the professor's job to grade exams. Ron makes a few statements in hopes of not having to correct his own exams. Because his exams are objective, requiring a correct answer, Ron believes it's not necessary for him to personally grade the exams. He also points out that across the campus, and across the country, other faculty members are using graduate assistants to teach entire courses and to correct subjective papers and exams. Ron states that he does not think it fair to tell him that he cannot use graduate assistants to grade objective exams when others are doing so. He also states that the department does not need to have a policy, and requests that the department not set a policy. However, Jean states that she wants a policy. Ron holds a single, minority view during the meeting. But, after the meeting, one other member, Eddie Accorsi, who said nothing during the meeting, tells Ron he agrees that it is not fair to deny him this use of a graduate assistant.

There was no department consensus, as Jean hoped there would be. Jean says that she will draft a department policy, which will be discussed at a future DA meeting. The next day, Ron sends a memo to department members asking if it is ethical and legal to deny him the same resources as others are using across the campus. He also states that if the department sets a policy stating that he can no longer use graduate assistants to correct objective exams, he will appeal the policy decision to the dean, vice president, and president.

Support your answers to the following questions with specific information from the case and text, or with other information you get from the Web or other sources.

1. (a) What source of power does Jean have, and (b) what type of power is she using? (c) Which influencing tactic is Jean using during the meeting? (d) Is negotiation and/or the (e) exchange tactic appropriate in this situation?

2. (a) What source of power does Ron have, and (b) what type of power is he using during the meeting? (c) Which two influencing tactics is Ron primarily using during the meeting? (d) Which influencing tactic is Ron using with the memo? (e) Is the memo a wise political move for Ron? What might he gain and lose by sending it?

3. What would you do if you were Jean? (a) Would you talk to the dean, letting him know that Ron said he would appeal the policy decision? (b) Which influencing tactic would this discussion involve? (c) Which political behavior would the discussion represent? (d) Would you draft a policy directly stating that graduate assistants cannot be used to grade objective exams? (e) Would your answer to (d) be influenced by your answer to (a)?
4. (a) If you were Ron, knowing you had no verbal supporters during the meeting, would you have continued to defend your position or agreed to stop using a graduate assistant? (b) What do you think of Ron sending the memo? (c) As a tenured full professor, Ron is secure in his job. Would your answer change if you (as Ron) had not received tenure or promotion to the top rank?
5. (a) If you were Ron, and Jean drafted a policy and department members agreed with it, what would you do? Would you appeal the decision to the dean? (b) Again, would your answer change if you had not received tenure or promotion to the top rank?
6. If you were the dean of SAS, knowing that the vice president does not want to set a college-wide policy, and Ron appealed to you, what would you do? Would you develop a school-wide policy for SAS?
7. At what level (college-wide, by schools, or by departments within each school) should a graduate assistants policy be set?
8. (a) Should Eddie Accorsi have spoken up in defense of Ron during the meeting? (b) If you were Eddie, would you have taken Ron's side against the other seven members? (c) Would your answer change if you were or were not friends with Ron, and if you were or were not a tenured full professor?

CUMULATIVE CASE QUESTIONS

9. Which level(s) of analysis of leadership theory is (are) presented in this case (Chapter 1)?
10. Is it ethical for graduate students to correct undergraduate exams (Chapter 2)?
11. Which of the four Ohio State University leadership styles did Jean use during the department meeting (Chapter 3)?

CASE EXERCISE AND ROLE-PLAY

Preparation: Read the case and think about whether you agree or disagree with using graduate assistants to correct objective exams. If you do this exercise, we recommend that you complete it before discussing the questions and answers to the case.

In-Class DA Meeting: A person who strongly agrees with Ron's position volunteers to play his or her role (women can use the name Ronnie) during a leadership department DA meeting. A second person who also agrees with the use of graduate assistants correcting exams plays the role of Eddie (or Freddie). However, recall that Eddie/Freddie cannot say anything during the meeting to support Ron/Ronnie. One person who strongly disagrees with Ron—who doesn't want graduate assistants to correct exams, and who also feels strongly that there should be a policy stating what graduate assistants can and cannot do—volunteers to play the role of the department chair (Jean) who runs the DA meeting. Six others who strongly disagree with graduate assistants grading exams play the roles of other department members.

The ten role-players sit in a circle in the center of the room, with the other class members sitting around the outside of the circle. Observers just quietly watch and listen to the meeting discussion.

Role-Play: *(about 15 minutes)* Jean opens the meeting by simply stating that the agenda item is to set a graduate assistants policy stating what they can and cannot do, and that he or she hopes the department can come to a consensus on a policy. Jean states his or her position on why graduate students should not be allowed to correct exams, and then asks for other views. Ron/Ronnie and the others, except Eddie/Freddie, jump in anytime with their opinions.

Discussion: After the role-play is over, or when time runs out, the person playing the role of Ron/Ronnie expresses to the class how it felt to have everyone against him or her. Other department members state how they felt about the discussion, followed by observers' statements as time permits. A discussion of the case questions and answers may follow.

VIDEO CASE

Employee Networks at Whirlpool Corporation

Since 1911, Whirlpool Corporation has grown from a small company to a global corporation with manufacturing locations on every major continent and over 68,000 employees worldwide. Like many organizations, one of Whirlpool's strategies for creating a culture of pluralism is encouraging the formation of employee network groups. These are voluntary groups formed around primary dimensions such as gender and ethnicity, and which meet regularly to focus on business issues. The groups are also a resource to the employees by providing a supportive community, decreasing social isolation, and promoting career development. Further, they help retain employees by providing them a forum for expressing ideas. These discussions often spark new ideas that benefit the company as a whole.

1. Using the Whirlpool Corporation Web site (**http://www.whirlpoolcorp.com**), identify the employee network groups at Whirlpool and the mission of each.
2. Do you think Whirlpool's encouragement of employee networks works for or against creating a culture of diversity? Explain your answer.

Skill-Development Exercise 1

Influencing Tactics

Preparing for Skill-Development Exercise 1

Below are three situations. For each situation, select the most appropriate influencing tactic(s) to use. Write the tactic(s) on the lines following the situation. At this time, don't write out how you would behave (what you would say and do).

1. You are doing a college internship, which is going well. You would like to become a full-time employee in a few weeks, after you graduate.

   Which influencing tactic(s) would you use? ______

   Who would you try to influence? ______

   How would you do so (behavior)? ______

2. You have been working at your job for six months, and you are approaching the elevator. You see a powerful person who could potentially help you advance in your career waiting for the elevator. You have never met her, but you do know that her committee has recently completed a new five-year strategic plan for the company and that she plays tennis and is active at the same religious organization (church, synagogue, mosque) as you. Although you only have a couple of minutes, you decide to try to develop a connection.

   Which influencing tactic(s) would you use? ______

   How would you strike up a conversation? What topic(s) do you raise? ______

3. You are the manager of the production department. Some of the sales staff has been scheduling deliveries for your product that your department can't meet. Customers are blaming you for late delivery. This is not good for the company, so you decide to talk to the sales staff manager about it over lunch.

   Which influencing tactic(s) would you use? ______

   How would you handle the situation (behavior)? ______

Now select one of the three situations that seems real to you—you can imagine yourself in the situation. Or briefly write in a real-life situation that you can quickly explain to a small group. Now, briefly write out the behavior (what you would do and say) that you would use in the situation to influence the person to do what you want.

Situation # ______ Or, my situation: ______________________

____

Influencing tactic(s) to use: ______________________

Behavior: ______________________________________

____

____

____

Doing Skill-Development Exercise 1 In-Class

Objective

To develop your persuasion skills by using influencing tactics.

The primary AACSB learning standard skills developed through this exercise are analytic and strategic management skills—students learn to achieve their goals by influencing others.

Experience

You will discuss which influencing tactics are most appropriate for the preparation situations. You may also be given the opportunity to role-play how you would handle the one situation you selected; you will also play the role of the person to be influenced, and observer.

Procedure 1 *(10–20 minutes)* Break up into groups of three, with one or two groups of two if needed. Try not to have two members in a group who selected the same situation; use people who selected their own situation. First, try to quickly agree on which influencing tactics are most appropriate in each situation. Select a spokesperson to give group answers to the class. In preparation to role-play, have each person state the behavior selected to handle the situation. The others give feedback for improvement: suggestions to delete, change, and/or add to the behavior (e.g., I would not say . . . , I'd say it this way . . . , I'd add . . . to what you have now).

Procedure 2 *(5–10 minutes)* One situation at a time, each group spokesperson tells the class which influencing styles it would use, followed by brief remarks from the professor. The professor may also ask people who selected their own situation to tell the class the situation.

Conclusion

The instructor may lead a class discussion and/or make concluding remarks.

Apply It *(2–4 minutes)* What did I learn from this exercise? How will I use this knowledge in the future?

____

____

____

Sharing

In the group, or to the entire class, volunteers may give their answers to the "Apply It" questions.

Skill-Development Exercise 2

Influencing, Power, and Politics

Preparing for Skill-Development Exercise 2

Your instructor will tell you to select one, two, or all three of the following topics (influencing, power, and/or politics) for this preparation.

To get what you want, you need to develop your ability to influence others and gain power through politics. It is helpful to read about these topics and how to improve your skills, but unless you apply the concepts in your personal and professional life, you will not develop these skills.

This preparation covers three skills, each with two activities. The first activity is to develop a general guide to daily actions you can take to increase your influence, power, and/or understanding of politics. The second is to think of a specific situation in the future, and develop a plan to get what you want. Use additional paper if you need more space to write your plan.

Influencing

Write down the influencing tactic that you are the strongest at using: __________. The weakest: __________. The one you would like to improve on: __________ (it does not have to be your weakest). Review the ideas for using this tactic, and write down a few ways in which you will work at developing your skill.

____

____

____

Think of a specific situation in the near future in which you can use this tactic to help you get what you want. Briefly describe the situation, and explain how you will use this tactic—what you will say and do, and so on.

____

____

____

Power

Write down the one type of your power you would like to improve on: __________. Review the ideas for increasing this type of power, and write down a few ways in which you will work at developing your power.

Think of a specific situation in the near future in which you can use this type of power to help you get what you want. Briefly describe the situation, and explain how you will use this tactic—what you will say and do, and so on.

Politics

Write down the one area of politics you would like to improve on: ___________ . Review the ideas for using this type of politics, and write down a few ways in which you will work at developing your skill.

Think of a specific situation in the near future in which you can use this type of politicking to help you get what you want. Briefly describe the situation, and explain how you will use this tactic—what you will say and do, and so on.

Doing Skill-Development Exercise 2 in Class

Objective

To develop your ability to influence others and gain power through politics.

The primary AACSB learning standard skills developed through this exercise are analytic and strategic management skills—students learn to achieve their goals by influencing others.

Experience

You will develop a general guide to daily actions you can take to increase your influence, power, and/or understanding of politics. You'll also develop a plan to get what you want.

Preparation

You should have completed the preparation for this exercise, unless told not to do so by your instructor.

Procedure 1 *(10–20 minutes)* Break into groups of three, with some groups of two if necessary. If group members developed plans for more than one skill area, select only one to start with. One group member volunteers to share first and states his or her preparation for influencing, power, or politics. The other members give input into how effective they think the plan is and offer ideas on how to improve the plan. After the first member shares, the other two have their turn, changing roles with each round. If there is time remaining after all have shared, go on to another skill area until the time is up.

Procedure 2 *(2–3 minutes)* Each member commits to implementing his or her plan by a set time, and to telling the others how well the influence, power, or politics went by a specific date—before or after the class ends.

Name ___________
Date of implementation ___________
Date to report results ___________

Name ___________
Date of implementation ___________
Date to report results ___________

Name ___________
Date of implementation ___________
Date to report results ___________

Conclusion

The instructor may make concluding remarks.

Apply It *(2–4 minutes)* What did I learn from this experience? How will I use this knowledge in the future?

Sharing

In the group, or to the entire class, volunteers may give their answers to the "Apply It" questions.

Skill-Development Exercise 3

*Networking Skills**

Preparing for Skill-Development Exercise 3

Based on the section "Networking" and the subsection on the networking process, complete the following steps.

1. Perform a self-assessment and set goals. List two or three of your accomplishments and set a goal. The goal can be to learn more about career opportunities in your major; to get an internship, part-time, summer, or full-time job; and so on.

2. Create your one-minute self-sell. Write it out. See page 130 for a written example.

   History: ____________________

   Plan: ____________________

   Question: ____________________

3. Develop your network. List at least five people to be included in your network, preferably people who can help you achieve your goal.

   ____

   ____

   ____

4. Conduct networking interviews. To help meet your goal, select one person for a personal 20-minute interview or to interview by phone if it is difficult to meet in person. List the person and write questions to ask during the interview. This person can be a person in your college career center or a professor in your major.

   ____

   ____

   ____

*Source: This exercise was developed by Andra Gumbus, assistant professor, College of Business, Sacred Heart University. © Andra Gumbus, 2002. It is used with Dr. Gumbus's permission.

Doing Skill-Development Exercise 3 in Class

Objective

To develop networking skills by implementing the steps in the networking process.

The primary AACSB learning standard skills developed through this exercise are analytic and strategic management skills—students learn to achieve their goals by networking.

Experience

You will deliver your one-minute self-sell from the preparation and get feedback for improvement. You will also share your network list and interview questions and get feedback for improvement.

Procedure 1 *(7–10 minutes)*

A. Break into groups of two. Show each other your written one-minute self-sell. Is the history, plan, and question clear (do you understand it), concise (60 seconds or less to say), and compelling (does it promote interest to help)? Offer suggestions for improvement.

B. After perfected, each person states (no reading) the one-minute self-sell. Was it stated clearly, concisely, and with confidence? Offer improvements. State it a second and third time, or until told to go on to the next procedure.

Procedure 2 *(7–10 minutes)* Break into groups of three with people you did not work with during procedure 1. Follow procedures A and B above in your triad. Repeating your self-sell should improve your delivery and confidence.

Procedure 3 *(10–20 minutes)* Break into groups of four with people you did not work with during procedures 1 and 2, if possible. Share your answers from steps 3 (your network list) and 4 (your interview questions). Offer each other improvements to the questions and new questions. You should also get ideas for writing new questions for your own interview.

Applications (done outside of class)

Expand your written network list to at least 25 names. Conduct the networking interview using the questions developed through this exercise.

Conclusion

The instructor may make concluding remarks, including requiring the network lists and/or networking interview in the "Applications" section. Written network lists and/or interview questions and answers (following the name, title, and organization of interviewee; date, time, and type of interview—phone or in person) may be passed in.

Apply It *(2–4 minutes)* What did I learn from this experience? How will I use this knowledge in the future?

____

____

____

Sharing

In groups, or to the entire class, volunteers may give their answers to the "Apply It" questions.

Skill-Development Exercise 4

*Car Dealer Negotiation**

Preparing for Skill-Development Exercise 4

You should have read and should understand the negotiation process.

Doing Skill-Development Exercise 4 in Class

Objective

To develop your negotiation skills.

The primary AACSB learning standard skills developed through this exercise are analytic and strategic management skills—students learn to achieve their goals through negotiating.

Experience

You will be the buyer or seller of a used car.

Procedure 1 *(1–2 minutes)* Break up into groups of two and sit facing each other, so that you cannot read each other's confidential sheet. Each group should be as far away from other groups as possible, to avoid overhearing each other's conversations. If there is an odd number of students in the class, one student will be an observer or work with the instructor. Select who will be the buyer and who will be the seller of the used car.

Procedure 2 *(1–2 minutes)* The instructor goes to each group and gives each buyer and seller their confidential sheet.

Procedure 3 *(5–6 minutes)* Buyers and sellers read their confidential sheets and write down some plans (what will be your basic approach, what will you say) for the lunch meeting.

Procedure 4 *(3–7 minutes)* Negotiate the sale of the car. Try not to overhear your classmates' conversations. You do not have to buy or sell the car. After you make the sale, or agree not to sell, read the confidential sheet of your partner in this exercise and discuss the experience.

Integration *(3–7 minutes)* Answer the following questions:

1. Which of the nine influencing tactics (see Exhibit 4.1 on page 111) did you use during the negotiations?
2. Which of the seven types of power (Exhibit 4.1) did you use during the negotiations? Did both parties believe that they got a good deal?
3. During your planning, did you (1) research the other party, (2) set an objective (price to pay or accept), (3) develop options and trade-offs, and (4) anticipate questions and objections and prepare answers?
4. During the negotiations, did you (1) develop a rapport and focus on obstacles, not the person; (2) let the other party make the first offer; (3) listen and ask questions to focus on meeting the other party's needs; and (4) were you too quick to give in and did you ask for something in return?
5. Did you reach an agreement to sell/buy the car? If yes, did you get exactly, more than, or less than your target price?
6. When negotiating, is it a good practice to ask for more than you expect to receive, or to offer less than you expect to pay?
7. When negotiating, is it better to be the one to give or receive the initial offer?
8. When negotiating, is it better to appear to be dealing with strong or weak power? In other words, should you try to portray that you have other options and don't really need to make a deal with this person? Or, should you appear to be in need of the deal?
9. Can having the power to intimidate others be helpful in negotiations?

Conclusion

The instructor leads a class discussion, or simply gives the answers to the "Integration" questions, and makes concluding remarks.

Apply It *(2–4 minutes)* What did I learn from this experience? How will I use this knowledge in the future? What will I do differently?

Sharing

In the group, or to the entire class, volunteers may give their answers to the "Apply It" questions.

**Source:* The car dealer negotiation confidential information is from Arch G. Woodside, Tulane University. The Car Dealer Game is part of a paper, "Bargaining Behavior in Personal Selling and Buying Exchanges," that was presented at the 1980 *Eighth Annual Conference of the Association for Business Simulation and Experiential Learning (ABSEL)*. It is used with Dr. Woodside's permission.

5 Contingency Leadership Theories

Chapter Outline

Contingency Leadership Theories and Models

Leadership Theories versus Leadership Models

Contingency Theory and Model Variables

Global Contingency Leadership

Contingency Leadership Theory and Model

Leadership Style and the LPC

Situational Favorableness

Determining the Appropriate Leadership Style

Research

Leadership Continuum Theory and Model

Path-Goal Leadership Theory and Model

Situational Factors

Leadership Styles

Research

Normative Leadership Theory and Models

Leadership Participation Styles

Model Questions to Determine the Appropriate Leadership Style

Selecting the Time-Driven or Development-Driven Model for the Situation

Determining the Appropriate Leadership Style

Research

Putting the Behavioral and Contingency Leadership Theories Together

Prescriptive and Descriptive Models

Leadership Substitutes Theory

Substitutes and Neutralizers

Leadership Style

Changing the Situation

Research

Learning Outcomes

After studying this chapter, you should be able to:

1. State the major difference between behavioral and contingency leadership theories, and explain the behavioral contribution to contingency theories. p. 152
2. Describe the contingency leadership theory variables. p. 152
3. Identify the contingency leadership model styles and variables. p. 154
4. State the leadership continuum model major styles and variables. p. 159
5. Identify the path-goal leadership model styles and variables. p. 161
6. State the normative leadership model styles and the number of variables. p. 165
7. Discuss the major similarities and differences between the behavioral and contingency leadership theories. p. 171
8. Compare and contrast four major differences among the four contingency leadership models. p. 171
9. List which leadership models are prescriptive and descriptive, and explain why they are classified as such. p. 173
10. Explain substitutes and neutralizers of leadership. p. 173
11. Define the following **key terms** (in order of appearance in the chapter):

leadership model
contingency leadership model
leadership continuum model
path-goal leadership model
normative leadership model
prescriptive leadership models
descriptive leadership models
substitutes for leadership

Opening Case APPLICATION

PepsiCo was ranked 63rd in the 2007 *Fortune 500* list of the largest companies (ranked by revenues) and is number 1 in the Food and Consumer Products category (ahead of Kraft Foods, Sara Lee, Conagra Foods, and General Mills).[1] Its two primary lines of business are snack foods (Frito-Lay—its largest unit) and beverages (Pepsi, Tropicana, Gatorade),[2] with some cereal products (Quaker Oats). Although Coca-Cola sells more carbonated soft drinks than Pepsi, PepsiCo moved into the noncarbonated beverages (bottled water, sports drinks, and teas) market before Coke and it now commands half the U.S. market share, about twice as much as Coke.[3] Coca-Cola was ranked lower (94th) than PepsiCo in the 2007 *Fortune 500* list.[4]

Indra K. Nooyi is Chairman and Chief Executive Officer of PepsiCo, and according to *Fortune,* Nooyi is ranked as the most powerful woman.[5] Beginning in the mid-1990s, Nooyi was the chief strategist that dramatically reshaped PepsiCo.[6] The company got out of the restaurant business by selling Pizza Hut, Taco Bell, and KFC in 1997. It got into the juice business by buying the world's largest brand juice producer Tropicana in 1998. PepsiCo entered the sports drink business in 2001 by acquiring the bestseller Gatorade, through the purchase of its maker Quaker Oats, which also gave PepsiCo a line of cereal products, including breakfast and other types of granola bars that complement its snacks. PepsiCo also acquired Izze sparkling juice drinks in 2006 and Naked Juice smoothies and other fruit drinks in 2007.[7] PepsiCo also has joint ventures with partners, including Lipton (ice teas) and Starbucks (frappuccino). Nooyi expects to continue to expand PepsiCo through acquisitions.[8]

Nooyi is a different kind of CEO. She says her approach boils down to balancing the profit motive with making healthier snacks (in a speech to the food industry, she pushed the group to tackle obesity), striving for a net-zero impact on the environment, and taking care of your workforce. She was one of the first executives to realize that the health and green movements were not just fads, and she demanded true innovation. As stated earlier, PepsiCo is now the leading seller of noncarbonated beverages. It is gradually shifting its percentage of "better for you" and "good for you" snacks and widening its product portifolio with grains, nuts, and fruits. The company was one of the first to invest in green capital expenditures for water- and heat-related conservation projects. Executives originally questioned Nooyi's spending, but not today with $55 million in annual savings. Her new motto, "Performance with Purpose," is both a means of herding the organization and of presenting PepsiCo globally. So far Nooyi has been a great success at PepsiCo, but cola wars, higher energy costs, and rising ingredient costs will test her leadership.[9]

Opening Case Questions:

1. What does climbing the corporate ladder to CEO of PepsiCo have to do with contingency leadership? What life, educational, and job experiences qualified Indra Nooyi for her job as CEO?
2. What do colleagues say about Indra Nooyi's leadership—is it task or relationship, does she have a life outside of PepsiCo, and does she have any future career plans?
3. Which continuum leadership style does Indra Nooyi tend to use in making acquisitions at PepsiCo?
4. Which path-goal leadership styles does Indra Nooyi tend to use at PepsiCo?
5. Which normative leadership styles does Indra Nooyi tend to use at PepsiCo?

Can you answer any of these questions? You'll find answers to these questions about PepsiCo and Indra Nooyi throughout the chapter.

To learn more about PepsiCo, visit the company's Web site at **http://www.pepsico.com**.

As you read this chapter, you will learn more about leadership style as it relates to four contingency leadership theories. We begin with an overview of contingency leadership theories. Next we present four contingency leadership models: contingency leadership, leadership continuum, path-goal leadership, and normative leadership, listed in historical sequence by the date each model was published. Then we put the behavioral (Chapter 3) and contingency leadership theories together. We end by discussing leadership substitutes theory.

Learning Outcome 1 *State the major difference between behavioral and contingency leadership theories, and explain the behavioral contribution to contingency theories.*

Contingency Leadership Theories and Models

Both the trait and behavioral leadership theories were attempts to find the one best leadership style in all situations. In the late 1960s, it became apparent that there is no one best leadership style in all situations. Managers need to adapt different leadership styles,[10] as leadership success requires adapting leadership styles to meet the situation.[11] Thus, contingency leadership theory became the third major leadership paradigm (Chapter 1), and the leadership styles used in its models are based on the behavioral leadership theories. Although there are no new leadership models, researchers continue to try to better understand and predict which leadership styles are the most appropriate in a given situation.[12]

In this section, we discuss theories versus models, the contingency theory factors, and the need for global contingency leadership.

Leadership Theories versus Leadership Models

As defined in Chapter 1, a *leadership theory* is an explanation of some aspect of leadership; theories have practical value because they are used to better understand, predict, and control successful leadership. *A* **leadership model** *is an example for emulation or use in a given situation.* In earlier chapters we talked about leading by example, which is emulation or the hope that followers will imitate the leader's behavior.[13] In this chapter we discuss using models in a given situation to improve performance of leaders, followers, or both.

All of the contingency leadership theories in this chapter have leadership models. The leadership theory is the longer text that explains the variables and leadership styles to be used in a given contingency situation. The leadership model is the short (one page or less) summary of the theory to be used when selecting the appropriate leadership style for a given situation. Models have been compared to baseball in this way. A model can't teach you to get a hit everytime at bat, but if you use the model, it will improve your batting average.

Learning Outcome 2 *Describe the contingency leadership theory variables.*

Contingency Theory and Model Variables

Contingency means "it depends." One thing depends on other things, and for a leader to be effective there must be an appropriate fit between the leader's behavior and style and the followers and the situation.[14] Recent research supports that the number 1 and number 2 posts in organizations often require a very different type of leader.[15] Recall from Chapter 1 that *contingency leadership theories* attempt to explain the appropriate leadership style based on the leader, followers, and situation.

Different individuals and groups prefer different leadership styles.[16] Leaders display a range of behavior in different situations, because leadership is largely shaped by contextual factors that not only set the boundaries within which leaders and followers interact but also determine the demands and constraints confronting the leader.[17]

See Exhibit 5.1 for a list of general contingency leadership variables that can be used as a framework in which to place all the contingency leadership model variables for analyzing leadership. Throughout this chapter, each contingency leadership model's variables are described in terms of this framework. For each model, the *leader* variable also includes the leadership styles of each model.

EXHIBIT 5.1 Framework for Contingency Leadership Variables

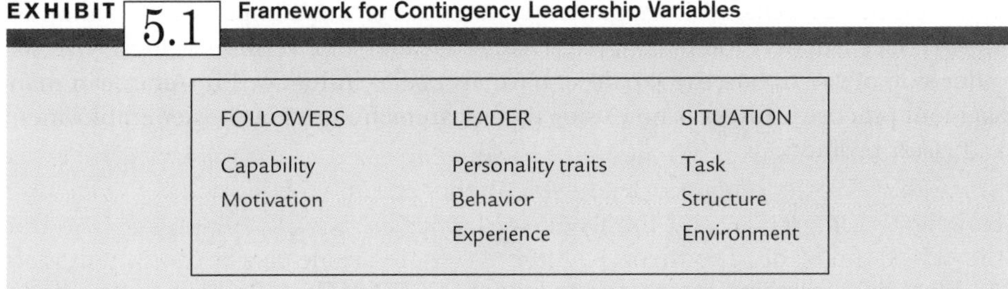

FOLLOWERS	LEADER	SITUATION
Capability	Personality traits	Task
Motivation	Behavior	Structure
	Experience	Environment

Ethical Dilemma 1

Leadership Gender

Should gender be a contingency variable in leadership? Developing leadership is a challenge for most young managers, but particularly for young women.[18] Are there differences in the leadership of men and women? Some researchers say that women tend to be more participative, relationship-oriented leaders and men are more assertive and task oriented. However, others say that men and women leaders are more alike than different because they do the same things, so they are equally effective leaders.[19]

1. Do you think that men and women lead the same or differently?
2. Are men or women more ethical and socially responsible leaders?
3. Would you prefer to have a man or woman for a boss?
4. Is it ethical and socially responsible to say that one gender makes better leaders?
5. Should global companies appoint women as managers in countries that believe in equal rights for women, but not allow women to be managers in countries that don't have these beliefs?

Global Contingency Leadership

Before we get into all the theories, let's take a minute to quickly help you realize how important contingency leadership is in the global economy of today.[20] Global companies like McDonald's, with restaurants all over the world, realize that successful leadership styles can vary greatly from place to place.[21] In Europe and other parts of the world, managers have more cultural than technical variables to deal with as they encounter diverse value systems and religious backgrounds among employees. Employees in some countries prefer domineering, self-centered, autocratic leaders, whereas other countries prefer a more democratic and participative leadership style.[22] More companies are now looking for graduates with an international openness and flexibility who can master the complexity of the global economy.[23]

Back in the 1970s, Japan was increasing its rate of productivity at a faster pace than that of the United States. William Ouchi found that Japanese firms were managed and led differently than U.S. organizations. He identified seven major differences between the two countries. The Japanese had (1) longer periods of employment, (2) more collective decision making, (3) more collective responsibility, (4) slower process of evaluating and promoting employees, (5) more implicit mechanisms of control, (6) more unspecialized career paths, and (7) more holistic concern for employees. Ouchi combined practices of U.S. and Japanese companies in what he called *Theory Z*.[24] Over the years, many American companies have adopted more collective decision-making and shared-leadership responsibilities. On the other side of the ocean, the Japanese have also been influenced by American management practices. Toyota is now using American techniques of shorter employment and faster promotions.

Opening Case APPLICATION

1. What does climbing the corporate ladder to CEO of PepsiCo have to do with contingency leadership? What life, educational, and job experiences qualified Indra Nooyi for her job as CEO?

Contingency theory is about using the right style in the right situation to succeed, which Indra Nooyi continues to do. Growing up in India, Nooyi was the right person to continue to take PepsiCo global, as 40 percent of its total revenue ($39 billion in 2007) now comes from international sales. On special occasions, Nooyi wears a traditional Indian sari. Her South Asian heritage gives her a wide-angle view on the world. She grew up in Chennai (formerly Madras), on the southeast coast of India, the daughter of a stay-at-home mom and an accountant father. Although her family is Hindu, Nooyi attended a Catholic school, was an avid debater, played cricket and the guitar, and formed an all-girl rock band. She earned a BS degree from Madras Christian College, an MBA from the Indian Institute of Management in Calcutta, and a Masters of Public and Private Management from Yale University. Before coming to PepsiCo, Nooyi was Senior VP and Director of Corporate Strategy and Planning at Motorola from 1986–1990 and Senior VP of Strategy and Strategic Marketing at Asea Brown Bovri from 1990–1994. She spent 12 years climbing the corporate ladder at PepsiCo. Nooyi started as Senior VP of Strategic Planning in 1994, was promoted to Senior VP of Corporate Strategy and Development in 1996, was promoted to President and CFO in 2001, and was promoted to CEO in 2006.

Learning Outcome 3 *Identify the contingency leadership model styles and variables.*

Contingency Leadership Theory and Model

In 1951, Fred E. Fiedler began to develop the first situational leadership theory. It was the first theory to specify how situational variables interact with leader personality and behavior. He called the theory "Contingency Theory of Leader Effectiveness."[25] Fiedler believed that leadership style is a reflection of personality (trait theory–oriented) and behavior (behavioral theory–oriented), and that leadership styles are basically constant. Leaders do not change styles, they change the situation. *The* **contingency leadership model** *is used to determine if a person's leadership style is task- or relationship-oriented, and if the situation (leader–member relationship, task structure, and position power) matches the leader's style to maximize performance.* In this section we discuss Fiedler's leadership styles, situational favorableness, determining the appropriate leadership style for the situation, and research by Fiedler and others. See Exhibit 5.2 to see how Fiedler's model fits into the framework of contingency leadership variables.

EXHIBIT 5.2 Contingency Leadership Model Variables Within the Contingency Leadership Framework

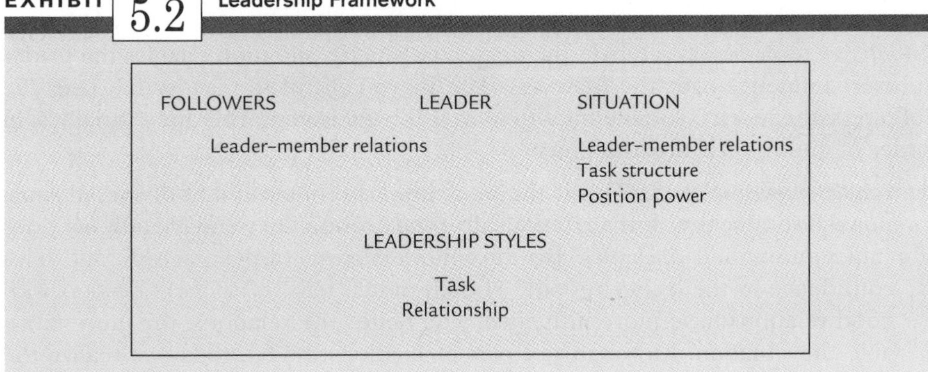

Leadership Style and the LPC

Although you may be able to change your behavior with different followers, you also have a dominant leadership style. The first major factor in using Fiedler's model is to determine whether your dominant leadership style is task-motivated or relationship-motivated. People primarily gain satisfaction from task accomplishment or from forming and maintaining relationships with followers. To determine leadership style, using Fiedler's model, you must complete the least preferred coworker (LPC) scales. The LPC essentially answers the question, "Are you more task-oriented or relationship-oriented?" The two leadership styles are (1) *task* and (2) *relationship.*

Note that Fiedler developed two leadership styles, which is a one-dimensional model. The leadership styles part of Fiedler's model is similar to the University of Michigan Leadership Model, in that it is based on only two leadership styles: one focusing on the task (job-centered leadership) and the other focusing on relationship (employee-centered). To determine your Fiedler leadership style, complete Self-Assessment 1.

SELF-ASSESSMENT 1

Leadership Style

Your Fiedler LPC

Return to Chapter 3, Self-Assessment 1 on page 71, and place your score for tasks on the following Task line and your score for people on the Relationship line.

10 — 9 — 8 — 7 — 6 — 5 — 4 — 3 — 2 — 1
High Task Leadership Style

10 — 9 — 8 — 7 — 6 — 5 —4 — 3 — 2 — 1
High Relationship Leadership Style

According to Fiedler, you are primarily either a task- or relationship-oriented leader. Your highest score is your primary leadership style. Neither leadership style is the one best style. The one appropriate leadership style to use is based on the situation—our next topic.

Situational Favorableness

After determining your leadership style, determine the situational favorableness. *Situational favorableness* refers to the degree to which a situation enables the leader to exert influence over the followers. The more control the leader has over the followers, the more favorable the situation is for the leader. The three variables, in order of importance, are as follows:

1. *Leader–member relations.* This is the most powerful determinant of overall situational favorableness. Is the relationship good (cooperative and friendly) or poor (antagonistic and difficult)? Do the followers trust, respect, accept, and have confidence in the leader (good)? Is there much tension (poor)? Leaders with good relations have more influence. The better the relations, the more favorable the situation. Although not part of Fiedler's model, today we realize the importance of relationships to getting the job done.[26]
2. *Task structure.* This is second in potency: Is the task structured or unstructured? Do employees perform repetitive, routine, unambiguous, standard tasks that are easily understood? Leaders in a structured situation have more influence. The more structured the jobs are, the more favorable the situation.
3. *Position power.* This is the weakest factor: Is position power strong or weak? Does the leader have the power to assign work, reward and punish, hire and fire, give raises and promotions? The leader with position power has more influence. The more power, the more favorable the situation.

The relative weights of these three factors together create a continuum of situational favorableness of the leader. Fiedler developed eight levels of favorableness, going from 1 (highly favorable) to 8 (very unfavorable). See Exhibit 5.3 for an adapted model.[27]

Determining the Appropriate Leadership Style

To determine whether task or relationship leadership is appropriate, the user answers the three questions pertaining to situational favorableness, using the Fiedler contingency theory model (Exhibit 5.3). The user starts with question 1 and follows the decision tree to Good or Poor depending on the relations. The user then answers question 2 and follows the decision tree to Repetitive or Nonrepetitive. When answering question 3, the user ends up in one of eight possible situations. If the LPC leadership style matches, the user does nothing, since they may be successful in that situation.

Changing the Situation

However, if the leadership style does not match the situation, the leader may be ineffective. One option is to change to a job that matches the leadership style. Fiedler recommends (and trains people to) change the situation, rather than their leadership styles. Here are a few general examples of how to change the situation variables to make a more favorable match for the leader's style:

- The leader generally would not want to change the *relationship* from good to poor, but rather the task structure or position power. If relations are poor, the leader can work to improve them by showing interest in followers, listening to them, and spending more time getting to know them personally.
- The *task* can be more or less structured by stating more or less specific standards and procedures for completing the task, and giving or not giving clear deadlines.
- A leader with strong *position power* does not have to use it; he or she can downplay it. Leaders with weak power can try to get more power from their manager and play up the power by being more autocratic.

EXHIBIT 5.3 Fiedler Contingency Leadership Model

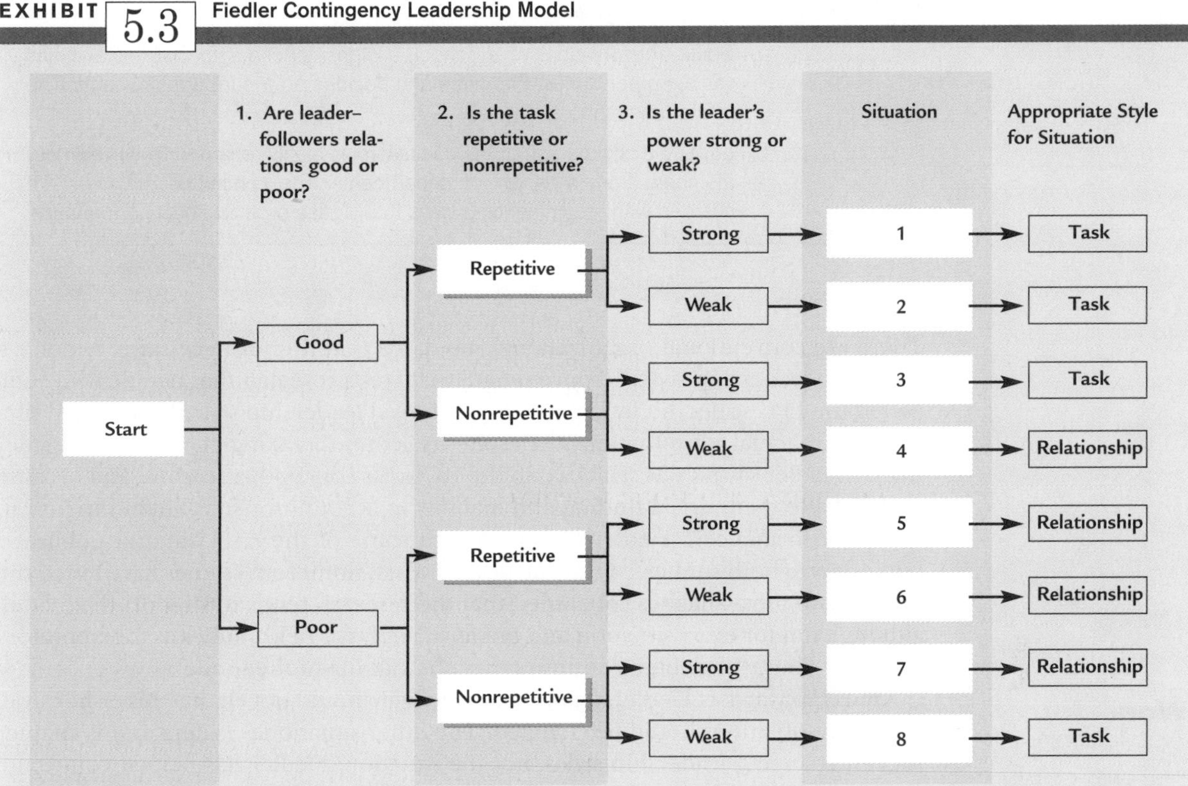

If the manager's LPC leadership style matches the situation, the manager does nothing. If the LPC leadership style does not match the situation, the manager changes the situation to match his or her LPC leadership style.

Source: Adapted from Fred E. Fiedler, A Theory of Leadership Effectiveness *(New York: McGraw-Hill, 1967).*

Applying the **Concept 1**

Contingency Leadership Theory

Using Exhibit 5.3, determine the situation number with its corresponding appropriate leadership style. Select two answers, writing the appropriate letters in the blanks before each item.

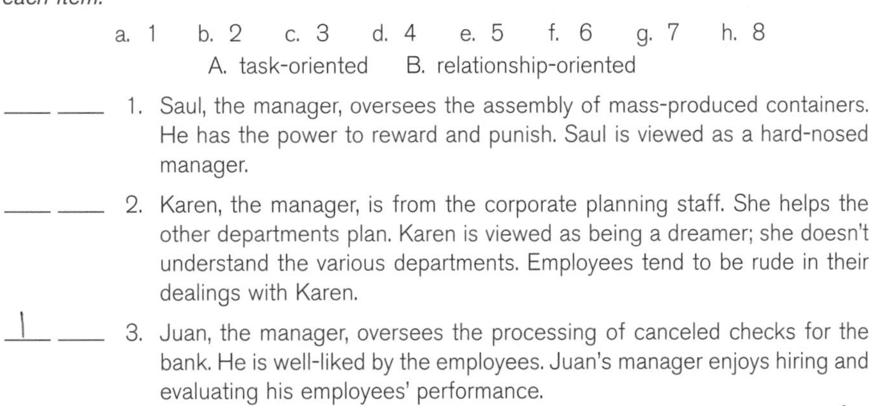

a. 1 b. 2 c. 3 d. 4 e. 5 f. 6 g. 7 h. 8

A. task-oriented B. relationship-oriented

___ ___ 1. Saul, the manager, oversees the assembly of mass-produced containers. He has the power to reward and punish. Saul is viewed as a hard-nosed manager.

___ ___ 2. Karen, the manager, is from the corporate planning staff. She helps the other departments plan. Karen is viewed as being a dreamer; she doesn't understand the various departments. Employees tend to be rude in their dealings with Karen.

___ ___ 3. Juan, the manager, oversees the processing of canceled checks for the bank. He is well-liked by the employees. Juan's manager enjoys hiring and evaluating his employees' performance.

continued

(Applying the Concept 1 continued)

____ ____ 4. Sonia, the principal of a school, assigns teachers to classes and has various other duties. She hires and decides on tenure appointments. The school atmosphere is tense.

____ ____ 5. Louis, the chairperson of the committee, is highly regarded by its volunteer members from a variety of departments. The committee members are charged with recommending ways to increase organizational performance.

Research

There are conventional organizational standards that do not necessarily endorse a change in leadership style.[28] Approximately 200 tests revealed that people who completed the LPC scales did in fact use the preferred leadership style in simulated situations and actual job situations.[29] Despite its groundbreaking start to contingency theory, Fiedler's work was criticized in the 1970s for conceptual reasons, and because of inconsistent empirical finding and inability to account for substantial variance in group performance.[30] Fiedler disagreed with some of the criticism and published rejoinders to both studies.[31] Over the past 20 years, numerous studies have tested the model. Two meta-analyses concluded that the research tends to support the model, although not for every situation and not as strongly for field studies as for laboratory studies.[32] Thus, the debate continues over the validity of the model.

One criticism is of Fiedler's view that the leader should not change his or her style, rather the situation should be changed. The other situational writers in this chapter suggest changing leadership styles, not the situation. Fiedler has helped contribute to the other contingency theories. Based on the contingency leadership model, Fiedler teamed up with J. E. Garcia to develop cognitive resources theory (CRT).[33]

CRT is a person-by-situation interaction theory in which the person variables are leader intelligence and experience, and the situational variable is stress, experienced by leaders and followers. CRT has important implications for leader selection and for situational management. Fiedler recommends a two-step process for effective utilization of leaders: (1) recruiting and selecting individuals with required intellectual abilities, experience, and job-relevant knowledge, and (2) enabling leaders to work under conditions that allow them to make effective use of the cognitive resources for which they were hired.[34] Fiedler has empirical support for his new CRT, but again, it is not without critics.[35]

Despite the critics, Fiedler's contingency leadership model and cognitive resources theory are considered the most validated of all leadership theories by some scholars.[36] However, if there were only one accepted valid motivation theory (Chapter 3) and only one leadership theory, this book would not be presenting several of them.

Work Application 1

Select a present or past manager. Which LPC leadership style is or was dominant for that manager? Using the Fiedler model (see Exhibit 5.3 on page 157), which situation number is the manager in? What is the appropriate leadership style for the manager in this situation? Does it match his or her style? How successful a leader is your manager? Do you think there is a relationship between the manager's leadership style and the situation?

If you are a manager, you may want to repeat this work application, using yourself as the manager.

Opening Case APPLICATION

2. What do colleagues say about Indra Nooyi's leadership—is it task or relationship, does she have a life outside of PepsiCo, and does she have any future career plans?

Her colleagues say Indra Nooyi is intense, decisive, an excellent negotiator, very open and very direct, demanding, and she challenges you. Nooyi is charismatic. She can rouse an audience and rally them around any project. Although she is task oriented, Nooyi also has strong relationships with her colleagues. She insists that everybody's birthday is celebrated with a cake. She has a supportive husband (Raj) and two daughters (Preetha and Tara), and she enjoys being a soccer mom. Nooyi is a karaoke fan, and her karaoke machine is the ubiquitous party game at every PepsiCo gathering. Being CEO of PepsiCo will not be Nooyi's last job. She wants to give back by going to Washington to work for the government.

Learning Outcome 4 *State the leadership continuum model major styles and variables.*

Leadership Continuum Theory and Model

Robert Tannenbaum and Warren Schmidt also developed a contingency theory in the 1950s.[37] They stated that leadership behavior is on a continuum from boss-centered to subordinate-centered leadership. Their model focuses on who makes the decisions. They noted that a leader's choice of a leadership pattern should be based on forces in the boss, forces in the subordinates, and forces in the situation. Look at Exhibit 5.4 to see how Tannenbaum and Schmidt's variables fit within the framework of contingency leadership variables.

EXHIBIT 5.4 Leadership Continuum Model Variables Within the Contingency Leadership Framework

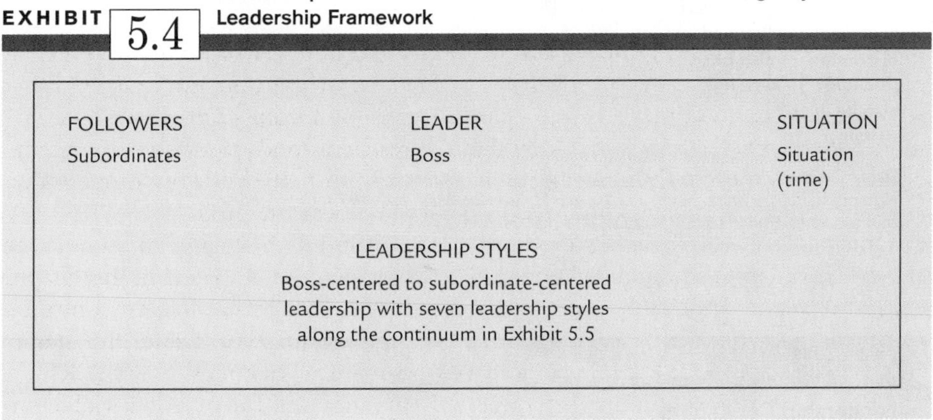

FOLLOWERS
Subordinates
LEADER
Boss
SITUATION
Situation
(time)
LEADERSHIP STYLES
Boss-centered to subordinate-centered
leadership with seven leadership styles
along the continuum in Exhibit 5.5

Tannenbaum and Schmidt identify seven major styles the leader can choose from. Exhibit 5.5 on the next page is an adaptation of their model, which lists the seven styles.[38] *The* **leadership continuum model** *is used to determine which one of seven styles to select, based on the use of boss-centered versus subordinate-centered leadership, to meet the situation (boss, subordinates, situation/time) in order to maximize performance.*

Before selecting one of the seven leadership styles, the leader must consider the following three forces or variables:

- *Boss.* The leader's personality and behavioral preferred style—based on experience, expectation, values, background, knowledge, feeling of security, and confidence in the subordinates—is considered in selecting a leadership style. Based on personality and behavior, some leaders tend to be more autocratic and others more participative.
- *Subordinates.* The followers' preferred style for the leader is based on personality and behavior, as with the leader. Generally, the more willing and able the followers are to participate, the more freedom of participation should be used, and vice versa.
- *Situation (time).* The environmental considerations, such as the organization's size, structure, climate, goals, and technology, are considered in selecting a leadership style. Upper-level managers also influence leadership styles. For example, if a middle manager uses an autocratic leadership style, the leader may tend to use it too.

  The *time* available is another consideration. It takes more time to make participative decisions. Thus, when there is no time to include followers in decision making, the leader uses an autocratic leadership style.

EXHIBIT 5.5 Tannenbaum and Schmidt's Leadership Continuum Model

Autocratic Style — Participative Style

1.	2.	3.	4.	5.	6.	7.
Leader makes decision and announces it to followers individually or in a group without discussion (it could also be in writing).	Leader makes decision and sells it to followers through a presentation of why it's a good idea (it could also be in writing).	Leader presents ideas and invites follower questions.	Leader presents tentative decision subject to change	Leader presents problem, gets suggested solutions, and makes the decision.	Leader defines limits and asks the followers to make a decision.	Leader permits followers to make ongoing decisions within defined limits

Source: Adapted and reprinted by permission of Harvard Business Review. *From "How to Choose a Leadership Pattern" by Robert Tannenbaum and Warren H. Schmidt, May–June 1973. Copyright © 1973 by the Harvard Business School Publishing Corporation, all rights reserved.*

Applying the Concept 2

Leadership Continuum

Using Exhibit 5.5, identify these five statements by their style. Select two answers, writing the appropriate letters in the blank before each item.

a. 1 b. 2 c. 3 d. 4 e. 5 f. 6 g. 7

____ 6. "Chuck, I selected you to be transferred to the new department, but you don't have to go if you don't want to."

____ 7. "Sam, go clean off the tables right away."

____ 8. "From now on, this is the way it will be done. Does anyone have any questions about the procedure?"

____ 9. "These are the two weeks we can go on vacation. You select one."

____ 10. "I'd like your ideas on how to stop the bottleneck on the production line. But I have the final say on the solution we implement."

Work Application 2

Using the leadership continuum model (Exhibit 5.5), identify your manager's most commonly used leadership style by number and description. Would you say this is the most appropriate leadership style based on the leader, the followers, and the situation? Explain.

In a 1986 follow-up by Tannenbaum and Schmidt to their original 1958 and 1973 articles, they recommended that (1) the leader become a group member when allowing the group to make decisions; (2) the leader clearly state the style (follower's authority) being used; (3) the leader not try to trick the followers into thinking they made a decision that was actually made by the leader; and (4) it's not the number of decisions the followers make, but their significance that counts.[39]

Note that Tannenbaum and Schmidt developed two major leadership styles, with seven continuum styles, which is a one-dimensional model. The leadership styles part of their model is similar to the University of Michigan Leadership Model in that it is based on two major leadership styles: one focusing on boss-centered behavior (job-centered leadership) and the other focusing on subordinate-centered behavior (employee-centered).

Although the leadership continuum model was very popular, it did not undergo research testing like the contingency leadership model. One major criticism of this model is that the three factors to consider when selecting a leadership style are very subjective. In other words, determining which style to use, and when, is not clear in the model. The normative leadership model thus took over in popularity, most likely because it clearly identified which leadership style to use in a given, clearly defined situation.

You will determine your major leadership continuum style later in Self-Assessment 4 on page 185, which puts together three of the contingency leadership styles (continuum, path-goal, and normative).

APPLICATION

3. Which continuum leadership style does Indra Nooyi tend to use in making acquisitions at PepsiCo?

Nooyi tends to use #5—the leader presents problem, gets suggested solutions, and makes the decision. She has others look into possible acquisition targets and gets recommendations from them, but Nooyi has the final say on which companies will be acquired.

Learning Outcome 5 *Identify the path-goal leadership model styles and variables.*

Path-Goal Leadership Theory and Model

The path-goal leadership theory was developed by Robert House, based on an early version of the theory by M. G. Evans, and published in 1971.[40] House formulated a more elaborate version of Evans's theory, one that included situational variables. House intended to reconcile prior conflicting findings concerning task- and relationship-oriented leader behavior. His theory specified a number of situational moderators of relationships between task- and person-oriented leadership and their effects.[41] House attempted to explain how the behavior of a leader influences the performance and satisfaction of the followers (subordinates). Look at Exhibit 5.6 on the next page to see how House's model fits into the framework of contingency leadership variables. Note that unlike the earlier contingency leadership models, House's model does not have a leader trait and behavior variable. The leader is supposed to use the appropriate leadership style (one of four), regardless of preferred traits and behavior.

The **path-goal leadership model** *is used to select the leadership style (directive, supportive, participative, or achievement-oriented) appropriate to the situation (subordinate and environment) to maximize both performance and job satisfaction.* Note that path-goal leadership theory is based on motivation theories of goal setting and expectancy theory. The leader is responsible for increasing followers' motivation to attain personal and organizational goals. Motivation is increased by (1) clarifying the follower's path to the rewards that are available, or (2) increasing the rewards that the follower values and desires. *Path clarification* means that the leader works with followers to help them identify and learn the behaviors that will lead to successful task accomplishment and organizational rewards.

EXHIBIT 5.6 Path-Goal Leadership Model Variables Within the Contingency Leadership Framework

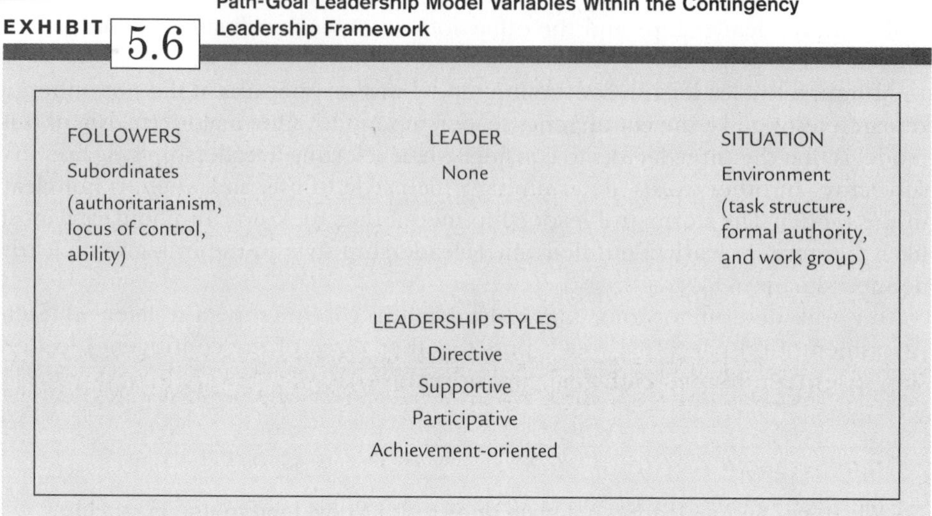

The path-goal model is used to determine employee objectives and to clarify how to achieve them using one of four leadership styles. It focuses on how leaders influence employees' perceptions of their goals and the paths they follow toward goal attainment. As shown in Exhibit 5.7 (an adaptation of the model), the situational factors are used to determine the leadership style that affects goal achievement through performance and satisfaction.

EXHIBIT 5.7 House Path-Goal Leadership Model

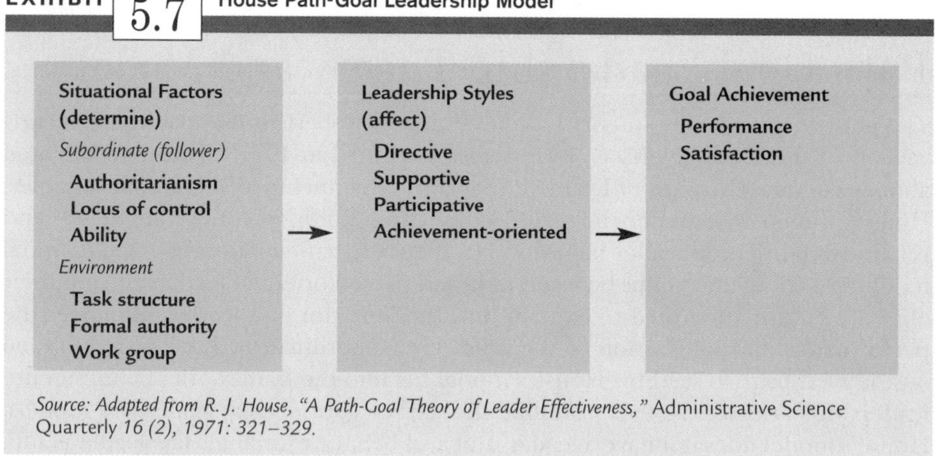

Source: Adapted from R. J. House, "A Path-Goal Theory of Leader Effectiveness," Administrative Science Quarterly *16 (2), 1971: 321–329.*

Situational Factors

Subordinate

Subordinate situational characteristics follow:

1. *Authoritarianism* is the degree to which employees defer to others, and want to be told what to do and how to do the job.
2. *Locus of control* (Chapter 2) is the extent to which employees believe they control goal achievement (internal) or if goal achievement is controlled by others (external).
3. *Ability* is the extent of the employees' ability to perform tasks to achieve goals.

Environment

Environment situational factors follow:

1. *Task structure* is the extent of repetitiveness of the job.
2. *Formal authority* is the extent of the leader's position power. Note that task structure and formal authority are essentially the same as Fiedler's.
3. *Work group* is the extent to which coworkers contribute to job satisfaction or the relationship between followers. Note that House identifies work group as a situational variable. However, under the contingency framework, it would be considered a follower variable.

Ethical **Dilemma 2**

Drug Research

Several drug companies, including Glaxo-SmithKline (Paxil antidepressant drug) and Merck (Vioxx arthritis pain medication) have been accused of situationally favorable research reporting. When results support the use of the drug, they are reported; when they don't, results are not reported. Although all medications have side effects, some drug users have died because of medication. As a result, the Food and Drug Administration (FDA) has been criticized for its process of approving drugs and monitoring their safety.

1. Is it ethical and socially responsible to report only the results that help gain FDA approval of drugs?
2. If you worked for a drug company and knew that the results of a study showed negative effects, but were not included in a report, what would you do?
3. If you worked for a drug company and your boss asked you to change negative results into positive results, or to make results even better, what would you do?
4. What would you do if you gave your boss a negative report on a drug and found out the results were changed to positive results?
5. Is the FDA doing a good job of monitoring the safety of drugs? If not, what else should it do?

Leadership Styles

Based on the situational factors in the path-goal model, the leader can select the most appropriate leadership style by using the following general guidelines for each style. The original model included only the directive (based on initiating structure, job-centered style) and supportive (based on consideration and employee style) leadership styles (from the Ohio State and University of Michigan behavioral leadership studies). The participative and achievement-oriented leadership styles were added in a 1974 publication by House and Mitchell.[42]

Directive

The leader provides high structure. Directive leadership is appropriate when the followers want authority leadership, have external locus of control, and the follower ability is low. Directive leadership is also appropriate when the environmental task is complex or ambiguous, formal authority is strong, and the work group provides job satisfaction.

Supportive

The leader provides high consideration. Supportive leadership is appropriate when the followers do not want autocratic leadership, have internal locus of control, and follower ability is high. Supportive leadership is also appropriate when the environmental tasks are simple, formal authority is weak, and the work group does not provide job satisfaction.

Participative

The leader includes employee input into decision making. Participative leadership is appropriate when followers want to be involved, have internal locus of control, and follower ability is high; when the environmental task is complex, authority is either strong or weak, and job satisfaction from coworkers is either high or low.

Achievement-Oriented

The leader sets difficult but achievable goals, expects followers to perform at their highest level, and rewards them for doing so. In essence, the leader provides both high directive (structure) and high supportive (consideration) behavior. Achievement-oriented leadership is appropriate when followers are open to autocratic leadership, have external locus of control, and follower ability is high; when the environmental task is simple, authority is strong, and job satisfaction from coworkers is either high or low.

Applying the **Concept 3**

Path-Goal Leadership

Using Exhibit 5.7 on page 162, and text descriptions, identify the appropriate leadership style for the five situations. Write the appropriate letter in the blank before each item.

a. directive
b. supportive
c. participative
d. achievement-oriented

____ 11. The manager has a new, complex task for her department, and she is not sure how it should be done. Her employees are experienced and like to be involved in decision making.

____ 12. The manager is putting together a new task force that will have an ambiguous task to complete. The members all know each other and get along well.

____ 13. The manager has decided to delegate a new task to an employee who has been doing a good job. The employee, however, tends to be insecure and may feel threatened by taking on a new task, even though it is fairly easy and the manager is confident that the employee can do the job easily.

____ 14. The department members just finished the production quarter and easily met the quota. The manager has strong position power and has decided to increase the quota to make the job more challenging.

____ 15. The manager has an employee who has been coming in late for work, with no apparent good reason. The manager has decided to take some corrective action to get the employee to come in on time.

Research

A meta-analysis based on 120 studies examined directive and supportive behavior and showed that support for path-goal theory was significantly greater than chance, but results were quite mixed. An extensive review of the research on moderator variables in leaders also had inconclusive findings.[43] Recent reviews of the history of path-goal theory have concluded that it has not been adequately tested, possibly because it is such a complex model. It continues to be tested; a recent study used a survey of 1,000 respondents from a governmental and public auditing sample.[44]

Although path-goal theory is more complex and specific than leadership continuum, it is also criticized by managers because it is difficult to know which style to use when. As you can see, there are many situations in which not all six situational factors are exactly as presented in the guidelines for when to use the style. Judgment calls are required to select the appropriate style as necessary.

Despite its limitations, the path-goal model has already made an important contribution to the study of leadership by providing a conceptual framework to guide researchers in identifying potentially relevant situational variables. It also provides a useful way for leaders to think about motivating followers.

Charismatic Leadership and Value-Based Leadership Theory

Path-goal leadership theory led to the development of the theory of charismatic leadership in 1976. You will learn about charismatic leadership in Chapter 9. Path-goal theory was considerably broadened in scope, and in 1996 House referred to it as value-based leadership theory.[45] Because value-based leadership theory is new and relatively untested, we do not present it here. However, see note 45 for House's further-developed theory.

You will determine your path-goal leadership style in Self-Assessment 4 on page 185, which puts together the contingency leadership styles.

Work Application 3

Identify your manager's most commonly used path-goal leadership style. Would you say this is the most appropriate leadership style based on the situational factors? Explain.

Opening Case APPLICATION

4. Which path-goal leadership styles does Indra Nooyi tend to use at PepsiCo?

Nooyi tends to use the achievement-oriented and participative styles. She sets high standards and expects everyone around her to measure up. She has red, green, and purple pens and uses them liberally to mark up everything that crosses her desk. Her scribbles are legendary, and include the following, "I have never seen such gross incompetence," and "This is unacceptable," with "unacceptable" underlined three times. Nooyi believes in people; you give them an objective and get them all to buy into it, and they can move mountains. She uses input from others, including her second in command Mike White, who she treats like a partner; her "Team Pepsi" members; and three prior Pepsi CEOs.

Learning Outcome 6 *State the normative leadership model styles and the number of variables.*

Normative Leadership Theory and Models

An important leadership question today is, "When should the manager take charge and when should the manager let the group make the decision?" In 1973, Victor Vroom and Philip Yetton published a decision-making model to answer this question while improving decision-making effectiveness.[46] Vroom and Arthur Jago refined the model and expanded it to four models in 1988. The four models are based on two factors: individual or group decisions and time-driven or development-driven decisions.[47]

In 2000, Victor Vroom published a revised version entitled "Leadership and the Decision-Making Process." The current model is based on the research of Vroom and colleagues at Yale University on leadership and decision-making processes, with more than 100,000 managers making decisions.[48] We present the latest version with a focus on time- and development-driven decisions.

The **normative leadership model** *has a time-driven and development-driven decision tree that enables the user to select one of five leadership styles (decide, consult individually, consult group, facilitate, and delegate) appropriate for the situation (seven questions/variables) to maximize decisions.* See Exhibit 5.8 to see how the normative leadership model fits into the contingency leadership framework variables. It is called a *normative model* because it provides a sequential set of questions that are rules (norms) to follow to determine the best leadership style for the given situation.

EXHIBIT 5.8 Normative Leadership Model Variables Within the Contingency Leadership Framework

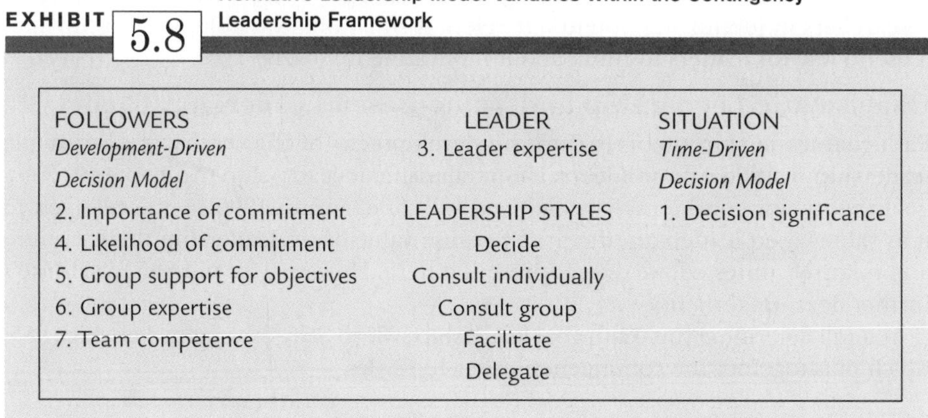

FOLLOWERS
Development-Driven
Decision Model
2. Importance of commitment
4. Likelihood of commitment
5. Group support for objectives
6. Group expertise
7. Team competence
LEADER
3. Leader expertise
LEADERSHIP STYLES
Decide
Consult individually
Consult group
Facilitate
Delegate
SITUATION
Time-Driven
Decision Model
1. Decision significance

To use the normative model, you must have a specific decision to make, have the authority to make the decision, and have specific potential followers to participate in the decision.

Leadership Participation Styles

Vroom identified five leadership styles based on the level of participation in the decision by the followers. Vroom adapted them from Tannenbaum and Schmidt's leadership continuum model (see Exhibit 5.5 on page 160), ranging from autocratic to participative styles. Vroom's five leadership styles follow.

Decide

The leader makes the decision alone and announces it, or sells it, to the followers. The leader may get information from others outside the group and within the group without specifying the problem.

Consult Individually

The leader tells followers individually about the problem, gets information and suggestions, and then makes the decision.

Consult Group

The leader holds a group meeting and tells followers the problem, gets information and suggestions, and then makes the decision.

Facilitate

The leader holds a group meeting and acts as a facilitator to define the problem and the limits within which a decision must be made. The leader seeks participation and concurrence on the decision without pushing his or her ideas.

Delegate

The leader lets the group diagnose the problem and make the decision within stated limits. The role of the leader is to answer questions and provide encouragement and resources.

Model Questions to Determine the Appropriate Leadership Style

To determine which of the five leadership styles is the most appropriate for a given situation, answer a series of diagnostic questions based on seven variables. The seven variables presented in Exhibit 5.8 are repeated in Exhibit 5.9 and in Exhibit 5.10 on the next page.

EXHIBIT 5.9 Normative Leadership Time-Driven Model

Instructions: The model is a decision tree that works like a funnel. Define the problem statement, then answer the questions from left to right as high (H) or low (L), skipping questions when not appropriate to the situation and avoiding crossing any horizontal lines. The last column you come to contains the appropriate leadership participation decision-making style for the situation.

	1. Decision Significance?	2. Importance of Commitment?	3. Leader Expertise?	4. Likelihood of Commitment?	5. Group Support?	6. Group Expertise?	7. Team Competence?	Leadership Style
PROBLEM STATEMENT	H	H	H	H	–	–	–	Decide
				L	H	H	H	Delegate
							L	Consult (Group)
						L	–	
					L	–	–	
			L	H	H	H	H	Facilitate
							L	Consult (Individually)
						L	–	
					L	–	–	
				L	H	H	H	Facilitate
							L	Consult (Group)
						L	–	
					L	–	–	
		L	H	–	–	–	–	Decide
			L	–	H	H	H	Facilitate
							L	Consult (Individually)
						L	–	
					L	–	–	
	L	H	–	H		–	–	Decide
				L	–	–	H	Delegate
							L	Facilitate
		L	–	–	–	–	–	Decide

Source: Adapted from Organizational Dynamics *28, Victor H. Vroom, "Leadership and the Decision-Making Process," p. 87, Copyright © 2000 with permission from Elsevier.*

EXHIBIT 5.10 Normative Leadership Development-Driven Model

Instructions: The model is a decision tree that works like a funnel. Define the problem statement, then answer the questions from left to right as high (H) or low (L), skipping questions when not appropriate to the situation and avoiding crossing any horizontal lines. The last column you come to contains the appropriate leadership participation decision-making style for the situation.

	1. Decision Significance?	2. Importance of Commitment?	3. Leader Expertise?	4. Likelihood of Commitment?	5. Group Support?	6. Group Expertise?	7. Team Competence?	Leadership Style
PROBLEM STATEMENT							H	Delegate
					H	H	L	Facilitate
				H		L	–	Consult (Group)
		H	–		L	–	–	
							H	Delegate
	H			L	H	H	L	Facilitate
						L	–	
					L	–	–	Consult (Group)
							H	Delegate
						H	L	Facilitate
		L	–	–	H	L	–	Consult (Group)
					L	–	–	
				H	–	–	–	Decide
	L	H	–	L	–	–	–	Delegate
		L	–	–	–	–	–	Decide

Source: Adapted from Organizational Dynamics *28, Victor H. Vroom, "Leadership and the Decision-Making Process," p. 88, Copyright © 2000 with the permission from Elsevier.*

We now explain how to answer the questions, based on the variables, when using the two models:

1. *Decision Significance.* How important is the decision to the success of the project or organization? Is the decision of high (H) importance or low (L) importance to the success? When making highly important decisions, leaders need to be involved.

2. *Importance of Commitment.* How important is follower commitment to implement the decision? If acceptance of the decision is critical to effective implementation, importance is high (H). If commitment is not important, it's low (L). When making highly important commitment decisions that followers may not like and may not implement, followers generally need to be involved in making the decision.

3. *Leader Expertise.* How much knowledge and expertise does the leader have with this specific decision? Is expertise high (H) or low (L)? The more expertise the leader has, the less need there is for follower participation.
4. *Likelihood of Commitment.* If the leader were to make the decision alone, is the certainty that the followers would be committed to the decision high (H) or low (L)? When making decisions that followers will like and want to implement, there is less need to involve them in the decision.
5. *Group Support for Objectives.* Do followers have high (H) or low (L) support for the team or organizational goals to be attained in solving the problem? Higher levels of participation are acceptable with high levels of support.
6. *Group Expertise.* How much knowledge and expertise do the individual followers have with this specific decision? Is expertise high (H) or low (L)? The more expertise the followers have, the greater the individual or group participation can be.
7. *Team Competence.* Is the ability of the individuals to work together as a team to solve the problem high (H) or low (L)? With high team competence, more participation can be used.

Not all seven variables/questions are relevant to all decisions. All seven or as few as two questions are needed to select the most appropriate leadership style in a given situation. Tying questions 1, 3, and 6 together, when making important decisions it is critical to include the leader and/or followers with the expertise to solve the problem. Then, the issue of commitment (questions 2 and 4) becomes relevant. Tying questions 5, 6, and 7 together in decision making, the leader should not delegate decisions to groups with low support for objectives, low group expertise, and low team competence. The great thing about the models is that they tie the relevant variables together as you answer the questions to determine the most appropriate leadership style for the given situation.

Selecting the Time-Driven or Development-Driven Model for the Situation

The first step is actually to select one of the two models, based on whether the situation is driven by the importance of time or development of followers. The characteristics of the decision are focus, value, and orientation.

The Time-Driven Model

See Exhibit 5.9 on page 167 for the three characteristics:

1. *Focus.* The model is concerned with making effective decisions with minimum cost. Time is costly, as it takes longer for groups to make decisions than the leader alone.
2. *Value.* Value is placed on time, and no value is placed on follower development.
3. *Orientation.* The model has a short-term horizon.

The Development-Driven Model

See Exhibit 5.10 for the three characteristics:

1. *Focus.* The model is concerned with making effective decisions with maximum development of followers. Follower development is worth the cost.
2. *Value.* Value is placed on follower development, and no value is placed on time.
3. *Orientation.* The model has a long-term horizon, as development takes time.

Computerized Normative Model

Vroom has developed a computerized CD-ROM model that is more complex and more precise, yet easier to use. It combines the time-driven and development-driven models into one model, includes 11 variables/questions (rather than seven), and has five variable measures (rather than H or L). It guides users through the process of analyzing the situation with definitions, examples, and other forms of help as they progress through the use of the model. The computerized model is beyond the scope of this course, but you will learn how to use the time-driven and development-driven models below and in Skill-Development Exercise 2.

Determining the Appropriate Leadership Style

Work Application 4

Recall a specific decision you or your boss has or had to make. Is or was the decision time-driven or development-driven? Using Exhibit 5.9 on page 167 or 5.10 on page 168, select the appropriate participation style for the situation. Be sure to state the questions you answered and how (H or L) you answered each.

To determine the appropriate style for a specific situation, use the best model (time-driven or development-driven) for the situation and answer the questions, some of which may be skipped based on the model used and prior questions. The questions are sequential and are presented in a decision-tree format similar to the Fiedler model, in which you end up with the appropriate style to use. Use both models for the same situations; for some decisions the appropriate style will be the same, and it will be different for others.

Research

Numerous studies have tested the normative leadership model.[49] In general, the results found in the empirical research have supported the model. Vroom and Jago conducted research concluding that managers using the style recommended in the model have a 62 percent probability of a successful decision, while not using the recommended style allows only a 37 percent probability of a successful decision.[50] However, the model is not without its critics.[51]

In summary of prior research based on six separate studies conducted in three different countries—contrary to Fiedler—managers do change their style to meet the situation. Managers using the decision style recommended by the normative model were almost twice as likely to be successful as were managers using decisions not recommended by the model. Higher-level managers use more participation in decision making. Women managers tend to use more participation than men. Almost all managers view themselves as using a higher level of participation than do their followers. Over the 25 years of research, there has been a move toward higher levels of participation, greater empowerment, and use of teams.[52]

The Vroom and Vroom Yetton/Jago model tends to be popular in the academic community because it is based on research. However, it is not as popular with managers because they find it cumbersome to select models and to pull out the model and follow a seven-question decision tree every time they have to make a decision. In his defense, Vroom states that his models are not tools to be slavishly embraced and used in all decisions.[53] Besides, once you learn how to use the model, you can better mentally judge the most appropriate style for the situation without the model. Thus, Vroom agrees with other researchers who state that leadership styles evolve,[54] and that leaders can develop their leadership skill[55] by using his normative leadership models.

You will determine your major normative leadership style in Self-Assessment 3 on pages 180–181.

Opening Case APPLICATION

5. Which normative leadership styles does Indra Nooyi tend to use at PepsiCo?

Based on the decision to be made, Nooyi consults and facilitates others. As chairman and CEO, she has the final say in major decisions affecting PepsiCo. However, she also delegates some decisions down the chain of command that involve specific products in American and international markets.

Learning Outcomes 7 and 8

Discuss the major similarities and differences between the behavioral and contingency leadership theories.

Compare and contrast four major differences among the four contingency leadership models.

Putting the Behavioral and Contingency Leadership Theories Together

Exhibit 5.11 is a review of different words that are used to describe the same two leadership behavior concepts. It includes the number of leadership styles based on the two behavior concepts and the different names given to the leadership styles. You should realize that all the leadership styles are based on the same two behavior concepts. We developed Exhibit 5.11 and Exhibit 5.12 on the next page to put all these contingency leadership theories together with behavioral leadership styles. These exhibits should help you to better understand the similarities and differences between these theories.

As we put the leadership theories together, we acknowledge the brilliant synthesizer Russell Ackoff, founder of systems theory, and present his advice on leadership. Ackoff warns against the continued reliance by management on fads, and he advocates systems leadership. Systems leadership requires an ability to bring the will of followers into agreement with that of the leader so they follow him or her voluntarily, with enthusiasm and dedication.[56]

Work Application 5

1. Identify the one contingency leadership model you prefer to use on the job, and state why.
2. Describe the type of leader that you want to be on the job. Identify specific behavior you plan to use as a leader. You may also want to identify behavior you will not use.

EXHIBIT 5.11 Names Given to the Same Two Leadership Behavior Concepts

	Leadership & Behavior/Style		Number of Leadership Styles Based on Behavior Concepts
Behavioral Theories			
University of Iowa	Autocratic	Democratic	2
University of Michigan	Job-centered	Employee-centered	2
Ohio State University	Structure	Consideration	4
Leadership Grid®	Concern for production	Concern for people	5
Contingency Theories			
Contingency model	Task	Relationship	2
Leadership continuum	Boss-centered	Subordinate-centered	7
Path-goal model	Directive	Supportive	4
Normative model	Autocratic	Group	5

EXHIBIT 5.12 Putting the Behavioral and Contingency Leadership Theories Together

BEHAVIORAL THEORIES	LEADERSHIP STYLES				CONTINGENCY VARIABLES	CONTINGENCY CHANGE	DESIRED OUTCOME
U of Michigan	Job-Centered		Employee-Centered				
Ohio State U	High Structure/ Low Consideration	High Structure/ High Consideration	Low Structure/ High Consideration	Low Structure/ Low Consideration			
CONTINGENCY THEORIES							
Contingency Leadership Model	Task		Relationship		Leader/Follower Relations Task Structure Position Power	Situation	Performance
Leadership Continuum Model	1	2 & 3	4 & 5	6 & 7	Manager Subordinates Situation/time	Leadership Style	Performance
Path-Goal Model	Directive	Achievement	Supportive	Participative	Subordinate (authoritarianism, locus of control, ability) Environment (task structure, formal authority, work group)	Leadership Style	Performance Job Satisfaction
Normative Leadership Model	Decide	Consult Individual or Group	Facilitate	Delegate	Development-Driven or Time-Driven Models: (1) Decision significance (2) Importance of commitment (3) Leader expertise (4) Likelihood of commitment (5) Group support for objectives (6) Group expertise (7) Team competence	Leadership Style	Decisions

Learning Outcome 9 *List which leadership models are prescriptive and descriptive, and explain why they are classified as such.*

Prescriptive and Descriptive Models

One last difference between models, not shown in any exhibits is the difference between prescriptive and descriptive models. The contingency leadership model and the normative leadership model are prescriptive models. **Prescriptive leadership models** *tell the user exactly which style to use in a given situation.* However, the continuum and path-goal leadership models are descriptive models. **Descriptive leadership models** *identify contingency variables and leadership styles without specifying which style to use in a given situation.* In other words, users of the descriptive model select the appropriate style based more on their own judgment. Look at all the leadership models and you will see what we mean.

Many managers prefer prescriptive models; this is a reason why the normative leadership model is more commonly used in organizational leadership training programs than the descriptive leadership models. On the other hand, many academic researchers scoff at prescriptive models, especially simple ones, and prefer the more complex descriptive models based on solid theoretical foundations.

Learning Outcome 10 *Explain substitutes and neutralizers of leadership.*

Leadership Substitutes Theory

The four leadership theories presented assume that some leadership style will be effective in each situation. However, in keeping with contingency theory, there are factors outside the leader's control that have a larger impact on outcomes than do leadership actions.[57] Contingency factors provide guidance and incentives to perform, making the leader's role unnecessary in some situations.[58] Steven Kerr and John Jermier argued that certain situational variables prevent leaders from affecting subordinates' (followers') attitudes and behaviors.[59] **Substitutes for leadership** *include characteristics of the subordinate, task, and organization that replace the need for a leader or neutralize the leader's behavior.*

Substitutes and Neutralizers

Thus, *substitutes* for leadership make a leadership style unnecessary or redundant. Highly skilled workers do not need a leader's task behavior to tell them how to do their job. *Neutralizers* reduce or limit the effectiveness of a leader's behavior. For example, managers who are not near an employee cannot readily give task-directive behavior. See Exhibit 5.13 to see how the substitutes for leadership fit into the

EXHIBIT 5.13 Substitutes for Leadership Variables Within the Contingency Leadership Framework

FOLLOWERS	LEADER	SITUATION
Subordinates	None	Task Organization

framework of contingency leadership variables. Then, read a description of each substitute.

The following variables may substitute or neutralize leadership by providing task-oriented direction and/or people-oriented support rather than a leader:

1. *Characteristics of followers.* Ability, knowledge, experience, training. Need for independence. Professional orientation. Indifference toward organizational rewards.
2. *Characteristics of the task.* Clarity and routine. Invariant methodology. Provision of own feedback concerning accomplishment. Intrinsic satisfaction. This characteristic is similar to Fiedler's and others' task behavior.
3. *Characteristics of the organization.* Formalization (explicit plans, goals, and areas of responsibility). Inflexibility (rigid, unbending rules and procedures). Highly specified and active advisory and staff functions. Closely knit, cohesive work groups. Organizational rewards not within the leader's control. Spatial distance between leader and followers.

Leadership Style

Leaders can analyze their situation and better understand how these three characteristics substitute or neutralize their leadership style and thus can provide the leadership and followership most appropriate for the situation. The leader role is to provide the direction and support not already being provided by the task, group, or organization. The leader fills the gaps in leadership.

Changing the Situation

Like Fiedler suggested, leaders can change the situation rather than their leadership style. Thus, substitutes for leadership can be designed in organizations in ways to complement existing leadership, to act in leadership absence, and to otherwise provide more comprehensive leadership alternatives. After all, organizations have cut middle-management numbers, and something has to provide the leadership in their absence. One approach is to make the situation more favorable for the leader by removing neutralizers. Another way is to make leadership less important by increasing substitutes such as job enrichment, self-managing teams, and automation.[60]

Work Application **6**

Identify your present or past manager. Can the characteristics of followers, task, and/or the organization substitute for this leader? In other words, is his or her leadership necessary? Explain.

Research

A study of nursing work indicated that the staff nurses' education, the cohesion of the nurses, and work technology substituted for the head nurse's leadership behavior in determining the staff nurses' performance. Another study found that situational variables directly affect subordinate satisfaction or motivation; however, it also found little support for moderating effects of situational variables on the relationship between leader behavior and subordinate motivation. Another study found that need for supervision moderates the relationship between task-oriented leadership and work stress, but not between task-oriented leadership and job satisfaction; however, a robust relationship between human-oriented leadership and job satisfaction was found.[61]

A meta-analysis was conducted to estimate more accurately the bivariate relationships among leadership behaviors, substitutes for leadership, followers' attitudes, and role perceptions and performance; and to examine the relative strengths of the relationships among these variables. It was based on 435 relationships obtained from 22 studies containing 36 independent samples. Overall, the theory was supported. In summary, as with the other theories, results are mixed. Research has found support for some aspects of the theory, but other aspects have not been tested or supported. Therefore, it is premature to assess the validity and utility of leadership substitutes theory.[62] To close this chapter, complete Self-Assessment 2 to determine how your personality influences your use of contingency leadership theory.

SELF-ASSESSMENT 2

Your Personality and Contingency Leadership Theories

In Self-Assessment 1 on page 155, were you more task or relationship oriented? Your being more task or relationship oriented is based very much on your personality. Based on surgency, if you have a high need for power, you may tend to be more task oriented. Based on agreeableness, if you are a real "people" person with a high need for affiliation, you may tend to be more relationship oriented. Based on conscientiousness, if you have a high need for achievement, you may tend to be more task oriented to make sure the job gets done, and done your way.

Based on your personality profile, does it match Fiedler's contingency leadership theory, as presented in Self-Assessment 1? If you have a higher need for power, do you tend to use the autocratic (1–3) leadership continuum styles, the directive and achievement path-goal leadership styles, and the decide and consult normative leadership styles?

If you have a higher need for affiliation, do you tend to use more participative leadership continuum styles, the supportive and participative path-goal styles, and the facilitate and delegate normative leadership styles?

You will better be able to understand which leadership style you do tend to use when you complete Self-Assessment 3 on pages 180–182, "Determining Your Preferred Normative Leadership Style." The leadership continuum and path-goal styles are explored in Self-Assessment 4 on page 185. It is important to realize that your personality does affect your leadership style. However, you can use the leadership style that is most appropriate for the situation. You will learn how in Skill-Development Exercises 1 and 2.

Go to the Internet (www.cengage.com/management/lussier)
where you will find a broad array of resources to help maximize your learning.

- **Review the vocabulary**
- **Try a quiz**
- **Find related links**

Chapter Summary

The chapter summary is organized to answer the 11 learning outcomes for Chapter 5.

1. **State the major difference between behavioral and contingency leadership theories, and explain the behavioral contribution to contingency theories.**

   Behavioral theories attempt to determine the one best leadership style for all situations. Contingency leadership theories contend that there is no one best leadership style for all situations. Behavioral theories contributed to contingency theories because their basic leadership styles are used in contingency leadership models.

2. **Describe the contingency leadership theory variables.**

   The contingency leadership variables used to explain the appropriate leadership style are the leader, followers, and situation. The leader factor is based on personality traits, behavior, and experience. The followers factor is based on capability and motivation. The situational factor is based on task, structure, and environment.

3. **Identify the contingency leadership model styles and variables.**

The contingency leadership model styles are task and relationship. The variables include (1) the leader–follower relationship, (2) the leadership styles—task or relationship, and (3) the situation—task structure and position power.

4. **State the leadership continuum model major styles and variables.**

The two major continuum leadership model styles are boss-centered and subordinate-centered. The variables include (1) the boss, (2) the subordinates, and (3) the situation (time).

5. **Identify the path-goal leadership model styles and variables.**

The path-goal leadership model styles include directive, supportive, participative, and achievement-oriented. Variables used to determine the leadership style are the subordinate and the environment.

6. **State the normative leadership model styles and the number of variables.**

The five normative leadership model styles are decide, consult individually, consult group, facilitate, and delegate. The model has seven variables.

7. **Discuss the major similarities and differences between the behavioral and contingency leadership theories.**

The primary similarity between these theories is that their leadership styles are all based on the same two leadership concepts, although they have different names. The major difference is that the contingency leadership models identify contingency variables on which to select the most appropriate behavioral leadership style for a given situation.

8. **Compare and contrast four major differences among the four contingency leadership models.**

Using Exhibit 5.12 on page 172, the first difference is in the number of leadership styles used in the four models, which ranges from 2 (contingency) to 7 (continuum). The second difference is in the number of contingency variables used to select the appropriate leadership style, which ranges from 2 (path-goal) to 7 (normative). The third difference is what is changed when using the model. When using the contingency model, the leader changes the situation; with the other three models, the leader changes behavior (leadership style). The last difference is the desired outcome. Contingency and continuum leadership models focus on performance, and the path-goal model adds job satisfaction. The normative model focuses on decisions.

9. **List which leadership models are prescriptive and descriptive, and explain why they are classified as such.**

The contingency and normative leadership models are prescriptive models, because they specify exactly which leadership style to use in a given situation. The continuum and path-goal leadership models are descriptive models, because users select the appropriate leadership style for a given situation based on their own judgment.

10. **Explain substitutes and neutralizers of leadership.**

Substitutes for leadership include characteristics of the subordinate, task, and organization that make leadership behavior unnecessary or redundant; neutralizers reduce or limit the effectiveness of a leader's behavior.

11. **Define the following key terms (in order of appearance in the chapter).**

Select one or more methods: (1) fill in the missing key terms from memory; (2) match the key terms from the following list with their definitions below; (3) copy the key terms in order from the list at the beginning of the chapter.

__________ is an example for emulation or use in a given situation.

__________ determines if a person's leadership style is task- or relationship-oriented, and if the situation (leader–member relationship, task structure, and position power) matches the leader's style to maximize performance.

__________ determines which one of seven styles to select, based on the use of boss-centered versus subordinate-centered leadership, to meet the situation (boss, subordinates, situation/time) in order to maximize performance.

__________ determines the leadership style (directive, supportive, participative, or achievement-oriented) appropriate to the situation (subordinate and environment) to maximize both performance and job satisfaction.

__________ has a time-driven and development-driven decision tree that enables the user to select one of five leadership styles (decide, consult individually, consult group, facilitate, and delegate) appropriate for the situation.

__________ tell the user exactly which style to use in a given situation.

__________ identify contingency variables and leadership styles without specifying which style to use in a given situation.

__________ include characteristics of the subordinate, task, and organization that replace the need for a leader or neutralize the leader's behavior.

Key Terms

contingency leadership model, 154

descriptive leadership models, 173

leadership continuum model, 159

leadership model, 152

normative leadership model, 166

path-goal leadership model, 161

prescriptive leadership models, 173

substitutes for leadership, 173

Review Questions

1. What is the difference between a theory and a model?
2. What contingency leadership variables are common to all of the theories?
3. How does the global economy relate to contingency leadership?
4. What are the two contingency leadership theory leadership styles?
5. Do the three situational favorableness factors of the contingency leadership model (see Exhibit 5.3 on page 157) fit in only one of the three variables (follower, leader, situation) of all contingency leadership variables (see Exhibit 5.1 on page 153)? Explain.
6. What is the difference in the outcomes of the contingency leadership and the continuum leadership models and that of the path-goal model?
7. What are the three subordinate and environment situational factors of the path-goal model?
8. What are the path-goal theory leadership styles?
9. What are the normative leadership theory leadership styles?
10. What is the primary difference between the contingency leadership model and the other leadership models (leadership continuum, path-goal, and normative leadership)?
11. What are the three substitutes for leadership?

Communication Skills

The following critical-thinking questions can be used for class discussion and/or as written assignments to develop communication skills. Be sure to give complete explanations for all questions.

1. Is Theory Z still relevant today?
2. Do you agree with Fiedler's belief that people have one dominant leadership style and cannot change styles? Explain.
3. Do you believe that managers today are using more boss- or subordinate-centered leadership styles?
4. Do you agree that time is an important situational factor to consider in selecting a leadership style for the situation? Explain.
5. The normative leadership model is the most complex. Do more variables improve the model?
6. One group of authors believes that Fiedler's contingency leadership model is the model best supported by research. However, a different author believes that it is the normative leadership model. Which model do you believe is best supported by research? Why?
7. Which contingency leadership theory do you think is the best?
8. Which contingency leadership theory do you actually plan to use, and how? If you don't plan to use any, give a detailed reason for not wanting to use any of the models.

CASE

Rick Parr—Archer Daniels Midland (ADM) Company

Archer Daniels Midland (ADM) was ranked 59th on the 2007 *Fortune 500* list.[63] ADM is one of the largest agricultural processors in the world, with 27,600 employees globally. Because everything ADM does begins with agriculture, its partnership with the farming community is vital. Farmers are essential to the overall world economy, and that's why ADM's work is essential to them; ADM creates thousands of products from their crops, and serves hundreds of markets for their crops. Serving as a vital link between farmers and consumers, ADM takes crops and processes them to make food ingredients, animal feed ingredients, renewable fuels, and naturally derived alternatives to industrial chemicals. Four of its primary resources it gets from farmers to turn into products are: cocoa (all kinds of chocolate goodies), corn (food, ethanol fuel for your car, and alcohol), wheat (flower and food products), and oilseeds (soybean, canola, cottonseeds, sunflower seed, palm, and also biodiesel fuel for cars and trucks).

As you know, with the high price of gasoline, people are looking for an alternative to fuel their motor vehicles. ADM is placing a big bet on the business of turning farm crops into fuel and chemicals. To lead this new strategic initiative into more profitable industrial products, in 2006 ADM broke company tradition by appointing a woman and energy-savvy outsider as its new CEO—Patricia A. Woertz. She left her position as executive VP at Chevron Corporation seeking a CEO position. With annual revenues around $70 billion, ADM is the largest publicly traded U.S. company headed by a woman.[64] Woertz increased her power by being appointed as chairman of the board of directors in 2007.[65] She has been ranked 4th and 6th on *Fortune*'s list of "Most Powerful Women."[66] Although Woertz's story in interesting, in this case we focus on a lower-level manager, Rick Parr.[67] (Please note: ADM is an existing company. However, Rick Parr, Ed Carlton, and Jose Goizueta are not the names of actual managers at ADM; they are used to illustrate contingency leadership.)

Rick Parr worked his way up to become the manager in a department making small parts. Parr's job was to supervise the production of one part that is used as a component in other products. Running the machines to make the standard parts is not complicated, and his employees generally find the job to be boring with low pay. Parr closely supervised the employees to make sure they kept production on schedule. Parr believed that if he did not watch the employees closely and keep them informed of their output, they would slack off and miss production goals. Parr's employees viewed him as an okay boss to work for, as he did take a personal interest in them, and employees were productive. Parr did discipline employees who did not meet standard productivity, and he ended up firing some workers.

Ed Carlton, the manager of a larger department that designs instruments to customer specifications, retired and Parr was given a promotion to manage this department because he did a good job running his old department. Parr never did any design work himself nor supervised it. The designers are all engineers who are paid well and who were doing a good job according to their prior supervisor Carlton. As Parr observed workers in his usual manner, he realized that all of the designers did their work differently. So he closely observed their work and looked for good ideas that all his employees could follow. It wasn't long before Parr was telling employees how to do a better job of designing the custom specifications. Things were not going too well, however, as employees told Parr that he did not know what he was talking about. Parr tried to rely on his authority, which worked while he was watching employees. However, once Parr left one employee to observe another, the workers went back to doing things their own way. Parr's employees were complaining about his being a poor manager behind his back.

The complaints about Parr being a poor manager got to his boss, Jose Goizueta. Goizueta also realized that performance in the design department had gone down since Parr took over as manager. Goizueta decided to call Parr into his office to discuss how things are going.

GO TO THE INTERNET: To learn more about ADM, visit its Web site **(http://www.admworld.com)**.

Support your answers to the following questions with specific information from the case and text or with other information you get from the Web or other sources.

1. Which leadership style would Fiedler say Rick Parr uses?
2. Using Exhibit 5.3 on page 157, Fiedler's contingency leadership model, what situation and leadership style are appropriate for the production department and for the custom design department?
3. Why isn't Parr doing an effective job in the design department?
4. What would Fiedler and Kerr and Jermier recommend that Parr do to improve performance?
5. Which of the two basic continuum leadership styles would Tannenbaum and Schmidt recommend for the manager of the design department?
6. Which path-goal leadership style would House recommend for the manager of the design department?

CUMULATIVE CASE QUESTIONS

7. Describe Parr's personality based on the Big Five model of personality (Chapter 2). How does Parr's personality influence his leadership style?
8. How is Parr's leadership style and behavior affecting employee needs and motivation (Chapter 3)?
9. Which source and type of power does Parr use? Is Parr using the appropriate power? If not, which power should Parr use (Chapter 4)?

CASE EXERCISE AND ROLE-PLAY

Preparation: Put yourself in the role of Jose Goizueta. Which normative leadership style would you use with Parr during the meeting? How would you handle the meeting with Parr? What will you say to him?

In-Class DA Meeting: Break into groups of four to six members, and discuss the three preparation questions.

Role-Play: One person (representing themselves or a group) meets with Parr to role-play the meeting for the class to observe. The person does not identify which normative leadership style they are using. You can discuss the role-play, as discussed next. More than one role-play may also take place.

Observer Role: As the rest of the class members watch the role-play, they should: (1) Identify the leadership style used by the person playing the role of Goizueta. (2) State if it is the appropriate leadership style for this situation. (3) Look for things that Goizueta does well, and not so well. For your suggested improvements, be sure to have alternative behaviors that are coaching.

Discussion: After the first role-play, the class (1) votes for the leadership style used by the person role-playing Goizueta, (2) determines the appropriate leadership style, and (3) discusses good behavior and better behavior that could be used. If additional role-plays are used, skip step 2.

VIDEO CASE

Leadership at McDonald's

McDonald's has achieved the status of one of the most recognizable franchises across the globe through a mixture of successful marketing, consistent service and products, and strong leadership. Ray Kroc was a visionary leader who inspired others through his charisma. He saw the potential for standardizing an efficient, systematized restaurant model and replicating it across the country. Kroc is quoted as saying, "If you've got time to lean, you've got time to clean," which highlights his goal-oriented and task-focused leadership style that still exists in the corporation today. McDonald's espouses a commitment to investing in the growth and job satisfaction of its employees so they can realize their full potential.

1. As a leader in the first years of McDonald's, what kind of normative leadership style do you think Ray Kroc likely used? Explain your answer.
2. What are the benefits of a corporate leadership strategy?

SELF-ASSESSMENT 3

Determining Your Preferred Normative Leadership Style

Following are 12 situations. Select the one alternative that most closely describes what you would do in each situation. Don't be concerned with trying to pick the right answer; select the alternative you would really use. Circle a, b, c, or d. Ignore the S ____ part, which will be explained later in Skill-Development Exercise 1.

1. Your rookie crew seems to be developing well. Their need for direction and close supervision is diminishing. What do you do?
   a. Stop directing and overseeing performance unless there is a problem. S ____
   b. Spend time getting to know them personally, but make sure they maintain performance levels. S ____
   c. Make sure things keep going well; continue to direct and oversee closely. S ____
   d. Begin to discuss new tasks of interest to them. S ____
2. You assigned Jill a task, specifying exactly how you wanted it done. Jill deliberately ignored your directions and did it her way. The job will not meet the customer's standards. This is not the first problem you've had with Jill. What do you decide to do?
   a. Listen to Jill's side, but be sure the job gets done right. S ____
   b. Tell Jill to do it again the right way, and closely supervise the job. S ____
   c. Tell her the customer will not accept the job, and let Jill handle it her way. S ____
   d. Discuss the problem and possible solutions to it. S ____
3. Your employees work well together; the department is a real team. It's the top performer in the organization. Because of traffic problems, the president okayed staggered hours for departments. As a result, you can change your department's hours. Several of your workers have suggested changing. You take what action?
   a. Allow the group to decide its hours. S ____
   b. Decide on new hours, explain why you chose them, and invite questions. S ____
   c. Conduct a meeting to get the group members' ideas. Select new hours together, with your approval. S ____
   d. Send around a memo stating the hours you want. S ____
4. You hired Bill, a new employee. He is not performing at the level expected after one month's training. Bill is trying, but he seems to be a slow learner. What do you decide to do?
   a. Clearly explain what needs to be done and oversee his work. Discuss why the procedures are important; support and encourage him. S ____
   b. Tell Bill that his training is over and it's time to pull his own weight. S ____
   c. Review task procedures and supervise Bill's work closely. S ____
   d. Inform Bill that his training is over, and tell him to feel free to come to you if he has any problems. S ____
5. Helen has had an excellent performance record for the last five years. Recently you have noticed a drop in the quality and quantity of her work. She has a family problem. What do you do?
   a. Tell Helen to get back on track and closely supervise her. S ____
   b. Discuss the problem with Helen. Help her realize that her personal problem is affecting her work. Discuss ways to improve the situation. Be supportive and encourage her. S ____
   c. Tell Helen you're aware of her productivity slip, and that you're sure she'll work it out soon. S ____
   d. Discuss the problem and solution with Helen, and supervise her closely. S ____
6. Your organization does not allow smoking in certain areas. You just walked by a restricted area and saw Joan smoking. She has been with the organization for 10 years and is a very productive worker. Joan has never been caught smoking before. What action do you take?

continued

(Self-Assessment 3 continued)

a. Ask her to put it out, and then leave. S ____
b. Discuss why she is smoking, and ask what she intends to do about it. S ____
c. Give her a lecture about not smoking, and check up on her in the future. S ____
d. Tell her to put it out, watch her do it, and tell her you will check on her in the future. S ____

7. Your department usually works well together with little direction. Recently a conflict between Sue and Tom has caused problems. As a result, you take what action?
   a. Call Sue and Tom together and make them realize how this conflict is affecting the department. Discuss how to resolve it and how you will check to make sure the problem is solved. S ____
   b. Let the group resolve the conflict. S ____
   c. Have Sue and Tom sit down and discuss their conflict and how to resolve it. Support their efforts to implement a solution. S ____
   d. Tell Sue and Tom how to resolve their conflict and closely supervise them. S ____
8. Jim usually does his share of the work with some encouragement and direction. However, he has migraine headaches occasionally and doesn't pull his weight when this happens. The others resent doing Jim's work. What do you decide to do?
   a. Discuss his problem and help him come up with ideas for maintaining his work; be supportive. S ____
   b. Tell Jim to do his share of the work and closely watch his output. S ____
   c. Inform Jim that he is creating a hardship for the others and should resolve the problem by himself. S ____
   d. Be supportive, but set minimum performance levels and ensure compliance. S ____
9. Barbara, your most experienced and productive worker, came to you with a detailed idea that could increase your department's productivity at a very low cost. She can do her present job and this new assignment. You think it's an excellent idea; what do you do?
   a. Set some goals together. Encourage and support her efforts. S ____
   b. Set up goals for Barbara. Be sure she agrees with them and sees you as being supportive of her efforts. S ____
   c. Tell Barbara to keep you informed and to come to you if she needs any help. S ____
   d. Have Barbara check in with you frequently, so that you can direct and supervise her activities. S ____
10. Your boss asked you for a special report. Frank, a very capable worker who usually needs no direction or support, has all the necessary skills to do the job. However, Frank is reluctant because he has never done a report. What do you do?
    a. Tell Frank he has to do it. Give him direction and supervise him closely. S ____
    b. Describe the project to Frank and let him do it his own way. S ____
    c. Describe the benefits to Frank. Get his ideas on how to do it and check his progress. S ____
    d. Discuss possible ways of doing the job. Be supportive; encourage Frank. S ____
11. Jean is the top producer in your department. However, her monthly reports are constantly late and contain errors. You are puzzled because she does everything else with no direction or support. What do you decide to do?
    a. Go over past reports with Jean, explaining exactly what is expected of her. Schedule a meeting so that you can review the next report with her. S ____
    b. Discuss the problem with Jean, and ask her what can be done about it; be supportive. S ____
    c. Explain the importance of the report. Ask her what the problem is. Tell her that you expect the next report to be on time and error free. S ____
    d. Remind Jean to get the next report in on time without errors. S ____
12. Your workers are very effective and like to participate in decision making. A consultant was hired

continued

(Self-Assessment 3 continued)

to develop a new method for your department using the latest technology in the field. What do you do?

a. Explain the consultant's method and let the group decide how to implement it. S ____

b. Teach them the new method and closely supervise them. S ____

c. Explain the new method and the reasons that it is important. Teach them the method and make sure the procedure is followed. Answer questions. S ____

d. Explain the new method and get the group's input on ways to improve and implement it. S ____

To determine your preferred normative leadership style, follow these steps:

1. In this chart, circle the letter you selected for each situation.

   The column headings (S1 through S4) represent the style you selected.

   S1=Decide, S2=Consult (Individually or Group), S3=Facilitate, S4=Delegate

	S1 D	**S2 C**	**S3 F**	**S4 DL**
1	c	b	d	a
2	b	a	d	c
3	d	b	c	a
4	c	a	d	b
5	a	d	b	c
6	d	c	b	a
7	d	a	c	b
8	b	d	a	c
9	d	b	a	c
10	a	c	d	b
11	a	c	b	d
12	b	c	d	a
Totals	____	____	____	____

2. Add up the number of circled items per column. The column with the highest total is your preferred leadership style. There is no correct or best normative leadership style. Below is an explanation about each style.

S1 Decide Leadership Style. The decide style includes making the decision alone. As a decider, you autocratically tell people how to implement your decision and follow up to make sure performance is maintained, or you tell people what to do and make sure they continue to do it.

S2 Consult (Individually or Group) Leadership Style. As they are both consult styles, we combine individual and group styles for this exercise. The consult style includes talking to individuals or groups for input in a supportive way before you make the decision. As a consulter, after making the decision, you also tell people how to implement your decision and follow up to make sure performance is maintained, while you support and encourage them as they implement your decision.

S3 Facilitate Leadership Style. The facilitate style includes having a group meeting to get input from members as you attempt to support the group to agree on a decision within boundaries set by you; in other words, you still have the final say on the decision. As a facilitator, you are supportive and encouraging to the group members to both make the decision and implement the decision.

S4 Delegate Leadership Style. The delegate style includes letting the group make the decision within limits. As a delegater, you don't tell the group what to do or facilitate the group during the decision making and its implementation.

To determine your flexibility to change styles, do the following. Look at your total score for each column leadership style. The more evenly distributed the totals (for example 4, 4, 4, 4), the more flexible you appear to be at changing your leadership style. Having high numbers in some columns and low in others indicates a strong preference to use or avoid using one or more leadership styles.

Note: There is no right, correct, or best normative leadership style. What this self-assessment exercise does is allow you to know your preferred leadership style and your flexibility at changing styles. In Skill-Development Exercise 1, you will develop your skill to identify the normative leadership styles. In Skill-Development Exercise 2, you will learn to use the normative leadership models to select the most appropriate leadership style for a given situation.

Skill-Development Exercise 1

Identifying Normative Leadership Styles

Preparing for Skill-Development Exercise 1

Return to the 12 situations in Self-Assessment 3. This time, instead of selecting one of the four options, a–d, identify the normative leadership style used in each option, with the aid of the leadership style definitions in Self-Assessment 3 above. Let's do the following example.

Example

Your rookie crew seems to be developing well. Their need for direction and close supervision is diminishing. What do you do?

a. Stop directing and overseeing performance unless there is a problem. S __DL__

b. Spend time getting to know them personally, but make sure they maintain performance levels. S __C__

c. Make sure things keep going well; continue to direct and oversee closely. S __D__

d. Begin to discuss new tasks of interest to them. S __F__

Answers

a. As indicated on the S __DL__ line, this is the *delegate* leadership style. As in the definition of *delegate,* you are leaving the group alone—unless there is a problem (limits)—to make and implement its own decisions about work.

b. As indicated on the S __C__ line, this is the *consult* leadership style. As in the definition of *consult,* you are being supportive by getting to know them, yet you are still following up to make sure they get the job done.

c. As indicated on the S __D__ line, this is the *decide* leadership style. As in the definition of *decide*, you are following up to make sure performance is maintained.

d. As indicated on the S __F__ line, this is the *facilitate* leadership style. As in the definition of *facilitate*, you are facilitating a group decision on possible new tasks for the group to perform.

Now, complete situation numbers 2–12 by determining the leadership style and placing the letters D, C, F, and DL on each of the a–d S __ lines as illustrated above. All four alternative behaviors do represent a different normative leadership style.

Doing Skill-Development Exercise 1 in Class

Objective

To develop the skill of identifying normative leadership styles.

The primary AACSB learning standard skill developed through this exercise is analytic skills.

Procedure *(5–30 minutes)* Select an option:

A. The instructor goes over the answers.

B. The instructor calls on students and goes over the answers.

C. Break into groups of three and come up with group answers for the 11 situations. This is followed by the instructor going over the answers.

Skill-Development Exercise 2

Using the Normative Leadership Models

Preparing for Skill-Development Exercise 2

You should have studied the normative leadership model text material. Using Exhibits 5.9 and 5.10 on pages 167–168, determine the appropriate leadership style for the given problem statements below. Follow these steps:

1. Determine which normative leadership model to use for the given situation.
2. Answer the variable questions (between 2 and 7) for the problem.
3. Select the appropriate leadership style from the model.

1. Production department manager. You are the manager of a mass-produced manufactured product. You have two major machines in your department with ten people working on each. You have an important order that needs to be shipped first thing tomorrow morning. Your boss has made it very clear that you must meet this deadline. It's 2:00 and you are right on schedule to meet the order deadline. At 2:15 an employee comes to tell you that one of the machines is smoking a little and making a noise. If you keep running the machine, it may make it until the end of the day and you will deliver the important shipment on time. If you shut down the machine, the manufacturer will not be able to check the machine until tomorrow and you will miss the deadline. You call your boss and there is no answer, and you don't know how else to contact the boss or how long it will be before the boss gets back to you if you leave a message. There are no higher-level managers than you or anyone with more knowledge of the machine than you. Which leadership style should you use?

Step 1 Which model should you use? (_____ time-driven _____ development-driven)

Step 2 Which questions did you answer and how? (H=high, L=low, NA=not answered/skipped)

1. H L or NA 3. H L or NA 5. H L or NA 7. H L or NA

2. H L or NA 4. H L or NA 6. H L or NA

Step 3 Which leadership style is the most appropriate?

____ decide ____ consult individually ____ consult group ____ facilitate ____ delegate

2. Religious leader. You are the top religious leader of your church with 125 families and 200 members. You have a Doctor of Religious Studies degree with just two years' experience as the head of a church, and no business courses. The church has one paid secretary, three part-time program directors for religious instruction, music, and social activities, plus many volunteers. Your paid staff serve on your advisory board with ten other church members who are primarily top-level business leaders in the community. You make a yearly budget with the board's approval. The church source of income is weekly member donations. The board doesn't want to operate in the red, and the church has very modest surplus funds. Your volunteer accountant (CPA), who is a board member, asked to meet with you. During the meeting, she informed you that weekly collections are 20 percent below budget and the cost of utilities has increased 25 percent over the yearly budget figure. You are running a large deficit, and at this rate your surplus will be gone in two months. Which leadership style will you use in this crisis?

Step 1 Which model should you use? (____ time-driven ____ development-driven)

Step 2 Which questions did you answer and how? (H=high, L=low, NA=not answered/skipped)

1. H L or NA 3. H L or NA 5. H L or NA 7. H L or NA

2. H L or NA 4. H L or NA 6. H L or NA

Step 3 Which leadership style is the most appropriate?

____ decide ____ consult individually ____ consult group ____ facilitate ____ delegate

3. School of business dean. You are the new dean of the school of business at a small private university. Your faculty includes around 20 professors, only two of whom are nontenured, and the average length of employment at the school is 12 years. Upon taking the job, you expect to leave for a larger school in three years. Your primary goal is to start a business school faculty advisory board to improve community relations and school alumni relations, and to raise money for financial aid scholarships. You have already done this in your last job as dean. However, you are new to the area and have no business contacts. You need help to develop a network of alumni and other community leaders fairly quickly if you are to show achieved results on your resume in 2½ years. Your faculty gets along well and is talkative, but when you approach small groups of them they tend to become quiet and disperse. Which primary leadership style would you use to achieve your objective?

Step 1 Which model should you use? (____ time-driven ____ development-driven)

Step 2 Which questions did you answer and how? (H=high, L=low, NA=not answered/skipped)

1. H L or NA 3. H L or NA 5. H L or NA 7. H L or NA

2. H L or NA 4. H L or NA 6. H L or NA

Step 3 Which leadership style is the most appropriate?

____ decide ____ consult individually ____ consult group ____ facilitate ____ delegate

4. Dot.com president. You are the president of a dot.com company that has been having financial problems for a few years. As a result, your top two managers left for other jobs. One left four months ago and the other two months ago. With your networking contacts you replaced both managers within a month; thus, they don't have a lot of time on the job and haven't worked together for very long. Plus, they currently do their own thing to get their jobs done. However, they are both very bright, hard-working, and dedicated to your vision of what the company can be. You know how to turn the company around and so do your two key managers. To turn the company around, you and your two managers will have to work together, with the help of all your employees. Virtually all the employees are high-tech specialists who want to be included in decision making. Your business partners have no more money to invest. If you cannot turn a profit in four to five months, you will most likely go bankrupt. Which primary leadership style would you use to achieve your objective?

Step 1 Which model should you use? (____ time-driven ____ development-driven)

Step 2 Which questions did you answer and how? (H=high, L=low, NA=not answered/skipped)

1. H L or NA 3. H L or NA 5. H L or NA 7. H L or NA

2. H L or NA 4. H L or NA 6. H L or NA

Step 3 Which leadership style is the most appropriate?

____ decide ____ consult individually ____ consult group ____ facilitate ____ delegate

Doing Skill-Development Exercise 2 in Class

Objective

To develop your skill at determining the appropriate leadership style to use in a given situation using the normative leadership models, Exhibits 5.9 and 5.10.

The primary AACSB learning standard skills developed through this exercise are leadership and analytic skills.

Experience

You will use the normative leadership models in four given problem situations.

Procedure 1 *(10–15 minutes)* The instructor goes over the normative leadership models and uses the models to illustrate how to select the appropriate leadership style for problem situation 1.

Procedure 2 *(10–20 minutes)* Break into groups of two or three and use the models to determine the appropriate leadership style for situations 2–4 in the preparation above. This is followed by the instructor going over or just stating the answers to situations 2–4.

Conclusion

The instructor may lead a class discussion and/or make concluding remarks.

Apply It *(2–4 minutes)* What did I learn from this experience? How will I apply normative leadership in the future?

Sharing

In the group, or to the entire class, volunteers may give their answers to the "Apply It" questions.

SELF-ASSESSMENT 4

Your Leadership Continuum and Path-Goal Leadership Styles

You have already determined your preferred LPC contingency leadership style (Self-Assessment 1 on page 155) and your preferred normative leadership style (Self-Assessment 3 on pages 180–182). Using Self-Assessment 4, you can determine your other preferred styles by checking your preferred normative leadership style in the first column. In the same row, the columns to the right show your continuum and path-goal preferred leadership styles. Does your preferred leadership style match your personality for Self-Assessment 2 on page 175?

NORMATIVE LEADERSHIP STYLE	LEADERSHIP CONTINUUM STYLE	PATH-GOAL LEADERSHIP STYLE
Decide	1 Boss-centered	Directive
Consult (individually or group)	2 or 3	Achievement-oriented
Facilitate	4 or 5	Supportive
Delegate	6 or 7 Subordinate-centered	Participative

Team Leadership

part two

chapter 6
Communication, Coaching, and Conflict Skills 188

chapter 7
Leader–Follower Relations 238

chapter 8
Team Leadership and Self-Managed Teams 278

Chapter Outline

Communication

Communication and Leadership

Sending Messages and Giving Instructions

Receiving Messages

Feedback

The Importance of Feedback

Common Approaches to Getting Feedback on Messages—and Why They Don't Work

How to Get Feedback on Messages

360-Degree Multirater Feedback

Coaching

Coaching and Leadership

How to Give Coaching Feedback

What Is Criticism and Why Doesn't It Work?

The Coaching Model for Employees Who Are Performing Below Standard

Mentoring

Managing Conflict

The Psychological Contract

Conflict and Leadership

Conflict Management Styles

Collaborating Conflict Management Style Models

Initiating Conflict Resolution

Responding to Conflict Resolution

Mediating Conflict Resolution

6 Communication, Coaching, and Conflict Skills

Learning Outcomes

After studying this chapter, you should be able to:

1. List the steps in the oral message-sending process. p. 190
2. List and explain the three parts of the message-receiving process. p. 194
3. Describe paraphrasing and state why it is used. p. 197
4. Identify two common approaches to getting feedback, and explain why they don't work. p. 198
5. Describe the difference between criticism and coaching feedback. p. 206
6. Discuss the relationship between the performance formula and the coaching model. p. 207
7. Define the five conflict management styles. p. 210
8. List the steps in the initiating conflict resolution model. p. 215
9. Define the following **key terms** (in order of appearance in the chapter):

communication	attribution theory
oral message-sending process	performance formula
message-receiving process	mentoring
feedback	conflict
paraphrasing	initiating conflict resolution model
360-degree feedback	BCF model
coaching	mediator
job instructional training	arbitrator
coaching feedback	

Opening Case APPLICATION

The Ranch Golf Club, where every player is a special guest for the day, opened in 2001 in Southwick, Massachusetts. Prior to being a golf club, it was a dairy farm owned by the Hall family. The Hall family wanted to turn the farm into a golf club with the help of Rowland Bates as project coordinator. The Halls were to provide the land, and investors would provide the capital.

Peter and Korby Clark were part owners of nearly 50 Jiffy Lubes, selling most to Pennzoil in 1991. Through the 1990s, the Clarks had a variety of opportunities to invest in new and ongoing businesses. Nothing interested the Clarks until the late 1990s. Unlike other businesses looking simply for investors, Bates offered Peter Clark the opportunity to create and help manage a new golf club. Although Clark played golf, it was not so much the golf but the challenge of creating a new course and also playing an ongoing part in its management that interested him. Bates found two more investors, Bernard Chiu and Ronald Izen, to provide the additional funding, creating a one-third ownership by the Halls, Clarks, and Chiu and Izen.

The Clarks were happy to have the professional golf management team of Willowbend. First, they realized that they could not create and run a successful golf club business without expertise. Neither of them had ever worked for a golf club, and they only played recreational golf. Secondly, they would not have to manage The Ranch full time. However, in 2005 Willowbend stopped managing golf courses and sold its business. By then the Clarks had gained enough experience running The Ranch and no longer needed professional management. Peter Clark increased his management role to become the managing partner, overseeing day-to-day operations, and Korby works full time too.

The Ranch's competitive advantage is its upscale public course with links, woods, and a variety of elevations with unsurpassed service in New England. The Ranch is striving to be the best golf club in New England. In less than a year, The Ranch earned a 4-star course rating, one of only four in New England. In the January 2003 issue of *Golf Digest,* The Ranch was rated number 3 in the country in the new upscale public golf course category, and it was ranked as the best public golf course in Massachusetts in 2007.[1]

Opening Case Questions:

1. Why is communication important to the management of The Ranch?
2. How does management use feedback at The Ranch?
3. Is there a difference in managing an oil change business, a golf course, and a sports team; and how does Peter Clark use coaching at The Ranch?
4. Which conflict management style does Peter Clark tend to use at The Ranch?
5. What types of conflict resolutions do the Clarks deal with at The Ranch?

Can you answer any of these questions? You'll find answers to these questions and learn more about The Ranch Golf Club and its leadership throughout the chapter.

To learn more about The Ranch Golf Club, or take a virtual tour of the course, visit its Web site at **http://www.theranchgolfclub.com**.

The focus of this chapter is on three related topics. We begin with sending and receiving communications, because it is the foundation for coaching and managing conflict. Next, we discuss feedback as it relates to both communication and coaching. Based on this foundation, you will learn how to coach followers, and then how to manage conflicts.

Communication

Communication *is the process of conveying information and meaning.* True communication takes place only when all parties understand the message (information) from the same perspective (meaning). Thus, communications are critical to organizational success,[2] and vocabulary affects the bottom line.[3] Your ability to speak, read, and write will have a direct impact on your career success.[4] In this section, we discuss the importance of communication in leadership and examine the communication process of sending and receiving messages.

Communication and Leadership

Managers spend around 40 percent of their time communicating.[5] Leadership is about influencing others, and we do so through communications.[6] Leadership is also about building relationships, which is also based on communications. Thus, there is a positive relationship between communication competency and leadership performance.[7] Organizations are training employees to communicate better to influence others to get their jobs done.[8] Two important parts of leadership communication are sending and receiving messages.

Sending Messages and Giving Instructions

Managers use the communication process of sending a variety of messages in person, on the phone, and in writing—primarily e-mail. An important part of a manager's job is to give instructions, which is sending a message. Have you ever heard a manager say, "This isn't what I asked for"? When this happens, it is usually the manager's fault. Managers often make incorrect assumptions and do not take 100 percent of the responsibility for ensuring their message is transmitted with mutual understanding. As a manager, how well you give instructions directly affects your ability to motivate your employees, as well as their satisfaction with your supervisory leadership. Before sending a message, you should carefully plan the message using persuasive language.[9] Then, give the message orally using the message-sending process, or send the message in writing.

Planning the Message

Before sending a message, you should plan it, answering these questions:

- *What is the goal of the message?* Is it to influence, to inform, to express feeling, or all of these things? What do you want as the end result of the communication? Set an objective.[10] After considering the other planning dimensions, determine exactly what you want to say to meet your objective, and speak plainly to be understood.[11]
- *Who should receive the message?* Have you included everyone who needs to receive your message?
- *How will you send the message?* With the receivers in mind, plan how you will convey the message so that it will be understood. Select the appropriate method for the audience and situation (see Applying the Concept 1 for a list). As a general guide, use rich oral channels for sending difficult and unusual messages, less rich written channels for transmitting simple and routine messages to several people, and combined channels for important messages that employees need to attend to and understand.
- *When will the message be transmitted?* Timing is important. For example, if it is going to take 15 minutes to transmit a message, don't approach an employee 5 minutes before quitting time. Wait until the next day. Make an appointment when appropriate.
- *Where will the message be transmitted?* Decide on the best setting—your office, the receiver's workplace, and so forth. Remember to keep distractions to a minimum.

Learning Outcome 1 *List the steps in the oral message-sending process.*

The Oral Message-Sending Process

Be careful not to talk too fast when sending oral messages over the phone or in person. It is helpful to follow these steps in the **oral message-sending process**: (1) *develop* *rapport;* (2) *state your communication objective;* (3) *transmit your message;* (4) *check the receiver's understanding; and* (5) *get a commitment and follow up.* Model 6.1 lists these steps.

MODEL 6.1 The Oral Message-Sending Process

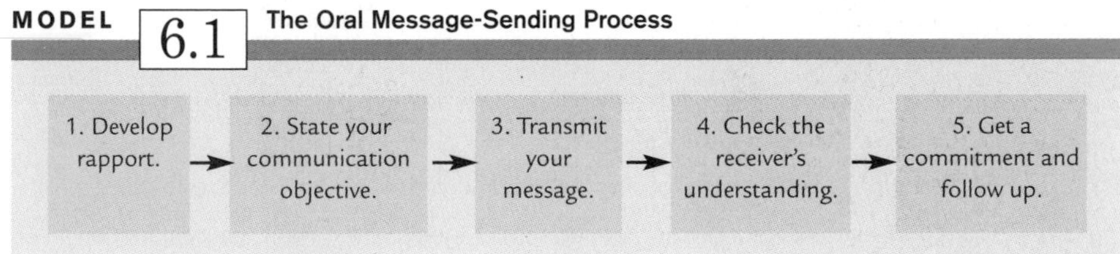
1. Develop rapport.
2. State your communication objective.
3. Transmit your message.
4. Check the receiver's understanding.
5. Get a commitment and follow up.

Step 1. Develop rapport. Put the receiver at ease. It is usually appropriate to begin communications with small talk correlated to the message. It helps prepare the person to receive the message.

Step 2. State your communication objective. The common business communication objectives are to influence, inform, and express feelings. With the goal of influencing, it is helpful for the receiver to know the desired end result of the communication before covering all the details.[12]

Step 3. Transmit your message. If the communication objective is to influence, tell the people what you want them to do, give instructions, and so forth. Be sure to set deadlines for completing tasks. If the objective is to inform, tell the people the information. If the objective is to express feeling, do so.

Step 4. Check the receiver's understanding. When influencing and giving information, you should ask direct questions and/or use paraphrasing. To simply ask, "Do you have any questions?" does not check understanding. In the next section of this chapter, you will learn how to check understanding by using feedback.

Step 5. Get a commitment and follow up. When the goal of communication is to inform or express feelings, a commitment is not needed. However, when the goal of communication is to influence, it is important to get a commitment to the action. The leader needs to make sure that followers can do the task and have it done by a certain time or date. For situations in which the follower does not intend to get the task done, it is better to know this when sending the message, rather than to wait until the deadline before finding out. When followers are reluctant to commit to the necessary action, leaders can use persuasive power within their authority.[13] When communicating to influence, follow up to ensure that the necessary action has been taken.

Work Application 1

Recall a specific task that your manager assigned to you. Identify which steps the manager did and did not use in the oral message-sending process.

Applying the Concept 1

Methods of Sending Messages

For each of these ten communication situations, select the most appropriate channel for transmitting the message. Write the appropriate letter in the blank before each item.

Oral communication

a. face-to-face
b. meeting
c. presentation
d. telephone

Written communication (includes e-mail and traditional methods)

e. memo
f. letter
g. report
h. bulletin board
i. poster
j. newsletter

continued

(Applying the Concept 1 continued)

____ 1. You are waiting for an important letter to arrive by FedEx, and you want to know if it is in the mail room yet.

____ 2. Employees have been leaving the lights on in the stock room when no one is in it. You want them to shut the lights off.

____ 3. José, Jamal, and Sam will be working on a new project as a team. You need to explain the project to them.

____ 4. John has come in late for work again, and you want this practice to stop.

____ 5. You have exceeded your departmental goals. You want your manager to know about it, because it should have a positive influence on your upcoming performance appraisal.

____ 6. Your spouse sells Avon products and wants you to help her advertise where you work. However, you don't want to ask anyone directly to buy Avon.

____ 7. People in another department sent a message asking for some numbers relating to your work.

____ 8. You have been asked to be the speaker for a local nonprofit organization.

____ 9. You enjoy writing, and you want to become better known by more people throughout your firm.

____ 10. You have been given a written complaint from a customer and asked to take care of it.

Written Communication and Writing Tips

With information technology and the Internet, you can communicate with anyone in the world—in real time. Because the use of e-mail will continue to increase, your written communication skills are more important than ever. Even if people aren't telling you that you're using incorrect grammar, they are evaluating you and may conclude you're not intelligent.[14] So we have included some simple but important writing tips that can help you to improve your writing:

- Lack of organization is a major writing problem. Before you begin writing, set an objective for your communication. Keep the audience in mind. What do you want them to do? Make an outline, using letters and/or numbers, of the major points you want to get across. Now put the outline into written form. The first paragraph states the purpose of the communication. The middle paragraphs support the purpose of the communication: facts, figures, and so forth. The last paragraph summarizes the major points and clearly states the action, if any, to be taken by you and other people.
- Write to communicate, not to impress. Keep the message short and simple.[15] Follow the 1-5-15 rule. Limit each paragraph to a single topic and an average of five sentences. Sentences should average 15 words. Vary paragraph and sentence length. Write in the active voice (I recommend...) rather than the passive voice (it is recommended...).
- Edit your work and rewrite where necessary. To improve sentences and paragraphs, add to them to convey full meaning, cut out unnecessary words and phrases, and/or rearrange the words. Check your work with the computer spelling and grammar checkers. Have others edit your important work as well.

Work Application **2**

Select two or three of the tips that you can use to improve your written communication. Explain how using the tip will improve your writing.

Ethical **Dilemma 1**

Advertising

Companies use oral, nonverbal, and written communications to advertise their products in order to increase sales. Selecting the best words to sell a product or service is important. However, some of the terms used in ads are misleading and even deceptive, although in some cases the words are legal.

For example, some companies use the word "natural" on foods that are highly processed, such as products including white sugar. So some question the use of the term "natural." Bags of chips are advertised as being "all natural," which leads people to think they are healthy, when in fact others classify them as junk food. Because obesity has become such a major health problem, the Food and Drug Administration (FDA) obesity task force is trying to crack down on misleading labels and ads, and is calling for warnings and fines for violators.

1. Is it ethical and socially responsible for food companies to use terms (like "natural") that can be misleading to increase sales and profits?
2. Should companies use terms that are considered misleading by some but are not illegal?
3. How would you define "natural"?
4. How should the FDA define "natural" so that it is not used to mislead people to buy food thinking that it is healthy, when in fact it is not?

Receiving Messages

The second communication process that leaders are involved in is receiving messages. With oral communications, the key to successfully understanding the message is listening. In fact, failure to listen is one of the top five reasons leaders fail, and Warren Bennis said it is the most common reason CEOs fail.[16] Thus, you need to listen to others.[17] Complete Self-Assessment 1 to determine how good a listener you are, then read the tips for improving listening skills in the message-receiving process.

SELF-ASSESSMENT 1

Listening Skills

Select the response that best describes the frequency of your actual behavior. Write the letter A, U, F, O, or S on the line before each of the 15 statements.

A—almost always U—usually F—frequently
O—occasionally S—seldom

_____ 1. I like to listen to people talk. I encourage others to talk by showing interest, smiling, nodding, and so forth.

_____ 2. I pay closer attention to people who are more similar to me than I do to people who are different from me.

_____ 3. I evaluate people's words and their nonverbal communication ability as they talk.

_____ 4. I avoid distractions; if it's noisy, I suggest moving to a quiet spot.

_____ 5. When people come to me and interrupt me when I'm doing something, I put what I was doing out of my mind and give them my complete attention.

_____ 6. When people are talking, I allow them time to finish. I do not interrupt, anticipate

continued

(Self-Assessment 1 continued)

what they are going to say, or jump to conclusions.

_____ 7. I tune people out who do not agree with my views.

_____ 8. While the other person is talking, or professors are lecturing, my mind wanders to personal topics.

_____ 9. While the other person is talking, I pay close attention to the nonverbal communication to help me fully understand what they are trying to communicate.

_____ 10. I tune out and pretend I understand when the topic is difficult for me to understand.

_____ 11. When the other person is talking, I think about and prepare what I am going to say in reply.

_____ 12. When I think there is something missing or contradictory, I ask direct questions to get the person to explain the idea more fully.

_____ 13. When I don't understand something, I let the other person know I don't understand.

_____ 14. When listening to other people, I try to put myself in their position and to see things from their perspective.

_____ 15. During conversations I repeat back to the other person what has been said in my own words to be sure I correctly understand what has been said.

If people you talk to regularly were to answer these questions about you, would they have the same responses that you selected? To find out, have friends fill out the questions with you in mind rather than themselves. Then compare answers.

To determine your score, give yourself 5 points for each A, 4 for each U, 3 for each F, 2 for each O, and 1 for each S for statements 1, 4, 5, 6, 9, 12, 13, 14, and 15. Place the numbers on the line next to your response letter. For items 2, 3, 7, 8, 10, and 11 the score reverses: 5 points for each S, 4 for each O, 3 for each F, 2 for each U, and 1 for each A. Place these score numbers on the lines next to the response letters. Now add your total number of points. Your score should be between 15 and 75. Place your score on the continuum below. Generally, the higher your score, the better your listening skills.

15–20–25–30–35–40–45–50–55–60–65–70–75
Poor listener *Good listener*

When asked, "Are you a good listener?" most people say yes. In reality, 75 percent of what people hear, they hear imprecisely—and 75 percent of what they hear accurately, they forget within three weeks. In other words, most people are really not good listeners. One of the skills we need to develop most is listening. Listening's greatest value is that it gives the speaker a sense of worth. People have a passionate desire to be heard.

Learning Outcome 2 *List and explain the three parts of the message-receiving process.*

The Message-Receiving Process

The **message-receiving process** *includes listening, analyzing, and checking understanding.* To improve your listening skills, spend one week focusing your attention on listening by concentrating on what other people say and the nonverbal communications they send when they speak. Notice if their verbal and nonverbal communication are consistent. Do the nonverbal messages reinforce the speaker's words or detract from them? Talk only when necessary, so that you can listen and "see" what others are saying. If you apply the following tips, you will improve your listening skills. The tips are presented in the depiction of the message-receiving process (Exhibit 6.1): We should listen, analyze, and then check understanding.

EXHIBIT 6.1 The Message-Receiving Process

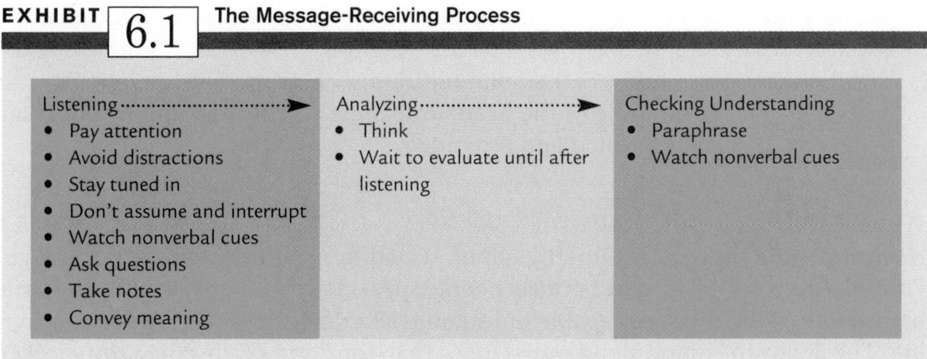

Listening
• Pay attention
• Avoid distractions
• Stay tuned in
• Don't assume and interrupt
• Watch nonverbal cues
• Ask questions
• Take notes
• Convey meaning
Analyzing
• Think
• Wait to evaluate until after listening
Checking Understanding
• Paraphrase
• Watch nonverbal cues

Listening

Listening is the process of giving the speaker your undivided attention. As the speaker sends the message, you should listen by

- *Paying attention.* When people interrupt you to talk, stop what you are doing and give them your complete attention immediately. Quickly relax and clear your mind, so that you are receptive to the speaker. This will get you started correctly. If you miss the first few words, you may miss the message.
- *Avoiding distractions.* Keep your eye on the speaker. Do not fiddle with pens, papers, or other distractions. For important messages, put your phone on "take a message." If you are in a noisy or distracting place, suggest moving to a quiet spot.
- *Staying tuned in.* While the other person is talking or the professor is lecturing, do not let your mind wander to personal topics. If it does wander, gently bring it back. Do not tune out the speaker because you do not like something about the person or because you disagree with what is being said. If the topic is difficult, do not tune out; ask questions. Do not think about what you are going to say in reply; just listen.
- *Not assuming and interrupting.* Do not assume you know what the speaker is going to say, or listen to the beginning and jump to conclusions. Most listening mistakes are made when people hear the first few words of a sentence, finish it in their own minds, and miss the second half. Listen to the entire message without interrupting the speaker.
- *Watching nonverbal cues.* Understand both the feelings and the content of the message. People sometimes say one thing and mean something else. So watch as you listen to be sure that the speaker's eyes, body, and face are sending the same message as the verbal message. If something seems out of sync, get it cleared up by asking questions.
- *Asking questions.* When you feel there is something missing, contradictory, or you just do not understand, ask direct questions to get the person to explain the idea more fully.
- *Taking notes.* Part of listening is writing important things down so you can remember them later, and document them when necessary. This is especially true when you're listening to instructions. You should always have something to take notes with, such as a pen and a notebook or some index cards.

- *Conveying meaning.* The way to let the speaker know you are listening to the message is to use verbal clues, such as, "you feel...," "uh huh," "I see," and "I understand." You should also use nonverbal communication such as eye contact, appropriate facial expressions, nodding of the head, or leaning slightly forward in your chair to indicate you are interested and listening.

Analyzing

Analyzing is the process of thinking about, decoding, and evaluating the message. Poor listening occurs in part because people speak at an average rate of 120 words per minute, while they are capable of listening at a rate of over 500 words per minute. The ability to comprehend words more than four times faster than the speaker can talk often results in minds wandering. As the speaker sends the message, you should analyze by

- *Thinking.* To help overcome the discrepancy in the speed between your ability to listen and people's rate of speaking, use the speed of your brain positively. Listen actively by organizing, summarizing, reviewing, interpreting, and critiquing often. These activities will help you to do an effective job of decoding the message.
- *Waiting to evaluate until after listening.* When people try to listen and evaluate what is said at the same time, they tend to miss part or all of the message. You should just listen to the entire message, then come to your conclusions. When you evaluate the decision, base your conclusion on the facts present rather than on stereotypes and generalities.

Checking Understanding

Checking understanding is the process of giving feedback. After you have listened to the message—or during the message if it's a long one—check your understanding of the message by

- *Paraphrasing.* Begin speaking by giving feedback, using paraphrasing to repeat the message to the sender. When you can paraphrase the message correctly, you convey that you have listened and understood the other person. Now you are ready to offer your ideas, advice, solution, decision, or whatever the sender of the message is talking to you about.
- *Watching nonverbal cues.* As you speak, watch the other person's nonverbal cues. If the person does not seem to understand what you are talking about, clarify the message before finishing the conversation.

Work Application **3**

Refer to Self-Assessment 1 and the listening tips. What is your weakest listening skill area on the job? How will you improve your listening ability?

Do you talk more than you listen? To be sure your perception is correct, ask your manager, coworkers, and friends who will give you an honest answer. If you spend more time talking than listening, you are probably failing in your communications, and boring people too. Regardless of how much you listen, if you follow these guidelines, you will improve your conversation and become a person that people want to talk to, instead of a person they feel they have to listen to. To become an active listener, take the responsibility for ensuring mutual understanding.

Work to change your behavior to become a better listener. Review the 15 statements in Self-Assessment 1 on pages 193–194. To improve your listening skills, practice doing items 1, 4, 5, 6, 9, 12, 13, 14, and 15; and avoid doing items 2, 3, 7, 8, 10, and 11. Effective listening requires responding to the message to ensure mutual understanding takes place.

Opening Case APPLICATION

1. Why is communication important to the management of The Ranch?

The key to success at The Ranch is clear, open communications of expectations. Peter Clark has to continually communicate with his partners and department heads, and nothing takes the place of sitting down face-to-face during regular weekly meetings and listening to each other to continually improve operations. Meetings of department managers with employees continually focus on the importance of communicating the philosophy of unsurpassed professional service. To communicate professionalism, all employees wear The Ranch uniforms and name tags, and they are trained with instructions on how to perform high-quality service. Even the words used are chosen to communicate professionalism. For example, The Ranch has player assistants (PAs), not rangers; golf cars, not golf carts; and it has a golf shop, not a pro shop.

Learning Outcome 3 *Describe paraphrasing and state why it is used.*

Feedback

In this section, we discuss the importance of feedback, the common approaches to getting feedback—and why they don't work, and how to get feedback. We end with formal 360-degree feedback. In the next section we discuss how to give feedback as part of coaching.

The Importance of Feedback

Feedback *is the process of verifying messages and determining if objectives are being met.* In essence, any time a person is sending or receiving job-related information that affects performance, they are giving or getting feedback.

The Role of Feedback in Verifying Messages

Questioning, paraphrasing, and allowing comments and suggestions are all forms of feedback that check understanding. Recall that checking receiver understanding is the fourth step in the oral message-sending process. Feedback motivates employees to achieve high levels of performance.[18] Organizations train employees to give effective feedback, because it is an essential part of leadership communication.[19]

Mutual understanding of the meaning of the message must exist for communication to take place. The best way to make sure communication has taken place is to get feedback from the receiver of the message through questioning and paraphrasing. **Paraphrasing** *is the process of having the receiver restate the message in his or her own words.* If the receiver of the message can answer the questions or paraphrase the message, communication has taken place.

The Role of Feedback in Meeting Objectives

Feedback is also essential to knowing how the leader and organization are progressing to meet objectives.[20] Recall from Chapter 3 that objectives must be measurable. Feedback is used to measure performance. And giving and receiving feedback must be an ongoing process to be effective. Thus, leaders should set specific measurable objectives and monitor the process through feedback.[21]

The Need to Be Open to Feedback—Criticism

Work Application 4

Are you really open to feedback—criticism from others at work? How can you improve on accepting criticism?

To improve your performance and get ahead in an organization, you have to be open to feedback—commonly called *criticism.*[22] You should actually solicit feedback.[23] However, if you're asking for personal feedback, remember that you are asking to hear things that may surprise, upset, or insult you, and even hurt your feelings. If you become defensive and emotional—and it is tough not to when you feel attacked—feedback will stop. People do not really enjoy being criticized, even when it is constructive. You should realize that criticism from your manager, peers, or others is painful. Keep the phrase, "no pain, no gain" in mind when it comes to criticism. When you get criticism, whether you ask for it or not, view it as an opportunity to improve.[24] Stay calm (even when the other person is emotional), don't get defensive, and don't blame others.[25]

Ethical **Dilemma 2**

Academic Grades

Grades are a form of feedback and are often criticism. (Recall Ethical Dilemma "Academic Standards" in Chapter 3.) Successful managers set and maintain high expectations for all their employees, and as Lou Holtz said, we need to set a higher standard. While students are doing less work than in prior years, grades continue to increase, which is called grade inflation. At one time, most colleges had a set grade point average (GPA) to determine honors. But today, most colleges use a ranking system of GPA, because of grade inflation, to limit the number of students graduating with honors.

1. How do you react when you get a grade that is lower than you wanted or expected?
2. Do you use the feedback of correcting and grades to help you improve? Why or why not, and if yes, how?
3. Why are professors giving higher grades today than were given 5, 10, or 20 years ago?
4. Are students who are putting in less time and getting higher grades being well prepared for a career with high standards after graduation?
5. Is it ethical and socially responsible for professors to drop standards and for colleges to award degrees with higher grades today than 5, 10, or 20 years ago?

Learning Outcome 4 *Identify two common approaches to getting feedback, and explain why they don't work.*

Common Approaches to Getting Feedback on Messages—and Why They Don't Work

One common approach that ignores feedback is to send the entire message and then assume that the message has been conveyed with mutual understanding. A second approach is to give the entire message and then ask "Do you have any questions?" Feedback usually does not follow, because people have a tendency "not" to ask questions. There are at least four good reasons why people do not ask questions:

1. *Receivers feel ignorant.* To ask a question, especially if no one else does, is often considered an admission of not paying attention or not being bright enough to understand the issue.
2. *Receivers are ignorant.* Sometimes people do not know enough about the message to know whether it is incomplete, incorrect, or subject to interpretation. There are no questions, because what was said sounds right. The receiver does not understand the message or does not know what to ask.
3. *Receivers are reluctant to point out the sender's ignorance.* Employees often fear that asking a question suggests that the manager has done a poor job of preparing and sending the message. Or it suggests that the manager is wrong.
4. *Receivers have cultural barriers.* For example, in many Asian countries it is considered impolite to disagree with the manager, so the employee would answer yes when asked by the manager if the message was understood.

After managers send a message and ask if there are questions, they then proceed to make another common error. Managers assume that no questions being asked means communication is complete, that there is mutual understanding of the message. In reality, the message is often misunderstood. When "this isn't what I asked for" happens, the task has to be done all over again. The end result is often wasted time, materials, and effort.

The most common cause of messages not resulting in communication is the lack of getting feedback that ensures mutual understanding. The proper use of questioning and paraphrasing can help you ensure that your messages are communicated.

How to Get Feedback on Messages

Here are four guidelines appropriate for managers and nonmanagers that you should use when getting feedback on messages:

- *Be open to feedback.* There are no dumb questions. When someone asks a question, you need to be responsive, and patiently answer questions and explain things clearly. If people sense that you get upset if they ask questions, they will not ask questions.
- *Be aware of nonverbal communication.* Make sure that your nonverbal communications encourage feedback. For example, if you say, "I encourage questions," but when people ask questions you look at them as though they are stupid, or you act impatient, people will learn not to ask questions. You must also be aware of, and read, people's nonverbal communications. For example, if you are explaining a task to Larry and he has a puzzled look on his face, he is probably confused but may not be willing to say so. In such a case, you should stop and clarify things before going on.
- *Ask questions.* When you send messages, it is better to know whether the messages are understood before action is taken, so that the action will not have to be changed or repeated. Communicating is the responsibility of both the message sender and receiver. Ask questions to check understanding, rather than simply asking, "Do you have any questions?" Direct questions dealing with the specific information you have given will indicate if the receiver has been listening, and whether he or she understands enough to give a direct reply. If the response is not accurate, try repeating, giving more examples, or elaborating further on the message.

You can also ask indirect questions to attain feedback. You can ask "how do you feel?" questions about the message. You can also ask "if you were me" questions, such as, "If you were me, how would you explain how to do it?" Or you can ask third-party questions, such as, "How will employees feel about this?" The response to indirect questions will often tell you other people's attitudes.

- *Use paraphrasing.* The most accurate indicator of understanding is paraphrasing. How you ask the receiver to paraphrase will affect his or her attitude. For example, if you say "Joan, tell me what I just said so that I can be sure you will not make a mistake as usual," this will probably result in defensive behavior on Joan's part. Joan will probably make a mistake. Here are two examples of proper requests for paraphrasing:

  "Now tell me what you are going to do, so we will be sure that we are in agreement."

  "Would you tell me what you are going to do, so that I can be sure that I explained myself clearly?"

  Notice that the second statement takes the pressure off the employee. The sender is asking for a check on *his or her* ability, not that of the employee. These types of requests for paraphrasing should result in a positive attitude toward the message and the sender. They show concern for the employee and for communicating effectively.

Work Application 5

Recall a past or present manager. Did or does your manager use the common approach to getting feedback on messages regularly? Was or is he or she open to feedback and aware of nonverbal communication on a regular basis? Did the manager regularly ask questions and ask you to paraphrase?

360-Degree Multirater Feedback

So far, we have discussed the informal methods of getting feedback. We now turn to a formal evaluation process using 360-degree multirater feedback. The use of feedback from multiple sources has become popular as a means of improving performance. As the name implies, **360-degree feedback** *is based on receiving performance evaluations from many people.* Most 360-degree evaluation forms are completed by the person being evaluated, his or her manager, peers, and subordinates when applicable. Customers, suppliers, and other outside people are also asked for an evaluation when applicable. See Exhibit 6.2 for an illustration of the 360-degree feedback process.

EXHIBIT 6.2 360-Degree Feedback Sources

	may be customers	
	Manager	
Peers	360-degree multirater feedback form results	Self
	Employees	
	may be suppliers	

If you are serious about getting ahead, it is critical for you to focus on the feedback from your manager and do what it takes to receive a good evaluation. You should work together with your manager to develop and implement a plan for improvement during the next evaluation period.

Opening Case APPLICATION

2. How does management they use feedback at The Ranch?

Feedback is critical to success at The Ranch, because it is how the Clarks and the managers know if the players are getting quality service and learn how to improve service. The Clarks, managers, and employees are open to player criticism because they realize that the only way to improve is to listen and make changes to improve performance. In fact, Peter and Korby Clark spend much of their time at The Ranch talking to players about their experience, with the focus on listening for ways to make improvements. The Clarks and managers set clear objectives and have regular meetings with employees to get and give feedback on how The Ranch is progressing toward meeting its objectives.

Although it is a small business, during the summer 80 people work at The Ranch, and it has a sophisticated information system for its three departments—golf (greens and practice, tournaments/outings, golf shop), maintenance (the course and other facilities), and food and beverage (The Ranch Grille, bar, and functions) that include many performance measures. The Ranch does not have a formal 360-degree feedback system. However, managers who evaluate employee performance do interact regularly with each employee, employee peers, the players, and other managers at The Ranch; and they use the feedback from others in their performance appraisals.

Coaching

Coaching is based on feedback and communications: It involves giving feedback, which requires communication. In this section we discuss coaching and leadership, how to give coaching feedback, and what criticism is—and why it doesn't work. We then present a coaching model you can use on the job, and end by briefly discussing mentoring, which may be considered a form of coaching.

Coaching and Leadership

Coaching *is the process of giving motivational feedback to maintain and improve performance.* Coaching is designed to maximize employee strengths and minimize weaknesses. As a means of improving performance, organizations are training their managers to be coaches, and this trend is expected to continue because coaching boosts performance.[26] Developing your coaching skills is an important part of your leadership development.[27] Whether you are a manager or not, you can be a leader and coach others, including your manager. Coaching is especially important when an employee is new to the job and organization. Capital One Financial pairs managers with coaches to hone leadership skills.[28]

How to Give Coaching Feedback

When people hear the word *coaching,* they often think of athletes, but managers should also be looking for steady performance and continual improvement. Athlete-coaching skills are being used successfully in the business world. If you have ever had a good coach, think about the behavior he or she used that helped to maintain and improve your performance and that of other team members. The next time you watch a sporting event, keep an eye on the coaches and learn some ways to coach employees.

We next discuss some guidelines that will help you to be an effective coach; the guidelines are also shown in Exhibit 6.3 on the next page. The guidelines are designed primarily for use with employees who are doing a good job. As in the

EXHIBIT 6.3 Coaching Guidelines

1. Develop a supportive working relationship.
2. Give praise and recognition.
3. Avoid blame and embarrassment.
4. Focus on the behavior, not the person.
5. Have employees assess their own performance.
6. Give specific and descriptive feedback.
7. Give coaching feedback.
8. Provide modeling and training.
9. Make feedback timely, but flexible.
10. Don't criticize.

definition of coaching, the focus is on maintaining and continually improving performance. In the next section we present more specific guidelines and a coaching model for leading employees who are not performing as expected.

Develop a Supportive Working Relationship

The experienced boss should be a coach to rookies.[29] Research has shown that the most important contributor to employee success and retention is their relationship with their manager.[30] The manager and employee do not have to be personal friends and socialize together—it's about having a good working relationship. Your relationship with followers needs to convey your concern for them as individuals and your commitment to coach them to success. A supportive working relationship can build enthusiasm and commitment to continual performance improvement.

You should periodically ask employees if there is anything you can do to help them do a better job. Take the time to listen to them.[31] There will seldom be big problems. Problems are often caused by petty annoyances that an employee believes are too trivial to bother the manager with. Your job as a manager is to run interference and to remove the stumbling blocks for the employees to improve their performance and that of the business unit.

Give Praise and Recognition

Why should you give recognition to employees for doing their job? The reason is simple: It motivates employees to maintain and increase performance. In Chapter 3 you learned the importance of giving praise, and how to use the giving praise model. We cannot overemphasize the importance of giving praise and recognition. Recognition includes praise, awards, and recognition ceremonies. Awards include certificates of achievement, a letter of commendation, a pin, a plaque, a trophy, a medal, a ribbon, clothing, cash, trips, meals, employee of the month, and so on.

Awards are symbolic acts of thanks for contributions to the success of the organization. Recognition ceremonies ensure that individual, team, and work-unit achievements are acknowledged by others in the organization. Most highly successful organizations celebrate their success in some way. Mary Kay owes much of the success of its cosmetics business to its elaborate recognition systems, with the ultimate award of the pink Cadillac. True leaders are always quick to give recognition to their followers.

Avoid Blame and Embarrassment

The objective of coaching is to develop employees' knowledge, abilities, and skills. Thus, any leadership behavior that focuses on making the person feel bad does not help to develop the employee. Some things are best not said. For example, if an employee makes a mistake and realizes it, verbalizing it is not needed; doing so only makes them feel bad. Statements like, "I'm surprised that you did XYZ," or "I'm disappointed in you" should also be avoided. Besides, effective leaders treat mistakes as learning experiences.[32]

Focus on the Behavior, not the Person

The purpose of coaching is to achieve desirable behavior, not to belittle the person. Let's use examples to illustrate the difference between coaching by focusing on changing behavior rather than by focusing on the person. Notice that the statements focusing on the person place blame and embarrassment—or belittle the person:

- *Situation 1.* The employee is dominating the discussion at a meeting.

  Focus on person—You talk too much; give others a chance.

  Focus on behavior—I'd like to hear what some of the other group members have to say.

- *Situation 2.* The employee is late for a meeting again.

  Focus on person—You are always late for meetings; why can't you be on time like the rest of us?

  Focus on behavior—This is the second time in a row that you arrived late for our meeting. The group needs your input right from the start of the meeting.

Work Application 6

Recall the best and worst manager you ever had. With which manager did you have the best working relationship? Which one gave you the most encouragement, praise, and recognition for a job well done? Which one gave you the most negative criticism? Was your performance at a higher level for your best or worst manager?

Have Employees Assess Their Own Performance

Here are some examples of criticism and self-evaluation coaching feedback to help explain the difference:

- *Situation 3.* The employee has been making more errors lately.

  Criticism—You haven't been working up to par lately; get on the ball.

  Self-evaluation—How would you assess the number of errors you have been making this week?

- *Situation 4.* The employee is working on a few reports, and one is due in two days. The manager believes the employee may not meet the deadline.

  Criticism—Are you going to meet the deadline for the report?

  Self-evaluation—How are you progressing on the cost-cutting report that's due this Thursday? Is there something I can do to help?

Can the criticism statements result in defensive behavior, not listening, feeling bad about oneself, and disliking the task and the manager? Do the self-evaluation statements create different feelings and behavior?

Give Specific and Descriptive Feedback

Specific feedback is needed to avoid confusion over which particular behavior needs to be improved. Compare the preceding criticism statements, which are not specific, to the self-evaluation statements, which are specific. Can you understand how the person being criticized may not understand specifically what the manager is talking about, and therefore may be unable to change even if they are willing to do so?

Descriptive feedback can be based on *facts* or *inferences.* Facts can be observed and proven; inferences cannot. In situation 3, the manager can observe and prove that the employee made more errors this week than in prior weeks. However, the manager cannot observe or prove why. The manager may infer many reasons for the changed behavior, such as laziness, illness, a personal problem, and so on. In situation 4, the manager cannot prove that the report will be late; the manager is inferring that it will be and attempting to coach the employee to make sure it is completed on time. Give factual rather than inferential feedback, because factual feedback tends to be positive, while inferential feedback tends to be more negative criticism.

Give Coaching Feedback

Self-assessment can work well, especially when performance needs to be maintained rather than improved. However, it is not always appropriate; if overused, it can have limited success. There are often times when you will want to offer coaching feedback without self-assessment. It is important to respond positively to negative behavior and outcomes, and the way to do this is not by pointing out mistakes but by selling the benefits of positive behavior.[33] Here are some examples of how to coach versus criticize:

- *Situation 5.* The manager just saw an employee, who knows how it should be done, incorrectly pick up a fairly heavy box.

  Criticism—You just picked up the box wrong. Don't let me catch you again.

  Coaching feedback—If you don't want to injure your back, use your legs—not your back.
- *Situation 6.* A student sees a fellow student going to the Yahoo! Web site by typing in the entire address, **http://www.yahoo.com.**

  Criticism—You just wasted time typing in the entire Yahoo! Web site address. Don't use the entire address, or make it a favorite address.

  Coaching feedback—Would you like me to show you a faster way to get to the Yahoo! home page?
- *Situation 7.* A worker is completing a task by following an inefficient, step-by-step procedure.

  Criticism—You're not doing that the best way. Do X, Y, then Z from now on.

  Coaching feedback—Have you given any thought to changing the sequence of steps for completing that task to X, Y, then Z?

Provide Modeling and Training

A good manager leads by example. If employees see the manager doing things in an effective manner, they will tend to copy the manager. As illustrated in situations 4 and 5, coaching often requires some training. Failing to train and coach new employees is failing to lead.[34] The job instructional training method is widely used (see Model 6.2). *The* **job instructional training** (JIT) *steps include* (1) *trainee receives preparation;* (2) *trainer presents the task;* (3) *trainee performs the task; and* (4) *trainer follows up.* Remember that tasks we know well seem very simple, but they are usually difficult for the new trainee. You can also use coleadership and have others do the training, especially if they are better at training than you are.

Step 1. **Trainee receives preparation.** Put the trainee at ease as you create interest in the job and encourage questions. Explain the quantity and quality requirements and why they are important.

MODEL 6.2 Job Instructional Training Steps

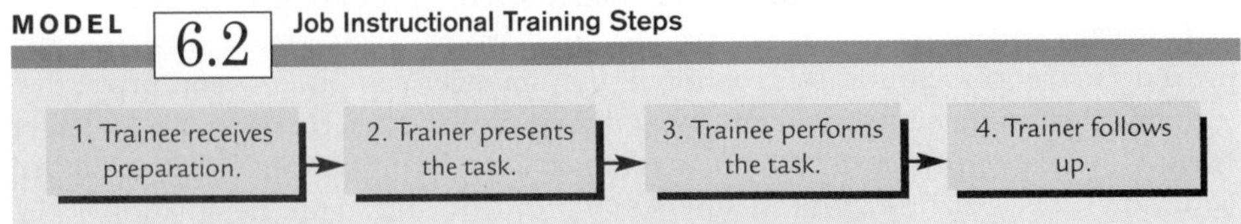
1. Trainee receives preparation.
2. Trainer presents the task.
3. Trainee performs the task.
4. Trainer follows up.

Step 2. **Trainer presents the task.** Perform the task yourself at a slow pace, explaining each step several times. Once the trainee seems to have the steps memorized, have the trainee explain each step as you slowly perform the task again. For complex tasks with multiple steps, it is helpful to write them out and to give a copy to the trainee.

Step 3. **Trainee performs the task.** Have the trainee perform the task at a slow pace, while explaining each step to the trainer. Correct any errors and be patiently willing to help the trainee perform any difficult steps. Continue until the trainee is proficient at performing the task.

Step 4. **Trainer follows up.** Tell the trainee who to ask for help with any questions or problems. Gradually leave the trainee alone. Begin by checking quality and quantity frequently, and decrease checks based on the trainee's skill level. Observe the trainee performing the task, and be sure to correct any errors or faulty work procedures before they become a habit. As you follow up, be sure to be patient and encouraging. Praise a good effort at first, and good performance as skills develop.

Make Feedback Timely, but Flexible

Feedback should be given *as soon as possible* after the behavior has been observed. For example, in situation 5 you will want to give the coaching feedback as soon as you see the employee lift the box incorrectly. To tell the employee about it a few days later will have less impact on changing the behavior, and the employee could be injured by then. The *flexibility* part comes into play (1) when you don't have the time to do the full coaching job, and (2) when emotions are high. For example, if you were late for an important meeting and wanted to sit down with the employee to fully discuss the problem of lifting incorrectly, a later date could be set. If you were really angry and yelled at the employee and the employee yelled back, it is usually a good idea to make an appointment to discuss it later when emotions have calmed; then you can rationally discuss the matter using coaching feedback. Besides, yelling rarely works; it is a form of criticism. Even if you shouted in anger while following every other coaching guideline, it would be criticism.

Don't Criticize

Jack Falvey, management consultant and author, takes the positive versus negative feedback to the point of recommending only positive feedback:

> *Criticism is to be avoided at all costs (there is no such thing as constructive criticism; all criticism is destructive). If you must correct someone, never do it after the fact. Bite your tongue and hold off until the person is about to do the same thing again and then challenge the person to make a more positive contribution.*[35]

Work Application 7

Recall a present or past manager. Which of the ten guidelines does or did the manager use most frequently and least frequently?

Remember that everyone can be a coach. Coaches can be effective by following the simple guidelines presented here. So don't criticize, start coaching—today. These general guidelines apply to any leadership situation, such as being a parent or guardian.

What Is Criticism and Why Doesn't It Work?

Falvey's statement may seem a bit extreme, but it is true. Placing blame and embarrassment and focusing on the person are types of criticism. Criticism is rarely effective. Criticism involves a judgment, which is that either the person is right or wrong. Criticism is also the process of pointing out mistakes, which places blame and is embarrassing. Once you tell people they are wrong or made a mistake, directly or indirectly, four things usually happen: (1) They become defensive and justify their behavior, or they blame it on someone or something. (2) They don't really listen to so-called constructive feedback. (3) They are embarrassed and feel bad about themselves, or they view themselves as losers. (4) They begin to dislike the task or job, as well as the critic.

The more criticism employees receive, the more defensive they become. They listen less, they are in conflict as their self-concept is threatened or diminishes, they eventually hate the task or job and usually the critic, and they often quit the job, get a transfer, or are fired. Giving praise has an opposite, positive effect on employees, their behavior, and their performance.

Demotivating

Employees with overly critical managers tend to develop the attitude of, "My manager doesn't care about me or appreciate my work, so why should I work hard to do a good job?" They play it safe by doing the minimum, taking no risks, focusing on not making errors, and covering up any errors so they aren't criticized. They avoid contact with the manager and they feel stress just seeing the manager approach them. They think, "What did I do this time?"

Applying the **Concept 2**

Criticism or Coaching Feedback

Identify each of these five statements as criticism or coaching feedback. For each criticism only, write a coaching feedback statement to replace it.

a. criticism b. coaching feedback

____ 11. You just dropped it on the floor.

____ 12. This is still dirty. You are going to have to clean it again.

____ 13. I couldn't help overhearing your conflict with Jack. Would you like me to tell you how you can minimize this problem in the future?

____ 14. You are a poor speller. Make sure you don't forget to use the spell check before you pass in your work.

____ 15. *In a loud, angry voice:* Let me help you with that.

Learning Outcome 5 *Describe the difference between criticism and coaching feedback.*

The Difference Between Criticism and Coaching Feedback

By now you probably agree that criticism usually does not work; in fact, it often makes the behavior worse. But you may be thinking that you can't always catch an employee in the act and challenge them to perform better. What do you do? The major difference between criticism and coaching feedback is that **coaching feedback** *is based on a good, supportive relationship; it is specific and descriptive; and it is not judgmental criticism.* And coaching is often based on the employee doing a self-assessment of performance. Criticism makes employees feel like losers; praise and coaching feedback makes them feel like winners. And nothing breeds success like good coaches. Next, we focus on how to coach the employee who is performing below expected standards.

Learning Outcome 6 *Discuss the relationship between the performance formula and the coaching model.*

The Coaching Model for Employees Who Are Performing Below Standard

When managers are giving feedback to employees who are performing below standard, all ten of the coaching guidelines are important. However, most managers are more apt to use embarrassment, to focus on the person, and to criticize the person who is performing below standard than to focus on the person who is doing a good job. Avoid this temptation, because it doesn't really work. Don't exclude poor performers and develop negative relationships with them. They need your one-on-one coaching at its best. Be patient but persistent; don't give up on them. Before getting into the coaching model, let's discuss attribution theory and the performance formula because they affect the coaching model.

Attribution Theory

Attribution theory *is used to explain the process managers go through in determining the reasons for effective or ineffective performance and deciding what to do about it.* The reaction of a manager to poor performance has two stages. First, the manager tries to determine the cause of the poor performance, and then he or she selects an appropriate corrective action. To help you determine the cause of poor performance, we provide you with the performance formula; and to take corrective action, the coaching model.

Managers tend to attribute the cause of poor performance by certain employees to internal reasons (ability and/or motivation) within their control, and poor performance by other employees to external reasons (resources) beyond their control. Managers are less critical of those employees whose poor performance is attributed to external reasons beyond their control. Effective leaders try to avoid this problem. (Chapter 7 examines these "in-group" and "out-group" relationships in depth.)

Determining the Cause of Poor Performance and Corrective Coaching Action

The **performance formula** *explains performance as a function of ability, motivation, and resources.* Model 6.3 is a simple model that can help you determine the cause of poor performance and the corrective action to take based on the cause. When ability, motivation, or resources are low, performance will be lower.

When the employee's *ability* is the reason for keeping performance from being optimal, the corrective coaching action is training (JIT). When *motivation* is

MODEL 6.3 The Performance Formula

Performance (*f*)*
Ability, Motivation, and Resources

*(*f*) = is a function of

lacking, motivational techniques (discussed in Chapter 3) such as giving praise might help. Coach the employee, and work together to develop a plan to improve performance. When *resources* (tools, material, equipment, information, others did not do their part, bad luck or timing, and so on) are the problem, you need to get the resources. When obstacles are getting in the way of performance, you need to overcome them.

Improving Performance with the Coaching Model

The steps in the coaching model are (1) describe current performance; (2) describe desired performance; (3) get a commitment to the change; and (4) follow up. Again, use all ten guidelines to coaching within the framework of the coaching model.

Step 1. **Describe current performance.** In detail, using specific examples, describe the current behavior that needs to be changed.

For example, for an ability or motivation problem, say something like, "There is a way to lift boxes that will decrease your chances of getting injured."

Step 2. **Describe desired performance.** Tell the employee exactly what the desired performance is, in detail. If *ability* is the reason for poor performance, modeling and training the employee with JIT are very appropriate. If the employee knows the proper way, the reason for poor performance is *motivational*. Demonstration is not needed; just describe desired performance as you ask the employee to state why the performance is important.

For example: *Ability*—"If you squat down and pick up the box using your legs instead of your back, it is easier and there is less chance of injuring yourself. Let me demonstrate for you." *Motivation*—"Why should you squat and use your legs rather than your back to pick up boxes?"

Step 3. **Get a commitment to the change.** When dealing with an *ability* performance issue, it is not necessary to get employees to verbally commit to the change if they seem willing to make it. However, if employees defend their way, and you're sure it's not as effective, explain why your proposed way is better. If you cannot get the employee to understand and agree based on rational persuasion, get a verbal commitment through coercive power, such as a threat of discipline. For *motivation* performance issues, this is important because, if the employee is not willing to commit to the change, he or she will most likely not make the change.

For example: *Ability*—the employee will most likely be willing to do it correctly, so skip the step. *Motivation*—"Will you squat rather than use your back from now on?"

Step 4. **Follow up.** Remember, some employees do what managers inspect, not what they expect. You should follow up to ensure that the employee is behaving as desired.

When you are dealing with an *ability* performance issue, the person was receptive, and you skipped step 3, say nothing. But watch to be sure the task is done correctly in the future. Coach again, if necessary. For a *motivation* problem, make a statement that you will follow up, and describe possible consequences for repeated poor performance.

For example: *Ability*—say nothing, but observe. *Motivation*—"Picking up boxes with your back is dangerous; if I catch you doing it again, I will take disciplinary action."

See Model 6.4 for a review of the steps in the coaching model.

MODEL 6.4 Coaching Model

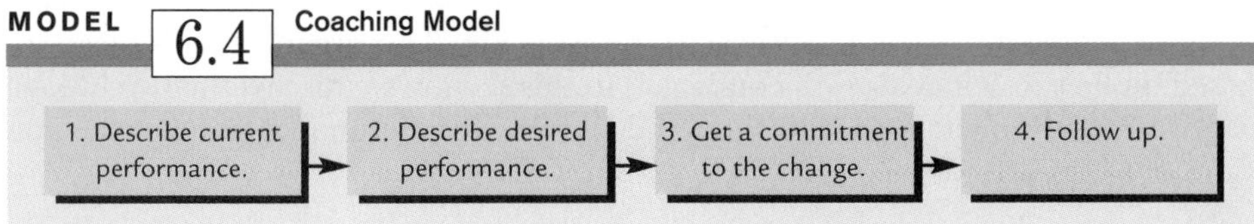
1. Describe current performance.
2. Describe desired performance.
3. Get a commitment to the change.
4. Follow up.

Mentoring

Mentoring *is a form of coaching in which a more-experienced manager helps a less-experienced protégé.* Thus, the ten tips for coaching apply to mentoring. However, mentoring includes more than coaching, and it is more involved and personal than coaching. The formal mentor is usually at a higher level of management and is not the protégé's immediate manager. Family, friends, and peers can also be mentors. The primary responsibility is to coach the protégé by providing good, sound career advice and to help develop leadership skills necessary for a successful management career.[36] However, the protégé should not try to become just like the mentor; we all need to learn from others, yet we need to be ourselves to be effective.

Research studies have found that mentoring results in more career advancement and job satisfaction for the protégé. Based on the success of mentoring, many organizations—including the IRS, Hewlett-Packard, and IBM—have formal mentoring programs, while others have informal mentoring. Nokia takes mentoring so serious that it creates a mentoring mentality by having its top 200 executives' evaluations include how subordinates rate their ability to lead, teach, and inspire.[37]

We all need mentors, so don't wait for someone to ask you. Seek out a good mentor.[38] If your organization has a formal mentoring program, try to sign up for it. If it is informal, ask around about getting a mentor, and remember that a mentor can be from another organization. Whenever you have job- or career-related questions and would like advice, contact your mentor.

Work Application 8

Recall a person who is or was a mentor to you. Briefly describe the relationship and type of advice you got from your mentor.

Opening Case APPLICATION

3. Is there a difference in managing an oil change business, a golf course, and a sports team; and how does Peter Clark use coaching at The Ranch?

Peter Clark says there are more similarities than differences in running a Jiffy Lube business and a golf club and coaching sports. The focus is the same—high-quality service. You have to treat the customer or player right. Clark uses the same 3 I's coaching philosophy for all three: You need Intensity to be prepared to do the job right, Integrity to do the right thing when no one is watching, and Intimacy to be a team player. If one person does not do the job right, everyone is negatively affected. In business and sports, you need to strive to be the best. You need to set and meet challenging goals.

Clark strongly believes in being positive and the need to develop a supportive working relationship, which includes sitting down to talk and really listening to the other person. He also strongly believes in the need for good training. Employees at The Ranch give high-quality service because they are thoroughly trained to do so, and they are continually coached to maintain and improve performance. Although The Ranch does not have a formal mentoring program, Clark clearly sees mentoring as an important role he plays at The Ranch.

Managing Conflict

A **conflict** *exists whenever people are in disagreement and opposition.* Conflict is inevitable because people don't see things exactly the same way.[39] An organization's success is based on how well it deals with conflicts.[40] In this section we discuss the psychological contract, conflict and leadership, and the five conflict management styles you can use to resolve conflicts.

The Psychological Contract

All human relations rely on the psychological contract.[41] The *psychological contract* is the unwritten implicit expectations of each party in a relationship. At work, you have a set of expectations of what you will contribute to the organization (effort, time, skills) and what it will provide to you (compensation, job satisfaction, and so on). We are often not aware of our expectations until they have not been met (for example, how you are treated by your manager).[42]

Conflict Arises by Breaking the Psychological Contract

The psychological contract is broken for two primary reasons: (1) We fail to make explicit our own expectations and fail to inquire into the expectations of the other parties. (2) We further assume that the other party(ies) has the same expectations that we hold. So as long as people meet our expectations, everything is fine; when they don't meet our expectations, we are in conflict. Thus, it is important to share information and negotiate expectations assertively.[43] After all, how can you expect others to meet your expectations when they don't know what they are?

Conflict and Leadership

Many leaders are constantly exposed to conflict. Executives say their managers spend an average of more than seven hours a week sorting out conflicts among their staff members.[44] Thus, handling conflict constructively is an important leadership skill.[45] Your ability to resolve conflicts will have a direct effect on your leadership success. With the trend toward teamwork, conflict skills are increasingly important to team decision making.[46] In the global economy, you need to be sensitive to cultural differences so that you don't create additional conflicts.[47]

Conflict Can Be Dysfunctional or Functional

People often think of conflict as fighting and view it as disruptive. When conflict is not resolved effectively, negative consequences occur.[48] When conflict prevents the achievement of organizational objectives, it is negative or *dysfunctional conflict.* However, it can be positive. *Functional conflict* exists when disagreement and opposition supports the achievement of organizational objectives. Functional conflict increases the quality of group decisions and leads to innovative changes.[49] The question today is not whether conflict is negative or positive, but how to manage conflict to benefit the organization.

Learning Outcome 7 *Define the five conflict management styles.*

Conflict Management Styles

Conflict management skills can be developed with appropriate training. In this discussion, we focus on resolving conflicts in your own personal and professional life.

When you are in conflict, you have five conflict management styles to choose from. The five styles are based on two dimensions of concern: concern for others' needs and concern for your own needs. These concerns result in three types of behavior:

1. A low concern for your own needs and a high concern for others' needs results in passive behavior.
2. A high concern for your own needs and a low concern for others' needs results in aggressive behavior.
3. A moderate or high concern for your own needs and others' needs results in assertive behavior.

Each conflict style of behavior results in a different combination of win-lose situations. The five styles, along with concern for needs and win-lose combinations, are presented in Exhibit 6.4 and discussed here in order of passive, aggressive, and assertive behavior. The conflict style that you tend to use the most is based on your personality and leadership style. There is no one best conflict management style for all situations. In this section you will learn the advantages and disadvantages and the appropriate use of each conflict management style.

EXHIBIT 6.4 Conflict Management Styles

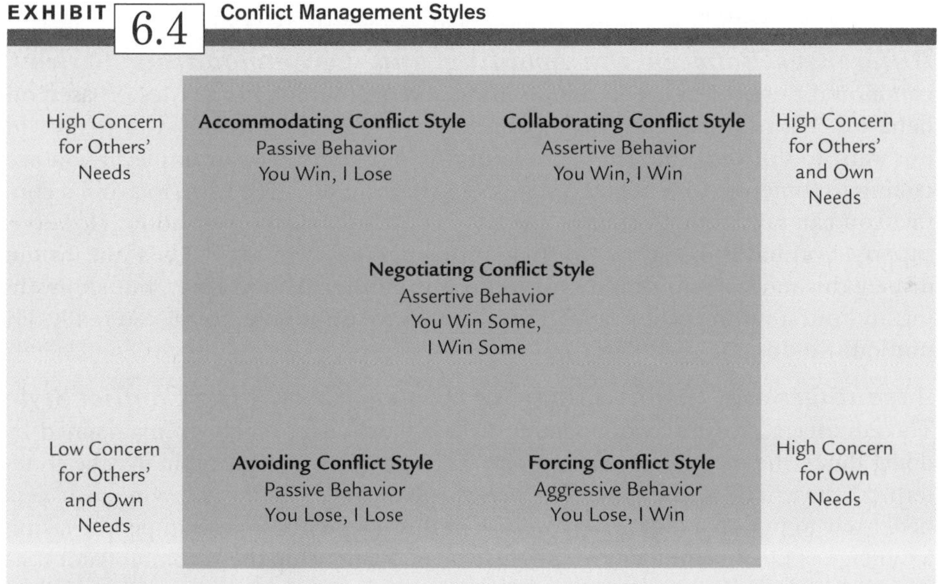

Avoiding Conflict Style

The *avoiding conflict style* user attempts to passively ignore the conflict rather than resolve it. When you avoid a conflict, you are being unassertive and uncooperative. People avoid conflict by refusing to take a stance, or escape conflict by mentally withdrawing and physically leaving. A lose-lose situation is created because the conflict is not resolved.

Advantages and Disadvantages of the Avoiding Conflict Style The advantage of the avoiding style is that it may maintain relationships that would be hurt through conflict resolution. The disadvantage of this style is that conflicts do not get resolved. An overuse of this style leads to conflict within the individual.

People tend to walk all over the avoider. Some managers allow employees to break rules without confronting them. Avoiding problems usually does not make them go away; the problems usually get worse. And the longer you wait to confront others, the more difficult the confrontation usually is.[50]

Appropriate Use of the Avoiding Conflict Style The avoiding style is appropriate to use when (1) the conflict is trivial; (2) your stake in the issue is not high; (3) confrontation will damage an important relationship; (4) you don't have time to resolve the conflict; or (5) emotions are high. When you don't have time to resolve the conflict or people are emotional, you should confront the person(s) later. However, it is inappropriate to repeatedly avoid confrontation until you get so upset that you end up yelling at the other person(s). This passive-aggressive behavior tends to make the situation worse by hurting human relations. Often people do not realize they are doing something that bothers you (that you are in conflict), and when approached properly, they are willing to change.

Accommodating Conflict Style

The *accommodating conflict style* user attempts to resolve the conflict by passively giving in to the other party. When you use the accommodating style, you are being unassertive but cooperative. You attempt to satisfy the other party, neglecting your own needs by letting others get their own way. A win-lose situation is created, as you try to please everyone.

Differences Between the Avoiding and Accommodating Styles A common difference between the avoiding and accommodating styles is based on behavior. With the avoiding style, you don't have to do anything you really did not want to do; with the accommodating style, you do. For example, if you are talking to someone who makes a statement that you disagree with, to avoid a conflict you can say nothing, change the subject, or stop the conversation. However, suppose you have to put up a display with someone who says, "Let's put up the display this way." If you don't want to do it the other person's way, but say nothing and put it up the other person's way, you have done something you really did not want to do.

Advantages and Disadvantages of the Accommodating Conflict Style The advantage of the accommodating style is that relationships are maintained by doing things the other person's way. The disadvantage is that giving in may be counterproductive. The accommodating person may have a better solution, such as a better way to put up a display. An overuse of this style tends to lead to people taking advantage of the accommodator, and the type of relationship the accommodator tries to maintain is usually lost.

Appropriate Use of the Accommodating Conflict Style The accommodating style is appropriate when (1) the person enjoys being a follower; (2) maintaining the relationship outweighs all other considerations; (3) the changes agreed to are not important to the accommodator, but are to the other party; or (4) the time to resolve the conflict is limited. This is often the only style that can be used with an autocratic manager who uses the forcing style.

Forcing Conflict Style

The *forcing conflict style* user attempts to resolve the conflict by using aggressive behavior to get his or her own way. When you use the forcing style, you are uncooperative and aggressive, doing whatever it takes to satisfy your own needs—at the expense of others, if necessary. Forcers use authority, threaten, intimidate, and call for majority rule when they know they will win. Forcers commonly enjoy dealing with avoiders and accommodators. If you try to get others to change without being willing to change yourself, regardless of the means, then you use the forcing style. A win-lose situation is created.

Advantages and Disadvantages of the Forcing Style The advantage of the forcing style is that better organizational decisions will be made, when the forcer is correct, rather than less-effective compromised decisions. The disadvantage is that overuse of this style leads to hostility and resentment toward its user. Forcers tend to have poor human relations.

Appropriate Use of the Forcing Style Some managers commonly use their position power to force others to do what they want them to do. The forcing style is appropriate to use when (1) unpopular action must be taken on important issues; (2) commitment by others to proposed action is not crucial to its implementation—in other words, people will not resist doing what you want them to do; (3) maintaining relationships is not critical; or (4) the conflict resolution is urgent.

Negotiating Conflict Style

The *negotiating conflict style* user attempts to resolve the conflict through assertive, give-and-take concessions. This is also called the *compromising style.* When you use the compromising approach, you are moderate in assertiveness and cooperation. An "I win some, you win some" situation is created through compromise. As discussed in Chapter 4, negotiation skills are important in both your personal and your professional life.[51]

Advantages and Disadvantages of the Negotiating Conflict Style The advantage of the negotiating style is that the conflict is resolved relatively quickly and working relationships are maintained. The disadvantage is that the compromise often leads to counterproductive results, such as suboptimum decisions. An overuse of this style leads to people playing games such as asking for twice as much as they need in order to get what they want. It is commonly used during management and labor collective bargaining.

Appropriate Use of the Negotiating Conflict Style The negotiating style is appropriate to use when (1) the issues are complex and critical, and there is no simple and clear solution; (2) parties have about equal power and are interested in different solutions; (3) a solution will be only temporary; or (4) time is short.

Collaborating Conflict Style

The *collaborating conflict style* user assertively attempts to jointly resolve the conflict with the best solution agreeable to all parties. It is also called the *problem-solving style.* When you use the collaborating approach, you are being assertive and cooperative. Although avoiders and accommodators are concerned about others' needs, and forcers are concerned about their own needs, the collaborator is concerned about finding the best solution to the problem that is satisfactory to all parties. Unlike the forcer, the collaborator is willing to change if a better solution is presented. While negotiating is often based on secret information, collaboration is based on open and honest communication. This is the only style that creates a true win-win situation.

Differences Between the Negotiating and Collaborating Styles A common difference between negotiating and collaborating is the solution. Let's continue with the example of putting up a display. With negotiation, the two people may trade off by putting up one display one person's way and the next display the other person's way. This way they each win and lose. With collaboration, the two people work together to develop one display method that they both like. It may be a combination of both, or simply one person's idea if after an explanation, the other person really agrees that the method is better. The key to collaboration is agreeing that the solution is the best possible one.

Work Application 9

Select a present or past manager. Which conflict management style did that manager use most often? Explain by giving a typical example. Which one of the five conflict management styles do you tend to use most often? Explain your answer.

Advantages and Disadvantages of the Collaborating Style The advantage of the collaborating style is that it tends to lead to the best solution to the conflict, using assertive behavior. The disadvantage is that the skill, effort, and time it takes to resolve the conflict are usually greater and longer than the other styles. There are situations, mentioned under "Negotiating Conflict Style," when collaboration is difficult, and when a forcer prevents its use. The collaborating style offers the most benefit to the individual, group, and organization.

Applying the Concept 3

Selecting Conflict Management Styles

For each of these five conflict situations, identify the most appropriate conflict management style. Write the appropriate letter in the blank before each item.

a. avoiding
b. accommodating
c. forcing
d. negotiating
e. collaborating

____ 16. You have joined a committee in order to meet people. Your interest in what the committee does is low. While serving on the committee, you make a recommendation that is opposed by another member. You realize that you have the better idea. The other party is using a forcing style.

____ 17. You are on a task force that has to select a new computer. The four alternatives will all do the job. It's the brand, price, and service that people disagree on.

____ 18. You are a sales manager. Beth, one of your competent salespeople, is trying to close a big sale. The two of you are discussing the next sales call she will make. You disagree on the strategy to use to close the sale.

____ 19. You're late and on your way to an important meeting. As you leave your office, at the other end of the work area you see Chris, one of your employees, goofing off instead of working.

____ 20. You're over budget for labor this month. It's slow, so you ask Kent, a part-time employee, to leave work early. Kent tells you he doesn't want to go because he needs the money.

Appropriate Use of the Collaborating Conflict Style The collaborating style is appropriate when (1) you are dealing with an important issue that requires an optimal solution, and compromise would result in suboptimizing; (2) people are willing to place the group goal before self-interest, and members will truly collaborate; (3) maintaining relationships is important; (4) time is available; and (5) it is a peer conflict.

Of the five styles the most difficult to implement successfully, due to the complexity and level of skill needed, is the collaborative style. It is most likely to be underutilized when it would have been appropriate. Organizations around the globe are training employees to resolve conflicts using collaboration.[52]

Therefore, in order to develop your conflict skills, the collaborative style is the only one that we cover in detail in the next section. You learned how to negotiate in Chapter 4.

Opening Case APPLICATION

4. Which conflict management style does Peter Clark tend to use at The Ranch?

At The Ranch, with partners and managers, conflict is inevitable. Peter Clark prefers to use the collaborating conflict style, which goes back to the importance he places on open communications and a good supportive working relationship. He prefers to sit down and work through problem issues together and agree on solutions. He believes that when you have a conflict problem, ignoring it using the avoiding conflict style usually does not solve the problem. When Clark is in conflict with a manager, he does not like to simply accommodate when he does not agree with what the manager wants to do, but he has accommodated, such as in the case of building a waterfall on the course.

Clark does not like to use the forcing conflict style, but there are times when he says no to managers, such as operating an expensive waterfall on the course—he stopped it based on his guiding question: Will spending the money clearly improve player satisfaction enough to pay for itself? Having a waterfall is attractive, but it will not be a deciding factor in playing golf at The Ranch.

Clark also has to negotiate with outside organizations.

Collaborating Conflict Management Style Models

Effective leaders encourage conflict resolution and build collaboration throughout the organization.[53] They challenge all of us to learn to get along with each other. Although you can help prevent conflict, you will not eliminate it completely—nor should you try to, because it can be functional.[54] You will develop your skill to assertively confront (or be confronted by) people you are in conflict with, and in a manner that resolves the conflict without damaging interpersonal relationships. The model of conflict management can be used to develop conflict skills. We provide a model with the steps you can follow when initiating, responding to, and mediating a conflict resolution. The same steps for resolving conflict effectively are applicable to coworkers, people we live with, and international political situations.

Learning Outcome 8 *List the steps in the initiating conflict resolution model.*

Initiating Conflict Resolution

An initiator is the person who confronts the other person(s) to resolve the conflict. Confronting others you are in conflict with is usually the better solution to conflict, rather than avoiding or accommodating.[55] When initiating a conflict resolution using the collaborating style, use the following model: *The* **initiating conflict resolution model** *steps are* (1) *plan a BCF statement that maintains ownership of the problem;* (2) *present your BCF statement and agree on the conflict;* (3) *ask for, and/or give,* *alternative conflict resolutions; and* (4) *make an agreement for change.* This model is part of behavior modeling, which is an effective training method to develop your conflict resolution leadership skills.

Step 1. Plan a BCF statement that maintains ownership of the problem. Planning is the starting management function and the starting point of initiating a conflict resolution. Let's begin by stating what *maintains ownership of the problem* means. Assume you don't smoke, and someone visits you while smoking. Is it you or the smoker who has a problem? The smoke bothers you, not the smoker. It's your problem. Open the confrontation with a request for the respondent to help you solve your problem. This approach reduces defensiveness and establishes an atmosphere of problem solving that will maintain the relationship.

The **BCF model** *describes a conflict in terms of behavior, consequences, and feelings.* When you do B (behavior), C (consequences) happens, and I feel F (feelings). For example, when you smoke in my room (behavior), I have trouble breathing and become nauseous (consequence), and I feel uncomfortable and irritated (feeling). You can vary the sequence by starting with a feeling or consequence to fit the situation and to provide variety. For example, I fear (feeling) that the advertisement is not going to work (behavior), and that we will lose money (consequences).

When developing your opening BCF statement, as shown in the examples just given, be descriptive, not evaluative. Keep the opening statement short. The longer the statement, the longer it will take to resolve the conflict. People get defensive when kept waiting for their turn to talk. Avoid trying to determine who is to blame for something or who is right and wrong. Both parties are usually partly to blame or correct. Fixing blame or correctness only makes people defensive, which is counterproductive to conflict resolution. Timing is also important. If others are busy, see them later to discuss the conflict. In addition, don't confront a person on several unrelated issues at once.

After planning your BCF statement, you should practice saying it before confronting the other party. In addition, think of some possible alternatives you can offer to resolve the conflict. However, be sure your ideas show high concern for others rather than just for yourself; create a win-win situation. Try to put yourself in the other person's position. If you were the other person, would you like the ideas presented by the confronter?

Step 2. Present your BCF statement and agree on the conflict. After making your short, planned BCF statement, let the other party respond. If the other party does not understand or avoids acknowledgment of the problem, persist. You cannot resolve a conflict if the other party will not even acknowledge its existence. Repeat your planned statement several times by explaining it in different terms until you get an acknowledgment or realize it's hopeless. But don't give up too easily. If you cannot agree on a conflict, you may have to change your approach and use one of the other four conflict management styles.

Step 3. Ask for, and/or give, alternative conflict resolutions. Begin by asking the other party what can be done to resolve the conflict. If you agree, great; if not, offer your resolution. However, remember that you are collaborating, not simply trying to change others. When the other party acknowledges the problem, but is not responsive to resolving it, appeal to common goals. Make the other party realize the benefits to him or her and the organization as well.

Step 4. **Make an agreement for change.** Try to come to an agreement on specific action you will both take to resolve the conflict. Clearly state—or better yet for complex change, write down—the specific behavior changes necessary by all parties to resolve the conflict. Again, remember that you are collaborating, not forcing. The steps are also listed in Model 6.5.

Work Application 10

Use the BCF model to describe a conflict you face or have faced on the job.

Responding to Conflict Resolution

As the responder, an initiator has confronted you. Here's how to handle the role of the responder to a conflict. Most initiators do not follow the model. Therefore, the responder must take responsibility for successful conflict resolution by following the conflict resolution model steps, which are also listed in Model 6.5:

1. Listen to and paraphrase the conflict using the BCF model.
2. Agree with some aspect of the complaint.
3. Ask for, and/or give, alternative conflict resolutions.
4. Make an agreement for change.

Mediating Conflict Resolution

Frequently, conflicting parties cannot resolve their dispute alone.[56] In these cases, a mediator should be used. A **mediator** *is a neutral third party who helps resolve a conflict.* In nonunionized organizations, managers are commonly the mediators. But some organizations have trained and designated employees as mediators. In unionized organizations, the mediator is usually a professional from outside the organization. However, a conflict resolution should be sought internally first. As a manager or leader, you will mediate conflicts.[57]

Before bringing the conflicting parties together, you should decide whether to start with a joint meeting or conduct individual meetings. If one employee comes to complain, but has not confronted the other party, or if there is a serious discrepancy in employee perceptions, meet one-on-one with each party before bringing them together. On the other hand, when both parties have a similar awareness of the problem and motivation to solve it, you can begin with a joint meeting when all parties are calm.[58] The manager should be a mediator, not a

MODEL 6.5 **The Collaborating Conflict Style**

Initiating Conflict Resolution	Responding to Conflict Resolution	Mediating Conflict Resolution
Step 1. Plan a BCF statement that maintains ownership of the problem.	Step 1. Listen to and paraphrase the conflict using the BCF model.	Step 1. Have each party state his or her complaint using the BCF model.
Step 2. Present your BCF statement and agree on the conflict.	Step 2. Agree with some aspect of the complaint.	Step 2. Agree on the conflict problem(s).
Step 3. Ask for, and/or give, alternative conflict resolutions.	Step 3. Ask for, and/or give, alternative conflict resolutions.	Step 3. Develop alternative conflict resolutions.
Step 4. Make an agreement for change.	Step 4. Make an agreement for change.	Step 4. Make an agreement for change.
		Step 5. Follow up to make sure the conflict is resolved.

judge. Get the employees to resolve the conflict, if possible. Remain impartial, unless one party is violating company policies. Do a good job of coaching. Avoid blame and embarrassment. Don't make comments such as, "I'm disappointed in you two," or "you're acting like babies."

When bringing conflicting parties together, follow the mediating conflict model steps. These steps are listed in Model 6.5.

If either party blames the other, make a statement such as, "We are here to resolve the conflict; placing blame is not productive." Focus on how the conflict is affecting their work. Discuss the issues by addressing specific behavior, not personalities. If a person says, "We cannot work together because of a personality conflict," ask the parties to state the specific behavior that is bothering them. The discussion should make the parties aware of their behavior and the consequences of their behavior. The mediator may ask questions or make statements to clarify what is being said. The mediator should develop one problem statement that is agreeable to all parties, if possible.

If the conflict has not been resolved, an arbitrator may be used. *An* ***arbitrator*** *is a neutral third party who makes a binding decision to resolve a conflict.* The arbitrator is like a judge, and his or her decision must be followed. However, the use of arbitration should be kept to a minimum because it is not a collaborative conflict style. Arbitrators commonly use a negotiating style in which each party wins some and loses some. Mediation and then arbitration tend to be used in management–labor negotiations, when collective bargaining breaks down and the contract deadline is near.

Opening Case APPLICATION

5. What types of conflict resolutions do the Clarks deal with at The Ranch?

At The Ranch, Peter Clark more often responds to conflict than initiating conflict resolutions since, when problems arise, he is asked for solutions or to approve actions. Clark also has to occasionally mediate a conflict between partners or between managers and employees.

As we end this chapter, you should understand how important communication, feedback, coaching, and conflict resolution are to leadership effectiveness in all organizations. Self-Assessment 2 will help you to understand how your personality traits affect your communication, feedback, coaching, and conflict management style.

SELF-ASSESSMENT 2

Your Personality Traits and Communication, Feedback, Coaching, and Conflict Management Style

Let's tie personality traits from Chapter 2 together with what we've covered in this chapter. We are going to present some general statements about how your personality may affect your communication, feedback, coaching, and conflict management styles. For each area, determine how the information relates to you. This will help you better understand your behavior strengths and weaknesses, and identify areas you may want to improve.

continued

(Self-Assessment 2 continued)

Communication

If you have a high *surgency* personality, you most likely are an extrovert and have no difficulty initiating and communicating with others. However, you may be dominating during communication and may not listen well and be open to others' ideas. Be careful not to use communications simply as a means of getting what you want; be concerned about others and what they want. If you are low in surgency, you may be quiet and reserved in your communications. You may want to be more vocal.

If you are high in *agreeableness* personality trait, you are most likely a good listener and communicator. Your *adjustment* level affects the emotional tone of your communications. If you tend to get emotional during communications, you may want to work to keep your emotions under control. We cannot control our feelings, but we can control our behavior. If you are high in *conscientiousness*, you tend to have reliable communications. If you are not conscientious, you may want to work at returning messages quickly. People who are *open to new experience* often initiate communication, because communicating is often part of the new experience.

Feedback and Coaching

If you have a high *surgency* personality, you have a need to be in control. Watch the tendency to give feedback, but not listen to it. You may need to work at *not* criticizing. If you have low surgency, you may want to give more feedback and do more coaching. If you have a high *agreeableness* personality, you are a people person and probably enjoy coaching others. However, as a manager, you must also discipline when needed, which may be difficult for you.

If you are high on the *adjustment* personality trait, you may tend to give positive coaching; people with low *adjustment* need to watch the negative criticism. If you have a high *conscientiousness* with a high need for achievement, you may tend to be more concerned about your own success. This is also true of people with a high *surgency* personality. Remember that an important part of leadership is coaching others. If you have a low *conscientiousness*, you may need to put forth effort to be a good coach. Your *openness to experience* personality affects whether you are willing to listen to others' feedback and make changes.

Conflict Styles

Generally, the best conflict style is collaboration. If you have a high *surgency* personality, you most likely have no problem confronting others when in conflict. However, be careful not to use the forcing style with others; remember to use social, not personal power. If you have a high *agreeableness* personality, you tend to get along well with others. However, be careful not to use the avoiding and accommodating styles to get out of confronting others; you need to satisfy your needs too.

Adjustment will affect how to handle a conflict situation. Try not to be low in adjustment and get too emotional. If you are *conscientious*, you may be good at conflict resolution; but again, be careful to meet others' needs too. *Openness to experience* affects conflicts, because their resolution often requires change; be open to new things.

Action Plan

Based on your personality, what specific things will you do to improve your communication, feedback, coaching, and conflict management style?

____

____

____

Go to the Internet (www.cengage.com/management/lussier)
where you will find a broad array of resources to help maximize your learning.

- **Review the vocabulary**
- **Try a quiz**
- **Find related links**

Chapter Summary

This chapter summary is organized to answer the nine learning outcomes for Chapter 6.

1. **List the steps in the oral message-sending process.**

   The five steps in the oral message-sending process are (1) develop rapport; (2) state your communication objective; (3) transmit your message; (4) check the receiver's understanding; (5) get a commitment and follow up.

2. **List and explain the three parts of the message-receiving process.**

   The three parts of the message-receiving process are listening, analyzing, and checking understanding. Listening is the process of giving the speaker your undivided attention. Analyzing is the process of thinking about, decoding, and evaluating the message. Checking understanding is the process of giving feedback.

3. **Describe paraphrasing and state why it is used.**

   Paraphrasing is the process of having the receiver restate the message in his or her own words. Paraphrasing is used to check understanding of the transmitted message. If the receiver can paraphrase the message accurately, communication has taken place. If not, communication is not complete.

4. **Identify two common approaches to getting feedback, and explain why they don't work.**

   The first common approach to getting feedback is to send the entire message and to assume that the message has been conveyed with mutual understanding. The second approach is to give the entire message followed by asking, "Do you have any questions?" Feedback usually does not follow because people have a tendency not to ask questions. There are at least four good reasons why people do not ask questions: receivers feel ignorant, receivers are ignorant, receivers are reluctant to point out the sender's ignorance, and receivers have cultural barriers.

5. **Describe the difference between criticism and coaching feedback.**

   Criticism is feedback that makes a judgment about behavior being wrong. Coaching feedback is based on a supportive relationship and offers specific and descriptive ways to improve performance. Criticism focuses on pointing out mistakes, while coaching feedback focuses on the benefits of positive behavior.

6. **Discuss the relationship between the performance formula and the coaching model.**

   The performance formula is used to determine the reason for poor performance and the corrective action needed. The coaching model is then used to improve performance.

7. **Define the five conflict management styles.**

   (1) The *avoiding conflict style* user attempts to passively ignore the conflict rather than resolve it. (2) The *accommodating conflict style* user attempts to resolve the conflict by passively giving in to the other party. (3) The *forcing conflict style* user attempts to resolve the conflict by using aggressive behavior to get his or her own way. (4) The *negotiating conflict style* user attempts to resolve the conflict through assertive, give-and-take concessions. (5) The *collaborating conflict style* user assertively attempts to jointly resolve the conflict with the best solution agreeable to all parties.

8. **List the steps in the initiating conflict resolution model.**

   The initiating conflict resolution model steps are (1) plan a BCF statement that maintains ownership of the problem; (2) present your BCF statement and agree on the conflict; (3) ask for, and/or give, alternative conflict resolutions; and (4) make an agreement for change.

9. **Define the following key terms (in order of appearance in the chapter).**

   Select one or more methods: (1) fill in the missing key terms from memory; (2) match the key terms from the following list with their definitions below; (3) copy the key terms in order from the list at the beginning of the chapter.

__________ is the process of conveying information and meaning.

__________ steps include (1) develop rapport; (2) state your communication objective; (3) transmit your message; (4) check the receiver's understanding; and (5) get a commitment and follow up.

__________ includes listening, analyzing, and checking understanding.

__________ is the process of verifying messages and determining if objectives are being met.

__________ is the process of having the receiver restate the message in his or her own words.

__________ is a formal evaluation process based on receiving performance evaluations from many people.

__________ is the process of giving motivational feedback to maintain and improve performance.

__________ steps include (1) trainee receives preparation; (2) trainer presents the task; (3) trainee performs the task; and (4) trainer follows up.

__________ is (1) based on a good, supportive relationship; (2) specific and descriptive; and (3) not judgmental criticism.

__________ is used to explain the process managers go through in determining the reasons for effective or ineffective performance and deciding what to do about it.

__________ explains performance as a function of ability, motivation, and resources.

__________ is a form of coaching in which a more-experienced manager helps a less-experienced protégé.

__________ exists whenever people are in disagreement and opposition.

__________ steps are (1) plan a BCF statement that maintains ownership of the problem; (2) present your BCF statement and agree on the conflict; (3) ask for, and/or give, alternative conflict resolutions; (4) make an agreement for change.

__________ describes a conflict in terms of behavior, consequences, and feelings.

__________ is a neutral third party who helps resolve a conflict.

__________ is a neutral third party who makes a binding decision to resolve a conflict.

Key Terms

arbitrator, 218
attribution theory, 207
BCF model, 216
coaching, 201
coaching feedback, 206
communication, 189
conflict, 210
feedback, 197
initiating conflict resolution model, 215
job instructional training, 204
mediator, 217
mentoring, 209
message-receiving process, 194
oral message-sending process, 190
paraphrasing, 197
performance formula, 207
360-degree feedback, 200

Review Questions

1. What should be included in your plan to send a message?
2. What are the three parts of a written outline?
3. As an average, how many words should a sentence have, and how many sentences should there be in a paragraph?
4. Which personality traits are associated with being closed to feedback?
5. What are the four guidelines to getting feedback on messages?
6. What is 360-degree feedback, and are many organizations using it?
7. Should a supportive working relationship be a true friendship?
8. Why doesn't criticism work?
9. Are all managers mentors?
10. How do you know when you are in conflict?
11. What is the difference between functional and dysfunctional conflict, and how does each affect performance?
12. What is meant by *maintaining ownership of the problem?*
13. How is the BCF model used?
14. What is the difference between a mediator and an arbitrator?

Communication Skills

The following critical-thinking questions can be used for class discussion and/or as written assignments to develop communication skills. Be sure to give complete explanations for all questions.

1. How would you assess communications in organizations? Give examples of good and poor communications in organizations.
2. How did you score on Self-Assessment 1 on pages 193–194, "Listening Skills"? State your plan for improving your listening skills.
3. How would you assess managers at giving feedback? Specifically, what should managers do to improve?

4. Is 360-degree multirater feedback really better than a boss-based assessment? As a manager, would you elect to use 360?
5. Do you agree with the statement, "Don't criticize"? Do managers tend to give criticism or coaching feedback? How can managers improve?
6. Women and minorities are less likely to have mentors, so should they get mentors? Will you seek out career mentors?
7. What are your psychological contract expectations of your boss and coworkers? Give examples of conflicts you have had at work, listing the expectation that was not met.
8. What percentage of the time do you think a manager can actually use the collaborating conflict management style? Give detailed examples of when managers have used collaboration at work.

CASE

Lawrence Weinbach—from Unisys Corporation to Yankee Hill Capital Management

This is a case about a rising-star leader who flew for a while, but fell. Unisys Corporation has been in business for more than 130 years. Unisys contributed to the computer revolution with the first commercial large-scale system, its 29,000-pound UNIVAC computer back in 1951. As you know, the mainframe computer business gradually declined as smaller computers and PCs took over. Like IBM, Unisys had to change its business focus. Larry Weinbach took over as CEO of Unisys with the strategy of steering the company away from mainframes and toward services, and de-emphasizing commodity PCs.[59]

Lawrence Weinbach understands the importance of good communications. In fact, he won the Excellence in Communication Leadership (EXCEL) Award. The EXCEL Award is the highest honor the International Association of Business Communicators (IABC) gives to nonmembers, usually to CEOs of major companies. Weinbach's communications strategy was credited as a principal factor in his success in boosting employee morale and productivity while at the same time generating a financial turnaround.

Here are some of the communications methods Weinbach used to transform Unisys from primarily a computer company to a full-service IT company. A major challenge was to change the culture through communications. Within three or four days after taking over as CEO, Weinbach sent a letter to customers and shareholders introducing himself and telling them that if they had any questions or concerns, to write to him and he would personally respond to them. Weinbach also hired a vice president of corporate communications, who reported directly to him.

As an outsider, Weinbach realized that the employees had lost some confidence in the company and themselves. To regain their confidence, he went on the road and talked to 12,000 employees, asking them to send him ideas to improve Unisys. Within six weeks, Weinbach received 4,500 e-mails, and he answered about 2,000 of them himself before the task became too difficult for him. He then developed "Ask Larry" on the intranet in order to respond to more generic questions, and he followed this with a monthly newsletter to all employees so that employees could feel like they were a part of what was going on in the company.

Weinbach transformed Unisys from a hierarchical flow of information to a more decentralized flow of authority and communications, in which the person with the information needed could be contacted. Having been in the service business, Weinbach knew that the key to success was first, getting people motivated and then ensuring that they were willing to follow where he wanted the company to go; that is, to follow his vision. Weinbach believed the vision had to be simple.

The vision of Unisys is illustrated through its "three-legged stool," which focuses on customers, employees, and reputation. All three values are equally important and each is represented by a leg; if any one is missing, the stool (Unisys) falls. In fact, all employees were given a three-legged-stool pin to remind them of the Unisys vision. Weinbach always wore the pin, and if anyone asked him what his vision for the company was, he just pointed to the pin.

Unisys managed to sign up Compaq Computer, Hewlett-Packard (HP), and Dell Computer to resell its breakthrough server, called the ES7000. However, a few years later they stopped selling it to focus on their own designs, and Unisys was struggling to make the leap from being a computer company to an e-business services company. Unisys was not competing effectively with IBM and HP IT services. It was losing money again, and Unisys replaced Weinbach with a new CEO; its current CEO is Joseph McGrath, who plans to step down at the end of 2008.[60] Unisys is still in the *Fortune 500* (number 400 in 2007).[61]

Rather than look for another job as CEO, Weinbach decided to start a business with his son Peter Weinbach—Yankee Hill (YH) Capital Management, with offices in Connecticut and New York. YH is a service industry specialists advisory and investment firm.

Go to the Internet: To learn more about Larry Weinbach and YH, visit their Web site **(http://www.yankeehillcapital.com)**, and to learn more about Unisys Corporation, visit its Web site **(http://www.unisys.com)**.

Support your answers to the following questions with specific information from the case and text or with other information you get from the Web or other sources.

1. Which major topic of this chapter (communication, feedback, coaching, conflict) was Weinbach's primary focus as he took over as CEO of Unisys?
2. Which communication method did CEO Weinbach use within his first few days, with customers and shareholders, and then with employees? Which method of communication did he primarily use with all three groups?
3. Was Weinbach's communication focus on sending or receiving messages?
4. How would you assess Weinbach's use of feedback?
5. Did Weinbach use coaching? If yes, how?
6. Using Exhibit 6.3 on page 202, "Coaching Guidelines," did Weinbach use each of the ten guidelines as a new CEO at Unisys? Be sure to explain your answers.
7. Did Weinbach use criticism or coaching feedback when he took over as CEO?
8. Which conflict management style did Weinbach use as CEO?
9. Weinbach got off to a good start, so what do you think led to his downfall?
10. What advice would you give to others to improve their communication skills? To come up with an answer, you may want to think about a person you know who is a very effective communicator. What makes that person successful?

CUMULATIVE CASE QUESTIONS

11. Which level of analysis and leadership paradigm are presented in this case, and did Weinbach use the management or leadership paradigm (Chapter 1)?
12. What do the Pygmalion effect and job satisfaction have to do with this case (Chapter 2)?
13. What role did Weinbach's leadership behavior and ability to motivate employees play in the Unisys turnaround (Chapter 3)?
14. Which one of the contingency leadership theories do you think Weinbach used as CEO (Chapter 5)?

CASE EXERCISE AND ROLE-PLAY

Preparation: An important part of getting ideas for improving Unisys comes from asking customers questions and then listening to them. Your role is an executive at Unisys. List some questions that you would ask customers to get ideas for improvement.

In-Class Groups: Break into groups of four to six members, and develop a list of questions to ask customers to get ideas for improving Unisys. Select a spokesperson to record the questions and then ask them of a customer in front of the class.

Role-Play: One person (representing him- or herself or a group) asks question of a customer to get ideas for improving Unisys.

VIDEO CASE

Communication at Navistar International

The decision to dedicate the resources needed to fund and support the Department of Communications within Navistar International sends a signal that corporate communication is seen as vital to the health of this $12 billion truck and engine manufacturing and financial services corporation. The Department of Communications functions as a business partner with the company's three major business units. Each plant has a communications manager who reports to both the plant manager and the corporate director of the Department of Communications. The role of the communications manager is to drive the message to the target audience. The manager uses different approaches depending on the audience and the direction of the message, whether it's heading up or down the corporate ladder or across business units.

1. Explain why the communication skills and techniques used within a business unit (department) are not always effective in communicating across business units or up and down the corporate ladder.
2. Explain why conflict resolution communication skills are not always present in everyday workplace situations and how a skilled communications professional would add value to that workplace.

Skill-Development Exercise 1

Giving Instructions

Doing Skill-Development Exercise 1 in Class

Objective

To develop your ability to give and receive messages (communication skills).

The primary AACSB learning standard skill developed through this exercise is communication abilities.

Preparation

No preparation is necessary except reading and understanding the chapter. The instructor will provide the original drawings that must be drawn.

Experience

You will plan, give, and receive instructions for completing a drawing of three objects.

Procedure 1 *(3–7 minutes)* Read all of procedure 1 twice. The task is for the manager to give an employee instructions for completing a drawing of four objects. The objects must be drawn to scale and look like photocopies of the originals. You will have up to 15 minutes to complete the task.

The exercise has four separate parts or steps:

1. The manager plans.
2. The manager gives the instructions.
3. The employee does the drawing.
4. Evaluation of the results takes place.

Rules: The rules are numbered to correlate with the four parts of the exercise.

1. *Planning.* While planning, the manager may write out instructions for the employee, but may not do any drawing of any kind.
2. *Instructions.* While giving instructions, the manager may not show the original drawing to the employee. (The instructor will give it to you.) The instructions may be given orally, and/or in writing, but no nonverbal hand gestures are allowed. The employee may take notes while the instructions are being given, but cannot do any drawing with or without a pen. The manager must give the instructions for all four objects before drawing begins.
3. *Drawing.* Once the employee begins the drawing, the manager should watch but no longer communicate in any way.
4. *Evaluation.* When the employee is finished or the time is up, the manager shows the employee the original drawing. Discuss how you did. Turn to the "Integration" section of this exercise, and answer the questions. The manager writes the answers, not the employee. The employee will write when playing the manager role.

Procedure 2 *(2–5 minutes)* Half of the class members will act as the manager first and give instructions. Managers move their seats to one of the four walls (spread out). They should be facing the center of the room with their backs close to the wall.

Employees sit in the middle of the room until called on by a manager. When called on, bring a seat to the manager. Sit facing the manager so that you cannot see any managers' drawing.

Procedure 3 *(Up to 15 minutes for drawing and integration)* The instructor gives each manager a copy of the drawing, being careful not to let any employees see it. The manager plans the instructions. When a manager is ready, she or he calls an employee and gives the instructions. It is helpful to use the message-sending process. Be sure to follow the rules. The employee should do the drawing on an 8½" by 11" sheet of paper, not in this book. If you use written instructions, they may be on the reverse side of the page that the employee draws on or on a different sheet of paper. You have up to 15 minutes to complete the drawing and about 5 minutes for integration (evaluation). When you finish the drawing, turn to the evaluation questions in the "Integration" section.

Procedure 4 *(Up to 15 minutes)* The employees are now the managers, and they sit in the seats facing the center of the room. New employees go to the center of the room until called for.

Follow procedure 3, with the instructor giving a different drawing. Do not work with the same person; change partners.

Integration

Evaluating Questions: You may select more than one answer. The manager and employee discuss each question; and the manager, not the employee, writes the answers to the questions.

1. The goal of communication was to:

   a. influence b. inform c. express feelings

2. The manager transmitted the message through __________ communication channel(s).

   a. oral b. written

   c. nonverbal d. combined

3. The manager spent __________ time planning.

   a. too much b. too little

   c. the right amount of

Questions 4 through 8 relate to the steps in the message-sending process.

4. The manager developed rapport. (Step 1)

   a. true b. false

5. The manager stated the communication objective. (Step 2)

   a. true b. false

6. The manager transmitted the message __________. (Step 3)

   a. effectively b. ineffectively

7. The manager checked understanding by using __________. (Step 4)

   a. direct questions b. paraphrasing

   c. both d. neither

   The amount of checking was __________.

   a. too frequent b. too infrequent

   c. about right

8. The manager got a commitment and followed up. (Step 5)

   a. true b. false

9. The employee did an __________ job of listening, an __________ job of analyzing, and an __________ job of checking understanding through the receiving message process.

   a. effective b. ineffective

10. When going over this integration, the manager was __________ and the employee was __________ to criticism that can help improve communication skills.

    a. open b. closed

11. Were the objects drawn to approximate scale (same size)? If not, why not?

12. Did you follow the rules? If not, why not?

13. If you could do this exercise again, what would you do differently to improve communications?

Conclusion

The instructor leads a class discussion and/or makes concluding remarks.

Apply It *(2–4 minutes)* What did I learn from this experience? How will I use this knowledge in the future? When will I practice?

Sharing

Volunteers may give their answers to the "Apply It" questions.

Behavior Model Skills Training 1

Session 1

In this behavior model skills training session, you will perform four activities:

1. Complete Self-Assessment 3 (to determine your preferred communication style).
2. Read "The Situational Communications Model."
3. Watch Behavior Model Video 6.1, "Situational Communications."
4. Complete Skill-Development Exercise 2 (to apply the model to various situations).

For practice, use the situational communications model in your personal and professional communication.

SELF-ASSESSMENT 3

Determining Your Preferred Communication Style

To determine your preferred communication style, select the one alternative that most closely describes what you would do in each of the 12 situations described. Do not be concerned with trying to pick the correct answer; select the alternative that best describes what you would actually do. Circle the letter a, b, c, or d.

For now, ignore these three types of lines:

- ____ 1. (before each number)
- _______ time _______ information
  _______ acceptance _______ capability
  _______ communication style
- S____ (following each letter)

They are explained later, and will be used during the in-class part of Skill-Development Exercise 2.

_____ 1. Wendy, a knowledgeable person from another department, comes to you, the engineering supervisor, and requests that you design a special product to her specifications. You would:

_______ time _______ information

_______ acceptance _______ capability

_______ communication style

a. Control the conversation and tell Wendy what you will do for her. S _____

b. Ask Wendy to describe the product. Once you understand it, you would present your ideas. Let her realize that you are concerned and want to help by offering your ideas. S _____

c. Respond to Wendy's request by conveying understanding and support. Help clarify what is to be done by you. Offer ideas, but do it her way. S _____

d. Find out what you need to know. Let Wendy know you will do it her way. S _____

_____ 2. Your department has designed a product that is to be fabricated by Saul's department. Saul has been with the company longer than you have; he knows his department. Saul comes to you to change the product design. You decide to:

_______ time _______ information

_______ acceptance _______ capability

_______ communication style

a. Listen to the change and why it would be beneficial. If you believe Saul's way is better, change it; if not, explain why the original design is superior. If necessary, insist that it be done your way. S _____

b. Tell Saul to fabricate it any way he wants to. S _____

c. You are busy; tell Saul to do it your way. You don't have time to listen and argue with him. S _____

d. Be supportive; make changes together as a team. S _____

_____ 3. Upper management has a decision to make. They call you to a meeting and tell you they need some information to solve a problem they describe to you. You:

_______ time _______ information

_______ acceptance _______ capability

_______ communication style

continued

(Self-Assessment 3 continued)

a. Respond in a manner that conveys personal support and offer alternative ways to solve the problem. S _____

b. Just answer their questions. S _____

c. Explain how to solve the problem. S _____

d. Show your concern by explaining how to solve the problem and why it is an effective solution. S _____

_____ 4. You have a routine work order. The work order is to be placed verbally and completed in three days. Sue, the receiver, is very experienced and willing to be of service to you. You decide to:

_______ time _______ information

_______ acceptance _______ capability

_______ communication style

a. Explain your needs, but let Sue make the order decision. S _____

b. Tell Sue what you want and why you need it. S _____

c. Decide together what to order. S _____

d. Simply give Sue the order. S _____

_____ 5. Work orders from the staff department normally take three days; however, you have an emergency and need the job today. Your colleague Jim, the department supervisor, is knowledgeable and somewhat cooperative. You decide to:

_______ time _______ information

_______ acceptance _______ capability

_______ communication style

a. Tell Jim that you need it by three o'clock and will return at that time to pick it up. S _____

b. Explain the situation and how the organization will benefit by expediting the order. Volunteer to help in any way you can. S _____

c. Explain the situation and ask Jim when the order will be ready. S _____

d. Explain the situation and together come to a solution to your problem. S _____

_____ 6. Danielle, a peer with a record of high performance, has recently had a drop in productivity. Her problem is affecting your performance. You know Danielle has a family problem. You:

_______ time _______ information

_______ acceptance _______ capability

_______ communication style

a. Discuss the problem; help Danielle realize the problem is affecting her work and yours. Supportively discuss ways to improve the situation. S _____

b. Tell the manager about it and let him decide what to do about it. S _____

c. Tell Danielle to get back on the job. S _____

d. Discuss the problem and tell Danielle how to solve the work situation; be supportive. S _____

_____ 7. You are a knowledgeable supervisor. You buy supplies from Peter regularly. He is an excellent salesperson and very knowledgeable about your situation. You are placing your weekly order. You decide to:

_______ time _______ information

_______ acceptance _______ capability

_______ communication style

a. Explain what you want and why. Develop a supportive relationship. S _____

b. Explain what you want, and ask Peter to recommend products. S _____

c. Give Peter the order. S _____

d. Explain your situation and allow Peter to make the order. S _____

_____ 8. Jean, a knowledgeable person from another department, has asked you to perform a routine staff function to her specifications. You decide to:

_______ time _______ information

_______ acceptance _______ capability

_______ communication style

a. Perform the task to her specifications without questioning her. S _____

b. Tell her that you will do it the usual way. S _____

c. Explain what you will do and why. S _____

d. Show your willingness to help; offer alternative ways to do it. S _____

continued

(Self-Assessment 3 continued)

_____ 9. Tom, a salesperson, has requested an order for your department's services with a short delivery date. As usual, Tom claims it is a take-it-or-leave-it offer. He wants your decision now, or within a few minutes, because he is in the customer's office. Your action is to:

________ time ________ information

________ acceptance ________ capability

________ communication style

a. Convince Tom to work together to come up with a later date. S _____

b. Give Tom a yes or no answer. S _____

c. Explain your situation, and let Tom decide if you should take the order. S _____

d. Offer an alternative delivery date. Work on your relationship; show your support. S _____

_____ 10. As a time-and-motion expert, you have been called regarding a complaint about the standard time it takes to perform a job. As you analyze the entire job, you realize that one element of the job should take longer, but other elements should take less time. The end result is a shorter total standard time for the job. You decide to:

________ time ________ information

________ acceptance ________ capability

________ communication style

a. Tell the operator and foreman that the total time must be decreased and why. S _____

b. Agree with the operator and increase the standard time. S _____

c. Explain your findings. Deal with the operator and/or foreman's concerns, but ensure compliance with your new standard. S _____

d. Together with the operator, develop a standard time. S _____

_____ 11. You approve budget allocations for projects. Marie, who is very competent in developing budgets, has come to you. You:

________ time ________ information

________ acceptance ________ capability

________ communication style

a. Review the budget, make revisions, and explain them in a supportive way. Deal with concerns, but insist on your changes. S _____

b. Review the proposal and suggest areas where changes may be needed. Make changes together, if needed. S _____

c. Review the proposed budget, make revisions, and explain them. S _____

d. Answer any questions or concerns Marie has and approve the budget as is. S _____

_____ 12. You are a sales manager. A customer has offered you a contract for your product, but the contract has a short delivery date—only two days. The contract would be profitable for you and the organization. The cooperation of the production department is essential to meet the deadline. Tim, the production manager, and you do not get along very well because of your repeated request for quick delivery. Your action is to:

________ time ________ information

________ acceptance ________ capability

________ communication style

a. Contact Tim and try to work together to complete the contract. S _____

b. Accept the contract and convince Tim in a supportive way to meet the obligation. S _____

c. Contact Tim and explain the situation. Ask him if he and you should accept the contract, but let him decide. S _____

d. Accept the contract. Contact Tim and tell him to meet the obligation. If he resists, tell him you will go to his manager. S _____

To determine your preferred communication style: (1) Circle the letter you selected as the alternative you chose in situations 1 through 12. The column headings indicate the style you selected. (2) Add up the number of circled items per column. The total for all the columns should not be more than 12. The column with the highest number represents your preferred communication style. There is no one best style in all situations. The more evenly distributed the numbers are between the four styles, the more flexible are your communications. A total of 0 or 1 in any column may indicate a reluctance to use the style(s). You could have problems in situations calling for the use of this style.

continued

(Self-Assessment 3 continued)

	Autocratic (S1A)	Consultative (S2C)	Participative (S3P)	Empowerment (S4E)
1.	a	b	c	d
2.	c	a	d	b
3.	c	d	a	b
4.	d	b	c	a
5.	a	b	d	c
6.	c	d	a	b
7.	c	a	b	d
8.	b	c	d	a
9.	b	d	a	c
10.	a	c	d	b
11.	c	a	b	d
12.	d	b	a	c
	Totals			

The Situational Communications Model

The Interactive Process System

Communication has the following five dimensions, which are each on a continuum:

Initiation______________________________Response

- *Initiation.* The sender starts, or initiates, the communication. The sender may or may not expect a response to the initiated message.
- *Response.* The receiver's reply or action to the sender's message. In responding, the receiver can become an initiator. As two-way communication takes place, the role of initiator (sender) and responder (receiver) may change.

Presentation______________________________Elicitation

- *Presentation.* The sender's message is structured, directive, or informative. A response may not be needed, although action may be called for. ("We are meeting to develop next year's budget." "Please open the door.")
- *Elicitation.* The sender invites a response to the message. Action may or may not be needed. ("How large a budget do we need?" "Do you think we should leave the door open?")

Closed______________________________Open

- *Closed.* The sender expects the receiver to follow the message. ("This is a new form to fill out and return with each order.")
- *Open.* The sender is eliciting a response as a means of considering the receiver's input. ("Should we use this new form with each order?")

Rejection______________________________Acceptance

- *Rejection.* The receiver does not accept the sender's message. ("I will not fill out this new form for each order!")
- *Acceptance.* The receiver agrees with the sender's message. ("I will fill out the new form for each order!")

Strong______________________________Mild

- *Strong.* The sender will use force or power to have the message acted upon as directed. ("Fill in the form or you're fired.")
- *Mild.* The sender will not use force or power to have the message acted upon as directed. ("Please fill in the form when you can.")

Situational Communication Styles

Following is the interactive process. Acceptance or rejection can come from any of the styles because, to a large extent, it is out of the sender's control.

***The Autocratic Communication Style* (S1A).** This style demonstrates high task/low relationship behavior (HT-LR), initiating a closed presentation. The other party has little, if any, information and is low in capability.

- *Initiation/Response.* You initiate and control the communication with minimal, if any, response.
- *Presentation/Elicitation.* You make a presentation letting the other parties know they are expected to comply with your message; there is little, if any, elicitation.
- *Closed/Open.* You use a closed presentation; you will not consider the receiver's input.

The Consultative Communication Style **(S2C)** This style demonstrates high task/high relationship behavior (HT-HR), using a closed presentation for the task with an open elicitation for the relationship. The other party has moderate information and capability.

- *Initiation/Response.* You initiate the communication by letting the other party know that you want him or her to buy into your influence. You desire some response.
- *Presentation/Elicitation.* Both are used. You use elicitation to determine the goal of the communication. For example, you may ask questions to determine the situation and follow up with a presentation. When the communication goal is known, little task elicitation is needed. Relationship communication is elicited in order to determine the interest of the other party and acceptance of the message. The open elicitation should show your concern for the other party's point of view and motivate him or her to follow your influence.
- *Closed/Open.* You are closed to having the message accepted (task), but open to the person's feelings (relationship). Be empathetic.

The Participative Communication Style **(S3P)** This style demonstrates low task/high relationship behavior (LT-HR), responding with open elicitation, some initiation, and little presentation. The other party is high in information and capability.

- *Initiation/Response.* You respond with some initiation. You want to help the other party solve a problem or get him or her to help you solve one. You are helpful and convey personal support.
- *Presentation/Elicitation.* Elicitation can occur with little presentation. Your role is to elicit the other party's ideas on how to reach objectives.
- *Closed/Open.* Open communication is used. If you participate well, the other party will come to a solution you can accept. If not, you may have to reject the other party's message.

The Empowerment Communication Style **(S4E)** This style demonstrates low task/low relationship behavior (LT-LR), responding with the necessary open presentation. The other party is outstanding in information and capability.

- *Initiation/Response.* You respond to the other party with little, if any, initiation.
- *Presentation/Elicitation.* You present the other party with information, structure, and so forth, which the sender wants.
- *Closed/Open.* Open, you convey that the other party is in charge; you will accept the message.

Situational Variables

When selecting the appropriate communication style, you should consider four variables: time, information, acceptance, and capability. Answering the questions related to each of these variables can help you select the appropriate style for the situation.

Time. Do I have enough time to use two-way communication—yes or no? When there is no time, the other three variables are not considered; the autocratic style is appropriate. When time is available, any of the other styles may be appropriate, depending on the other variables. Time is a relative term; in one situation, a few minutes may be considered a short time—in another situation, a month may be a short time.

Information. Do I have the necessary information to communicate my message, make a decision, or take action? When you have all the information you need, the autocratic style may be appropriate. When you have some of the information, the consultative style may be appropriate. When you have little information, the participative or empowerment style may be appropriate.

Acceptance. Will the other party accept my message without any input? If the receiver will accept the message, the autocratic style may be appropriate. If the receiver will be reluctant to accept it, the consultative style may be appropriate. If the receiver will reject the message, the participative or empowerment style may be appropriate to gain acceptance. There are situations in which acceptance is critical to success, such as in the area of implementing changes.

Capability. Capability has two parts. *Ability:* Does the other party have the experience or knowledge to participate in two-way communications? Will the receiver put the organization's goals ahead of personal needs or goals? *Motivation:* Does the other party want to participate? When the other party is low in capability, the autocratic style may be appropriate; moderate in capability, the consultative style may be appropriate; high in capability, the participative style may be appropriate; outstanding in capability, the empowerment style may be appropriate. In addition, capability levels can change from one task to another. For example, a professor may have outstanding capability in classroom teaching but be low in capability for advising students.

Selecting Communication Styles

Successful managers rely on different communication styles according to the situation. There are three steps to follow when selecting the appropriate communication style in a given situation. After reading these steps and looking at Model 6.6, you will get to practice this selection process in the section, "Determining the Appropriate Communications Style for Situation 1."

Step 1. Diagnose the situation. Answer the questions for each of the four situational variables (time, information, acceptance, and capability). In Self-Assessment 3 at the beginning of this training session, you were asked to select an alternative to 12 situations. You were told to ignore certain lines. When completing the in-class part of Skill-Development Exercise 2, you will place the style letters (S1A, S2C, S3P, S4E) on the lines provided for each of the 12 situations.

Step 2. Select the appropriate communication style for the situation. After analyzing the four variables, you select the appropriate communication style for the situation. In some situations, variables may have conflicting styles; you should select the style of the most important variable for the situation. For example, capability may be outstanding (S4E) but you have all the information needed (S1A). If the information is more important, use the autocratic style even though the capability is outstanding. When doing the in-class part of Skill-Development Exercise 2, place the letters (S1A, S2C, S3P, S4E) for the appropriate communication styles on the style lines (S _____).

Step 3. Use the appropriate communication style for the situation. During the in-class part of Skill-Development Exercise 2, you will identify one of the four communication styles for each alternative action; place the S1A, S2C, S3P, or S4E on the S _____ lines. Select the alternative (a, b, c, or d) that represents the appropriate communication style for each of the 12 situations, and place it on the line before the number of the situation.

Model 6.6 summarizes the material in this preparation for the exercise. Use it to determine the appropriate communication style in situation 1 and during the in-class part of Skill-Development Exercise 2.

Determining the Appropriate Communication Style for Situation 1

Step 1. Diagnose the situation. Answer the four variable questions from the model, and place the letters on the four variable lines for situation 1.

____ 1. Wendy, a knowledgeable person from another department, comes to you, the engineering supervisor, and requests that you design a special product to her specifications. You would:

____ time ____ information

____ acceptance ____ capability

____ communication style

a. Control the conversation and tell Wendy what you will do for her. S _____

b. Ask Wendy to describe the product. Once you understand it, you would present your ideas. Let her realize that you are concerned and want to help by offering your ideas. S _____

MODEL 6.6 Situational Communication

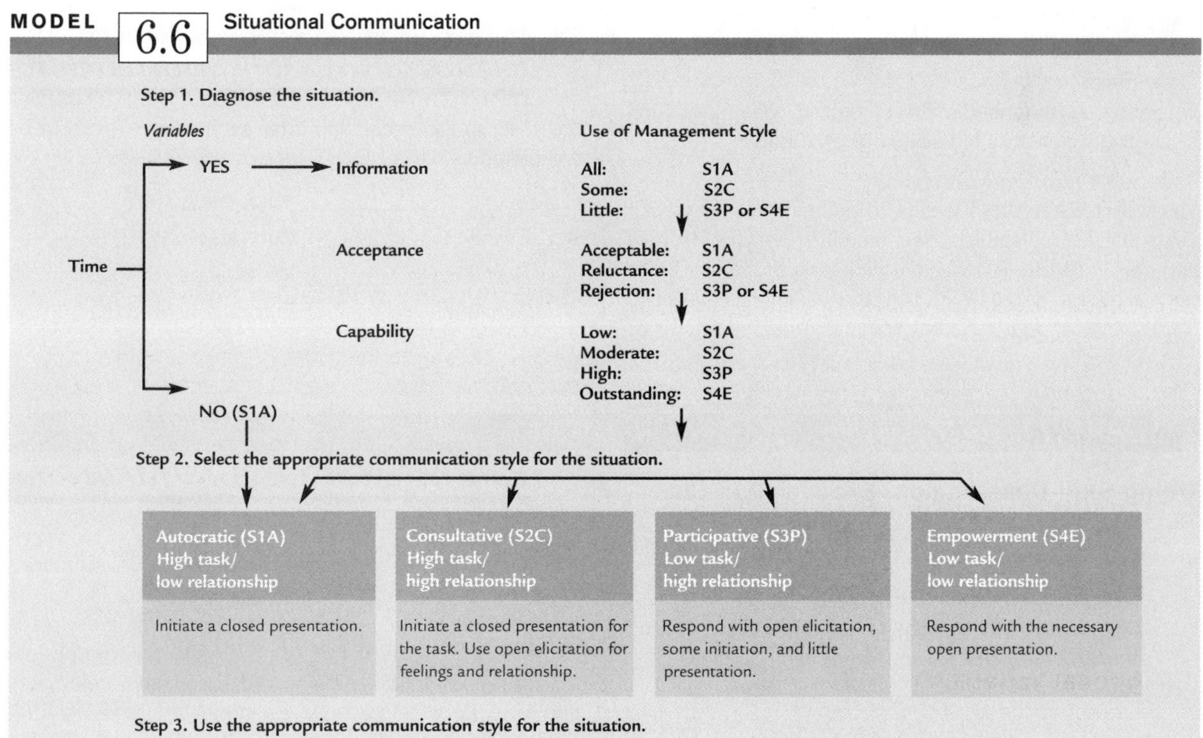

c. Respond to Wendy's request by conveying understanding and support. Help clarify what is to be done by you. Offer ideas, but do it her way. S _____

d. Find out what you need to know. Let Wendy know you will do it her way. S _____

Step 2. Select the appropriate communication style for the situation. Review the four variables. If they are all consistent, select one style. If they are conflicting, select the most important variable as the style to use. Place its letters (S1A, S2C, S3P, or S4E) on the style line.

Step 3. Use the appropriate communication style for the situation. Review the four alternative actions. Identify the communication style for each, placing its letters on the S _____ line, then place the appropriate match (a, b, c, d) on the line before the number.

Let's See How You Did

1. *Time:* Time is available (or yes, you have time); it can be any style. *Information:* You have little information, so you need to use a participative or empowerment style to find out what Wendy wants done (S3P or S4E). *Acceptance:* If you try to do it your way rather than Wendy's way, she will most likely reject it. You need to use a participative or empowerment style (S3P or S4E). *Capability:* Wendy is knowledgeable and has a high level of capability (S3P).
2. Reviewing the four variables, you see that there is a mixture of S3P and S4E. Because you are an engineer, it is appropriate to participate with Wendy to give her what she needs. Therefore, the choice is S3P.
3. Alternative (a) is S1A; this is the autocratic style, high task/low relationship. Alternative (b) is S2C; this is the consultative style, high task/high relationship. Alternative (c) is S3P; this is the participative style, low task/high relationship. Alternative (d) is S4E; this is empowerment style, low task/low relationship behavior. If you selected (c) as your action, you chose the most appropriate action for the situation. This was a three-point answer. If you selected (d) as your answer, this is also a good alternative; it scores two points. If you selected (b), you get one point for overdirecting. If you selected (a), you get zero points; this is too much directing and will most likely hurt communications.

The better you match your communication style to the situation, the more effective you will be at communicating. In the in-class part of Skill-Development Exercise 3, you will apply the model to the other 11 situations in Self-Assessment 3 to develop your ability to communicate as a situational communicator.

Behavior Model Video 6.1

Situational Communications

Objectives

To better understand the four situational communication styles and which style to use in a given situation.

Video *(12 minutes)* Overview

You will first listen to a lecture to understand how to use the situational communications model. Then, you will view two managers, Steve and Darius, meeting to discuss faulty parts. You are asked to identify the communication style Darius uses in four different scenes. Write the letters of the style on the scene line after each scene. This may be completed as part of Skill-Development Exercise 2.

Scene 1. ________	Autocratic (S1A)
Scene 2. ________	Consultative (S2C)
Scene 3. ________	Participative (S3P)
Scene 4. ________	Empowerment (S4E)

Skill-Development Exercise 2

Situational Communications

Doing Skill-Development Exercise 2 in Class

Objectives

To develop your ability to communicate using the appropriate style for the situation.

The primary AACSB learning standard skill developed through this exercise is communication abilities.

Preparation

You should have competed Self-Assessment 3, and finished the reading about situational communications. You may also want to view Behavior Model Video 6.1.

Experience

You will select the appropriate style for the 12 situations in Self-Assessment 3. On the *time* line, place Y (yes); on the *information*, *acceptance*, and *capability* lines, place the letters S1A, S2C, S3P, or S4E that are appropriate for the situation. Based on your diagnoses, select the one style you would use by placing its letters (S1A, S2C, S3P, or S4E) on the *communication style* line. On the four *S* lines, write the letters S1A, S2C, S3P, or S4E to identify each style being used. Place the letter a, b, c, or d on the line before the exercise number that represents the most appropriate communication style for the situation.

Procedure 1 *(10–20 minutes)* The instructor shows the video and then reviews the situational communications model, explaining how to apply it to determine the appropriate style for situation 2.

Procedure 2 *(4–8 minutes)* Students, working alone, complete situation 3 of Self-Assessment 3 using the model. The instructor then goes over the recommended answers.

Procedure 3 *(20–50 minutes)*

A. Break into groups of two or three. As a team, apply the model to situations 4 through 8. The instructor will go over the appropriate answers when all teams are finished, or the time is up.

B. Break into new groups of two or three and do situations 9 through 12. The instructor will go over the appropriate answers.

Conclusion

The instructor leads a class discussion and/or makes concluding remarks.

Apply It *(2–4 minutes)* What did I learn from this experience? How will I use this knowledge in the future? When will I practice using the model?

Sharing

In the group, or to the entire class, volunteers may give their answers to the "Apply It" questions.

Behavior Model Skills Training 2

Session 2

In this behavior model skills training session, you will perform three activities:

1. Read "Improving Performance with the Coaching Model" on pages 208–209 (to review how to use the model).
2. Watch Behavior Model Video 6.2, "Coaching."
3. Complete Skill-Development Exercise 3 (to develop your coaching skills).

For further practice, use the coaching model in your personal and professional life.

The Coaching Model

In the text, on pages 208–209, read about the coaching model and review Model 6.4.

Behavior Model Video 6.2

Coaching

Objective

To assist you in coaching to improve performance of employees who are not performing to standard.

Video *(3½ minutes)* **Overview**

You will watch a Web development manager coach an employee who has missed deadlines for completing Web sites.

Skill-Development Exercise 3

Coaching

Preparing for Skill-Development Exercise 3

You should have read and understood the text material on coaching. You may also view Behavior Model Video 6.2.

Doing Skill-Development Exercise 3 in Class

Objective

To develop your skill at improving performance through coaching.

The primary AACSB learning standard skill developed through this exercise is leadership.

Experience

You will coach, be coached, and be observed coaching using Model 6.4 from the text.

Procedure 1 *(2–4 minutes)* Break into groups of three. Make some groups of two, if necessary. Each member selects one of the following three situations in which to be the manager, and a different one in which to be the employee. In each situation, the employee knows the standing plans, but is not motivated to follow them. You will take turns coaching and being coached.

Three Employee-Coaching Situations

1. *Employee 1 is a clerical worker.* The person uses files, as do the other ten employees in the department. The employees all know that they are supposed to return the files when they are finished so that others can find the files when they need them. Employees should have only one file out at a time. The supervisor notices that employee 1 has five files on the desk, and another employee is looking for one of them. The supervisor thinks that employee 1 will complain about the heavy workload as an excuse for having more than one file out at a time.
2. *Employee 2 is a server in an ice cream shop.* The person knows that the tables should be cleaned up quickly after customers leave so that new customers do not have to sit at dirty tables. It's a busy night. The supervisor finds dirty dishes on two of this employee's occupied tables. Employee 2 is socializing with some friends at one of the tables. Employees are supposed to be friendly; employee 2 will probably use this as an excuse for the dirty tables.
3. *Employee 3 is an auto technician.* All employees at the garage where this person works know that they are supposed to put a paper mat on the floor of each car so that the carpets don't get dirty. When the service supervisor got into a car repaired by employee 3, the car did not have a mat and there was grease on the carpet. Employee 3 does excellent work and will probably mention this fact when coached.

Procedure 2 *(3–7 minutes)* Prepare for coaching to improve performance. On the following lines, each group member writes an outline of what he or she will say when coaching employee 1, 2, or 3, following the coaching steps listed:

1. Describe current performance. ______________________

____

____

2. Describe the desired behavior. ______________________

____

____

3. Get a commitment to the change. ______________________

____

____

4. Follow up. ______________________

____

____

Procedure 3 *(5–8 minutes)*

A. Role-playing. The manager of employee 1, the clerical worker, coaches him or her as planned. (Use the actual name of the group member playing employee 1. Talk—do not read your written plan.) Employee 1, put yourself in the worker's position. You work hard; there is a lot of pressure to work fast. It's easier when you have more than one file. Refer to the workload while being coached. Both the manager and the employee will have to improvise their roles.

The person not playing a role is the observer. He or she takes notes using the observer form. Try to make positive coaching feedback comments for improvement. Give the manager alternative suggestions for what he or she could have said to improve the coaching session.

Observer Form

1. How well did the manager describe current behavior?

____

____

____

2. How well did the manager describe desired behavior?

____

____

____

3. How successful was the manager at getting a commitment to the change? Do you think the employee would change?

____

____

____

4. How well did the manager describe how he or she was going to follow up to ensure that the employee performed the desired behavior?

____

____

____

B. Feedback. The observer leads a discussion on how well the manager coached the employee. (This should be a coaching discussion, not a lecture.) Focus on what the manager did well, and on how the manager could improve. The employee should also give feedback on how he or she felt, and what might have been more effective in getting him or her to change.

Do not go on to the next interview until you are told to do so. If you finish early, wait for the others to finish.

Procedure 4 *(5–8 minutes)* Same as procedure 3, but change roles so that employee 2, the server, is coached. Employee 2 should make a comment about the importance of talking to customers to make them feel welcome. The job is not much fun if you can't talk to your friends.

Procedure 5 *(5–8 minutes)* Same as procedure 3, but change roles so that employee 3, the auto technician, is coached. Employee 3 should comment on the excellent work he or she does.

Conclusion

The instructor leads a class discussion and makes concluding remarks.

Apply It *(2–4 minutes)* What did I learn from this experience? How will I use this knowledge in the future? When will I practice?

Sharing

In the group, or to the entire class, volunteers may give their answers to the "Apply It" questions.

Behavior Model Skills Training 3

Session 3

In this behavior model skills training session, you will perform three activities:

1. Read "Initiating Conflict Resolution" on pages 215–217 (to review how to use the model).
2. Watch Behavior Model Video 6.3, "Initiating Conflict Resolution."
3. Complete Skill-Development Exercise 4 (to develop your conflict resolution skills).

For further practice, use the conflict resolution model in your personal and professional life.

The Initiating Conflict Resolution Model 6.5

In the text, on pages 215–217, read the initiating conflict resolution model and review Model 6.5.

Behavior Model Video 6.3

Initiating Conflict Resolution

Objective

To assist you in resolving conflicts.

Video ***(4½ minutes)*** **Overview**

You will watch an advertising agency's employees. Alex initiates a conflict resolution with Catherine to resolve a conflict over a client.

Skill-Development Exercise 4

Initiating Conflict Resolution

Preparing for Skill-Development Exercise 4

During class you will be given the opportunity to role-play a conflict you face, or have faced, in order to develop your conflict skills. Students and workers have reported that this exercise helped prepare them for a successful initiation of a conflict resolution with roommates and coworkers. Fill in the following information.

Other party(ies) (You may use fictitious names.)

Describe the conflict situation:

List pertinent information about the other party (i.e., relationship with you, knowledge of the situation, age, background, and so on).

Identify the other party's possible reaction to your confrontation. (How receptive will they be to collaborating? What might they say or do during the discussion to resist change?)

How will you overcome this resistance to change?

Following the initiating conflict resolution model steps, write out your planned opening BCF statement that maintains ownership of the problem.

Doing Skill-Development Exercise 4 in Class

Objective

To experience and develop skills in resolving a conflict.

The primary AACSB learning standard skill developed through this exercise is communication abilities.

Preparation

You should have completed the questionnaire in "Preparing for Skill-Development Exercise 4."

Experience

You will initiate, respond to, and observe a conflict role-play, and then evaluate the effectiveness of its resolution.

Procedure 1 *(2–3 minutes)* Break into as many groups of three as possible. If there are any people not in a triad, make one or two groups of two. Each member selects the number 1, 2, or 3. Number 1 will be the first to initiate a conflict role-play, then 2, followed by 3.

Procedure 2 *(8–15 minutes)*

A. Initiator number 1 gives his or her information from the preparation to number 2 (the responder) to read. Once number 2 understands, proceed with role-play (see item B). Number 3 is the observer.

B. Role-play the conflict resolution. Number 3, the observer, writes his or her observations on the feedback form at the end of this exercise.

C. Integration. When the role-play is over, the observer leads a discussion on the effectiveness of the conflict resolution. All three should discuss the effectiveness. Number 3 is not a lecturer. Do not go on until told to do so.

Procedure 3 *(8–15 minutes)* Same as procedure 2, only number 2 is now the initiator, number 3 is the responder, and number 1 is the observer.

Procedure 4 *(8–15 minutes)* Same as procedure 2, only number 3 is the initiator, number 1 is the responder, and number 2 is the observer.

Conclusion

The instructor leads a class discussion and/or makes concluding remarks.

Apply It *(2–4 minutes)* What did I learn from this experience? How will I use this knowledge in the future? When will I practice?

Sharing

In the group, or to the entire class, volunteers may give their answers to the "Apply It" questions.

Feedback Form

Try to have positive coaching improvement feedback comments for each step in initiating conflict resolution. Remember to be *specific* and *descriptive*, and for all improvements have an alternative positive behavior (APB). (For example: "If you would have said/done…, it would have improved the conflict resolution by…")

Initiating Conflict Resolution Model Steps

Step 1. Plan a BCF statement that maintains ownership of the problem. (Did the initiator have a well-planned, effective BCF statement?)

Step 2. Present your BCF statement and agree on the conflict. (Did the initiator present the BCF statement effectively? Did the two agree on the conflict?)

Step 3. Ask for, and/or give, alternative conflict resolutions. (Who suggested alternative solutions? Was it done effectively?)

Step 4. Make an agreement for change. (Was there an agreement for change?)

Behavior Model Video 6.4

Mediating Conflict Resolution

Objective

To view the process of mediating a conflict resolution between employees.

Video *(6½ minutes)* Overview

This is a follow-up to the advertising agency conflict (Video 6.3). The two employees end up in conflict again. Their manager, Peter, brings them together to resolve the conflict by following the steps in "Mediating Conflict Resolution" on pages 217–218 (Model 6.5 in text).

Note: There is no skill-development exercise.

7

Leader–Follower Relations

Chapter Outline

Evolution of the Dyadic Theory
Vertical Dyadic Linkage (VDL) Theory
Leader–Member Exchange (LMX) Theory
Team Building
Systems and Networks

Leader–Member Exchange Theory
The Influence of LMX on Follower Behavior
The Three-Stage Process for Developing Positive LMX Relations
Factors that Determine LMX Quality
Effective Leader–Follower Feedback
Limitations of LMX Theory Application
Bias in LMX: Employee Career Implications

Followership
The Effective Follower, and Follower Types
Guidelines to Becoming an Effective Follower
Determinants of Follower Influence
Dual Role of Being a Leader and a Follower

Delegation
Delegating
Delegation Decisions
Delegating with the Use of a Model

Learning Outcomes

After studying this chapter, you should be able to:

1. List the four stages of development of the dyadic approach. p. 240
2. Define the two kinds of relationships that can occur among leaders and followers under the vertical dyadic linkage model. p. 241
3. Describe the main focus of team building from a Leader–Follower perspective. p. 244
4. Discuss the focus of the systems and networks approach from a Leader–Follower perspective. p. 245
5. Describe three determining factors of high-quality LMX relationships. p. 250
6. Discuss the key limitation or drawback with LMX application. p. 252
7. Explain the cycle that leads to the Pygmalion effect. p. 254
8. Explain how LMX relationships can lead to unintended bias in HR practices. p. 254
9. Discuss the three follower influencing characteristics. p. 261
10. List five things a leader should delegate. p. 265
11. Define the following **key terms** (in order of appearance in the chapter):

dyadic	followership
dyadic theory	follower
vertical dyadic linkage (VDL) theory	alienated follower
in-group	conformist follower
out-group	passive follower
leader–member exchange (LMX)	effective follower
impressions management	pragmatic follower
ingratiation	locus of control
self-promotion	delegation
	delegation model

Opening Case APPLICATION

Lakewood Church is the largest and fastest-growing church in America today. The leader of the church is Pastor Joel Osteen. He is one of a new generation of evangelical entrepreneurs/leaders who has transformed his church into a mega-empire using smart marketing tools traditionally employed by for-profit organizations.[1] The highly diverse, nondenominational church he inherited from his late father in 1999 has more than quadrupled in size, welcoming upward of 40,000 visitors a week.

A youthful-looking, forty-something-year-old with a ready smile, Osteen is media savvy and knows how to use technology to reach his followers. Osteen's relationship with his followers and his approach to delivering the message is anything but conventional. He does not yell or cry for sinners to repent. He preaches a positive, upbeat gospel of hope and prosperity. Almost immediately, Osteen is able to win the trust of those who hear him. As Mr. Osteen himself puts it, "I don't condemn and I don't believe in being judgmental."[2] Osteen believes that encouraging and lifting people's spirits will gain their respect, admiration, and loyalty—a message that business leaders can apply with their employees, customers, or colleagues.

Joel Osteen's services are surprisingly intimate considering the size of the congregation. People who need a special prayer are invited up front to counsel with a "prayer partner"—who could be a member of the Osteen family and leadership team or a volunteer trained for the job. These dyadic relationships allow for meaningful exchanges between church leaders and followers. The church service and the meet-and-greet are the only opportunities Osteen's followers have to get close to him personally. Unlike his father, Osteen does not perform weddings or funerals. He avoids sickbeds and does not do personal counseling. He has delegated these tasks to his assistants. Members seem to be fine with the arrangement.[3]

Music and entertainment are a big part of Joel Osteen's service. Many have criticized him for reducing the serious business of preaching biblical doctrine to simply putting on a show. Yet, Osteen's popularity continues to grow. He has been featured on *60 Minutes, Larry King Live, Good Morning America,* and other major network shows as well as in countless magazine and newspaper articles.

Opening Case Questions:

1. Explain the dyadic relationship between Pastor Osteen and his followers and how this affects the way he is perceived.
2. What leadership action/decision by Pastor Osteen might create in-groups and out-groups at Lakewood Church?
3. What leadership qualities does Pastor Osteen possess, and how have those qualities affected the level of teamwork between church leaders and followers?
4. Describe the quality of the LMX relationship between Osteen and his leadership team and how this has in turn influenced their ability to counsel and minister to church members.
5. If there were some concerns that Osteen's staff/ministers were not meeting the needs of church members in the one-on-one counseling sessions, how should Pastor Osteen conduct an effective feedback session to ensure greater success?

Can you answer any of these questions? You'll find answers to these questions and learn more about Pastor Osteen and his leadership at the Lakewood Church throughout the chapter.

To learn more about Pastor Osteen and the Lakewood Church, visit the church's Web site at **http://www.lakewood.cc**.

In this chapter, you will explore the intricate nature of dyadic relationships. We will discuss the evolution of dyadic theory, including the vertical dyadic linkage (VDL) theory and leader–member exchange (LMX) theory. Then we will turn our attention to followership, an often ignored but relevant component of effective leadership. The last section of the chapter covers delegation, including a model that can help you develop your delegation skills.

Evolution of the Dyadic Theory

Most of the early theory and research on leadership has focused on leaders and not paid much attention to followers. However, it is evident that good or effective leadership is in part due to good relationships between leaders and followers. Relationship-based approaches to leadership theory have been in development over the past 25 years, and they continue to evolve. Each unique association between a leader and a follower is called a *dyad.* For our purposes, **dyadic** *refers to the individualized relationship between a leader and each follower in a work unit.* Dyadic theorists focus on the development and effects of separate dyadic relationships between leaders and followers. **Dyadic theory** *is an approach to leadership that attempts to explain why leaders vary their behavior with different followers.*

The dyadic approach concentrates on the heterogeneity of dyadic relationships, arguing that a single leader will form different relationships with different followers. For instance, if we were to sample the opinions of different followers about one leader, they would reveal different dyadic relationships. One group of followers may characterize their relationship with the leader in positive terms, while another group characterizes their relationship with the same leader in negative terms. A central theme in dyadic leadership is the notion of "support for self-worth" that leaders provide to followers, and the return performance that followers provide to leaders. Support for self-worth is defined as a leader's support for a follower's actions and ideas; building the follower's confidence in his or her ability, integrity, and motivation; and paying attention to the follower's feelings and needs.

Opening Case APPLICATION

1. Explain the dyadic relationship between Pastor Osteen and his followers and how this affects the way he is perceived.

The nature of the dyadic relationship between Pastor Osteen and his followers will influence how he treats each member. The inner circle consists of the Osteen family and a team of 4,000 volunteers. Also, Pastor Osteen is very close with the music director and the songwriter, two individuals who are instrumental in setting the mood prior to Pastor Osteen's grand appearance during each service. There is no evidence that he treats the members of his inner circle of leadership differently than other members of the church. Because of Osteen's charismatic personality, each church member feels like he or she has a positive, one-on-one relationship with him. This feeling could be part of the reason why the church is experiencing such phenomenal growth.

Learning Outcome 1 *List the four stages of development of the dyadic approach.*

As shown in Exhibit 7.1, the four stages of evolution in the dyadic approach are vertical dyadic linkage theory (VDL), leader–member exchange theory (LMX), team building, and systems and networks theory. The first evolutionary stage (VDL) is the awareness of a relationship between a leader and a follower, rather than between a leader and a group of followers. The second stage (LMX) proposes that the quality of the relationship between a leader and a follower is an important determinant of how each follower will be treated. The third stage (team building) explores the relationship between the leader and the followers as a team concept rather than as a dyad, and the fourth stage (systems and networks) examines relationships at a much broader scale involving multiple levels and structural units within the organization. The four evolutionary stages of dyadic theory are presented separately.

EXHIBIT 7.1 Dyadic Approach: Stages of Development

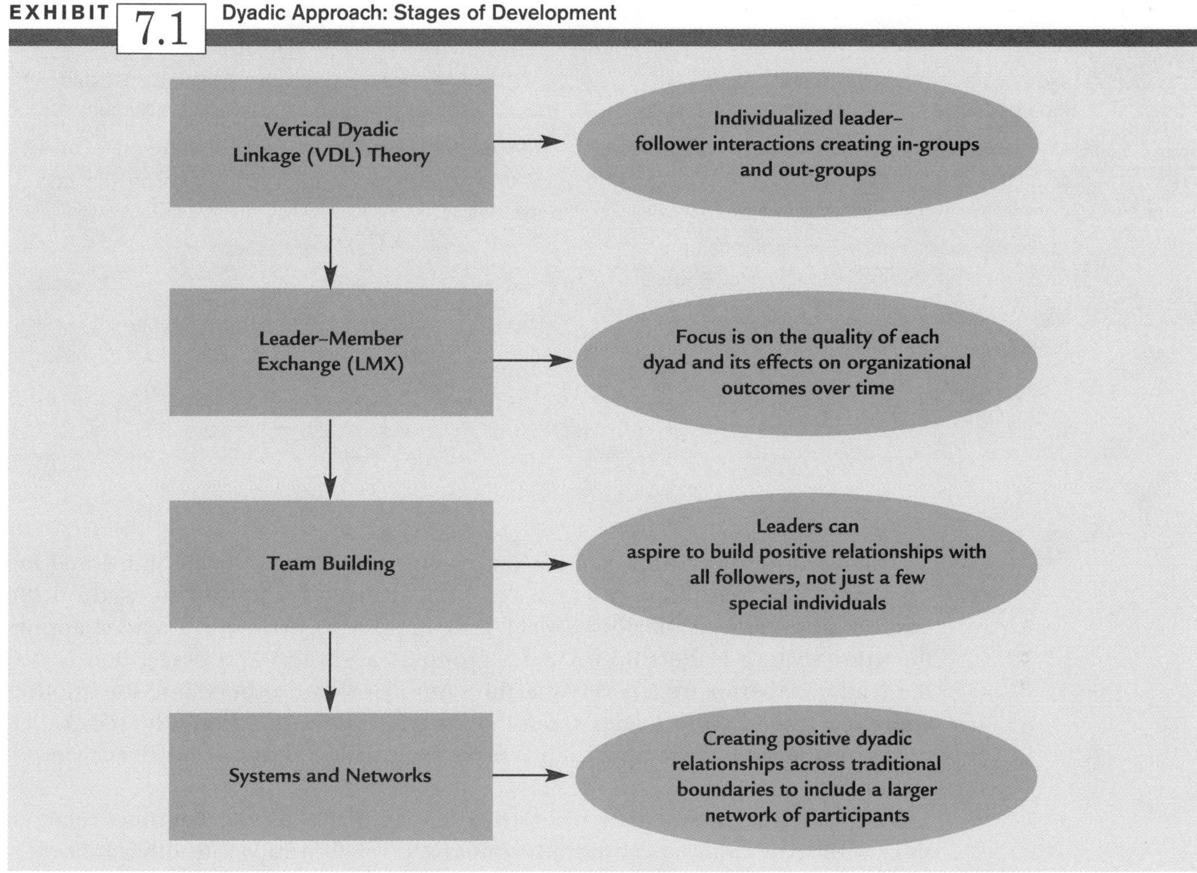

Learning Outcome 2 *Define the two kinds of relationships that can occur among leaders and followers under the vertical dyadic linkage model.*

Vertical Dyadic Linkage (VDL) Theory

Before we begin, determine the dyadic relationship with your manager by completing Self-Assessment 1.

SELF-ASSESSMENT 1

Dyadic Relationship with Your Manager

Select a present or past manager and answer each question describing your relationship using the following scale:

1 — 2 — 3 — 4 — 5

Is descriptive of our relationship ... *Is not descriptive of our relationship*

__1__ 1. I have quick, easy access to talk with my manager anytime I want to.

__1__ 2. I get along well with my manager.

__3__ 3. I can influence my manager to get things done my way—to get what I want.

__4__ 4. When I interact with my manager, our conversation is often relationship-oriented (we talk on a personal level), rather than just task-oriented (we talk only about the job).

continued

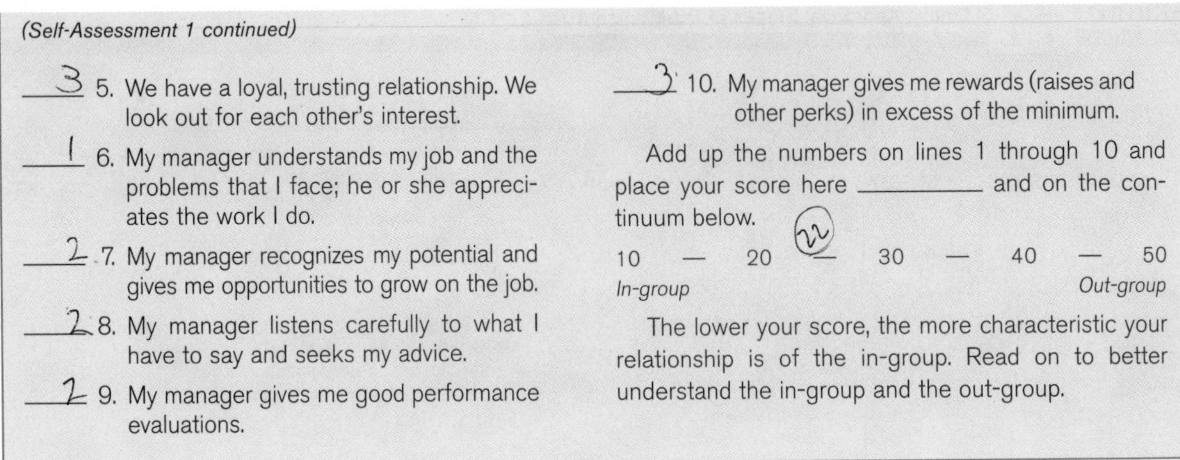

(Self-Assessment 1 continued)

__3__ 5. We have a loyal, trusting relationship. We look out for each other's interest.

__1__ 6. My manager understands my job and the problems that I face; he or she appreciates the work I do.

__2__ 7. My manager recognizes my potential and gives me opportunities to grow on the job.

__2__ 8. My manager listens carefully to what I have to say and seeks my advice.

__2__ 9. My manager gives me good performance evaluations.

__3__ 10. My manager gives me rewards (raises and other perks) in excess of the minimum.

Add up the numbers on lines 1 through 10 and place your score here ________ and on the continuum below.

10 — 20 — (22) — 30 — 40 — 50

In-group ... Out-group

The lower your score, the more characteristic your relationship is of the in-group. Read on to better understand the in-group and the out-group.

The vertical dyad approach is an evolutionary phase from individualized leadership research. Early research on individualized leadership focused on the traditional average leadership style (ALS) approach, in which a leader applies the same style of leadership toward a group as a whole.[4] The perception is that the leader/superior treats everyone the same. However, others describe another approach whereby the leader treats his or her followers differently. It is called the vertical dyad linkage approach. This is essentially a dyads-within-dyads view of leadership.[5]

VDL describes a situation whereby a leader forms dyadic in-group relationships with some followers and dyadic out-group relationships with other followers. Therefore, **vertical dyadic linkage (VDL) theory** *examines how leaders form one-on-one relationships with followers, and how these often create in-groups and out-groups within the leader's work unit.*

Central to VDL theory is the notion of "support for self-worth" that one individual provides for another. A leader provides support for feelings of self-worth to a follower.[6] For example, a leader may provide closer attention, guidance, feedback, and consideration to a follower. The follower in turn renders exceptional performance to the leader—for example, a follower performing above standards and always willing to go the extra mile for the leader. Studies have revealed that relationships developed in these dyads may occur at a formal or informal level, whereby some dyads are linked to assigned work groups and others are independent of formal work groups. Also, a leader may link (one-on-one) with many individuals, or only a few individuals, and not others. This selective association or differentiation by leaders with subordinates leads to in-groups and out-groups that tend to remain stable over time.[7] These relationships affect the types of power and influence tactics leaders use.

The **in-group** *includes followers with strong social ties to their leader in a supportive relationship characterized by high mutual trust, respect, loyalty, and influence.* Leaders primarily use expert, referent, and reward power to influence members of the in-group. *The* **out-group** *includes followers with few or no social ties to their leader, in a strictly task-centered relationship characterized by low exchange and top-down influence.* Leaders mostly use reward, as well as legitimate and coercive power, to influence out-group members. (These types of power were discussed in more detail in Chapter 4.) To satisfy the terms of the exchange relationship, out-group followers need only comply with formal role requirements (such as duties, rules, standard procedures, and legitimate direction from the leader). As long as such compliance is forthcoming, the out-group follower receives the standard benefits for the job (such as a salary) and no more.[8]

Opening Case APPLICATION

2. What leadership action/decision by Pastor Osteen might create in-groups and out-groups at Lakewood Church?

It is said that Pastor Osteen does not perform weddings or funerals and that he avoids sickbeds and does not do personal counseling. He decided to delegate these needs to ministers the church employs. If Pastor Osteen were to suddenly start performing these services for some members and not for others, it would certainly give the impression of him favoring some members over others, and this would likely create in-groups and out-groups within the church.

Members of the in-group are invited to participate in important decision making, are given added responsibility, and have greater access to the leader. Members of the out-group are managed according to the requirements of the employment contract. They receive little inspiration, encouragement, or recognition. In terms of influence and support, in-group members experience greater support and positive influence from the leader, while out-group members tend not to experience positive relationships and influence. The in-group versus out-group status also reveals an element of reciprocity or exchange in the relationship. The leader grants special favors to in-group members in exchange for their loyalty, commitment, and outstanding performance. This creates mutual reinforcement based on common needs and interests. Ultimately, these formations create stronger social ties within the groups as well as intergroup biases between the groups. Thus, individuals will be more likely to share with members of their own group (in-group) than with members of other groups (out-groups).[9]

Work Application 1

Recall a work unit or organization you worked at that had both in-groups and out-groups. Describe some of the ways in which the manager's behavior and actions toward in-group and out-group members varied.

Applying the Concept 1

In-Groups versus Out-Groups

From each of the following statements from a subordinate, identify the group to which he or she belongs. Write the appropriate letter in the blank before each item.

a. in-group b. out-group

____ 1. My boss and I are similar in a lot of ways.

____ 2. When I am not sure what is going on, I can count on my boss to tell me the truth even if it will hurt my feelings.

____ 3. When I have a major problem at work or in my personal life, my boss would do only that which is required of him or her as my manager without going out of his or her way.

____ 4. As far as my feelings toward my boss go, we relate to each other strictly along professional lines and work.

____ 5. I seldom have any direct contact with my boss unless something is wrong with the way I have done my job.

Leader–Member Exchange (LMX) Theory

The next evolutionary stage in the dyadic approach is the LMX theory. Face-to-face leader–member interaction plays a critical role in organizational life. Unfortunately, such exchanges can also be a leading cause of employee distress. The underlying assumption of LMX theory is that leaders or superiors have limited amounts of social, personal, and organizational resources (such as energy, time, attention, and discretion), and as a result tend to distribute them among followers selectively.[10] Leaders do not interact with all followers equally, which ultimately results in the formation of LMXs that vary in quality.

In high-quality LMX relationships, followers tend to receive better social support, more resources, and more guidance for career development. The relationship is characterized by greater follower input in decision making and greater negotiating latitude. Low-quality LMX relationships are characterized by less support, more formal supervision, and little or no involvement in decision making.[11] Therefore, **leader–member exchange (LMX)** *is defined as the quality of the exchange relationship between an employee and his or her superior.*[12] LMX theory and research offer an alternative way of examining organizational leadership, arguing that the quality of the social exchange between a leader and a follower would be more predictive of follower performance than traits or behaviors of superiors.

Ethical **Dilemma 1**

LMX at Work

Leader–member exchange theory states that in each work group some employees belong to the in-group and others belong to the out-group. Think about your present or past employment. Can you identify members of the in-group and the out-group? Which group were you in?

1. Is it ethical to exclude employees from the in-group?
2. Do you think people in the in-group tend to think exclusion is ethical and those in the out-group tend to think it is unethical?
3. Is your answer to question 1 based on whether you were a member of the in-group or the out-group?
4. Is it possible for all employees to be in the in-group?
5. Should managers work to overcome LMX theory by including all employees in the in-group?

Learning Outcome 3 *Describe the main focus of team building from a Leader–Follower perspective.*

Team Building

Given the increasingly complex and uncertain environment in which organizations find themselves, many have responded by using teams as their fundamental unit of organizational design in an effort to decentralize decision making and respond more effectively to external opportunities and threats.[13] There is no question that team dynamics does influence both task performance and the quality of interpersonal relations.[14] Therefore, team leadership involves a primary concern to motivate a group of individuals to work together to achieve a common objective, while alleviating any conflicts or obstacles that may arise while striving toward that objective.[15] The emphasis is on forming relationships with all group members, not just with a few special individuals. Effective leaders know that while it is not possible to treat all followers in exactly the same way, it is important that each person perceive that he or she is an important and respected member of the team rather than a non-entity. For instance, not every employee may desire greater responsibility, but each should feel that there is equal opportunity based on competence rather than on being part of some in-group in the organization.

Leader–member exchange relationships can result in greater teamwork, because employees pursue cooperation with other team members as a way to reciprocate to the leader who desires such behavior.[16] Therefore, workplace social exchanges between individual employees, work groups, and managers are critical to team building. The concept of social capital is used to describe group members' social relationships within and outside their groups and how these relationships affect group effectiveness.[17] As a result, some see team building as a multilevel social exchange concept wherein the interface of leadership and team processes is quite evident.[18]

Opening Case APPLICATION

3. What leadership qualities does Pastor Osteen possess, and how have those qualities affected the level of teamwork between church leaders and followers?

Pastor Osteen is described as a charming person with a smile that captivates everyone he encounters. He is an effective communicator. Some have called him the "smiling preacher." Osteen's friendly personality and upbeat message of self-help reach everyone in a personal way. As Osteen puts it, "I don't condemn; I don't believe in being judgmental." He is obviously a very people-oriented leader.

Studies have shown that when leaders are trained to develop and nurture high-quality relationships with all of their followers, the results on follower performance are dramatic. Followers who feel they have developed a positive one-on-one relationship with the leader tend to exhibit higher productivity and performance gains. As these relationships mature, the entire work group becomes more cohesive, and the payoffs are evident to all participants. In some sense, partnership building enables a leader to meet both the personal and work-related needs of each group member, one at a time. Through the leader's support, encouragement, and training, the followers feel a sense of self-worth, appreciation, and value for their work, and they respond with high performance. The concept of leading teams is covered in detail in Chapter 8.

Learning Outcome 4 *Discuss the focus of the systems and networks approach from a Leader–Follower perspective.*

Systems and Networks

Across all sectors of our economy, there is a noticeable trend of organizations seeking and getting involved in a variety of collaborative arrangements (such as partnerships, consortia, alliances, and networks) for the purposes of entering new markets and gaining innovations or new products. By collaborating, organizations hope to exchange strengths (such as skills, capabilities, knowledge, and resources) with others, which will allow all partners to develop timely, innovative, synergistic solutions to complex problems they could not address on their own. From a network perspective, the focus is on relations among actors, whether they are individuals, work units, or organizations. The actors are embedded within networks of interconnected relationships that provide opportunities and constraints on behavior.[19]

Effective LMX at this level would determine the extent to which individual participants are able to draw on their group ties and, at the same time, transcend those ties to act collectively. A systems-oriented perspective focuses on how the quality of the LMX relationship affects followers at the interpersonal, group, and organizational levels. For instance, studies have found that the quality of LMX strongly influences subordinates' communication satisfaction at the interpersonal (personal feedback and supervisory communication), group (coworker exchange and organizational integration in the workgroup), and organizational (corporate communications and communications climate) levels.[20,21]

Proponents of the systems and networks view contend that leader relationships are not limited to followers, but include peers, customers, suppliers, and other relevant stakeholders in the collectives of workgroups and organization-wide networks. The organization is viewed as a system of interrelated parts. To be effective, groups need to manage "boundary-spanning" relationships with other groups and external members in their organization in order to gain access to information and political resources. Accomplishing this outcome requires effective leadership.

Today, organizations are structured along functional, divisional, product, customer, and geographic lines. Research on group dynamics and culture does reveal that such organizational structures also affect employee cognitive structures. In other words, these structures form departmental boundaries that create stronger social ties within the group as well as intergroup biases between the groups. Individuals and groups are connected to certain people (and not to others), and this pattern of connection creates a network of interdependent social exchanges wherein certain people become trusted exchange partners who can be called upon for resources and support.[22] As a result, individuals will be more inclined to align or associate with members of their own functional group (in-group) than with members of other functional groups (out-groups). Such alliance networks may provide members such benefits as access to knowledge, information, referrals, and career opportunities.[23,24]

However, it should also be noted that organizational group boundaries create actual and perceived difficulties in integrating and coordinating organizational activities. A study comparing perceptual sharing to actual sharing between employees revealed that individuals understated the extent of their sharing with out-group members and overstated their sharing with in-group members. Therefore, there is a need for groups to more actively manage their cooperation and coordination with other organizational units. Leaders must create processes and networks that bring all workers (across functional lines) together to talk to one another, listen to one another's stories, and reflect together. Developing relationships of trust, where people from various backgrounds, disciplines, and hierarchies talk to one another, would no doubt avoid the polarization that dominates organizations characterized by in-groups and out-groups.[25] Cisco Systems is a leading provider of networking technologies that optimize collaborations within and between organizations. The way Cisco sees it, collaboration across functions, geographies, and corporate boundaries is imperative and the way of the future.[26]

Applying the **Concept 2**

Stages of Development of the Dyadic Approach

Which stage is described by the following statements? Write the appropriate letter in the blank before each item.

a. vertical dyadic linkage theory
b. leader–member exchange theory
c. team building
d. systems and networks

____ 6. A dyadic approach that focuses on creating positive dyadic relationships across traditional boundaries to include more participants.

____ 7. A hierarchical relationship in which leader–follower dyads develop, and the emphasis is on the quality of each relationship and its effects on organizational outcomes over time.

____ 8. A dyadic approach that encourages leaders to aspire to having positive relationships with all followers, not just a few special individuals.

____ 9. A relationship in which leader–follower interactions lead to the creation of in-groups and out-groups.

Leader–Member Exchange Theory

As defined earlier, leadership is the ability to influence others to contribute toward the achievement of organizational goals. Leader–member exchange is one theory that examines how leaders influence member behaviors. According to this theory, leaders form high-quality social exchanges (based on trust and liking) with some members and low-quality economic exchanges with others that do not extend beyond the employment contract.[27,28] The quality of LMX affects employees' work ethics, productivity, satisfaction, and perceptions. There is a sense among followers in the exchange relationship to reciprocate their leader's trust and liking through "citizenship behaviors" and excellent performance. Studies that have used leader–member exchange theory to examine the effects of the employee–supervisor relationship on important job-related outcomes have come to the same conclusion: Employees who perceive themselves to be in supportive relationships with their supervisors tend to have higher performance, job satisfaction, and organizational commitment.[29,30] For an expanded discussion of the theory, this section will examine the following: the influence of LMX quality on follower behavior, the three-stage process for developing positive LMX relations, factors that determine LMX quality, effective leader–follower feedback, limitations of LMX theory application, and bias in LMX with employee career implications.

The Influence of LMX on Follower Behavior

The underlying assumption of LMX is that leaders do not interact with all followers equally, which ultimately results in the formation of leader–member exchange relations that vary in quality. Followers with strong social ties to the leader (high LMX) are said to belong to the in-group while those with weak social ties to the leader (low LMX) are said to belong to the out-group. As revealed earlier, being a member of the in-group puts you in a very favorable position. For example, in-group followers routinely receive higher performance ratings than out-group followers; out-group followers routinely show higher levels of turnover than in-group followers; and, finally, when asked to evaluate organizational climate, in-group followers give more positive ratings than out-group followers.

However, the special relationship with in-group followers creates certain obligations and constraints for the leader.[31] To maintain the relationship, the leader must continuously pay attention to in-group members, remain responsive to their needs and feelings, and rely more on time-consuming influence methods such as persuasion and consultation. The leader cannot resort to coercion or heavy-handed use of authority without endangering the quality of the relationship. The followers are therefore said to have developed *social capital,* defined as the set of resources that inheres in the structure of relations between members of the group, which helps them get ahead.[32,33]

The basis for establishing a deeper exchange relationship with in-group members is the leader's control over outcomes that are desirable to the followers. These outcomes include such benefits as helping with a follower's career (for example, recommending advancement), giving special favors (bigger office, better work schedule), allowing participation in decision making, delegating greater responsibility and authority, more sharing of information, assigning in-group members to interesting and desirable tasks, and giving tangible rewards such as a pay increase. In return for these benefits, in-group members have certain obligations and expectations beyond those required of out-group members. In-group members are expected to be loyal to the leader, to be more committed to task objectives, to work harder, and to share some of the leader's administrative duties.

To the leader this also represents social capital that gives him or her power and influence over followers. Unless this cycle of reciprocal reinforcement of leader and member behavior is interrupted, the relationship is likely to develop to a point where there is a high degree of mutual dependence, support, and loyalty. Organizational culture, and more specifically respect for people, plays a key role in protecting the cycle and strengthening the relationship between perceptions of fairness and LMX.[34]

A number of studies have demonstrated that the quality of LMX is central in influencing followers' affective, cognitive, and behavioral experiences; roles; and fate in their organizations.[35,36] Studies focusing on these outcomes have explored such factors as communication frequency, turnover, job satisfaction, performance, job climate, and commitment.[37,38] High-quality LMX relationships are characterized by higher levels of leader support and guidance, higher levels of follower satisfaction and performance, wide latitude of discretion for followers, and lower levels of follower turnover.[39,40,41] Also, the positive relationship between LMX and follower job satisfaction is stronger when leaders have high perceived organizational support (POS) because these leaders feel they have more resources to exchange with followers.[42] Compared to employees in low-quality LMXs, high-quality LMX employees exhibit greater organizational citizenship behavior.[43]

Opening Case APPLICATION

4. Describe the quality of the LMX relationship between Osteen and his leadership team and how this has in turn influenced their ability to counsel and minister to church members.

Pastor Osteen has a high-quality LMX relationship with his leadership team. Evidence of this can be seen in the close ties he has with his team of volunteers, ministers, and the church board. A high level of trust exists between them. There is a high level of involvement in decisions regarding church matters and support for each other. As a result, the entire team is focused on the mission of the church, thanks to the leadership of their pastor.

Now that you understand LMX, complete Self-Assessment 2.

SELF-ASSESSMENT 2

In-Group and Out-Group

Based on Self-Assessment 1 on pages 241–242 and your reading of VDL and LMX theory, place the people who work or have worked for your present or past manager in the in-group or out-group. Be sure to include yourself.

In-Group Members	Out-Group Members
________________	________________
________________	________________
________________	________________

The Three-Stage Process for Developing Positive LMX Relations

The development of relationships in a leader–member exchange dyad has been described as a "life-cycle model" with three possible stages. Each of these stages is described below.

Stage 1

At this early stage, the leader and follower conduct themselves as strangers, testing each other to identify what kinds of behavior are acceptable. Each relationship is negotiated informally between each follower and the leader. The definition of each group member's role determines what the leader expects the member to do. Here, impressions management by the follower plays a critical role in influencing how the leader perceives him or her. **Impressions management** *is a follower's effort to project a favorable image in order to gain an immediate benefit or improve a long-term relationship with the leader.* Employees seeking to form a positive relationship with the leader will often be the ones seeking feedback on how to improve their work performance. Researchers have identified two kinds of motives associated with follower feedback-seeking behavior: performance-driven motive and impressions-driven motive. The performance-driven motive is the follower's genuine attempt to seek information from the leader that will help improve work performance, while the impressions-driven motive refers to the desire to control how one appears to the leader.[44]

Work Application 2

Recall an occasion when you had the opportunity to make a positive first impression on your manager. Describe what tactics you employed and their effects on your manager.

Another tactic for influencing a leader is ingratiation. **Ingratiation** *is the effort to appear supportive, appreciative, and respectful.* Ingratiatory influence tactics include favor rendering, self-promotion, and behavioral conformity. In this instance, followers go beyond the call of duty to render services to the leader and to conform their behavior to the expectations of the leader. **Self-promotion** *is the effort to appear competent and dependable.* Studies have found a positive correlation between ingratiation by a follower and affection (or liking) of the leader for the follower. Affection, in turn, is positively related to the quality of the exchange relationship and the leader's assessment of the follower's competence, loyalty, commitment, and work ethic. These tactics are valuable tools that can enhance the visibility of the follower's strengths and performance. However, others caution that these tactics can have a negative effect on the LMX relationship in that leaders may discount or devalue the follower's attempts, if deemed to be self-serving.[45] Therefore, one's social skills are critical in influencing the leader–member relations.

Stage 2

As the leader and follower become acquainted, they engage in further refining the roles they will play together. Mutual trust, loyalty, and respect begin to develop between leader and follower. During this stage, the perceived fairness of leaders is crucial. When the the leader is perceived as fair and benevolent in his or her intentions, followers will infer from this that the leader is committed to them, and high-quality exchanges result.[46] Followers in this type of relationship are more likely to be very proactive. Some have argued that high-quality social exchanges can give organizations a competitive advantage in retaining and motivating talented employees. Relationships that do not mature beyond the first stage may deteriorate and remain at the level of an out-group. As described earlier, in the out-group exchange, there is less social interaction and followers are afforded limited opportunities to influence decisions or interact informally with leaders.

Stage 3

Some exchange relationships advance to a third stage as the roles reach maturity. Here, exchange based on self-interest is transformed into mutual commitment to the mission and objectives of the work unit. It would appear from examining these three stages that the end result of the life cycle model of LMX relationships is the creation of actual and perceived differences between in-group (high-quality LMX) and out-group (low-quality LMX) members. Critics point out that these differences could lead to intergroup conflicts and undermine teamwork within the broader work unit.[47]

Learning Outcome 5 *Describe three determining factors of high-quality LMX relationships.*

Factors that Determine LMX Quality

Behavioral and situational factors influence the creation of high- or low-quality leader–member exchange relationships. LMX relationship antecedents include (1) follower attributes, (2) leader and follower perceptions of each other, and (3) situational factors. Each is briefly discussed.

Follower Attributes

The difference between contingency theories and LMX is that while the former emphasizes how a good leader facilitates employee job performance, the latter emphasizes how a good employee facilitates leader job performance.[48] The leader–member exchange model suggests that proactive followers show initiative even in areas outside their immediate responsibility, possess a strong sense of commitment to work unit goals, and show a greater sense of responsibility for unit success. These follower attributes influence leaders to show support, delegate more, allow greater discretion, engage in open communication, and encourage mutual influence between themselves and their followers.[49]

Work Application 3

Recall two leaders you have worked with over a period of time. Identify specific attributes that would describe the true nature of your relationship with these leaders. Identify one leader with whom you feel you had a high-quality relationship, and one with whom you had a low-quality relationship. What attributes describe the high-quality and the low-quality relationships with these leaders?

Leader–Follower Perceptions of Each Other

The leader's first impressions of the follower can influence the leader's behavior toward the follower. A positive relationship is more likely when the follower is perceived to be competent and dependable, and when the follower's values and attitudes are similar to those of the leader. The same is true for the follower's perceptions of the leader. A favorable exchange relationship is said to correlate with more supportive behavior by the leader toward the follower, less close monitoring, more mentoring, and more involvement and delegation. From the follower's perspective, leaders that are perceived to be competent, experienced, fair, and honest are more likely to be supported, encounter fewer pressure tactics (for example, threats and demands), and receive more honest input.[50] One study's findings revealed that transformational leadership relationships were significantly stronger for followers who perceived high-quality leader–member exchange.[51]

Situational Factors

Situational factors are used here to refer to random or planned events that provide the opportunity for leaders to evaluate a follower's work ethic or character. Follower reaction to "tryouts," described as "role episodes," will give leaders clues about employees.[52,53] For example, a manager asks a new employee to do something beyond what the formal employment agreement calls for. The new employee's reaction ("sure, glad to help," versus a grumble, or "that's not my job" attitude) indicates potential loyalty, support, and trustworthiness, and leads to more—versus fewer—opportunities for responsibility, personal growth, and other positive experiences. The perception of the leader from this tryout will greatly influence the type of relationship or social exchange that ensues between the leader and the follower. Followers perceived to be hardworking and willing to go the extra mile for the leader have a higher-quality exchange relationship with the leader than those who are perceived to be lazy or unwilling to go the extra mile for the leader.[54]

Work Application 4

Recall a work situation in which you were required to do something that was beyond your employment contract. How did you respond to your manager's request, and what consequences did it have on your relationship with him or her?

Effective Leader–Follower Feedback

Followers are responsible for implementing whatever plans the leader formulates. They are judged on their effectiveness and efficiency. However, when this does not happen, it is the leader's responsibility to provide appropriate feedback to the followers on their performance.[55] As most leaders will attest, this is an important but difficult managerial responsibility. People in general tend to be defensive about criticism because it questions their abilities and threatens their self-esteem. Many leaders avoid confronting followers about below-average performance because of the potential for such actions to turn into personal conflict that fails to deal with the underlying problem, or does so only at the cost of shattered respect and trust between the leader and follower.

While some leaders can use threats to bring about desired behavior, the effective leader prefers to use position or referent power to effect positive change in followers. Correcting a follower's performance deficiencies may be required to help the follower improve, but the way it is done can preserve or strain the leader–follower relationship. Some of the supporting principles of trust that may facilitate effective follower feedback include authentic caring, ethical actions, good leadership, and personal character. Much of the sociological and psychological literature on this topic reveals that followers seek, admire, and respect leaders who, through the feedback process, produce within them three emotional responses: a feeling of significance, a sense of belonging, and a sense of excitement. Leaders must recognize the significance of this aspect of their job and take it seriously.

Work Application 5

Recall the last time you were evaluated on the job by your manager. Describe how you felt at the end of the session. What factors accounted for your feelings? See if some of the factors discussed in this section apply in your particular situation.

Leaders must learn to stay calm and professional when followers overreact to corrective feedback. Leaders must avoid a rush to judgment when followers don't perform. The leader must be specific in stating the deficiency, calmly explaining the negative impact of ineffective behavior, involving the follower in identifying the reasons for poor performance, and suggesting remedies for change. At the conclusion of an evaluation session, the follower must come away believing that the leader showed a genuine desire to be of help, and that both parties arrived at a mutual agreement on specific action steps for improvement. The follower's self-confidence should remain intact or be enhanced through feedback, rather than being shattered.[56]

Exhibit 7.2 presents 12 guidelines for effective leader feedback. It should be noted that these 12 guidelines are not in sequential order; however, they have been organized in a three-step process to underscore the importance of careful planning prior to undertaking any feedback activity.

EXHIBIT 7.2 Guidelines for Effective Leader Feedback

Pre-Feedback—Leader should:
- remind self to stay calm and professional
- gather accurate facts on follower performance
- remind self to avoid rush to judgment

During Feedback Session—Leader should:
- be specific in stating performance deficiency
- explain negative impact of ineffective behavior
- help follower identify reasons for poor performance
- ask follower to suggest remedies
- arrive at mutual agreement on specific action steps

Post-Feedback Session—Leader should:
- follow up to ensure implementation of action steps
- show desire to be of help to follower
- build follower's self-confidence

Opening Case APPLICATION

5. If there were some concerns that Osteen's staff/ministers were not meeting the needs of church members in the one-on-one counseling sessions, how should Pastor Osteen conduct an effective feedback session to ensure greater success?

This situation is a real possibility because Pastor Osteen does not do personal counseling. He relies on the over 60 ministers hired by the church. Members rely on these ministers for counseling on all sort of issues—relationship difficulties, sickness, death of loved ones, loneliness, and depression, to name a few. If ministers don't do their jobs well and church member satisfaction declines, it could result in loss of members. Using the guidelines for effective feedback in Exhibit 7.2 should significantly increase Pastor Osteen's chances of success with the process.

Learning Outcome 6 *Discuss the key limitation or drawback with LMX application.*

Limitations of LMX Theory Application

A major limitation of LMX is measurement difficulty. LMX theory deals with attitudes and perceptions of individuals; two issues that are often difficult to quantify and measure. For this reason, recent research efforts on LMX have focused on instrumentation of the theory.[57] The way in which the attributes of high-quality LMX relationships have been defined and measured have varied somewhat from study to study. Most studies have measured LMX with a scale based on a questionnaire filled out by the follower. The LMX-7 scale is the most commonly used instrument for defining and measuring the quality of relationships. Examples of questions featured on the LMX-7 scale included structured questions, such as the following:

- How well does your leader understand your job problems and needs? (Not a bit, a little, a fair amount, quite a bit, and a great deal)
- How well does your leader recognize your potential? (Not at all, a little, moderately, mostly, and fully)
- How would you characterize your working relationship with your leader? (Extremely ineffective, worse than average, average, better than average, and extremely effective)

In studies using this scale, the quality of relationships is usually assumed to involve attributes such as mutual trust, respect, affection, and loyalty. Complete Self-Assessment 3 to determine your LMX relationship with your manager.

SELF-ASSESSMENT 3

Your LMX Relationship with Your Manager

Self-Assessment 1 is a form of measuring your LMX relationship with your manager. Note that some of the questions are similar to the LMX-7 questions. The score, ranging from 10 to 50, gives you more than a simple in-group or out-group assessment. Place your score here ________ and on the following continuum.

10 — 20 — 30 — 40 — 50

High-quality LMX relationship *Low-quality LMX relationship*

The lower your score, generally, the better is your relationship with your manager. We say generally, because you could have a manager who does not have a good relationship with any employee. Thus, a good LMX can be a relative measure.

LMX-7 measures vertical dyad linkages and not social exchanges. Other measures employ more diverse questionnaires in an attempt to identify separate dimensions of LMX relationships and unique attributes. A new scale called leader–member social exchange (LMSX) proposes to assess different components of the leader–subordinate realtionship.[58] These new measures appear to combine quality of the relationship with determinants of the relationship, such as perceived competence or behavior of the other person. It is not clear yet whether the newest scales offer any advantages over a single scale in identifying and measuring attributes that can be described as more broad-based or universal. Only a few studies have measured LMX from the perception of both the leader and the follower.[59,60]

Characteristics of LMX deemed positive to the exchange relationship may vary among leaders and followers, depending on key influencing factors.[61] Contrary to expectations of high correlation on LMX attributes, the correlation between leader-rated LMX and follower-rated LMX is weak enough to raise questions about scale validity for one or both sources. It is unclear whether the low correlation reflects instrument reliability or actual differences in perception. Despite recent research support for LMX theory, it is evident from the above discussion that further research on instrumentation is needed.

Embedded in LMX theory is the question of bias. To what extent does bias affect the quality of relationships between leaders and followers, and how does it influence their affective, behavioral, and organization-related performance? The next section examines this question.

Learning Outcome 7 *Explain the cycle that leads to the Pygmalion effect.*

Bias in LMX: Employee Career Implications

Work Application **6**

Identify a particular leader–follower working relationship that you have had with a manager. To what extent did the Pygmalion effect play a role in the quality of this relationship? How did it affect your career development within the organization?

As mentioned in Chapter 2, the Pygmalion effect occurs when managers reciprocate the friendship and loyalty from some followers with higher performance ratings. Here we apply it to LMX and consider how it applies to a leader's performance evaluation of a follower. The Pygmalion effect occurs when selected group members demonstrate loyalty, commitment, dedication, and trust, and as a result, win the liking of leaders who subsequently give them higher performance ratings. These ratings, which may or may not be tied to actual performance, then influence the member's reputation and often become a matter of record. The ratings may ultimately be used—formally or informally—in future selection, development, and promotion decisions. Generally, employees with a history of high performance ratings are those who get promoted to higher-level positions.

Learning Outcome 8 *Explain how LMX relationships can lead to unintended bias in HR practices.*

On its face, the idea of promoting those who consistently score high in their performance evaluations seems harmless and even rational were it not for the possible adverse implications it might have for the development and career advancement of other group members who (regardless of their work performance) are not similar to, familiar to, and well liked by their leader. The out-group members may be paying a price for not maintaining the same social equity with their leaders as in-group members.

The conclusion to be drawn from this discussion is that leaders, managers, and human resource management specialists need to be made aware of the potential biasing processes inherent in high-quality LMX relationships. Procedural checks and balances need to be applied to minimize such biases, if indeed possible. Otherwise, the development of high-quality LMX relations could result in negative consequences and discrimination against out-group followers. One possible approach to minimizing this type of bias is simply to train and encourage leaders to maintain high-quality LMX relationships with all followers, not just a few.

Followership

Most scholars would agree that there is increasing use of the words *follower* and *followership* in discussions of organizational leadership. This trend represents a shift away from early theories that focused on the internal dispositions associated with effective leadership.[62] Past leadership research has focused on leaders and ignored the role of followers in explaining organizational successes or failures. This has led to criticism of extant leadership theories for being too "leader-centric."[63] The focus of these theories has been almost exclusively on the impact of leader traits and behaviors on followers' attitudes and behaviors. However, there is increasing recogniton of the notion that leadership is a relationship that is jointly produced by leaders and followers, and that to adequately understand it, we must know more about the often-nameless persons who comprise the followers of leaders.[64] The emphasis in the current literature is on the cognitions, attributes, behaviors, and contexts in which leaders and followers interact.[65]

Followership *refers to the behavior of followers that results from the leader–follower influence relationship.* Much less has been done to advance understanding of the follower component and the psychological processes and mechanisms that connect leaders and followers.[66] To a large extent, societal views about followers have contributed to our limited understanding of followership. From an early age we are taught to focus on becoming a leader, not a follower.

Webster defines a follower as "one that follows the opinions or teachings of another." This definition implies that followers are passive partners of the leader–follower dyad until they receive explicit instructions from a leader and then proceed to follow those instructions in an unquestioning manner.[67] There is increasing recognition that leaders are just one part of a duality, because there can be no leaders without followers. Effective leadership requires effective followership, because without followers, there are no leaders. No work unit or organized effort can succeed and be sustained without followers.

Effective followers do more than fulfill the vision laid out by their leader; they are partners in creating the vision. They take responsibility for getting their jobs done, take the initiative in fixing problems, and question leaders when they think they are wrong.[68] These types of followers exhibit what some have called self-leadership and perform at high levels in their teams. They have a high need for autonomy and welcome empowering leadership from their leaders.[69,70]

Recall from Chapter 1 that we defined leadership as "the influencing process of leaders and followers to achieve organizational objectives through change." *A* **follower** *is a person who is being influenced by a leader.* However, there is growing awareness that the influencing process is a two-way street, with followers also influencing leaders. Effective followers can help leaders lead without threatening the leader's position. Good followers who give input that influences managers are vital to the success of any organization. In this section we discuss followership styles, guidelines for effective followership, follower influencing characteristics, and the dual roles of being a leader and follower.

The Effective Follower, and Follower Types

Organizational successes and failures are often attributed to effective or ineffective leaders without fully recognizing the contributions of followers. Unfortunately, due to the limited research focusing on the role of followers, there does not appear to be much evidence supporting a strong correlation between effective followership and effective leadership. However, when examining the question of what distinguishes high-performing organizations from average ones, most scholars and practitioners agree that high-performing organizations have good leaders and good followers. Competent, confident, and motivated followers are key to the successful performance of any leader's work group or team. Rather than the conforming and passive role in which followers have been cast, effective followers are described as courageous, responsible, and proactive.[71]

Like leaders, there are different types of followers. Based on individual characteristics, motivations, and behaviors, some followers may be more active and involved than others. Some of the names that have been used to describe different types of followers include isolates, bystanders, participants, activists, and diehards.[72] The best conceptualization of follower types is Kelley's model.[73] Using a combination of two types of behavior—critical thinking and level of involvement in organizational affairs—Kelley groups followers into five categories based on their specific behavioral mix.

The behavioral mix can be summarized into two components: the follower's ability to think or not think critically and his or her level of involvement or lack of it.

Exhibit 7.3 depicts these two variables on the vertical and horizontal axes, where level of involvement is on a continuum from low to high and critical thinking is on a continuum from low to high as well. The high critical thinker refers to the follower's ability to examine, analyze, and evaluate matters of significance in the organization's life. Conversely, the opposite of this person is someone who is low on critical thinking. The second behavior variable—level of involvement—refers to the follower's willingness to be a visible and active participant. The opposite of this person is someone who is low on involvement. She or he is barely noticeable within the work unit.

EXHIBIT 7.3 Followership Types

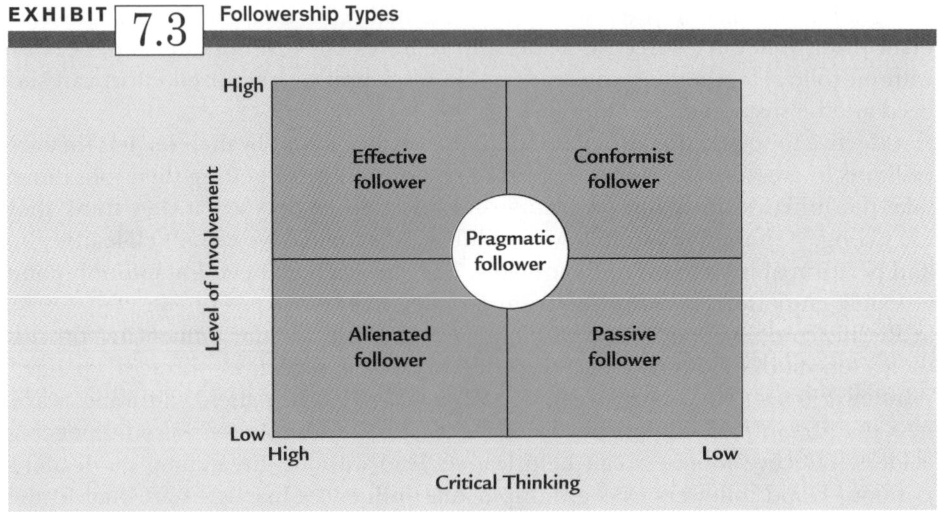

According to Kelley, the extent to which a follower is active or passive—and is an independent, critical thinker or a dependent, noncritical thinker—determines whether he or she is an alienated follower, a passive follower, a conformist follower, a pragmatic follower, or an effective follower (see Exhibit 7.3):[74]

- *The* **alienated follower** *is someone who is low on involvement yet is high on critical thinking.* The alienated follower is someone who feels cheated, or unappreciated, by his or her organization for exemplary work. Often cynical in their behavior, alienated followers are capable but unwilling to participate in developing solutions to problems. They are just happy to dwell on the negatives and ignore the positives as far as organizational life goes.
- *The* **conformist follower** *is someone who is high on involvement but low on critical thinking.* In other words, conformists are the "yes people" of the organization. They carry out all orders without considering the consequences of such orders. A conformist would do anything to avoid conflict. Authoritarian leaders prefer conformist followers.
- *The* **passive follower** is someone who is *neither high on critical thinking nor involvement.* The passive follower looks to the leader or others to do all the thinking and does not get involved. Lacking in initiative and commitment to the team, the invisible follower requires constant supervision and never goes beyond the job description. They are often described by their leaders as lazy, unmotivated, and incompetent.
- *The* **effective follower** *is someone who is high on critical thinking and involvement.* Effective followers are not risk-averse nor do they shy from conflict. They have the

courage to initiate change and put themselves at risk or in conflict with others, even their leaders, to serve the best interest of the organization. As such, they are often described as proactive. Effective followers tend to function very well in self-managed teams. They are a manager's best asset in that they complement the leader's efforts and can be relied upon to relieve the leader of many tasks.

- *The* **pragmatic follower** *exhibits a little of all four styles—depending on which style fits the prevailing situation.* Pragmatic followers are "stuck in the middle" most of the time. Because it is difficult to discern just where they stand on issues, they present an ambiguous image, with positive and negative sides. On the positive side, when an organization is going through desperate times, the pragmatic follower knows how to "work the system to get things done." On the negative side, this same behavior can be interpreted as "playing political games," or adjusting to maximize self-interest.

To be effective as a follower, it is important to acquire the skills necessary to combine two opposing follower roles; namely, to execute decisions made by a leader, and to raise issues about those decisions when they are deemed misguided or unethical. Although not always practical, followers must be willing to risk the leader's displeasure with such feedback. Moral integrity and a willingness to take stands based on principle are distinguishing characteristics of the effective follower. Developing a high level of mutual trust and respect between the leader and follower can mitigate the risk of falling out of favor with the leader. In such a relationship, a leader is likely to view criticism and dissenting views as an honest effort to facilitate achievement of shared objectives and values, rather than as an intentional expression of personal disagreement or disloyalty.

How followers perceive a leader plays a critical role in their ability to help the leader grow and succeed. Just as leaders make attributions about follower competence, followers make attributions about leader competence and intentions. Followers assess whether the leader's primary motivation is more for his or her personal benefit or career advancement than their own welfare and the organization's well-being. Credibility is increased and follower commitment is enhanced when the leader makes self-sacrifices to gain support for his or her ideas, rather than imposing on followers. Leaders who appear insincere, or motivated only by personal gain, create an atmosphere in which integrating the two opposing follower roles is impossible. Here, followers would play the passive role of conforming to the leader's expectations without offering any constructive criticism, even when it is called for in a leader's decisions and actions. Complete Self-Assessment 4 to learn how effective you are as a follower.

SELF-ASSESSMENT 4

Effective Followership

Select a present or past boss and answer each question describing your behavior using the following scale.

5 — 4 — 3 — 2 — 1

I do this regularly *I do not do this*

_____ 1. I offer my support and encouragement to my boss when things are not going well.

_____ 2. I take initiative to do more than my normal job without having to be asked to do things.

_____ 3. I counsel and coach my boss when it is appropriate, such as with a new, inexperienced boss, and in a unique situation in which the boss needs help.

continued

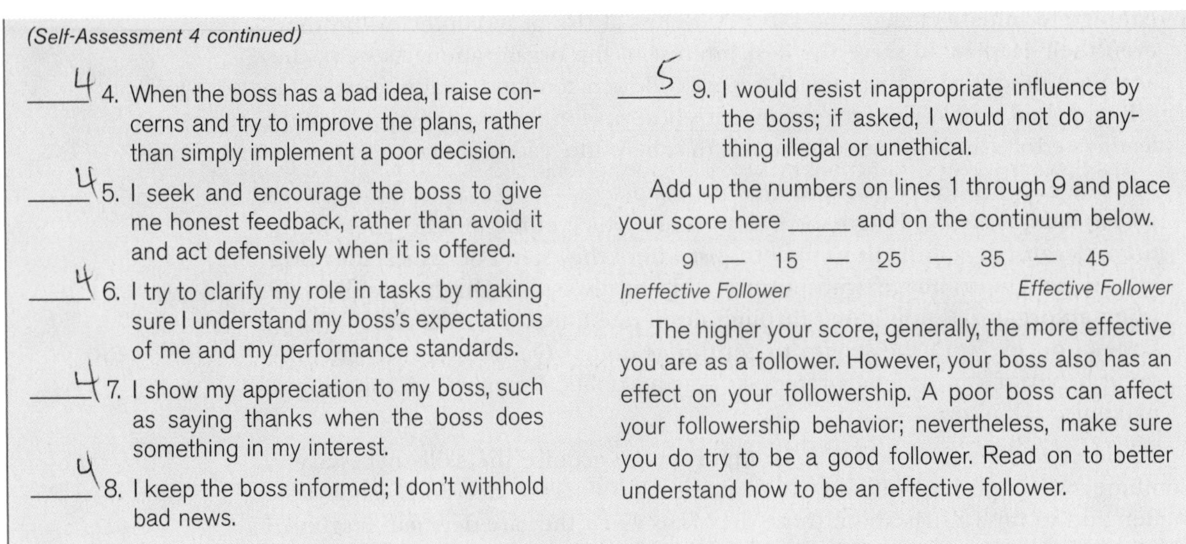

(Self-Assessment 4 continued)

______ 4. When the boss has a bad idea, I raise concerns and try to improve the plans, rather than simply implement a poor decision.

______ 5. I seek and encourage the boss to give me honest feedback, rather than avoid it and act defensively when it is offered.

______ 6. I try to clarify my role in tasks by making sure I understand my boss's expectations of me and my performance standards.

______ 7. I show my appreciation to my boss, such as saying thanks when the boss does something in my interest.

______ 8. I keep the boss informed; I don't withhold bad news.

______ 9. I would resist inappropriate influence by the boss; if asked, I would not do anything illegal or unethical.

Add up the numbers on lines 1 through 9 and place your score here ______ and on the continuum below.

9 — 15 — 25 — 35 — 45

Ineffective Follower *Effective Follower*

The higher your score, generally, the more effective you are as a follower. However, your boss also has an effect on your followership. A poor boss can affect your followership behavior; nevertheless, make sure you do try to be a good follower. Read on to better understand how to be an effective follower.

Guidelines to Becoming an Effective Follower

Research focused on followership has identified certain behaviors that work and others that don't. This has led to a formulation of guidelines on how to become an effective follower. The guidelines, it is argued, distinguish followers on top-performing teams from their counterparts on marginally performing teams. Issues such as how to improve the leader–follower relationship, how to resist improper influence, and how to challenge flawed plans and actions are dealt with through these guidelines. Also underlying these guidelines are ethical and moral themes, such as maintaining credibility and trust, adhering to your own values and convictions, and taking personal responsibility for team performance and for your own life. Exhibit 7.4 presents nine guidelines for effective followership; note that the nine questions in Self-Assessment 4 are based on these guidelines.

EXHIBIT 7.4 Guidelines to Becoming an Effective Follower

a. Offer support to leader.
b. Take initiative.
c. Play counseling and coaching roles to leader when appropriate.
d. Raise issues and/or concerns when necessary.
e. Seek and encourage honest feedback from the leader.
f. Clarify your role and expectations.
g. Show appreciation.
h. Keep the leader informed.
i. Resist inappropriate influence of leader.

Offer Support to Leader

A good follower looks for ways to express support and encouragement to a leader who is encountering resistance in trying to introduce needed change in his or her organization. Successful organizations are characterized by followers whose work ethic and philosophy are in congruence with those of the leader.

Take Initiative

Effective followers take the initiative to do what is necessary without being told, including working beyond their normally assigned duties. They look for opportunities to make a positive impact on the organization's objectives. When serious problems arise that impede the organization's ability to accomplish its objectives, effective followers take the risk to initiate corrective action by pointing out the problem to the leader, suggesting alternative solutions, or if necessary, resolving the problem outright. While taking the initiative often involves risks, if done carefully and properly, it can make the follower a valuable part of the team and a member of the leader's in-group.

Counsel and Coach the Leader When Appropriate

Contrary to the myth that leaders have all the answers, most people now recognize that followers also have opportunities to coach and counsel leaders, especially when a leader is new and inexperienced. A mutually trusting relationship with a leader facilitates upward coaching and counseling. An effective follower must be alert for opportunities to provide helpful advice, and ask questions, or simply be a good listener when the leader needs someone to confide in. Because some leaders may be reluctant to ask for help, it is the follower's responsibility to recognize such situations and step in when appropriate. For example, a leader whose interpersonal relationship with another follower may be having a different effect than the leader intended could be counseled to see the ineffectiveness of his approach or style by another follower: "I am sure you intended for Bob to see the value of being on time when you said…, but that is not how he took it." When coaching and counseling a leader is done with respect, it is most effective. Respect creates symmetry, empathy, and connection in all kinds of relationships, including that between a leader and a follower.[75]

Raise Issues and/or Concerns When Necessary

When there are potential problems or drawbacks with a leader's plans and proposals, a follower's ability to bring these issues or concerns to light is critical. How the follower raises these issues is crucial, because leaders often get defensive in responding to negative feedback. Followers can minimize such defensiveness by acknowledging the leader's superior status and communicating a sincere desire to be of help in accomplishing the organization's goals, rather than personal objectives. When challenging a leader's flawed plans and proposals, it is important for the follower to pinpoint specifics rather than vague generalities, and to avoid personalizing the critique. This guideline corresponds with the emerging view of the proactive employee as a follower who is highly involved and very much an independent thinker with initiative and a well-developed sense of responsibility.

Seek and Encourage Honest Feedback from the Leader

Followers can play a constructive role in how their leaders evaluate them. Some leaders are uncomfortable with expressing negative concerns about a follower's performance, so they tend to focus only on the follower's strengths. One way to build mutual trust and respect with the leader is to encourage honest feedback in his or her evaluation of your performance. Encourage the leader to point out the strongest and weakest aspects of your work. To ensure that you have a comprehensive evaluation, consult the leader for his or her input on other things you can do to be more effective, and find out if he or she has concerns about any other aspects of your work performance.

Clarify Your Role and Expectations

Where there is some question of role ambiguity or uncertainty about job expectations, this must be clarified with the leader. As will be revealed in Chapter 8 on leading effective teams, it is the leader's responsibility to clearly communicate role expectations for followers. Nevertheless, some leaders fail to communicate clear job expectations, followers' scope of authority and responsibility, performance targets that must be attained, and deadlines. Followers must insist on clarification in these areas by their leaders. In some cases the problem is that of role conflict. The leader directs a follower to perform mutually exclusive tasks and expects results on all of them at the same time. Followers should be assertive but diplomatic about resolving role ambiguity and conflict.

Show Appreciation

Everyone, including leaders, loves to be appreciated when they perform a good deed that benefits others. When a leader makes a special effort to help a follower, such as helping to protect the follower's interest, or nurturing and promoting the follower's career, it is appropriate for the follower to show appreciation. Even if the leader's actions don't directly benefit a particular follower but represent a significant accomplishment for the organization (for example, negotiating a difficult joint venture, completing a successful restructuring task, securing a greater share of resources for the group), it is still an appropriate gesture for followers to express their appreciation and admiration for the leader. Recognition and support of this kind only reinforce desirable leadership behavior. Although some may argue that praising a leader is a form of ingratiation easily used to influence the leader, when sincere, it can help to build a productive leader–follower exchange relationship.

Keep the Leader Informed

Leaders rely on their followers to relay important information about their actions and decisions. Accurate and timely information enables a leader to make good decisions and to have a complete picture of where things stand in the organization. Leaders who appear not to know what is going on in their organizations do feel and look incompetent in front of their peers and superiors. It is embarrassing for a leader to hear about events or changes taking place within his or her unit from others. This responsibility of relaying information to the leader includes both positive and negative information. Some followers tend to withhold bad news from their leaders; this is just as detrimental as providing no information at all.

Work Application 7

Give examples of how you, or someone you worked with, implemented three of the nine guidelines to effective followership.

Resist Inappropriate Influence of Leader

A leader may be tempted to use his or her power to influence the follower in ways that are inappropriate (legally or ethically). Despite the power gap between the leader and follower, the follower is not required to comply with inappropriate influence attempts, or to be exploited by an abusive leader. Effective followers challenge the leader in a firm, tactful, and diplomatic way. Reminding the leader of his or her ethical responsibilities, insisting on your rights, and pointing out the negative consequences of complying are various ways in which a follower can resist inappropriate influence attempts by a leader. It is important to challenge such behavior early, before it becomes habitual, and to do it without personal hostility.

Applying the **Concept 3**

Guidelines to Becoming an Effective Follower

Identify each guideline using the letters a–i from Exhibit 7.4 on page 258:

____ 10. We started a new project today, and I did not understand what I was supposed to do. So I went to talk to my boss about what to do.

____ 11. We have a new boss, and I've been filling her in on how we do things in our department.

____ 12. My boss and I have short daily meetings.

____ 13. Employees have not been following safety rules as they should, and the boss hasn't done anything about it. So I went to talk to my boss about it.

____ 14. We only have performance reviews once a year. But I wanted to know what my boss thinks of my work, so we had a meeting to discuss my performance.

____ 15. My boss gave me a new assignment that I wanted, so I thanked him.

____ 16. I showed up early for the meeting and the conference room was messy, so I cleaned up.

____ 17. My boss hinted about having a sexual relationship, so I reminded her that I was happily married and clearly told her I was not interested and not to talk about it again.

Learning Outcome 9 *Discuss the three follower influencing characteristics.*

Determinants of Follower Influence

In every organization or work setting, some followers seem to have more influence over their peers (and even their leaders) than others. These are the followers that command respect, obedience, and loyalty from their peers and thus are considered of higher status than the rest. The status of a follower within an organization will affect how he or she is treated by other followers. It is not uncommon for a follower with high status to exert greater influence on other followers than even a leader. Leaders who understand this follower–follower dynamic can use it to their advantage.

It is not the case that all influential followers are effective followers. They can employ their influence in negative ways to make the leader's job of influencing followers difficult. This section examines the factors that determine follower influence. The three determining factors that have been found to distinguish influential followers from their peers are: follower's relative power position, locus of control, and education and experience (see Exhibit 7.5 on the next page).

Follower Relative Power Position

Leaders need to realize that they are no longer the sole possessors of power and influence in their work units. The new reality is that no matter what position a person holds in the workplace, they are a force for change. Followers are often recognized as innovators, self-managers, or risk-takers. These are terms that were traditionally reserved for describing leaders, not followers. Some followers may have personal, referent, expert, information, and connection-based sources of power that can be used to boost upward influence. These power sources were discussed in Chapter 4. Any of these types of powers can give the follower the ability to influence others at different levels of the organization. As more and more employees come to rely on a particular follower for information, expertise, or simply because of his

EXHIBIT 7.5 Factors that Determine Follower Influence

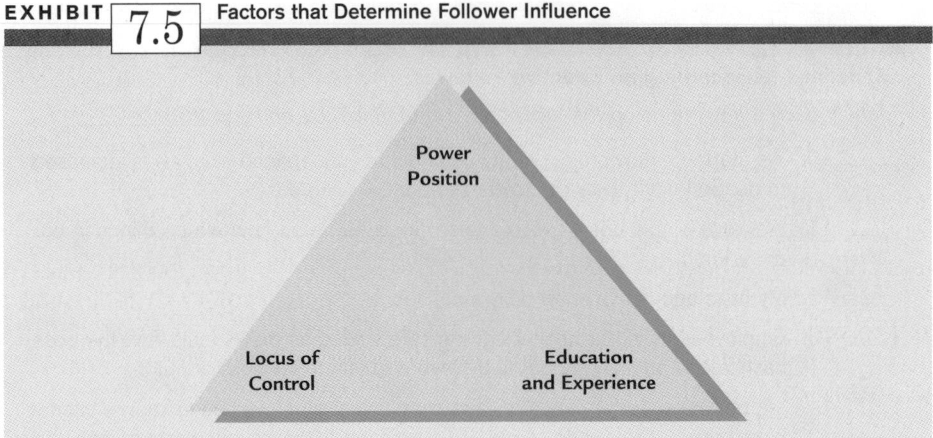

or her personality, the follower's relative power position increases. These are the followers that can influence other followers to slow down performance, file grievances, stage demonstrations, or even sabotage operations—all actions that can hurt a leader's reputation.

Follower Locus of Control

As discussed in Chapter 2, **locus of control** *is on a continuum between an external and internal belief over who has control of a person's destiny.* People who believe they are "masters of their own destiny" are said to have an *internal locus of control;* they believe that they can influence people and events in their workplace. People who believe they are "pawns of fate" (*external locus of control*) tend to believe they have no influence or control at work. Followers with an internal locus of control prefer a different type of work environment than those who have an external locus of control.

Internal locus of control followers prefer a work environment that facilitates communication with leaders, participation in decision making, and opportunities to be creative. Research relating to this proposition found that followers' locus of control did influence their choice of preferred leadership style. Followers with an internal locus of control preferred a participative style, while followers with an external locus of control preferred a directive style. Therefore, conflict is likely to occur when followers with an internal locus of control are led by leaders wanting to exercise directive leadership. Followers with an internal locus of control are likely to be more influential with other followers than those with external locus of control.

Follower Education and Experience

Not all followers have the same level of education or experience. These differences can have a major impact on the relationships among followers, and between leaders and followers. Followers in new job positions with little or no experience tend to need more guidance, coaching, and feedback, whereas followers in long-term employment positions with experience often need only minimal guidance and periodic feedback in order to achieve high levels of performance. To improve their performance, inexperienced employees often seek the assistance of experienced employees. Followers with valuable skills and experience may be able to use their expert power to influence other followers and even the leader. To be more effective, leaders will need to understand and appreciate their followers' education, experience, training, and background—and how these factors influence their behavior.

Leaders have to allow themselves room to learn from followers in the modern global economy. This requirement is dictated by the fact that leaders and followers today work in an environment of constant change. Today's workers—most of them followers—are far more educated, mobile, diverse, and younger than the workforce of 20 years ago; yet, the need for continuing education and training on the job will only increase. Leaders have to shift away from the top-down directive style of leading that was common when tasks were highly structured and power tended to be centralized and move toward a more decentralized, participative style of managing. As workers' education and experience increase, they tend to reject this style of leadership. Leaders who ignore this fact will face higher employee dissatisfaction and turnover.[76] The era of the passive follower, it would appear, is a thing of the past. The experienced and educated follower can be much more influential with other followers than the leader.

Work Application 8

Recall a work-related incident when you felt more qualified to do the job than your boss because of your education and experience. Describe how this characteristic enabled you to influence your boss.

Applying the **Concept 4**

Determinants of Follower Influence

Identify the specific follower influencing characteristic in each of these statements.

a. relative power position b. locus of control c. education and experience

____ 18. When it comes to selling my points to peers, I easily get them to see things my way rather than the boss's way due to my seniority and popularity in this division.

____ 19. Many of my peers depend on me for direction because I am the only one in the department who has been trained to work with this new machine successfully.

____ 20. It's not what you know; it's who you know around here that counts.

We conclude this section on followership with a brief discussion of the dual role of being a leader and a follower and the challenges it presents.

Dual Role of Being a Leader and a Follower

As mentioned earlier, leadership is not a one-way street. And as the guidelines for effective followership revealed, good leadership is found in highly effective followers. It is important to recognize that even when someone is identified as a leader, the same person often holds a complementary follower role.[77] It is not at all uncommon to switch between being a leader and being a follower several times over the course of a day's work. For example, within an organization, middle managers answer to vice presidents, who answer to the CEO, who answers to the board of directors; within the school system, teachers answer to the principal, who answers to the school superintendent, who answers to school board members. Regardless of one's position on the corporate ladder, we are all in a follower role to someone else.

There is research proposing that the leader's relationship with his or her superior (leader–leader exchange) moderates the effects of the leader's relationship with the subordinate (leader–member exchange). Proponents argue that leader–member exchange has a stronger positive effect on employees' attitudes toward the organization and its customers when leader–leader exchange is higher.[78] This signals organizational support for high-quality LMX relationships at all levels of the organization and some indication of the organization's culture.

Research on high-performance teams reveals that some organizations are moving toward the use of self-managed teams, in which team members alternate between playing leadership and followership roles. The duality of playing both leader and follower roles is further examined in Chapter 8 with self-managed teams.

To execute both roles effectively is a challenge. It is not an easy task, given the high potential for role conflicts and ambiguities. Leaders are held responsible for everything that happens in their work unit, yet they are also required to delegate much responsibility and authority to their followers to empower them in resolving problems on their own. In effect, leaders are asked to train and develop followers, who may eventually want the leader's job—even if the leader is not ready to give it up. How to balance these often conflicting demands and perform the dual roles of leader and follower effectively is a subject that deserves much more research focus than it has received.

Delegation

We now focus on developing followers by delegating tasks to them. **Delegation** *is the process of assigning responsibility and authority for accomplishing objectives.* Telling employees to perform the tasks that are part of their job design is issuing orders, not delegating. *Delegating* refers to giving employees new tasks. The new task may become a part of a redesigned job, or it may simply be a one-time task. The true art of delegation lies in a manager's ability to know what cannot be delegated and what should be delegated.[79] Some management experts believe that if there were a top ten list of managerial mistakes, failure to delegate would be one of them.[80] In this section we discuss delegating, delegation decisions, and delegating with a model.

Delegating

Effective delegation requires that a leader should carefully consider several factors relating to the task, time requirement, and follower characteristics before delegating.[81] A leader should delegate work when there is not enough time to attend to priority tasks, when followers desire more challenges and opportunities, and when the tasks match follower skill levels and experiences. Also a leader must find the proper person for the job and provide careful instructions. Effective delegation allows people to prosper in their own uniqueness.

Let's begin by discussing the benefits of delegation, the obstacles to delegation, and signs of delegating too little.

Benefits of Delegation

When managers delegate, they have more time to perform high-priority tasks. Delegation gets tasks accomplished and increases productivity. It enables leaders to mobilize resources and secure better results than they could have gotten alone. Delegation trains employees and improves their self-esteem, as well as eases the stress and burden on managers.[82] By delegating responsibilities, leaders can focus on doing a few tasks well instead of many tasks less effectively. Consequently, they improve their management and leadership potential while training others to succeed them. It is a means of developing followers by enriching their jobs. From the organization's perspective, delegating can result in increased performance and work outcomes. It can also lead to more communication between leaders and followers, thus encouraging followers to voice their opinions on how to improve the work environment.[83]

Obstacles to Delegation

Managers become used to doing things themselves. Managers fear that employees will fail to accomplish tasks. You can delegate responsibility and authority, but not your accountability. Managers believe they can perform tasks more efficiently than others.[84] Some managers don't realize that delegation is an important part of their job, others don't know what to delegate, and some don't know how to delegate.

Effective delegation greatly improves a leader's time management, without which efficiency and effectiveness suffer.[85,86] If you let these or other reasons keep you from delegating, you could end up like Dr. Rudenstine, former president of Harvard University, who became ill due to job stress by trying to do too much by himself.

Signs of Delegating Too Little

Certain behaviors are associated with leaders who are reluctant to delegate to their subordinates. These behaviors are signs that a leader is delegating too little. Some of these behaviors include taking work home, performing employee tasks, being behind in work, a continual feeling of pressure and stress, rushing to meet deadlines, and requiring that employees seek approval before acting. Leaders who can't disengage from the office and delegate authority and responsibility undermine employees' confidence to make decisions and take responsibility for their actions.[87] Unfortunately, in many of today's cost-cutting environments, you don't always have someone you can delegate some of your tasks to.

Work Application 9

Describe an obstacle to delegation, or sign of delegating too little, that you have observed on the job.

Learning Outcome 10 *List five things a leader should delegate.*

Delegation Decisions

As mentioned earlier, an important part of delegation is knowing which tasks to delegate.[88] Successful delegation is often based on selecting what task to delegate and who to delegate it to.[89]

What to Delegate

As a general guide, use your prioritized to-do list and delegate anything that you don't have to be personally involved with because of your unique knowledge or skill.[90] Some possibilities include the following:

- *Paperwork.* Have others prepare reports, memos, letters, and so on.
- *Routine tasks.* Delegate checking inventory, scheduling, ordering, and so on.
- *Technical matters.* Have top employees deal with technical questions and problems.
- *Tasks with developmental potential.* Give employees the opportunity to learn new things. Prepare them for advancement by enriching their jobs.
- *Employees' problems.* Train employees to solve their own problems; don't solve problems for them, unless their capability is low.

What Not to Delegate

As a general guide, do not delegate anything that you need to be personally involved with because of your unique knowledge or skill. Here are some typical examples:

- *Personnel matters.* Performance appraisals, counseling, disciplining, firing, resolving conflicts, and so on.
- *Confidential activities.* Unless you have permission to do so.
- *Crises.* There is no time to delegate.
- *Activities delegated to you personally.* For example, if you are assigned to a committee, do not assign someone else without permission.

Determining to Whom to Delegate

Once you have decided what to delegate, you must select an employee to do the task. When selecting an employee to delegate to, be sure that he or she has the capability to get the job done right by the deadline. Consider your employees' talents and interests when making a selection.[91] You may consult with several employees to determine their interests before making the final choice.

Before you learn how to delegate with the use of a model, complete Self-Assessment 5 to learn how your personality may affect your followership and delegation.

SELF-ASSESSMENT 5

Followership and Personality

Personality Differences

Generally, if you have an agreeableness Big Five personality type, which is a high need for affiliation, you will have a good relationship with your manager, because having a good relationship with everyone helps you to meet your needs. If you have a lower need for power, you prefer to be a follower, rather than a leader. Generally, you will be willing to delegate authority.

If you have a surgency/high need for power, you may have some problems getting along with your manager. You prefer to be in control, or to be a leader rather than a follower. However, if you don't get along well with your manager, you will have difficulty climbing the corporate ladder. You may have some reluctance to delegate authority because you like to be in control—and when you delegate, you lose some control.

If you have a conscientiousness/high need for achievement, you may not be concerned about your relationship with your manager, other than getting what you want to get the job done. However, if you don't get along well with your manager, you will have difficulty getting what you want. You may also be reluctant to delegate tasks that you like to do, because you get satisfaction from doing the job itself, rather than having someone else to do it.

Being well adjusted also helps you to have a good relationship with your manager. Being open to experience, which includes an internal locus of control (Chapter 2), helps you to get along with others since you are willing to try new things.

Gender Differences

Although there are exceptions, generally, women tend to seek relationships that are on a more personal level than men. For example, two women who work together are more apt to talk about their family lives than two men. Men do socialize, but it is more frequently about other interests such as sports. It is not unusual for women who have worked together for months to know more about each other's personal and family lives than men who have worked together for years. Men who do enjoy talking about their personal lives tend to talk more about their families in dyads with women than in those with men. One of the reasons men enjoy working with women is because they often bring a personal-level relationship to the job.

How does your personality affect your dyadic relationships, followership, and delegation?

____

____

____

____

Ethica **Dilemma 2**

Delegating the Destruction of Documents

Arthur Andersen, a consulting company, and Global Crossing, a multimedia communications company, were both taken to court for destroying evidence that could have been used in a court of law to support charges of illegal activities. Arthur Andersen destroyed evidence related to Enron, to protect both companies from being found guilty of conducting illegal business practices. Arthur Andersen claimed that it was not

continued

(Ethical Dilemma 2 continued)

trying to destroy incriminating evidence, that it was simply destroying records, which is done periodically. Destroying documents is routine; the question therefore becomes, what is being destroyed and why is it being destroyed?

1. Is it ethically responsible to delegate the task of destroying documents that may potentially be used as evidence of wrongdoing?
2. What would you do if your boss asked you to destroy documents that you thought might be to cover up wrongdoing (evidence) by the firm? (Some options include: just do it, don't say anything but don't do it, question the motives, look closely at what you are asked to destroy, go to your boss's boss to make sure it's okay to do it, tell the boss you will not do it, ask the boss to do it him- or herself, blow the whistle to an outside source like the government or media, and so on.)
3. If you went to court for destroying evidence, do you believe you would have a good ethical defense by saying "I was only following orders?"

Delegating with the Use of a Model

After determining what to delegate and to whom, you must plan for and delegate the tasks. *The* **delegation model** *steps are* (1) *explain the need for delegating and the reasons for selecting the employee;* (2) *set objectives that define responsibility, level of authority, and deadline;* (3) *develop a plan; and* (4) *establish control checkpoints and hold employees accountable.*[92,93] Following these four steps can increase your chances of successfully delegating. As you read on, you will see how the delegation model is used with the job characteristics model, core job dimensions, and critical psychological states to influence performance and work outcomes.

Step 1. **Explain the need for delegating and the reasons for selecting the employee.** It is helpful for the employee to understand why the assignment must be completed. In other words, how will the department or organization benefit? Informing employees helps them realize the importance of the task (experienced meaningfulness of work). Telling the employee why he or she was selected should make him or her feel valued. Don't use the "it's a lousy job, but someone has to do it" approach. Be positive; make employees aware of how they will benefit from the assignment. If step 1 is completed successfully, the employee should be motivated, or at least willing, to do the assignment.

Step 2. **Set objectives that define responsibility, level of authority, and deadline.** The objectives should clearly state the end result the employee is responsible for achieving by a specific deadline. You should also define the level of authority the employee has, as the following choices illustrate:

- Make a list of all supplies on hand, and present it to me each Friday at 2:00 (inform authority).
- Fill out a supply purchase order, and present it to me each Friday at 2:00 (recommend authority).
- Fill out and sign a purchase order for supplies; send it to the purchasing department with a copy put in my in-basket each Friday by 2:00 (report authority).

- Fill out and sign a purchase order for supplies, and send it to the purchasing department each Friday by 2:00, keeping a copy (full authority).

Step 3. Develop a plan. Once the objective is set, a plan is needed to achieve it. It is helpful to write out the objective, specifying the level of authority and the plan. When developing a plan, be sure to identify the resources needed to achieve the objectives, and give the employee the authority necessary to obtain the resources. Inform all parties of the employee's authority and with whom the employee must work. For example, if an employee is doing a marketing report, you should contact the marketing department and tell them the employee must have access to the necessary information.

Step 4. Establish control checkpoints and hold employees accountable. For simple, short tasks, a deadline without control checkpoints is appropriate. However, it is often advisable to check progress at predetermined times (control checkpoints) for tasks that have multiple steps or will take some time to complete. This builds information flow into the delegation system right from the start. You and the employee should agree on the form (phone call, visit, memo, or detailed report) and time frame (daily, weekly, or after specific steps are completed but before going on to the next step) for information regarding the assignment. When establishing control, consider the employee's capability level. The lower the capability, the more frequent the checks; the higher the capability, the less frequent the checks.

It is helpful to list the control checkpoints in writing on an operational planning sheet, making copies of the finished plan so that the parties involved and you as the delegating manager have a record to refer to. In addition, all parties involved should record the control checkpoints on their calendars. If the employee to whom the task was delegated does not report as scheduled, follow up to find out why the person did not report, and get the information. You should evaluate performance at each control checkpoint, and upon completion provide feedback that develops knowledge of the results of work.

Work Application 10

Select a manager you work or have worked for, and analyze how well he or she implements the four steps of delegation. Which steps does the manager typically follow and not follow?

Providing praise for progress and completion of the task motivates employees to do a good job. You will recall that Chapter 6 discussed how to give praise.

The four steps of the delegation process are summarized in Model 7.1. In Skill-Development Exercise 2, you will have the opportunity to use the model to delegate a task and to develop your delegation skills.

MODEL 7.1 Steps in the Delegation Model

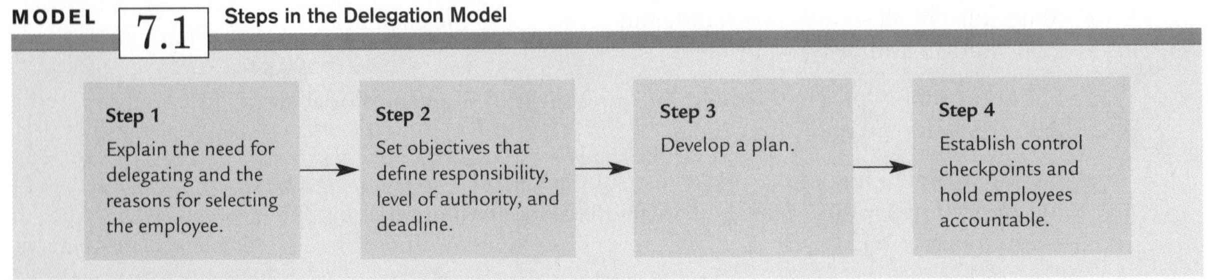

Step 1
Explain the need for delegating and the reasons for selecting the employee.
Step 2
Set objectives that define responsibility, level of authority, and deadline.
Step 3
Develop a plan.
Step 4
Establish control checkpoints and hold employees accountable.

Go to the Internet (www.cengage.com/management/lussier)
where you will find a broad array of resources to help maximize your learning.

- Review the vocabulary
- Try a quiz
- Find related links

Chapter Summary

The chapter summary is organized to answer the 11 learning outcomes for Chapter 7.

1. **List the four stages of development of the dyadic approach.**

   The first conception of dyadic theory was the awareness of a relationship between a leader and a follower, rather than between a leader and a group of followers. The second stage of dyadic theory describes specific attributes of exchange between a leader and a follower that lead to high- or low-quality relationships. The third and fourth stages of dyadic theory emphasize team building and systems and networks. Organizations strive for team building among all employees (managers and nonmanagers) and to create valuable systems and networks across traditional boundaries of the organization. Leaders and followers begin to see themselves as part of a larger network rather than as isolated units.

2. **Define the two kinds of relationships that can occur among leaders and followers under the vertical dyadic linkage model.**

   The two types of relationships that can occur among leaders and followers under the VDL model are in-group and out-group members. In-groups include followers with strong social ties to their leader in a people-oriented relationship, characterized by high mutual trust, respect, loyalty, and influence. Out-groups include followers with little or no social ties to their leader in a strictly task-oriented relationship, characterized by low exchange, lack of trust and loyalty, and top-down influence.

3. **Describe the main focus of team building from a Leader–Follower perspective.**

   The emphasis of the team-building view is the notion that effective leaders should aspire to establish relationships with all followers, not just with a few special individuals. It is about forging a partnership with each group member without alienating anyone.

4. **Discuss the focus of the systems and networks approach from a Leader–Follower perspective.**

   The systems and networks version of the dyadic approach examines how a dyadic relationship can be created across traditional boundaries to include everyone in the organization. It emphasizes creating relationships that cut across functional, divisional, and even organizational boundaries, rather than including leaders and followers in only a limited section of the organization.

5. **Describe three determining factors of high-quality LMX relationships.**

   High-quality LMX relationships may be influenced by the following three antecedent factors: (1) *Follower attributes*—Attributes such as commitment, trust, respect, and loyalty will influence leaders to show support, delegate more, allow followers more discretion in conducting their work, and engage in open communication with followers. (2) *Leader's perceptions and behavior*—The leader's first impressions of a group member's competency plays an important role in defining the quality of the relationship. (3) *Situational factors*—Factors such as tryouts or tests of a new employee may be key determinants of a follower's in-group or out-group status.

6. **Discuss the key limitation or drawback with LMX application.**

   A major limitation of LMX is measurement difficulty. LMX theory deals with attitudes and perceptions of individuals; two issues that are often difficult to quantify and measure. For this reason, recent research efforts on LMX have focused on instrumentation of the theory. The way in which the attributes of high-quality LMX relationships have been defined and measured have varied somewhat from study to study.

7. **Explain the cycle that leads to the Pygmalion effect.**

   The Pygmalion effect occurs when selected followers demonstrate loyalty, commitment, and trust, as a result winning the favor of leaders who subsequently give those followers higher performance ratings. These ratings, which may or may not be tied to actual performance, then influence the follower's reputation, and often become a matter of record. The ratings may ultimately be used—formally or informally—in future selection, development, and promotion decisions. Consequently, followers with a history of high performance ratings (positive Pygmalion effect) are often promoted to higher-level positions, and those with a history of low performance ratings (negative Pygmalion effect) may never be promoted or, even worse, may be demoted.

8. **Explain how LMX relationships can lead to unintended bias in HR practices.**

   In LMX relationships, leaders develop strong social ties with in-group members. Whether intentionally or unintentionally, this positive relationship has been known to correlate with higher performance ratings for in-group members compared to out-group members. HR decisions regarding promotions, demotions, reassignments, layoffs, and salary increases are often based on information accumulated in employee files. An employee's performance evaluation from his or her manager may influence the decision on who gets promoted, demoted, or worse, laid off. If the evaluation was based on a manager liking or not liking a follower in the first place, rather than on actual job performance, then it may seem unfair to use it as the basis for any action; and yet it happens everyday.

9. **Discuss the three follower influencing characteristics.**

The three follower influencing characteristics are: (1) *Relative power position*—Leaders need to realize that followers also have the power to influence them. (2) *Locus of control*—Followers can have an internal or external locus of control, based on their belief about who is the master of their destiny. Thus, leader–member exchanges should be different based on locus of control. (3) *Education and experience*—Leaders need to realize that followers may have different levels of education and experience, and that they need to supervise them differently.

10. **List five things a leader should delegate.**

A leader should delegate paperwork, routine tasks, technical matters, tasks with developmental potential, and employee problems.

11. **Define the following key terms (in order of appearance in the chapter).**

Select one or more methods: (1) fill in the missing key terms from memory; (2) match the key terms from the following list with their definitions below; (3) copy the key terms in order from the list at the beginning of the chapter.

__________ refers to the individualized relationship between a leader and each follower in a work unit.

__________ is an approach to leadership that attempts to explain why leaders vary their behavior with different followers.

__________ examines how leaders form one-on-one relationships with followers, and how these often create in-groups and out-groups within the leader's work unit.

__________ includes followers with strong social ties to their leader in a supportive relationship characterized by high mutual trust, respect, loyalty, and influence.

__________ includes followers with few or no social ties to their leader, in a strictly task-centered relationship characterized by low exchange and top-down influence.

__________ is the quality of the exchange relationship between an employee and his or her superior.

__________ is a follower's effort to project a favorable image in order to gain an immediate benefit or improve a long-term relationship with the leader.

__________ is the effort to appear supportive, appreciative, and respectful.

__________ is the effort to appear competent and dependable.

__________ refers to the behavior of followers that results from the leader–follower influence relationship.

__________ is a person who is being influenced by a leader.

__________ is someone who is low on involvement yet is high on critical thinking.

__________ is someone who is high on involvement but low on critical thinking.

__________ is someone who is neither high on critical thinking nor involvement.

__________ is someone who is high on critical thinking and involvement.

__________ exhibits a little of all four styles—depending on which style fits the prevailing situation.

__________ is on a continuum between an external and internal belief over who has control over a person's destiny.

__________ is the process of assigning responsibility and authority for accomplishing objectives.

__________ steps are (1) explain the need for delegating and the reasons for selecting the employee; (2) set objectives that define responsibility, level of authority, and deadline; (3) develop a plan; and (4) establish control checkpoints and hold employees accountable.

Key Terms

alienated follower, 256
conformist follower, 256
delegation, 264
delegation model, 267
dyadic, 240
dyadic theory, 240
effective follower, 256
follower, 255
followership, 255
impressions management, 249
ingratiation, 249
in-group, 242
leader–member exchange (LMX), 244
locus of control, 262
out-group, 242
passive follower, 256
pragmatic follower, 257
self-promotion, 249
vertical dyadic linkage (VDL) theory, 242

Review Questions

1. What are the differences between in-groups and out-groups?
2. How do quality leader–member exchange relationships influence follower behavior?
3. How does a leader's first impression and perception of a follower influence the quality of their relationship?
4. What are the three stages of the life-cycle model of LMX theory?
5. How can a follower's perception or attribution of a leader influence their relationship?
6. What is the presence of bias in the LMX relationship? What is its potential impact on out-group and in-group members of the organization?
7. How do education and experience, described as follower influencing characteristics, affect effective followership?
8. What are some of the benefits of delegating?
9. What are some things that a leader should not delegate?

Communication Skills

The following critical-thinking questions can be used for class discussion and/or as written assignments to develop communication skills. Be sure to give complete explanations for all questions.

1. In your opinion, can a leader maintain a personal friendship with some members of his or her work group or team without creating the perception of in-groups (those in his or her social circle) and out-groups (those outside his or her social circle)?
2. What should a leader do to dispel any notion or misperception that there are in-groups and out-groups in his or her work unit?
3. High-quality LMX relationships create a circle of reciprocity where followers feel like they should go the extra mile for a leader who supports them and the leader feels like he or she should offer the followers more support and benefits to keep their loyalty. Do you believe this is the case in the real world or is it something different?
4. Movies dealing with the prison or college environment often depict one or two prisoners or students who seem to have more influence over other prisoners or students than even the guards or administrators. Can you think of one such case and explain why the individual was influential over other prisoners or students?
5. What do you say to those who argue that tactics used by followers to get noticed by their leader (such as impressions management, ingratiation, and self-promotion) are shameful and self-serving and should be avoided?
6. Can someone have a successful career by aspiring to be an effective follower? Explain.
7. As a leader, how will you motivate the alienated follower?

CASE

W. L. Gore & Associates

Founded in 1958, W. L. Gore & Associates has become a modern-day success story as a uniquely managed, privately owned, family business. Founders Bill and Vieve Gore set out to explore opportunities for fluorocarbon polymers, especially polytetrafluoroethylene (PTFE). Today Gore is best known for its Gore-Tex fabric and Elixir Strings for guitars. Gore is the leading manufacturer of thousands of advanced technology products for the medical, electronics, industrial, and fabrics markets. With sales of over $2 billion, the company employs approximately 8,000 associates at more than 45 facilities around the world.

Terri Kelly replaced Chuck Carroll as the president and CEO of W. L. Gore & Associates in April 2005. In 2008, Gore was named one of the nation's best companies to work for by *Fortune* magazine. It was the 11th consecutive year that Gore appeared on the list. CEO Kelly said 2008's selection was particularly meaningful because Gore was celebrating its 50th anniversary. According to Kelly, all of Gore's practices and ways of doing business reflect the innovative and entrepreneurial spirit of its founders. "Our practices stress maximizing individual potential, cultivating an environment that fosters creativity, and operating with high integrity in everything we do," she said.[94] CEO Kelly attributes Gore's success to its unique culture.

How work is conducted at Gore and how employees relate to one another sets Gore apart. There are no formal job titles. Compensation and promotions are determined by peer rankings of each other's performance. To avoid dampening employee creativity, the company has an organizational structure and culture that goes against conventional wisdom. W. L. Gore & Associates has been described as not only unmanaged but also unstructured. Bill Gore (the founder) referred to the company's structure as a "lattice organization." Gore's lattice structure includes the following features:

- Direct lines of communication—person to person—with no intermediary
- No fixed or assigned authority
- Sponsors, not bosses
- Natural leadership as evidenced by the willingness of others to follow
- Objectives set by those who must "make them happen"
- Tasks and functions organized through commitments
- Complete avoidance of the hierarchical command and control structure

The lattice structure as described by the people at Gore encourages hands-on innovation and discourages bureaucratic red tape by involving those closest to a project in decision making. Instead of a pyramid of bosses and managers, Gore has a flat organizational structure. There are no chains of command, no predetermined channels of communication. It sounds very much like a self-managed team at a much broader scale.

Why has Gore achieved such remarkable success? W. L. Gore & Associates prefers to think of the various people who play key roles in the organization as being *leaders, not managers.* While Bill Gore did not believe in smothering the company in thick layers of formal management, he also knew that as the company grew, he had to find ways to assist new people and to follow their progress. Thus, W. L. Gore & Associates came up with its "sponsor" program. The sponsor program is a dyadic relationship between an incumbent, experienced employee and a newly hired, inexperienced employee. Before a candidate is hired, an associate has to agree to be his or her sponsor or what others refer to as a mentor. The sponsor's role is to take a personal interest in the new associate's contributions, problems, and goals, acting as both a coach and an advocate. The sponsor tracks the new associate's progress, offers help and encouragement, points out weaknesses and suggests ways to correct them, and concentrates on how the associate might better exploit his or her strengths.

Sponsoring is not a short-term commitment. All associates have sponsors, and many have more than one. When individuals are hired, at first they are likely to have a sponsor in their immediate work area. As associates' commitments change or grow, it's normal for them to acquire additional sponsors. For instance, if they move to a new job in another area of the company, they typically gain a sponsor there. Sponsors help associates chart a course in the organization that will offer personal fulfillment while maximizing their contribution to the enterprise. Leaders emerge naturally by demonstrating special knowledge, skill, or experience that advances a business objective.

An internal memo describes the three kinds of sponsorship and how they might work:

- *Starting sponsor*—a sponsor who helps a new associate get started on his or her first job at Gore, or helps a present associate get started on a new job.
- *Advocate sponsor*—a sponsor who sees to it that the associate being sponsored gets credit and recognition for contributions and accomplishments.
- *Compensation sponsor*—a sponsor who sees to it that the associate being sponsored is fairly paid for contributions to the success of the enterprise.

An associate can perform any one or all three kinds of sponsorship. Quite frequently, a sponsoring associate is a good friend, and it's not uncommon for two associates to sponsor each other as advocates.

Being an associate is a natural commitment to four basic principles articulated by Bill Gore and still a key belief of the company: fairness to each other and everyone we come in contact with; freedom to encourage, help, and allow other associates to grow in knowledge, skill, and scope of responsibility; the ability to make one's own commitments and keep them; and consultation with other associates before undertaking actions that could affect the reputation of the company.

Over the years, W. L. Gore & Associates has faced a number of unionization drives. The company neither tries to dissuade associates from attending organizational meetings nor retaliates against associates who pass out union flyers. However, Bill Gore believes there is no need for third-party representation under the lattice structure. He asks, "Why would associates join a union when they own the company? It seems rather absurd."

Commitment is seen as a two-way street at W. L. Gore & Associates—while associates are expected to commit to making a contribution to the company's success, the company is committed to providing a challenging, opportunity-rich work environment, and reasonable job security. The company tries to avoid laying off associates. If a workforce reduction becomes necessary, the company uses a system of temporary transfers within a plant or cluster of plants, and requests voluntary layoffs. According to CEO Kelly, Gore's structure, systems, and culture have continued to yield impressive results for the company. Gore, she said, has consistently grown revenues at a 7 to 9 percent rate for the past decade and voluntary turnover is just 5 percent—a strikingly low number for an industrial company with more than 45 manufacturing plants worldwide.

GO TO THE INTERNET: To learn more about W. L. Gore & Associates, visit its Web site **(http://www.gore.com)**.

Support your answers to the following questions with specific information from the case and text or with other information you get from the Web or other sources.

1. What theories from this chapter are revealed through the case?
2. How did Gore's "sponsors" program facilitate the creation of high-quality relationships among leaders, sponsors, and associates?
3. Evaluate followership at W. L. Gore & Associates. What company actions and/or policies account for the quality of followership?

CUMULATIVE CASE QUESTIONS

4. Would you characterize the leadership style at W. L. Gore & Associates as job-centered or employee-centered (Chapter 3)? Support your answer.
5. Based on the types of power discussed in the text, what type(s) of power do sponsors have in their relationships with associates (Chapter 4)?
6. What role, if any, does coaching play in W. L. Gore's lattice structure (Chapter 6)?

CASE EXERCISE AND ROLE-PLAY

Preparation: You are part of an organization that evaluates its employees at the end of each year. The month of the year when evaluations need to be completed by all leaders and managers is approaching. Your task is to play the role of a leader evaluating your followers, and then play the role of follower being evaluated by your own manager. Based on your understanding of the discussion of guidelines for effective leader feedback and guidelines for effective followership, (1) present a scenario of an effective and an ineffective feedback session, applying at least three of the guidelines discussed in the text, and (2) present a scenario of effective and ineffective followership, applying at least three of the guidelines discussed in the text.

Role-Play: The instructor forms students into leader–follower pairs and has each pair dramatize scenarios 1 and 2 in front of the rest of the class. After each scenario, the class is to contrast the two approaches (effective versus ineffective feedback) by identifying the guidelines that the presenters or actors employed in making their points. Different student teams should try the exercise by employing different guidelines to both scenarios.

VIDEO CASE

Delegation at Boyne USA Resorts

Detroit native Everett Kircher moved to northern Michigan in 1947 and purchased land (for the price of $1) necessary to start his first ski resort known today as Boyne Mountain. Kircher practiced a traditional chain of command in a vertical organizational structure. Every decision came from his desk. As his company expanded, additional people were needed to manage the different locations. For Kircher, it was the beginning of a partial decentralization and delegation of his leadership and decision making. In 2002, Everett Kircher died at the age of 85, but his legacy lives on. The company's reorganization in 2004 paved the way for the "Boyne Brand" to grow while maintaining organizational integrity. General managers were hired at each resort location to oversee operations. In addition, vice presidents known as "subject matter experts" were hired. The VPs share critical information with the general managers to help each resort operation. The general managers fold these experts into the decision-making process and help provide policy.

1. Describe leader–follower relations at Boyne USA Resorts.
2. Why was decentralization and delegation necessary to Boyne's future despite the success with Everett Kircher at the helm of a vertical structure?

Skill-Development Exercise 1

Improving Dyadic Relationships—Followership

Preparing for Skill-Development Exercise 1

Based on your reading of effective leader–member exchange relationships, how can you improve your current or future relationship with your manager?

Be sure to list specific things you plan to do.

Based on Self-Assessment 4 on pages 257–258, "Effective Followership," how can you improve your followership skills with your present or future manager? Be sure to list specific things you plan to do.

Doing Skill-Development Exercise 1 in Class

Objective

To develop a plan to improve your dyadic relationship with your manager and to improve your followership skills.

The primary AACSB learning standard skills developed through this exercise are reflective thinking and self-management and analytic skills.

Preparation

You should have completed a plan in the preparation part of this exercise.

Experience

You will share your plan in a small group to provide further development.

Procedure 1 *(8–12 minutes)*

Option A: Break into groups of 3 or 4 and share your plans. Offer each other ideas for improving plans.

Option B: Same as Option A, but add a spokesperson to record some of the best ideas from each group member.

Procedure 2 *(10–20 minutes)* Option B, each spokesperson reports to the entire class.

Conclusion

The instructor leads a class discussion and/or makes concluding remarks.

Apply It *(2–4 minutes)* What did I learn from this exercise? When will I implement my plan?

Sharing

In the group, or to the entire class, volunteers may give their answers to the "Apply It" questions.

Behavior Model Skills Training

In this behavior model skills training session, you will perform three activities:

1. Read the section, "Delegation," in this chapter (to learn how to use Model 7.1, page 268).
2. Watch Behavior Model Video 7.1, "Delegating."
3. Complete Skill-Development Exercise 2 (to develop your delegating skills).

For further practice, use the delegation model in your personal and professional life.

The Delegation Model

Step 1 Explain the need for delegating and the reasons for selecting the employee.

Step 2 Set objectives that define responsibility, level of authority, and deadline.

Step 3 Develop a plan.

Step 4 Establish control checkpoints and hold employees accountable.

Behavior Model Video 7.1

Delegating

Objective
To observe a manager delegating a task to an employee.

Video *(4½ minutes)* Overview
You will watch a production manager, Steve, delegate the completion of a production output form to Dale.

Skill-Development Exercise 2

Delegating

Preparing for Skill-Development Exercise 2

You should have read and understood the material on delegation.

Doing Skill-Development Exercise 2 in Class

Objective

To experience and develop skills in delegating a task.

The primary AACSB learning standard skills developed through this exercise are leadership and communication abilities.

Experience
You will delegate, be delegated to, and observe the delegation of a task, and then evaluate the effectiveness of the delegated task. You may also see a video example of how to delegate using the delegation model.

Procedure 1 *(4–8 minutes)* Break into as many groups of three as possible with the remainder in groups of two. Each person in the group picks a number 1, 2, or 3. Number 1 will be the first to delegate a task, then 2, and then 3. The level of difficulty of the delegation will increase with the number.

Each person then reads his or her delegation situation below (1, 2, or 3) and plans how he or she will delegate the task. If you prefer, you can use an actual delegation from a past or present job. Just be sure to fully explain the situation to the delegatee. Be sure to follow the four delegation steps in this chapter. An observer sheet is included at the end of this exercise for giving feedback on each delegation.

Delegation Situation 1
Delegator 1, you are a college student with a paper due in three days for your 10:00 a.m. class. It must be typed. You don't type well, so you have decided to hire someone to do it for you. The going rate is $1.50 per page. Think of an actual paper you have written in the past or will write in the future. Plan to delegate. Be sure to include the course name, paper title, special typing instructions, and so on. Assume that you are meeting the typist for the first time. He or she doesn't know you and doesn't expect you.

Delegator 2, assume that you do typing and are willing to do the job if the delegation is acceptable to you.

Delegation Situation 2
Delegator 2, you are the manager of a fast-food restaurant. In the past, you have scheduled the workers. Your policy is to keep changing the workers' schedules. You have decided to delegate the scheduling to your assistant manager. This person has never done any scheduling, but appears to be

very willing and confident about taking on new responsibility. Plan your delegation.

Delegator 3, assume that you are interested in doing the scheduling if the manager delegates the task effectively.

Delegation Situation 3

Delegator 3, you own and manage your own business. You have eight employees, one of whom is the organization's secretary. The secretary currently uses an old computer, which needs to be replaced. You have not kept up with the latest technology and don't know what to buy. You can spend $1,200. You try to keep costs down and get the most for your money. Because the secretary will use the new machine, you believe that this employee should be involved or maybe even make the decision. The secretary has never purchased equipment, and you believe he or she will be somewhat insecure about the assignment. Plan your delegation.

Delegator 1, assume that you are able to do the job but are somewhat insecure. Accept the task if the delegator "participates" effectively.

Procedure 2 *(7–10 minutes)*

A. *Delegation 1.* Delegator 1 delegates the task (role-play) to number 2. Number 3 is the observer. As the delegation takes place, the observer uses the form at the end of this exercise to provide feedback on the effectiveness of the delegator. Answer the questions on the form.

B. *Integration.* The observer (or number 3) leads a discussion of the effectiveness of the delegation, although all team members should participate. Do not continue until you are told to do so.

Procedure 3 *(7–10 minutes)*

A. *Delegation 2.* Follow procedure 2A, except number 2 is now the delegator, number 3 is the delegatee, and number 1 is the observer.

B. *Integration.* Follow procedure 2B with number 1 as the observer. Do not continue until you are told to do so.

Procedure 4 *(7–10 minutes)*

A. *Delegation 3.* Follow procedure 2A, except number 3 is now the delegator, number 1 is the delegatee, and number 2 is the observer. If you are in a group of two, be an additional observer for another group.

B. *Integration.* Follow procedure 2B with number 2 as the observer.

Conclusion

The instructor may lead a class discussion and make concluding remarks.

Apply It *(2–4 minutes)* What did I learn from this experience? When will I delegate using the model?

____

____

Sharing

In the group, or to the entire class, volunteers may give their answers to the "Apply It" questions.

Note: Remember that the process does not end with delegating the task; you must control (check progress at control points and help when needed) to ensure that the task is completed as scheduled.

OBSERVER FORM

During the delegation process, the observer checks off the items performed by the delegators. Items not checked were not performed. After the delegation, the delegator and delegatee also check off the items.

This sheet is used for all three situations. Use the appropriate column for each situation.

Delegation items for all situations	Situation 1	2	3
Did the delegator follow these steps?			
Step 1. Explain the need for delegating and the reasons for selecting the person.			
Step 2. Set an objective that defines responsibility, level of authority, and deadline.			
Step 3. Develop a plan.			
Step 4. Establish control checkpoints and hold the person accountable.			

Process

Did the delegate clearly understand what was expected of him or her and know how to follow the plan?

Improvements

How could the delegation be improved if done again?

Chapter Outline

The Use of Teams in Organizations

Groups Versus Teams: What Is the Difference?

Advantages and Disadvantages of Teamwork

Characteristics of Effective Teams

Types of Teams

Functional Team

Cross-Functional Team

Virtual Team

Self-Managed Team (SMT)

Decision Making in Teams

Leader-Centered Decision-Making Model

Team-Centered Decision-Making Model

Normative Leadership Model

Leadership Skills for Effective Team Meetings

Planning Meetings

Conducting Meetings

Handling Problem Members

Self-Managed Teams

The Nature of Self-Managed Teams

The Benefits of Self-Managed Teams

Guidelines for Improving Self-Managed Team Effectiveness

The Changing Role of Leadership in Self-Managed Teams

The Challenges of Implementing Self-Managed Teams

8 Team Leadership and Self-Managed Teams

Learning Outcomes

After studying this chapter, you should be able to:

1. Discuss the advantages and disadvantages of working in teams. p. 282
2. Briefly describe the seven characteristics of effective teams. p. 286
3. Describe top management's and the team leader's roles in fostering creativity. For each, list activities they should undertake to promote creativity. p. 291
4. Outline the three parts of conducting effective meetings. p. 303
5. Explain the differences between conventional and self-managed teams. p. 306
6. Describe how team member characteristics impact self-managed team effectiveness. p. 306
7. Describe the benefits of using self-managed teams in organizations. p. 308
8. Describe the guidelines for improving self-managed team effectiveness. p. 309
9. Describe the challenges of implementing effective self-managed teams. p. 313
10. Define the following **key terms** (in order of appearance in the chapter):

team
teamwork
social loafing
groupthink
team effectiveness
team learning
team norms
team cohesion
team creativity
functional team
cross-functional team
virtual team
self-managed teams (SMTs)
self-managed team champion
distributed leadership
self-managed team facilitator

Opening Case APPLICATION

John Chambers is the CEO of Cisco Systems. His legacy at Cisco will not soon be forgotten. As one writer puts it, "Perhaps no CEO in history has risen so high, fallen so hard and come back so quickly."[1] After Chambers became CEO in January 1995, Cisco's dominance and competitiveness in the industry was so strong that it led to the early exit of quite a few competitors. *BusinessWeek* named Cisco one of the Top 50 market performers, *Fortune* magazine designated Cisco one of America's "Most Admired Companies," and *Forbes* magazine called Cisco one of the "Leading Companies in the World." *Business Ethics Magazine* listed Cisco as one of its "Business Ethics 100 Best Corporate Citizens."[2]

However, it has not been a smooth ride the whole way. Beginning in early 2001, things started to change. A number of telecom companies and Internet service providers—some of them Cisco's biggest customers—were experiencing major declines in sales and profitability. As a result, they stopped buying Cisco equipment. The negative effect on Cisco's performance caused some industry experts to question Chambers' leadership abilities. Chambers remained unmoved. His strategy for resurrecting Cisco was twofold: first to downsize the company by making deep staffing cuts immediately, and second to implement a new organizational structure focused on cross-divisional teamwork and collaboration at all levels of the company. Underperforming products were eliminated as part of Cisco's recovery.

In making his case for change, Chambers said the future belongs to those who collaborate. There is a great need for the type of collaboration that bridges traditional geographic, institutional, and functional boundaries, he said. In a world characterized by the need for corporate agility, global competition, and the rise of emerging markets, the focus on collaboration both within and among organizations is imperative. Chambers maintains that collaboration among functional groups and organizations will help companies become more productive and innovative.[3]

Cisco's recovery is largely attributed to Chambers' leadership and brilliant strategic mind. He is said to be an excellent communicator and motivator. Cisco's comeback has caused some analysts to suggest that Chambers has ascended to a rarefied level, up with the likes of former CEOs Jack Welch of General Electric and Andy Grove of Intel.[4]

Opening Case Questions:

1. What would be the evidence that Cisco is a team of employees and not just a group of workers?
2. What characteristics of team leadership does John Chambers possess that make him so effective?
3. What role did organizational support play in the success of cross-divisional teams at Cisco?
4. One of the characteristics of effective teams is that they are creativity driven. How important is creativity to Cisco's success?
5. Why did John Chambers see cross-divisional teams and collaboration as the solution to Cisco's problems?
6. What evidence is there that the cross-divisional team structure at Cisco has worked so far?
7. Do you think John Chambers is the type of leader who would embrace self-managed teams? Explain your answer.

Can you answer any of these questions? You'll find answers to these questions and learn more about Cisco Systems and team leadership throughout the chapter.

To learn more about John Chambers and Cisco Systems visit Cisco's Web site at **http://www.cisco.com**.

The focus of this chapter is on how organizations can develop and use effective teams to achieve organizational goals. We will explore the importance of incorporating teams into the organization's structure and the different types of teams commonly found in organizations. Decision making in teams and leadership skills for conducting effective team meetings are addressed. The chapter concludes with a discussion of self-managed teams.

The Use of Teams in Organizations

Teamwork is a way of life in the postmodern organization.[5,6] Teams have become the basic structure through which work is done in organizations.[7,8] Early discussions of the concept came from post–World War II Japanese management approaches and led to greater academic scrutiny in the human relations movement before being embraced by major U.S. corporations. Through the years, many studies have documented the importance of teams for achieving organizational success.[9] The basic premise of teamwork is that teams offer the best opportunity for better organizational performance in the form of increased productivity and profits. In other words, the synergistic benefits of teamwork are such that members of a team working cooperatively with one another can achieve more than working independently. Thus, teams have become the basic unit of empowerment—large enough for the collective strength and synergy of diverse talents and small enough for effective participation and bonding.

Since the early 1990s, various studies have reported greater numbers of U.S. corporations using teams to accomplish organizational tasks.[10,11] The reasons for this trend are obvious. Many companies, large and small, face serious challenges from a dynamic and complex global economy—challenges that have put in question the effectiveness of traditional management methods. Some of these challenges include growing demands from customers for better quality products and services at lower prices, globalization, technological advances, and pressure from competitors and suppliers.[12] Because of this trend, many more organizations are seeking employees who possess team leadership skills.

According to some estimates, over 50 percent of all organizations and 80 percent of organizations with more than 100 employees use some form of teams.[13] Many organizations have reengineered their work processes and procedures to accommodate teams. There is growing evidence that the use of teams has led to desirable performance improvements for many organizations in a variety of industries. Some specific examples of team outcomes include the following:

- A large stamping plant created empowered maintenance teams that took it upon themselves to improve the functionality of specific machines in the operation, for both preventive and rapid response maintenance, resulting in a 28 percent reduction in machine downtime.
- Using self-managed teams, an appliance manufacturing plant increased productivity by 22 percent.
- A large warehousing operation reduced the procurement cycle time by a full day through the creation of an operational improvement team that had the full backing of top management.
- By creating and empowering a new safety team, a mid-sized furniture factory reduced lost time for on-the-job injuries by 30 percent.

However, not all team efforts have resulted in success. In some cases, the use of teams has resulted in such negative outcomes as increased costs, stress, and lower group cohesion.[14] To avoid these outcomes, it is recommended that an organization ask critical questions of itself before embracing the team concept, such as whether teams will diffuse important organizational capabilities, how much infrastructure realignment will be required, whether leaders will embrace the team concept and change their styles to suit, whether teams can carry out tasks previously performed by individuals, and how difficult it will be to develop team problem-solving capabilities.[15] This chapter addresses several important issues pertaining to conventional teams and the emerging trend toward self-managed teams. This section will address the definitional question of whether a team is the same as a group and examine the advantages and disadvantages of using teams.

Groups Versus Teams: What Is the Difference?

All teams are groups, but not all groups are teams. A manager can put together a group of people and never build a team. *A* **team** *is a unit of interdependent individuals with complementary skills who are committed to a common purpose and set of performance goals and to common expectations, for which they hold themselves accountable.*[16] Extensive research in the workplace has confirmed that some differences do indeed exist between teams and groups. The team concept implies a sense of shared mission and collective responsibility. Whereas groups focus on individual performance and goals, and reliance on individual abilities, teams have a collective mentality that focuses on (1) sharing information, insights, and perspectives; (2) making decisions that support each individual to do his or her own job better; and/or (3) reinforcing each other's individual performance standards.

Team members tend to have shared responsibilities, whereas group members sometimes work slightly more independently with greater motivation to achieve personal goals. The leadership style in a group tends to be very hierarchical, while in a team it is more likely to be participative or empowerment-oriented. In a team, performance measures create direct accountability for the team and incentives are team-based; in contrast, a group is characterized by individual self-interest, with a mentality of "what's in it for me." A group, some say, is simply a collection of people working together. Teams strive for equality between members; in the best teams, there are no stars, and everyone suppresses individual ego for the good of the whole. Given this background, it would appear that the terms "team" and "group" are not interchangeable, though some authors have not distinguished between them. It is important to bear in mind that these distinctions probably reflect matters of degree. One might consider teams to be highly specialized groups.

Work Application **1**

Think of a past or present job. Based on your knowledge of the distinction between a group and a team, would you say you were part of a team or a group? Explain.

Opening Case APPLICATION

1. What would be the evidence that Cisco is a team of employees and not just a group of workers?

CEO John Chambers sets the agenda for transforming Cisco into a team of employees, not just a group. He institutionalized the concept of teamwork from the top down. At present, part of executives' compensation is based on how they work as a team. The message has been passed down as the company now emphasizes cross-divisional work teams. Chambers himself spent a lot of time communicating his policy changes to all employees and making sure that they bought into the rationale for making the shift to teamwork. High-scoring employee satisfaction surveys and Chambers' popularity with his employees are evidence that they have embraced the change wholeheartedly.

Applying the **Concept 1**

Group or Team

Based on each statement, identify it as characteristic of a group or a team. Write the appropriate letter in the blank before each item.

a. group b. team

____ 1. My boss conducts my performance appraisals, and I get good ratings.

____ 2. We don't have any departmental goal; we just do the best we can to accomplish the mission.

____ 3. My compensation is based primarily on my department's performance.

____ 4. I get the assembled product from Jean; I paint it and send it to Tony for packaging.

____ 5. There are about 30 people in my department.

Learning Outcome 1 *Discuss the advantages and disadvantages of working in teams.*

Advantages and Disadvantages of Teamwork

Teamwork *is an understanding and commitment to group goals on the part of all team members.* The increased acceptance and use of teams suggests that their usage offers many advantages. However, teams also present organizations with many challenges, including the need for effective communication; resolving personality conflicts and egos; establishing unifying goals, direction, and focus; establishing appropriate rewards and incentives; clarity about team structure; effective leadership; and organizing the team's work to ensure timely decisions. Clearly, teamwork skills and knowledge are imperative as organizations learn to compete in the information and knowledge economy.[17] Failure to effectively handle these challenges often results in dysfunctional teams, which means there are disadvantages that come with using teams in organizations.[18,19]

Advantages of Teamwork

There are several advantages of teamwork:

- First, in a team situation it is possible to achieve synergy, whereby the team's total output exceeds the sum of the various members' contributions. Synergy involves the creative cooperation of people working together to achieve something beyond the capacities of individuals working alone.
- Second, team members often evaluate one another's thinking, so the team is likely to avoid major errors. This tendency of mutual support and peer review of ideas helps teams make better decisions and can provide immunity for an organization against disruptive surprises.
- Third, teams can and do contribute well to continuous improvement and innovation. Besides speeding up decision making and innovation, team members report greater satisfaction with their jobs.[20]
- Fourth, teams create a work environment that encourages people to become self-motivated, empowered, and satisfied with their jobs. Job satisfaction is important because it has, in turn, been associated with other positive organizational outcomes. For example, employees who are satisfied with their jobs are less likely to quit, are absent less, and are more likely to display organizational citizenship behavior.[21]

- Fifth, being a member of a team makes it possible to satisfy more needs than if one worked alone; among these are the needs for affiliation, security, self-esteem, and self-fulfillment. Team members develop trust for each other and come to see the team as a social unit that fulfills other needs.[22]

Research on teamwork does provide support for the proposition that people's perceptions of their own interdependence with others (such as in a team) influences both their beliefs about group members' trustworthiness and their attitude toward group members. Thus, interpersonal trust is seen as an important social resource that can facilitate cooperation and enable coordinated social interactions. This adds to team member commitment and motivation. Employees who are more committed and motivated are less likely to leave their jobs, less likely to experience stress, and more likely to perform well and behave pro-socially.[23]

Work Application 2

Identify a team you were or are a part of and describe the advantages that you derived from being a member of the team.

Disadvantages of Teamwork

Teamwork has some potential disadvantages for both organizations and individuals:

- A common problem may be that members face pressure to conform to group standards of performance and conduct. For example, a team member may be ostracized for being much more productive than his or her coworkers.
- Situations exist in which working in teams is perceived by some individuals to impinge on their autonomy, thus creating resistance to the team effort.[24] Shirking of individual responsibility, also known as *social loafing*, is another problem frequently noted in groups. **Social loafing** *is the conscious or unconscious tendency by some team members to shirk responsibilities by withholding effort toward group goals when they are not individually accountable for their work.* Many students who have worked on team projects (like group term papers) have encountered a social loafer. Some believe it is a naturally occurring process of project teams.[25] Social loafing is likely to result when individual effort is not recognized and assessed.[26]

  Individual performance appraisal helps to discourage social loafing by providing each team member with feedback on the quality of his or her work; however, it goes against the popular view that implementing team-based performance measures is necessary for a strong team identity, and a strong team identity leads to greater coordination.[27] In other words, individual-level performance appraisal helps reduce social loafing, but it risks jeopardizing the interaction and synergistic benefits that are characteristic of effective teams.
- Another well-known disadvantage associated with highly cohesive groups or teams is groupthink. **Groupthink** *is when members of a cohesive group tend to agree on a decision not on the basis of its merit but because they are less willing to risk rejection for questioning a majority viewpoint or presenting a dissenting opinion.* The group culture values getting along more than getting things done. The group often becomes more concerned with striving for unanimity than with objectively appraising different courses of action. Dissenting views are suppressed in favor of consensus.[28] These problems may explain why some studies have not found consistent support for the strong belief in the effectiveness of teams. The problem of groupthink can be remedied by training team members to become effective participants in the decision-making process—something that is taken for granted when a team is formed.[29,30,31]
- Though cohesiveness is a desirable quality of teams, teams that are extremely cohesive can also become, at their worst, a source of conflict with other teams. They may become so cohesive that they resemble cliques with minimal outside

Work Application 3

Based on Self-Assessment 1, list some things that a team could do to improve its level of teamwork. Use experiences associated with a present or past job.

interaction or influence, thus creating the potential for significant intergroup conflicts. There is pressure for workers to stand by their teammates and to achieve the team's goals. High levels of pressure can contribute to high levels of stress, which ultimately affect team performance if left unmanaged.[32] Also, within the team, groupthink—described earlier as the tendency for members of cohesive teams to agree on a decision not on the basis of its merit, but because they don't want to disagree with fellow teammates and risk rejection—may dominate team decision making.

Effective team leaders find ways to maximize the advantages of teams and to minimize the disadvantages of teams. Complete Self-Assessment 1 to evaluate teamwork from your own work experience.

SELF-ASSESSMENT 1

Assessing Teamwork in Your Group

Based on experiences you have or have had with teams, indicate whether your team has (or had) the following characteristics by placing a check mark in the appropriate column:

In my team:	Mostly True	Mostly False
1. There is a common understanding and commitment to group goals on the part of all team members.	___	___
2. Members support and provide constructive feedback to one another's ideas.	___	___
3. Members do not feel the pressure to conform to group standards of performance and conduct.	___	___
4. Dissenting views are accepted and discussed rather than suppressed in favor of consensus.	___	___
5. The level of interpersonal interaction among members is high.	___	___
6. Much of the responsibility and authority for making important decisions is turned over to the team.	___	___
7. There is an open communication channel for all members to voice their opinions.	___	___
8. Members are provided with the opportunity for continuous learning and training in appropriate skills.	___	___
9. Every team member is treated equally.	___	___
10. Members are more likely to provide backup and support for one another without the team leader's instruction.	___	___
11. Rewards and recognition are linked to individual as well as team results.	___	___
12. Roles and responsibilities for performing various tasks are clearly established.	___	___

Scoring

Add up the number of mostly true answers and place the total on the continuum below.

12—11—10—9—8—7—6—5—4—3—2—1

Effective teamwork *Ineffective teamwork*

Interpreting the Score

The higher the score, the more effective is the teamwork. Self-assessment exercises like this can be used by groups during team building to improve teamwork. You will learn more about the team leader's role in building effective teams in the next section and about self-managed teams later in the chapter.

Ethical **Dilemma 1**

Team Players

JetBlue Airways is not structured around teams. However, teamwork knowledge, skills, and attitudes are important to the success of JetBlue. In fact, JetBlue gives extensive screening interviews to make sure job candidates are team players. In addition to checking the six or seven references the job candidate provides, JetBlue recruiters ask the reference people for the names of people who can give insights into the candidate, and they call them as well.

1. Is being a team player really necessary to be a successful employee at JetBlue?
2. Is it ethical and socially responsible of JetBlue to reject job candidates because they are considered not to be good team players?

Characteristics of Effective Teams

Teams vary in terms of their effectiveness. Some are effective and some are not. The obvious question therefore becomes, what makes one team successful and another unsuccessful? According to one author, there are five dysfunctions that every team must overcome to be effective: lack of trust, fear of conflict, lack of commitment, lack of accountability, and inattention to results.[33] Much of the literature portrays team effectiveness as a function of both internal and external factors. Supporting this viewpoint, one model of team effectiveness focused on internal team processes such as group learning, self-leadership, interdependency, and team cohesion (also referred to as group potency) as influencing factors of team effectiveness.[34,35,36] Another model examined three contextual factors—team design, organizational resources and rewards, and process assistance—as determinants of team effectiveness.[37] **Team effectiveness** *has three components:* (1) *task performance—the degree to which the team's output (product or service) meets the needs and expectations of those who use it;* (2) *group process—the degree to which members interact or relate in ways that allow the team to work increasingly well together over time; and* (3) *individual satisfaction—the degree to which the group experience, on balance, is more satisfying than frustrating to team members.*[38]

This definition embodies a number of performance outcomes that others have used as a basis for evaluating team effectiveness. These include innovation, efficiency, quality, and employee satisfaction. Innovative teams are those with the capability to rapidly respond to environmental needs and changes with creative solutions. They are teams that have mastered what some scholars refer to as "team learning." **Team learning** *is the collective acquisition, combination, creation, and sharing of knowledge.*[39] Efficient teams enable the organization to attain goals with fewer resources. Quality pertains to the team's ability to achieve superior results with fewer resources and exceed customer expectations. Satisfaction measures the team's ability to maintain employee commitment to and enthusiasm for the team effort by meeting not just the team's goals but also the personal needs of its members.

Understanding what makes teams effective is of obvious importance to organizational leaders. Based on the relevant literature on team effectiveness, this section summarizes the following factors as characteristic of effective teams: team norms, team leadership, team cohesiveness and interdependence, team composition, team structure, and organizational support.[40,41,42] The final characteristic of effective teams that demands particular attention is the last one discussed in this section: an effective team is also a very creative team.

Learning Outcome 2 *Briefly describe the seven characteristics of effective teams.*

Team Norms

Team norms is an important characteristic of effective teams because norms guide team members' behavior. Norms determine what behavior is acceptable and unacceptable. **Team norms** *are acceptable standards of behavior that are shared by team members.* Norms influence how a team's members perceive and interact with one another, approach decisions, and solve problems. An effective team must possess an appropriate set of norms that govern all members' behavior. For example, a team norm might specify cooperative over competitive behavior. To the outside observer, this may be reflected by the level of importance members place on shared pursuits, objectives, and mutual interests rather than personal interests. The reward structure must match the cooperative norm.[43]

At the early stages of a team's formation, norms begin to develop and often gain acceptance and significance in every team member's work life. Team leaders can play a major role in helping to shape norms that will help the team successfully realize its goals and also keep members satisfied and committed to the team. There are many ways by which team norms get formed; the two most common are critical events and symbols. Norms often emerge out of critical events in the team's history and way(s) in which team members responded. This sets a precedent and becomes the standard for future behavior.

Ethical **Dilemma 2**

Norms

One or a few employees can break the norms and cause disastrous consequences for not only one organization but also entire industries. On the other hand, one or a few people can blow the whistle to disclose illegal and unethical business practices, which can lead to decreasing unethical behavior, such as at Enron. On the micro-team level, employees influence each other's behavior through developing and enforcing norms; we can also call it peer pressure.

1. Should employees be able to do their own thing without the group enforcing norms?
2. Is it ethical and socially responsible for groups to develop and enforce norms? If so, what type of ethical standards should a group have?

Team Leadership

Given the increasing use of teams to organize work activities in many organizations, the role of leaders in facilitating productive behaviors among team members is critical. The need for leadership still exists, because teams are made up of many personalities, mindsets, motives, and agendas.[44] Having a team leader who can effectively influence the whole team can mean the difference between success and failure. To be an effective team leader requires a shift in mindset and behavior for those who are accustomed to working in traditional organizations in which managers make all the decisions.[45] Team-based organizations need leaders who are knowledgeable in the team process and are capable of developing a productive and effective team.[46]

If they are to have satisfied, productive, and loyal team members, team leaders must recognize that not everyone knows how to be a team player. The team leader must model the behavior that he or she desires. A leader's self-sacrificing behavior and display of self-confidence does influence team members. Self-sacrificing leaders are those who go above and beyond what's expected of them. They don't just issue orders; they get involved in making things happen.[47] The results of a laboratory experiment revealed that productivity levels, effectiveness ratings, and perceived leader group-orientedness and charisma were positively affected by leader's self-sacrifice.[48] Therefore, team leaders have an important personal role to play in building effective teams.[49,50]

Effective teams typically have effective team leaders who employ multiple influencing tactics to control and direct team member actions toward the achievement of organizational goals.[51,52,53] Effective team leaders encourage norms that positively affect the team's goals and alter those that are negative.[54] In order to foster the development of team spirit, leaders should observe with a keen eye what's going on in the team, make contributions when necessary, encourage a climate of dialogue, turn obstacles into opportunities, and see themselves and others as part of the team's pool of knowledge, skills, and ideas.[55,56] An effective team leader must be adaptive, knowing when to play different roles—manager, facilitator, or coach. For example, empowering leadership has a stronger effect on team members or followers who have a high need for autonomy than directive leadership.[57,58] Also empowering leadership has been found to positively affect both knowledge sharing and team efficacy, which in turn, positively affects team performance.[59,60]

Being an effective team leader means understanding people.[61] This is also referred to as having social skills.[62] Researchers are interested in how social network structures of team leaders and members help or hinder team effectiveness. There is support for the proposition that social networks of leaders and members do improve team effectiveness.[63] According to one study, four dimensions determine whether an individual has high or low social skills: *influence, interpersonal facilitation, relational creativity,* and *team leadership.*[64] Focusing on creativity alone, another study argues that social influences resulting from group interactions are important antecedents to creativity.[65] Leaders with high social skills tend to have greater influencing abilities and interpersonal skills, and relate well with team members. When a leader or a team member can leverage his social skills to obtain resources for the team, he or she is said to possess social capital.[66] Without effective leadership, teams can get off course, go too far or not far enough, lose sight of their mission, and become blocked by interpersonal conflict.

The key responsibilities a leader should undertake in order to create an effective team are summarized in Exhibit 8.1 on the next page.[67]

Opening Case APPLICATION

2. What characteristics of team leadership does John Chambers possess that make him so effective?

It is evident that Chambers employs all or most of the team leader roles for creating effective teams listed in Exhibit 8.1. For example, communication is one of his greatest strengths, and he uses it to inspire and motivate teams toward higher goals. Employees and investors, it is said, give him standing ovations at company events. This is indicative of the type of relations he has with his employees and shareholders. He has high social skills.

Work Application 4

Interview someone you have worked with or know who is a team leader. Ask him or her to provide specific examples for some of the roles outlined in Exhibit 8.1 that he or she employed.

EXHIBIT 8.1 The Team Leader's Role in Creating Effective Teams

- Emphasize group recognition and rewards.
- Identify and build on the team's strengths.
- Develop trust and a norm of teamwork.
- Develop the team's capabilities to anticipate and deal with change effectively.
- Empower teams to accomplish their work with minimal interference.
- Inspire and motivate teams toward higher levels of performance.
- Recognize individual and team needs and attend to them in a timely fashion.
- Encourage and support team decisions.
- Provide teams with challenging and motivating work.

Team Cohesiveness and Interdependence

Effective teams typically have high levels of cohesion, interdependence, and autonomy.[68] **Team cohesion** *is the extent to which team members band together and remain committed to achieving team goals.* Highly cohesive teams are also described as having high group potency (the collective belief of a group that it can be effective) and a strong self-efficacy (an internal belief held by an individual or group about how well an impending situation can be handled).[69] Some of the factors that have been found to increase team cohesion include shared purpose and goals, team reputation for success, interteam competition, and personal attraction to the team. Team cohesion is increased when

- team members agree on a common purpose and direction;
- external parties give high praise and recognition for the team's success;
- the organization encourages and motivates teams to compete with each other for rewards;
- members find they have common ground and similar attitudes and values and enjoy being on the team.

The presence of all these factors has been shown to have strong correlations with team member satisfaction and commitment. Teams experiencing cohesion are less likely to engage in affective disagreement and more likely to remain together longer and to make more effective decisions. Also, in highly cohesive teams, the quality of interpersonal relations and member self-identification with the team is strong.[70]

The degree to which team members depend on each other for information, resources, and other inputs to complete their tasks affects the level of interdependence or mutual influences within the team. With interdependence comes the need for coordination to insure that the team functions as a unified whole.[71] In effective teams, interdependence and coordination are built into the team's goal, reward system, and job structure. Among teams, three types of interdependence have been identified: pooled, sequential, and reciprocal interdependence. Without describing each type in detail, it should be noted that the level of team member interaction and dependency increases successively as one goes from pooled, to sequential, to reciprocal interdependence.

Team Composition

Team composition focuses on the diversity in knowledge, background, and experiences of team members. Deciding who to put on a team is one of the toughest challenges facing a leader and should not be taken lightly.[72] Research on team diversity has revealed that team members' differences can enhance learning and creativity under the right circumstances.[73] Effective teams must have the right mix of complementary skills, knowledge, and ability to perform the team's job.[74,75,76]

Recognizing the heterogeneous nature of today's workforce, organizational researchers have increasingly focused on teams with multicultural, multifunctional, and multinational characteristics. According to one study, there are three fundamental descriptors of team members—multifunctional knowledge, teamwork skills, and an established good working relationship.[77] Teams with experience of working together tend to demonstrate greater task proficiency and teamwork effectiveness.[78,79]

Team diversity brings diverse points of view to bear on problems.[80,81] Another benefit of diversity is the reduced likelihood of groupthink because of greater opportunities for differing points of view. However, it should be noted that not all diverse teams perform well.[82,83] Teams that do not manage diversity well may suffer from intrateam conflicts, stalemate, lack of communication, an absence of collegiality, and ultimately lack of any team spirit.[84,85] Successful teams are both proactive in anticipating the need for conflict resolution and pluralistic in developing conflict resolution strategies that apply to all team members.[86]

To have a good working relationship with peers requires good social skills.[87] According to one study, four dimensions determine an individual's level of social skills—influence, interpersonal facilitation, relational creativity, and team leadership.[88] Where team members have strong social interactions with each other, there is more likely to be strong team comraderie and thus greater cooperation.

Another aspect of team composition is the size of the team. Small teams, typically under 12 people, are generally more effective than larger teams. In small teams, conflicts and differences are more manageable, and the team is able to rally around its mission. Size affects team members' ability to relate closely with other members. In larger teams, it is much more difficult for members to interact and share ideas with each other. Teams made up of more than 12 people have been successful in some cases, but do tend to break into subteams rather than functioning as a single unit. In general, teams that participants perceive as too small or too large relative to the task at hand have been shown to be less effective. In a study conducted at Hewlett-Packard to identify key success factors for cross-functional teams, HP researchers found that successful teams were those with under 25 members. Thus, team size is relative.

Team Structure

Team structure refers to interrelations that determine the assignment of tasks, responsibilities, and authority. In other words, team structure may determine if the team employs a hierarchical model or a "flat," horizontal model. The horizontal (decentralized decision making) model is designed for high performance teams with much decision-making clout and accountability. Team members' degree of interdependence and autonomy have been identified as key structural components that influence team effectiveness.[89] Teams that possess high autonomy, broad participation in team decisions, and variety in tasks performed by individual members, are said to have motivational job design characteristics. When teams perceive their tasks as motivating, they are generally more effective.

Along the same line of thought, another study proposes that team structure determines the extent to which team members directly control the actions of each other (horizontal incentive system) or report observations of their peers' efforts to management (vertical incentive system). The study concluded that team structures that allow for horizontal incentive systems show higher levels of team identity and coordination than team structures that insist on vertical incentive systems.[90]

Organizational Support

Effective teams are those that have strong support from the top of the organization. Assessing team effectiveness as it relates to the overall performance of the organization should be an important part of top management's responsibility. When teams are not achieving expected results, top management must ask itself some key questions. First, do the teams fully understand their mission? Second, are teams getting enough support from top management in the form of training, rewards, information, and material resources that they need? Third, have the appropriate leadership, communication, and task structures been set up for team operations? And, finally, does the organizational culture/environment support teamwork and have reward programs that motivate and reinforce team behavior?[91] These questions address the role of the organization in providing an infrastructure that supports effective teamwork. Exhibit 8.2 summarizes the key responsibilities of an organization in creating an effective team.[92,93]

Work Application 5

Recall a team you have worked with that you would characterize as effective. What role(s) did your leader and/or organization play in making the team effective?

EXHIBIT 8.2 The Organization's Role in Creating Effective Teams

- Top management's unconditional support.
- Adequate information and other resources.
- Flexible task structure.
- Appropriate size and membership mix.
- Clearly defined mission and goals.
- Appropriate power sharing structure—shared leadership.
- Competent team leadership.
- Evaluation and solicitation of feedback on team effectiveness.
- Adequate socialization of team members.

Opening Case APPLICATION

3. What role did organizational support play in the success of cross-divisional teams at Cisco?

Because it was a concept advocated by the CEO himself, cross-divisional teams had organizational support from the get-go. Exhibit 8.2 lists the key features of the organization's role in creating effective teams. It is not surprising that the very first feature is top management's unconditional support.

Learning Outcome 3 *Describe top management's and the team leader's roles in fostering creativity. For each, list activities they should undertake to promote creativity.*

Creativity Driven

Effective teams are also characterized by higher levels of creativity. Creativity feeds innovation, which has become increasingly valuable for organizations, particularly in turbulent and uncertain times.[94] Today's economy has been rightly described as a knowledge economy because more companies are gaining competitive advantages based on knowledge rather than on physical or financial resources. The companies that will survive and thrive will not be those that have the greatest financial resources, but those that can make use of the creativity of their workforce.[95] **Team creativity** *is the creation of a valuable, useful, and novel product, service, idea, procedure, or process carried out via discovery rather than a predetermined step-by-step procedure, by individuals working together in a complex social system.*[96]

Research reveals that a number of enabling factors—team autonomy, performance measurement and incentive systems, team bonuses, team continuity, a stable team composition, and sufficient resource endowment—can assist in improving team knowledge management and thus creativity.[97] These are the factors that directly bear on the role that top leaders can play in designing teams that exemplify creativity. For teams to maximize their creative potential, the organization must rethink its work structures and leadership approaches. Organizations with advanced communication systems that connect teams to knowledgeable sources and relevant information will not only be more innovative but also more efficient.[98] Creating an organizational structure and climate that supports and encourages creativity provides the backdrop against which managerial practices can take hold.[99] Social networks, for example, have been found to greatly enhance creativity.[100] This discussion can be summarized into four simple instructions for fostering team creativity:[101,102]

1. Provide adequate and quality resources.
2. Provide appropriate recognition and rewards.
3. Provide flexibility and a minimum amount of structure.
4. Provide supportive climate and culture.

As a point of emphasis, it should also be understood that a team leader's actions can support or kill creativity within the team despite the organization's best intentions. Just because senior management establishes supportive policies and practices does not mean that they will automatically be implemented at the team level. That's why it is still important to emphasize team leader responsibilities, which must be carefully executed for creativity to flourish. As mentioned earlier, a distinguishing characteristic of effective teams is the quality and personality of the team leader. With respect to the role of the team leader in fostering creativity, researchers have identified specific actions that can ensure that a creative team spirit is not quashed, including matching people with the right assignments; giving team members greater autonomy to do the job; ensuring the availability of adequate time, money, and other resources for the team; and protecting against "creativity blockers."[103] While this list is not exhaustive, it highlights many of the operational decisions and actions team leaders have to make to keep their team's creativity juices flowing.

Self-Assessment 2 on the next page should help you assess the climate for creativity in your organization or institution.

Work Application 6

Think of a work situation in which you were required to do a lot of creative thinking, or in which your job required doing a lot of very creative things. In what ways did the organization and your immediate supervisor or leader facilitate or hinder your effectiveness? Use the discussion of top management and the team leader's roles in facilitating creativity as your guide.

SELF-ASSESSMENT 2

Assessing the Climate for Creativity

Place a checkmark in the appropriate column for each question.

	Mostly Agree	Mostly Disagree
1. Organizational practices generally encourage creativity.	___	___
2. The reward system has been carefully designed to encourage creativity.	___	___
3. People are not restricted by rules and regulations or many layers of approval when they want to try new ideas.	___	___
4. "Doing things the way they have always been done" is not a slogan that applies in this organization.	___	___
5. People are able to experiment and dream outside their regular functional area on company time.	___	___
6. The organization's culture values and appreciates input from members.	___	___
7. People feel they have been properly matched with tasks that fit their skills, interests, and experiences.	___	___
8. Employees have greater autonomy to think and act freely than they would in another organization.	___	___
9. In looking around, it is certain that the work environment has been carefully designed to encourage creativity.	___	___
10. Managerial practices in this organization would lead to the conclusion that creativity and innovation are highly valued at all levels.	___	___

Scoring

Begin by placing a checkmark in the appropriate column for each question. Add up the number of "mostly agree" checkmarks and place the sum on the continuum below.

10—9—8—7—6—5—4—3—2—1

Supportive climate *Unsupportive climate*

Interpreting the Score

The higher the score, the more supportive the organizational climate is of creativity and innovation. Self-assessment exercises like this can be used to encourage students to relate their work environments to the concepts in ways that others can benefit from the experience of their peers.

Opening Case APPLICATION

4. One of the characteristics of effective teams is that they are creativity driven. How important is creativity to Cisco's success?

According to information from Cisco's Web site, Cisco's technology leadership is based on three differentiators. The company is committed to creating networks that are smarter, faster, and longer lasting. Creativity and innovation are the driving forces behind Cisco's success. According to CEO John Chambers, "what we can achieve is limited not by technology but by our creativity and willingness to act." There is no doubt that he understands the power of teams and creativity.

Applying the **Concept 2**

Managing Creative Teams

Identify which strategy for creative teams each statement relates to:

a. quality resources
b. recognition and rewards
c. flexibility
d. free time

____ 6. They gave me this pin for five years of service to the company.

____ 7. How does management expect us to make a quality product when they get these cheap parts from our supplier?

____ 8. There sure are a lot of rules and regulations to know to work here.

____ 9. I wish I could take my break, and take it on time, regularly.

____ 10. I don't know why the boss keeps checking to make sure I'm doing my job according to the proper company procedures.

Types of Teams

Structural metamorphosis seems to be the one constant in organizational life today. Traditional organizational structures, known for their stable designs, are changing in favor of more fluid designs that can respond to external environmental trends. These flexible designs include a flatter and more horizontal structure, a focus on new ways to motivate employees, and the use of teams instead of functional structures. A manufacturing enterprise might, for example, make use of a variety of teams, including quality improvement teams, problem-solving teams, self-managed productive teams, cross-functional teams, technology integration teams, virtual cross-functional teams, and safety teams. Over the years, increasing competition stemming from the global and technological nature of markets has forced organizations to adopt different team types—going from functional teams to cross-functional teams and then to self-managed teams. We will examine all three types in this section.

Functional Team

One hundred years ago, Frederick Taylor, called the "father of scientific management," espoused a leadership approach whereby managers made themselves functional experts, divided work processes into simple repetitive tasks, and treated workers as interchangeable parts. The functional team is mostly made up of the functional manager and a small group of frontline employees within that department. *A* **functional team** *is a group of employees belonging to the same functional department, such as marketing, R&D, production, human resources, or information systems, who have a common objective.*

Over time, the drawbacks of this approach became evident, as workers suffered from boredom due to the repetitive nature of their jobs. The structure of the functional team is generally more hierarchical with the functional leader making all the decisions and expecting his or her followers to implement them. Another drawback of the functional team, although unintended, is the tendency for team members to focus on their local area of specialization and ignore or downplay the overall organizational mission. This can lead to a lack of cooperation between functional groups, resulting in poor quality of decisions and overall organization performance. In fact, rivalry rather than cooperation is what often happens between functional groups that don't interact with each other. A study examining the quality of the relationship between R&D and marketing in a functional organizational structure found that interfunctional rivalry had the following consequences: It severely reduced R&D's use of information supplied by marketing personnel, it lowered the perceived quality of information transferred between the two departments, and it increased political pressures to ignore useful information provided by marketing.

As discussed in Chapter 5, there is no one best leadership style to use in all functional teams. However, in many situations, the size of the team, task description, and membership mix may play a role in determining what leadership style is employed. For instance, functional team leaders in small- to medium-sized teams, performing standardized tasks, generally tend to have a more centralized and directive leadership style in place. In one study, the leader of a functional team at an electronics firm describes how he made the transition from a traditional command-and-control leadership style to an empowered workforce style. Over the lifetime of the project, the leader slowly transformed what started as a rigid functional group of engineers into a team. Along the way, his leadership style also changed to match the situation, following four phases: traditional, direct involvement, team advisor, and observer.

Over the years, the use of functional structure has been in decline. Cross-functional teams became popular in the late 1980s, when companies started to readjust their organizational structures to make them more flexible and competitive.

Cross-Functional Team

Increasingly, organizations are encountering complex and very dynamic external environments requiring flexible and less hierarchical structures. In today's flatter organizations, completing tasks often requires cooperation across boundaries, such as functional areas or divisions. Individuals are continually asked to cross functional boundaries and form teams with individuals of other functional disciplines for the purpose of accomplishing a common objective. The multifunctional team is composed of various members with different backgrounds, knowledge, experience, and expertise, who can solve problems and also help in decision making. Another name for this type of team is the cross-functional team. *A* **cross-functional team** *is made up of members from different functional departments of an organization who are brought together to perform unique tasks to create new and nonroutine products or services.*[104] Team members may also include representatives from outside organizations, such as suppliers, clients, and joint-venture partners.[105]

The premise behind the cross-functional team concept is that interaction, cooperation, coordination, information sharing, and cross-fertilization of ideas among people from different functional areas (production, marketing, R&D, and so on) produces better quality products/services with shorter developmental cycles.[106,107] This is especially true for cross-functional teams charged with developing innovative products/services or new technologies.[108,109] Here, managing human interactions and coordinating the transfer of knowledge and ideas among individuals and functional groups can be the most challenging aspect of the job.[110] While functional diversity has potentially beneficial results, there is also the likelihood that individual team members may perceive the team's task differently, thus affecting team success.[111]

As cross-functional team applications continue to grow, research studies attempting to identify key factors responsible for ensuring success have also kept pace. In one study, researchers interviewed 75 current and previous leaders of cross-functional teams in Hewlett-Packard's marketing, R&D, manufacturing, and information systems units. The interviews focused on identifying factors that were critical to the optimal functioning of cross-functional teams.[112] In another study, a survey of frontline managers regarding the barriers and gateways to management cooperation and teamwork revealed a consensus around five keys or gateways proposed by respondents for getting frontline managers to work effectively in cross-functional teams.[113] Combined, these two studies highlight key success traits of effective cross-functional teams. Exhibit 8.3 summarizes six key success factors for cross-functional team effectiveness.

EXHIBIT 8.3 Key Success Factors for Effective Cross-Functional Teams

1. Develop consensus around a common vision or mission as well as goals that focus on organizational outcomes.
2. Implement team-based performance measures, feedback, and reward systems.
3. Ensure effective leadership and top management support.
4. Promote the use of team building, skill development, and team training as common practices.
5. Assemble the right skills.
6. Organize at the right size.

Cross-functional teams offer many potential benefits to an organization. For example,

- bringing together the right people gives the team a rich and diverse base of knowledge and creative potential that far exceeds anything a single functional team could come up with;
- coordination is improved and many problems are avoided when people from different functions come together to work on a project at the same time, rather than working in separate units;
- the cross-functional makeup of the team provides the benefit of multiple sources of information and perspectives, contacts outside of one's functional specialty, and speed to market, which are critical for success in globally competitive, high-technology markets;
- members learn new skills that are carried back to their functional units and to subsequent teams;
- finally, the positive synergy that occurs in effective cross-functional teams can help them achieve a level of performance that far exceeds the sum of the individual performances of members.[114]

Cross-functional teams are often an organization's first step toward greater employee participation and empowerment. These teams may gradually evolve into self-managed teams, which represent a fundamental change in how work is organized.

Work Application 7

Recall any experience you have had or currently have, working with individuals from different disciplines or technical specialties from yours. How did you get along with these individuals? Describe the positives and negatives of your experience.

Opening Case APPLICATION

5. Why did John Chambers see cross-divisional teams and collaboration as the solution to Cisco's problems?

As Chambers puts it, Cisco had been organized around "silos" of products, which often had nothing to do with each other. Cross-divisional teams encourage interaction, cooperation, coordination, information sharing, and cross-fertilization of ideas among people from different divisions and produce better quality products/services with shorter developmental cycles. Also, Chambers believes that companies are facing a new imperative to form collaborative relationships because of the increasingly dynamic global environment they face.

Virtual Team

With modern communication technology have come virtual teams. In particular, new and advanced technologies are providing the means for work that is dispersed (carried out in different locations) and asynchronous (carried out at different times) to still be performed in team settings. This work structure is called the virtual team and can be organized along functional or cross-functional lines. *A* **virtual team** *is one whose members are geographically distributed, requiring them to work together through electronic means with minimal face-to-face interaction.*[115] An increasing number of organizations are using virtual teams to provide human resource flexibility, customer service responsiveness, innovation, and speed in project completion.[116] Virtual teams present significant collaboration, communication, and leadership challenges that if not handled properly can potentially hinder team interaction, information sharing, and knowledge integration—all critical to success.[117,118] Recommendations for dealing with these challenges include focusing attention on both technological and interpersonal issues, with team leaders staying alert to relational and communication issues.[119] Leaders of successful virtual teams establish and maintain trust and commitment within the team by making sure that the necessary infrastructure is in place.[120,121]

A key infrastructural requirement is usually the adoption of advanced information and communications technologies. These tools have been found to be very effective in building trust and cooperation among members of self-managed teams.[122,123] Virtual cross-functional teams are growing in companies with global operations. Global virtual team leaders are counseled to employ success strategies, such as building trust-based relationships, encouraging members to show respect for other cultures and languages, and promoting diversity as a team strength and not a weakness.[124,125,126]

The fourth type of team is called the self-managed team and commonly calls for Vroom's facilitate and delegate leadership styles.

Self-Managed Team (SMT)

The challenges of succeeding in a global economy have reached new levels, as companies strive to develop and sustain competitive advantages with an intensity not seen before, and with the knowledge that the business environment has become ever more turbulent. To meet these challenges and become more competitive, U.S. companies of all types and sizes are acknowledging the need for changes in their internal structures and culture. They will have to create alternatives to command and control hierarchical structures, change the way decisions are made, redefine jobs, and change assumptions managers have about how to lead. To meet these challenges, one novel approach that has been gaining ground is the self-managed work team (SMT).[127,128]

Work Application 8

Recall a present or past job. Describe what type of team you are in or have been in—functional, cross-functional, or self-managed.

Self-managed teams (SMTs) *are relatively autonomous teams whose members share or rotate leadership responsibilities and hold themselves mutually responsible for a set of performance goals assigned by higher management.* Self-managed teams are usually cross-functional in membership makeup, and have wide latitude in decision areas such as managing themselves, planning and scheduling work, and taking action on problems. Within the team, members set task goals for their specific areas of responsibility that support the achievement of overall team goals. The general perception is that these characteristics make self-managed teams more adaptive and proactive in their behavior than the traditional team.[129]

The self-managed team concept is the second primary topic of interest in this chapter and will be discussed later in greater depth.

Opening Case APPLICATION

6. What evidence is there that the cross-divisional team structure at Cisco has worked so far?

At every level of analysis, it seems Cisco is a better company now than it was in 2001 after the beginning of the tech meltdown. Financially, Cisco is doing well. Employees are happy and satisfied with the leadership and strategies of CEO John Chambers. Analysts are comparing him to some of the great ones, like Jack Welch and Andy Grove.

Applying the **Concept 3**

Type of Team

Identify each statement as characteristic of the following team types:

a. functional
b. cross-functional
c. virtual
d. self-managed

____ 11. We are developing a team to speed up processing our orders, and we are including two of our major customers.

____ 12. Our team has been charged with developing a new product within three months, and we get to come up with it any way we want to.

____ 13. Members of my team are dispersed all over the country and even overseas, yet we conduct meetings and get our work done using the Internet and videoconferencing technologies.

____ 14. We don't really have a boss in our team.

____ 15. The manager is setting up a team with three of her employees to come up with ideas to increase productivity.

Decision Making in Teams

The uncertainty, ambiguity, and ever-changing circumstances of today's environment require that leaders know when to make the decisions and when to allow the team to make the decisions. In this section, we will examine decision making under three models: leader-centered decision making, team-centered decision making, and normative leadership model.

Leader-Centered Decision-Making Model

The way a leader runs a team meeting greatly affects whether the ideas of team members are expressed. If a team leader takes a power position and uses a top-down directive approach, team member responses will tend to be guarded and cautious. According to this model of decision making, the leader exercises his or her power to initiate, direct, drive, instruct, and control team members. This focus on the leader points to the following prescriptions for success:

- The leader should focus on the task and ignore personal feelings and relationships whenever possible.
- The leader should seek opinions and try to get agreement but never relinquish the right to make final choices.

- The leader should stay in control of the group discussion at all times and should politely but firmly stop disruptive acts and irrelevant discussion.
- The leader should discourage members from expressing their feelings and should strive to maintain a rational, logical discussion without any emotional outbursts.
- The leader should guard against threats to his or her authority in the group and should fight if necessary to maintain it.

While this kind of leadership role produces some favorable results in certain situations, some behavioral scientists argue that it comes at a price. Meetings are conducted in an orderly fashion and decisions get made, but members become apathetic and resentful, which leads to a decrease in participation and a reduction in quality of decisions. Acceptance of decisions by team members may also be jeopardized if members feel pressured and unable to influence the decisions significantly.

Team-Centered Decision-Making Model

The team-centered decision-making model is preferred when relevant information and expertise are scattered among different people, when participation is needed to obtain necessary commitment, when concentrating power in a single individual hurts the team, and when unpopular decisions need to be made.[130] The team-centered approach empowers team members to make decisions and follow through. Advocates of the team-centered approach argue that empowerment results in a more dedicated, energetic, and creative workforce.[131] Empowerment is described as recognizing the untapped talents and human potential that lie in the knowledge, experience, and internal motivation of the people in an organization, and releasing that power. One way of releasing this potential is by replacing hierarchical management approaches that are leader-centered with teams.[132] The premise of the team-centered approach is that employees can be trusted to make decisions about their work, that they can be trained to acquire the skills and abilities needed to do so, and that organizational effectiveness is enhanced through this approach. The team-centered approach offers team leaders the following prescriptions for success:

- The leader should listen attentively and observe nonverbal cues to be aware of member needs, feelings, interactions, and conflict. In doing so, the leader should view the group as a collective entity or social system rather than a collection of individuals.
- The role of the leader should be to serve as a consultant, advisor, teacher, and facilitator, rather than as a director or manager of the team.
- The leader should model appropriate leadership behaviors and encourage members to learn to perform these behaviors themselves.
- The leader should establish a climate of approval for expression of feelings as well as ideas.[133]
- The leader should relinquish control to the team and allow it to make the final choice in all appropriate kinds of decisions.[134]

The advantages of team-centered decision making are that it can improve decision quality; it shifts much of the decision-making action away from the leader, thereby freeing him or her to think more strategically; it allows responsibility to be diffused among several people, thereby facilitating support for some types of unpopular decisions; and it results in higher commitment by team members to implement decisions as compared to decisions made alone by a leader.[135]

The disadvantages of team-centered decision making are that it can take longer than decisions made alone by a manager; it can be self-serving and contrary to the best interests of the organization, if team members have objectives and/or priorities that are different from those of the leader; and it can end up being a poor compromise rather than an optimal solution, when team members cannot agree among themselves.

Challenges occur when an organization has to transition from a leader-centered to a team-centered decision-making approach. Leaders who are accustomed to the leader-centered approach may be afraid to risk sharing control with team members, or fear that if they do, they will appear weak or incompetent. Also, resistance may come from team members who prefer to avoid assuming more responsibility for leadership functions in the team. Despite these challenges, the team-centered decision-making model has received much more attention among scholars than the leader-centered model. When both approaches have been examined, the team-centered model has been found to be more effective in some teams, although further research is needed to determine the extent and limits of its usefulness. It is more likely the case that neither approach is inherently good or bad, but rather that it all depends on the situation and circumstances. This is the contingency theory of leadership skills discussed in Chapter 5.

There is broad support among scholars that personality traits affect team decision-making performance. Team members with similar traits and values will more likely have a common frame of reference when making decisions.[136] We should note that the characteristics of effective teams discussed earlier will also contribute to effective decision making. Complete Self-Assessment 3 to better understand how your personality will affect your teamwork.

Work Application 9

Recall a team decision that you were a part of, and describe the team leader's role during the process leading up to the final decision. Would you characterize the leader's role as belonging to the leader-centered or team-centered approach to decision making?

SELF-ASSESSMENT 3

Personality Traits and Teams

Answer the following two questions, and then read how your personality profile can affect your teamwork.

I enjoy being part of a team and working with others more than working alone.

7—6—5—4—3—2—1
Strongly agree *Strongly disagree*

I enjoy achieving team goals more than individual accomplishments.

7—6—5—4—3—2—1
Strongly agree *Strongly disagree*

The stronger you agree with the two statements, the higher the probability that you will be a good team player. However, lower scores do not mean that you are not a good team player. The following is some information on how Big Five personality dimensions and their related motive needs can affect your teamwork.

Surgency—high need for power. If you have a high need for power, whether you are the team leader or not, you have to be careful not to dominate the group. Seek others' input, and know when to lead and when to follow. Even when you have great ideas, be sensitive to others so they don't feel that you are bullying them, and stay calm (adjustment) as you influence them. Be aware of your motives to make sure you use socialized rather than personalized power. You have the potential to make a positive contribution to the team with your influencing leadership skills. If you have a low need for power, try to be assertive so that others don't take advantage of you, and speak up when you have good ideas.

Agreeableness—high need for affiliation. If you have a high need for affiliation, you tend to be a good team player. However, don't let the fear of hurting relationships get in your way of influencing the team when you have good ideas. Don't be too quick to give in to others; it doesn't help the performance of the team when you have a better idea that is not implemented. You have the potential to be a valuable asset to the

continued

(Self-Assessment 3 continued)

team as you contribute your skills of working well with others and making them feel important. If you have a low need for affiliation, be careful to be sensitive to others.

Conscientiousness—high need for achievement. If you have a high need for achievement, you have to watch your natural tendency to be more individualistic than team oriented. It's good to have your own goals; but if the team and organization fail, so do you. Remember that there is usually more than one good way to do anything; your way is not always the best. In a related issue, don't be a perfectionist, as you can cause problems with team members. Being conscientious, you have the potential to help the team do a good job and reach its full potential. If you have a low need for achievement, push yourself to be a valuable contributor to the group, or pull your own weight.

Normative Leadership Model

Recall that in Chapter 5, "Contingency Leadership Theories," we discussed the normative leadership model. Recall that the normative models (Exhibits 5.9 and 5.10 on pages 167-168) and Chapter 5's Skill-Development Exercise 2 (on pages 183-185) apply to group decision making, because the models are used to determine the level of participation to use in a given decision. Skill-Development Exercise 1 in this chapter (on pages 323-325) presents a contingency leadership decision-making model that is adapted from the normative leadership model. It is a simpler model and uses the same leadership styles as situational communications (Skill-Development Exercise 2 in Chapter 6 on pages 232-233) to help you determine the appropriate level of participation to use in a given situation.

An important part of a leader's job is conducting team meetings. The next section focuses on strategies for conducting effective meetings.

Leadership Skills for Effective Team Meetings

With a group structure, managers spend a great deal of time in management meetings. Most meetings include employees, and it is common for teams to have daily meetings. With the trend toward teams, meetings are taking up an increasing amount of time. Therefore, the need for meeting management skills is stronger than ever.[137] The success of meetings depends on the leader's skill at managing the group process. The most common complaints about meetings are that there are too many of them, they are too long, and they are unproductive.[138] Meeting leadership skills can lead to more productive meetings. Ford Motor Company spent $500,000 to send 280 employees to a three-day training session on developing meeting leadership skills, with three one-day sessions to follow. After the training, fewer employees complained of meetings being too long or unproductive. Managers had gained the necessary meeting leadership skills and were putting this knowledge into practice. Ford's investment had obviously paid off. In this section, we learn how to plan and conduct a meeting and how to handle problem group members.

Planning Meetings

Leader and member preparations for a meeting have a direct effect on the meeting. Unprepared leaders tend to conduct unproductive meetings. Planning is needed in at least five areas: objectives, selecting participants and making assignments, the agenda, the time and place for the meeting, and leadership.[139] A written copy of the plan should be sent to members prior to the meeting (see Exhibit 8.4).

EXHIBIT 8.4 Meeting Plans

- **Time.** List date, place (if it changes), and time (both beginning and ending).
- **Objective.** State the objectives and/or purpose of the meeting. The objectives can be listed with agenda items, as shown below, rather than as a separate section. However, be sure objectives are specific.
- **Participation and Assignments.** If all members have the same assignment, list it. If different members have different assignments, list their names and assignments. Assignments may be listed as agenda items, as shown below for Ted and Karen.
- **Agenda.** List each item to be covered, in order of priority, with its approximate time limit. Accepting the minutes of the preceding meeting may be an agenda item. Here is an example agenda:

GOLD TEAM MEETING

November 22, 2010, Gold room, 9:00 a.m. to 10:00 a.m.

Participation and Assignments

All members will attend and should have read the six computer brochures enclosed before the meeting. Be ready to discuss your preferences.

Agenda

1. Discussion and selection of two PCs to be presented to the team at a later date by PC representatives—45 minutes. (Note that this is the major objective: the actual selection takes place later.)
2. Ted will give the Venus project report—5 minutes.
3. Karen will present an idea for changing the product process slightly, without discussion—5 minutes. Discussion will take place at the next meeting, after members have given the idea some thought.

Objectives

Probably the single greatest mistake made by those who call meetings is that they often have no clear idea and purpose for the meeting. Before calling a meeting, clearly define its purpose and set objectives to be accomplished during the meeting. The only exceptions may be at regularly scheduled information-dissemination or brainstorming meetings.

Participants and Assignments

Before calling the meeting, decide who should attend the meeting. The more members who attend a meeting, the less the chance that any work will get done. Does the full group/team need to attend? Should some nongroup specialist be invited to provide input? On controversial issues, the leader may find it wiser to meet with the key members before the meeting to discuss the issue. Participants should know in advance what is expected of them at the meeting. If any preparation is expected (read material, do some research, make a report, and so forth), they should have adequate advance notice.

Agenda

Before calling the meeting, identify the activities that will take place during the meeting in order to achieve the objective. The agenda tells the members what is expected and how the meeting will progress. Having a set time limit for each agenda item helps keep the group on target; needless discussion and getting off the subject are common at all meetings. However, you need to be flexible and allow more time when really needed. Agenda items may also be submitted from members to include. If you get agenda items that require action, they should have objectives.

Place agenda items in order of priority. That way, if the group does not have time to cover every item, the least important items carry forward. In meetings in which the agenda items are not prioritized, the tendency is for the leader to put all the so-called quick items first. When this happens, the group gets bogged down and either rushes through the important items or puts them off until later.

Date, Time, and Place

To determine which day(s) and time(s) of the week are best for meetings, get members' input. Members tend to be more alert early in the day. When members are close, it is better to have more frequent shorter meetings focusing on one or just a few items. However, when members have to travel, fewer but longer meetings are needed. Be sure to select an appropriate place for the meeting, and plan for the physical comfort of the group. Be sure seating provides eye contact for small discussion groups, and plan enough time so that the members do not have to rush. If reservations are needed for the meeting place, make them far enough in advance to get a proper meeting room.

With advances in technology, telephone conferences are becoming quite common. Videoconferences are also gaining popularity. These techniques have saved travel costs and time and have resulted in better and quicker decisions. Companies using videoconferencing include Aetna, Arco, Boeing, Ford, IBM, TRW, and Xerox. The personal computer has been said to be the most useful tool for running meetings since *Robert's Rules of Order.* The personal computer can be turned into a large-screen "intelligent chalkboard" that can dramatically change meeting results. Minutes (notes on what took place during the last meeting) can be taken on the personal computer and distributed at the end of the meeting.

Leadership

The leader should determine the appropriate leadership style for the meeting. It is recommended that leaders play the role of facilitators, which involves guiding the process of the meeting while not influencing the content.[140] Each agenda item may need to be handled differently. For example, some items may simply call for disseminating information; others require a discussion, vote, or consensus; while other items require a simple, quick report from a member, and so forth. An effective way to develop group members' ability is to rotate the role of the group moderator/leader for each meeting.

Conducting Meetings

The First Meeting

At the first meeting, the group is in the orientation stage. The leader should use the high-task role. However, the members should be given the opportunity to spend some time getting to know one another. Introductions set the stage for subsequent interactions. A simple technique is to start with introductions, then move on to the group's purpose and objectives, and members' job roles. Sometime during or following this procedure, have a break that enables members to interact informally. If members find that their social needs will not be met, dissatisfaction may occur quickly.

Learning Outcome 4 *Outline the three parts of conducting effective meetings.*

The Three Parts of a Meeting

Each meeting should cover the following:

1. *Identifying objectives.* Begin the meeting on time; waiting for late members penalizes the members who are on time and develops a norm for arriving late. Begin by reviewing progress to date, the group's objectives, and the purpose/objective for the specific meeting. If minutes are recorded, they are usually approved at the beginning of the next meeting. For most meetings it is recommended that a secretary be appointed to take minutes.
2. *Covering agenda items.* Be sure to cover agenda items in priority order. Try to keep to the approximate times, but be flexible. If the discussion is constructive and members need more time, give it to them; however, if the discussion becomes more of a destructive argument, move ahead.
3. *Summarizing and reviewing assignments.* End the meeting on time. The leader should summarize what took place during the meeting. Were the meeting's objectives achieved? Review all of the assignments given during the meeting. Get a commitment to the task that each member should perform for the next or a specific future meeting. The secretary and/or leader should record all assignments. If there is no accountability and follow-up on assignments, members may not complete them.

Leadership

The team leader needs to focus on group structure, process, and development. As stated, the leadership style needs change with the group's level of development. The leader must be sure to provide the appropriate task and/or maintenance behavior when it is needed.

Handling Problem Members

As members work together, personality types tend to emerge. Certain personality types can cause the group to be less efficient than possible. Some of the problem members you may have in your group are the following: silent, talker, wanderer, bored, and arguer.

Silent

To have a fully effective meeting, all group members should participate. If members are silent, the group does not get the benefit of their input. It is the leader's responsibility to encourage the silent member to participate without being obvious or overdoing it. One technique the leader can use is the rotation method, in which all members take turns giving their input. This method is generally less threatening than directly calling on people. However, the rotation method is not always appropriate. To build up the silent member's confidence, call on them with questions they can easily answer. When you believe they have convictions, ask them to express them. Watch their nonverbal communication as indicators of when to call on them. If you are a silent type, try to participate more often. Know when to stand up for your views and be assertive. Silent types generally do not make good leaders.

Talker

Talkers have something to say about everything. They like to dominate the discussion. However, if they do dominate, the other members do not get to participate. The talker can cause intragroup problems, such as low cohesiveness and conflicts. It is the leader's responsibility to slow talkers down, not to shut them up. Do not let them dominate the group. The rotation technique is also effective with talkers. They have to wait their turn. When not using a rotation method, gently interrupt the talker and present your own ideas or call on other members to present their ideas. Prefacing questions with statements like "let's give those who have not answered yet a chance" can also slow the talker down. If you tend to be a talker, try to slow down. Give others a chance to talk and do things for themselves. Good leaders develop others' abilities in these areas.

Wanderer

Wanderers distract the group from the agenda items; they tend to change the subject and often like to complain. The leader is responsible for keeping the group on track. If the wanderer wants to socialize, cut it off. Be kind, thank the member for the contribution, then throw a question out to the group to get it back on track. If the wanderer has a complaint that is legitimate and solvable, allow the group to discuss it. Group structure issues should be addressed and resolved. However, if an issue is not resolvable, get the group back on track. Griping without resolving anything tends to reduce morale and commitment to task accomplishment. If the wanderer complains about unresolvable issues, make statements like, "We may be underpaid, but we have no control over our pay. Complaining will not get us a raise; let's get back to the issue at hand." If you tend to be a wanderer, try to be aware of your behavior and stay on the subject at hand.

Bored

Your group may have one or more members who are not interested in the job. The bored person may be preoccupied with other issues and not pay attention or participate in the group meeting. The bored member may also feel superior and wonder why the group is spending so much time on the obvious.

The leader is responsible for keeping members motivated. Assign the bored member a task like recording ideas on the board and recording the minutes. Call on bored members; bring them into the group. If you allow them to sit back, things may get worse and others may decide not to participate either. If you tend to be bored, try to find ways to help motivate yourself. Work at becoming more patient and in control of behavior that can have negative effects on other members.

Arguer

Like the talker, the arguer likes to be the center of attention. This behavior can occur when you use the devil's advocate approach, which is helpful in developing and selecting alternative courses of action. However, arguers enjoy arguing for the sake of arguing, rather than helping the group. They turn things into a win-lose situation, and they cannot stand losing.

The leader should resolve conflict, but not in an argumentative way. Do not get into an argument with arguers; that is exactly what they want to happen. If an argument starts, bring others into the discussion. If it is personal, cut it off. Personal attacks only hurt the group. Keep the discussion moving on target. If you tend to be an arguer, strive to convey your views in an assertive debate format, not as an aggressive argument. Listen to others' views and be willing to change if they have better ideas.

Applying the Concept 4

Group Problem People

Identify the problem type as:

a. silent b. talker c. wanderer d. bored e. arguer

____ 16. Charlie is always first or second to give his ideas. He is always elaborating on ideas. Because Charlie is so quick to respond, others sometimes make comments to him about it.

____ 17. One of the usually active group members is sitting back quietly today for the first time. The other members are doing all the discussing and volunteering for assignments.

____ 18. As the group is discussing a problem, Billy asks the group if they heard about the company owner and the mailroom clerk.

____ 19. Eunice is usually reluctant to give her ideas. When asked to explain her position, Eunice often changes her answers to agree with others in the group.

____ 20. Dwayne enjoys challenging members' ideas. He likes getting his own way. When a group member does not agree with Dwayne, he makes wisecracks about the member's prior mistakes.

Working with Group Members

Whenever you work in a group, do not embarrass, intimidate, or argue with any members, no matter how they provoke you. If you do, the result will make a martyr of them and a bully of you to the group. If you have serious problem members who do not respond to the above techniques, confront them individually outside of the group. Get them to agree to work in a cooperative way.

The remainder of this chapter will focus on the concept of self-managed teams, an innovative extension of the team concept.

Work Application 10

Recall a meeting you attended. Did you receive an agenda prior to the meeting? How well did the leader conduct the meeting? Give ideas on how the meeting could have been improved. Did the group have any problem members? How well did the leader handle them?

Self-Managed Teams

Worldwide, companies big and small face serious challenges from a dynamic and complex global economy—challenges that render traditional work methods ineffective.[141] To effectively and efficiently address these challenges, organizations are rethinking the way work is done. Old concepts of hierarchical leadership, centralized decision making, functional specialization, and individualized reward systems are being replaced with new, more flexible and adaptive structures.[142,143] As discussed earlier in the chapter, management styles have shifted from the "Lone Ranger" model of leadership to participatory management practices, and task structures have gone from functional specialization to cross-functional team models. The use of teams has become the competitive weapon of choice for many business and nonbusiness organizations, with many of these companies opting for a new form of performing work called the *self-managed team*. In self-managed teams, decision-making authority is left up to the individual members who make up the team.

Self-managed teams go by many different names: self-directed, self-leading, self-maintaining, and self-regulating teams, to name a few. The concept itself is not new. It has its roots in sociotechnical systems theory and design, developed by Eric Trist and his colleagues in England in the 1960s.[144] The theory contends that organizations intimately combine people and technology in complex forms to produce outputs. The sociotechnical systems approach worked through sectional design teams, which were usually charged with implementing planned change programs, initiating improvement programs, and encouraging learning. For the concept to work, team members must understand the team's goals and be committed to achieving them. The major contribution of sociotechnical systems theory is the belief that team members involved in formulating tasks are more likely to feel invested in the process and be dedicated to accomplishing the stated goals. This laid the groundwork for self-managed teams, which have become more common as the evolution of total quality management (TQM) has continued.

Because of the increasing use of self-managed teams in organizations, much attention has been devoted to understanding how best to design and launch them in order to maximize their efficiency and effectiveness. This section examines the unique nature of self-managed teams, their benefits, guidelines for improving their effectiveness, leadership issues, and the challenges of implementation.

Learning Outcome 5 *Explain the differences between conventional and self-managed teams.*

The Nature of Self-Managed Teams

In the quest to remain competitive in new product/service development, companies are finding out that effectively managing human interactions and the rapid transfer of technology and ideas among individuals and functional teams is a prerequisite to success. Studies of the human interaction processes that characterize new product/service development reveal that effective leadership as well as followership, equitable distribution of power, and collaboration among functional groups can make such human interactions more productive, thus enhancing performance and efficiency. This quest to maximize the human potential represents the essence or rationale for the self-managed team concept. To understand the nature of SMTs, two key questions need to be posed and addressed: (1) What makes them different from conventional teams? and (2) How widespread is their use in organizations?

Learning Outcome 6 *Describe how team member characteristics impact self-managed team effectiveness.*

How Are SMTs Different from Conventional Teams?

Self-managed teams differ from conventional teams in a number of ways. In conventional teams, a leader (or leaders) provides the team with direction and maintains control over work-related issues. In contrast, self-managed teams have a significant amount of decision-making authority. Members are charged with duties such as managing themselves, assigning jobs, planning and scheduling work, making production- or service-related decisions, and taking action on problems. Members take responsibility for outlining how they will achieve the team's objectives. Often teams will focus on what some have described as the 5Ts: project *targets* (milestones), specific project *tasks, team* membership (roles and responsibilities), *time* issues (both team and individual), and *territories* (of personal and collective focus) that would lead to successful planning, design, and completion of specific projects.

Self-managed team members share or rotate leadership responsibilities and hold themselves mutually responsible for a set of performance goals assigned by senior management. Roles interchange frequently as members learn to be followers as well as leaders. Rather than being specialized, SMT members develop multiskilled capabilities that make them very flexible in performing various tasks within the team. Self-managed teams give workers, especially non-managerial workers, a voice in making decisions about the design of work, as well as greater autonomy and discretion in the structure of their work. Members operate without direct managerial supervision—an idea almost unthinkable a generation ago.

The nature of self-managed teams is one of team rather than individual empowerment and accountability. Team accountability is a significant responsibility, especially since SMT members determine how they will organize themselves to get the work done, and are responsible not only for their own performance but for that of other team members as well. In successful SMTs, members have come to see that what they collectively gain is greater than what they personally sacrifice. Therefore, assigning members to self-managed teams must provide for a complementary fit that balances team member characteristics such as concientiousness, introversion, and extroversion.[145] A review of the literature on member characteristics that have been identified with effective SMTs does reveal a general consensus on at least seven characteristics. It should be noted that these following characteristics are not exclusive to SMT members alone; they can apply to members of other types of teams discussed earlier:

- A strong belief in personal accountability
- An internal locus of control coupled with emotional stability
- Openness to new ideas/viewpoints
- Effective communication
- Good problem-solving skills
- Ability to engender trust
- Good conflict resolution skills

Depending on the types of decisions, the amount of authority vested in a team varies greatly from one organization to another. For instance, in some organizations, the teams are given the primary responsibility for personnel decisions such as hiring and firing team members, conducting performance appraisals, and determining compensation (within specified limits); while in other organizations, such decisions are left to top management. Teams are usually allowed to make small expenditures for supplies and equipment without prior approval, but in most organizations, any action involving large purchases must be approved by top management. Exhibit 8.5 summarizes the key differences between conventional teams and self-managed teams.

Work Application 11

Using your own experience, or asking someone who has been part of an SMT, describe some of the self-managing activities of the team that made it a truly self-managing team as opposed to a traditional team.

EXHIBIT 8.5 Differences Between Conventional and Self-Managed Teams

Characteristics	Self-Managed Teams	Conventional Teams
Leadership	Within the team	Outside the team
Team member role	Interchangeable	Fixed
Accountability	Team	Individual
Work effort	Cohesive	Divided
Task design	Flexible	Fixed
Skills	Multiskilled	Specialized

Applying the **Concept 5**

Types of Teams

Identify each statement below with one of these key terms.

a. group
b. functional team
c. cross-functional team
d. self-managed team

____ 21. In my department, a couple of us sometimes get together to discuss ways of improving our work processes.

____ 22. In my organization, I work in a team where leadership roles are rotated and shared, with each of us taking initiative at appropriate times for the good of the group.

____ 23. At the Appalachian Ice Cream factory, the quality control department headed by a unit supervisor is in charge of testing all incoming ingredients to make sure only the best products go into the company's ice cream.

____ 24. At Norton Telecom International, a team with members from information technology, finance, customer service, and quality control oversaw an ambitious system—an integration project that spanned operations in the United States and Canada.

Learning Outcome 7 *Describe the benefits of using self-managed teams in organizations.*

The Benefits of Self-Managed Teams

A primary reason for growth in popularity of the self-managed team concept is the reported benefits by organizations that have adopted it. Self-managed work teams are praised for bringing about results such as increased productivity, accelerated new product development and process improvements, improved worker participation, and decreased hierarchy.[146,147] These results have led to increases in job satisfaction, which in turn have been associated with other positive organizational and employee outcomes, such as lower absenteeism rates, less turnover, more interdependence of objectives, and, ultimately, increased levels of profitability.[148]

Self-managed teams inspire their members to connect with the company's vision and mission in a special way. A sense of belonging and ownership in one's work help to create a linkage between individual goals and aspirations and the company's long-term vision and mission. Employee motivation levels and self-esteem are much higher in SMTs. In the service sector, where there has been some debate as to whether self-managed teams can produce the same positive results as found in manufacturing, there is now strong empirical support that participation in self-managed teams is also associated with significant improvements in service quality.[149] In a study examining whether self-managed teams increased productivity in automobile service garages, it was found that service garages that used self-managed teams increased productivity compared to service garages that did not use teams.[150] More and more, the service sector is employing self-managed teams in service delivery with great results. A recent Finnish study of home health care workers found that self-designed teams improved productivity and the quality of work life of the agency staff.[151]

In exploring the question of how self-managed teams in high-velocity environments handle unexpected critical incidents, one study found that they responded effectively. Not only did the self-managed team create a context for a shared and emotionally grounded identity, it also allowed for a shared set of guiding principles for decision making and action.[152] SMTs bring "a collective seeing and knowing" to the job that surpasses the capability of any individual team member. Any agreed-upon course of action is taken collectively and so has the strong commitment of all team members to make it successful.

Self-managed teams reduce costs because of the reductions in managerial ranks throughout the organization. In a study examining the economic benefits of organizing field technicians into self-managed teams, it was found that SMTs absorb the monitoring and coordination tasks of supervisors, substantially reducing indirect labor costs but without adversely affecting objective measures of quality and labor productivity. Also, operating costs are greatly reduced with self-managed teams because they tend to focus on product and process improvement. The focus on a single process, taking time to fully understand it, and collectively identifying opportunities to improve it, is what usually makes SMTs successful at reducing operational costs. It should be noted that self-managed teams do exhibit the same general advantages of teamwork discussed earlier in the chapter. Exhibit 8.6 summarizes the benefits of self-managed teams. The next section discusses guidelines for improving SMT effectiveness and addresses organizational-level factors that can impact SMT effectiveness.

Work Application 12

If you have been part of an SMT, describe the benefits that you derived from being part of the team. Be specific, matching your description to the list in Exhibit 8.6.

EXHIBIT 8.6 Benefits of Self-Managed Teams

- Greater improvements in quality, speed, process, and innovation.
- A sense of belonging and ownership in one's work.
- Greater employee motivation.
- Accelerated new product development.
- Greater employee participation.
- Reduced operational costs because of reductions in managerial ranks and greater efficiencies.
- Greater employee job satisfaction, commitment, and productivity, and lower turnover and absenteeism rates.

Opening Case APPLICATION

7. Do you think John Chambers is the type of leader who would embrace self-managed teams? Explain your answer.

John Chambers has been described as a "relentlessly optimistic" individual who has a lot of confidence in himself. Organizations that have instituted SMTs have said it is the best vehicle for achieving creativity and innovation. Given Chambers' personality and emphasis on innovation and creativity, he would most likely embrace the self-managed team concept. Chambers wants to set Cisco apart from its competitors through innovative technologies. As the text has illustrated, the progression for teamwork has been from functional teams to cross-functional teams to self-managed teams. SMTs will make a logical next step for a forward-thinking CEO like Chambers.

Learning Outcome 8 *Describe the guidelines for improving self-managed team effectiveness.*

Guidelines for Improving Self-Managed Team Effectiveness

Despite the documented successes and benefits of SMTs, there is still much that needs to be done to improve their effectiveness. Many things can go wrong with self-managed teams, and adjusting to new behavioral expectations can be difficult. Many SMT initiatives are eventually abandoned.[153] For this reason, studies have focused on identifying factors or conditions that are key to building high-performance management teams. As part of a larger survey, managers from various manufacturing industries were asked what they considered to be key factors in getting managers to cooperate with each other and to function as a team. Their responses focused on the significant role that senior management must play to ensure SMT effectiveness and success. At the organizational level, important policy and procedural changes can greatly enhance the effectiveness of SMTs.[154] In planning the transition to SMTs, top management should ensure that the following policies, procedures, and actions are implemented:

- Ensure that the whole organization has changed its culture, structure, and climate to support SMTs. This will address questions such as: Does the SMT have sufficient autonomy to perform its task and have access to information? Have conditions been created in which authority can shift between members to appropriately match the demands of their task? Are SMT participants motivated, stimulated, and supported in a fashion that breaks down walls and creates unity of purpose and action?
- Have a champion to support and defend the SMT from opponents who are threatened by the new concept and what it represents. *A* **self-managed team champion** *is an advocate of the self-managed team concept whose responsibility is to help the team obtain necessary resources, gain political support from top management and other stakeholders of the organization, and defend it from enemy attacks.* This advocacy role is especially critical when the self-managed team concept is being applied on a broader scale throughout the company, and when there is hostility and distrust by other managers who are afraid the self-managed teams will cause major shifts of power and authority in the organization. The SMT champion is therefore constantly engaged in getting others to "buy in" and gaining commitment at all levels, while communicating the benefits of the SMT.
- Have a well thought-out vision of the way in which SMTs will fit into the scheme of the entire organization.
- Allow time after training for the team members to bond with one another and form team skills. Effective team-building interventions can be used to break down barriers and create opportunities for cooperation.
- Provide adequate training so team member skills and experiences match task requirements. Identify specific areas that need improvement and develop solutions from a team-based perspective.
- Provide objective goals, incentives, and appropriate infrastructure. Self-managed team participants should have a vested interest in clarifying team goals, designing team-based incentive and reward systems, understanding each other's roles, and improving their understanding of processes and systems that will be used.
- Ensure that the organization has the necessary resources to commit to this kind of change in time, money, and people.
- Create a sense of empowerment so SMTs take ownership of what they are doing and how they are going to do it. For example, designating a team leader may help ensure that critical team management functions are accomplished in a timely fashion; however, if leadership responsibilities are rotated among

members, a climate of shared leadership may be fostered and this should lead to the team feeling empowered.[155]

- Pay close attention to team design decisions. As mentioned earlier, teams with peer evaluations and rotating leadership among members tend to have higher levels of cooperation, performance, and member satisfaction.
- Develop team-based measurements and corresponding feedback methods that address team performance.
- Recruit and train managers to act as team facilitators or coaches. This will be further elaborated on later in the chapter, as we explore the changing role of leadership in self-managed teams.
- Avoid overreacting at the first sign of crisis. Team-building experts say company leaders should "keep a stiff upper lip" when an SMT starts experiencing problems, because the tendency is to overreact by pulling the plug on the new program or getting too involved. SMTs, they say, fluctuate like stocks—even the blue chips with excellent long-term prospects experience short-term troughs.

The best example to illustrate how the lack of managerial action in these areas can create problems during the implementation of SMT programs is captured in this statement by Asea Brown Boveri's former CEO, Percy Barnevik: "I found myself trying to implement third-generation strategies through second-generation organizations run by first-generation managers."[156] (Asea Brown Boveri is a manufacturer of power transformers and other large, expensive equipment.) Implementing these guidelines will help eliminate mismatches such as this one. The next sections examine the changing role of leadership in SMTs and the challenges of implementing SMTs.

Applying the **Concept 6**

Guidelines for Improving SMT Effectiveness

Identify which factor is missing in the scenarios based on the statements below.

a. top management support and commitment
b. unambiguous goals and objectives
c. appropriate compensation structure
d. appropriate task design and measurement system
e. appropriate scope of authority
f. adequate information system
g. strong and experienced facilitator

____ 25. I get frustrated with this team because no one seems to know what we are doing.

____ 26. Management expects us to give input into which products we should make. However, they don't give us the numbers we need to make effective decisions.

____ 27. The thing that bothers me is the fact that we don't have a clear agreement on the quality of the product.

____ 28. We really need a better manager if we are going to improve our team performance.

____ 29. The team members are not taking our new self-directed status seriously, because they believe SMTs are just the latest fad, that management will drop it for the next hot topic.

The Changing Role of Leadership in Self-Managed Teams

It seems contradictory that a self-managed team would need a leader. After all, the concept implies that the team leads itself. However, the concept of a self-managed team does not mean "without management." Rather, it implies self-responsibility and self-accountability. Self-managed teams require a different kind of leadership. At the organizational level, the self-managed team must still receive direction and instruction from higher levels in the organization. And it must report to that hierarchy through a person who is ultimately held accountable for the team's performance.

Many managers find themselves in a conflicting position when called upon to function as external leaders for self-managed teams. Most receive conflicting signals on how to go about it. For example, how involved should they be in their team's decision-making process? How can they get involved without compromising the team's autonomy? Studies have focused on investigating such issues for answers. Contrary to what many would have predicted, a study on the subject revealed that the best external leaders were not necessarily the ones who employed a hands-off approach; instead, the external leaders who had contributed most to their team's success excelled at one skill: managing the boundary between the team and the larger organization.[157] Several studies of empowered teams have emphasized that managing this boundary is the central focus of the external leader's role.

Effective external leaders are able to develop strong relationships both inside the team and across the organizational landscape. External leaders play the role of facilitators, while allowing team members to manage themselves through a process some have described as distributed or shared leadership. *In* **distributed leadership**, *multiple leaders take complementary leadership roles in rotation within the same SMT, according to their area of expertise or interest.*[158] In other words, different members of the SMT assume different leadership roles as circumstances and task requirements warrant. Studies investigating the relationship between shared leadership and team effectiveness have found that teams employing shared leadership were more effective.[159] Teams with shared leadership offered advantages ranging from support and shared functions to higher ratings from clients on performance.[160]

Teams will vary in how quickly they can transition into distributed leadership practice, based on such factors as their prior experience with teams, the quality of relationships among team members, and their collective orientation and interest. For example, some individuals simply do not like working with others, preferring to work alone on tasks. Other individuals crave attention or compete for power within the team, such as the opportunity to direct and control discussions, or the prerogative to confirm or dispute others' views.[161] This is where the SMT facilitator can play a significant role.

The **self-managed team facilitator** *is the external leader of a self-managed team, whose job is to create optimal working conditions so team members take on responsibilities to work productively and solve complex problems on their own.*[162] Effective facilitators must be good at coaching, influencing, and empowering the team. For example, a self-managed team facilitator collected data from the accounting department to persuade his failing team to think of ways to improve its performance. Using the data, the facilitator, playing the role of external leader, impressed upon his team how much the organization lost in profits every minute because of downtime caused by some workers leaving the manufacturing line. The facilitator told the team, "This is money that we didn't make." He reiterated that someone's decision to cut off the line to eat a sandwich or indulge in a habit was costing everybody. Three months later, the team's performance improved markedly. Remarkably, the team members were going the extra mile without their external leader having to ask (let alone demand) that they do so.[163] The team facilitator had simply influenced their decision by showing them the data from accounting and then allowing the team to decide on what to do.

A summary of the facilitator's team-building activities is presented in Exhibit 8.7. These activities should ensure that there is strong identification with the team, especially as pride in the team's accomplishments grows. These activities will also strengthen cohesiveness and the level of mutual cooperation among team members.

Work Application 13

Describe which of the facilitator's team-building activities (see Exhibit 8.7) your SMT or other type of team facilitator employed in leading the team.

EXHIBIT 8.7 SMT Facilitator Team-Building Activities

- Opening forums for resolving interpersonal conflicts.
- Creating opportunities for social interaction.
- Increasing mutual acceptance and respect among diverse team members.
- Maintaining an open communication policy.
- Highlighting mutual interest, not differences, of team members.
- Increasing team identification through the use of ceremonies, rituals, and symbols.
- Using team-oriented incentives to foster teamwork.

Learning Outcome 9 *Describe the challenges of implementing effective self-managed teams.*

The Challenges of Implementing Self-Managed Teams

When an organization transitions into self-managed work teams, what is the response among the managerial and nonmanagerial ranks of the organization's workers? A study examining the differential outcomes of team structures for 1,200 workers, including supervisors and middle managers of a large unionized telecommunications company, found that participation in self-managed teams was associated with significantly higher levels of perceived discretion, employment security, and satisfaction for workers, and the opposite for supervisors.[164] This supports the perception held by some in the managerial ranks that managers fear their jobs will disappear if work teams become self-directed.

However, in many organizations where there has been careful planning, former managers become SMT facilitators and are retrained to function differently than they did in their previous role. Many of the drawbacks associated with SMTs stem from the difficulties of transitioning from a traditional command-and-control work environment to self-managed teams. Teambuilding experts maintain that managers who have become accustomed to traditional, autocratic management and jaded at management fads that come and go may resist or undermine a team approach.

Even among members of the nonmanagerial ranks, the transition to SMTs has as much potential for frustrations and problems as it does for managers. This is usually due to unfamiliarity with the new structure and new routines, and adjusting to team responsibilities. Team members must learn new behaviors, like putting aside differences in order to make decisions that benefit the team. The need to adapt to a new working environment, in which the definition of teamwork requires a personal, cultural, and behavioral adjustment, may be too much for some members and thus lead to personality and behavior conflicts.[165] Thus, the greatest challenge may lie in setting and enforcing new behavioral expectations, made necessary by the absence of a traditional leader and the presence of new employee rights and responsibilities.

Work Application 14

Have you worked in a team in which former managers have been reassigned to function simply as members of the team? What was your experience with the behavior and attitude of these former managers in their new role as team members?

When managers do not cooperate with other team members in an SMT environment, coordination suffers and breakdowns in planning increase. When SMT members are not working together, counterproductive workplace conflict and political activity increases, as does ill will and decrease in morale. Ultimately, when former managers now working as team members in SMTs worry more about their egos and avoid communicating with other members, they set a poor example for the rest of the team. Some of the disadvantages of working in teams in general discussed earlier in the chapter—such as social loafing and groupthink—are also likely to occur in self-managed teams.

The lesson, therefore, is that the decision to use self-managed teams as a tool for re-engineering work in an organization is not always a guaranteed success. It requires a great deal of commitment, effort, and support from all members of the organization. As described earlier, in the long run, the benefits of SMTs to employee morale, efficiency, product quality, economic savings, and overall organizational performance are well worth the growing pains.

As for the future of self-managed teams, they undoubtedly pose very serious challenges to organizations that experiment with them; however, they probably will continue to ride a growth curve of popularity among employers and new generations of workers because of the productivity gains that they bring.

Go to the Internet (www.cengage.com/management/lussier)
where you will find a broad array of resources to help maximize your learning.

- Review the vocabulary
- Try a quiz
- Find related links

Chapter Summary

The chapter summary is organized to answer the ten learning outcomes for Chapter 8.

1. **Discuss the advantages and disadvantages of working in teams.**

   Advantages: In a team situation it is possible to achieve synergy, whereby the team's total output exceeds the sum of individual member contributions. Team members often evaluate and add to one another's thinking, so there are fewer chances of errors and the quality of the decisions is improved. A team atmosphere contributes well toward effective problem solving, continuous improvement, and innovation. Also, being a team member makes it possible for someone to satisfy more needs than working alone; among these are the need for affiliation, security, self-esteem, and self-fulfillment.

   Disadvantages: Some teams have the unhealthy practice of pressuring members to conform to lower group standards of performance and conduct. For example, a team member may be ostracized for being more productive than his or her coworkers. Shirking of individual responsibility, or social loafing, is another problem frequently noted in groups. Another well-known problem common in teams is the practice of groupthink, which happens when the team values getting along so much that dissenting views are quickly suppressed in favor of group consensus.

2. **Briefly describe the seven characteristics of effective teams.**

   The seven characteristics of effective teams are: (1) team norms, (2) team leadership, (3) team cohesiveness and interdependence, (4) team composition, (5) team structure, (6) organizational support, and (7) creativity driven. Team norms influence how a team's members perceive and interact with one another, approach decisions, and solve problems; they guide team members' behavior. Teams need effective leaders who will monitor the progress of the team to make sure that the team does not go off track, go too far or not far enough, lose sight of its goal, or become bogged down by conflict. Effective teams have high levels of cohesion and interdependence. Highly cohesive teams are characterized by high group potency and strong self-efficacy.

Members of highly effective teams are more interactive and dependent on one another to get tasks done. Effective teams must have the appropriate mix of complementary skills, knowledge, and ability to successfully realize the team's objectives. Effective teams have structures that provide team members with broad participation in decision making. Effective teams have strong support from top management. Management support, both tangible and intangible, is critical for team success. It is management's responsibility to create a work climate that supports and rewards teamwork. Finally, effective teams are also characterized by higher levels of creativity.

3. **Describe top management's and the team leader's roles in fostering creativity. For each, list activities they should undertake to promote creativity.**

Top management's role in encouraging creativity is significant. Creativity does not work in hierarchical command-and-control environments. Top management has the responsibility to create the appropriate setting and support systems that foster and nourish creativity.

Top management activities that can enhance creativity include providing teams with the following: (1) adequate and quality resources, (2) appropriate recognition and rewards, (3) flexibility and a minimum amount of structure, and (4) supportive climate and culture.

Team leader activities that can help to enhance team creativity include (1) matching members with the right assignments; (2) giving team members greater autonomy to do the job; (3) ensuring the availability of adequate time, money, and other resources for the team; and (4) protecting against "creativity blockers."

4. **Outline the three parts of conducting effective meetings.**

Each meeting should cover the following:

1. *Identify objectives.* Begin the meeting on time. Begin by reviewing progress to date, the group's objectives, and the purpose/objective for the specific meeting. If minutes are recorded, they are usually approved at the beginning of the next meeting.
2. *Cover agenda items.* Be sure to cover agenda items in priority order. Try to keep to the approximate times, but be flexible. If the discussion is constructive and members need more time, give it to them; however, if the discussion is more of a destructive argument, move ahead.
3. *Summarize and review assignments.* End the meeting on time. The leader should summarize what took place during the meeting. Were the meeting's objectives achieved? Review all of the assignments given during the meeting. Get a commitment to the task that each member should perform for the next or a specific future meetings. The secretary and/or leader should record all assignments.

5. **Explain the differences between conventional and self-managed teams.**

Self-managed teams differ from traditional teams in a number of ways. In self-managed teams, roles interchange frequently as members learn to be followers as well as leaders. Rather than functioning in their specialized units, SMT members develop multiskilled capabilities that make them very flexible in performing various tasks within the team. The nature of self-managed teams is one of group empowerment and accountability rather than individual empowerment and accountability. Team accountability is a significant responsibility, especially since SMT members determine how they will organize themselves to get the work done and are responsible not only for their own performance but for that of other team members as well.

6. **Describe how team member characteristics impact self-managed team effectiveness.**

An SMT is no better than the quality of the members that make up the team. Certain qualities associated with members of effective SMTs have been identified through research. They are (1) a strong belief in personal accountability, (2) an internal locus of control coupled with emotional stability, (3) openness to new ideas/viewpoints, (4) effective communication, (5) good problem-solving skills, (6) ability to engender trust, and (7) good conflict resolution skills. The nature of SMTs is such that they are empowered to plan and schedule their own work, track performance, and do self-evaluations. This presumes that individual team members possess all these qualities in order for the above-mentioned activities to be successfully performed.

7. **Describe the benefits of using self-managed teams in organizations.**

Self-managed teams (1) create a stronger sense of commitment to the work effort among team members; (2) improve quality, speed, and innovation; (3) have more satisfied employees and lower turnover and absenteeism; (4) facilitate faster new-product development; (5) allow cross-trained team members greater flexibility in dealing with personnel shortages due to illness or turnover; and (6) keep operational costs down because of reductions in managerial ranks and increased efficiencies.

8. **Describe the guidelines for improving self-managed team effectiveness.**

Senior management has the principal responsibility to create the right environment in which self-managed teams can grow and thrive. This involves undertaking activities to ensure that the whole organization has a changed culture, structure, and climate to support SMTs. This requires providing sufficient responses to questions such as whether the SMT has sufficient autonomy to perform its task and has access to information; whether conditions have been created in which authority can shift between members to appropriately match the demands of their task; and whether SMT participants are motivated, stimulated, and supported in a fashion that breaks down walls and creates unity of purpose and action.

Management must have a well thought-out vision of the way in which SMTs will fit into the scheme of the entire organization; allow time after training for the team members to bond with one another and form team skills; provide adequate training, so team member skills and experiences match task requirements; provide objective goals, incentives, and appropriate infrastructure; ensure that the organization has the necessary resources to commit to this kind of change (not only in time but also in money and people); and create a sense of empowerment, so SMTs take ownership of what they are doing and how they are going to do it.

9. **Describe the challenges of implementing effective self-managed teams.**

Many of the challenges of implementing SMTs stem from the difficulties of transitioning from a traditional command-and-control work environment to self-managed teams. Team-building experts contend that managers who have become accustomed to traditional, autocratic management and jaded at management fads that come and go may resist or undermine a team approach. Even among members of the nonmanagerial ranks, the transition to SMTs has as much potential for frustrations and problems as it does for managers. This is usually due to unfamiliarity with the new structure and new routines, and adjusting to team responsibilities. Team members must learn new behaviors, like putting aside differences in order to make decisions that benefit the team. The need to adapt to a new working environment in which the definition of teamwork requires a personal, cultural, and behavioral adjustment may be too much for some members and thus lead to personality and behavior conflicts. Thus, the greatest challenge may lie in setting and enforcing new behavioral expectations, made necessary by the absence of a traditional leader and the presence of new employee rights and responsibilities.

10. **Define the following key terms (in order of appearance in the chapter).**

Select one or more methods: (1) fill in the missing key terms from memory; (2) match the key terms from the following list with their definitions below; (3) copy the key terms in order from the list at the beginning of the chapter.

__________ is a unit of interdependent individuals with complementary skills who are committed to a common purpose and set of performance goals and to common expectations, for which they hold themselves accountable.

__________ is an understanding and commitment to group goals on the part of all team members.

__________ is the conscious or unconscious tendency by some team members to shirk responsibilities, by withholding effort toward group goals when they are not individually accountable for their work.

__________ happens when members of a cohesive group tend to agree on a decision not on the basis of its merits but because they are less willing to risk rejection for questioning a majority viewpoint or presenting a dissenting opinion.

__________ has three components: (1) task performance—the degree to which the team's output (product or service) meets the needs and expectations of those who use it; (2) group process—the degree to which members interact or relate in ways that allow the team to work increasingly well together over time; and (3) individual satisfaction—the degree to which the group experience, on balance, is more satisfying than frustrating to team members.

__________ is the collective acquisition, combination, creation, and sharing of knowledge.

__________ are acceptable standards of behavior that are shared by team members.

__________ is the extent to which team members band together and remain committed to achieving team goals.

__________ is the creation of a valuable, useful, and novel product, service, idea, procedure, or process carried out via discovery rather than by a predetermined step-by-step procedure, by individuals working together in a complex social system.

__________ is a group of employees belonging to the same functional department, such as marketing, R&D, production, human resources, or information systems, who have a common objective.

__________ is made up of members from different functional departments of an organization who are brought together to perform unique tasks to create new and nonroutine products or services.

__________ is a team whose members are geographically distributed, requiring them to work together through electronic means with minimal face-to-face interaction.

__________ are relatively autonomous teams whose members share or rotate leadership responsibilities and hold themselves mutually responsible for a set of performance goals assigned by higher management.

__________ is an advocate of the self-managed team concept whose responsibility is to help the team obtain necessary resources, gain political support from top management and other stakeholders of the organization, and defend from enemy attacks.

__________ is the process by which multiple leaders take complementary leadership roles in rotation within the same SMT, according to their area of expertise or interest.

__________ is the external leader of a self-managed team, whose job is to create optimal working conditions so team members take on responsibilities to work productively and solve complex problems on their own.

Key Terms

cross-functional team, 294
distributed leadership, 312
functional team, 293
groupthink, 283
self-managed team champion, 310
self-managed team facilitator, 312
self-managed teams (SMTs), 296
social loafing, 283
team, 281
team cohesion, 288
team creativity, 291
team effectiveness, 285
team learning, 285
team norms, 286
teamwork, 282
virtual team, 296

Review Questions

1. What is groupthink, and under what conditions is it most likely to occur?
2. Describe the factors that generally contribute high levels of team cohesion.
3. Creativity is usually thought of as a characteristic of individuals, but are some teams more creative than others?
4. What is team-centered leadership, and how does it differ from the leader-centered approach?
5. Describe how a leader can avoid conducting nonproductive meetings.
6. What is the depth of decision-making latitude commonly found in self-managed teams?
7. Briefly discuss some of the potential benefits and drawbacks of using self-managed teams.

Communication Skills

The following critical-thinking questions can be used for class discussion and/or as written assignments to develop communication skills. Be sure to give complete explanations for all questions.

1. Teams are often credited with making better decisions than individuals, yet they are also criticized for groupthink. What are some strategies for creating effective teams that are not victims of the groupthink phenomenon?
2. Identify and describe any team you have been a member of, or know about otherwise, that has a strong norm of teamwork that all members buy into. What role did the team leader play in making this possible?
3. What are some of the key indicators of team dysfunction?
4. What is the key to creating cross-functional teams in which team members put the good of the team ahead of functional self-interest?
5. How can virtual teams work well together from far apart?
6. What would you describe as some of the do's and don'ts of team leadership?
7. Describe an organization whose culture, structure, and leadership philosophy clearly support creativity and innovation.

CASE

Frederick W. Smith—FedEx

Thirty-eight years along, Federal Express, now known as simply FedEx, remains the market leader in an industry it helped create. The name FedEx is synonymous with overnight delivery. The person in charge of providing the strategic direction for all FedEx Corporation companies is its founder, Frederick W. Smith, the Chairman, President, and Chief Executive Officer. To position the company for the twenty-first century, Smith has organized FedEx into the following Strategic Business Units: FedEx Express, FedEx Ground, FedEx Freight, FedEx Office, FedEx Custom Critical, FedEx Trade Networks, and FedEx Services. These companies serve more than 220 countries and territories with operations that include 672 aircraft and more than 80,000 vehicles. With more than 290,000 team members worldwide, FedEx handles more than 7.5 million shipments each business day.

FedEx has expanded far beyond what Smith started with back in 1971. FedEx has continued to strengthen its industry leadership over the past 38 years and has been widely acknowledged for its commitment to total quality service. Federal Express was the first service company to win the Malcolm Baldrige National Quality Award in 1990. In addition, FedEx has consistently been ranked on *Fortune* magazine's industry lists, including "World's Most Admired Companies," "America's Most Admired Companies," "100 Best Companies to Work For," and "Blue Ribbon Companies."

With growth comes difficulties of coordination, maintaining efficiency, meeting customer expectations, and managing employees. Smith realized that a rigid hierarchy of command-and-control groups would only magnify these difficulties. To give his employees the flexibility and freedom they need to move quickly and help FedEx remain the dominant overnight delivery service in the world, Smith decided to restructure FedEx by emphasizing the team approach to getting work done. He directed his leadership team to empower these groups by giving them the authority and the responsibility to make the changes needed to improve productivity and customer satisfaction throughout the FedEx system.

An example of the successful implementation of this new FedEx approach to organizing work can be found in Springfield, Virginia. With strong support from its managers, employees formed the Quality Action Team to overhaul their package-sorting techniques. The improvements they introduced put couriers on the road 12 minutes earlier than before, and halved the number of packages they delivered late. The success of teams at departmental or local levels encouraged Smith and his leadership team to also assign employee teams to companywide projects. Facing growing competition from United Parcel Service, the U.S. Postal Service, and Airborne Express, FedEx organized its clerical employees into "superteams" of up to 10 people. These teams operated as self-managed teams with little direct supervision from managers. One team cut service glitches, such as incorrect bills and lost packages, by 13 percent. Another team spotted—and worked until they eventually solved—a billing problem that had been costing the company $2.1 million a year.

FedEx teams have worked so well because Fred Smith sets standards and reinforces them. He spearheaded the concept of the "golden package," the idea that every package FedEx handles is critical and must be delivered on time. Whenever there's a crisis, whether due to competitive pressure or to Mother Nature threatening to ground the company's planes, the team with the golden package takes charge to figure out how to make the delivery on time. Smith reinforces group performance by presenting a monthly Circle of Excellence award to the best FedEx station. He encourages innovative thinking by creating a "job-secure environment." He takes the position that "if you hang people who try to do something that doesn't quite work, you'll get people who don't do anything."

Managers are by no means obsolete at FedEx. Smith has redefined their roles. There has been a shift in mindset from the traditional leader-centered to the team-centered leadership approach. Managers are expected to formulate clear, attainable goals for their teams, to solicit employee ideas, and to act on the best employee suggestions. FedEx managers perceive their role as facilitators—and sometimes they are players. During emergencies at the Memphis hub, senior managers have been known to hurry down from the executive suite to help load packages onto the conveyor belts that feed the company's planes. They practice team leadership by doing, not by telling.

According to one company executive, "FedEx has built what is the most seamless global air and ground network in its industry, connecting more than 90 percent of the world's economic activity." It is evident that Smith's leadership in pushing for a much more open, flexible, team-based organization has been instrumental in keeping FedEx's lead position in overnight package service. It is also one of the reasons that FedEx has continuously earned high marks as one of the top companies to work for in the United States.

GO TO THE INTERNET: To learn more about Fred Smith and FedEx, visit their Web site **(http://www.fedex.com)**.

Support your answers to the following questions with specific information from the case and text or with other information you get from the Web or other sources.

1. How do the standards set by Fred Smith for FedEx teams improve organizational performance?
2. What motivates the members of FedEx to remain highly engaged in their teams?
3. Describe the role FedEx managers play in facilitating team effectiveness.
4. What type of teams does FedEx use? Provide evidence from the case to support your answer.
5. Leaders play a critical role in building effective teams. Cite evidence from the case that FedEx managers performed some of these roles in developing effective teams.

CUMULATIVE CASE QUESTIONS

6. The Big Five model of personality categorizes traits into dimensions of surgency, agreeableness, adjustment, conscientiousness, and openness to experience (Chapter 2). Which of these dimensions do you think Fred Smith possesses?
7. The normative leadership model identifies five leadership styles appropriate for different situations that users can select to maximize decisions (Chapter 5). Which of the five leadership styles is practiced by FedEx team leaders?
8. The case reveals that at the Memphis hub senior managers have been known to hurry down from the executive suite to help load packages during emergencies in order to get the plane off on time. FedEx leaders want to be seen as coaches, not managers. Specific guidelines can help a leader become an effective coach (Chapter 6). Which of the guideline(s) does the example above represent?
9. Research on followership describes five types of followership (see Exhibit 7.3, Chapter 7). Which of these types will work best in FedEx's team environment as described in the case, and why?

CASE EXERCISE AND ROLE-PLAY

Preparation: You are senior vice president for operations at FedEx. FedEx's monthly Circle of Excellence Award is presented to the best FedEx station. This time the best station was one that truly represented the spirit of teamwork in problem solving. The station manager spotted a loading problem that was costing the company millions of dollars a year and decided to leave it up to the station as a group to find ways of solving the problem. After a series of group meetings and key decisions, a solution was found that successfully took care of the loading problem and was adopted by the rest of the company. It has come to Fred Smith's attention that a key reason for the station's success is the leadership role played by the team leader during this process. Smith has asked that you use the award ceremony as an opportunity to highlight the virtues of the group-centered approach of leadership, particularly with respect to decision making in teams. Develop the key parts of the speech you will give on this occasion.

Your instructor may elect to break the class into groups to share ideas and put together the speech or simply ask each student to prepare an independent speech. If you do a group speech, select one leader to present the speech to the entire class.

Role-Play: One person (representing oneself or a group) may give the speech to the entire class, or break into groups of five or six and deliver speeches one at a time.

VIDEO CASE

The NEADS Team: People and Dogs

The National Education for Assistance Dog Services (NEADS) functions with teams of people. But another type of teamwork is also central to the mission of NEADS: the team of human and dog. NEADS acquires, raises, trains, and matches service dogs to meet the needs of people with limited physical mobility or deafness. It takes about two years to train a service dog—and that requires a lot of teamwork. Volunteer families become part of the team when, at four months of age, the puppies are placed in foster care. These families agree to feed, love, and raise the puppies so they become accustomed to the distractions and energy of the real world. Professional dog trainers from NEADS visit regularly to work with the families and dogs to ensure that the dogs receive the proper training in preparation for their later work. The puppies live in their foster homes until they are about a year and a half old; then they return to the NEADS farm to continue their education. Here, they receive advanced training from professional dog trainers. When a dog's training is complete, its new owner arrives on campus for a two-week stay, during which the person and the dog become a team. The person and dog have been matched through an extensive interview process that involves a team of people interviewers and dog trainers.

1. Describe the characteristics of a typical NEADS team, using the information discussed in the chapter.
2. What factors determine the cohesiveness of NEADS teams?

Behavior Model Skills Training

This behavior model skills training on leadership decision making has four parts. You should first read how to use the model. Then, you may view the behavior model video that illustrates all four decision-making styles for the same decision. Parts three and four are together in Skill-Development Exercise 1, which gives you the opportunity to develop your ability to select the leadership decision-making style most appropriate for a given situation. Lastly, you further develop this skill by using the model in your personal and professional life.

Leadership Decision-Making Model

(PART I)

Deciding Which Leadership Decision-Making Style to Use

Read the instructions for using the leadership decision-making model, and see Model 8.1 on the next page. You may want to refer to the model as you read.

Managers today realize the trend toward participation in decision making, and managers are open to using participation. It is frustrating for managers to decide when to use participation and when not to, and what level of participation to use. You are about to learn how to use a model that will develop your skill at selecting the appropriate leadership style to meet the needs of the situation. First, let's examine ways in which groups can be used to generate solutions.

Selecting the Appropriate Leadership Decision Style

We have the same four variables as in the Situational Communication Model 6.6—time, information, acceptance, and capability level.

Step 1 Diagnose the situation. The first step you follow as a leader involves diagnosing the situational variables, including time, information, acceptance, and follower capability.

Time. You must determine whether there is enough time to include followers in decision making. Time is viewed as yes (you have time to use participation) or no (there is no

MODEL 8.1 Leadership Decision Making

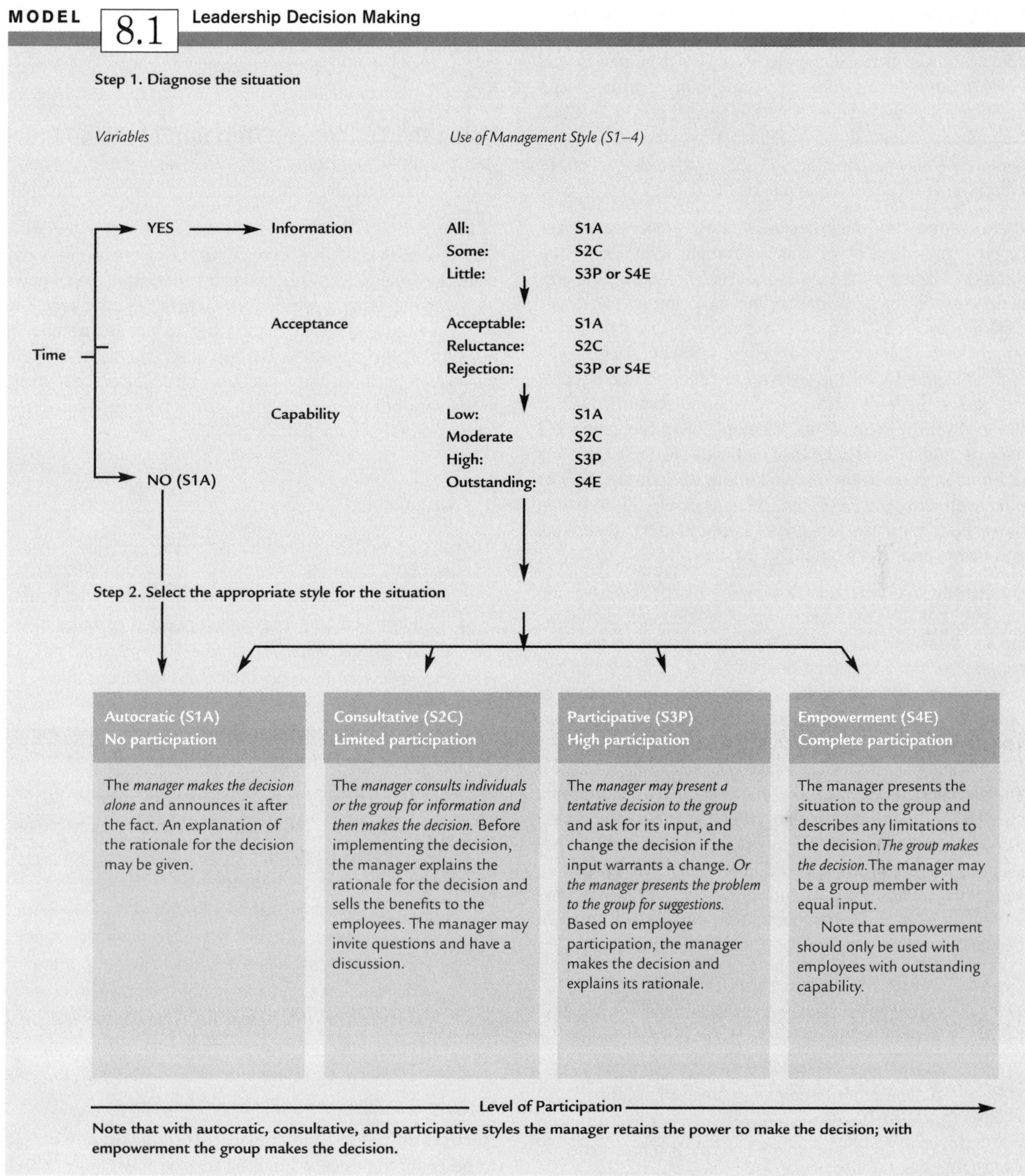

time to use participation). If there is no time, you should use the autocratic style (S1A), regardless of preference. When there is no time to include employees in problem solving and decision making, you ignore the other three variables; they are irrelevant if there is no time. If you say yes there is time, then the consultative, participative, or empowerment styles may be appropriate. You use the other three variables to select the style.

Step 1. Diagnose the situation
Variables
Use of Management Style (S1–4)
Time
YES
Information
All: S1A
Some: S2C
Little: S3P or S4E
Acceptance
Acceptable: S1A
Reluctance: S2C
Rejection: S3P or S4E
Capability
Low: S1A
Moderate S2C
High: S3P
Outstanding: S4E
NO (S1A)
Step 2. Select the appropriate style for the situation
Autocratic (S1A)
No participation
The manager makes the decision alone and announces it after the fact. An explanation of the rationale for the decision may be given.
Consultative (S2C)
Limited participation
The manager consults individuals or the group for information and then makes the decision. Before implementing the decision, the manager explains the rationale for the decision and sells the benefits to the employees. The manager may invite questions and have a discussion.
Participative (S3P)
High participation
The manager may present a tentative decision to the group and ask for its input, and change the decision if the input warrants a change. Or the manager presents the problem to the group for suggestions. Based on employee participation, the manager makes the decision and explains its rationale.
Empowerment (S4E)
Complete participation
The manager presents the situation to the group and describes any limitations to the decision. The group makes the decision. The manager may be a group member with equal input.
Note that empowerment should only be used with employees with outstanding capability.
Level of Participation
Note that with autocratic, consultative, and participative styles the manager retains the power to make the decision; with empowerment the group makes the decision.

Time is a relative term. In one situation, a few minutes may be considered a short time period, but in another a month may be a short period of time. Time is not wasted when the potential advantages of using participation are realized.

Information. You must decide if you have enough information to make a quality decision alone. The more information you have, the less need for participation; the less information you have, the greater the need for participation. If you have all the necessary information, there is no need for follower participation, and the autocratic style (S1A) is appropriate. When you have some information, but need more, which can be obtained by asking questions, the consultative style (S2C) may be appropriate. If you have little information, the appropriate style may be participative (S3P—group discussion) or empowerment (S4E—group makes the decision).

Acceptance. You must decide whether employee acceptance of the decision is critical to implementation of the decision. The more the followers will like a decision, the less need there is for participation; the more the followers will dislike a decision, the greater the need for participation. If you make the decision alone, will the follower or group willingly implement it? If the follower or group will be accepting, the appropriate style is probably autocratic (S1A). If the follower or group will be reluctant, the appropriate style may be consultative (S2C) or participative (S3P). If they will probably reject the decision, the participative (S3P) or empowerment style (S4E) may be appropriate. When teams make decisions, they are more understanding, accepting, and committed to implementing the decision.

Capability. You must decide whether the follower or group has the ability and motivation to be involved in problem solving and decision making. Does the follower or group have the experience and information needed to be involved? Will followers put the organization's or department's goals ahead of personal goals? Do the followers want to be involved in problem solving and decision making? Followers are more willing to participate when the decisions personally affect them. If the follower or group capability level is low (C1), an autocratic style (S1A) may be appropriate. When capability is moderate (C2), a consultative style (S2C) may be appropriate. If capability level is high (C3), a participative style (S3P) might be adopted. If capability is outstanding (C4), choose the empowerment style (S4E). Remember that an employee's or group's capability level can change from situation to situation.

Step 2 Select the appropriate leadership style. After considering the four variables, you select the appropriate style. In some situations, all variables will indicate that the same style is appropriate, whereas in other cases, the appropriate style is not so clear. For example, you could be in a situation in which you have time to use any style, may have all the information necessary (autocratic), followers may be reluctant (consultative or participative), and their capability may be moderate (consultative). In situations where different styles are indicated for different variables, you must determine which variables should be given more weight. In the above example, assume that acceptance was critical for successful implementation of the decision. Acceptance takes precedence over information. Because the followers involved have moderate capability, the consultative style would be appropriate. Again, Model 8.1 summarizes use of the four situational communication styles in decision making.

Using the Leadership Decision-Making Model

We will apply the model to the following situation; additional similar situations are presented later with the skill-development exercise.

Manager Ben can give one of his followers a merit pay raise. He has a week to make the decision. Ben knows how well each employee performed over the past year. The followers really have no option but to accept getting or not getting the pay raise, but they can complain to upper management about the selection. The followers' capability levels vary, but as a group they have a high capability level under normal circumstances.

___ time ___ information ___ acceptance ___ capability

Leadership style ____________________

Step 1 Diagnose the situation. Ben has plenty of time to use any level of participation (place a Y for yes on the "time" line below the situation). He has all the information needed to make the decision (place S1A on the "information" line). Followers have no choice but to accept the decision (place S1A on the "acceptance" line). And the group's capability level is normally high (place S3P on the "capability" line).

Step 2 Select the Appropriate Style for the Situation. There are conflicting styles to choose from (autocratic and participative): *yes* time; *S1A* information; *S1A* acceptance; *S3P* capability.

The variable that should be given precedence is information. The followers are normally capable, but in a situation like this they may not put the department's goals ahead of their own. In other words, even if followers know who deserves the raise, they may fight for it anyway. Such a conflict could cause future problems. Some ways to make the decision could include the following:

Autocratic (S1A). The manager would select the person to be given the raise without discussing it with any followers. Ben would simply announce the decision after submitting it to the payroll department.

Consultative (S2C). The manager would get information from the followers concerning who should get the raise. Ben would then decide who would get the raise. He would announce the decision and explain the rationale for it. He may invite questions and discussion.

Participative (S3P). The manager could tentatively select the employee who gets the raise, but be open to change if a group member convinces him that someone else should. Or

Ben could explain the situation to the group and lead a discussion concerning who should get the raise. After considering their input, Ben would make the decision and explain the rationale for it. Notice that the consultative style does not allow for discussion as the participative style does.

Empowerment (S4E). The manager would explain the situation and allow the group to decide who gets the raise. Ben may be a group member. Notice that this is the only style that allows the group to make the decision.

The autocratic style is appropriate for this situation. The consultative style is also a good approach. However, the participative and empowerment styles use too much participation for the situation. Your skill at selecting the appropriate decision-making leadership style should improve through using the model for the 10 situations in the skill-development exercise. However, the next step is to view the behavior video model.

Behavior Model Video 8.1 and Video Exercise

(PART II)

Deciding Which Leadership Decision-Making Style to Use

Objectives

To better understand the four leadership decision-making styles, and to select the most appropriate style for a given situation.

Video *(13 minutes)* Overview

The video begins by telling you how to use the model. Then it shows the human resources director, Richard, meeting with a supervisor, Denise, to discuss training changes. Each of the four styles is shown to illustrate how all four styles can be used in the same situation. Thus, you gain a better understanding of the four styles. During the video you will be asked to identify each of the four styles being used by Richard. The answers will be given by your instructor during or at the end of the video. In viewing the video, you should also realize that some styles are more appropriate than others for this situation. As a class, you may discuss which style would be the most effective, and at the end of the video, the recommended style is stated.

Preparation

You should have read the "Leadership Decision-Making Model" section of this leadership behavior-modeling skills training.

Procedure 1 *(10–20 minutes)* The instructor shows (or you view on your own) the video, "Decision Making." As you view each of the four scenes, identify the four leadership decision-making styles being used by Richard. Write the letters and number of the style on the line after each scene.

Scene 1. ________	Autocratic (S1A)
Scene 2. ________	Consultative (S2C)
Scene 3. ________	Participative (S3P)
Scene 4. ________	Empowerment (S4E)

Option A: View all four scenes and identify the style used by Richard. Select the one style that you would use in this situation. Are other styles also appropriate? Which style would you not use (is not appropriate) for this situation? Next to each style listed above, write the letter "a" for appropriate or "n" for not appropriate. After everyone is finished the instructor leads a class discussion and/or gives the correct answers.

Option B: After each scene the class discusses the style used by Richard. The instructor states the correct answer after each of the four scenes. Then discuss which style is the most effective for the situation.

Option C: Simply view the entire video without any discussion.

Conclusion

The instructor may lead a class discussion and/or make concluding remarks.

Skill-Development Exercise 1

(PARTS III & IV)

Deciding Which Leadership Decision-Making Style to Use

Preparation for Skill-Development Exercise 1

Below are 10 situations calling for a decision. Select the appropriate decision-making style for each. Be sure to use Model 8.1 when determining the style to use. First determine the answers to the variables (S1A, S2C, S3P, S4E) and write them on the lines below the situation. Then place the selected style on the "Leadership style" line.

S1A autocratic	S2C consultative
S3P participative	S4E empowerment

1. You have developed a new work procedure that will increase productivity. Your boss likes the idea and wants you to try it in a few weeks. You view your followers as fairly capable, and believe that they will be receptive to the change.

   ___ time ___ information ___ acceptance ___ capability

   Leadership style ______________________

2. There is new competition in your industry. Your organization's revenues have been dropping. You have been told to lay off three of your 15 followers in two weeks. You have been supervisor for over three years. Normally, your followers are very capable.

   ___ time ___ information ___ acceptance ___ capability

   Leadership style ______________________

3. Your department has been facing a problem for several months. Many solutions have been tried and have failed. You've finally thought of a solution, but you're not sure of the possible consequences of the change required, or of acceptance by your highly capable followers.

   ___ time ___ information ___ acceptance ___ capability

   Leadership style ______________________

4. Flextime has become popular in your organization. Some departments let each employee start and end work when he or she chooses. However, because of the cooperation required of your followers, they must all work the same eight hours. You're not sure of the level of interest in changing the hours. Your followers are a very capable group and like to make decisions.

   ___ time ___ information ___ acceptance ___ capability

   Leadership style ______________________

5. The technology in your industry is changing too fast for the members of your organization to keep up. Top management hired a consultant who has made recommendations. You have two weeks to decide what to do about the recommendations. Your followers are usually capable; they enjoy participating in the decision-making process.

   ___ time ___ information ___ acceptance ___ capability

   Leadership style ______________________

6. Top management has handed down a change. How you implement it is your decision. The change takes effect in one month. It will affect everyone in your department. Their acceptance is critical to the success of the change. Your followers are usually not interested in making routine decisions.

   ___ time ___ information ___ acceptance ___ capability

   Leadership style ______________________

7. Your boss called to tell you that someone requested an order for your department's product; the delivery date is very short. She asked you to call her back in 15 minutes with a decision about taking the order. Looking over the work schedule, you realize that it will be very difficult to deliver the order on time. Your followers will have to push hard to make it. They are cooperative, capable, and enjoy being involved in decision making.

   ___ time ___ information ___ acceptance ___ capability

   Leadership style ______________________

8. Top management has decided to make a change that will affect all of your followers. You know that they will be upset because it will cause them hardship. One or two may even quit. The change goes into effect in 30 days. Your followers are very capable.

   ___ time ___ information ___ acceptance ___ capability

   Leadership style ______________________

9. You believe that productivity in your department could be increased. You have thought of some ways to increase it, but you're not sure of them. Your followers are very experienced; almost all of them have been in the department longer than you have.

   ___ time ___ information ___ acceptance ___ capability

   Leadership style ______________________

10. A customer offered you a contract for your product with a quick delivery date. The offer is open for two days. To meet the contract deadline, followers would have to work nights and weekends for six weeks. You cannot require them to work overtime. Filling this profitable contract could help get you the raise you want and feel you deserve. However, if you take the contract and don't deliver on time, it will hurt your chances of getting a big raise. Your followers are very capable.

    ___ time ___ information ___ acceptance ___ capability

    Leadership style ______________________

Doing Skill-Development Exercise 1 in Class

Objective

To develop your skill at knowing which level of participation to use in a given decision-making situation. You will learn to use the leadership decision-making model.

The primary AACSB learning standard skills developed through this exercise are leadership, analytic skills, and teamwork.

Experience

You will try to select the appropriate decision-making style for each of 10 situations in preparation for this exercise.

Preparation

You should have completed the preparation for this exercise, unless told not to do so by your instructor. There is an option to do the preparation in class as part of the exercise.

Procedure 1 *(8–12 minutes)* The instructor may review the leadership decision-making model (Model 8.1), and will explain how to use it to select the appropriate leadership style for the first situation.

Procedure 2 *(4–8 minutes)* Students, working alone, complete situation 2 using the model, followed by the instructor going over the recommend answers. If the instructor will be testing you on leadership decision making, you may be told the details.

Procedure 3 *(10–20 minutes)* Break into teams of two or three. Apply the model to situations 3 through 5 as a team. You may decide to change your original answers. The instructor goes over the recommended answers and scoring for situations 3 through 5. Your instructor may tell you not to continue on to situation 6 until he or she goes over the answers to situations 3 through 5.

Procedure 4 *(10–20 minutes)* In the same teams, select decision-making styles for situations 6 through 10. The instructor will go over the recommended answers and scoring.

Conclusion

The instructor may lead a class discussion and/or make concluding remarks.

Apply It *(2–4 minutes)* What did I learn from this experience? How will I use this knowledge in the future? Identify when you will practice this skill.

Sharing

In the group, or to the entire class, volunteers may give their answers to the "Apply It" questions.

Skill-Development Exercise 2

Individual Versus Group Decision Making

Preparation for Skill-Development Exercise 2

To complete this exercise you must answer the questions in Applying the Concept parts 1 through 4 in the chapter.

Doing Skill-Development Exercise 2 in Class

Objective

To compare individual and group decision making, to better understand when to use a group to make decisions.

The primary AACSB learning standard skills developed through this exercise are analytic skills and teamwork.

Preparation

As preparation, you should have answered the questions in Applying the Concept parts 1 through 4.

Experience

You will work in a group, each member of which will answer the same 20 questions, and then analyze the results to determine if the group or one (or more) of its members had the higher score.

Procedure 1 *(1–2 minutes)* Place your answers to the 20 questions in the "Individual Answer" column in the table on page. 326.

Procedure 2 *(15–20 minutes)* Break into teams of five, with smaller or larger groups as necessary. As a group, come to an agreement on the answers to the 20 questions. Place the group answers in the "Group Answer" column. Try to use consensus rather than voting or majority in arriving at the answers.

Procedure 3 *(4–6 minutes)* **Scoring.** The instructor will give the recommended answers. Determine how many you got right as an individual and as a group. Total your individual and the group's score.

Compute the *average* individual score by adding all the individual scores and dividing by the number of group members. Write it here: _____.

Now calculate the difference between the average individual score and the group score. If the group's score is higher than the average individual score, you have a gain (+)

of points; if the group score is lower, you have a loss (−) of points. Write it here, _____ and circle one (+ or −).

Determine the highest individual score. Write it here: _____.

Determine the number of individuals who scored higher than the group's score: _____.

Procedure 4 *(5–10 minutes)* **Integration.** As a group, discuss the advantages or disadvantages of being in a group while making the decisions in this exercise. Go back to the text and review the advantages and disadvantages of team-centered decision making listed on pages 298–299 and discuss. Then try to agree on which of the advantages and disadvantages your group had.

Overall, were the advantages of using a group greater than the disadvantages? If your group were to continue to work together, how could it improve its decision-making ability? Write your answer below.

Conclusion

The instructor may lead a class discussion and/or make concluding remarks.

Apply It *(2–4 minutes)* What did I learn from this experience? How will I use this knowledge in the future? Specifically, what will I do the next time I'm in a group to help it make better decisions? When will I have the opportunity?

Sharing

In the group, or to the entire class, volunteers may give their answers to the "Apply It" questions.

Question Number	Individual Answer	Group Answer	Recommended Answer	Individual Score	Group Score
AC 1: 1					
2					
3					
4					
5					
AC 2: 6					
7					
8					
9					
10					
AC 3: 11					
12					
13					
14					
15					
AC 4: 16					
17					
18					
19					
20					
Total scores					

Organizational Leadership

part three

chapter 9
Charismatic and Transformational Leadership 328

chapter 10
Leadership of Culture, Ethics, and Diversity 368

chapter 11
Strategic Leadership and Change Management 416

chapter 12
Crisis Leadership and the Learning Organization 450

Chapter Outline

Personal Meaning

Factors That Influence Personal Meaning

Charisma

Weber's Conceptualization of Charisma

Differentiating Between Charismatic and Noncharismatic Leaders

Charismatic Leadership

Locus of Charismatic Leadership

The Effects of Charismatic Leadership

Qualities of Charismatic Leaders

How One Acquires Charismatic Qualities

Charisma: A Double-Edged Sword

Transformational Leadership

The Effects of Transformational Leadership

Charismatic versus Transformational Leadership

Transformational Leader Behaviors and Attributes

Transformational versus Transactional Leadership

The Transformation Process

Stewardship and Servant Leadership

The Nature of Stewardship and Servant Leadership

Framework for Stewardship

Framework for Servant Leadership

9 Charismatic and Transformational Leadership

Learning Outcomes

After studying this chapter, you should be able to:

1. Describe personal meaning and how it influences attributions of charismatic qualities. p. 330
2. Briefly explain Max Weber's conceptualization of charisma. p. 334
3. Describe the behavioral qualities that differentiate charismatic from noncharismatic leaders. p. 335
4. Explain the locus of charismatic leadership. p. 337
5. Discuss the effects of charismatic leadership on followers. p. 338
6. Describe the characteristics that distinguish charismatic from noncharismatic leaders. p. 341
7. Discuss how one can acquire charismatic qualities. p. 344
8. Explain the difference between socialized and personalized charismatic leaders. p. 345
9. Distinguish between charismatic and transformational leadership. p. 349
10. Explain the difference between transformational and transactional leadership. p. 352
11. Explain the four phases of the transformation process. p. 354
12. Explain the basis of stewardship and servant leadership. p. 356
13. Define the following **key terms** (in order of appearance in the chapter):

    personal meaning
    self-belief
    legacy
    selflessness
    spirituality
    values
    charisma
    vision
    socialized charismatic leader (SCL)
    personalized charismatic leader (PCL)
    transformational leadership
    transactional leadership
    stewardship
    servant leadership

Opening Case APPLICATION

In 1986, Oprah Winfrey launched Harpo Productions, Inc. Two years later, in October 1988, television history was made when Harpo Productions announced that it was taking over all production responsibilities for the *Oprah Winfrey Show* from Capitol Cities/ABC, making Winfrey the first woman in history to own and produce her own talk show. The *Oprah Winfrey Show* has remained the number one talk show for 22 consecutive seasons. The show is seen by more than 48 million viewers weekly in the United States and airs in more than 120 countries. Oprah has differentiated her show from the rest of daytime talk shows by offering a self-empowering vision of hope and uplift. To capitalize on her name brand, Discovery Communications has formed an alliance with Winfrey to launch a new network that will go by the acronym, "OWN"—Oprah Winfrey Network—due to begin airing in 2009. Oprah will be the creative force behind the channel, developing programs on topics familiar to her predominantly female audience.[1] Her popular magazine, *O,* sold an average of 2.4 million copies per month in 2007. Her Book Club can turn any title into a best seller. She has a satellite show, "Oprah & Friends," on XM Satellite Radio.

When it comes to popularity of celebrities, Oprah tops the list in name recognition and likeability. When people are asked whether they believe she is "an influence in today's world," she beats everyone else on the list. She is unmatched as a celebrity spokesperson. In an AP poll taken in 2006, Oprah was selected the best celebrity role model of the year.[2]

From her humble beginnings in rural Mississippi, Oprah is not only America's richest celebrity, she is also one of the most charitable. In 1987, she created the Oprah Winfrey Foundation to aid women, children, and families. Oprah's Angel Network, formed in 1998, also raises money for charitable causes. In January 2007, she opened the Oprah Winfrey Leadership Academy in Johannesburg, South Africa. Oprah's goal for the academy is to find talented girls who come from difficult economic backgrounds and give them education and leadership training.[3] Oprah's legacy has established her as one of the most important figures in popular culture. Through her television, publishing, and film endeavors, Oprah entertains, enlightens, and empowers millions of viewers around the world.

Opening Case Questions:

1. Why is Oprah such a popular and admired figure on TV?
2. Oprah seems to have a clear sense of her personal meaning or purpose in life. What factors do you think have contributed to her understanding?
3. What is the locus of Oprah's charisma?
4. What effects has Oprah's charisma had on her followers?
5. What qualities of charismatic leadership does Oprah possess?
6. Does Oprah embody the example of a socialized charismatic leader or a personalized charismatic leader?
7. Is Oprah a transformational leader, a charismatic leader, or both?

Can you answer any of these questions? You'll find answers to these questions and learn more about Oprah Winfrey's businesses and leadership style throughout the chapter.

To learn more about Oprah Winfrey, visit her Web site at **http://www.oprah.com**.

The last 20 years have witnessed a renewed interest in and scholarship focus on charismatic and transformational leadership.[4] This growth in interest has coincided with significant geopolitical, social, and economic change. Much higher levels of turbulence, uncertainty, discontinuous change, and global competition characterize today's work environment.

The challenge many institutions face is how to continually cope with new situations in order to survive and prosper. Organizations are faced with the need to adapt or perish. Adaptation requires that organizations learn to do things differently, such as the need to transform internal cultures, empower organizational members, adapt or develop new technologies, restructure personnel and workflow patterns, eliminate concrete and artificial boundaries, pave the path to continuous innovation, and foster a high-involvement and risk-taking organizational climate.[5]

The charismatic and transformational leader, according to many scholars and practitioners, represents a new paradigm of leadership that may be capable of steering organizations through the chaos of the twenty-first century.[6,7,8] In the literature, both charismatic and transformational forms of leadership are commonly discussed from two separate but interrelated perspectives: in terms of the effects that leaders have upon followers, and in terms of the relationships that exist between leaders and followers.

Charismatic and transformational theories return our focus to the leader. These theories shine the light on exemplary leaders who have extraordinary effects on their followers and ultimately on entire social, cultural, economic, and political systems. According to this new paradigm of leadership theories, such leaders transform the needs, aspirations, and values of followers from a focus on self-interest to a focus on collective interest. They practice trust building to create strong commitment to a common mission. They generate emotion, energy, and excitement that cause followers to make significant personal sacrifices in the interest of the mission, and to perform above and beyond the call of duty. According to some scholars, charismatic and transformational leadership represents a shift from an emphasis on financial capital to human capital. It's a leadership philosophy in which strategy, structure, and systems thinking are replaced with purpose, process, and people thinking—"purpose leadership."[9]

Charismatic and transformational leaders often have a more heightened sense of who they are than most people do. They seem to have a clearer picture of their personal meaning or purpose in life much sooner, and seek to actualize it through active leadership. To lay the foundation for charisma and charismatic leadership, we will focus the discussion first on the concept of personal meaning. Then we will discuss the unique and complementary qualities of charisma, charismatic leadership, transformational leadership, stewardship, and servant leadership, focusing on the impact of each on individuals and the organization.

Opening Case APPLICATION

1. Why is Oprah such a popular and admired figure on TV?

Oprah possesses the charisma and transformational qualities alluded to above. She has already left an indelible mark on the face of television. She has used her celebrity status to push for social change in our society. She has championed the cause for child abuse, poverty, domestic violence, illiteracy, and much more. Her audience represents a cross-section of the American ethnic landscape. As supervising producer and host of the *Oprah Winfrey Show,* Oprah entertains, enlightens, and empowers millions of viewers not just in the United States, but around the world.

Learning Outcome 1 *Describe personal meaning and how it influences attributions of charismatic qualities.*

Personal Meaning

Personal meaning is described in terms of meaningfulness or purpose in life. A more formal definition is *the degree to which people's lives make emotional sense and to which the demands confronted by them are perceived as being worthy of energy and commitment.* It is the "work–life balance" or the achievement of equilibrium in personal and official life.

One scholar described charismatic leaders as "meaning makers."[10] Thus, personal meaning is that which makes one's life most important, coherent, and worthwhile for him or her.

The theoretical basis of personal meaning is derived from research on purpose in life (PIL). PIL represents a positive attitude toward possessing a transcendent vision for life.[11] The depth (i.e., strength) and type (i.e., content of meaning associated with a goal) of personal meaning are major determinants of motivation, especially for individuals facing challenges. There is a general recognition that compared to noncharismatic leaders, charismatic leaders have a heightened sense of their personal meaning and are willing to act on it. Therefore the question becomes, what factors influence and differentiate leaders who are willing to act to realize their personal meaning or PIL from others who are less inclined to actively pursue the journey?

Factors That Influence Personal Meaning

Exhibit 9.1 lists a variety of factors that influence personal meaning, derived from a review of the literature. Each factor is briefly discussed below in terms of its contribution to the personal meaning of leaders.

EXHIBIT 9.1 Factors That Influence Personal Meaning

a. Self-belief
b. Legacy
c. Selflessness
d. Cultural heritage and traditions
e. Activist mind-set
f. Faith and spirituality
g. Personal interests
h. Values

Source: Based on G. T. Reker, and P. T. P. Wong (1988), Meaning and Purpose in Life and Well-Being: A Life-Span Perspective. Journal of Gerontology *42 (1992): 44–49.*

Self-Belief

Self-belief *is knowing who you are based on your lifespan of experiences, motivation states, and action orientation.* The search for meaning involves finding opportunities to express the aspects of one's self that motivate subsequent behavior. Closely related to self-belief is a trait called positive self-concept. Individuals with a positive self-concept possess emotional stability, believe in their self-worth (high self-esteem), see themselves as generally capable of accomplishing things (high generalized self-efficacy), and feel they are in control of their lives (internal locus of control). In many cases, the charismatic leader is a person who has overcome an inner conflict to realize his or her full potential and, through this process, developed a strong belief in himself or herself. The resolution of this conflict serves as a stimulus and model for followers.[12]

Legacy

The need to leave behind something of enduring value after one's death can be both a powerful motivator and a source of personal meaning. **Legacy** *is that which allows an individual's accomplishments to "live on" in the ideals, actions, and creations of one's followers, long after his or her death.*[13] Charismatic leaders are driven to leave their personal mark on the society they serve. Gandhi advocated passive resistance and passion for truth. His legacy has influenced many subsequent social and political activists and leaders, including Martin Luther King, Jr., and Nelson Mandela. These leaders derived meaning from a realization that their legacy may provide their followers with a framework for self-development, harmony and fellowship, and a more socially desirable future.

Selflessness

Selflessness *is an unselfish regard for or devotion to the welfare of others.* Therefore, a leader with an unselfish attitude derives motivation through concern for others rather than for oneself. Servant leadership is rooted in providing service to followers. For example, helping followers to develop and work toward collective goals may satisfy a charismatic leader's motives and therefore make sacrifices and suffering meaningful. Examples of selfless charismatic leaders include Bishop Desmond Tutu, Mother Teresa, and Princess Diana. They were all driven by a concern for others.

Cultural Heritage and Traditions

Rites and ceremonies may be used as vehicles to transfer charisma to others. Charismatic leaders of religious organizations (e.g., Martin Luther King, Jr.; Rev. Billy Graham) derive personal meaning by leading their churches, while their personal meaning helps define rites, doctrine, and ceremonies. Also, oral and written traditions may make the charismatic leader's vision meaningful over time. For example, Frederick Douglass sought to preserve the traditions and heritage of African people by emphasizing the value of education as a vehicle for self-empowerment and growth. His determination not to live as a slave but to live proudly as a black American is part of the heritage of the African-American culture today and has added meaning to his life.

Activist Mind-Set

Charismatic leaders tend to have a more activist mind-set than noncharismatic leaders. They use political and social causes as opportunities to influence change and provide a better life for their followers. These accomplishments provide charismatic leaders with meaning for their existence and satisfy their motives. Charismatic leaders have a greater sensitivity to political, societal, and organizational situations that are ripe for change. They magnify a climate of dissatisfaction by encouraging activism that heightens followers' willingness to change the status quo. When followers are going through periods of turmoil and collective stress, they may respond to a leader who is able to give meaning to their experiences in terms of a new social or political order. For example, Oprah's commitment to children led her to initiate the National Child Protection Act in 1991, when she testified before the U.S. Senate Judiciary Committee to establish a national database of convicted child abusers. On December 20, 1993, President Clinton signed the national "Oprah Bill" into law.

Faith and Spirituality

Spirituality *concerns an individual's awareness of connections between human and supernatural phenomena, which provide faith explanations of past and present experiences and, for some, predict future experiences.* Supporters believe that religion and spirituality endow individuals' lives with meaning and purpose and give them hope for a better future. Charismatic leaders face hardship and suffering while leading missions of change. They often rely on their faith for support. Faith and spirituality influence one's meaning and purpose in life, and some argue that without meaning and purpose there would be no reason for charismatic leaders to endure their struggles. In addition, charismatic leaders sustain faith by linking behaviors and goals to a "dream" or utopian ideal vision of a better future. Followers may be driven by such faith because it is internally satisfying. Billy Graham, Martin Luther King, Jr., and Gandhi illustrate charismatic leaders whose purpose in life is or was influenced by their spirituality. In the end-of-book Appendix, "Leadership and Spirituality in the Workplace," we provide more details on this topic.

Personal Interests

Personal pursuits may reflect aspects of one's personality. By engaging in meaningful personal pursuits, we may establish and affirm our identity as either extroverts or introverts, high or low risk-takers, and open- or close-minded. Hobbies and other activities of personal interest have been linked to sets of personally salient action that add meaning to individuals' lives and leader behavior.

Values

Values *are generalized beliefs or behaviors that are considered by an individual or a group to be important.* Values provide basis for meaning. Charismatic leadership has been described as values-based leadership. By aligning their values with those of followers, and appealing to followers' subconscious motives, charismatic leaders may derive personal meaning from their actions.

Opening Case APPLICATION

2. Oprah seems to have a clear sense of her personal meaning or purpose in life. What factors do you think have contributed to her understanding?

Much has been published about Oprah in books and on the Internet. It is apparent from reading through these materials that her sense of personal meaning has been influenced by all the factors described above and listed in Exhibit 9.1 on page 331. The following examples illustrate Oprah's selflessness, values, activist mind-set, and legacy. The Oprah Winfrey Foundation was established to support the inspiration, empowerment, education, and well-being of women, children, and families around the world. Through this private charity, Oprah has directly served the needs of low-opportunity people and has awarded hundreds of grants to organizations that carry out this vision. She has contributed millions of dollars toward providing a better education for underserved students who have merit but no means. She created the "Oprah Winfrey Scholars Program," which gives scholarships to students determined to use their education to give back to their communities in the United States and abroad. The Oprah Winfrey Foundation continues to expand Oprah's global humanitarian efforts in developing countries. In December 2002, Oprah brought a day of joy to tens of thousands of children with "ChristmasKindness South Africa 2002," an initiative that included visits to orphanages and rural schools in South Africa where children received gifts of food, clothing, athletic shoes, school supplies, books, and toys. Sixty-three rural schools received libraries and teacher education, which continued throughout 2003. In addition, Oprah announced a partnership with South Africa's Ministry of Education to build a model leadership school for girls. The Oprah Winfrey Leadership Academy for Girls–South Africa is now up and running. Oprah speaks openly of her strong faith and spirituality on her show every day.

From a conceptual standpoint, the stronger one's perception of his or her personal meaning or purpose in life, the greater the likelihood that such an individual will act to realize his or her PIL. We propose a two-step process by which this can happen:

- First, a leader's personal meaning influences his or her behavior to act. In turn, the leader's behavior is reflected in the formulation and articulation of a vision or rationale for action.
- Second, the leader's extraordinary actions or compelling vision garner attributions of charisma from followers.

Therefore, a key aspect of the charismatic leadership process involves the perceptions and evaluations—that is, attributions—made by followers about a leader's behaviors and effects.

From a follower perspective, charismatic leaders are viewed as out-of-the-ordinary persons who can satisfy a need for finding meaning in life.[14] The extraordinary quality or image of the charismatic leader is seen not only as a source of influence but also a symbol of the realization of the meaning that is constructed in an appealing and/or evocative vision.[15] Vision is the leader's idealized goal that he or she wants the organization to achieve in the future. Based on this interconnection between a leader's personal meaning, behavior, and attributions of charisma, some scholars have argued that charismatic leaders are "meaning makers" who "interpret reality to offer us images of the future that are irresistible."[16] The next section focuses on this concept of charisma.

Applying the **Concept 1**

Sources of Personal Meaning

Referring to the sources of personal meaning in Exhibit 9.1 on page 331, match each statement to its source using the letters a–h.

____ 1. A desire to leave your personal mark on history long after you are dead.

____ 2. A collection of lifespan experiences, motivation states, and action orientation that serves as a source of personal meaning.

____ 3. Faith in a higher power that motivates one to endure hardships and struggles and thus serves as a source of personal meaning.

____ 4. A leader derives personal meaning by being very sensitive to societal, political, and organizational situations that are ripe for change and acting on them.

____ 5. Rites and ceremonies used as vehicles to transfer charisma to others or to define one's personal meaning.

Charisma

The Greek word *charisma* means "divinely inspired gift." Like the term *leadership* itself, charisma has been defined from various organizational perspectives by researchers studying political leadership, social movements, and religious cults.[17] Nevertheless, there is enough consistency among these definitions to create a unifying theme. This section will focus on Max Weber's early conceptualization of the concept and the differences between charismatic and noncharismatic leaders.

Learning Outcome 2 *Briefly explain Max Weber's conceptualization of charisma.*

Weber's Conceptualization of Charisma

Of the early theories of charisma, the sociologist Max Weber made what is probably the single most important contribution. Weber used the term "charisma" to explain a form of influence based not on traditional or legal–rational authority systems but rather on follower perceptions that a leader is endowed with the gift of divine inspiration or supernatural qualities.[18]

Charisma has been called "a fire that ignites followers' energy and commitment, producing results above and beyond the call of duty."[19] Weber saw in a charismatic leader someone who single-handedly visualizes a transcendent mission or course of action that is not only appealing to potential followers, but compels them to act on it because they believe the leader is extraordinarily gifted.[20] Other attributes of charisma identified in the political and sociological literature include acts of heroism, an ability to inspire and build confidence, espousing of revolutionary ideals, oratorical ability, and a "powerful aura." Combining these attributes with relational dynamics between leaders and followers provides a comprehensive picture of this phenomenon. Therefore, **charisma** *is "a distinct social relationship between the leader and follower, in which the leader presents a revolutionary idea, a transcendent image or ideal which goes beyond the immediate . . . or the reasonable; while the follower accepts this course of action not because of its rational likelihood of success . . . but because of an effective belief in the extraordinary qualities of the leader."*[21]

Work Application 1

Think of a leader from your work experience or education who you believe has charisma. Explain why.

Learning Outcome 3 *Describe the behavioral qualities that differentiate charismatic from noncharismatic leaders.*

Differentiating Between Charismatic and Noncharismatic Leaders

Attribution theory states that followers make attributions of heroic or extraordinary leadership abilities when they observe certain behaviors in their leader. These attributions form the basis on which a leader is seen as possessing or not possessing charismatic qualities, which explains why the theory of charismatic leadership is seen as an extension of attribution theory.[22,23,24] It is argued that such attributions of charisma are either concomitants or early indicators of the onset of other psychological and behavioral outcomes, such as unconditional loyalty, devotion, self-sacrifice, obedience, and commitment to the leader and to the cause the leader represents.[25,26] Noncharismatic leaders will find it much harder to garner the same behavioral attributes from their followers.

If the followers' attribution of charisma depends on observed behavior of the leader, the question then becomes: what are the behavioral qualities responsible for such attributions? Some studies have gone so far as to propose that if these attributions can be identified and operationalized, the knowledge gained can then be used to develop charismatic qualities in noncharismatic leaders. The attribution of charisma to some leaders is believed to depend on four behavior attributes that distinguish charismatic from noncharismatic leaders. They are listed and discussed below:

1. Dissatisfaction with status quo
2. Compelling nature of the vision
3. Use of unconventional strategies for achieving desired change
4. A realistic assessment of resource needs and other constraints for achieving desired change

Disatisfaction with Status Quo

The discrepancy between charismatic and noncharismatic leaders is such that the former is very much opposed to the status quo and strives to change it, while the latter essentially agrees with the status quo and strives to maintain it. For the charismatic leader, the more idealized or discrepant the future goal is from the present status quo, the better. And the greater the gap from the status quo, the more likely followers will attribute extraordinary vision to the leader.

Vision Formulation and Articulation

Charismatic leaders have the ability to articulate an ideological and inspirational vision—a transcendent vision that paints or promises a better future than the present.[7] The question that persists is why a few possess this quality or ability to visualize a future that many other leaders fail to see or grasp. Effective articulation of vision is measured in what is said (content and context) and how it is said (oratorical abilities).

Charismatic leaders articulate the context of their message by highlighting positive images of the future vision and negative images of the present situation. The present situation is often presented as unacceptable, whereas the vision is presented as the most attractive alternative in clear, specific terms. This makes the case for change very strong and convincing.[27]

Effective communication skills are an imperative in the successful articulation of a compelling vision and maintenance of a leadership role. Through verbal and nonverbal means, charismatic leaders communicate their self-confidence, convictions, and dedication in order to give credibility to what they advocate. They are often described as great orators who know how to incite passion and action among their followers. Followers tend to model the charismatic leader's high energy and persistence, unconventional and risky behavior, heroic actions, and personal sacrifices.

Use of Unconventional Strategies

The noncharismatic leader's expertise lies in using available or conventional means to achieve existing goals, whereas the charismatic leader's expertise lies in using unconventional means to transcend the existing order. Unconventional leader behavior is perceived as novel—that is, original or new. Research linking unconventional leader behavior with subordinate satisfaction and perception of leader effectiveness revealed positive correlation between the variables. In other words, unconventional behavior was found to be significantly related to follower satisfaction with the overall experience and perceptions of leader effectiveness.[28]

Admirers of charismatic leaders believe that such individuals possess heroic qualities that enable them to persist in spite of the odds against them. Charismatic leaders are thought to possess heroic characteristics such as courage, determination, and persistence to face and prevail against those who would resist their noble efforts. Follower perceptions of such heroic qualities evoke sentiments of adoration, especially when the leader's activities exemplify acts of heroism involving personal risk and self-sacrificing behavior. Thus, the behavior of the noncharismatic leader is seen as standard and conforming to existing norms while that of the charismatic leader is unconventional and counter to the norm.[29]

Work Application 2

Think of a leader in our society today who is generally perceived to be a charismatic leader. In your opinion, which of the behavioral components of charisma described in the text can be attributed to him or her?

Awareness for Resource Needs and Constraints

Charismatic leaders are also very good strategists. They understand the need to perform a realistic assessment of environmental resources and constraints affecting their ability to effect major change within their organization. They are sensitive to both the capabilities and emotional needs of followers, and they understand the resources and constraints of the physical and social environment in which they operate. They are aware of the need to align organizational strategies with existing capabilities to ensure a successful transformation. This need is low for noncharismatic leaders—fitting with their focus on maintaining the status quo. From the basic concept of charisma, we now turn our attention to the broader concept of charismatic leadership.

Applying the Concept 2

Charismatic versus Noncharismatic Behavior

Identify which behavior corresponds to either the charismatic or the noncharismatic leader.

a. charismatic behavior b. noncharismatic behavior

____ 6. Relies on using unconventional means to transcend the existing order.

____ 7. Accepts the status quo and seeks to maintain it.

____ 8. Models the values and beliefs to which you want your followers to subscribe.

____ 9. Relies on using conventional means to achieve existing goals.

____ 10. Opposes the status quo and seeks to change it.

Charismatic Leadership

The term *charismatic leadership* has generally been defined in terms of the effects of the leader on followers, or in terms of the relationship between leaders and followers.[30] It is a complex paradigm that has generated a number of theories regarding its nature, causes, and implications for organizational performance.

From Weber's early conceptualization of the theory as a distinct style of leadership, contemporary leadership theorists have taken the view that charismatic leadership is a variable—that is, a matter of degree—and have made significant advances in discovering the unique patterns of behavior, psychological motives, and personality traits of leaders that are correlated with varying levels of charismatic effects on followers.[31] Some of these effects include the charismatic leader's ability to

- garner strong personal attraction from followers;
- articulate a compelling and evocative vision;
- and enhance followers' self-conceptions.[32,33]

Among charismatic leaders of different cultural backgrounds, similarities may be attributable to their intrinsic and universal human desires for autonomy, achievement, and morality.[34] This section will focus on the following topics: the locus of charismatic leadership, the effects of charismatic leadership, qualities of charismatic leaders, how other leaders can develop charismatic qualities, and the notion of charisma as a double-edged sword.

Learning Outcome 4 *Explain the locus of charismatic leadership.*

Locus of Charismatic Leadership

Over the years, scholars from different schools of thought have commented on Weber's conceptualization of charismatic leadership. Perhaps the most controversial concerns the locus of charismatic leadership. The question at the center of the debate is whether charisma is primarily the result of

1. the situation or social climate facing the leader;
2. the leader's extraordinary qualities; or
3. an interaction of the situation and the leader's qualities.

Proponents of the view that charismatic leadership could not take place unless the society was in a crisis argue that before an individual with extraordinary qualities could be perceived as a charismatic leader, the social situation must be such that followers would recognize the need for the leader's qualities. The sociological literature, led by Weber, supports this viewpoint, emphasizing that charismatic leadership is born out of stressful situations. It is argued that under stressful situations, charismatic leaders are able to express sentiments that are different from the established order, and deeply felt by followers. Proponents of this view would argue that neither Martin Luther King, Jr., nor Gandhi would have emerged as charismatic leaders to lead their followers without the prevailing social crises in their respective countries.

However, others argue that charisma need not be born out of distress but rather that charisma is primarily the result of leader attributes as seen by their followers. These attributes include a strong sense of vision, exceptional communication skills, strong conviction, trustworthiness, high self-confidence and intelligence, and high energy and action orientation. Proponents of this view would argue that Martin Luther King, Jr., and Gandhi possessed these qualities, and without them would never have emerged as leaders of their respective followers regardless of the situation.

Finally, there are those who believe that charismatic leadership does not depend on the leader's qualities or the presence of a crisis alone, but rather that it is an interactional concept. There is increasing acceptance of this view. Most theorists now view charisma as the result of follower perceptions and reactions, influenced not only by actual leader characteristics and behavior but also by the context of the situation. The next section discusses the effects of charismatic leadership on individuals and organizations.

Opening Case APPLICATION

3. What is the locus of Oprah's charisma?

The locus of Oprah's charisma can be attributed more to her extraordinary qualities than to any external factor in her environment. "Knowledge is power! With knowledge you can soar and reach as high as your dreams can take you," said Oprah. This belief has guided Oprah Winfrey on her brilliant journey from a troubled youth to international fame. Oprah Gail Winfrey was born in Kosciusko, Mississippi. Oprah lived with her grandmother until age six, when she moved to Milwaukee to live with her mother, Vernita Lee. At the age of nine she was sexually abused by a teenage cousin. Over the next five years, she was molested several times by a family friend and once by her uncle. Without a doubt, she became a rebellious child and was reportedly headed toward a juvenile-detention center. Fortunately, at the age of fourteen, she went to live with her father, Vernon Winfrey, a strict disciplinarian. This, she said, was the turning point in her life. Oprah Winfrey is a success story that the everyday person can relate to. She has worked hard to gain success. Oprah's achievements came after a lot of hard work, determination, and education.

Learning Outcome 5 *Discuss the effects of charismatic leadership on followers.*

The Effects of Charismatic Leadership

An area of interest for many scholars of charisma concerns the effects that charismatic leadership has on follower motivations, effectiveness, and satisfaction as well as organizational performance.[35,36] The relationship between the charismatic leader and followers is often described as very emotional.[37] This emotional element involves feelings of fulfillment and satisfaction derived from the pursuit of worthwhile activities and goals and from positive beliefs and values about life. The relationship between the charismatic leader and the followers is comparable to that of disciples to a master. Though not always the case, followership is not out of fear or monetary inducement, but out of love, passionate devotion, and commitment.[38] Such a strong emotional bond is possible because the charismatic leader is believed to have the power to effect radical change by virtue of a transcendent vision that is different from the status quo. The strong belief in the vision of the charismatic leader is a key factor in distinguishing followers of charismatic leaders from those of other types of leaders.

Charismatic leaders are seen as generally more positive in their personality than noncharismatic leaders. Research on positiveness as a personality trait has found that people enhance their own feelings of well-being by sharing positive experiences with others and, as a consequence, treat others more positively because they themselves are in a positive mood.[39] Charismatic leaders generally possess this type of positiveness and have the capacity to spread it. When this happens, a positive atmosphere permeates the organization and fuels excitement and energy for the leader's cause.[40]

The charismatic leader is seen as an object of identification by followers who try to emulate his or her behavior. Thus, an effect of charismatic leadership is to cause followers to imitate the leader's behavior, values, self-concept, and cognitions.[41] Charismatic leadership has been found to affect the general risk propensities of followers. Followers tend to assume greater risk with charismatic leaders than they would with other types of leaders.[42] They are willing to suffer whatever fate awaits the leader as he or she fights to change the status quo. This was the case with Gandhi and Martin Luther King's followers, as they fought to bring about equality and freedom for all. Therefore, on the upside, charismatic leadership can be very effective in encouraging followers to buy into the future vision and potential change in an organization; however, the downside is that a parent/child relationship can develop with followers switching off and not challenging leadership decisions.[43]

Another effect of charismatic leadership on followers is to cause them to set or accept higher goals and have greater confidence in their ability to contribute to the achievement of such goals.[44] By observing the leader display self-confidence, followers develop self-confidence as well. Also, the leader's character has an effect on followers. When the character of the leader is grounded on such core values as integrity, trust, respect, and truth, it influences the leader's vision, ethics, and behavior. The leader is also empowered through his or her character to serve as a mentor. We are all aware of business leaders—such as Steve Jobs (Apple), Richard Branson (the Virgin Group), and Jack Welch (former GE CEO)—who command an extraordinary level of respect from their followers and have effectively initiated change and innovation for their respective companies. According to some scholars, the effect of the leader's character on followers is more critical than charisma itself.[45] Character, more than charisma, is seen as the basis for leadership excellence.

Focusing on the effect of charismatic leadership on external support for an organization, some scholars observed that the use of charismatic appeals and charismatic leadership may indeed make the organization more attractive to outside stakeholders. There is an ongoing debate in academic circles about charismatic CEOs and organizational performance. The question is whether charismatic CEOs achieve better organizational performance than their less charismatic counterparts. One study found that organizational performance was associated with subsequent perceptions of CEO charisma, but that perceptions of CEO charisma were not associated with subsequent organizational performance.[46]

According to a study conducted by researchers at the University of Pittsburgh and Yale University, CEO charisma had little lasting effect on a company's financial performance. Further, the study revealed that while a charismatic CEO can in fact boost shareholder value between 10 and 12 percent during the first five years of his or her tenure, the effect on performance becomes negligible after that.[47] The May 15, 2000, edition of *Fortune* asked the question: "Is John Chambers the best CEO on earth? Is it too late to buy his stock?"[48] There are those who believe that much of a company's stock market value these days depends on the image and reputation of the CEO. There are more questions than answers in this area because of limited research interest; instead the focus has almost exclusively been on the effects of charisma on organizational members—an internal focus. An important function of the executive is to manage the external environment of the firm; therefore, research support for the effects of charismatic leadership on external stakeholders is critical.[49] Exhibit 9.2 summarizes these effects.

EXHIBIT 9.2 Effects of Charismatic Leadership

- Follower trusts in the "rightness" of the leader's vision
- Similarity of follower's beliefs and values to those of the leader
- Heightened sense of self-confidence to contribute to accomplishment of the mission
- Acceptance of higher or challenging goals
- Identification with and emulation of the leader
- Unconditional acceptance of the leader
- Strong affection for the leader
- Emotional involvement of the follower in the mission
- Unquestioning loyalty and obedience to the leader

Source: Based on R. J. House, and M. L. Baetx (1979). "Leadership: Some Empirical Generalizations and New Research Directions." In B. M. Staw (ed.), Research in Organizational Behavior, *vol. 1 (Greenwich, CT: JAI Press, 1979), 399–401.*

Opening Case APPLICATION

4. What effects has Oprah's charisma had on her followers?

The effects of charismatic leadership summarized in Exhibit 9.2 are very much applicable to Oprah and her followers. Oprah's followers and supporters seem to have an unquestioning loyalty to her and all that she stands for. There is a strong affection and unconditional acceptance of her, and a willingness to trust in the "rightness" of whatever cause she champions. For example, in a 1997 episode of the *Oprah Winfrey Show,* Oprah encouraged viewers to use their lives to make a difference in the lives of others, which led to the creation of the public charity Oprah's Angel Network in 1998. To date, Oprah's Angel Network has raised more than $30 million, with 100 percent of audience donations going to nonprofit organizations across the globe. Oprah's Angel Network has helped establish scholarships and schools, support women's shelters, and build youth centers and homes—changing the future for people all over the world. As John Grace, executive director of Interbrand Group, a New York-based brand consultant, puts it, "Oprah stands for a certain set of very specific American values that very few of her celebrity competitors can claim, like honesty, loyalty, and frankness. It's a value set that is rare in business institutions and celebrities."

Learning Outcome 6 *Describe the characteristics that distinguish charismatic from noncharismatic leaders.*

Qualities of Charismatic Leaders

A number of studies have identified qualities that differentiate charismatic and noncharismatic leaders, and have described the behaviors and personal attributes that help charismatic leaders achieve remarkable results. These attributions, based on leader behaviors, constitute the personality profile of charismatic leaders.[50] Attribution theorists have thus used behaviors as distinguishing characteristics for charismatic and noncharismatic leaders.[51] (Many of these characteristics also apply to transformational leaders because charisma is a key component of transformational leadership, which is discussed later in this chapter.)

A study exploring charismatic leadership in the public sector focused on four qualities: (1) energy and determination, (2) vision, (3) challenge and encouragement, and (4) risk taking.[52] Another study narrowed charismatic leadership attributes to three core components—envisioning, empathy, and empowerment.[53]

The charismatic leader is seen as someone who has a compelling vision or sense of purpose; the ability to effectively communicate that vision; the ability to motivate others to join the cause; and is consistent and focused, highly confident, and understands what it will take to accomplish the mission.

Exhibit 9.3 summarizes these qualities, along with other distinguishing characteristics of charismatic leaders, and is followed by an explanation of each. You will realize that many of these characteristics have already been featured throughout the discussion so far. Therefore, the purpose of this section is to bring all the qualities together.

EXHIBIT 9.3 Qualities of Charismatic Leaders

a. Vision
b. Superb communication skills
c. Self-confidence and moral conviction
d. Ability to inspire trust
e. High risk orientation
f. High energy and action orientation
g. Relational power base
h. Minimum internal conflict
i. Ability to empower others
j. Self-promoting personality

Vision

Research has consistently emphasized the role of vision in charismatic leadership. Charismatic leaders articulate a transcendent vision that becomes the rallying cry of a movement or a cause. Charismatic leaders are future-oriented. They have the ability to articulate an idealized vision of a future that is significantly better than the present. They quickly recognize fundamental discrepancies between the status quo and the way things can (or should) be.[54] ***Vision*** *is the ability to imagine different and better conditions and the ways to achieve them.* A vision uplifts and attracts others. For this to happen, the leader's vision must result from a collaborative effort. Charismatic leaders formulate their vision by synthesizing seemingly disparate issues, values, and problems from many sources of the organization or work unit. They have a compelling picture of the future and are very passionate about it.

Superb Communication Skills

In addition to having a vision, charismatic leaders can communicate complex ideas and goals in clear, compelling ways, so that everyone from the top management level to the bottom level of the organization can understand and identify with their message. Their eloquent, imaginative, and passionate manner heightens followers' emotional levels and inspires them to embrace the leader's vision.[55] Charismatic leaders use their superior rhetorical skills to stir dissatisfaction with the status quo while they build support for their vision of a new future. They employ rhetorical techniques such as metaphors, analogy, and stories to drive home their points so that their message will have a profound impact on followers. Fitting examples here include Martin Luther King, Jr.'s "I Have a Dream" speech, Hitler's "Thousand-year Reich," or Gandhi's vision of an India in which Hindus and Muslims live in harmony independent from British rule.

While metaphors and analogies are inspiring, charismatic leaders are also adept at tailoring their language to particular groups, thereby better engaging them mentally and emotionally. For example, a CEO attempting to inspire vice presidents may use an elevated language style; but that same CEO attempting to inspire first-line employees to keep working hard may speak on a colloquial level. Another significant aspect of the communication style of charismatic leaders is that they make extensive use of anecdotes to get their message across. Communicating through anecdotes tells inspiring stories.

Self-Confidence and Moral Conviction

Charismatic leaders build trust in their followers through unshakable self-confidence, an abiding faith, strong moral conviction, and optimism. The importance of self-confidence in everyday interactions is critical, and all the more so for a leader who must convince others to join his or her cause. Studies examining the role and influence of self-confidence and optimism on the growth and performance of a leader have found it to be a critical ingredient for success.[56,57] Self-confidence increases one's level of performance.

Optimism, according to some experts, is an essential component behind charismatic leaders because followers feel connected to leaders who are themselves optimistic and positive about their mission.[58] Martin Luther King, Jr.'s "I Have a Dream" speech is an example of how a leader's self-confidence, faith, optimism, and strong moral conviction can inspire hope and faith in a better future, and move an entire nation.

Ability to Inspire Trust

Constituents believe so strongly in the integrity of charismatic leaders that they will risk their careers to pursue the leader's visions. Charismatic leaders build support and trust by showing commitment to followers' needs over self-interest and by being fair. These qualities inspire followers and often result in greater cooperation between a leader and followers. Also, a leader's credibility could result from modeling desired behavior and projecting an image of being likable and knowledgeable.

Research supports the proposition that leaders with charisma tend to model the values and beliefs to which they want their followers to subscribe. That is, the leader "role models" a value system that is congruent with the articulated vision for the followers. Gandhi represents an outstanding example of such systematic and intentional role modeling. He preached self-sacrifice, brotherly love, and nonviolent resistance to British rule. Repeatedly he engaged in self-sacrificing behaviors, such as giving up his lucrative law practice to live the life of a peasant, engaging in civil disobedience, fasting, and refusing to accept the ordinary conveniences offered to him by others.

High Risk Orientation

Charismatic leaders earn followers' trust by being willing to incur great personal risk. It is said that charismatic leaders romanticize risk. People admire the courage of those who take high risk. Putting themselves on the line is one way charismatic leaders affirm self-advocacy for their vision and thus gain the admiration and respect of their followers. It has been reported that Martin Luther King, Jr., received death threats against himself and his family almost every day during the civil rights movement. Yet, he persisted with his mission until his assassination.

In addition to assuming great risk, charismatic leaders use unconventional strategies to achieve success. Herb Kelleher, former CEO of Southwest Airlines, is a leader who was well known for inspiring employees with his unconventional approach, thus helping to make the airline consistently profitable. Kelleher encouraged employees to break the rules, maintain their individuality, and have fun—a style he called "management by fooling around." It is a style that has made Southwest Airlines' employees the most productive in the industry.

High Energy and Action Orientation

Charismatic leaders are energetic and serve as role models for getting things done on time. They engage their emotions in everyday work life, which makes them energetic, enthusiastic, and attractive to others. Charismatic leaders tend to be emotionally expressive, especially through nonverbal means, such as warm gestures, movement, tone of voice, eye contact, and facial expressions. It is partly through their nonverbal behaviors that charismatic leaders are perceived to have a magnetic personality.

Relational Power Base

A key dimension of charismatic leadership is that it involves a relationship or interaction between the leader and the followers. However, unlike other types of leadership, it is intensely relational and based almost entirely upon referent and expert power (Chapter 4), even when the leader occupies a formal organizational role. Charismatic leadership involves an emotionalized relationship with followers. Followers are often in awe of the leader. There is a powerful identification with and emulation of the leader and an unquestioning acceptance of and affection for the leader.

Minimum Internal Conflict

Typically, charismatic leaders are convinced they are right in their vision and strategies, which explains why they persist and stay the course, even through setbacks. Because of this conviction, they experience less guilt and discomfort in pushing followers to stay the course even when faced with threats.

Ability to Empower Others

Charismatic leaders understand that they cannot make the vision come true alone. They need help and support from their followers. Charismatic leaders empower followers by building their self-efficacy. They do this by assigning followers tasks that lead to successively greater positive experiences and heightened self-confidence, thus persuading followers of their capabilities and creating an environment of

Work Application 3

Identify a leader from your past or current employment that you believe is or was a charismatic leader. Which of the characteristics described in the text did he or she possess? Support your answer.

positive emotions and heightened excitement. Charismatic leaders also empower followers by role modeling and coaching, providing feedback and encouragement, and persuading followers to take on more responsibilities as their skills and self-confidence grow.[59]

Self-Promoting Personality

Even if no one will take up their cause, charismatic leaders are frequently out promoting themselves and their vision. Richard Branson has relied on self-promotion to help build his empire. Charismatic leaders are not "afraid to toot their own horn."

Opening Case APPLICATION

5. What qualities of charismatic leadership does Oprah possess?

"I am guided by the vision of what I believe this show can be. Originally our goal was to uplift, enlighten, encourage and entertain through the medium of television. Now, our mission statement for 'The Oprah Winfrey Show' is to use television to transform people's lives, to make viewers see themselves differently and to bring happiness and a sense of fulfillment into every home" (Oprah Winfrey).[60] Not only does Oprah have a vision, she is a superb communicator with a strong self-confidence and moral conviction in everything she does. She has inspired and empowered millions of people through her show. She is of high energy and does not shy away from self-promotion. As revealed in the opening case, Oprah is described by those close to her as confident, brilliant, and personable. She is considered a sister by many of her key employees. She is one of the richest women in America; yet, she finds it hard to let all of her success go to her head. Oprah exemplifies all the qualities of charismatic leaders summarized in Exhibit 9.3 on page 341.

Applying the Concept 3

Qualities of Charismatic Leaders

Referring to the characteristics listed in Exhibit 9.3 on page 341, identify each statement by its characteristic using the letters a–j.

____ 11. We don't need a committee to evaluate the plan. I'm ready to implement it next week. Let's get going before we miss the opportunity.

____ 12. Last month our department had the highest level of productivity in the organization.

____ 13. The odds of hitting that high a sales goal are maybe 70 percent. Are you sure you want to set this goal?

____ 14. Cutting our plant pollution is the right thing to do. I'm sure we can exceed the new EPA standards, not just meet the minimum requirements.

____ 15. Will you do me a favor and . . . for me, right away?

Learning Outcome 7 *Discuss how one can acquire charismatic qualities.*

How One Acquires Charismatic Qualities

There are those who believe that charisma is inborn and cannot be trained into someone. They argue that those without charisma are "not off the leadership track ... just in a slower, more challenging lane."[61] However, there are also those who believe charisma can be developed or enhanced.[62,63] Several of the qualities of charismatic leaders described in this chapter are capable of enhancement. For example, it is possible through training to enhance communication skills, build self-confidence, and learn techniques to inspire and empower others.[64,65] Suggested strategies for acquiring or enhancing one's charismatic qualities follow:

- Through practice and self-discipline, you can develop your visionary skills by practicing the act of creating a vision in a college course like this one. This would be a key factor in being perceived as charismatic. The role-play exercise at the end of this chapter is directed at this issue.
- You can practice being candid. Although not insensitive, the charismatic person is typically forthright in giving his or her assessment of a situation, whether the assessment is positive or negative. Charismatic people are direct rather than indirect in their approach, so that there is no ambiguity about their position on issues.
- You can develop a warm, positive, and humanistic attitude toward people rather than a negative, cool, and impersonal attitude. Charisma, as mentioned earlier, is a relational and emotional concept and ultimately results from the perception of the followers.
- You can develop an enthusiastic, optimistic, and energetic personality. A major behavior pattern of charismatic people is their combination of enthusiasm, optimism, and a high energy level.

Work Application 4

Identify a leader you have worked with or currently work with who you think has charismatic potential. Describe one trait or characteristic of this individual that, if developed, can transform him or her into an effective charismatic leader.

Learning Outcome 8 *Explain the difference between socialized and personalized charismatic leaders.*

Charisma: A Double-Edged Sword

Most people agree that charisma can be a double-edged sword capable of producing both positive and negative outcomes. It is possible in reading about the personal magnetism, vision, self-confidence, masterful rhetorical skills, and empowering style of charismatic leaders to conclude that they are all good moral leaders that others should emulate. As one observer warns, it can be foolish, futile and even dangerous to follow leaders just because they are charismatic.[66,67] Be careful of hero worship.[68]

It is important to remind ourselves that not all charismatic leaders are necessarily good leaders. Leaders such as Gandhi, Martin Luther King, Jr., John F. Kennedy, and Winston Churchill exhibited tremendous charisma. So did leaders such as Charles Manson, David Koresh, Adolph Hitler, and the Reverend Jim Jones of the People's Temple. This second group of charismatic leaders represents the dark side of charisma. These leaders and many others like them are prone to extreme narcissism that leads them to promote highly self-serving and grandiose goals.[69] Therefore, charisma can cut both ways; it is not always used to benefit others.[70]

One method for differentiating between positive and negative charisma is in terms of the values and personality of the leader. The key question for determining classification is whether the leaders are primarily oriented toward their own needs or the needs of followers and the organization.[71]

Valuation theory proposes that two opposing but complementary basic motives drive an individual's behavior: self-glorification and self-transcendence. The self-glorification motive, based on self-maintenance and self-enhancement, influences one's meaning in life by protecting, maintaining, and aggrandizing one's self-esteem and is consistent with negative or destructive charisma. On the other hand, the self-transcendence motive, based on collective interest, provides meaning through supportive relationships with others and is consistent with altruistic and empowering orientations of positive or constructive charisma.[72]

Based on this notion of positive and negative charisma, two types of charismatic leaders are identified—the socialized or positive charismatic leader and the personalized or negative charismatic leader.[73] *The* **socialized charismatic leader (SCL)** *is one who possesses an egalitarian, self-transcendent, and empowering personality. The* **personalized charismatic leader (PCL)** *is one who possesses a dominant, Machiavellian, and narcissistic personality.* This leader is exploitative, nonegalitarian, and self-aggrandizing. SCLs pursue organization-driven goals and promote feelings of empowerment, personal growth, and equal participation in followers; whereas PCLs pursue leader-driven goals and promote feelings of obedience, dependency, and submission in followers. In the former, rewards are used to reinforce behavior that is consistent with the vision and mission of the organization; in the latter, rewards and punishment are used to manipulate and control followers, and information is restricted and used to preserve the image of leader infallibility or to exaggerate external threats to the organization.[74,75] Socialized charismatic leaders are said to have work groups that are more cohesive and team oriented.[76]

Work Application 5

Describe a leader in your work experience that mainfested positive or negative charismatic qualities. How did this affect your relationship with the leader?

Some charismatic leaders intentionally seek to instill commitment to their ideological goals and, either consciously or unconsciously, seek follower devotion and dependency.[77] Negative charismatic leaders emphasize devotion to themselves more than to ideals. Decisions of these leaders are often self-serving. Group accomplishments are used for self-glorification.

In terms of affect, negative charismatic leaders emphasize personal identification rather than internalization. Personal identification is leader-centered while internalization is follower-centered. Ideological appeals are only a ploy to gain power, after which the ideology is ignored or arbitrarily changed to serve the leader's self-interest. In contrast, positive charismatic leaders seek to instill devotion to ideology more than devotion to self. In terms of affect, they emphasize internalization rather than personal identification. Therefore, outcomes of their leadership are more likely to be beneficial to followers and society.[78]

Opening Case APPLICATION

6. Does Oprah embody the example of a socialized charismatic leader or a personalized charismatic leader?

Oprah's philanthropic activities and the way she conducts herself would suggest that she is more of a socialized than a personalized charismatic leader. As explained above, the socialized charismatic leader is driven by a self-transcendence motive. The self-transcendence motive focuses on collective interest, provides meaning through supportive relationships with others, and is consistent with altruistic and empowering orientations of positive or constructive charisma. The Oprah Winfrey Foundation was established to support the inspiration, empowerment, education, and well-being of women, children, and families around the world. Through this private charity, Oprah has directly served the needs of low-opportunity people and has awarded hundreds of grants to organizations that carry out this vision. She has contributed millions of dollars toward providing a better education for underserved students who have merit but no means. She created the "Oprah Winfrey Scholars Program," which gives scholarships to students determined to use their education to give back to their communities in the United States and abroad.

Ethical **Dilemma 1**

Obesity and Charismatic Ads

The federal government has reported that obesity might overtake tobacco as the leading cause of death in the United States.[79] Some social activists are blaming part of the obesity problem on marketing junk food to kids,[33] and food makers and ad agencies are defending advertising to children.[80] Some companies use charismatic star performers and athletes to promote their junk food products to get people to eat more. At the same time, American health officials are trying to persuade people to lose weight. The government has taken out public service ads to convince people to get in shape and eat right. Part of the ads' success depends on whether people take personal responsibility for their own health and weight.[81]

1. What is the reason for the increase in obesity in the United States? Are junk food ads using charismatic stars to promote their products contributing to the obesity problem?
2. Is it ethical for junk food sellers to use charismatic stars to promote their products?
3. Is it ethical and socially responsible for the government to try to get people to lose weight, through ads and other methods?

Despite the contributions of charismatic theorists to the field of leadership, charisma is not without its limitations. Charismatic leadership theories emphasize the role of an individual leader who takes the initiative for developing and articulating a vision to followers. In this "heroic leadership stereotype," the leader is omnipotent and followers are submissive to the leader's will and demands.[82] However, it is more likely the case that in times of crisis (such as an organization facing significant external challenges or serious internal weaknesses), greater success comes from a shared strategic leadership approach than a lone star individualistic approach.

Most of the descriptive literature on effective leaders suggests that charisma in its individualized form may be inadequate to achieve major changes in an organization's performance. In fact, it is more likely the case that positive organizational change is the result of transformational leadership by individuals not perceived as charismatic. Thus, charismatic theories that emphasize "lone star" leadership by extraordinary individuals may be most appropriate for describing a visionary entrepreneur who establishes a new organization. Examples include Richard Branson of the Virgin Group, Stephen Case of America Online, and Jeff Bezos of Amazon.com, and the exceptional "turnaround manager" Al Dunlap, former CEO of Sunbeam Corporation. Lone star leadership is not a panacea for the problems of every organization. The second half of this chapter focuses on transformational leadership.

Transformational Leadership

J. M. Burns first articulated the idea of transformational leadership in 1978 before Bernard Bass expanded on it almost a decade later. Burns proposed two leadership approaches for getting work done: transactional or transformational.[83] Transformational leadership focuses largely on the leader's vision rather than on follower attributions. Transformational leaders are known for moving and changing things "in a big way," by communicating to followers a special vision of the future, tapping into followers' higher ideals and motives.[84] They seek to alter the existing structure and influence people to buy into a new vision and new possibilities.[85]

As is the case with charismatic leaders, followers trust, admire, and respect the transformational leader. There is a collective "buy in" to the organizational vision put forth by the leader and, as such, followers willingly expend exceptional effort in achieving organizational goals. **Transformational leadership** *serves to change the status quo by articulating to followers the problems in the current system and a compelling vision of what a new organization could be.* **Transactional leadership** *seeks to maintain stability within an organization through regular economic and social exchanges that achieve specific goals for both the leaders and their followers.*

We will examine the effects of transformational leadership; the similarities and differences between charismatic, transactional, and transformational leadership; transformational leader behaviors and attributes; and the transformation process.

The Effects of Transformational Leadership

As organizations continue to face global challenges, the need for leaders who can successfully craft and implement bold strategies that will transform or align the organization's strengths and weaknesses with emerging opportunities and threats is ever greater. Increased volatility and uncertainty in the external environment is seen as one of the contributing factors to the emergence of transformational leadership.[86] Transformational leadership describes a process of positive influence that changes and transforms individuals, organizations, and communities. Research studies have consistently revealed that transformational leadership is positively related to individual, group, and organizational performance.[87,88,89]

At the individual level, transformational leaders influence their constituencies to make the shift from focus on self-interests to a focus on collective interests. Transformational leaders understand the importance of trust building as a means to creating a strong commitment to mission-driven outcomes. Effective transformational leaders use their charisma and power to inspire and motivate followers to trust and follow their example. They generate excitement and energy by focusing on the future.[90]

Researchers investigating these proposed linkages have found support for some proposed correlations and not for others. For example, transformational leadership has been found to be positively related to employee service performance, organizational commitment, and job satisfaction.[91,92] Examining the effects of transformational and change leadership on employees' commitment to change, researchers found a positive relationship between the two variables, especially when the change had significant personal impact.[93] Another study found that employees with supervisors high on transformational leadership experienced more positive emotions throughout the workday, including interactions with coworkers and customers, and also reported increased job satisfaction.[94] Relating back to Chapter 7, one study found that transformational leadership relationships are significantly stronger for followers who perceive a high-quality leader–member exchange relationship.[95] Relating the effects of transformational leadership to empowerment and team effectiveness, transformational leadership increased subordinates' self-reported empowerment and team effectiveness.[96] Another study investigating the effects of self-awareness of empowering and transformational leadership found that self-awareness of transformational leadership was related to leader effectiveness and followers' supervisory satisfaction.[97]

At the group level, transformational leadership was found to influence team performance and team potency.[98,99] At the organizational level, there is broad support for the proposition that transformational leadership can change both an organization's climate and culture.[100] A number of studies have found that transformational leadership has a strong, significant influence on organizational learning.[101,102,103] Organizational learning, as we will see in Chapter 12, has direct effect on firm innovation.

Learning Outcome 9 *Distinguish between charismatic and transformational leadership.*

Charismatic versus Transformational Leadership

Some authors make no distinction between the charismatic and the transformational leader, preferring to combine them into one theory. They refer to the two theories as charismatic because charisma is a central concept in both of them, either explicitly or implicitly. Others have conceptualized charisma as one of several attributes that may define the transformational leader. The other attributes include honesty, optimism, communication skills, confidence, and consideration. It adds another dimension of behavior traits of the leader. Charisma is seen as just one of a collection of attributes that may explain transformational leadership behavior. Yet, charisma is relational in nature. It is not something found solely in the leader as a psychological phenomenon, nor is it totally situationally determined. Instead, charisma manifests itself in the interplay between the leader (his or her traits and behaviors) and the follower (his or her values, needs, perceptions, and beliefs).

There is general agreement that charismatic leaders by nature are transformational, but not all transformational leaders achieve their transforming results through the charismatic effects of their personalities. According to this viewpoint, some transformational leaders lacking in charisma may still be able to influence and inspire others by meeting the emotional needs of their followers through individualized consideration, and/or they may intellectually stimulate their followers through rationalizing the need for change, involvement of followers into possible solutions, and the passion to bring about resolution. One prominent leader who comes to mind is Bill Gates. Many will agree that he is definitely a transformational leader, but few will label him as a charismatic leader. He has led not only the transformation of Microsoft as a leader in the computer software industry, but also transformed our society in the way we use computer technology to better our lives.

From a power and moral leadership perspective, charismatic and transformational leadership overlap as well as support and reinforce each other. A leader like Nelson Mandela has been described as charismatic and transformational. Mandela is known to live by the tenets of consultation, persuasion, and cohabitation, and shuns coercion and domination. Transformational leaders seek to transform or change the basic values, beliefs, and attitudes of followers so that they are willing to perform beyond the minimum levels specified by the organization. Transformational leaders are similar to charismatic leaders in that they can articulate a compelling vision of the future and influence followers by arousing strong emotions in support of the vision.

Transformational leaders can emerge from different levels of the organization. Therefore, an organization may have many transformational leaders. In contrast, charismatic leaders are few in number. Charismatic leaders are most likely to emerge in the throes of a crisis, when an organization is in turmoil because of conflicting value and belief systems. The response by people to a charismatic or transformational leader is often highly polarized, because those with the most to lose by abandoning the old system will put up the most resistance to any change initiative. Additionally, it would appear that the emotional levels of resistance toward charismatic leaders are more extreme than those toward transformational leaders. This may be the underlying cause for the untimely, violent deaths of some charismatic leaders (such as Malcolm X, Martin Luther King, Jr., John F. Kennedy, and Mahatma Gandhi). Both charismatic and transformational leadership always involve conflict and change, and both types of leaders must be willing to embrace conflict, create enemies, make unusual allowances for self-sacrifice, and be extraordinarily focused in order to achieve and institutionalize their vision.

Transformational Leader Behaviors and Attributes

Although much remains to be learned about transformational leadership, there is enough consensus from the many years of research to suggest that there are common behaviors associated with transformational leaders. Like charismatic leaders, effective transformational leadership requires an ability to initiate change and challenge the status quo, recognize opportunities for the organization as well as for others, take risks, and encourage others to do the same. Transformational leadership requires an ability to effectively inspire a shared vision.[104] Such leaders rally others around a common dream and are adept at envisioning the future and enlisting others in seeing and moving toward the vision. They must be able to model the way—that is, set the example of commitment to shared vision and values.[105]

Bass and Avilio proposed that transformational leadership is composed of four behavior dimensions, and referred to them as the "four I's"—idealized influence, inspirational motivation, individual consideration, and intellectual stimulation.[106] The "four I's" have been used in other disciplines and cultures to explain the transformational leader–follower relationship:[107,108,109]

- Though not required to be a successful transformational leader, *idealized influence (charisma)* is still a fundamental factor in the transformation process. Transformational leaders with charisma possess the ability to develop great symbolic power that is then used to influence followers. Followers idealize such a leader and often develop a strong emotional attachment.
- The next attribute associated with charisma is *inspirational motivation.* Transformational leaders tend to be inspirational individuals as well. Inspiration describes how the leader passionately communicates a future idealistic goal or situation that is a much better alternative to the status quo and can be shared. The transformational leader employs visionary explanations to depict what the workgroup can accomplish. Excited followers are then motivated to achieve organizational objectives.
- The third attribute, *individual consideration,* is a factor that reveals the mentoring role often assumed by transformational leaders. The leader serves as a mentor to followers. He or she treats followers as individuals and uses a developmental orientation that responds to follower needs and concerns.
- Finally, *intellectual stimulation* describes the transformational leader's creative and out-of-the-box thinking style. He or she encourages followers to approach old and familiar problems in new ways. By stimulating novel employee thinking patterns, the leader inspires followers to question their own beliefs and learn to solve problems creatively by themselves.

Transformational leaders understand that in order to get followers to fully contribute to the transformation process, they have to empower them and offer support in getting things done, encourage creativity, challenge followers to rethink old ways of doing things and to re-examine old assumptions, foster collaboration, motivate, and reinforce positive behavior (such as recognizing and acknowledging the accomplishments of others and celebrating small wins).[110,111] Nelson Mandela led the change that is depolarizing a nation racially polarized for decades. Mandela's transformational leadership humanized apartheid South Africa and led to the emergence of a nation deserving of global recognition. His charismatic effect softened the hardest stances of the haves and have-nots and aligned them in pursuit of a constructive common cause. In summary, transformational leaders

- See themselves as change agents
- Are visionaries who have a high level of trust for their intuition
- Are risk-takers, but not reckless
- Are capable of articulating a set of core values that tend to guide their own behavior
- Possess exceptional cognitive skills and believe in careful deliberation before taking action
- Believe in people and show sensitivity to their needs
- Are flexible and open to learning from experience

Exhibit 9.4 highlights key transformational leader behaviors. It should be noted that some of these behaviors have received broad conceptual support among researchers while others have only been partially supported. For example, creating and articulating a vision has been identified by virtually every study on the subject as an important component of the transformational leadership process. Also, facilitating acceptance for team goals and modeling appropriate behavior have been identified by a majority of studies as key elements of transformational leadership.

Martin Luther King, Jr. was both a charismatic and a transformational leader like Nelson Mandela. A study focused on examining his legacy concluded that he personified all the attributes of transformational leadership listed above. The study

EXHIBIT 9.4 Transformational Leader Behaviors

Behavioral Components	Description
Creation and articulation of vision	Leader behavior that is directed at finding new opportunities for the organization; formulating, articulating, and inspiring followers with the vision of a better future
Role modeling	Setting an example for followers that is consistent with the organizational values and expectations
Fostering a "buy in" of team goals	Behavior aimed at encouraging and building teamwork among followers and commitment to shared goals
High performance expectations	Behavior that conveys the leader's expectations for everyday excellence and superior performance on the part of followers
Personalized leader-member exchange	Behavior that indicates that the leader trusts, respects, and has confidence in each follower, and is concerned about their personal needs, not just organizational needs
Empowerment	Behavior on the part of the leader that challenges followers to think "outside of the box" and re-examine old ways and methods

Source: Based on P. M. Podsakoff, S. B. Mackenzie, R. H. Moorman, R. Fetter, "Transformational Leader Behaviors and Their Effects on Followers' Trust in Leader, Satisfaction, and Organizational Citizenship Behavior," Leadership Quarterly *1(2) (1990): 107–142.*

emphasized the importance of building follower confidence, challenging taken-for-granted assumptions, developing follower needs, and upholding high moral values.[112] Martin Luther King, Jr. embodied all these things, and that is why his status as a transformational leader who changed America is unquestioned.

Opening Case APPLICATION

7. Is Oprah a transformational leader, a charismatic leader, or both?

A cursory review of the creation and evolution of the *Oprah Winfrey Show* and Harpo Productions is enough to conclude that Oprah is definitely a transformational leader. In 1986, Oprah formed her own production company, Harpo Productions, to bring quality entertainment projects into production. Two years later, television history was made when Harpo Productions announced that it had assumed ownership and all production responsibilities for the *Oprah Winfrey Show* from Capitol Cities/ABC, making Oprah Winfrey the first woman in history to own and produce her own talk show. Today, Harpo is well on its way to becoming a formidable force in film and television production. That growth has meant financial success. Oprah's Harpo Entertainment Group, the corporate umbrella over her film and TV production operations, is privately held and executives do not publicly talk about its finances. However, published reports say Oprah is well on her way to becoming the first African-American billionaire, with an estimated net worth of $675 million, according to *Forbes* magazine.

Oprah's venture into magazine publishing is another example that she has the ability to start and transform any venture she embarks upon. In April 2000, Oprah and Hearst Magazines introduced *O, The Oprah Magazine,* a monthly magazine that has become one of today's leading women's lifestyle publications. It is credited as being the most successful magazine launch in recent history and currently has an audience of over 2 million readers each month. *O, The Oprah Magazine,* is another medium through which Oprah connects with her audience and provides possibilities for transforming their lives. In April 2002, Oprah launched the first international edition of *O, The Oprah Magazine,* in South Africa. Oprah is a transformational leader with charismatic qualities. She embodies both leadership styles.

Learning Outcome 10 *Explain the difference between transformational and transactional leadership.*

Transformational versus Transactional Leadership

Begin this section by completing Self-Assessment 1 to determine if you are more of a transactional or transformational leader.

SELF-ASSESSMENT 1

Are You More of a Transactional or Transformational Leader?

Complete the following questions based on how you will act (or have acted) in a typical work or school situation. Use the following scale:

1 — 2 — 3 — 4 — 5
Disagree *Agree*

_____ 1. I enjoy change and see myself as a change agent.

_____ 2. I am better at inspiring employees toward a new future than motivating them to perform their current jobs.

continued

(Self-Assessment 1 continued)

_____ 3. I have/had a vision of how an organization can change for the better.

_____ 4. I see myself as someone who is comfortable encouraging people to express ideas and opinions that differ from my own.

_____ 5. I enjoy taking risks, but am not reckless.

_____ 6. I enjoy spending time developing new solutions to old problems rather than implementing existing solutions.

_____ 7. I deliberate carefully before acting; I'm not impulsive.

_____ 8. I like to support change initiatives, even when the idea may not work.

_____ 9. I learn from my experience; I don't repeat the same mistakes.

_____ 10. I believe the effort to change something for the better should be rewarded, even if the final outcome is disappointing.

Add up the numbers on lines 1–10 and place your total score here _____ and on the continuum below.

10 — 20 — 30 — 40 — 50

Transactional leader *Transformational leader*

The higher the score, generally, the more you exhibit transformational leader qualities. However, transformational leaders also perform transactional behaviors. It is also generally easier to be transformational at higher levels of management than at lower levels.

Using Weber's seminal work on charismatic leaders as his base, Burns conceptualized that leadership occurs in one of two ways—transformational or transactional.[113] The transactional leadership process involves an exchange of valued benefits, based on present values and motivations of both leaders and followers. It therefore revolves around the leader–follower exchange (LMX), in which the leader rewards the follower for specific behaviors and performance that meets with the leader's expectations and punishes or criticizes behavior or performance that does not meet expectations.[114] Such exchanges cater to the self-interest of followers, while transformational leadership inspires followers to go beyond self-interest and act for the good of the organization.[115,116] Transformational leadership motivates followers by appealing to higher ideals and moral values.

Some scholars refer to transactional leaders as managers and transformational leaders as leaders. These scholars hold the view that leadership and management are not interchangeable. They argue that leadership is about developing and communicating a vision and the objectives and strategies for realizing such a vision; while management's role is to plan, organize, and implement the leader's vision. Managers, it is argued, serve as the means to achieve the leader's ends.[117] Leaders rated as transformational are described as influential, inspirational, and charismatic, whereas leaders rated as transactional are described as task- and reward-oriented, structured, and passive.[118,119]

Transformational leadership serves to change the status quo by articulating to followers the problems in the current system and a compelling vision of what a new organization could be. The transactional leader enters into specific contractual arrangements with followers. In exchange for meeting specified objectives or performing certain duties, the leader provides benefits that satisfy followers' needs and desires.[120] An example of transactional leadership occurs when managers give monthly bonuses to salespeople for meeting and exceeding their monthly sales quotas, or to production people for exceeding quality standards.

Transactional leadership is conceptually similar to the cultural maintenance form of leadership, which acts to clarify or strengthen existing tasks, work standards, and outcomes. Some scholars have proposed that transactional leadership consist of three dimensions—contingent reward, management by exception, and passive leadership. Depending on a leader's personality traits, each dimension represents an option that can be employed to shape strategies and structures, reward subordinates' efforts and commitment, and take corrective action to address mistakes and deviations from expectations; all efforts aim at achieving established organizational performance goals.[121]

Transactional leadership tends to be transitory, in that once a transaction is completed the relationship between the parties may end or be redefined. Transformational leadership is more enduring, especially when the change process is well designed and implemented. Transactional leaders promote stability, while transformational leaders create significant change in both followers and organizations.

Managing knowledge effectively can provide firms with sustainable competitive advantages. The process of managing knowledge involves three processes—creating, sharing, and exploiting knowledge. Leaders play a critical role in each of these processes. A study of these constructs concluded that transformational leadership may be more effective in creating and sharing knowledge at the individual and group levels, while transactional leadership is more effective at exploiting knowledge at the organizational level.[122] Research examining the degree to which cultural values and norms influence follower receptivity to different leadership styles found that transformational leaders inspire by emphasizing the importance of group values and focusing on collective interests, while transactional leaders tend to focus more on defining roles and task requirements and offering rewards that are contingent on task fulfillment.[123] This explains why transactional leadership is also referred to as contingent reward leadership.

Work Application 6

Identify your present or past manager as being more transformational or transactional. Explain why and include examples.

Despite these differences, it is worth mentioning that effective leaders exhibit both transactional and transformational leadership skills in appropriate situations.[124] Bernard Bass argued that contrary to Burns's assertion that transformational and transactional leadership are at opposite ends of a single continuum of leadership, the two approaches are actually interdependent and complementary. A meta-analytic test of the relative validity of transformational and transactional leadership styles confimed Bass's assertion. The study revealed that both are valid approaches for achieving organizational objectives, with transformational leadership showing the highest overall relations and transactional or contingent reward leadership a close second.[125,126]

Applying the Concept 4

Transformational or Transactional Leadership

Identify each statement as being more characteristic of one or the other style:

a. transformational leadership   b. transactional leadership

____ 16. We don't need a committee to work on a plan. Let's get going on this now.

____ 17. I'd say we have a 75 percent chance of being successful with the new product. Let's market it.

____ 18. The present inventory system is working fine. Let's not mess with success.

____ 19. That is a good idea, but we have no money in the budget to implement it.

____ 20. We need to monitor the demographics to make sure our products satisfy our customers.

Learning Outcome 11 *Explain the four phases of the transformation process.*

The Transformation Process

Transformational leaders are usually brought into an organization that is experiencing a crisis or approaching total collapse, to institute turnaround strategies that can rescue the organization. This often involves fundamental changes in followers' actions, thoughts, and work ethic to bring about profound and positive outcomes. There is some agreement among scholars and practitioners that certain transformational leadership practices are necessary for successful transformation. Key questions often used to highlight such practices include the transformational leader's ability to (1) challenge the status quo and make a convincing case for change, (2) inspire a shared vision for the future, (3) provide effective leadership during the transition, and (4) make the change a permanent and institutionalized part of the organization. Echoing a similar point of view, one study describes key managerial competencies necessary to lead an organization's transformation. These competencies include creativity, effective communication, vision, passion and charisma, and the ability to empower followers so that they feel valued.[127]

From this discussion, a four-stage process of transformation is developed. Exhibit 9.5 lists these four stages, with suggested activities to ensure effective and efficient execution of each stage.

EXHIBIT 9.5 The Transformation Process

Stages	Suggested Activities
1. Make a compelling case for change	Increase sensitivity to environmental changes and threats.
	Initiate change and challenge the status quo.
	Search for opportunities and take risks.
2. Inspire a shared vision	Encourage everyone to think of a new and brighter future.
	Involve others in seeing and moving toward the vision.
	Express new vision in ideological, not just economic, terms.
3. Lead the transition	Instill in managers a sense of urgency for the change.
	Empower, support, foster collaboration, and strengthen followers.
	Help followers understand need for change.
	Increase followers' self-confidence and optimism.
	Avoid the temptation of a "quick fix."
	Recognize and deal openly with emotional component of resisting change.
4. Implant the change	Enable and strengthen followers with a "greatness attitude"; for example, recognize and celebrate accomplishments.
	Help followers find self-fulfillment with new vision.
	Help followers look beyond self-interests to collective interests.
	Change reward systems and appraisal procedures.
	Implement team-building interventions and personnel changes.
	Appoint a special task force to monitor progress.
	Encourage top leaders and managers to model the way.

Source: Based on Carolyn Hines and William Hines Jr., "Seminar on the Essence of Transformational Leadership (Leadership Training Institute)," Nation's Cities Weekly *25(9) (March 4, 2002): 8 (1).*

Ethical **Dilemma 2**

Transforming Music and Movies

Transformational leaders at Grokster, StreamCast Networks, and Sharman Networks (Kazaa) have changed the way millions of people globally listen to music and watch movies, through file sharing. The music and movie industries claim copyright law violations and have tried to stop file sharing. Music companies claim that sharing music has led to multiyear declines in global music sales, and they have even taken people to court to collect damages. However, a lower court ruling that was upheld by a federal appeals court, in San Francisco, stated that online trading of movies and music allows creators of Internet file-sharing software to stay in operation, despite piracy by users of their programs. The ruling stated that providing file-sharing software that allows individuals to trade music, movies, and other digital content is not a violation of copyright law. However, in 2004 the Supreme Court ruled that Grokster illegally downloaded approximately 90 percent of its files, and Grokster closed in November 2005.[128]

1. When music and movies are downloaded, the artists/actors and companies don't get any money. Is it ethical for people to download music and movies without paying for them?
2. Would artists/actors tend to believe it's unethical while others don't?
3. Is it ethical for companies to provide file-sharing software so that people can get free music and movies?

Learning Outcome 12 *Explain the basis of stewardship and servant leadership.*

Stewardship and Servant Leadership

Stewardship and servant leadership are related to charismatic and transformational leadership, in that they focus on empowering followers to exercise leadership in accomplishing the organization's goals.[68] Traditional leadership theories emphasized the leader–follower structure in which the follower accepted responsibility from the leader and was accountable to the leader. However, proponents of stewardship and servant leadership view the leader as a steward and servant of the people and the organization. One study suggested that servant leadership leads to a spiritual generative culture while transformational leadership leads to an empowered dynamic culture.[129] Advocates of servant leadership and stewardship believe strongly in the positive relationship between spirituality and the conduct of business.

Stewardship and servant leadership represent a shift in the leadership paradigm toward followers. This shift represents the views of those who believe that leadership has less to do with directing other people and more to do with serving other people. Stewardship and servant leadership are about placing others ahead of oneself, and are viewed as a model for successful leadership in any field or profession.

Not everyone agrees with this model of leadership. To some the word "servant" implies a lower status for the person serving. Its use connotes negative feelings about leadership, especially for those who have traditionally thought of leaders as powerful visionaries leading the pack—the "greatman" theory of leadership. However, the servant as someone who is of assistance to, promotes the interests of, fights for, or aids another implies a much greater noble purpose and a sense of responsibility to others.[130] In this section, we discuss the nature and importance of stewardship and servant leadership, and the framework for establishing both.

The Nature of Stewardship and Servant Leadership

Stewardship *is an employee-focused form of leadership that empowers followers to make decisions and have control over their jobs.* **Servant leadership** *is leadership that transcends self-interest to serve the needs of others, by helping them grow professionally and personally.* Both leadership styles emphasize patience, kindness, humility, respectfulness, honesty, and commitment. In a study examining individual differences in servant leadership, followers' ratings of leaders' servant leadership were positively related to followers' ratings of leaders' values of empathy, integrity, and competence.[131] This is similar to the qualities of charismatic leaders such as Gandhi. These attributes are important because organizations that want to maintain a servant or stewardship leadership culture may benefit from recruiting leaders on the basis of these attributes.

Stewardship and servant leadership describe leaders who lead from positions of moral influence, not power, and are very follower-centered. Though some may view these two concepts of leadership as synonymous and use the terms interchangeably, subtle yet significant differences exist between the two concepts. While both shine the spotlight on those who actually perform the day-to-day tasks of producing goods and services for an organization's customers, servant leadership takes stewardship assumptions about leaders and followers one step further. Servant leadership calls for the highest level of selflessness—a level that some doubt exists in the real world.

At the core of servant leadership is self-sacrificing love of others without regard to what one might receive in return. The leader makes a conscious decision to hold followers in high regard. Servant leadership is described as an act of will and intellect, not of the fickleness of fleeting emotions. The leader is driven to serve, not to be served.[132,133] Robert Greenleaf first introduced the concept of the leader as a servant more than three decades ago. Today, there is a Greenleaf Center for Servant Leadership with a global reach that includes 11 branch offices located around the world.[134]

Framework for Stewardship

Leadership thinking based on stewardship prescribes a relationship between leaders and followers in which leaders lead without dominating or controlling followers. Leaders who embody the stewardship concept are sincerely concerned about their followers and assist them to grow, develop, and achieve both personal and organizational goals. An effective steward leader creates an environment in which everyone works together as a team to achieve organizational goals. Stewardship is more about facilitating than actively leading. We present four key values that describe stewardship; see Exhibit 9.6 on the next page.

Strong Teamwork Orientation

Stewardship works best in situations where self-managed teams of core employees and the leader work together to formulate goals and strategies for a changing environment and marketplace. Here, the leader's role is less dominant and more supportive of the process. Where a strong team spirit is absent, a leader must play a

EXHIBIT 9.6 Values of Stewardship

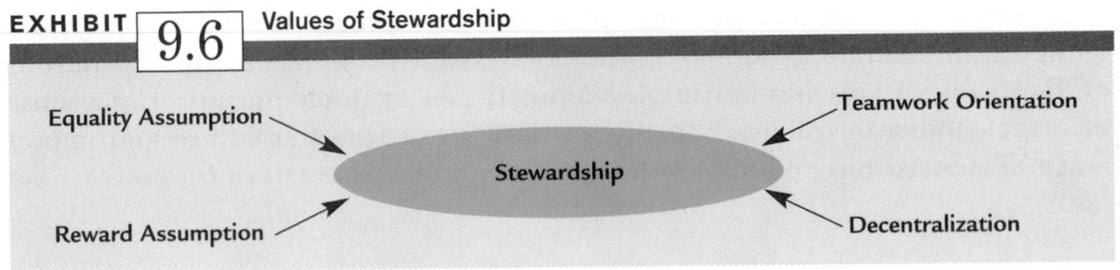

dominant role to push individuals in the right direction. However, this defeats the purpose of stewardship.

Decentralized Decision Making and Power

Stewardship is realized when authority and decision making are decentralized and brought down to where work gets done and employees interact with customers. In this environment, stewardship has a great chance to succeed, given the empowered status of employees and the closer relationship between managers and followers. The absence of this principle makes stewardship inoperable.

Equality Assumption

Stewardship works best when there is perceived equality between leaders and followers. It is a partnership of equals rather than a leader–follower command structure. The applicability of stewardship is enhanced as leaders find opportunities to serve rather than manage. Honesty, respect, and mutual trust prevail when there is equality, and these are values that enhance the success of stewardship.

Reward Assumption

Stewardship puts greater responsibility in the hands of employees. Therefore, to realize successful stewardship, the organization must redesign the compensation system to match rewards to actual performance. Employees with more responsibility and authority who are compensated accordingly flourish under stewardship because they are motivated and committed to the organization's mission. Without this value, it is hard to sustain stewardship.

Stewardship leaders are not known for their great deeds but for empowering others to achieve great deeds. Stewardship leaders offer the best chance for organizations to succeed and grow in today's dynamic environment, because these leaders don't just lead, they coach (Chapter 6) followers to do the leading. This focus on people is what encourages followers to be more creative, energetic, and committed to their jobs.[73]

Framework for Servant Leadership

Servant leaders approach leadership from a strong moral standpoint. The servant leader operates from the viewpoint that we all have a moral duty to one another and that as leaders, we have to both serve and lead.[135] Servant leadership emphasizes trust, fairness, and justice as means for achieving productive organizational citizenship behavior. One study's findings revealed that followers' ratings of leaders' servant leadership were positively related to followers' ratings of leaders' values of empathy, integrity, and competence. The study also concluded that servant leaders were high on the agreeableness personality trait.[136]

The servant leader sees leadership as an opportunity to serve at the ground level, not to lead from the top. It is a leadership approach characterized by a strong service orientation and a moral–spiritual emphasis.[137] An individual like Mother Teresa—through her humble and ordinary nature, strong moral values, and dedicated service to the poor and the afflicted—inspired hundreds of followers to join her order and emulate her example. The framework for servant leadership consists of the following basic guidelines,[138,139,140,141] as shown in Exhibit 9.7.

EXHIBIT 9.7 Guidelines of Servant Leadership

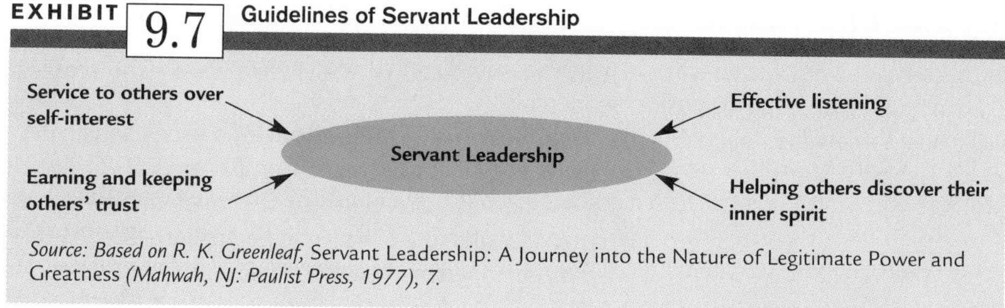

Source: Based on R. K. Greenleaf, *Servant Leadership: A Journey into the Nature of Legitimate Power and Greatness* (Mahwah, NJ: Paulist Press, 1977), 7.

Helping Others Discover Their Inner Spirit

The servant leader's role is to help followers discover the strength of their inner spirit and their potential to make a difference. This requires servant leaders to be empathetic to the circumstances of others. Servant leaders are not afraid to show their vulnerabilities.

Earning and Keeping Others' Trust

Servant leaders earn followers' trust by being honest and true to their word. They work hard to preserve their integrity. They don't have any hidden agendas, and they are willing to give up power, rewards, recognition, and control. It is how servant leaders build strong working relationships with followers. Servant leadership is about leadership influence that is based on trust, not hierachy.

Service Over Self-Interest

The hallmark of servant leadership is the desire to help others, rather than the desire to attain power and control over others. Doing what's right for others takes precedence over protecting one's position. Such leaders make decisions to further the good of the group rather than their own interests.

Effective Listening

Servant leaders do not impose their will on the group; rather, they listen carefully to the problems others are facing and then engage the group to find the best course of action. Servant leaders are more likely to express confidence and commitment in others than other types of leaders. They show love, acceptance, and encouragement for their followers and are very empathetic.[142]

Leaders like Gandhi, Martin Luther King, Jr., and Nelson Mandela possess both charismatic and servant leader qualities. They have all been described as leaders who put others' interests over self-interests, earned and kept the trust of followers, listened carefully to others' problems and concerns, and inspired followers to believe in their own inner strength and spirit. The discussion in this chapter has emphasized leadership approaches (charismatic, transformational, stewardship, and servant leadership) that operate under the premise that change is inevitable and not every leader is capable of managing it successfully. Thus, we have identified

Work Application 7

Explain how your present/past leader did, or did not, use stewardship and servant leadership.

the different leadership theories that equip leaders to deal with change effectively. Self-Assessment 2 provides the opportunity to link these leadership approaches to one personality type.

SELF-ASSESSMENT 2

Personality and Charismatic and Transformational Leadership

Charismatic leaders have charisma based on personality and other personal traits that cut across all of the Big Five personality types. Review the ten qualities of charismatic leaders in Exhibit 9.3 on page 341. Which traits do you have?

____

____

If you have a high surgency Big Five personality style and a high need for power, you need to focus on using socialized, rather than personalized, charismatic leadership.

Transformational leaders tend to be charismatic as well. In Self-Assessment 1 on pages 352-353 you determined if you were more transformational or transactional. How does your personality affect your transformational and transactional leadership styles?

____

____

Go to the Internet (www.cengage.com/management/lussier)
where you will find a broad array of resources to help maximize your learning.

- Review the vocabulary
- Try a quiz
- Find related links

Chapter Summary

The chapter summary is organized to answer the 13 learning outcomes for Chapter 9.

1. **Describe personal meaning and how it influences attributions of charismatic qualities.**

   Personal meaning is defined as the degree to which people's lives make emotional sense and to which the demands confronted by them are perceived as being worthy of energy and commitment. It provides a sense of purpose for one's life. Personal meaning influences attributions of charismatic qualities in that, first, a leader's personal meaning influences his or her behavior. In turn, the leader's behavior is reflected in the formulation and articulation of his or her vision. Second, the leader's behavior garners attributions of charisma from followers.

2. **Briefly explain Max Weber's conceptualization of charisma.**

   Weber used the term *charisma* to explain a form of influence based on follower perceptions that the leader is endowed with the gift of divine inspiration, not a traditional or legal mandate of authority. This gift of divine inspiration is the force behind a charismatic leader's ability to focus society's attention on both the crisis it faces and the leader's vision for a new and better future. According to Weber, charismatic individuals emerge as leaders during times of great social crisis and inspire people to do more than they would under normal circumstances.

3. **Describe the behavioral qualities that differentiate charismatic from noncharismatic leaders.**

   The attribution of charisma to leaders is believed to depend on four behavior variables:

- *Dissatisfaction with status quo.* The discrepancy between charismatic and noncharismatic leaders is such that the former is very much opposed to the status quo and strives to change it, while the latter essentially agrees with the status quo and strives to maintain it. For the charismatic leader, the more idealized or discrepant the future goal is from the present status quo, the better. And the greater the gap from the status quo, the more likely followers will attribute extraordinary vision to the leader.
- *Compelling nature of the vision.* Effective articulation of the vision is measured in terms of what is said (content and context) and how it is said (oratorical skills). Effective communication skills are an imperative in the successful articulation of a compelling vision

and maintenance of a leadership role. Through verbal and nonverbal means, charismatic leaders communicate their self-confidence, convictions, and dedication in order to give credibility to what they advocate.

- *The use of unconventional strategies for achieving desired change.* The charismatic leader's expertise lies in using unconventional means to transcend the existing order. Follower perceptions of the leader's revolutionary and unconventional qualities evoke sentiments of adoration, especially when the leader's activities exemplify acts of heroism involving personal risk and self-sacrificing behavior. Thus, the behavior of the noncharismatic leader is conventional and conforming to existing norms while that of the charismatic leader is unconventional and counter to the norm.
- *A realistic assessment of resource needs and other constraints for achieving desired change.* Charismatic leaders are also very good strategists. They understand the need to perform a realistic assessment of environmental resources and constraints affecting their ability to effect major change within their organization. They are sensitive to the capabilities and emotional needs of followers, and they understand the resources and constraints of the physical and social environment in which they operate. There is a high need to align organizational strategies and capabilities to ensure a successful transformation.

4. **Explain the locus of charismatic leadership.**

The question scholars have entertained since Weber's conception of charisma is whether charisma is a function of the prevailing social climate, the leader's extraordinary qualities, or an interaction between the two. Supporters of the view that charismatic leadership could not take place unless the society were in a tumultuous, unstable situation argue that without a crisis and followers' need for change, a leader's charismatic qualities would be hard to notice or appreciate. Therefore, the locus of charismatic leadership is the status of the society. Opponents argue that charismatic leadership is primarily the result of leader attributes, not the situation. They argue that without strong leader characteristics (such as vision, exceptional communication skills, trustworthiness, self-confidence, and focus on empowering others), leaders like Martin Luther King, Jr., or Gandhi would never have emerged as leaders of their respective followers, regardless of the situation. Finally, there is an emerging view that charismatic leadership is a convergence of follower perceptions and reactions influenced by leader characteristics and the prevailing social situation.

5. **Discuss the effects of charismatic leadership on followers.**

Charismatic leaders tend to have a strong emotional bond with their followers. The effects of such a bond are that followers are inspired enthusiastically to give unconditional loyalty, devotion, obedience, and commitment to the leader and to the cause the leader represents. A sense of fulfillment and satisfaction is derived from the pursuit of worthwhile activities and goals and having positive beliefs and values about life as presented by the charismatic leader. Implicitly, the charismatic leader is seen as an object of identification by which a follower emulates his or her behavior; thus, followers model their behavior, values, and cognitions after the leader. For example, followers are more likely to set or accept higher goals and have greater confidence in their ability to contribute to the achievement of such goals. By observing the leader display self-confidence, followers develop self-confidence as well.

6. **Describe the characteristics that distinguish charismatic from noncharismatic leaders.**

Charismatic leaders have a compelling vision of the future and are very passionate about it, while noncharismatic leaders are satisfied with the status quo and want to maintain it. The charismatic leader is gifted at communicating ideas and goals in very inspiring ways so that everyone can identify with the message. The charismatic leader is self-confident and has a strong moral conviction in his or her cause and the ability to inspire trust among followers and to empower them to achieve organizational goals. The charismatic leader possesses a high risk orientation, high energy and action orientation, minimum internal conflict, and a self-promoting personality. The charismatic leader's power base is intensely relational and based almost entirely on his or her referent and/or expert power.

7. **Discuss how one can acquire charismatic qualities.**

There are suggested strategies for acquiring or enhancing charismatic qualities. Through training and education, people can enhance their communication skills and learn techniques of crafting visionary statements, and how to empower followers. Through practice and self-discipline, an individual can build his or her self-confidence and develop a personality profile that is warm, positive, enthusiastic, and optimistic.

8. **Explain the difference between socialized and personalized charismatic leaders.**

The charismatic leader seeks to achieve the unconditional commitment and devotion of followers to his or her ideological goals. However, negative charismatic leaders emphasize devotion to themselves more than to ideals, and positive charismatic leaders seek the opposite. It is against this backdrop that negative charismatics are said to have a personalized power orientation and positive charismatics have a socialized power orientation. In the former, ideological appeals are only a ploy to gain power and manipulate and control followers. In the latter, ideological appeals are organization-driven and seek to empower followers to achieve the vision and mission of the organization. Personalized charismatic leaders seek self-glorification, and socialized charismatic leaders seek organizational transformation through empowerment of followers.

9. **Distinguish between charismatic and transformational leadership.**

Both charismatic and transformational leaders can convey a vision and form strong emotional bonds with followers, but not all charismatic leaders can motivate followers to transcend self-interest for the benefit of a higher ideal or societal need. On the other hand, transformational leaders take charismatic leadership one step further in that they, more often than not, can articulate a compelling vision of the future and also influence followers to transcend self-interest for the benefit of society. The vision and values of transformational leaders are more in line with the values and needs of followers. It is on this basis that some have argued that all transformational leaders are charismatic but not all charismatic leaders are transformational. Also, while charisma is in the eye of the beholder, transformational leaders have a more consistent definition.

10. **Explain the difference between transformational and transactional leadership.**

Transactional leadership tends to be transitory, in that once a transaction is completed, the relationship between the parties may end or be redefined. Transformational leadership is more enduring, especially when the change process is well designed and implemented. Transactional leaders promote stability, while transformational leaders create significant change in both followers and organizations. Transformational leadership inspires followers to go beyond their own self-interest for the good of the group. Transactional leadership seeks to satisfy followers' individual needs as a reward for completing a given transaction.

11. **Explain the four phases of the transformation process.**

A transformational leader who is brought into an organization facing a serious crisis or approaching total collapse has to institute a turnaround strategy. Turnaround strategies are often radical transformations that put the organization on a different path for future growth and prosperity. The magnitude of the task and the high risk of failure require that it be approached in a systematic fashion. Thus, the transformation process is a four-phase approach that starts with the recognition of the need for change. This provides the opportunity for the leader to formulate and introduce a new vision for the organization that promises a better and brighter future than the present. Once there is acceptance of the leader's vision, the third phase involves implementing the new vision and effectively managing the transition. Here, instilling in managers a sense of urgency for change, raising followers' self-confidence and optimism, and recognizing and dealing with resistance will greatly increase the chances of a successful transformation. The last phase is institutionalizing the change so that it is not a short-lived transformation. Effective strategies for institutionalizing change are outlined in the text.

12. **Explain the basis of stewardship and servant leadership.**

The basis of stewardship and servant leadership is serving rather than directing other people. It is leadership based on placing others ahead of oneself. Both shine the spotlight on the employees who actually perform the day-to-day task of meeting organizational goals and objectives. The key to successful stewardship is the presence of four supporting values: equal treatment for all, reward for work, teamwork attitude, and decentralized decision making and authority. The key to successful servant leadership is based on four guiding principles as well: service to others over self-interest, trust, effective listening, and empowering others to discover their inner strength.

13. **Define the following key terms (in order of appearance in the chapter).**

Select one or more methods: (1) fill in the missing key terms from memory; (2) match the key terms from the following list with their definitions below; (3) copy the key terms in order from the list at the beginning of the chapter.

__________ is the degree to which people's lives make emotional sense and to which the demands confronted by them are perceived as being worthy of energy and commitment.

__________ is knowing who you are based on your lifespan experiences, motivation states, and action orientation.

__________ is that which allows an individual's accomplishments to "live on" in the ideals, actions, and creations of one's followers, long after his or her death.

__________ is an unselfish regard for or devotion to the welfare of others.

__________ concerns an individual's awareness of connections between human and supernatural phenomena, which provide faith explanations of past and present experiences and, for some, predict future experiences.

__________ are generalized beliefs or behaviors that are considered by an individual or a group to be important.

__________ is a distinct social relationship between the leader and follower, in which the leader presents a revolutionary idea, a transcendent image or ideal which goes beyond the immediate or the reasonable; while the follower accepts this course of action not because of its rational likelihood of success, but because of an effective belief in the extraordinary qualities of the leader.

__________ is the ability to imagine different and better conditions and the ways to achieve them.

__________ is one who possesses an egalitarian, self-transcendent, and empowering personality.

__________ is one who possesses a dominant, Machiavellian, and narcissistic personality.

__________ serves to change the status quo by articulating to followers the problems in the current system and a compelling vision of what the new organization could be.

__________ seeks to maintain stability within an organization through regular economic and social exchanges that achieve specific goals for both the leaders and their followers.

__________ is an employee-focused form of leadership that empowers followers to make decisions and have control over their jobs.

__________ is leadership that transcends self-interest to serve the needs of others, by helping them grow professionally and personally.

Key Terms

charisma, 335

legacy, 331

personal meaning, 330

personalized charismatic leader (PCL), 346

self-belief, 331

selflessness, 332

servant leadership, 357

socialized charismatic leader (SCL), 346

spirituality, 332

stewardship, 357

transactional leadership, 348

transformational leadership, 348

values, 333

vision, 341

Review Questions

1. Describe the various sources from which one can draw his or her personal meaning.
2. Citing specific examples, explain how charismatic leaders of the past used vision and superb communication skills to make their case.
3. Describe the leading characteristics of charismatic leaders.
4. Martin Luther King, Jr., Gandhi, John F. Kennedy, Adolph Hitler, Nelson Mandela, David Koresh (of the Branch Davidians), Herb Kelleher (of Southwest Airlines), and Richard Branson (of the Virgin Group) are/were charismatic leaders. Can you associate with each name a characteristic (see Exhibit 9.3 on page 341) of charisma you think best describes the individual? *Note:* If you are not familiar with these individuals, do library or Internet research on them before attempting an answer.
5. Why is the theory of charisma described as a double-edged sword?
6. Describe the limitations of charismatic leadership theory.
7. Describe four key behaviors characteristic of transformational leaders.
8. Describe some key attributes of transformational leaders.
9. What is servant leadership?

Communication Skills

The following critical-thinking questions can be used for class discussion and/or as written assignments to develop communication skills. Be sure to give complete explanations for all questions.

1. A strong emotional attachment and loyalty to a charismatic leader can have both beneficial and detrimental effects on followers. Explain both types of effects on followers.
2. Charismatic leaders are said to possess special traits that influence their behaviors. Three such traits described in the chapter are envisioning, empathy, and empowerment. Explain how each of these traits influences how followers perceive the charismatic leader.
3. In Chapter 4, different types of power—legitimate, reward, coercive, referent, expert, connection, and information power—and influencing tactics were discussed. What type of power is the charismatic leader most likely to be associated with and why?
4. Explain the importance of effective communication skills for charismatic and transformational leaders.
5. Servant leadership emphasizes being able to serve and lead. In your opinion, is this contradictory or doable?
6. Do you believe everyone has the same capability to become a servant leader, or are some people by their nature more inclined to be servant leaders?

CASE

Anne Mulcahy and Ursula Burns: Xerox's Dynamic Duo

In 1999, Xerox appointed Rick Thoman to be its next CEO. A little more than a year later, with Xerox in financial crisis (as well as having accounting problems that resulted in a $10 million fine), Thoman's predecessor stepped back in to take control and turned to a surprise candidate, Anne Mulcahy, to be his Number 2. On paper, it looked like a desperation choice. *Fortune* magazine called her the "accidental CEO." But she immediately enlisted the strongest talent she could find. A key player was Ursula Burns, an engineering hotshot from Rochester who, despite her smarts, had an equally unlikely history. She had been raised in a housing project on Manhattan's Lower East Side by a hard-working single mother who cleaned, ironed, did child care—anything to see that Burns got a good Catholic education and eventually a graduate degree in engineering from Columbia.

Burns was promoted to first president of Xerox's Business Group Operations, becoming the first woman to hold that position. She was responsible for the engineering center and five separate divisions; together her group brought in 80 percent of Xerox's profits. African-Americans with Burns's background were not common at Xerox, but she never saw her race and low socioeconomic status as a liability. "My perspective comes in part from being a New York black lady, in part from being an engineer," she said. "I know that I'm smart and have opinions that are worth being heard."

While Mulcahy crisscrossed the country reassuring employees and shareholders and refining a plan to save the company, Burns began implementing the plan and streamlining the company. She successfully negotiated a contract with union workers. With Burns's streamlining and Mulcahy's finesse, Xerox went from a company in trouble to one poised to become the leader in sales in its industry. Many at the company placed Burns on the list of Mulcahy's potential successors. In 2007, it became official—CEO Anne Mulcahy named Ursula Burns president. The appointment was made with expectation that Burns would move up when Mulcahy steps down. Burns also became the only inside director on the Xerox board besides Mulcahy. Burns will lead Xerox's corporate strategy, marketing operations, and global accounts, while continuing to run research, engineering, marketing, and manufacturing of technology, supplies, and related services. Her promotion lays out a clear succession plan that eliminates uncertainty inside the organization.

Ursula Burns has been described by many as articulate, knowledgable, energetic, and a straight shooter when dealing with people. Burns has been credited with increasing Xerox's sales of color-capable printers and copiers, as the company brought to market 24 machines in the past two years amid competition from Hewlett-Packard and Canon. Because of Mulcahy's and Burns's leadership, Xerox today offers the broadest portfolio of document management systems and software in its industry and in the company's history. Mulcahy credits Burns with this achievement, saying that she drove a technology strategy that launched more than 100 products in the last three years and strengthened Xerox's business model, making it more efficient, competitive, and profitable.

Go to the Internet: To learn more about Anne Mulcahy and Ursula Burns and Xerox, visit their Web site (**http://www.xerox.com**).

Support your answers to the following questions with specific information from the case and text or with other information you get from the Web or other sources.

1. In your opinion, are Anne Mulcahy and Ursula Burns leaders who exemplify charismatic or transformational leadership qualities?
2. Immediately after Anne Mulcahy was appointed CEO, she tapped Ursula Burns to be her Number 2 and then president of Xerox. What transformational leadership qualities did Burns possess that made her the right person for the job?
3. A key attribute of servant leadership is that it transcends self-interest to serve the needs of others. Does Ursula Burns fit this bill?
4. Ursula Burns has already been picked as the next CEO to replace Anne Mulcahy when she steps down, likely making this the first time a woman CEO for a *Fortune 500* company has turned over the reins to another woman. How would her close working relationship with Mulcahy affect her leadership style?
5. Every leader has a sense of his or her personal meaning, described in the text as the degree to which people's lives make emotional sense and to which the demands confronted by them are perceived as being worthy of energy and commitment. Based on the facts of the case, what are the sources from which Burns derives her personal meaning?

CUMULATIVE CASE QUESTIONS

6. According to the leadership continuum model of Tannenbaum and Schmidt, where would you put Ursula Burns based on the facts of the case (Chapter 5)?
7. Communication is a major competency for leaders (Chapter 6). Would you agree that this is a quality that Burns likely possesses, to have been as effective as she has been so far?
8. Leader–member exchange theory describes the type of relationship that often develops between leaders and followers (Chapter 7). How would you describe the dyadic relationship between Anne Mulcahy and Ursula Burns?
9. One of the characteristics of effective teams is the presence of a capable and competent team leader (Chapter 8). Chapter 8 describes different activities of the team leader in creating an effective team (see Exhibit 8.1 on page 288), including turning obstacles into opportunities. Would you describe Ursula Burns as an effective team leader?

CASE EXERCISE AND ROLE-PLAY

Preparation: Assume you are part of the leadership of an organization or organizational unit that is in need of redirection in a changing market environment. Your task is to formulate a new vision and mission statement that would transform your organization.

Role-Play: The instructor forms students into small groups to develop an inspiring vision of no more than 15 words and a mission statement of no more than 100 words. Here are some guidelines:

1. Identify key environmental trends or changes that have influenced your group's vision.
2. Make up a list of core values that your organization holds, or you would want it to have, and incorporate these in your mission statement.
3. Share your vision and mission statement with other members of the class and vote on who has the most inspiring and compelling vision and mission.

VIDEO CASE

Timbuk2: Former CEO Sets a Course

Making decisions is a big part of any manager's job. Making decisions that determine the direction a company will take is the job of a CEO. Mark Dwight, former CEO of Timbuk2, a manufacturer of bicycle messenger bags, was comfortable with this role, even though it meant sometimes making unpopular decisions—or even making mistakes. Most of the decisions Dwight made at Timbuk2 were non-programmed decisions—such as the design of a new product or the type of fabric to use. These decisions can affect sales, the brand image, and even overall performance of the company. "Mark is the guy with the vision," said marketing manager Macy Allatt. "He will drive decision making, but he's very open to taking input from other people. When decisions need to be made, everyone sits down and we hash it out, and when we come out of the room, we feel like we're going to make some progress." Just about every decision Mark Dwight faced at Timbuk2 had some degree of uncertainty. He knew that he wanted Timbuk2 to achieve $25 million in sales in five years; he knew that he wanted the firm to reach new markets; he knew that the firm needed to find new distribution channels. But there was no guarantee that a single decision would be the right one.

1. Would you describe Timbuk2 former CEO Mark Dwight as a charismatic leader? Why or why not?
2. Does Mark Dwight possess any characteristics of a transformational leader? If so, what are they?

Skill-Development Exercise 1

Is the President of the United States a Charismatic Leader?

Preparing for Skill-Development Exercise 1

Rate the current president of the United States on each of the ten characteristics of charismatic leaders. For each characteristic, rate the president as high (H), medium (M), or low (L). Be sure to provide a specific example (what the president did or said) for why you rate the president as H, M, or L for each characteristic.

a. Vision
b. Superb communication skills
c. Self-confidence and moral conviction
d. Ability to inspire trust
e. High risk orientation
f. High energy and action orientation
g. Relational power base
h. Minimum internal conflict
i. Ability to empower others
j. Self-promoting personality

Based on the text, what specific things do you recommend the president do or say to improve his charismatic leadership?

____

____

____

Doing Skill-Development Exercise 1 in Class

Objective

To develop your ability to assess and advise a leader on charismatic leadership.

The primary AACSB learning standard skills developed through this exercise are analytic skills and teamwork.

Procedure *(10–30 minutes)*

Option A: As a class, go over the preparation and rate the president as high, medium, or low on each charismatic leadership characteristic, and give an overall rating.

Option B: Break into groups of 4 to 6, go over the preparation, and rate the president as high, medium, or low on each charismatic leadership characteristic, giving an overall rating. Be sure to provide a specific example (what the president did or said) for why your group rated the president as H, M, or L for each characteristic.

Option C: Same as B, but also select a spokesperson to present the group's answers to the entire class.

Conclusion

The instructor may lead a class discussion and/or make concluding remarks.

Apply It *(2–4 minutes)* What did I learn from this experience? How will I use this knowledge in the future?

Sharing In the group, or to the entire class, volunteers may give their answers to the "Apply It" questions.

10

Leadership of Culture, Ethics, and Diversity

Chapter Outline

Culture Creation and Sustainability

The Power of Culture

Low- and High-Performance Cultures

Characteristics of Low-Performance Cultures

Characteristics of High-Performance Cultures

The Role of Leadership in Culture Creation and Sustainability

Cultural Value Types

Values-Based Leadership

The Leader's Role in Advocating Ethical Behavior

National Culture Identities—Hofstede's Value Dimensions

Implications for Leadership Practice

Changing Demographics and Diversity

Current State of Workforce Diversity

The Impact of Globalization on Diversity

Reasons for Embracing Diversity

Obstacles to Achieving Diversity

Creating a Culture That Supports Diversity

Diversity Awareness Training and Leadership Education

Learning Outcomes

After studying this chapter, you should be able to:

1. Explain the power of culture in the strategy execution process. p. 371
2. Describe the characteristics of low- and high-performance cultures. p. 373
3. Distinguish between symbolic and substantive leadership actions for shaping organizational culture. p. 378
4. Differentiate between the four cultural value types. p. 382
5. Describe Hofstede's value dimensions of national culture. p. 391
6. Explain the primary reasons for embracing diversity. p. 396
7. Identify and briefly describe the obstacles that make it hard to achieve diversity objectives. p. 398
8. Describe the key indicators of a culture that supports diversity. p. 400
9. Define the following **key terms** (in order of appearance in the chapter):

culture
cooperative culture
adaptive culture
competitive culture
bureaucratic culture
values
ombudsperson
whistle blowing
individualism
collectivism
high uncertainty avoidance
low uncertainty avoidance
high power-distance culture
low power-distance culture
masculinity
femininity
demographic diversity
diversity
prejudice
ethnocentrism
glass ceiling

Opening Case APPLICATION

Andrea Jung has been CEO of Avon Company since November 1999. The oldest child of Chinese immigrants, Jung grew up speaking both English and Mandarin Chinese. Ten years ago, Avon, the world's largest direct seller of women's cosmetics, was experiencing some difficulties. Increasing sales in a market saturated with beauty products and savvy consumers was proving to be a daunting task even for a giant of Avon's stature. Jung gave the company what can only be described as "an extreme makeover," pouring millions into research and development, launching new lines of skin cream, expanding into overseas markets, and developing snazzy ads with celebrities like Salma Hayek. These strategy changes resulted in revenue and profit growth. However, in 2005, Avon was facing some tough times again. With growth slowing and its stock price plunging, Jung told investors in November 2005 that she was embarking on a bold multi-year restructuring plan that will cost about $500 million. Since that announcement, Andrea Jung has cut employee ranks by 10 percent and management by nearly 30 percent. She downsized on the number of product lines and only retained the most successful products. She almost tripled Avon's ad spending from 2005 to 2007 and gained some ground expanding Avon's presence in overseas markets, particularly Asia. She has won the first direct-selling license in China and already has a salesforce of more than 700,000. By all accounts, it appears Jung's strategies are once again paying off. Early results show positive gains in many areas. The share price, sales, and profits of the $15.6 billion company have been trending upward since 2007.

Avon embraces diversity in the workforce and continues to be a leader in taking affirmative action to ensure that doors are opened to talented individuals, and that all associates and employees have opportunities for development and advancement. Avon also strives to create a work environment that values and encourages the uniqueness of each individual, and is committed to creating a culture that supports associates as they balance their many, and sometimes competing, work and personal responsibilities. Andrea Jung has definitely transformed Avon and, in the process, some believe she has given herself a career makeover, with her name cropping up on shortlists of candidates to turn around bigger companies.

Opening Case Questions:

1. Is Avon's culture a contributing factor to its success? Explain.
2. The text points out that an organization's culture serves two important functions: (1) it creates internal unity, and (2) it helps the organization adapt to the external environment. Has this been the case at Avon?
3. The chapter discusses the characteristics of a high-performance (strong) culture. What is the evidence that Avon has a strong culture?
4. Is Avon's culture competitive, adaptive, bureaucratic, or cooperative? Support your answer.
5. What role has Andrea Jung played in fostering a climate of strict ethical standards at Avon?
6. What is Avon's stance on diversity, and has it lived up to it so far?

Can you answer any of these questions? You'll find answers to these questions and learn more about Avon and its leadership throughout the chapter.

To learn more about Avon and Andrea Jung, visit Avon's Web site at **http://www.avoncompany.com**.

In this chapter we examine issues of organizational culture, values, and diversity—and the leader's role in shaping them. A prevailing belief among researchers is that strong corporate cultures improve performance by facilitating internal behavioral consistency.[1] Regardless of the type of business or the size, the organizations that consistently achieve above-average growth and profits share a common characteristic. High-performance organizations have an unmistakable profile that sets them apart from average performers—a profile that includes distinctive characteristics of the corporate culture, the people, the structure, and the type of leadership.[2,3]

Culture Creation and Sustainability

All organizations have a culture, whether they acknowledge it or not. Every organization has a culture, distinguished by its own beliefs and approaches to problem solving and decision making. An organization's culture is manifested in the values, norms, and expectations that leaders preach and practice, in its employees' attitudes and behavior, in ethical standards and policies, in the "chemistry" that permeates its work environment, and in the stories people repeat about events in the organization.[4,5] An organization's position on diversity and multiculturalism, for example, can be attributed to its culture. Within an organization, culture gives meaning to each individual's membership in the workplace and, in so doing, defines the organization's essential purpose. An organization's culture is fairly enduring and can be described as warm and friendly, aggressive/passive, defensive/offensive, conservative/liberal, or innovative.[6]

Increasingly, culture is recognized as a source of competitive advantage.[7] Over the years, researchers have proposed a positive relationship between culture strength and performance.[8,9] Research supports the proposition that organizations with rich, healthy cultures perform better than those with less-defined cultures.[10,11] Studies investigating the effects of organizational culture on the performance of particular types of projects have found significant correlational effects between organizational culture and new product development.[12,13] **Culture** *is the aggregate of beliefs, norms, attitudes, values, assumptions, and ways of doing things that is shared by members of an organization and taught to new members.*[14] Culture is the operating system that brings to life the underlying core values of an organization.[15] Some have described organizational culture as a "shared mental model" or the "social glue" that holds an organization together.[16]

An organization's culture determines the way that it responds to problems of survival in its external and internal environments. The responses to problems in the external environment are reflected in the organization's vision, mission, objectives, core strategies, and ways of measuring success in attaining objectives.[17] The responses to internal problems underscore key aspects of the internal culture, such as revealing how power and status are determined in the organization, the criteria and procedure for allocating resources, the criteria for determining membership, and the guiding principles for interpreting and responding to unpredictable and uncontrollable forces in the external environment.[18]

The values, beliefs, and norms that derive from struggling to adapt to external and internal challenges serve as the basis for role expectations that guide behavior, become embedded in how the organization conducts its business, are shared by managers and employees, and then persist as new employees are encouraged to embrace them. As solutions are developed through experience, they become shared values, norms, and beliefs that are passed to new members. Over time, these elements become so deeply rooted in a culture that organizational members are no longer consciously aware of them. These basic underlying values, beliefs, and norms (whatever they are) become the building blocks of the culture. This evolutionary process is consistent with the view that an organization's culture emerges from the history and experiences of individuals and groups in that particular organization's context.[19]

In the process of culture creation, sustainability, and renewal, the past is often used as an indicator of things to come. The culture is sustained as each successive generation of leaders and followers embraces and passes it to the next through stories, artifacts, rituals, slogans, symbols, and special ceremonies.[20] An example of this would be Sam Walton's conception of Wal-Mart's culture from its early beginnings. The essence of Wal-Mart's culture is dedication to customer satisfaction, zealous pursuit of low costs, and strong work ethic. In addition to that are the ritualistic Saturday morning executive meetings at headquarters to exchange ideas and review problems, and company executives' commitment to visit stores, talk to customers, and solicit suggestions from employees. Creating and sustaining a high-performance culture such as Wal-Mart's is critical to organizational success.

In this section, we will examine the power of culture, high- versus low-performance cultures, the role of leadership in culture creation and sustainability, and cultural value types.

Opening Case APPLICATION

1. Is Avon's culture a contributing factor to its success? Explain.

It is evident in the opening case that organizational culture at Avon is a significant contributing factor to the company's success. Avon enjoys a proud legacy and commitment to women. By the very nature of its products and customer base, Avon has always had a special connection to women. Through the Avon Foundation, the company has created and significantly funded a number of global initiatives to further women's empowerment. Its philanthropic endeavors and diversity initiatives have received worldwide praise and recognition. The health issues that Avon has chosen to champion are the same issues that many of its customers and direct sales representatives care about, and thus a strong bond has developed between the company and its primary stakeholders. The culture of the organization is encapsulated in what it calls "The Five Values of Avon," which are trust, respect, integrity, belief, and humility. According to the company's management, these five values have served as a continuing source of strength throughout Avon's proud history and will remain at the heart of who they are as a company.

Learning Outcome 1 *Explain the power of culture in the strategy execution process.*

The Power of Culture

A deeply rooted culture that is well matched to strategy and external environmental trends is a strong recipe for successful strategy execution, while a weak or "shallow-root" culture can become an obstacle to successful strategy execution.[21] In this context, culture serves two important functions in organizations: (1) it creates internal unity, and (2) it helps the organization adapt to the external environment.[22,23]

Internal Unity

Organizational culture defines a normative order that serves as a source of consistent behavior within the organization. To the extent that culture provides organizational members with a way of making sense of their daily lives and establishes guidelines and rules for how to behave, it is a social control mechanism. A supportive culture provides a system of informal rules and peer pressures, which can be very powerful in determining behavior, thus affecting organizational performance. A strong culture provides a value system in which to operate and it promotes strong employee identification with the organization's vision, mission, goals, and strategy. Culture provides a shared understanding about the identity of an organization.[24] It can transform an organization's workforce into a source of creativity and innovative solutions. Culturally approved behavior thrives and is rewarded, while culturally disapproved behavior is discouraged and even punished. The right culture makes employees feel genuinely better about their jobs, work environment, and the mission of the organization; employees are self-motivated to take on the challenge of realizing the organization's objectives and to work together as a team.[25]

External Adaptation

Culture determines how the organization responds to changes in its external environment. Depending on the volatility in the business environment, some changes are significant enough to force members to question aspects of their organization's identity and purpose. Culture plays a role in informing and supporting sense-making by employees when external changes are severe enough to force members to re-evaluate aspects of their organizational identity and purpose.[26] The appropriate culture type can ensure that an organization responds quickly to rapidly changing customer needs or the offensive actions of a competitor. For example, if the competitive environment requires a strategy of superior customer service, the organizational culture should encourage such principles as listening to customers, empowering employees to make decisions, and rewarding employees for outstanding customer service deeds. The power of culture is in its potential to bring employees together to create a team rather than a collection of isolated individuals when faced with threats from the external environment.

In recent years, the airline industry has witnessed increased emphasis on the creation of a culture that fosters the effective implementation of a strong marketing orientation. This heightened interest stems from the knowledge that sound customer-focused marketing practices provide an important source of competitive advantage in the service sector, which is characterized by high levels of interaction between companies and their customers. This move to a marketing culture has strong support from those who maintain that a strong marketing culture leads to customer satisfaction and retention, which, in turn, yields higher profitability.

Opening Case APPLICATION

2. The text points out that an organization's culture serves two important functions: (1) it creates internal unity, and (2) it helps the organization adapt to the external environment. Has this been the case at Avon?

Avon's employee-centered culture is what helps to guide and sustain its employees' productive behavior. Its emphasis on social responsibility, participation, and empowerment appeals well to Avon's employees. Avon strives to create a work environment that values and encourages the uniqueness of each individual, and is committed to creating a culture that supports associates as they balance their many, and sometimes competing, work and personal responsibilities. The culture of Avon is certainly a factor in explaining the strong bond or internal unity that exists among company employees and also between sales representatives and their customers.

In terms of the culture facilitating external adaptation, Andrea Jung can be credited with directing the successful transformation of Avon Company by defining its vision as the company for women. She is revitalizing Avon's reputation as the world's foremost direct seller of beauty products while leading the company into exciting new lines of business, launching a series of bold and image-enhancing initiatives, and expanding career opportunities for women around the world. She expanded the number of products offered to longtime customers by introducing a line of lingerie and casual wear, proving that she was not afraid to take risks. This generated new revenue from an established consumer base. "We were the first to come out with an alpha hydroxide acid product," she says, as she explains the need to constantly be on the lookout for new products. Andrea Jung has undoubtedly created for Avon a culture that encourages internal unity and external adaptation.

Despite the importance of culture to strategy execution, not too many organizations have credible claims to a high-performance culture. A high-performance culture is a contributing factor to attaining a competitive advantage, while a low-performance culture is the reverse. Therefore, understanding the characteristics of each type is critical to the culture creation process.

Learning Outcome 2 *Describe the characteristics of low- and high-performance cultures.*

Low- and High-Performance Cultures

A growing body of literature documents the economic benefits of investing in a performance-oriented culture that focuses, to a large extent, on values and leadership.[27,28] Organizational cultures vary widely in the extent to which they are woven into the fabric of the organization's practices and behavioral norms. The strength of any culture depends on the degree to which a set of norms and values are widely shared and strongly held throughout the organization. A weak culture symbolizes a lack of agreement on key values and norms, and a strong culture symbolizes widespread consensus, with leadership playing a key role in both situations.[29] The best performers have a high-performance culture that is described as distinctive and very tight and strong; so much so, that members whose values don't match the organization's usually have a short tenure because they are either forced to quit or voluntarily quit.[30] The opposite is true of low-performance cultures. A unique corporate culture makes it difficult for competitors to duplicate or imitate a firm's capabilities and core competencies and thus increases the firm's competitive advantage.[31] This sections draws a distinction between low- and high-performance cultures by highlighting the characteristics of each type.

Characteristics of Low-Performance Cultures

Weak cultures are more likely to be associated with low performance. An organization's culture is weak when there is little agreement on the values, beliefs, and norms governing member behavior. This could be because the leader has not articulated a clear vision for the organization, or because members have not bought into the leader's vision for the organization. Members of the organization typically show no deeply felt sense of identity with the organization's vision, mission, long-term objectives, and strategy. In such organizations, culture has no meaning to the employees and managers. In a weak culture, negatives like gossiping, manipulation, favoritism, lack of communication, and internal conflict prevail. Without knowledge of what the organization stands for or allegiance to any common vision, weak cultures work against or hinder strategy implementation and thus are low performers.[32] Low-performance cultures have some common characteristics that can undermine performance. Exhibit 10.1 lists these characteristics.

EXHIBIT 10.1 Characteristics of Low-Performance Cultures

- Insular thinking
- Resistance to change
- Politicized internal environment
- Unhealthy promotion practices

Insular Thinking

In a low-performance culture, there is a tendency to avoid looking outside the organization for superior practices and approaches. Sometimes a company's past successes and status as an industry leader may lead to complacency. People within these organizations believe they have all the answers. Managerial arrogance and inward thinking often prevent the organization from making the necessary cultural adaptation as external conditions change, thus leading to a decline in company performance.

Enron is a company that exemplifies this characteristic. Up until the news media broke open the Enron case, it was a company wowing Wall Street with its growth and steady earnings gains. What many people did not know until it was too late was that the corporate culture at Enron contained the seeds of its demise, a culture of misstated earnings, highly questionable bookkeeping practices, and persistent effort to keep investors and employees in the dark. It was clearly a culture that promoted and supported insular thinking, with senior management being isolated from those at operational levels, individuals pursuing subgoals that were contrary to overall corporate goals, information flow restricted along a narrow linear channel that effectively foreclosed adverse information from getting to senior management, and a corporate culture of intimidation that discouraged open expression of doubt or skepticism.[33]

Resistance to Change

A second characteristic of low-performance cultures is one that can plague companies suddenly confronted with fast-changing domestic and global business conditions: resistance to change.[34] The lack of leadership in encouraging and supporting employees with initiative or new ideas destroys creativity. Low-performance cultures want to maintain the status quo; as a result, avoiding risk and not making mistakes become more important to a person's career advancement than entrepreneurial successes and innovative accomplishments.

Companies such as Ford, General Motors, Kmart, Sears, and Xerox enjoyed considerable success in years past. But when their business environments underwent significant change, they were burdened by a stifling bureaucracy and an inward-thinking mentality that rejected change. Today, these companies and many others like them are struggling to reinvent themselves and rediscover what caused them to succeed in the first place. As the Chapter 9 case revealed, Xerox seems to be on track in regaining its competitive position.

Politicized Internal Environment

An environment that allows influential managers to operate their units autonomously—like personal kingdoms—is more likely to resist needed change. In a politically charged culture, many issues or problems get resolved along the lines of power. Vocal support or opposition by powerful executives, as well as personal lobbying by key leaders and coalitions among individuals or departments with vested interests in a particular outcome, may stifle important change. Such a culture has low performance because what's best for the organization is secondary to the self-interests of individual players. An example of this is what happened at Enron. Many former Enron employees say that the company's culture became less welcoming with the rise of Jeffrey K. Skilling. Skilling's intense focus on the bottom line and making Enron a success at any cost, changed the culture, making it so competitive that employees were afraid to question irregularities for fear of reprisals. It is reported that on Skilling's watch, the Enron that once prided itself on its close team spirit metastasized into a more ruthless, less humane place where employees could be dismissed in an impersonal way. Enron had become a highly politicized environment in which groupthink was the norm.

Unhealthy Promotion Practices

Low-performance cultures tend to promote managers into higher leadership positions without serious consideration of a match between the job demands and the skills and capabilities of the appointee. For the purposes of rewarding a hard-working manager or a longtime employee, an organization may promote a manager who is good at managing day-to-day operations but is lacking in strategic leadership skills such as crafting vision, strategies, and capabilities or inspiring and developing the appropriate culture. This scenario represents a case of promoting a transaction-type manager into a senior executive position requiring transformation skills. While the former is adept at managing day-to-day operations, if he or she ascends to a senior executive position, the organization can find itself without a long-term vision and lack of leadership in forging new strategies, building new competitive capabilities, and creating a new culture—a condition that is ultimately harmful to long-term performance. Also, where promotions are based on personal considerations (friendship, family ties, favoritism, and so forth) rather than professional considerations, the wrong persons end up in leadership positions. This is symptomatic of a weak and low-performance culture.

Characteristics of High-Performance Cultures

Strong cultures are more likely to be associated with high performance.[35,36] Strong corporate cultures improve firm performance by facilitating internal behavioral consistency. An organization's culture is considered strong and cohesive when it conducts its business according to a clear and explicit set of principles and values. In this culture, management commits considerable time to communicating these principles and values and explaining how they relate to its mission and strategies. Also, these values are shared widely across the organization from top management to rank-and-file employees alike.[37] Trust, respect, honesty, responsibility, accountability, integrity, and high-quality relationships among organizational members characterize high-performance cultures.[38] These culture attributes are firm-specific assets that provide value, and because they are hard for competitors to imitate, help the firm build and sustain a competitive advantage.[39]

A strong culture has a bias for action. There is a desire to get things done, and more importantly, to do them the right way.[40] The right way involves the core values and principles that everyone adheres to.[41] Leaders teach and live the values they espouse.[42] The role of leadership in developing and sustaining a strong culture is critical and is the subject of a separate discussion in the next section.

Some organizations are so dedicated to their values that they terminate managers who perform well but who don't live according to the culture. An example is people who try to get ahead at the expense of others. In strong cultures, values and behavioral norms are so deeply ingrained that they do not change much even when a new leader takes over.

High-performance cultures are results oriented and tend to create an atmosphere in which there is constructive pressure to perform.[43] Also, there is unwavering commitment and support from the organization's key stakeholders—employees, customers, and shareholders.[44] Ultimately, high-performance cultures have what some have described as a culture of discipline—where everyone is responsible to the values of the company, to its standards, and to the purpose it serves.[45] Exhibit 10.2 on the next page lists the key characteristics of high-performance cultures, which are discussed next.[46,47,48]

EXHIBIT 10.2 Characteristics of High-Performance Cultures

- Culture reinforcement tools
- Intensely people oriented
- Results oriented
- Emphasis on achievement and excellence

Culture Reinforcement Tools

Some of these tools include ceremonies, symbols, stories, language, and policies. High-performance cultures pull together these mechanisms to produce extraordinary results with ordinary people. High-performance organizations have ceremonies that highlight dramatic examples of what the company values. Ceremonies recognize and celebrate high-performing employees and help create an emotional bond among all employees. Also, in high-performance cultures, leaders tell stories to new employees to illustrate the company's primary values and provide a shared understanding among workers. They also use symbols and specialized language (such as slogans) to convey meaning and values.

Intensely People Oriented

Organizations with high-performance cultures reinforce their concern for individual employees in many different ways; they

- treat employees with dignity and respect;
- grant employees enough autonomy to excel and contribute;
- cultivate a relationship with employees based on mutual respect and interdependency;
- initiate unique one-to-one relationships with top performers;
- give increased responsibility to the best employees;
- implement mentor programs;
- celebrate employee achievements;
- hold managers at every level responsible for the growth and development of the people who report to them;
- use the full range of rewards and punishment to enforce high performance standards;
- encourage employees to use their own initiative and creativity in performing their jobs;
- set reasonable and clear performance standards for all employees.[49,50,51,52]

An organization that treats its employees this way will generally benefit from higher morale and increased level of job satisfaction, greater employee loyalty, and higher retention rates. A reciprocal relationship develops when organizations are able to attract, retain, and reward outstanding performers. Such employees are more likely to behave in ways that help the organization succeed. The cycle of success that results is called a "virtuous spiral," and according to some, is the key to creating and sustaining a high-performance culture.[53] Intensely people-oriented organizations have decentralized management systems that consider employees an integral part of the organization and place much emphasis on their involvement in decision making.[54] It is the kind of inclusive culture that companies such as Corning, 3M, Microsoft, Google, and others have used to drive technology innovation and high performance.[55]

Results Oriented

High-performance cultures invest more time and resources to ensure that employees who excel or achieve performance targets are identified and rewarded. Control systems are developed to collect, analyze, and interpret employee performance data. Quantitative measures of success are used to identify employees who turn in winning performances. To insure accountability, emphasis is placed on individual goal setting, whereby employees draft performance goals and have them approved by their managers. All employees are trained in how to set goals, and managers are trained in the goal-setting process. There is commitment and motivation to achieve goals. These goals form the basis of manager–employee performance evaluation and feedback. In high-performance cultures, leaders seek out reasons and opportunities to give out pins, buttons, badges, certificates, and medals to those in ordinary or routine jobs who stand out in their performance.

While a discussion of a results-oriented culture tends to emphasize the positive, there are negative reinforcers too. In high-performance cultures, managers whose units consistently perform poorly are quickly replaced or reassigned. In addition, weak-performing employees who reject the cultural emphasis on high performance and results are weeded out. To lessen the use of negative reinforcers, high-performance organizations aim at hiring only motivated, ambitious applicants whose attitudes and work ethic mesh well with a results-oriented work culture.

Emphasis on Achievement and Excellence

High-performance cultures create an atmosphere in which there is constructive pressure to be the best. Achieving excellence requires a corporate culture that holds excellence above all and pursues processes that bring about persistent per-unit cost reductions, zero defects, improved product quality, and extraordinary customer service. Management pursues policies and practices that inspire people to do their best. The thinking is that linking a cultural change, for instance, with improved results, will remind managers of the importance of managing culture and will point to the most efficient way of doing so. When an organization performs consistently at or near peak capability, the outcome is not only more success but also a culture permeated with a spirit of high performance.

A strong culture is a valuable ally when it matches the requirements of a good strategy execution and a formidable enemy when it doesn't. While a shared set of values and beliefs does help in bringing a group of workers together, it can also stifle creative impulses and enforce conformist thinking. Therefore, a strong culture by itself is not a guarantee of success unless it is also aligned to strategy, leadership, and the external environment (a discussion that we will continue in Chapter 11). An organization could have a strong yet dysfunctional culture that hurts performance.[56,57] High-performing organizations place a higher degree of scrutiny on strategy attributes and place more emphasis on leadership and culture styles compared with low-performing organizations.[58] The extent to which an organization's culture supports or subverts internal management controls will determine if it is functional or dysfunctional.

As mentioned earlier, Enron represents a case where a strong corporate culture overcame a well-designed and sophisticated management control system and led to the largest corporate bankruptcy in U.S. history in 2001. With the appointment of Skilling as Enron's new CEO, the company's culture began a radical transformation. With Skilling at the helm, an aggressive performance-oriented culture emerged that not only fostered and rewarded fierce internal competition but also institutionalized and tolerated deviant behavior.[59] Enron's new leadership reshaped its culture in a way that celebrated those who exploited and bent the rules by undercutting management controls. A strong culture that is created through a reckless and aggressive leadership style will lead to followers taking actions that are unethical and even illegal like in the case of Enron.

Work Application 1

Would you describe the culture where you work or have worked as a low- or high-performance culture? Explain your answer.

Opening Case APPLICATION

3. The chapter discusses the characteristics of a high-performance (strong) culture. What is the evidence that Avon has a strong culture?

Andrea Jung has led the way in not only communicating but also modeling the principles and values that Avon espouses. As she puts it, "I have all the responsibilities running this public company, but I also have Avon's philanthropic work, which is so inextricably linked with what the company is at this point." The Avon story, according to Jung, is all about bringing together women from all walks of life who believe that when they join the company they can change their lives. Everyone at Avon seems to share the same dream and aspiration. There is an emotional bond with the mission of the company, and every employee works hard to realize the long-term goals set by Jung and her senior leadership team. She implores her senior leadership to communicate with the rank-and-file openly and frequently.

Applying the **Concept 1**

Low- or High-Performance Culture

Identify each statement as characteristic of a low- or high-performance culture. Write the appropriate letter in the blank before each item.

a. low-performance (weak) culture b. high-performance (strong) culture

____ 1. I think we spend too much time in meetings hearing about our mission.

____ 2. One thing I like about this place is that I can say and do whatever I want and no one says anything about my behavior.

____ 3. I think every department in the company has a copy of the mission statement on the wall somewhere.

____ 4. I know that Jean Claude started the company, but he died ten years ago. Do I have to keep hearing all these stories about him?

____ 5. I find it a bit frustrating because top management seems to change its mind about our priorities whenever it suits them.

____ 6. I wonder how many of the executives here ever climbed so high up the corporate ladder on merit.

____ 7. I enjoy being treated like a person, not like a number or piece of equipment.

____ 8. We get together regularly to celebrate one thing or another.

____ 9. Why do I hear "it's not in the budget" so often around here?

____ 10. I like the way management just tells us what it wants done. It lets us do the job our way, as long as we meet the goals.

Learning Outcome 3 *Distinguish between symbolic and substantive leadership actions for shaping organizational culture.*

The Role of Leadership in Culture Creation and Sustainability

Making sure an organization's culture is aligned with its strategies is among the most challenging responsibilities of leadership.[60] To build and maintain a strong culture, senior managers must have a clearly defined vision, mission, and culture statements that define the way things will be done.

One of the growing trends in the workplace today is toward a greater emphasis on a respectful and trusting environment. A culture that values employees, treats them with respect, and builds trusting relationships at all levels will almost always outperform one that treats its employees the opposite way.[61] This type of culture can transform an organization's workforce into a source of creativity and innovative solutions—an inspiring workplace.[62] Unfortunately, not too many organizations can make the claim of having this type of culture. Changing the culture of an organization to adapt to changes in the environment is a vital leadership responsibility. Effective leadership of culture should be proactive rather than reactive.[63]

To create strong, high-performing cultures, leaders can initiate many different types of organizational processes. Examples of organizational processes that have been studied as tools to embed and reinforce strong, high-performance cultures include the strategy formulation process, the leader's authority and influence, the motivation process, the management control process, the conflict management process, and the customer management process.[64,65] These processes represent actions that require significant leadership involvement or what some refer to as "engaging leadership."[66] Depending on the style or approach used, the outcomes of these processes can significantly influence the culture of the organization. Some of these actions are substantive, while others are primarily symbolic. However, they all have the same positive effect on followers when employed and the opposite when ignored.

Symbolic actions are valuable for the signals they send about the kinds of behavior and performance leaders wish to encourage and promote. The meaning is implied in the action taken. In his book, Schein uses the terms *primary* and *secondary mechanisms* to distinguish between symbolic and substantive actions.[67]

Substantive actions are explicit and highly visible and are indicative of management's commitment to new strategic initiatives and the associated cultural changes. These are actions that everyone will understand are intended to establish a new culture more in tune with the organization's strategy and environment. For example, a leader may set as his or her objective to create a culture that supports ethical behavior. Here the leader's actions in serving as a role model (symbolic), and/or developing a written values statement (substantive), may significantly influence the realization of the objective. Exhibit 10.3 summarizes the ten key leadership actions that offer the greatest potential for shaping organizational culture.[68,69]

EXHIBIT 10.3 Leadership Actions for Shaping Culture

Symbolic Actions
- Leaders serving as role models
- Celebrating achievements
- Interacting face-to-face with rank-and-file
- Matching organizational structure to culture

Substantive Actions
- Matching HR practices to culture
- Matching operating policies and practices to culture
- Creating a strategy–culture fit
- Aligning reward/incentive system with culture
- Matching work environment design to culture
- Developing a written values statement

Leaders Serving as Role Models

Senior executives are role models, and the stories they tell, decisions they make, and actions they take build an implicit cultural image for followers. Employees learn what is valued most in an organization by watching what attitudes and behaviors leaders pay attention to and reward and whether the leaders' own behaviors match the espoused values. Employees want to see that their leaders "walk the talk."[70] For example, top executives leading a cost-reduction effort by curtailing executive perks, and emphasizing the importance of responding to customers' needs by requiring all managers and executives to spend a portion of each week talking with customers and understanding their needs, sets a good example. The message employees get when a leader institutes a policy or procedure but fails to act in accordance with it is that the policy is really not important or necessary. The Enron case mentioned earlier revealed that CEO Skilling's leadership style included deliberate role modeling, teaching, and coaching; which is how he got close associates to align with his unethical and even illegal conduct.[71]

Celebrating Achievements

Leaders can schedule ceremonies to celebrate and honor people whose actions and performance exemplify what is called for in the new culture. Ceremonies reinforce specific values and create emotional bonds by allowing employees to share in important moments. This type of culture helps to retain valued employees. A ceremony often includes the presentation of an award. At Mary Kay Cosmetics, for example, awards and prizes ranging from ribbons to pink automobiles are given to beauty consultants who reach various sales targets.

Interacting Face-to-Face with Rank-and-File

Leaders who are sensitive to their role in creating a high-performance culture make a habit of appearing at ceremonial functions to praise individuals and groups who symbolize the values and practices of the new culture. Effective leaders will also make special appearances at nonceremonial events (such as employee training programs) to stress strategic priorities, values, cultural norms, and ethical principles. They understand the symbolic value of their presence at group gatherings and use the opportunity to reinforce the key aspects of the culture. To organization members, the mere appearance of the executive—and the things he or she chooses to emphasize—clearly communicates management's commitment to the new culture.[72]

Matching Organizational Structure to Culture

Organizational structure can symbolize culture. A decentralized structure reflects a belief in individual initiative and shared responsibility, whereas a centralized structure reflects the belief that only the leader knows what is best for the organization.

Matching HR Practices to Culture

The strongest sign that management is truly committed to creating a new culture is replacing old-culture members who are unwilling to change with a "new breed" of employees. Beyond immediate actions to replace old-culture employees, leaders can influence culture by establishing new criteria for recruiting, selecting, promoting, and firing employees. These new criteria should be consistent with the new culture of the organization. More and more, organizations are looking for employees who understand their culture and are willing to learn to work within it.

In high-performance cultures, policies on recruitment, selection, and training of new employees are different from those in low-performing cultures. For example, companies such as W. L. Gore & Associates, 3M, Southwest Airlines, and Nordstrom often employ careful and vigorous hiring practices. Chapter 7's end-of-chapter case featured W. L. Gore & Associates. As revealed in the case, new employees go through an extensive interviewing process, and when hired, a new employee is assigned a sponsor from within the company. The sponsor, who is usually a veteran of the company, will ensure that the new associate fully understands the company's culture and approach. This ensures that the employee and the organization's culture are compatible, something that more companies are now doing. Southwest Airlines looks first and foremost for a sense of humor in the prospective employee; at 3M, creativity and team spirit are critical, and at Nordstrom, "niceness" is an important cultural value.

Matching Operating Policies and Practices to Culture

Existing policies and practices that impede the execution of new strategies must be changed. Policies on budgets, planning, reports, and performance reviews can be used to emphasize aspects of the organization's culture. Through these actions, leaders let other members know what is important. Wal-Mart executives have had a long-standing practice of spending two to three days every week visiting Wal-Mart's stores and talking with store managers and employees. Sam Walton, Wal-Mart's founder, was dissatisfied with managerial practices that he observed in competitors' stores. To make sure it did not happen at his stores, he insisted on a different policy and practice. He made sure his managers understood his view on this issue. He believed that to be an effective manager, you have to get out into the store and listen to what the associates have to say, because the best ideas come from clerks and stockpersons. Over the years, this practice has become part of Wal-Mart's culture.

Creating a Strategy–Culture Fit

It is the leader's responsibility to select a strategy that is compatible with the prevailing culture or to change the culture to fit the chosen strategy. The lack of a fit will hinder or constrain strategy execution. In rapidly changing business environments, the capacity to introduce new strategies is a necessity if a company is to perform well over long periods of time.[73] Strategic agility and fast organizational response to new opportunities require a culture that quickly accepts and supports company efforts to adapt to environmental change rather than a culture that resists change.

A strategy–culture fit allows for easy adaptation, while a strategy–culture mismatch makes for a difficult adaptation. This is particularly true for high-tech firms that need to fast-track innovation in order to stay competitive. A study exploring the innovation process within the context of strategy, organizational culture, and leadership styles found close associations among these constructs.[74] Even during periods of stability and economic growth, it is still critical for the leader to pay attention to the existing culture. The culture of an organization naturally evolves over time, and without strong leadership it can change in the wrong direction. Key values or practices in a culture may gradually erode if no attention is paid to the culture. For example, incompatible subcultures may develop in various departments of the organization, leading to a culture of isolation rather than teamwork and cooperation.

With mergers and acquisitions dominating global business strategy, the integration of corporate cultures is often the deciding factor in whether a newly merged entity succeeds or fails. It is generally understood that following a merger, a culture assessment needs to be conducted to determine whether the acquired company's culture will mirror the acquiring company's culture, or a new culture will be formed from the merger. Senior leaders can improve the likelihood of a merger's success by ensuring that the two organizations' cultures are in sync, or that an attempt is made to develop a common culture that the two sides agree with.[75]

The damage that can be caused by culture incompatibility is underscored by a series of high-profile mergers and acquisitions that failed to meet expectations. The failed merger of Chrysler and Daimler-Benz comes to mind. Experts and scholars on mergers and acquisitions seem to favor the creation of a completely new corporate culture for merged organizations. They prefer a complete makeover rather than choosing to leave the cultures separate or permitting one culture to dominate. The creation of a new, shared culture in any merged organization may require a careful review of existing practices in the two organizations, the identification and retention of common practices, the introduction of new practices, and the discarding of old, unworkable practices.

Aligning Reward/Incentive System with Culture

Tying compensation incentives directly to new measures of strategic performance (i.e., strategic goals) is a culture-shaping undertaking, because it gives the leader leverage to reward only those performances that are supportive of the strategy and culture. It is often the case that in many organizations, when strategies change, changes to the reward structure tend to lag behind changes to the strategy. Imagine an organization in which the CEO and his or her top management team have articulated an integration-based strategy that will require middle-level leaders to think and act across boundaries and on behalf of the entire enterprise; however, imagine that the organization's reward system offers leaders incentives for achieving unit success, even when they fail to behave as enterprise leaders. Such reward/incentive misalignments weaken an organization's culture.[76]

Matching Work Environment Design to Culture

Leaders can design the work environment to reflect the values they want to promote within the organization. For example, having common eating facilities for all employees, no special parking areas, and similar offices is consistent with a value of equality. An open office layout with fewer walls separating employees is consistent with a value for open communication.

In designing its headquarters, Google wanted to provide open working spaces and an environment that promoted coworker contact and interaction. By providing a clear sense of place and purpose for its employees, Google succeeded in communicating an employee-friendly value through its facility, with the uniqueness and comfort of the setting reinforced by the cultural and aesthetic elements in the building.

Developing a Written Values Statement

Many leaders today set forth their organization's values and codes of ethics in written documents. Written statements have the advantage of explicitly stating the company's position on ethical and moral issues, and they serve as benchmarks for judging both company policies and actions and individual conduct. Value statements serve as a building block in the task of culture creation and maintenance. Exhibit 10.4 presents Starbucks' mission statement as it appears on its Web site. It first identifies the mission, then highlights six guiding value statements that symbolize the culture of the company.

The next section focuses on culture types, using a construct of two interacting elements.

Work Application 2

Identify and briefly explain which of the ten leadership actions for shaping culture have been used by a leader where you work or have worked.

Learning Outcome 4 *Differentiate between the four cultural value types.*

Cultural Value Types

Rather than looking at culture as either good or bad, some scholars view it as a construct that varies according to an organization's external environment and its

EXHIBIT 10.4 Starbucks' Mission Statement

Establish Starbucks as the premier purveyor of the finest coffee in the world while maintaining our uncompromising principles while we grow. The following six guiding principles will help us measure the appropriateness of our decisions:

1. Provide a great work environment and treat each other with respect and dignity.
2. Embrace diversity as an essential component in the way we do business.
3. Apply the highest standards of excellence to the purchasing, roasting and fresh delivery of our coffee.
4. Develop enthusiastically satisfied customers all of the time.
5. Contribute positively to our communities and our environment.
6. Recognize that profitability is essential to our future success.

Source: Used with permission. Copyright © 2008 Starbucks Corporation. **http://www.starbucks.com/aboutus/environment.asp.**

strategic focus. Organizational culture types or styles such as the clan, "adhocracy," hierarchy, and market cultures have been studied for their impact on employee outcome factors such as productivity, job satisfaction, or retention.[77] The variance associated with different culture types supports the view that organizational culture is not a singular, holistic concept. Rather, it is a multifaceted construct with distinct segments that share similar characteristics. Studies have shown that organizations that operate in similar environments will tend to reveal similar cultural value traits. An appropriate match of the right cultural value type, organizational strategy, and external environment can enhance organizational performance.[78]

Another framework for classifying culture types suggests that the match between an organization's environment and its strategic focus results in four types of cultures. The makeup of the culture types is based on two dimensions: (1) the degree of environmental turbulence (stable versus dynamic environment), and (2) the organization's strategic focus or orientation (internal versus external focus). The extent to which an organization's external environment is stable or changing will influence its culture. Also, top management's success strategy may be to focus on internal or external requirements as imperatives for achieving organizational objectives; this too will influence the organization's culture. As shown in Exhibit 10.5,

EXHIBIT 10.5 Types of Organizational Cultures

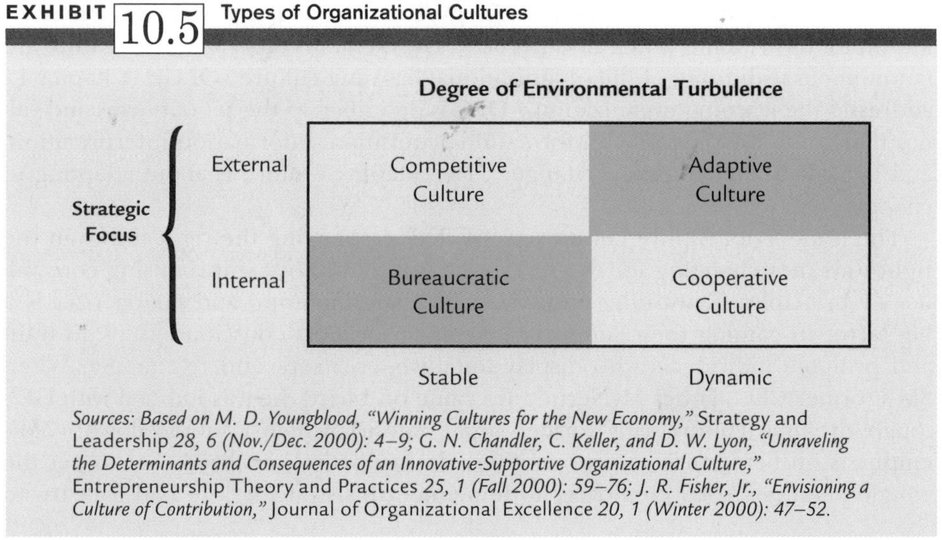

Sources: Based on M. D. Youngblood, "Winning Cultures for the New Economy," Strategy and Leadership *28, 6 (Nov./Dec. 2000): 4–9; G. N. Chandler, C. Keller, and D. W. Lyon, "Unraveling the Determinants and Consequences of an Innovative-Supportive Organizational Culture,"* Entrepreneurship Theory and Practices *25, 1 (Fall 2000): 59–76; J. R. Fisher, Jr., "Envisioning a Culture of Contribution,"* Journal of Organizational Excellence *20, 1 (Winter 2000): 47–52.*

the interaction of these two constructs—degree of environmental turbulence and management's strategic focus—creates four types of organizational cultures.[79]

The four types of organizational cultures are cooperative, adaptive, competitive, and bureaucratic. These cultural types are not mutually exclusive; an organization may have cultural values that fall into more than one group, or even into all groups. However, high-performance cultures with strong values tend to emphasize or lean more toward one particular culture type. The four cultural value types are discussed below.

Cooperative Culture

In a period of change and uncertainty, cooperative culture is seen by some leaders as the key to superior performance. **Cooperative culture** *represents a leadership belief in strong, mutually reinforcing exchanges and linkages between employees and departments.* In this type of culture, operating policies, procedures, standards, and tasks are all designed with one goal in mind—to encourage cooperation, teamwork, power sharing, and camaraderie among employees.[80] Management thinking is predicated on the belief that organizational success is influenced more by employee relationships inside the organization than by external relationships. It is an internally focused culture. Proponents of cooperative culture argue that in today's dynamic work environment, characterized by constant changes and fluid projects, creating a work environment in which workers feel empowered, support one another, share responsibilities and power, and are part of a team creates synergy and increases productivity. It is a culture where employees are trained to think like owners rather than hired hands.

Adaptive Culture

Adaptive culture *represents a leadership belief in active monitoring of the external environment for emerging opportunities and threats.* This culture is made up of policies, procedures, and practices that support employees' ability to respond quickly to changing environmental conditions. In adaptive cultures, members are encouraged to take risks, experiment, and innovate. Management thinking is based on the belief that organizational success is influenced more by events outside the organization than by internal factors. Therefore, employees are empowered to make decisions and act quickly to take advantage of emerging opportunities or avoid threats. There is greater individual autonomy and tolerance for failure. Responsiveness to customer needs is highly valued and rewarded. There is a spirit of doing what is necessary to ensure both short-term and long-term organizational success, provided core values and business principles are upheld in the process. The adaptive culture is generally known for its flexibility and innovativeness. The elements of an adaptive culture are synonomous with those of the organizational learning culture (OLC). (Chapter 12 addresses the learning organization.) OLC is described as the set of norms and values that guide the process of information acquisition, information interpretation, and behavioral and cognitive change.[81] The adaptive culture is about adapting to change.

The leaders of adaptive cultures are skilled at changing the right things in the right ways, not changing for the sake of change, and not compromising core values or principles. Rewarding employees for experimenting and taking risks is a big factor in gaining their support for change. Leaders consciously seek to train and promote individuals who display initiative, creativity, and risk taking. When 3M's former CEO, James McNerney, Jr., came on board, he was imbued with GE's tough dynamic culture (his former organization), which contrasted with 3M's emphasis on being nice to one another. He instinctively realized that to get the conglomerate's 75,000 employees to implement his strategies, he had to learn to work with the culture. He resisted barking orders and tried to win the hearts and minds of employees. His objective was to boost 3M's growth through cost cutting but preserve the company's hallmark of creativity. A company like 3M, where experimentation and risk-taking are a way of life, is a perfect example of the adaptive culture at work.

Competitive Culture

Competitive culture *represents a leadership that encourages and values a highly competitive work environment.* Organizational policies, procedures, work practices, rules, and tasks are all designed to foster both internal competition (employee versus employee, department versus department, or division versus division) and external competition (company versus competitors).[82] An organization with a competitive culture operates in a stable, mature external market environment in which competition for market share is intense. The organization's strategic focus is external because of the need to keep an eye on competitors who are constantly looking for weaknesses to exploit. The mature and saturated state of the consumer markets these firms operate in makes for intense competition.

Leaders of competitive cultures focus on the achievement of specific targets such as market share, revenue, growth, or profitability. This is a numbers-driven culture that values competitiveness, personal initiative, aggressiveness, achievement, and the willingness to work long and hard for yourself or for the team. The drive to win either against one another internally or against an external competitor is what holds the organization together.

PepsiCo and Coca-Cola are two companies that exemplify competitive culture. Both have the vision to be the best in the world. Each company socializes its members to view the other's employees as enemies and to do whatever is necessary to defeat them in the marketplace. High performance standards and tough reviews are used to weed out the weak and reward the strong. At PepsiCo, for example, former CEO Wayne Calloway was known to set backbreaking standards and then systematically raise them each year. Executives who met his standards were generously rewarded—stock options, bonuses, rapid promotions, and first-class air travel—and those who did not would feel the pressure to produce or risk negative consequences such as demotions, transfers, or job termination.

Bureaucratic Culture

Bureaucratic culture *represents a leadership that values order, stability, status, and efficiency.* Leaders in bureaucratic cultures perceive their environments as basically stable with an internal strategic focus. Bureaucratic culture emphasizes strict adherence to set rules, policies, and procedures, which ensure an orderly way of doing business.[83] Organizations with bureaucratic cultures are highly structured and efficiency driven. The bureaucratic culture may work for an organization pursuing a low-cost leadership strategy but not for one pursuing a differentiation strategy.

The bureaucratic culture is becoming increasingly difficult to sustain even for low-cost driven companies because of the growing level of environmental turbulence facing most organizations. Faced with increasing environmental threats, many leaders are forced to (or proactively) make the shift away from bureaucratic cultures because of the need for greater flexibility and responsiveness. In 2001, General Motors (GM) hired a new vice chairman for global product development, Robert Lutz. Lutz's instructions were clear and direct—transform GM's bureaucratic culture. Before Lutz's appointment, GM had been criticized for adapting slowly to changing consumer needs and imposing myriad restrictions on employees' efforts—issues characteristic of the bureaucratic culture. The jury is still out on Lutz's efforts so far.

Work Application 3

Describe which of the four types of organizational cultures (see Exhibit 10.5 on page 383) exist where you work or have worked.

Each of the four cultural value types can be successful under different environmental conditions and organizational orientations. The relative emphasis on various cultural values depends on the organization's strategic focus and on the level of environmental turbulence in its industry. It is the responsibility of strategic leaders to create the fit between strategy and culture, by ensuring that organizations do not persist in cultural types that worked in the past but are no longer relevant because of changing environmental conditions.

The challenge facing many leaders is how to sustain an organization's culture once it has been established or created; especially if it is working well. Several key steps to ensure that a culture is sustained have been proposed. They include

- defining a strategic plan for implementing the company culture;
- using well-trained and experienced employees to train new hires;
- making sure that employees at all levels know what the culture is and accept it;
- instituting a system by which new employees learn the written and unwritten parameters of the culture.[84,85]

Opening Case APPLICATION

4. Is Avon's culture competitive, adaptive, bureaucratic, or cooperative? Support your answer.

Avon's culture fits with three of the four culture types. Avon wants its saleswomen to share ideas with each other and to work together as a team. To facilitate this, Avon provides opportunities for employees to network among themselves. This qualifies Avon as having a cooperative culture. However, Avon is also cognizant of the need to adapt to market and technological changes. According to CEO Andrea Jung, these days, "you have to be part of a technology-driven and technology-resourced beauty company to win over the long run." Avon can also be described as having a competitive culture in the sense that the company is aware of its competitors and is constantly positioning and repositioning its marketing strategies vis-à-vis its competitors. The 2005 restructuring described in the opening case application was implemented with the competition in mind. Andrea Jung did not want to lose ground to her competitors, and that's why she took bold moves to cut costs, launch new products, and increase advertising. The one thing that cannot be said about Avon's culture is that it is bureaucratic. Jung wants broad participation in decision making and encourages managers to meet with followers face-to-face to solicit feedback.

Applying the **Concept 2**

Type of Organizational Culture

Identify each statement as characteristic of one of the types of organizational cultures. Write the appropriate letter in the blank before each item.

a. competitive c. bureaucratic
b. adaptive d. cooperative

____ 11. Things don't change much around here. We just focus on doing our functional tasks to standards.

____ 12. In the airline industry, we keep a close eye on ticket prices to make sure we are not underpriced.

____ 13. At Toyota, we focus on teamwork with much input into decision making to satisfy customers.

____ 14. Being a young Internet company, we go with the flow.

Values-Based Leadership

Values-based leadership examines the influence of an executive's values upon the strategic development of an organization.[86,87] It is a concept that applies not only to larger corporations but to small and medium enterprises as well.[88] **Values** *are generalized beliefs or behaviors that are considered by an individual or a group to be important.* Values permeate our lives and influence our actions.

A leader's decisions and actions reflect his or her personal values and beliefs. Integrity and strong values are considered to be vital traits of good leadership.[89] These traits influence the level of trust that followers have in a leader. Some have argued that trust is central to all transactions.[90] Relationships between leaders and members of an organization are based on shared values and trust. The impact of followers' trust in their leaders cannot be underestimated.

Values-based leadership is also about courage and character. Character provides the moral compass for decision making, especially the tough decisions.[91] Courageous leaders are able to speak out to right wrongs, admit to personal weaknesses, and own up to mistakes. How leaders' ethical values influence follower behavior and performance is the subject of values-based leadership.[92,93] Followers take their cue from the leader, which is why the role of the leader in developing the organization's culture is critical.[94]

The results of a study on the effect of leadership on values-based management revealed that the leader's values and behaviors were significantly related to the values and behaviors of subordinates.[95] Leaders are key in building a values-driven organization.[96] When it comes to upholding high moral values, Dr. Martin Luther King, Jr. was a leader who "talked the talk and walked the talk." He was the embodiment of charismatic, transformational, and values-based leadership.[97]

In some cases the values of the organization, espoused by the CEO, violate society's ethical standards or are not in line with the values of other members of top management. The effect of such perceived organizational value dissimilarity is that it can lead to relationship and task conflicts and affect follower satisfaction and commitment.[98]

In a recent *New York Times* article titled "Where Have All the Chief Financial Officers Gone?" the writer explored the dilemma that confronts some financial executives: what to do if your values do not reflect those of your organization. Lately, given the high-profile accounting scandals in the news, CFOs have found themselves in the position of being the culture's ethical benchmark in their organizations.

In this section, we will examine the leader's role in advocating and enforcing ethical behavior using such tools as a code of ethics handbook, ethics committees, training programs, and disclosure mechanisms. However, before we begin, complete Self-Assessment 1 to determine your personal values in eight areas.

SELF-ASSESSMENT 1

Personal Values

Below are 16 items. Rate how important each one is to you on a scale of 0 (not important) to 100 (very important). Write the number 0–100 on the line to the left of each item.

0—10—20—30—40—50—60—70—80—90—100
Not important *Somewhat important* *Very important*

_____ 1. An enjoyable, satisfying job

_____ 2. A high-paying job

_____ 3. A good marriage

_____ 4. Meeting new people, social events

_____ 5. Involvement in community activities

continued

(Self-Assessment 1 continued)

_____ 6. My relationship with God/my religion

_____ 7. Exercising, playing sports

_____ 8. Intellectual development

_____ 9. A career with challenging opportunities

_____ 10. Nice cars, clothes, home, and so on

_____ 11. Spending time with family

_____ 12. Having several close friends

_____ 13. Volunteer work for not-for-profit organizations like the cancer society

_____ 14. Meditation, quiet time to think, pray, and so on

_____ 15. A healthy, balanced diet

_____ 16. Educational reading, self-improvement programs, TV, and so on

Next, transfer your rating numbers for each of the 16 items to the appropriate columns. Then add the two numbers in each column.

	Professional	Financial	Family	Social
	1. _____	2. _____	3. _____	4. _____
	9. _____	10. _____	11. _____	12. _____
Totals:	_____	_____	_____	_____

	Community	Spiritual	Physical	Intellectual
	5. _____	6. _____	7. _____	8. _____
	13. _____	14. _____	15. _____	16. _____
Totals:	_____	_____	_____	_____

The higher the total in any area, the higher the value you place on that particular area. The closer the numbers are in all eight areas, the better rounded you are.

Think about the time and effort you put forth in your top three values. Is it sufficient to allow you to achieve the level of success you want in each of those areas? If not, what can you do to change? Is there any area in which you feel you should have a higher value total? If yes, which, and what can you do to change?

The Leader's Role in Advocating Ethical Behavior

Studies have found that many successful companies (those with measurable bottom-line revenue and profitability results) are distinguished by their commitment to strong organizational values that emphasize ethical behavior.[99,100] These are the companies that emphasize ethical and socially responsible behavior throughout the organization. Many values make up an organization's culture, but the one that is considered most critical for leaders is ethics. Recall from Chapter 2 that ethics consists of the standards of right and wrong that influence behavior; in Self-Assessment 6 on page 52–53 you determined how ethical your behavior is. Ethics provides guidelines for judging conduct and decision making. However, for an organization to display consistently high ethical standards, top leadership must model ethical and moral conduct.[101]

Values-based leaders cultivate a high level of trust and respect from members, based not just on stated values but on their willingness to make personal sacrifices for the sake of upholding values.[102] A leader's ethics reflect the contributions of diverse inputs, including personal beliefs, family, peers, religion, education, and experiences in the broader society. The family and religious upbringing of leaders often influence the principles by which they conduct business. A leader's personal beliefs may enable him or her to pursue an ethical choice even if the decision is unpopular. Some of the tools available for leaders to use in enforcing ethical behavior are discussed below.

Code of Ethics

Many leaders today set forth their organizations' values and codes of ethics in written documents. Written statements have the advantage of explicitly stating the company's position on ethical and moral issues, and they serve as benchmarks for judging both company policies and actions and individual conduct. A growing number of organizations have added a code of ethics to their list of formal statements and public pronouncements.

According to a study by the Center for Business Ethics, 90 percent of *Fortune 500* companies now have a code of ethics. The lesson from these companies is that it is never enough to assume that activities are being conducted ethically, nor can it be assumed that employees understand that they are expected to act with integrity.

Leaders must consistently communicate to members the value of not only observing ethical codes but also reporting ethical violations. "Gray areas" must be identified and openly discussed with members, and procedures created to offer guidance when issues in these areas arise. It is generally believed that the more an organization's employees are aware of proper conduct, the more likely they are to do the right thing. A code of ethics is of no consequence if an ethical corporate culture and top management support are lacking; it is more than just a formal document stipulating company policies and procedures.

Some organizations include ethics as part of their mission. Such mission statements generally define ethical values as well as corporate culture, and contain language about company responsibility, quality of product, and treatment of employees. Developing an effective code of ethics program should incorporate some key components: leaders model expected behaviors, ethics is a core element of the corporate culture, everyone participates in creating the guidelines, ethics is discussed openly, and rules are applied consistently. Exhibit 10.4 on page 383, featuring Starbucks Corporation's mission statement, contains a set of six guiding principles that illustrates how the company's mission and core values translate into ethical business practices.

Ethics Committees

In order to encourage ethical behavior, some organizations are setting up ethics committees charged with overseeing ethical issues. In other organizations the responsibility is given to an ombudsperson. *An ethics* **ombudsperson** *is a single person entrusted with the responsibility of acting as the organization's conscience.* He or she hears and investigates complaints and points out potential ethics failures to top management. In many large corporations, ethics departments with full-time staff are charged with helping employees deal with day-to-day ethical problems or questions.

Training Programs

Training provides the opportunity for everyone in the organization to be informed and educated on the key aspects of the culture. Training teaches employees how to incorporate ethics into daily behavior. In short, training helps to align member behaviors with the organization's values. Starbucks Corporation uses new employee training to ingrain values such as embracing diversity, taking personal responsibility, and treating everyone with respect.

Many scholars and practitioners now believe that business schools need to play a greater role in instilling ethical values in their students, who are, after all, future business practitioners.[103,104] Students must come to embrace a holistic view of business performance that involves not only the economic imperative of profit generation but also the fiduciary imperative of ethically anchored and socially responsible behavior.[105,106]

Disclosure Mechanisms

As part of enforcing ethical conduct, employees are encouraged to report any knowledge of ethical violations. **Whistle blowing** *is employee disclosure of illegal or unethical practices on the part of the organization.* In 2002, the scandals surrounding companies such as Enron and WorldCom left many people wondering why no one blew the whistle on these practices sooner. Later that year, *TIME Magazine* named

Work Application 4

Discuss which of the four mechanisms for advocating ethical behavior exist where you work or have worked.

three women, including Sherron Watkins of Enron Corporation, as People of the Year. Whistle blowing can be risky for those who choose to do it—they have been known to suffer consequences including being ostracized by coworkers, demoted or transferred to less-desirable jobs, and even losing their jobs.[107] Policies that protect employees from going through these setbacks will signal management's genuine commitment to enforce ethical behavior. Some organizations have done this by setting up hotlines to give employees a confidential way to report unethical or illegal actions. According to a report from nonprofit organization Public Concern at Work, employees are now twice as likely to blow the whistle on workplace wrongdoing as they were five years ago.[108]

Opening Case APPLICATION

5. What role has Andrea Jung played in fostering a climate of strict ethical standards at Avon?

In September 2004, Andrea Jung delivered the following message to Avon's Associates Worldwide that would seem to address this question. She described Avon's business environment as one that is continually more challenging and complex, particularly for a company such as Avon that conducts business in almost every country in the world. She indicated that only through the highest ethical conduct, and through a corporate culture that recognizes the value of compliance with these standards, can Avon look forward to continued success in the future. Avon's impeccable reputation, she said, is built upon a proud heritage of doing well by doing right. "For more than a century," she continued, "we have been setting the very highest example of integrity and ethics in all of our relationships—with our shareholders, associates, and representatives; our suppliers and competitors; governments; and the public. Our values and principles are the bedrock not only of Avon's past—but of its future."

On Avon's company Web site, the following declaration underscores its commitment to maintaining the highest ethical standards: "At Avon, we strive always to maintain the highest standards of integrity and ethical conduct, consistent with our Company values and in compliance with both the letter and spirit of all applicable laws and regulations. Each Avon Associate is individually responsible for strict compliance with the policies applicable to their work. Information published on this site reflects our commitment to upholding the highest of standards in the area of ethics, corporate governance and compliance." In 2004, Avon's Ethics Education Team created a new Code of Business Conduct and Ethics, as well as a mandatory ethics seminar for Avon's 47,700 associates around the world.

Avon continues to enjoy an unmatched reputation for integrity and business conduct. *Business Ethics* magazine has rated Avon one of the 100 Best Corporate Citizens for six consecutive years. In 2001, *TIME Magazine* declared Andrea Jung one of the 25 Most Influential Global Executives, and in January 2003, she was featured in *Business Week* as one of the best managers of the year. She has been ranked among *Fortune* magazine's "50 Most Powerful Women in Business" for the past five years, including being ranked at #3 for 2003 and 2004. In 2004, *The Wall Street Journal* named Jung one of "50 People to Watch in Business" and *Newsweek* magazine named her one of "10 Prominent People to Watch in 2005." One can safely assume that Andrea Jung's leadership actions are responsible for shaping Avon's culture and ethical climate.

When faced with difficult decisions, values-based leaders know what they stand for, and they have the courage to act on their principles regardless of external pressures. A manager's values, however, are shaped by differences in national or societal culture. The following section describes a framework for understanding the bases of broad national cultural differences.

Learning Outcome 5 *Describe Hofstede's value dimensions of national culture.*

National Culture Identities—Hofstede's Value Dimensions

Whether organizational or national, culture is a product of values and norms that people use to guide and control their behavior. Relationships between leaders and members of an organization are based on shared values. On a national level, a country's values and norms determine what kinds of attitudes and behaviors are acceptable or appropriate. The people of a particular culture are socialized into these values as they grow up, and norms and social guidelines prescribe the way they should behave toward one another.

Significant differences between national cultures exist and do indeed make a difference—often substantial—in the way people of that culture behave toward one another; especially employees in multinational corporations who have to travel and work in other cultures. Each unique culture has overt and subtle differences that influence how its members behave and interact with others.

Global Leadership and Organizational Behavior Effectiveness (GLOBE) is a research program dedicated to examining the relationship between national culture and attributes of effective leadership in 61 nations. GLOBE examines national cultures in terms of nine dimensions: performance orientation, future orientation, assertiveness, power distance, humane orientation, institutional collectivism, in-group collectivism, uncertainty avoidance, and gender egalitarianism.[109] GLOBE's nine value dimensions incorporate some of Geert Hofstede's dimensions. In this section, we explore national culture value types. We will focus on Hofstede's five key dimensions of national culture value types and the implications for leadership practice.[110] Exhibit 10.6 summarizes these values, which are briefly discussed in the following sections.

EXHIBIT 10.6 A Framework of Value Dimensions for Understanding Cultural Differences

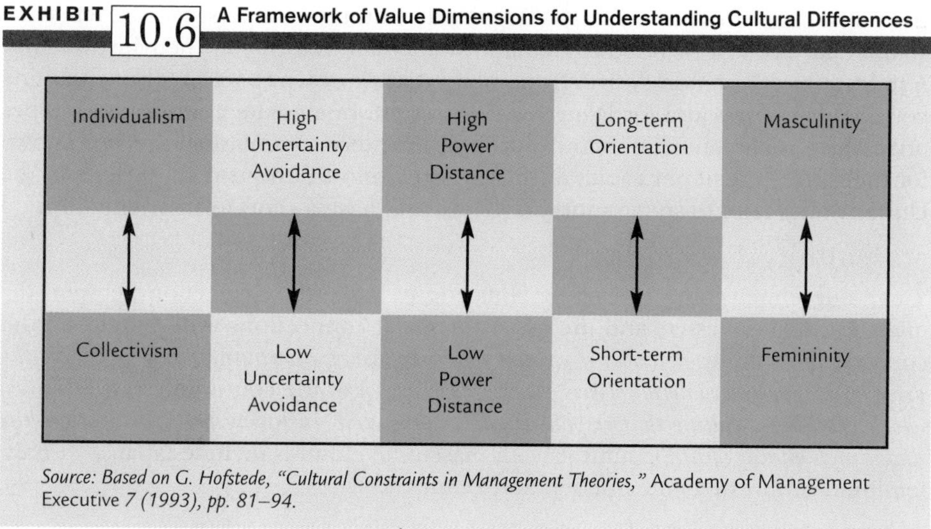

Source: Based on G. Hofstede, "Cultural Constraints in Management Theories," Academy of Management Executive *7 (1993), pp. 81–94.*

Individualistic to Collectivistic Cultures

This dimension involves a person's source of identity in society. Some societies value individualism more than collectivism, and vice versa. **Individualism** *is a psychological state in which people see themselves first as individuals and believe their own interest and values are primary.* **Collectivism** (at the other end of the continuum) *is the state* *of mind wherein the values and goals of the group—whether extended family, ethnic group, or company—are primary.*[111] The United States, Great Britain, and Canada have been described as individualistic cultures, while Greece, Japan, and Mexico are said to have collectivistic cultures.

High to Low Uncertainty Avoidance Cultures

A society with **high uncertainty avoidance** *contains a majority of people who do not tolerate risk, avoid the unknown, and are comfortable when the future is relatively predictable and certain.* In a high uncertainty avoidance country like Japan, managers prefer well-structured and predictable situations. The other end of the continuum is a society where the majority of the people have **low uncertainty avoidance;** *most people in this culture are comfortable with and accepting of the unknown, and tolerate risk and unpredictability.* The United States, Australia, and Canada are associated with low uncertainty avoidance cultures while Argentina, Italy, Japan, and Israel are associated with high uncertainty avoidance cultures.

High to Low Power-Distance Cultures

This dimension deals with society's orientation to authority. The extent to which people of different status, power, or authority should behave toward each other as equals or unequals is referred to as *power distance. In a* **high power-distance culture,** *leaders and followers rarely interact as equals; while in a* **low power-distance culture,** *leaders and their members interact on several levels as equals.* In an organization with a high power-distance culture, the leader is the primary decision maker while in a low power-distance culture, decision making is a group-oriented and participative activity.[112,113] High power-distance cultures include Mexico, Japan, Spain, and France. Low power-distance cultures include Germany, the United States, and Ireland.

Long-Term to Short-Term Oriented Cultures

This dimension refers to a society's long- or short-term orientation toward life and work. People from a culture with a long-term orientation have a future-oriented view of life and thus are thrifty (saving for the future) and persistent in achieving goals. They are less inclined to demand immediate returns on their investments. A short-term orientation derives from values that express a concern for maintaining personal happiness and for living for the present. Immediate gratification is a priority. Most Asian countries, known for their long-term orientation, are also known for their high rate of per capita savings, whereas most European countries and the United States tend to spend more, save less, and have a short-term orientation.

Masculinity–Femininity

This value dimension was used by Hofstede to make the distinction between the quest for material assets and the quest for social connections with people. In this context, **masculinity** *describes a culture that emphasizes assertiveness and a competitive drive for money and material objects.* At the other end of the continuum is **femininity,** *which describes a culture that emphasizes developing and nurturing personal relationships and a high quality of life.* Countries with masculine cultures include Japan and Italy; feminine cultures include Sweden and Denmark.

Work Application 5

Based on the five value dimensions discussed, briefly explain the level of cultural understanding that exists where you work or have worked.

Implications for Leadership Practice

The growing diversity of the workforce and the increasing globalization of the marketplace create the need for leaders with multicultural backgrounds and experiences. Multicultural leaders possess competencies (skills and abilities) that enable them to relate effectively to and motivate people across race, gender, age, social strata, and nationality.[114] Leaders have to recognize, for example, that although organizations in the United States may reward and encourage individual accountability, a different norm applies in industrialized Japan, where the group makes important decisions. In the United States, competition between work-group members for career advancement is desirable. In some other cultures, however, members resist competing with peers for rewards or promotions to avoid disrupting the harmony of the group or appearing self-interested.

Cross-cultural and international joint venture (IJV) studies often identify cultural differences as the cause of many interpersonal difficulties, including conflict and poor performance. Often, people on different sides of an issue see only their side as morally justifiable. Nonetheless, in today's global economy, people holding contrasting values need to work together. Dealing with diverse and divergent values will be an increasingly common challenge for leaders. Both leaders and followers will have to learn to minimize conflicts and tensions that may result from value differences.

Finally, it is important to note that people working across cultures are frequently surprised by cultural paradoxes that do not seem to fit the descriptions in Exhibit 10.6 on page 391. Here are two examples to illustrate this point:

1. Based on Hofstede's value dimensions of uncertainty avoidance, the Japanese have a low tolerance for uncertainty while Americans have a high tolerance. However, Japanese are known to intentionally incorporate ambiguous clauses into their business contracts, which are unusually short, while Americans dot every *i*, cross every *t*, and painstakingly spell out every possible contingency.
2. Americans are described as individualistic and believe deeply in self-reliance, yet they have the highest percentage of charitable giving in the world.

These examples contradict and confound attempts to neatly categorize cultures. For managerial applications, the way to reconcile these paradoxes or contradictions is through "value trumping." According to this concept, in a specific context, certain cultural values take precedence over others. The experts agree that culture is embedded in the context and cannot be understood fully without taking it into account. Another limitation of these constructs has to do with research efforts to measure and validate them accurately. So far results have been mixed.[115,116] Strategies for effectively managing multicultural work groups with value differences are discussed in the next section on diversity.

Ethical **Dilemma 1**

Buy American

Organizational culture is also based on national culture. People tend to believe their country or company is the best. You most likely have heard the slogan "Buy American." Unions tend to ask Americans to buy products made in the United States to help save their jobs. On the other hand, some Americans ask why they should buy American products, especially if they cost more or they are inferior in quality or style to foreign-made products. Many (or most) Americans don't know the country of ownership of many products they buy, and some products are made with more than half of the components coming from other countries—so is the product really made in America?

1. Is it ethical and socially responsible to ask people to buy American, or from their home country?
2. Is it ethical and socially responsible to buy foreign products?

Changing Demographics and Diversity

In the United States and many other societies of the industrialized world, multiculturalism is a fact of life.[117] A number of factors have contributed to make diversity a key leadership issue in the United States. Among these are the Civil Rights Acts, which outlawed most types of employment discrimination; increased immigration, which has resulted in a more racially and ethnically mixed population; and the trend of globalization, which has increased the need for multicultural awareness and understanding. Add to these factors the changing demographic landscape of the United States. **Demographic diversity** *is any characteristic that serves as a basis for social categorization and self-identification.*[118]

Diversity is a way of life in just about every organization today because of ongoing demographic trends reflected in the increasing number of Hispanics, African-Americans, and Asians in the workforce; an aging population; and a growing female labor force.[119,120] The population of these minority groups is growing at a faster rate than the overall society.[121] The U.S. Census Bureau projects that the number of Hispanics, already the largest minority group, will increase to 15 percent of the population by 2021. This group grew by over 40 percent in the 1990s. The percentage of African-Americans is expected to increase to 14 percent by 2021. Longer term, Caucasians are expected to become a minority by 2050. Four states (California, Hawaii, New Mexico, and Texas) currently have the distinction of having a combined minority population greater than white populations.[122]

The aging trend has now created what some are calling generational diversity in the workplace.[123] For the first time, four distinct generations comprise today's workforce—the Traditionalists (1900–1945), the Baby Boomers (1946–1964), the Generation Xers (1965–1980), and the Millennials (1981–2000). Summed up, these trends all point to one issue: diversity. Many CEOs of *Fortune 500* companies have acknowledged that diversity is a strategic business imperative. **Diversity** *is the inclusion of all groups at all levels in an organization.*

The United States has been described as the "melting pot" of cultures. The thinking not long ago was that to make it in this society, one had to blend in with the mainstream culture. Individuals from different cultures responded to this pressure by trying to lose or disguise their identity—adopting new names, changing accents, and abandoning old customs, traditions, and values. The prevailing belief was that to get ahead, one had to assimilate into mainstream culture. Job opportunities favored those who blended in. Now, however, it would appear that the *melting pot* concept has been replaced by the *salad bowl* concept. Rather than assimilation, the emphasis has shifted toward cultural integration without necessarily losing one's identity.

Diversity in the workplace, brought on by a multicultural society, is no longer viewed as a liability but an asset. Many organizations have found that tapping into diversity brings new and innovative ways of viewing traditional problems, and that diversity provides a rich mix of talents for today's globally competitive marketplace.

In this section, we explore the current state of diversity in the U.S. workforce, the impact of globalization on diversity, reasons for embracing diversity, obstacles to achieving diversity, and strategies organizations are employing to achieve full diversity.

Current State of Workforce Diversity

Diversity describes differences resulting from age, gender, race, ethnicity, religion, and sexual orientation. Dramatic changes are taking place in the workforce. National demographic changes, as well as greater minority representation in the workforce, have accounted for the most significant increase in workforce diversity.[124]

One study described the impact of African-American and Latino women in the U.S. labor movement as " a force to be reckoned with."[125] In 2005, African-American and Hispanic employees made up over 25 percent of the workforce, while the percentage of Caucasian males decreased from 51 percent to 44 percent.[126] A greater likelihood exists that individuals will find themselves leading or under the leadership of someone demographically different from them.

In the new work environment, workers must often share work duties and space with coworkers of diverse races, social backgrounds, and cultures.[127] The passage of the Americans with Disabilities Act (ADA) has further broadened the scope of diversity in the workplace. Today, the chances of working with a disabled coworker are much higher than a decade ago. In the last 25 years, attitudes toward diversity have and continue to change. There is now talk of diversity management competency in recruiting and training leaders. There is a growing interest in research on investigating the impact of diversity in management and firm performance.[128,129] Companies that can effectively manage diversity will be able to recruit from a larger pool, train and retain superior performers, and maximize the benefits of this diverse workforce.[130] More organizations are highlighting diversity in their advertising, because they are competing for talent in a tight labor market, and they recognize that demographic shifts are going to dramatically change their marketplace over the next 20 years.

Work Application 6

Describe diversity where you work or have worked. For example, approximately what percentage are male versus female, Caucasian versus non-Caucasian, older versus younger, and so on?

The Impact of Globalization on Diversity

The other factor that has led companies to value and manage diversity is globalization. Corporations are becoming more global and hence more ethnically diverse as well.[131,132] The economies of the world are interconnected, and changes in one economy quickly affect others. Corporations are becoming increasingly global,[133] pursuing merger and acquisition strategies around the world. Globalization has led firms to originate, produce, and market their products and services worldwide.

The emergence of a largely borderless economic world has created a new reality for organizations of all shapes and sizes. A global labor market is emerging, dominated by India and China.[134] United States-based companies such as Pepsi-Cola, Coca-Cola, Procter & Gamble, GE, GM, AT&T, Ford, Nike, General Mills, Boeing, McDonald's, and many others have established a significant presence in China and India; partly motivated by cheap labor and a sizable consumer market.[135] They face competition from European companies such as Daimler-Benz, Nestlé of Switzerland, Canada's Northern Telecom, Siemens of Germany, Sweden's Ericsson, and many others who also have a significant presence in the United States. These corporations are having to deal with a diverse cross-cultural workforce, customers, competitors, suppliers and financial institutions.[136] Collaboration among these companies has become a common way to meet the demands of global competition and to overcome the growing trend of consumer ethnocentrism, which is the tendency to want to purchase products from one's own country rather than a foreign country. Global strategic alliances between independent firms for the purpose of achieving common goals and overcoming domestic country bias are becoming quite prevalent. General Mills and Nestlé of Switzerland created Cereal Partners Worldwide for the purpose of fine-tuning Nestlé's European cereal and for marketing and distributing General Mills cereals worldwide.

In this global environment, understanding cultural differences and learning to deal effectively with partners from different cultures will be critical. This may partially explain why the number of foreign-born managers being appointed to lead U.S. companies is increasing. Multinational companies are interested in recruiting leaders who have multicultural experiences for obvious reasons. To be successful in the global marketplace, companies need to recruit executives with global mindsets and cross-cultural leadership abilities. Despite this reality, 85 percent of *Fortune 500* companies have reported a shortage of global managers with the necessary skills.[137]

Almost every employee in the workforce today is dealing with a wider range of cultures than ever before. The challenge for organizational leaders is to recognize that each person can bring values and strengths to the workplace based on his or her own unique backgrounds. Also, leaders must recognize that cultural values and norms can shape employee receptivity to leadership styles. For example, some argue that certain cultural value types (such as individualistic or collectivistic cultures) may enhance or weaken employee receptivity to transactional and transformational leadership styles.[138] As we discussed in Chapter 9, transformational leaders inspire their followers by focusing on the importance of team values and collective interests, while transactional leaders focus on clarifying roles and task requirements and offering specific rewards based on established performance standards.[139] By extension, we can assume that employees from a collectivistic culture may be more receptive to a transformational than a transactional leadership style.

Learning Outcome 6 *Explain the primary reasons for embracing diversity.*

Reasons for Embracing Diversity

Decades of research have confirmed what many in the business world already know—that diversity makes for good business.[140,141] From a purely humanistic perspective, some believe that there is an ethical and moral imperative to pursue a policy of inclusion rather than exclusion. Advocates of this position believe that it is a matter of fairness, and that an inclusionary policy signals a company's commitment to uphold the dignity of every person regardless of their circumstance.

From a legal perspective, embracing diversity is in compliance with laws that have precedent and historical foundations. From a practical perspective, shifting demographics and increasing globalization have significantly changed the composition of the workforce, forcing corporations to respond or suffer economic loss.[142] Organizations are forced to change their views and their approach to diversity in order to reflect this new reality. Regardless of the moral, legal, or practical imperative of diversity, it must also have a positive link to the "bottom line." Diversity initiatives that succeed in the short and long term are those that have a tangible impact on shareholder, customer, and employee values.

Some of the performance outcomes that make the case as to why organizations need to embrace diversity include the following:[143,144]

- Embracing diversity can offer a company a marketing advantage. There is much support for the view that having a multicultural workforce, supplier network, and customer base is good for business. A diversified workforce may offer insight into understanding and meeting the needs of diverse customers.[145] A representative workforce facilitates selling goods and services, because employees who share similar cultural traits with the customers may be able to develop better, longer-lasting customer relationships.[146] Diversity, therefore, can enable a company to gain access to and legitimacy in diverse markets.
- Embracing diversity can help a company to develop and retain talented people. When an organization has a reputation for valuing diversity, it tends to attract the best job candidates among women and other culturally diverse groups. For example, many HR recruiters have discovered that focusing on diversity in recruitment advertising helps attract more applicants from diverse areas. There

is some evidence that minority job seekers tend to look for companies with a proven diversity record.

- Embracing diversity can be cost effective. As organizations become more diversified, some are experiencing higher levels of job dissatisfaction and turnover among minority groups who are finding it hard to fit in with the old, Caucasian-male dominated culture. This has been the case with organizations that have not shown a total commitment and support for diversity. Organizations that wholeheartedly embrace diversity and make everyone feel valued for their contributions may increase the job satisfaction of diverse groups, thus decreasing turnover and absenteeism and their associated costs.
- Embracing diversity may provide a broader and deeper base of creative problem solving and decision making. Creative solutions to problems are more likely to be reached in diverse work groups than homogeneous groups.[147,148] In diverse groups, people bring different perspectives, knowledge, information, expertise, and skills to problems—resulting in better solutions and greater innovation.[149,150] In innovative companies, leaders are challenged to create organizational environments that nurture and support creative thinking and the sharing of diverse viewpoints.

There is no consensus on the effects of diversity on business performance—there are those who feel that diversity leads to better outcomes (such as those listed above) because of the richness of diverse perspectives, and those who feel that diversity impedes performance because diverse teams are less cohesive.[151] There is an implicit assumption that people are capable and willing to exchange ideas with little or no misunderstanding. However, this is not always the case as members in diverse teams may not feel safe or confident expressing their viewpoints. Therefore, the important factor is how people in diverse teams interrelate—part of the discussion in Chapter 8 on team effectiveness. Different experiences, functional backgrounds, and viewpoints without strong working relationships don't make for a productive or effective team.[152,153] This is what we describe as the downside of diversity, and it's the focus of the next section.

The Downside of Diversity

Despite its benefits, diversity can also bring about negative outcomes if not effectively managed. Research suggests that, left unmanaged, workforce diversity is more likely to damage morale, increase turnover, and cause communication difficulties and ultimately conflict.[154] This may occur because, in general, people feel more comfortable dealing with others who are like themselves. When individuals are brought together in a highly diverse work setting, member differences of any kind can complicate information exchange and coordination and result in stalemate or even conflict.[155,156] Rather than a unified team, competition with and even distrust toward one another may characterize a diverse work environment and ultimately lead to a decline in performance.[157]

A leader in a diverse work unit may spend more of his or her time and energy dealing with interpersonal conflicts rather than trying to achieve organizational objectives. Therefore, effective management of diversity requires creating an environment where all workers can succeed professionally and personally. Managing diversity has emerged as a much sought-after managerial skill and has spawned an industry of diversity training programs.[158]

Experts caution that simply responding to legislative mandates does not seem to automatically result in meaningful, substantive changes in behaviors and attitudes. Rather, change aimed at valuing diversity must have top management support and commitment, have broad participation through empowerment, involve multiple initiatives, and require constant reinforcement.

According to many diversity scholars, diversity management is now considered a new organizational paradigm that has moved beyond a human resource model based solely on meeting legal standards to one that promotes the inherent value of a multicultural workforce. This new model emphasizes that creating a culture of acceptance requires major, systematic, company-wide, planned change efforts, which are typically not part of standard affirmative action plans.[159] The next section examines obstacles to achieving diversity.

Learning Outcome 7 *Identify and briefly describe the obstacles that make it hard to achieve diversity objectives.*

Obstacles to Achieving Diversity

To increase performance, organizations have to unleash and take advantage of the potential of a diverse workforce; however, leaders often face a number of personal and organizational obstacles to realizing the full potential of diverse employees. Removing obstacles to diversity is in effect a transformation from an organizational culture characterized by exclusionary practices to one characterized by inclusionary practices. Exhibit 10.7 lists five obstacles to achieving diversity. Each is briefly discussed below.

EXHIBIT 10.7 Obstacles to Achieving Diversity

- Stereotypes and prejudice
- Ethnocentrism
- Policies and practices
- The glass ceiling
- Unfriendly work environment

Stereotypes and Prejudice

This is perhaps the most prevalent obstacle to achieving diversity in many organizations. **Prejudice** *is the tendency to form an adverse opinion without just cause about people who are different from the mainstream in terms of their gender, race, ethnicity, or any other definable characteristic.* It is an assumption, without evidence, that people who are not part of the mainstream culture (women, African-Americans, and other minorities) are inherently inferior, less competent at their jobs, and less suitable for leadership positions.[160]

A study designed to test the notion of whether there have been changes in the perception of women as leaders found mixed results. Male managers seemed to have changed their view about women over the past 30 years, perceiving them as capable of successful leadership; while stereotypes held by male students changed less, remaining strikingly similar to stereotypes held by male managers 15 years ago.[161] Stereotypes and prejudice often lead to discrimination and sexual harassment.[162,163]

Very few women and African-Americans are hired into the top executive ranks of major U.S. corporations. Stunned by highly publicized sexual harassment charges and costly lawsuits, many Wall Street firms have implemented strict sexual harassment policies with the hopes of changing their "old boys club" image.[164]

Another related problem involving workplace relationships that can create stereotypes and prejudice is stigmatization. This is the negative reactions that some members receive from other members because of personal characteristics or personality traits such as sexual orientation, race, physical attractiveness, or even one's socioeconomic status.[165] Leadership commitment toward eradicating stereotypes and prejudice of any kind will pave the way for a diverse workforce to thrive.[166]

Ethnocentrism

Ethnocentrism *is the belief that one's own group or subculture is naturally superior to other groups and cultures.* Ethnocentrism is an obstacle to diversity because it tends to produce a homogeneous culture, a culture where everyone looks and acts the same and shares the same set of values and beliefs. Removing ethnocentrism and replacing it with a belief that all groups, cultures, and subcultures are inherently equal will greatly enhance the achievement of a diverse workforce's full potential.

Policies and Practices

A third obstacle to diversity is embedded in organizational policies and practices that work against maintaining a diverse workforce. Policies express an organization's intentions and provide a blueprint for action. Policies document the organization's "diversity talk." Practices will represent the organization's "diversity walk."[167] Unfortunately, it is often the case that the two don't go hand-in-hand. The leader must perform an audit of the organization to determine if existing policies, rules, procedures, and practices work against minorities; for example, removing barriers (such as job requirements that are not valid or relevant to the job) to the selection of women and minorities.

Policies regarding human resource management issues such as hiring, training, promotion, compensation, and retirement or layoffs must be examined to make sure that minorities are not unfairly treated by actions taken in these areas. A gender and ethnicity pay-gap still exists where women and minorities continue to earn considerably less than white males because they tend to be segregated into lower-paying occupations, industries, and jobs.[168] This compounds the problem for women who have to contend with the "gender-gap." It is still the case that women earn less than men in general for the same job and skill requirements. Instituting policies that narrow or eliminate these gaps will bring more women and minorities into the workforce.[169]

Xerox Corporation, for example, has undertaken major initiatives to increase diversity by adopting practices that increase the proportion of women and minorities it recruits and promotes. Xerox has also established sophisticated support networks for minority employees (the Xerox Hispanic Professional Association is an example of such a support network). It is this kind of initiative that brought Ursula Burns to Xerox right out of college, and 27 years later she is poised to be the next CEO of the company.

The Glass Ceiling

In a newspaper headline titled "Where Are the Women?" the author laments the fact that despite a generation of Take-Our-Daughters-to-Work days, despite college and graduate school enrollments among women that exceed those of men, and despite a workforce participation rate since the mid-1960s that has resulted in three-fourths of all working-age women now in the labor force, the upper echelon of U.S. business is still a decidedly male bastion.[170] This statement depicts what is known as the glass ceiling. More than a decade after the Federal Glass Ceiling Commission recommended disclosure of diversity data to help shatter advancement barriers for woman, the phenomenon remains a pervasive problem in corporate America.[171] *The* **glass ceiling** *is therefore an invisible barrier that separates women and minorities from top leadership positions.* Evidence of the glass ceiling is seen in the concentration of women and minorities at the lower rungs of the corporate ladder, where their skills and talents are not fully utilized.[172]

A related concept to the glass ceiling is what some describe as the "glass cliff" phenomenon, which involves the experiences of women and minority employees when they take on positions of leadership.[173] Organizations with a token diversity policy may promote women and minority employees into top leadership positions but set them up to fail (thus the term *glass cliff*) just so the company will have an excuse for not hiring more minorities.

Women and minorities are still vastly underrepresented in the board rooms and upper management positions. According to a study on women in top executive positions in U.S. corporations, the pipeline to the CEO position shows a slow increase in the percentage of CEOs that will be women in the next five to ten years. The study went on to predict that if the trend continues, perhaps 6 percent of CEOs in *Fortune 1000* companies will be women by 2016; still a low percentage by any measure.[174] This trend is unfortunate given the increasing research evidence that companies with a high number of women executives deliver better financial results.[175,176]

Unfriendly Work Environment

Work Application 7

Identify and briefly explain which of the five obstacles to diversity exist and/or have been removed where you work or have worked.

The work environment for many minorities is a lonely, unfriendly, and stressful place, particularly in executive-level positions where Caucasian men outnumber women and minorities. Sexual harassment, intimidation, bullying, and social rejection are all examples of actions that make the work place unfriendly.[177,178] Minorities and women may be excluded from social activities in or out of the office, which often leads to feelings of alienation and despair. This in turn often leads to job dissatisfaction and high turnover among minority groups. Making the workplace friendly for everyone including women and other minorities will go a long way toward alleviating the problem of high turnover, and thus preserve diversity initiatives.

The next section focuses on the role of leadership and organizational processes that either enhance or handicap an organization's diversity initiatives.

Learning Outcome 8 *Describe the key indicators of a culture that supports diversity.*

Creating a Culture That Supports Diversity

Diversity starts at the top with board members and the senior executive team.[179] For organizations to embrace and value diversity, the concept itself must be embedded in the organization's business model. A company's business model defines its vision, mission, strategic objectives, and strategies for achieving those objectives. The process of creating these components of the business model is either centralized or decentralized. When diversity is part and parcel of the organizational mission, all employees are given equal opportunities to contribute their talents, skills, and expertise toward achieving organizational objectives, independent of their race, gender, ethnic background, or any other definable characteristic.

A successful diversity program requires a team approach; a strong commitment to attract, retain, and promote employees of minority backgrounds; and the creation of a culture that fully supports and rewards diversity initiatives throughout the organization.[180] The best companies look beyond diversity management (with its focus on simply managing the numbers) to diversity leadership (with its focus on performance).[181] Diversity experts and scholars have emphasized the importance of corporate leadership in ensuring the success of diversity initiatives.[182]

Leaders have a responsibility to create a work culture that accomodates the needs of a diverse workforce. Many companies never reap the benefits of diversity because of the lack of a supportive culture. They get candidates in the door but fail to retain them. They don't take the steps to encourage the unique contributions that new recruits bring to the workplace. They view diversity as a stand-alone function that ends once an employee is hired instead of a continuing process that is integrated into the business's mission, long-term goals, structure, and policies.[183]

A culture of multiculturalism is one that continuously values diversity and as a result has made it a way of life in the organization. An indication that diversity has become a way of life for a company can be found in what happens to diversity programs during an economic downturn. In the past, corporate leaders viewed diversity programs as luxuries, something to be indulged in when times were good but quickly eliminated when the going got tough. More and more, companies are sticking with their diversity programs even during an economic downturn, which indicates the seriousness with which they now take diversity. In one company where the executive team bonus is linked to a diversity scorecard, the CEO has committed that he will pay this bonus regardless of the financial performance of the company because, as he puts it, the inclusion culture change effort is a journey not limited to a company's financial cycle.[184]

Studies have identified factors related to diversity success. Exhibit 10.8 highlights these factors, which are briefly discussed below.

EXHIBIT 10.8 Factors Related to Diversity Success

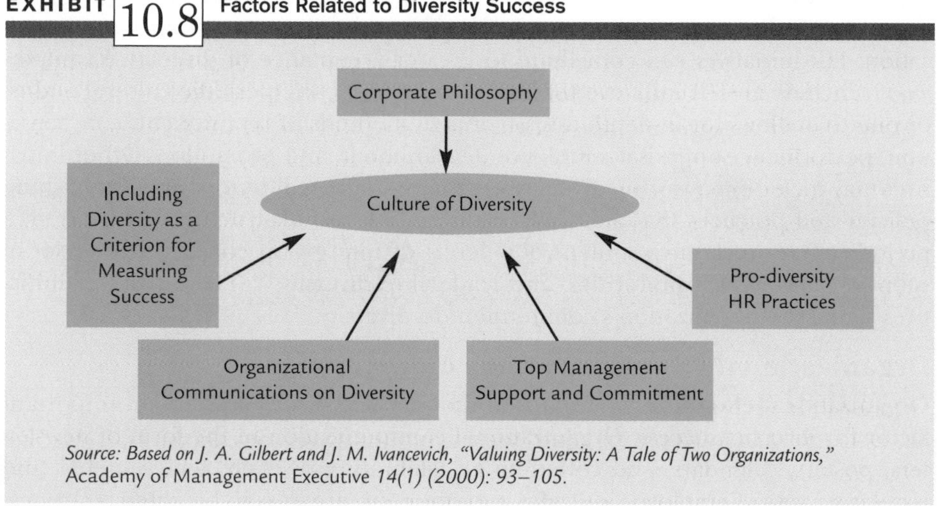

Source: Based on J. A. Gilbert and J. M. Ivancevich, "Valuing Diversity: A Tale of Two Organizations," Academy of Management Executive *14(1) (2000): 93–105.*

Top Management Support and Commitment

Achieving diversity success does not happen by chance. Many experts argue that support and commitment from senior management—and, especially, from the CEO—is imperative.[185] A major catalyst behind successful diversity management is the role played by the CEO and his or her management team. The CEO alone has the authority to make diversity part of the organizational mission and his or her vision. The commitment of the CEO and his or her top management team to diversity will filter down to individual operating units, thus making diversity an institutionalized concept. Leaders who talk diversity must "walk the talk." CEO commitment is considered to be the alpha and omega of organizational efforts to create a culture that supports diversity.[186] It is the cornerstone of any successful diversity initiative.[187,188]

To achieve full diversity, leaders are challenged to work to ensure that women, African-Americans, Hispanics, and other minorities have opportunities to move up the corporate ladder into leadership positions.[189] Though slowly changing, it is still the case that top leadership positions in most of corporate America are occupied by white males, despite the growing employee population made up of minorities. As recently as the mid-1980s, Wall Street was still a "men's club," with women relegated to roles such as secretaries or office assistants.[190] To achieve full diversity, top leaders must actively pursue the objective of changing the organizational culture to one that values diversity at every level of the organization—from the top to the bottom. Without effective diversity leadership, talk of diversity will remain just that: talk!

Corporate Philosophy

For diversity to succeed, there has to be an explicit corporate philosophy that unambiguously supports it. Success is achieved when the organization's diversity philosophy goes beyond simply responding to legislative mandates. Rather, a philosophy that views diversity as a strategic imperative strives to embed diversity into the daily practices and procedures of organizational operations. A corporate philosophy that values diversity will lead to a culture of openness, fairness, inclusion, and empowerment for all.

Pro-Diversity Human Resource Practices

In organizations that have achieved diversity success, several types of inclusionary measures are subelements of the HR department. The HR department is the gateway through which all employees pass in order to become members of an organization. HR initiatives can contribute to greater acceptance of diversity. Examples would include an HR initiative that stipulates conducting periodic cultural audits, or one that allows for in-depth assessments of methods of recruitment, compensation, performance appraisal, employee development, and promotion. Other initiatives may include sponsoring diversity workshops and conferences, and establishing policies and practices that aim for outcomes such as full structural integration, a prejudice-free work environment, low levels of intergroup conflict, strong social support networks for minorities, and leadership diversity.[191] These types of initiatives signal the organization's commitment to diversity.

Organizational Communications on Diversity

Organizational efforts to communicate the message of diversity are an important factor for diversity success. Organizational communication in the form of newsletters, posters, calendars, and coffee mugs celebrating diversity achievements, and regular surveys of employee attitudes and opinions, are ways to heighten awareness of diversity. Repeated exposure to diversity themes would help to promote the message that diversity is a normal and accepted part of everyday life in the organization. Also, such in-house communications and newsletters would encourage employee involvement and help transmit the diversity message.

Work Application **8**

Identify and briefly explain which of the five factors related to diversity success exist or do not exist where you work or have worked.

Including Diversity as a Criterion for Measuring Success

A final factor related to a successful diversity program is the extent to which diversity objectives are included among the criteria for measuring managerial performance. Compensation must be tied to diversity goals and on diversity metrics and progress.[192] An organizational objective to raise awareness of equality may include specific activities, such as writing an article for the company or department newsletter, recruiting more minorities into managerial positions, developing and implementing a discrimination refresher workshop, or addressing diversity concerns in a timely manner. By pursuing this course of action, success is measured not just in financial terms but also in a manager's ability to meet these specific goals. Multiple criteria for success, defined along multiple dimensions, will establish managerial accountability on multiple fronts. With such a system in place, managerial compensation can be easily tied to diversity success by requiring that a certain percentage of a manager's pay be dependent on meeting quantifiable diversity objectives. Not rewarding accomplishment of diversity goals could imply that diversity is not a top management priority.[193]

Diversity Awareness Training and Leadership Education

The benefits of diversity as we have demonstrated are enormous, but without a well-trained workforce that values diversity awareness and leadership commitment, increased cultural diversity may actually lead to decreased productivity and lower financial and strategic performance. As mentioned earlier, the notion that culturally diverse individuals coming into the workforce have to assimilate into the mainstream culture is a thing of the past. The challenge now is for organizations to make the necessary adjustments, such as removing obstacles to achieving diversity, and create a diversity-supportive culture that allows individuals to maintain their uniqueness and still be part of the team. As revealed in the preceding discussion, strong leadership commitment is needed to make these adjustments. Many of today's leaders belong to the baby-boom generation. Most of them grew up in segregated communities with little or no diversity in the institutions they attended. Some have little experience with managing and leading diverse work groups. For example, some leaders are uncertain how to handle communications with employees whose cultural backgrounds (values, beliefs, language) differ from the leaders' background. Various racial or ethnic groups may respond differently to the demands of their job responsibilities or to the approaches that leaders are using to manage and evaluate employees.[194] Similarly, some men still find it difficult to report to or be evaluated by a woman. Even managers who are sensitive to issues of diversity may not have the skills to deal with other, less obvious forms of discrimination.

Even if blatantly sexist, racist, or "ageist" acts do not occur, subtle forms of discrimination, such as exclusion from informal networks, conversations, and social interactions outside of work, will still occur, and, over time, may become standard behavior. These types of exclusionary tactics, if left unchecked, can lead to isolation and reduced opportunities for minorities. Employees of minority groups working in this type of environment often end up leaving, resulting in a loss of valuable human capital for the organization.

The ultimate objective of diversity training and education is to create a diversity sensitive orientation (DSO) within the entire workforce. Organizations that are significantly lacking in DSO are less likely to engage in diversity management practices that are considered the hallmark of excellence.[195,196] Underscoring the need for diversity training and education programs, one study on the subject revealed that awareness of racial and gender issues through education and training positively influenced leaders' attitudes toward diversity.[197] We will explore the role of diversity training and education in fostering a deeper cultural awareness among leaders and employees, and helping organizations effectively manage diversity.

Diversity Training

Diversity training can facilitate the management of a diverse workforce. The purpose of diversity training is to develop organizations as integrated communities in which every employee feels respected, accepted, and valued regardless of gender, race, ethnicity, or other distinguishing characteristic. Training sessions are aimed at increasing people's awareness of and empathy for people from different cultures and backgrounds. There are many diversity-training programs with many different objectives. Diversity training can include but is not limited to the following:[198]

- role-playing, in which participants act out appropriate and inappropriate ways to deal with diverse employees;
- self-awareness activities, in which participants discover how their own hidden and overt biases direct their thinking about specific individuals and groups;
- awareness activities, in which participants learn about others who differ from them in race, gender, culture, and so on.

Diversity training programs can last hours or days. They can be conducted by outside experts on diversity, or by existing members of an organization with expertise in diversity. Small organizations are more likely to rely on outside assistance while larger organizations often have their own in-house staff. The primary objectives of diversity training programs include one or more of the following:

- helping employees of varying backgrounds communicate effectively with one another;
- showing members how to deal effectively with diversity-related conflicts and tensions;
- exploring how differences might be viewed as strengths, not weaknesses, in the workplace;
- improving members' understanding of each other and their work relations.

Not all diversity-training programs are successful. Diversity training is most likely to be successful when it is not a one-time event, but an ongoing or repeated activity, and when there are follow-up activities to see whether the training objectives were accomplished.

Education

Sometimes effectively managing diversity requires that leaders of an organization receive additional education to make them better able to communicate and work with diverse employees. Through training and education, leaders develop personal characteristics that support diversity. Through education, leaders are taught to see diversity in the larger context of the organization's long-term vision. Managers should have long-term plans to include employees of different cultures at all levels of the organization. They should be educated on the strategic significance of linking diversity to the organization's competitiveness, rather than simply being told to do it.

To develop and implement diversity programs, leaders must first examine and change themselves. Through education, leaders learn how to communicate effectively and encourage feedback from all employees regardless of background, how to accept criticism, and how to adjust their behavior when appropriate. A broad knowledge base on multiculturalism and diversity issues helps. Also, through education, leaders learn how to mentor and empower employees of diverse cultures. They learn to appreciate their role in creating opportunities for all employees to use their unique abilities.

Work
Application 9

Does the organization you work or have worked for offer diversity awareness training and education? If you are not sure, contact the human resources department to find out. If it does, briefly describe the program.

Despite increased levels of diversity training initiatives in many organizations, there is concern that little is happening in terms of the impact of these initiatives on the hiring practices of many managers and the organizations they represent.[199] A healthcare diversity study revealed that although the main minority groups in the United States (Asians, African-Americans, Hispanics, and Native Americans) make up almost 30 percent of the population, they account for only about 10 percent of nursing staff, 6 percent of physicians, and less than 1 percent of healthcare executives.[200] Some reasons put forward for this lack of representation include the slow rate of college and graduate school graduations for African-Americans and Hispanics, CEO inertia, sexual harrassment, and racial discrimination. With respect to CEO inertia, there are still very few women CEOs in *Fortune 1000* companies. As recently as the year 2000, fewer than 50 percent of the *Fortune 1000* companies had women in their top executive ranks.[201] According to the U.S. Department of Justice, federal employment discrimination lawsuits increased by 300 percent from the years 1990 to 2000, with plaintiffs alleging discrimination related to hiring practices, pay, promotions, and harassment.[202,203] The American Hospital Association (AHA) is just one of many groups actively involved in helping the healthcare industry reflect the demographic diversity of the U.S. population. Through its Institute for Diversity in Health Management, the AHA has focused its attention on three key areas of diversity: leadership initiatives, HR strategies to change the workforce, and cultural adjustments.[204]

Without an educated and committed leadership team, the task of creating and managing a diverse workforce is unlikely to yield positive results. Everyone must be involved, including employees and managers at all levels, and top management commitment must be visible, for the benefits of diversity to be realized.

Opening Case APPLICATION

6. What is Avon's stance on diversity, and has it lived up to it so far?

Avon embraces diversity in the workforce, and continues to be a leader in taking affirmative action to ensure that doors are open to talented individuals, and that all associates and employees have opportunities for development and advancement. Avon has more women in management positions than any other *Fortune 500* company, and half of its board of directors is women. In the United States and elsewhere, Avon has internal networks of associates including a Parents' Network, a Hispanic Network, a Black Professional Association, an Asian network, and a Gay and Lesbian network. The networks act as liaisons between associates and management, to bring voice to critical issues that impact the workplace and the marketplace.

Avon's dedication and commitment to diversity has been honored by several organizations and media. Avon's awards and recognitions include appearances on *Fortune*'s "Most Admired Companies" list for over a decade, selection by *Business Week* as one of the "Top 100 Global Brands," recognition by *Business Ethics* among its "100 Best Corporate Citizens" for six consecutive years, the honor of being one of *Fortune*'s "50 Best Companies for Minorities," and ranking as the #1 company for executive women by the National Association for Female Executives. It is evident that Avon has established and continues to uphold its standards on diversity.

Ethical **Dilemma 2**

Gender Discrimination

Wal-Mart, the world's largest retailer, has been hit with a class action lawsuit. Wal-Mart has been accused, but not convicted, of denying women workers equal pay and opportunities for promotion. The suit claims that even if Wal-Mart policies are not clearly discriminatory, its organizational culture perpetuates gender stereotypes that lead to differences in pay and promotion between men and women. Up to 1.6 million women

continued

(Ethical Dilemma 2 continued)

could join the class action suit. Wal-Mart strongly disagreed with the court decision to proceed with a class action lawsuit, and is appealing. Wal-Mart also faces 30 lawsuits alleging it failed to pay workers overtime pay. CEO Lee Scott rebuts critics of pay scales, but he has initiated workplace-diversity moves to achieve full diversity. Wal-Mart hired a director of diversity and set diversity targets, and executive bonuses are cut if the company doesn't meet the objectives. Wal-Mart now posts management openings on its company-wide computer network.

1. Do you believe that organizational culture can lead to discrimination?
2. Do you believe Wal-Mart is innocent?
3. If Wal-Mart is guilty, do you think that it was intentional discrimination?

Now that you have learned about culture and diversity as described in this chapter, you may find it interesting to see how your own personality traits match up. Complete Self-Assessment 2.

SELF-ASSESSMENT 2

Personality, Culture, Values, and Diversity

Culture and Values

If you scored high on the Big Five personality dimension of conscientiousness (high need for achievement), you tend to be a conformist and will most likely feel comfortable in an organization with a strong culture. If you have a high agreeableness (high need for affiliation) personality, you tend to get along well with people, can fit into a strong culture, and would do well in a cooperative culture that values collectivism, low power distance, and femininity. If you have surgency (high need for power), you like to dominate and may not like to fit into a strong culture that does not reflect the values you have. You would tend to do well in a competitive culture that values individualism, high power distance (if you have it), and masculinity. On the Big Five, if you are open to new experience you will do well in an adaptive culture that values low uncertainty avoidance, whereas if you are closed to new experience, you will tend to do well in a bureaucratic culture that values high uncertainty avoidance. Would you like to work in an organization with a weak or strong culture? What type of culture and values interest you?

____

____

Diversity

If you have a Big Five agreeableness personality type (high need for affiliation), are open to experience, and are well adjusted, you will tend to embrace diversity and get along well with people who are different from you. However, if you have a surgency personality type (high need for power), are closed to experience, and are not well adjusted, you will tend to want to have things done your way (melting pot versus salad bowl) and may have problems with a diverse group of people who don't want to give you the power. If you have a conscientiousness personality type (high need for achievement), are well adjusted, and have openness to experience, you will tend to work with those who share your achievement values regardless of other differences. Do you enjoy working with a diversity of people?

____

____

Go to the Internet (www.cengage.com/management/lussier)
where you will find a broad array of resources to help maximize your learning.

- Review the vocabulary
- Try a quiz
- Find related links

Chapter Summary

The chapter summary is organized to answer the nine learning outcomes for Chapter 10.

1. **Explain the power of culture in the strategy execution process.**

   Strategy execution is a much smoother process when an organization's culture is in sync with its strategy. This strategy–culture match serves two important functions: (1) it creates internal unity, and (2) it helps the organization adapt to the external environment. Culture provides a value system in which to operate, and when all employees buy into such a value system, there is internal unity. Culture determines how the organization responds to changes in its external environment. Appropriate cultural values can ensure that the organization responds quickly or proactively to emerging trends, rather than reacting.

2. **Describe the characteristics of low- and high-performance cultures.**

   When there is little or no consensus on the values and norms governing member behavior, the culture of an organization is considered to be weak. The lack of common values and norms means that members of the organization may not show any sense of close identification with the organization's vision, mission, and strategy. On the other hand, a strong culture is one in which values are shared widely across the organization, from top management to rank-and-file employees. In strong cultures, values and behavioral norms are so deeply ingrained that they do not change much even when a new leader takes over. Weak cultures are associated with low performance and strong cultures are associated with high performance.

   The characteristics of low-performance cultures include insular thinking, resistance to change, a highly politicized internal environment, and poorly conceived promotion or advancement practices for employees. The characteristics of high-performance cultures include a reputation for valuing their employees, being very results-oriented, emphasizing everyday outstanding performance and excellence, and using diverse culture reinforcement tools such as ceremonies, symbols, slogans, stories, and language (ceremonies honor and recognize achievement; slogans, symbols, language, and stories communicate the organization's primary values and provide a shared understanding among members).

3. **Distinguish between symbolic and substantive leadership actions for shaping organizational culture.**

   Symbolic leadership actions are valuable for the signals they send about the kinds of behavior and performance leaders wish to encourage and promote. The meaning is implied in the actions taken. Examples of symbolic leadership actions include leaders serving as appropriate role models for employees; using ceremonies to highlight and honor members whose actions and performance exemplify espoused values; and making special appearances at nonceremonial events such as employee training or orientation programs, using the opportunity to stress strategic priorities, values, and norms.

   Substantive leadership actions are highly visible and concrete steps to show management's commitment to new strategic initiatives and cultural changes. The strongest evidence that management is truly committed to creating a new culture is a "shake-up" in both employee and managerial ranks, such as replacing change-resisting, old-culture members with a "new breed" of employees. Another example would be changing dysfunctional operating practices and policies that do not support the new culture.

4. **Differentiate between the four cultural value types.**

   The makeup of the four cultural value types is based on two dimensions: the degree of environmental turbulence (stable versus dynamic) and the organization's strategic focus or orientation (internal versus external). The interaction between these two dimensions creates four different types of cultures that researchers have identified in various organizations.

   The cooperative culture is found in organizations that operate in dynamic environments, yet emphasize an internal strategic focus. The belief is that empowering, respecting, rewarding, and trusting employees is the key to capitalizing on external opportunities. The adaptive culture is also found in organizations that operate in dynamic environments; however, the organization's strategic focus is external. Solutions for responding to external opportunities and threats are sought both inside and outside the firm. These organizations pursue outsourcing, strategic alliances, downsizing, and any other options that are available.

The adaptive and cooperative cultures are often referred to as cultures of innovation, for their flexibility and creativity in responding to environmental changes. The competitive culture is associated with organizations operating in a stable environment with an external strategic focus. Competitive cultures are common in mature markets in which the emphasis is on the achievement of specific targets (such as market share, revenue growth, and profitability). Last but not least is the bureaucratic culture associated with organizations that operate in stable environments with an internal strategic orientation. The bureaucratic culture emphasizes strict adherence to set rules, procedures, and authority lines. Organizations with bureaucratic cultures are highly structured and efficiency-driven. Change is slow in bureaucratic cultures.

5. **Describe Hofstede's value dimensions of national culture.**

The conceptual framework for understanding global cultural differences proposes that national cultures differ by the values they espouse. Researchers have associated different value dimensions with the cultures of different nationalities and/or regions of the world. Leading this effort is the work of Geert Hofstede, whose research, spanning almost two decades and involving more than 160,000 people from more than 60 countries, helped identify the first five value dimensions for understanding global cultural differences. Each value dimension represents a continuum, with selected countries and regions located at various points along the continuum. The five value dimensions making up the framework are:

- Individualism–collectivism
- High–low uncertainty avoidance
- High–low power distance
- Long-term–short-term orientation
- Masculinity–femininity

6. **Explain the primary reasons for embracing diversity.**

Changing demographics and increasing globalization have significantly changed the composition of the workforce. With more women and minorities entering the workforce and the growing interdependence between global companies, the need to embrace and value diversity is more critical than ever. The value of diversity is evident in studies that have found, among other things, that a diversified workforce (e.g., sales team) offers an advantage in understanding and meeting the needs of diverse customers; some of the best job candidates are found among women and other culturally diverse groups; embracing and valuing diversity can lower an organization's cost attributed to high turnover and/or absenteeism among minority groups; and diverse work groups are more creative and innovative than homogeneous work groups.

7. **Identify and briefly describe the obstacles that make it hard to achieve diversity objectives.**

To achieve full diversity, top management must remove obstacles such as stereotypes and prejudice, ethnocentricism, anti-diversity policies and practices, the glass ceiling, and an unfriendly work environment. Organizations that condone stereotypes and prejudice allow employees of minority backgrounds to be verbally assaulted and embarassed using stereotypical labels and comments. Ethnocentrists want to create a homogeneous work environment. The glass ceiling fosters the attitude that women are not capable of performing at the upper levels of leadership. An unfriendly work environment is very unwelcoming to employees of minority groups. They are not challenged and are excluded from formal and informal social networks. Work-related policies and practices favor some groups and not others.

8. **Describe the key indicators of a culture that supports diversity.**

A diversity-supportive culture is one that continuously values diversity and has made it a way of life in the organization. To achieve full diversity, organizations are challenged to create a diversity-supportive culture that ensures women and other minorities have equal opportunities to move up the corporate ladder into leadership positions. The leader's role in creating a diversity-supportive culture is to ensure that the following actions/practices are implemented: top management support and commitment; pro-diversity human resource practices; a corporate philosophy of diversity; regular organizational communications on diversity; and diversity as a criterion for measuring success.

9. **Define the following key terms (in order of appearance in the chapter).**

Select one or more methods: (1) fill in the missing key terms from memory; (2) match the key terms from the following list with their definitions below; and (3) copy the key terms in order from the list at the beginning of the chapter.

__________ is the aggregate of beliefs, norms, attitudes, values, assumptions, and ways of doing things that is shared by members of an organization and taught to new members.

__________ represents a leadership belief in strong, mutually reinforcing exchanges and linkages between employees and departments.

__________ represents a leadership belief in active monitoring of the external environment for emerging opportunities and threats.

__________ represents a leadership that encourages and values a highly competitive work environment.

__________ represents a leadership that values order, stability, status, and efficiency.

__________ are generalized beliefs or behaviors that are considered by an individual or a group to be important.

__________ is a single person entrusted with the responsibility of acting as the organization's conscience.

__________ is employee disclosure of illegal or unethical practices on the part of the organization.

__________ is a psychological state in which people see themselves first as individuals and believe their own interest and values are primary.

__________ is the state of mind wherein the values and goals of the group—whether extended family, ethnic group, or company—are primary.

__________ characterizes people who do not tolerate risk, avoid the unknown, and are comfortable when the future is relatively predictable and certain.

__________ refers to a culture in which most people are comfortable with and accepting of the unknown, and tolerate risk and unpredictability.

__________ is a society in which the leaders and followers rarely interact as equals.

__________ is a society in which leaders and their members interact on several levels as equals.

__________ describes a culture that emphasizes assertiveness and a competitive drive for money and material objects.

__________ describes a culture that emphasizes developing and nurturing personal relationships and a high quality of life.

__________ is any characteristic that serves as a basis for social categorization and self-identification.

__________ is the inclusion of all groups at all levels in an organization.

__________ is the tendency to form an adverse opinion without just cause about people who are different from the mainstream in terms of their gender, race, ethnicity, or any other definable characteristic.

__________ is the belief that one's own group or subculture is naturally superior to other groups and cultures.

__________ is an invisible barrier that separates women and minorities from top leadership positions.

Key Terms

adaptive culture, 384
bureaucratic culture, 385
collectivism, 391
competitive culture, 385
cooperative culture, 384
culture, 370
demographic diversity, 394
diversity, 394
ethnocentrism, 399
femininity, 392
glass ceiling, 399
high power-distance culture, 392
high uncertainty avoidance, 392
individualism, 391
low power-distance culture, 392
low uncertainty avoidance, 392
masculinity, 392
ombudsperson, 389
prejudice, 398
values, 387
whistle blowing, 389

Review Questions

1. What are the similarities and differences between the cooperative culture and the adaptive culture?
2. How does a code of ethics help enforce ethical behavior in an organization?
3. What potential problems could develop in a case in which a leader is from a high power-distance culture, but his followers are from a low power-distance culture?
4. Why has the "melting pot" mentality of multiculturalism been replaced with the "salad bowl" mentality?
5. What are the major obstacles often encountered in trying to achieve diversity?

Communication Skills

The following critical-thinking questions can be used for class discussion and/or as written assignments to develop communication skills. Be sure to give complete explanations for all questions.

1. Based on your knowledge of the Enron case, what part did culture play in its actions and ultimate demise?
2. Describe some of the practices, policies, and norms that you would expect to find in an organization that prides itself on building a culture of respect and trust.
3. Describe the different generations that make up what some people are now referring to as "generational diversity" and their unique characteristics. What are the implications of generational diversity on effective leadership?
4. Explain why diversity has been described by some as a "double-edged sword."
5. What is the difference between diversity management and diversity leadership?
6. In your opinion, what would be some strategies for developing a diversity sensitive orientation (DSO)?

CASE

Robert Stevens Continues Lockheed Martin's Diversity Initiatives

Lockheed Martin, a highly diversified, advanced technology multinational corporation with approximately $41.9 billion in annualized sales and approximately 140,000 employees worldwide, has one of the most successful diversity programs in the nation today. Lockheed Martin's varied businesses are organized into four broad strategic business units (SBUs): Aeronautics, Electronic Systems, Integrated Systems & Global Solutions, and Space Systems. Vance Coffman served as chairman of Lockheed Martin from 1998 to 2004. Coffman was replaced by Robert Stevens in August 2004. Prior to becoming CEO, Stevens served as Lockheed Martin's president and chief operating officer. He has also served as the corporation's chief financial officer, among other key positions. Coffman is most admired for his efforts at creating a work environment that fosters greater awareness and sensitivity to the needs of Lockheed's diverse employee population. These efforts include crafting a "mission success" statement that clearly delineates the corporation's commitment to diversity, and hiring executives with the skills and commitment to implement the corporation's diversity initiatives. Lockheed Martin's core values in its mission statement are ethics, excellence, "can-do," integrity, people, and teamwork. On people, Lockheed maintains that it will "embrace lifelong learning . . . combined with company-sponsored education and development programs." On teamwork, it will "multiply the creativity, talents, and contributions of . . . by focusing on team goals." Teams will "assume collective responsibility for . . . share trust and leadership, embrace diversity, and accept responsibility for prudent risk-taking." It is clear from the speeches and comments of Stevens that he intends to continue right where Coffman left off.

Upon receiving the "Executive of the Year" award from the National Management Association in November 2004, Stevens laid out what Lockheed Martin was looking for in its leaders as follows:

> *At Lockheed Martin, we want: . . . highly principled and ethical people who place a high priority on honesty and integrity, both in their personal and professional lives . . . advocates for diversity who actively foster an inclusive environment where individual respect and teamwork matters . . . disciplined hard workers who are fearless in their pursuit of excellence and who demonstrate great pride and loyalty toward their organization . . . "whole-system creative thinkers" who can pursue innovation, get to the root of a challenge, and commit themselves to the process of life-long learning . . . and valued colleagues who possess humor, humility, and common sense.*

At Lockheed Martin, the belief is that to attract the best of the best, the corporation must include all segments of the population. In this respect, the corporation's Equal Opportunity Office (EOO) has created a Workforce Diversity Initiative that provides guidelines for implementing diversity programs at the strategic business unit levels. The EOO is set up to provide information to Lockheed Martin's SBUs on how to achieve diversity. Many Lockheed Martin companies have diversity departments charged with ensuring, among other things, that their companies are flexible enough to meet the needs of all employees. A number of Lockheed Martin companies have enhanced their diversity efforts by creating employee councils that serve as the conduits to carry concerns from employees to the councils and from the councils to management. The councils, all of which work on a volunteer basis, carry out the goals and programs suggested by the diversity department and by fellow employees.

Another diversity initiative of Lockheed Martin has been the creation of employee networks. The following affinity groups were established by employees to foster career development and upward mobility through education, training and mentoring programs for employees in minority groups: the African American Mentoring and Information Network; the Gay, Lesbian, or Bisexual at Lockheed Martin (GLOBAL) Organization; the Asian American and Pacific-Islander American Lockheed Martin Association (ALMA); Lockheed Martin Employees with Disability; and the Lockheed Martin Latino Mentoring Network. Minority-based social networks such as these are important because they tailor their training and mentoring to the specific issues of a particular subculture.

Lockheed Martin has also actively advocated community outreach, which allows employees of the corporation to work with the community. Several community programs are sponsored by Lockheed. In Baltimore, teachers from around the country explore new, active, collaborative, and project-centered practices that bring math and science to life for kids. In Dallas, a special resource center gives indigent patients the care and guidance they might otherwise never receive; and in classrooms around the globe, students experience the thrill of space through virtual field trips and exciting hands-on activities.

From educational opportunities to career placement to leadership training, Lockheed Martin has made it a priority to reach students from underrepresented groups. Helping to advance minority youth participation in the fields of math, science, and technology is a corporate-wide effort. Lockheed Martin awards scholarships to minority students, and sponsors and participates in local and national conferences, such as the Emerald Honors Conference, the Black Engineer of the Year Awards Conference, the Asian American Engineer of the Year Awards, the Hispanic Engineer National Achievement Awards, and Women in Aerospace. Lockheed Martin's Math, Engineering, and Science Achievement (MESA) grants are aimed at developing academic and leadership skills, raising educational expectation, and instilling confidence in the nation's African-American, American Indian, Mexican-American, and Latino-American students within the fields of engineering, physical science, and other math-based fields. Its "INROADS" program develops and places talented minority students in business and industry, and prepares them for corporate and community leadership.

Diversity managers and volunteers at companies throughout Lockheed Martin take different approaches to assessing how big a role their diversity initiatives have played in helping current employees feel at home. One of the most quantifiable approaches for self-evaluation is the Diversity Progress Index, which measures improvements in diversity over time. The index, which was first piloted in 1997, evaluates a department's approach to advocacy, assessment, planning, and implementation—as they relate to diversity. The index also allows a department to evaluate the role diversity has played in its business success. Outstanding performers are honored with the prestigious President's Diversity Awards.

Because of strong leadership from Robert Stevens and his executive team and a highly motivated and committed group of managers, Lockheed Martin has received national attention and recognition for its diversity efforts. In 2005 alone, Lockheed Martin received the following recognitions:

- Sustained membership in the "Billion Dollar Roundtable" (BDR). Sponsored by *Minority Business News* and *Women's Enterprise Magazine*, the BDR recognizes companies that achieve annual spending of at least $1 billion with minority and women-owned suppliers.
- Voted #1 by readers of *Woman Engineer* magazine as the place they would most like to work or they believe provides the best working environment for women.
- Listed as one of the top ten employers for African-American College Graduates by *The Black Collegian*.
- Ranked #1 for the "Top Corporate Supporter of Historically Black Colleges and Universities".
- Ranked #1 for the "Top Corporate Supporter of the Hispanic Serving Institutions Engineering".
- Listed as one of the "Best Places to Work" by *Baltimore* magazine.
- Voted #5 by readers of *Minority Engineering* magazine in "Top 50 Companies".
- Ranked #5 on the Top 100 list by *Training Magazine*. Lockheed is in the top ten among the national elite of corporate training.

Lockheed Martin is the true embodiment of a company with a high-performance culture and a well-managed diversity program. Diversity at Lockheed Martin is an institutionalized concept, not just a principle on paper.

GO TO THE INTERNET: To learn more about Lockheed Martin, visit its Web site **(http://www.lockheedmartin.com)**.

Support your answers to the following questions with specific information from the case and text or with other information you get from the Web or other sources.

1. Would you say Lockheed Martin Corporation has a low- or high-performance culture? Support your answer with evidence from the case.
2. In what ways has Lockheed Martin taken a proactive approach toward supporting and encouraging diversity?
3. Based on the discussion of leadership actions that can help shape culture (see Exhibit 10.3 on page 379), what leadership actions has Lockheed Martin employed in shaping the corporation's culture?

CUMULATIVE CASE QUESTIONS

4. The self-managed team concept deals with the transfer of authority and responsibility to autonomous teams of employees who are responsible for complete, well-defined tasks that relate either to a final product or service or an ongoing process (Chapter 8). In your opinion, do you think the self-managed team structure can be used to implement Lockheed Martin's diversity initiatives? Support your answer.
5. Transformational versus transactional leadership describes two leadership styles commonly associated with senior leaders of corporations (Chapter 9). Which of these types of leadership do you think Robert Stevens represents? Support your answer.

CASE EXERCISE AND ROLE-PLAY

Preparation: Put yourself in Robert Stevens's position. You have been invited to make a special appearance at a ceremonial event honoring departments that have achieved the highest score on the Diversity Progress Index. Honorees will receive the President's Diversity Award. Develop an inspirational speech highlighting the value of diversity to your corporation and why it is necessary to continue the effort toward greater diversity. Your instructor may elect to form groups to share ideas and develop the speech. Groups should select one leader to present the speech to the entire class.

Role-Play: One student (representing themselves or their group) may give the speech to the entire class. Use information from this chapter on diversity for input.

VIDEO CASE

Diversity at PepsiCo

Imagine trying to manage and accommodate the needs of more than 185,000 people at once. Imagine a variety of voices, languages, cultures, ethnic backgrounds, families, lifestyles, ages, and geographies all vying for attention, all bearing the name PepsiCo. From the top down, PepsiCo embraces diversity and inclusion in its worldwide workforce. Top executives believe that nurturing diversity in the organization is not only a matter of responsible ethics but also good business. The Frito-Lay North American Diversity/Inclusion Model is a good example of how PepsiCo builds a measurable framework for diversity. The model addresses five key areas, ranging from "evolving the culture" to "leveraging our people systems." By following a structure, the human resources department and other managers can develop and implement specific programs to meet the needs of their employees.

1. Why is it important for upper-level managers at PepsiCo to receive diversity and inclusion training?
2. Do you think that PepsiCo's encouragement of employee networks actually works against diversity and the formation of multicultural teams? Why or why not?

Skill-Development Exercise 1

Identifying and Improving Organizational Culture

Preparing for Skill-Development Exercise 1

1. Select one organization you work for or have worked for. Identify its culture by answering Work Applications 1 (is it a high- or low-performance culture?), 2 (which of the ten leadership actions are used?), 3 (which of the four types of organizational cultures does it have?), and 5 (what are the five dimensions of the culture?). Your answers can be between the two poles for Work Applications 2 and 5 (on each of the five dimensions); however, try to identify which end of the spectrum the culture is closest to.
2. What are the mission and values of the organization? Does the culture support the mission and values of the organization? Explain why or why not. If the organization does not have a clearly written mission and values, that would be a good starting point.
3. Based on the organization's mission and values, how can the culture be improved? Be specific.

Doing Skill-Development Exercise 1 in Class

Objective

To improve your ability to identify and improve an organizational culture in order to support its mission and values.

The primary AACSB learning standard skill developed through this exercise is global and multicultural trends, diversity, and ethics.

Preparation

You should have completed the preparation for this exercise.

Procedure *(10–45 minutes)*

A. The instructor calls on students to give their answers to the preparation, with or without a class discussion.

B. Break into groups of 4–6 and share your answers to the preparation.

C. Same as B, but select one group member to present their answer to the entire class.

Conclusion

The instructor may lead a class discussion and/or make concluding remarks.

Apply It *(2–4 minutes)* What did I learn from this exercise? When will I implement my plan?

______

______

______

Sharing

In the group, or to the entire class, volunteers may give their answers to the "Apply It" questions.

Skill-Development Exercise 2

Diversity Training

Preparing for Skill-Development Exercise 2

In preparation for the in-class exercise, write out the answers to the following questions.

Race and Ethnicity

_____ 1. I am of _____ race and ethnicity(ies).
_____ 2. My name is _____. It is significant because it means _____ and/or I was named after _____.
_____ 3. One positive thing about being this race/ethnicity is _____.
_____ 4. One difficult or challenging thing is _____.

Religion

_____ 1. I am of _____ religion/nonreligious/atheist.
_____ 2. One positive thing about it is _____.
_____ 3. One difficult or challenging thing about it is _____.

Gender

_____ 1. I am of _____ gender.
_____ 2. One positive thing about being this gender is _____.
_____ 3. One difficult or challenging thing is _____.
_____ 4. Men and women are primarily different in _____ because _____.

Age

_____ 1. I am _____ years old.
_____ 2. One positive thing about this age is _____.
_____ 3. One difficult or embarrassing thing about being this age is _____.

Ability

_____ 1. I am of _____ (high, medium, low) ability in college and on the job. I do/don't have a disability.
_____ 2. One positive thing about being of this ability is _____.
_____ 3. One difficult or challenging thing about being of this ability is _____.

Other

_____ 1. The major other way(s) in which I'm different than other people is _____.
_____ 2. One positive thing about being different in this way is _____.
_____ 3. One difficult or challenging thing about being different in this way is _____.

Prejudice, Stereotypes, Discrimination
Identify how you have been prejudged, stereotyped, and discriminated against.

Objective

To increase your understanding of the value of diversity and being different. The more you value diversity, the more effort you will place on developing good human relations with a diversity of people.

The primary AACSB learning standard skill developed through this exercise is global and multicultural trends, diversity, and ethics.

Preparation
You should have answered the preparation questions for this exercise.

Procedure 1 *(2–3 minutes)* Break into groups of 4 to 6 with as much diversity as possible. The instructor will check the diversity levels and reassign people to groups to improve diversity, if necessary. Select a spokesperson to give the group's best one or two answers to the "Prejudice, Stereotype, Discrimination" question; it is not necessary to report on any other areas.

Procedure 2 *(10–30 minutes)* The instructor sets a time limit and selects the topics in the preparation to be discussed. Start with different areas first, but be sure to allow time (about 5 minutes) to complete the "Prejudice, Stereotypes, and Discrimination" question. If you finish the question to be reported before the time is up, go over other areas of difference that were not assigned by the instructor.

Procedure 3 *(5–20 minutes)* The spokesperson from each group gives the one or two best examples of prejudice, stereotypes, and discrimination.

Conclusion
The instructor may lead a class discussion and/or make concluding remarks.

Apply It *(2–4 minutes)* What did I learn from this experience? How will I use this knowledge in the future? More specifically, what will I do differently to personally embrace diversity? How will I encourage others to embrace diversity?

Sharing
In the group, or to the entire class, volunteers may give their answers to the "Apply It" questions.

Skill-Development Exercise 3

Developing an Effective Multicultural Team

Preparing for Skill-Development Exercise 3

Assume you are part of a team and your task is to develop a brand new product called the Mind Reader 2010. It will make it possible for you to tell what someone is thinking by simply focusing the device in their direction. There is currently no product like it on the market—or even substitutes—but time is of the essence and this product has to be on the market within a very short time; otherwise, other competing groups will beat you to it. You are a multicultural team with members from the following countries: United States, Japan, Argentina, Mexico, and Sweden. As discussed in the text section (pp. 391–393), "National Culture Identities—Hofstede's Value Dimensions," researchers have found key dimensions that explain broad cultural differences among selected nationalities. The table on the next page summarizes the value dimensions of five countries from which team members are to be selected.

Objective

To learn how to deal with the different values, norms, and attitudes that characterize different cultures. Leaders have to recognize that cultural differences can lead to conflicts in multicultural team settings, and finding common ground where value differences exist is key to effective teamwork.

The primary AACSB learning standard skills developed through this exercise are teamwork and global and multicultural trends, diversity, and ethics.

Preparation
Read and understand the meaning of each value dimension in Exhibit 10.6 on page 391. Review the table in this exercise for the particular value dimensions of each country.

Procedure 1 *(3–5 minutes)* Break up into groups of 4 to 6 with as much diversity as possible. The instructor will check to ensure that each group is well diversified and reassign students to groups needing more diversity, if possible. Select a leader who will present the findings of the group's deliberations.

Procedure 2 *(10–20 minutes)* The instructor sets a time limit on the deliberations. If quality, teamwork, and speed are critical to successfully completing this project, what adaptations in behavior would your group have to make, given the different countries your group members are from? Be mindful of the values associated with each country and team member. For example, somebody from an individualistic culture or a high uncertainty avoidance culture may have

Country	Masculinity	Femininity	Time Orientation		Individualism	Collectivism	Uncertainty Avoidance		Power Distance	
			Long Term	Short Term			High	Low	High	Low
United States			X		X					
Japan	X			X		X	X			
Argentina								X		
Mexico						X			X	
Sweden		X						X		X

difficulty working as part of a team or working with people who are comfortable with and accepting of the unknown, and who tolerate risk and unpredictability. What ideas does the group have to help this individual adapt to the needs of the team to finish the project on time? Other potential areas of conflict exist. Identify them based on the composition of your team, and deliberate on possible solutions, keeping the objective in mind.

Procedure 3 *(15–20 minutes)* The leader from each group presents the potential conflicts introduced by the differences in the value dimensions of team members, and the team's solutions for dealing with such conflicts in order to achieve the desired objectives.

Conclusion
The instructor may lead a class discussion and/or make concluding remarks.

Apply It *(2–4 minutes)* What did I learn from this experience? How will I use this knowledge in the future?

Sharing
In the group, or to the entire class, volunteers may give their answers to the "Apply It" questions.

Chapter Outline

Strategic Leadership
Strategic Leadership Failures
Strategic Management
The Strategic Management Process

Implementing Change
The Need for Change
The Role of Leadership in Implementing Change
The Change Management Process
Why People Resist Change
Strategies for Minimizing Resistance to Change

11 Strategic Leadership and Change Management

Learning Outcomes

After studying this chapter, you should be able to:

1. Discuss the role of strategic leadership in the strategic management process. p. 418
2. Describe the relevance of analyzing the internal and external environment to the strategic management process. p. 422
3. Explain the importance of a vision and a mission statement. p. 424
4. Explain the relationship between corporate goals and strategies. p. 426
5. Explain the importance of strategy evaluation in the strategic management model. p. 430
6. Describe the three phases of the change process. p. 435
7. Identify the major reasons for resisting change. p. 438
8. Discuss people- and task-centered recommendations for minimizing resistance to change. p. 441
9. Define the following **key terms** (in order of appearance in the chapter):

strategic leadership	value
strategic management	core competence
strategic vision	organizational change
mission statement	survival anxiety
strategy	learning anxiety

Opening Case APPLICATION

While attending Stanford University, Larry Page met Sergey Brin, a native of Moscow, and together they launched Google in 1998. With CEO Eric Schmidt, who joined in 2001, they have built Google into one of the industry's most powerful companies. Employing more than 16,000 employees, Google is available in 160 local country domains and 117 languages, and in 20 countries worldwide. Google's mission is to organize the world's information and make it universally accessible and useful. Since going public in 2004, Google has exceeded analyst estimates for its financial performance in all but one quarter, and profits topped $1 billion in the last quarter of 2006. Schmidt believes that it is the company's obligation to maximize shareholder value by maintaining a long-term focus. By providing the best user experience, Google and its leadership team believe that they can build a company that will create more value, not just for its user, but ultimately also for its shareholders.[1]

Page now holds the title of president of products; Brin is president of technology. Though Schmidt is the CEO, they still wield enormous influence over the way the company operates. Google's strength rests in its culture, which emphasizes teamwork, flexibility, transparency, and innovation. There is little in the way of corporate hierarchy. Google's hiring policy is aggressively nondiscriminatory and favors ability over experience. The result is a staff that reflects the global audience the search engine serves. In 2008, Google was named the best company to work for, for the second year running.[2]

Google continues to pursue an aggressive growth strategy. It has acquired more than 50 companies since its creation. Some of those acquisitions include YouTube (social networking software), Postini (enterprise e-mail software) that the company acquired in 2006, and DoubleClick (display advertising software) acquired in 2007.[3]

According to David Vise, co-author of the book *The Google Story,* Google has succeeded not only on the strength of technology, but because of its management style. It has focused on the end user and the quality of its search engine. Google's leaders aren't afraid to experiment—they are willing to question conventional wisdom and trust their own judgment.[4]

Opening Case Questions:

1. How effective has the executive leadership team of Schmidt, Page, and Brin been in providing the kind of strategic leadership that Google has utilized so far?
2. Describe Google's business environment. How well is Google adapting to it?
3. Critique Google's mission statement.
4. How well do Google's long-term objectives balance the interests of its stakeholders?
5. What type of growth strategy is Google pursuing, and why do you think the leadership team has chosen such a course rather than the alternatives?
6. What are some of the factors contributing to Google's effective strategy implementation?
7. Does a successful company like Google still need to change?
8. Why have Schmidt, Page, and Brin encountered less resistance in bringing about changes at Google than most companies experience?

Can you answer any of these questions? You'll find answers to these questions and learn more about Google and its leadership throughout the chapter.

To learn more about Google and its leadership team, visit the company's Web site at **http://www.google.com**.

Organizations are operating in increasingly complex environments, in which an adaptation to environmental changes is an imperative. The attempt by an organization to align its mission, goals, and strategies with the external environment is really the essence of strategic management, which is the domain of strategic (upper-level corporate) leadership. Many scholars and practitioners agree that the effectiveness of organizations is influenced by the degree of fit between their internal strengths and externalities in the macro-environment.[5] This process of adaptation is strongly influenced by the interpretations strategic leaders make of the environment. Interpretations of environmental trends play a large part in the future actions that strategic leaders employ to remain competitive.[6]

One area in which change is unmistakable is the increasingly global competitive landscape. Virtually every company, large or small, faces competition for critical resources and market opportunities, not just from competitors in the home market but also more and more from distant and often little-understood regions of the world. How successful a company is at exploiting emerging opportunities and dealing with associated threats depends crucially on leadership's ability to cultivate a global mindset among managers and their followers. It's all about reorienting the organization to see change not as a threat but as an opportunity. In some cases, change is triggered by a crisis—an unexpected incident with significant negative consequences.[7]

Also imperative for strategists operating in this era of hypercompetition, globalization, and technological revolution is the need to act fast. Strategists must respond quickly to marketplace demands for immediate action.[8] This is where the need for effective strategic planning comes into play. The pressures of the new competitive landscape are forcing some organizations to push planning aside and simply act faster. The focus of this chapter is on strategic leadership and the strategic management process, and change leadership.

Learning Outcome 1 *Discuss the role of strategic leadership in the strategic management process.*

Strategic Leadership

Achieving organizational success is not a chance occurrence. It is determined largely by the decisions strategic leaders make. It is the responsibility of top managers to monitor the organization's internal and external environments, build company resources and capabilities, track industry and competitive trends, spot emerging market opportunities, identify business threats, and develop a vision for the future that followers can believe in.[9] This series of activities makes up a major part of what is known as strategic leadership. It is hard to overstate the importance of strategic leadership in today's dynamic and uncertain business environment. It is one of the key factors considered critical to an organization's ability to adapt, evolve, and prevail amid turbulent disruptions.[10,11]

Although many authors have provided varying definitions of the concept of strategic leadership, they all seem to revolve around the same themes: **strategic leadership** *is a person's ability to anticipate, envision, maintain flexibility, think strategically, and work with others to initiate changes that will create a viable future for the organization.*[12] It is a process of providing the direction and inspiration necessary to create and implement a firm's vision, mission, and strategies to achieve organizational objectives.[13]

Strategic leadership must involve managers at the top, middle, and lower levels of the organization. However, of these three managerial classifications, top-level managers (strategists) are clearly held responsible for the organization's near-term performance, as well as for creating conditions that will ensure the organization's future survival.[14] The recent losses at companies such as Citigroup, American Express, Merrill Lynch, GM, Ford, and even the total collapse of Bears Stearns have been attributed to ineffective strategic leadership. Effective strategic leaders are skilled at[15,16,17,18]

- anticipating and forecasting events in the external environment that have the potential to impact business performance—they observe from the outside in;
- finding and sustaining competitive advantage by building core competencies and selecting the right markets in which to compete;
- evaluating strategy implementation and results systematically, and making strategic adjustments;
- building a highly effective, efficient, and motivated team of employees;
- selecting, developing, and mentoring a talented team of leaders;
- deciding on appropriate goals and priorities for achieving them;
- being an effective communicator.

A strategic leader can choose to concentrate decision-making power at the executive level or spread it throughout the organization. Each approach has implications on follower motivation and commitment.[19] For example, shifting much of the decision-making responsibility (especially operational decisions) away from the leader and onto other team members frees top leaders to think strategically and gives them more time to address key issues.[20]

Strategic Leadership Failures

Strategic decisions often fail due to decision-maker blunders. The one held responsible when strategic decisions fail is the CEO and his or her senior leadership team. Senior executives fail when their strategic vision for the organization favors their personal interests and not enough of their constituents' and organization's interests; they use failure-prone practices (such as illogical organization structures, culture, and compensation plans); they engage in or condone unethical conduct; they pay little or no attention to productivity, quality, and innovation; or they allocate time and money unwisely.[21,22] One study cites the loss of market focus as a leading cause of business failures. A loss of market focus results in missed opportunities.[23] A market-focused company ensures that its managers continuously focus and re-focus critical organizational resources on the ever-changing portfolio of market opportunities that create long-term value for all stakeholders.[24]

Failures have also been attributed to the fact that leaders, in the rush to make key decisions, have relied too much on intuition to the exclusion of rational analysis. Executive intuition is the instinctive ability to identify weak signals in the environment and respond without the benefit of concrete facts and information. Sometimes such intuition may fuel imagination, creativity, and innovation, and contribute to corporate success; other times it may result in spectacular blunders. While some see this as too risky, others argue that intuitive decisions are needed in highly volatile, globally competitive business environments in which time is of the essence. Many experts now believe that strategic decision making requires a balancing of intuition and rationality.[25,26]

Another reason why strategic leadership can derail is due to ethical and moral lapses in judgment. The recent corporate scandals underscore this fact. The ultimate goal of the strategic leader should be to build sustainable integrity programs into the strategic management framework that encourage positive self-regulation of ethical behavior as a matter of routine within the organization.[27,28] This will not happen unless the leader also demonstrates integrity. Integrity impacts the credibility and reputation of the strategic leader. Underscoring the significance of ethics and moral leadership, on July 9, 2002, the President of the United States announced in the wake of a series of business scandals that America's "greatest economic need" was "higher ethical standards to be upheld by responsible business leaders."

Opening Case APPLICATION

1. How effective has the executive leadership team of Schmidt, Page, and Brin been in providing the kind of strategic leadership that Google has utilized so far?

Together, this trio has put together a profitable business model built around keyword advertising. Since going public in 2004, Google has exceeded analysts' estimates for its financial performance in all but one quarter, and profits topped $1 billion in the last quarter of 2006 and continued into 2007. Google's stock is currently trading at over $350 per share. There is no doubt that its long-term objective of maximizing shareholder value is being met and exceeded. The Google team of strategic leaders is performing exceptionally well in all the areas of leadership responsibility identified above, especially as visionaries.

Strategic Management

In today's rapidly changing global world, leaders are bombarded with so much information, often conflicting, that making effective decisions becomes a challenge. The complexity of the environment and the uncertainty of the future make the task of the strategic leader more difficult. Effective strategists are said to perform four primary responsibilities: (1) conceptualize the organization's vision, mission, and core values; (2) oversee the formulation of objectives, strategies, policies, and structures that translate vision, mission, and core values into business decisions; (3) create an environment and culture for organizational learning and mutual exchange between individuals and groups; and (4) serve as steward and role model for the rest.[29,30,31]

Strategists pave the way for ethical behavior in organizations through the influence of leadership. All these activities fall under the domain of the strategic management framework.[32] The key question and central issue in strategic management is why some firms perform better than others. The answer lies in the role that strategic leadership plays in the life of the organization. Strategic leadership ensures that the strategic management process is successfully carried out and yields the desired results for the organization. **Strategic management** *is the set of decisions and actions used to formulate and implement specific strategies that will achieve a competitively superior fit between the organization and its environment, so as to achieve organizational goals.*[33]

A basic distinction between strategic leadership and strategic management is that strategic leadership envisions where the organization would like to be in five to ten years while strategic management focuses on how to achieve the vision. The two concepts should reinforce and support each other; however, this is not always the case. Strategic leadership failures are in the news every day.

This section focuses on the strategic management process shown in Exhibit 11.1. It is often summarized as a three-step process—strategy formulation, implementation, and evaluation. Great companies strategize, and the strategic management model is the tool that makes it possible. It greatly facilitates preparation and planning for the unpredictable.

EXHIBIT 11.1 Strategic Management Framework

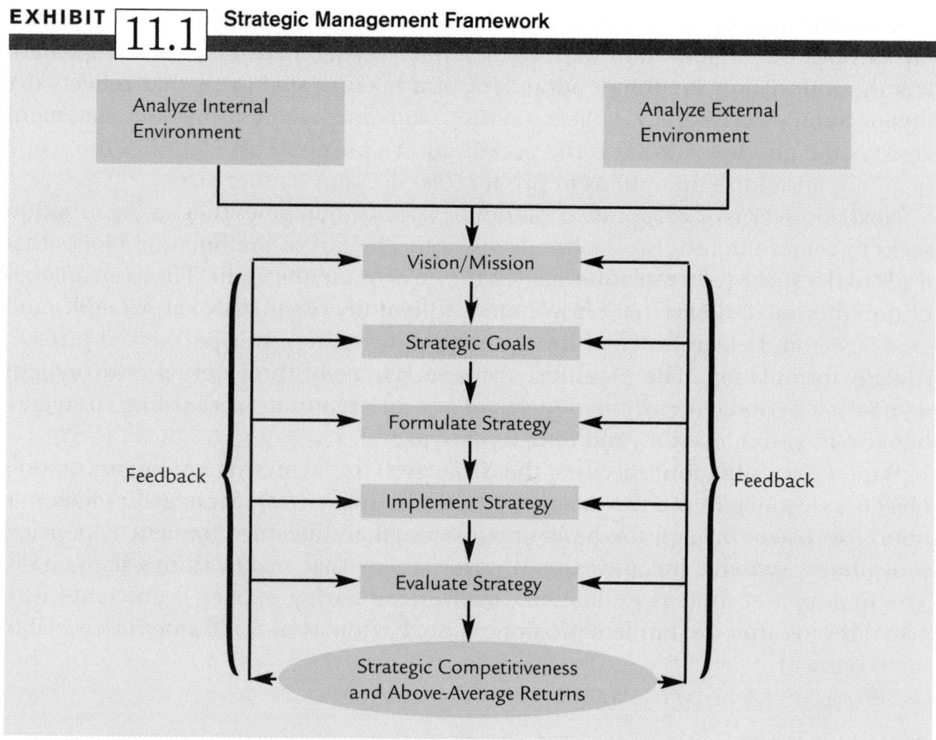

Ethical Dilemma 1

Strategic Leadership and Management

An important part of strategic leadership and management is creating the business model of how the business competes. The University of Miami Online High School (UMOHS) is in partnership with The University of Miami. UMOHS is for young athletes and performers (grades 8–12) who are too busy to attend traditional classes; it gives them more time to train, and to travel to compete/perform. It wants to become the establishment school in the sports and performing world. UMOHS also accepts international students who want an American diploma. Some argue that online high school deprives a child of a traditional education and prevents a kid from being a kid and enjoying childhood.

1. How do you feel about high school students enrolling in an online school and missing the experience of attending traditional classes?
2. Is it ethical and socially responsible to offer an online high school for athletes and performers?

The Strategic Management Process

Achieving strategic competitiveness and earning above-average returns for a company is not a matter of luck. It is determined by the decisions and actions of leaders throughout the strategic management process. As shown in Exhibit 11.1, the strategic management process begins with the strategist's vision. This is a vision statement of where the organization wants and needs to be in the future, given the nature of the environment in which it exists. The vision statement answers the question, "What does the organization want to or aspire to become?" The vision statement lays the foundation for the development of a mission statement that reflects the organization's core values, beliefs, culture, and purpose. The mission statement answers the question, "What is the organization's purpose?" It identifies the scope of an organization's operations in product/service and market terms.

Next, long-term or corporate goals define specific outcomes that an organization seeks to achieve in order to realize its mission. The last of the building blocks that leads to the strategy formulation stage is the environmental audit. This is an analysis of the internal and external environment to identify organizational strengths and weaknesses and environmental threats and opportunities. It is performed prior to strategy formulation. The ever-more dynamic nature of the external environment demands a periodic reexamination of not just an organization's existing strategies, but also its vision, mission, and long-term objectives.

Strategy formulation specifies the strategies for achieving an organization's objectives. Strategies are the means to the ends (objectives). Strategy implementation takes place through the basic organizational architecture (structure, policies, procedures, systems, incentives, and governance) that makes things happen.[34,35] The final phase, strategy evaluation, involves comparing expected outcomes with actual results after the implementation phase. Each part of this framework is elaborated on next.

Learning Outcome 2 *Describe the relevance of analyzing the internal and external environment to the strategic management process.*

Analyzing the Environment

One of the most important activities of strategic leadership is understanding the type of industry and general environment in which the organization operates. This involves being able to identify and interpret emerging trends before they become evident to everyone else. Organizations operate in highly uncertain and changing environments in which existing strategies quickly become outdated and ineffective—what others have described as environments characterized by turbulent disruptions.

Increasingly, leaders are confronted with environmental complexities, ambiguous situations, and conflicting demands from multiple constituencies. To survive and thrive, strategic leaders must be skilled at managing such environmental complexities and uncertainties.[36] Some describe it as strategic flexibility, which is an organization's capability to identify major changes in the external environment and respond promptly.[37,38]

It is essential to learn and understand the concerns of customers, the availability and bargaining power of suppliers and customers, the actions of competitors, market trends, economic conditions, government policies, and technological advances. From a competitive standpoint, knowing what your competitors are doing and how to respond is clearly important to a firm's survival. It is no surprise that competitive dynamics heavily influence the nature and content of a firm's strategies and its outcomes.[39] The underlying tenet of strategic management is that organizations need to formulate strategies to take advantage of external opportunities and to avoid or reduce the negative impact of external threats.[40]

Recent changes in communications technology and the labor force have created opportunities for forward-looking strategists to change the way work is done. Advances in telecommunications, the need to balance work–family life as more women enter the workforce, the rising cost of gasoline, increased traffic delays, and time scarcity are all trends that have led to a flexible and distributed working arrangement called telecommuting. With telecommuting, traditional hierachical bureaucratic structures are being replaced by flat structures that empower workers to work from home or even foreign country locations.[41] Companies that are slow to respond to these changes or have yet to respond are losing out on recruiting and utilizing talented employees who prefer this type of work structure. The discussion in Chapter 8 on the growing use of virtual self-managed teams is an example of this trend.

Analyzing the internal environment focuses on assessing an organization's market strength, financial position, capabilities, core competencies, culture, and structure. This process reveals an organization's strengths and weaknesses in its functional areas such as marketing, finance/accounting, HR, R&D, and production/operations. The combined analysis of the external environment (i.e., to identify opportunities and threats) and internal environment (i.e., to identify strengths and weaknesses) is commonly referred to as SWOT (Strengths, Weaknesses, Opportunities, and Threats), or situation, analysis. The effectiveness of an organization's strategies is influenced by the degree of fit or alignment between the organization's internal capabilities/resources and its environmental opportunities.[42]

Accurate interpretation of both types of environments requires considerable analytical and cognitive skills, such as the conceptual skills to think critically, identify and make sense of several complex trends, and streamline available information into a concise plan of action. Some have described this as the comprehensiveness of the strategy decision-making process.[43] Accurate and timely interpretation of environmental trends plays a large part in the future actions and the continuing effectiveness of an organization. The importance of speed in recognizing and responding to environmental opportunities and threats has been dramatically accentuated by the highly competitive landscape facing most organizations. As a result, some strategic leaders believe that it much better to be a first mover or pioneer and make mistakes occasionally than to be a follower.

Work Application 1

Think of your college or university. Prepare a SWOT analysis that identifies one opportunity and one threat facing your institution in the next five years. Also identify a strength and a weakness that you think your institution has.

Because environmental changes are often ambiguous, effective strategic leaders must rely on multiple sources of information for accurate interpretations, and also a balanced application of intuition and rationality. Intuition has been described as the interplay of knowing based on expertise and sensing based on feeling.[44] Executives make considerable use of intuition when strategizing. Intuition and rational analysis are viewed as two parallel systems of knowing that allow for high-quality strategic decision making.[45] They reinforce rather than oppose each other.

Opening Case APPLICATION

2. Describe Google's business environment. How well is Google adapting to it?

Google operates in the high-tech Internet environment, a sector that is undergoing significant transformations. The competition between Google, Yahoo!, and Microsoft for supremacy is intense. The technologies for serving user needs in the industry are constantly changing. Major demographic changes are taking place among the user market. The world's economy is now one boundaryless global market with as much universality as diversity in customer needs. Google has adapted well to this turbulent business environment. With math, science, and computer technology backgrounds, Brin and Page created an economical, distributed system, based on thousands of servers built around commodity PC hardware to support the gathering, storage, and analysis of Web content on a huge scale. Their focus on technological innovation and operating costs has created a search engine that is currently number one in its industry.

Learning Outcome 3 *Explain the importance of a vision and a mission statement.*

Vision Statement

Strategic leadership starts with the creation of meaning and purpose for the organization with a compelling vision and mission.[46] According to one expert, organizational leaders too often plunge into a long-term strategic planning process without first deliberating on certain fundamental questions relating to organizational beliefs and values. These questions include: Who are we (core ideology)? Why do we exist (core purpose)? What do we believe in (core values)? What inspires us (envisioned future)? Where are we going (vision statement)? And, finally, What will the future look like when we get there (vivid description)? These questions embody the essence of a strategic vision and mission statement.

A **strategic vision** *is an ambitious view of the future that everyone in the organization can believe in and that is not readily attainable, yet offers a future that is better in important ways than what now exists.*[47] It is important for the CEO to convey a vision of the organization's future and to do it in such a way that followers accept it as their vision as well. The leader must have a clear idea of what he or she wants to do and the strength to persist in the face of setbacks and even failures.[48]

John F. Kennedy demonstrated vision when he promised that an American would land on the moon during the 1960s, because at the time of his announcement, NASA was in its infancy and the state-of-the-art technology for space exploration was Sputnik. To be motivating, a vision must be expressed in ideological terms, not just in economic terms, to help people develop a personal connection with the organization.[49] A clear and inspiring vision serves a number of important functions, including[50]

- facilitating decision making, in that it helps people determine what is good or bad, important or trivial;
- inspiring followers by appealing to their fundamental human need to feel important and useful, and to be a part of something great;
- linking the present to the past by rationalizing the need for changing old ways of doing work;
- giving meaning to work by explaining not just what people do but why they do it;
- establishing a standard of excellence.

Work Application 2

Write an inspiring vision statement for an organization you work or worked for. If the company has one, you may use it or revise it. Explain why you think it has an inspirational appeal.

Effective leaders understand that creating a vision involves content, process, and implementation. To be widely accepted, vision creation should be a shared exercise. The role of the leader in bringing together all the key partners to the visioning process is critical.

To make a difference, a vision must be based on the input and values of followers and other key stakeholders. A well-crafted vision is one that is the result of teamwork, simple enough to be understood, appealing enough to energize and garner commitment, and credible enough to be accepted as realistic and attainable.[51] Some examples of companies with simple yet inspiring vision statements include the following:

- Komatsu: "Encircle Caterpillar"
- Coca-Cola: "People, Planet, Portfolio, Partners, and Profit—the five Ps"
- Citibank: "To be the most powerful, the most serviceable, the most far reaching world financial institution that has ever been"

- Nike: "To crush the enemy"
- American Express: "To be the world's most respected service brand"

Mission Statement

A vision statement provides the foundation for developing an organization's mission statement, which describes the general purpose of the organization. Research supports the proposition that managerial perceptions of the mission statement impact their implementation; also, that the mission statement's content and the process of creating it can lead to superior performance.[52] According to a *Business Week* report, firms with well-crafted mission statements have a 30 percent higher return on certain financial measures than firms that lack such documents.

A **mission statement** *is an enduring statement of purpose that distinguishes one organization from other similar enterprises.* It is the organization's core purpose and reason for existence. It answers the question, "What business are we in?" The two components that are often featured in a mission statement are the core values and the core purpose. The core values outline the guiding principles and ethical standards by which the company will conduct business, no matter the circumstance.

A well-crafted mission statement can provide many benefits to an organization, including providing direction and focus, forming the basis for objectives and strategies, inspiring positive emotions about the organization, ensuring unanimity of purpose, and helping resolve divergent views among managers.[53]

The core purpose doesn't just describe goods and services; it describes the broad needs (immediate and anticipated) of the people served by the organization. For 3M, the mission is "To solve unsolved problems innovatively"; for Merck, it is "To preserve and improve human life"; for the Army, it is "To be all that you can be"; and for Ford, it is to make "Quality job one." In these and many other examples, there is no mention of the specific products or services these organizations manufacture or serve.

Examples abound of organizations that have been adversely affected by poorly crafted mission statements. The railroad industry almost brought about its own demise by defining its mission as being in the railroad business rather than the transportation business. The March of Dimes' original mission was "to cure polio," until a cure was discovered and the organization found itself without a purpose. Today, its mission is to advance human health. Motorola and Zenith were once successful competitors in the manufacture and sale of televisions. Yet, while Zenith has lost ground, Motorola has continued to grow and expand. The difference is that Motorola, unlike Zenith, defined its mission as "applying technology to benefit the public," not as "making television sets."

A good mission statement should focus on the needs that the organization's products/services are meeting. The mission should be broad but not so broad that it does not distinguish the organization from its competitors. It should be specific but not so specific that it creates rigidity and resistance to new ideas. Finding an appropriate balance between specificity and generality is difficult, but worth the effort. It is generally believed that mission-driven organizations stand a better chance of succeeding and thus creating long-term shareholder value than those that are not mission-driven.[54]

A vision statement represents a future aspiration, whereas the mission statement represents the enduring character, values, and purpose of the organization in the present. The job of strategic leadership is to ensure that the vision and mission of the organization are effectively communicated and embraced by all employees.

Work Application 3

Write an inspiring mission statement for an organization you work or worked for. If the company has one, you may use it or revise it. Explain the core values and core purpose of your mission statement.

Opening Case APPLICATION

3. Critique Google's mission statement.

Google's mission is to organize the world's information and make it universally accessible and useful. It succinctly identifies Google's purpose. It focuses on the need (information) that Google's product/service (search engine technology) provides. It is neither too broad nor too narrow. Of the two components often featured in mission statements—core values and core purpose—Google's mission statement only identifies its core purpose; however, Google has a separate document called "Google's Code of Conduct" that identifies its core values. Overall, Google's mission statement is well-designed.

Learning Outcome 4 *Explain the relationship between corporate goals and strategies.*

Corporate-Level Goals

Goals are the desired long-term outcomes that an organization seeks to achieve for its various stakeholders—employees, customers, suppliers, stockholders, government agencies, activists, and other community groups.[55] Companies develop both financial and strategic goals. Financial goals may include measures such as return on investment, sales, profits, earnings per share, or return on equity. Strategic goals may include new customer, market, or product types to pursue. Corporate goals represent a clear and unambiguous articulation of what needs to be done.

Commitment to organizational goals is achieved when there is broad participation in goal setting, and rewards are linked to goal achievement. This is based on the underlying premise that one's conscious goals affect what one achieves. Goal-setting theory asserts that people with specific goals (often called "stretch" goals) perform better than those with vague goals (such as "do your best") or easily attained goals.[56] Stretch goals are difficult yet achievable goals. Stretch goals have been found to improve organizational effectiveness and enhance personal growth and professional development.[57]

Goals are essential because they help focus everyone in the same direction; they are the target against which actual performance is compared for strategy evaluation (feedback); they create synergy; they are the means by which organizations reveal their priorities; and they are the basis for effective planning, organizing, leading, and controlling activities.[58] Organizations must take the time to establish "SMART" goals (i.e., specific, measurable, achievable, results-based, and time-specific). Refer to Chapter 3 for details on how to write effective objectives (see Model 3.1).

Opening Case APPLICATION

4. How well do Google's long-term objectives balance the interests of its stakeholders?

CEO Eric Schmidt believes that in the long term, Google's obligation is to maximize shareholder and customer value by providing the best user experience. Google is a company that has remained relentlessly focused on the end user by continously improving on the quality of its search results. To accomplish this, Google has brought together a highly talented and motivated workforce. The media has regularly featured stories on Google touting its generous incentives and compensation package for its employees. For the second year running, *Fortune* named Google the best company to work for. The focus on quality has brought in more users and consequently more advertising revenues and profits. Google's philanthropic causes

continued

(Opening Case Application 4 continued)

include disease prediction and prevention, improvement of public services by informing and empowering people, and the increase of economic growth and job creation through stimulating small- and medium-sized enterprises. Google is a company that understands the needs and interests of its various stakeholders and is doing a great job trying to serve each group.

Strategy Formulation

Armed with a vision and mission statement, corporate objectives, and an assessment of the internal and external environment, a strategist can then select appropriate strategies or plans of action for his or her organization. Corporate strategy draws from all these elements.[59] *A* **strategy** *is an integrated, overarching plan of how an organization will achieve its objectives.* It represents the means to an end.

Examples of strategies include such actions as diversification, joint ventures, mergers and acquisitions, new product development, and entering new markets. Selecting among these options is a critical managerial activity, requiring careful consideration of various factors (including the results of SWOT analysis described earlier). For example, many companies have opted for external growth strategies such as mergers and acquisitions to avoid time-consuming and risky internal efforts.

For companies operating in high-velocity or turbulent environments, the desire to launch multiple product innovations in quick succession is the rationale behind large established firms acquiring small technology-based firms.[60,61] The opening case highlights Google's acquisition of several small technology-based firms as part of its aggressive growth strategy. Today's increasing competitive pressures require leaders to continuously seek opportunities for new strategies, to be aware of what reactions such strategies will incite from competitors, and to be prepared to defend their own interests when rivals attack.

A good strategy focuses on exploiting opportunities in the organization's external environment that match the organization's strengths.[62,63] In terms of an innovation strategy, studies have found that high-performing firms generally have stronger and more defined leadership and culture styles compared to low-performing firms.[64] A causal relationship exists among strategy, organizational culture, leadership, and innovation.[65,66] Some leading innovators, such as 3M, Microsoft, GE, Google, Nike, Procter & Gamble, and Whirlpool, to name a few, have validated this hypothesis.[67] Also, a good strategy must reflect the core mission and objectives of the organization. To maintain a competitive edge over rivals, effective strategic leaders develop strategies that

- enhance value to the customers;
- create synergistic opportunities;
- build on the company's core competence.[68,69]

Delivering value to the customer should be central to any strategy.[70] **Value** *is the ratio of benefits received to the cost incurred by the customer.* A strategy without this quality is sure to fail.[71,72] Synergy occurs when a chosen strategy (such as in related diversification) calls for organizational units or systems to interact and produce a joint result that is greater than the sum of the parts acting independently—the "2 + 2 = 5" phenomenon. Synergistic benefits include lower cost, greater market power, or superior employee skills and capabilities.

Strategies that are based on a company's core competencies have a better chance of improving the company's performance.[73] *A* **core competence** *is a capability that allows an organization to perform extremely well in comparison to competitors.* A strategic leader's job is to identify the organization's unique strengths—what differentiates the organization from its competitors in the industry. Core competencies are a source of sustainable competitive advantage when they are rare, hard to imitate, not easily substitutable, and create value for the firm.

Another factor that contributes to a firm's ability to sustain its competitive advantage is the extent to which core competencies match the opportunities available in the external environment and consistently generate higher customer value.[74] Arguably, the most distinctive and hard to imitate resource available to firms is knowledge, especially people-based knowledge.[75,76] There is a shared belief among scholars that an organization's financial and strategic success is partially dependent on the actions and interactions of employees as they share ideas and information across functional boundaries.[77]

Many of the companies considered leaders in their industry sector atrtribute a large part of their success to the knowledge base of their employees. A knowledge-based competitive advantage is hard to imitate or copy by rivals because it resides in people, not physical assets. Unlike physical resources, which are depleted when used, core competencies increase (in terms of their efficient application) as they are used. They represent the source of a company's competitive advantage over its rivals.[78,79]

Work Application 4

Identify a core competence of an organization you work or worked for. Explain how it differentiates the organization from its competitors.

A strategy is just the means to the end result of meeting customers' needs profitably. Many business failures can still be attributed to companies paying too much attention to the means and ignoring the customer. The customer must be central in strategy formulation because without consumers buying the products and services offered by a firm, strategy fails and performance suffers.[80] Creating a winning market leadership program that maximizes customer value creation is a precondition for firm profitability and survival.[81]

Opening Case APPLICATION

5. What type of growth strategy is Google pursuing, and why do you think the leadership team has chosen such a course rather than the alternatives?

Google is pursuing a growth strategy of mergers and acquisitions with other related businesses. This strategy is preferred because it allows Google to quickly adopt new technologies and processes rather than trying to develop them internally. Given the rapid changes the industry is undergoing, timing is critical. Acquisitions and partnerships make more sense.

Applying the **Concept 1**

Strategic Management Process

Identify each statement as part of the strategic management process.

a. analyze the environment
b. vision
c. mission
d. goal
e. strategy
f. value
g. core competence

____ 1. Springfield College: We educate students in spirit, mind, and body for leadership in service to humanity.

____ 2. Toyota: To become and remain the number 1 auto seller in the world.

____ 3. Motorola: The Apple iPhone is taking away sales.

____ 4. YMCA: We are the only child care provider to offer gym and swim classes as part of our programs.

continued

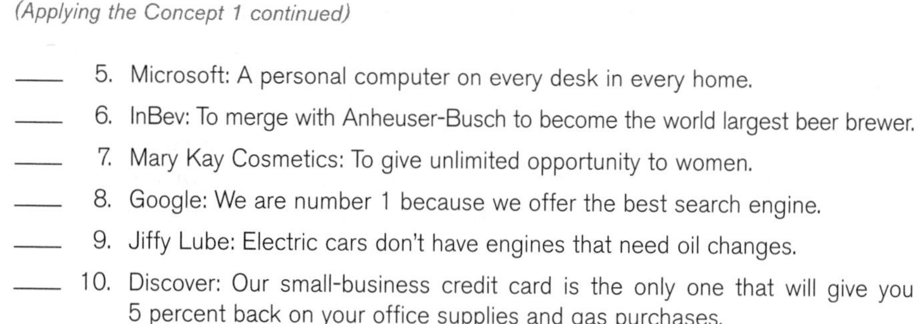

(Applying the Concept 1 continued)

____ 5. Microsoft: A personal computer on every desk in every home.

____ 6. InBev: To merge with Anheuser-Busch to become the world largest beer brewer.

____ 7. Mary Kay Cosmetics: To give unlimited opportunity to women.

____ 8. Google: We are number 1 because we offer the best search engine.

____ 9. Jiffy Lube: Electric cars don't have engines that need oil changes.

____ 10. Discover: Our small-business credit card is the only one that will give you 5 percent back on your office supplies and gas purchases.

Strategy Implementation

Effective strategy implementation means that objectives have a greater chance of being met and thus results in better firm performance.[82,83] Strategy implementation has been described as the most important and most difficult part of the strategic management process. Strong leadership is considered one of the most important tools for successful strategy implementation.[84,85] The style of leadership and an abundance of managerial skills make a difference. As was revealed in Chapter 2, some successful leaders employ a directive and task-oriented leadership style while others are equally successful by being more consultative, participative, and people-oriented. Managerial skills such as persuasiveness, administrative ability, communication, knowledge about team dynamics, social skills, creativity, and conceptual skills have been found to strongly affect strategy implementation efforts and ultimately firm performance.[86]

Strategy implementation requires galvanizing the organization's employees and managers at all levels to turn formulated strategies into action. An excellent strategy that is poorly executed will yield the same poor results as a bad strategy. Regardless of the strategy, careful consideration must be paid not just to its formulation but to its implementation as well.[87]

There are obstacles to effective strategy implementation.[88] Most strategies fail for lack of resources.[89] The leader must prioritize and make resources available during strategy implementation. Rewards and other forms of compensation must be aligned with the goals that employees are seeking to accomplish. Also, time is of the essence in strategy implementation. Being careful and rational during strategy formulation is important but not sufficient if managers are slow to initiate actions. Managers must avoid becoming trapped in the vicious cycle of rigidity and inaction that prevents them from acting in a timely fashion.[90]

Strategy implementation is considered the most difficult stage because it involves dealing with people who come with varying levels of motivation, commitment, and dedication. These differences often result in interpersonal conflicts that, if left unresolved, can significantly affect implementation efforts and performance.[91] Successful strategy implementation rests on the shoulders of managers who must be able to motivate employees to cooperatively perform at high levels—a task that is not always easy to undertake when the right employees are not in place or the leader lacks people skills.[92]

Another factor that makes strategy implementation a difficult process is related to the many components that need to be integrated in order to turn a chosen strategy into action. Leadership decisions on key issues such as appropriate annual objectives, structure, culture, pay or reward systems, budget allocation, and organizational rules, policies, and procedures will determine the success or failure of strategy implementation.[93] Decisions in these areas must match the requirements of the chosen strategy, mission, and objectives of the company.[94]

A company pursuing a strategy of differentiation through innovation in a bureaucratic, hierarchical organizational structure will be an example of a mismatch between strategy and structure. However, a company pursuing a strategy of internal efficiency and stability, aimed at offering customers lower prices than competitors, is more likely to succeed with this type of centralized hierarchical structure because of its strict controls on cost containment. A lack of fit between strategy elements (for example, a strategy–culture, strategy–structure, or strategy–environment misalignment) increases the chances of failure. Assessing the extent to which stated goals have been achieved or not achieved after implementation is strategy evaluation.

Opening Case APPLICATION

6. What are some of the factors contributing to Google's effective strategy implementation?

The following factors have supported and continue to support Google's effective strategy implementation:

- Its highly talented leadership team and workforce
- The strength of its culture that emphasizes teamwork, flexibility, transparency, and innovation
- Its structure—there is little in the way of corporate hierarchy
- Its aggressive hiring policy—it is nondiscriminatory and favors ability over experience

Applying the **Concept 2**

Strategic Thinking

Identify in each statement if the view expressed is reflective of a strategic or nonstrategic thinker.

a. strategic thinker b. nonstrategic thinker

____ 11. It makes good sense for top management to frequently ask themselves the question, "What will the future of this industry look like?"

____ 12. I spend my time focusing on solving the day-to-day problems.

____ 13. We are not concerned about developing skills or capabilities that cannot help us to perform the present job.

____ 14. A company cannot reach its full potential without an inspiring vision.

____ 15. In our business the environment changes very quickly. Therefore, we generally take things one week at a time.

Learning Outcome 5 *Explain the importance of strategy evaluation in the strategic management model.*

Strategy Evaluation

Strategy evaluation is the final stage in the strategic management process; it is the primary means of determining the effectiveness of the strategic management process. Effective strategy evaluation involves three fundamental activities:

(1) reviewing internal and external factors that are the bases for the current strategies, (2) measuring performance against stated objectives, and (3) taking corrective action.

What this three-step sequence of activities reveals is that strategy evaluation is a process that leaders use to assess the effectiveness of an organization's strategy used to achieve its objectives. When step two reveals discrepancies, it is the responsibility of senior leaders to support change efforts. It is the task of the strategic leader to encourage meaningful communication and interaction among managers and employees across hierarchical levels, so that feedback from strategy evaluation can be shared throughout the organization and necessary changes implemented. It is the job of strategic leadership to foster and promote a culture of openness and teamwork throughout the organization. A popular tool used to measure the effectiveness of the strategic management process is the balance scorecard. The balance scorecard translates mission and vision statements into a comprehensive set of objectives and performance measures that can be quantified and appraised.[95,96]

In 2004, Coca-Cola's board of directors called Neville Isdell out of retirement to lead the 122-year-old beverage company back to growth and profitability after two failed reorganization attempts. Isdell's first move was to bring in a new Human Resources Vice President, Cynthia McCague. Isdell reorganized the HR function so that instead of reporting to the general counsel's office, it reported directly to him. This move signaled the beginning of an important partnership between HR and strategic leadership at Coca-Cola. With this change in place, HR and senior managers embarked on a seven-month-long internal analysis of the company. A survey of the top 400 managers of Coca-Cola revealed some hard truths about the feelings of employees. For example, there was a feeling that the company and its people lacked a clear direction and a common purpose, had low employee morale, and demonstrated a lack of teamwork. Another group of 150 senior managers from around the globe met several times to review the survey results and interviews. Working in groups called "workstreams," they came up with solutions. Each workstream was led by two senior executives and included operational and functional managers. One workstream helped formulate new vision, mission, and values statements for Coca-Cola. The implementation plan was again a team effort. HR partnered with public affairs and communication specialists to roll out the plan. Communication was highly stressed with many interactions taking place via face-to-face meetings, intranet, webTV, and BlogBlast. The results so far have been positive. Isdell attributes the success to the process of looking inward, working collaboratively to create solutions, and engaging employees in implementation.[97] This example illustrates how strategic leadership and strategic management interact to bring about change. It is evident that Isdell and his team modeled the strategic management process described in this section.

Coca-Cola needed to change, and the board brought Isdell out of retirement to make it happen after two failed attempts. Implementing change is a key aspect of strategic leadership and is the subject of the next section.

Implementing Change

Strategy is often described as the management of change. Recall that change is part of our definition of leadership (Chapter 1); *leadership is the process of influencing leaders and followers to achieve organizational objectives through change.* As the discussion of charismatic, transformational, and strategic leadership has revealed, the focus of each of these three leadership disciplines is change, not status quo. The central issue in this section is to understand how change processes can be managed in order to improve the effectiveness of individual leaders and ultimately organizational success. **Organizational change** is defined as *an alteration in an organization's alignment with its external environment.*[98]

In today's turbulent environment, where change is a fact of life, organizations must constantly cope with unfamiliar events or situations in order to survive and stay competitive.[99] Corporations and government institutions spend millions of dollars on change efforts. Examples of change efforts include process improvement or re-engineering, restructuring, business acquisitions or mergers, business contractions or expansions, new technologies, a new organizational culture, or a change in leadership.

Change can be transformational or incremental, and sometimes an incremental change can emerge or amplify into a much larger and radical change than was anticipated.[100] In some cases, radical change may require a redefinition of an organization's vision and mission, and consequently a shift in the organization's objectives and strategies. In essence, organizational change is any transition that requires a change in human performance. Change is about people doing things differently. In this last section, we discuss the need for change, the role of leadership in implementing change, the change process, why people resist change, and strategies for minimizing resistance to change.

Ethical **Dilemma 2**

Change Through Upgrading

SAP is a world-leading software company, headquartered in Germany. Fluor Corporation is one of the world's largest publicly owned engineering, procurement, construction, and maintenance services organizations.

Fluor and other businesses have accused SAP and other software companies of forcing them to upgrade their software. Fluor claims that SAP upgrades are often minor and not needed, yet Fluor is required to purchase the upgrades. In fact, Fluor dropped part of the products it had licensed from SAP and tried to take over its own software, hiring its own Chief Information Officer (CIO) at a cost of about $13 million. However, SAP told Fluor that it would have to install a new version or pay even higher annual fees to get updates, fixes for bugs, and access to SAP's technicians.

1. Do you believe that companies come out with upgrades just to make more money (sometimes called *planned obsolescence*), or do you believe companies are being honestly innovative and customers are just resistant to change?
2. As a sales rep, would you push selling an upgrade to a customer who doesn't really need one so that you can make a commission?
3. What would you do if your boss pressured you to sell unneeded upgrades?
4. Is it ethical and socially responsible to "require" updates to continue using a product or service?

The Need for Change

In the past two decades, institutional theorists have been able to offer more insights into the processes that explain institutional stability than those that explain institutional change.[101] However, rapid environmental changes are causing fundamental transformations that are having a dramatic impact on organizations and presenting new opportunities and threats for leadership.[102] As a result, the literature on organizational change is increasingly viewed as an alteration of not only structures, systems, and processes, but also as a cognitive leadership reorientation.[103] Leaders must recognize the need to communicate a new mission and priorities to stakeholders when conditions warrant such actions.[104]

A key first step in managing change is to identify and analyze the need for change before embarking on any implementation plan. A comprehensive analysis that gives a clear and accurate assessment of prevailing conditions in the organization's internal and external environments should be a prerequisite step before any change in the management process is initiated.[105]

Just about every type of organization is facing an external environment characterized by rapid technological changes, a global economy, changing market requirements, and intense domestic and international competition. These changes have created opportunities such as larger, underserved markets in developing economies and falling trade barriers. Threats in the form of more domestic and foreign competition, increased rates of obsolescence in existing technologies, increased speed in new innovations, shortened product life cycles, and global competition are also evident in this type of environment.

Internally, the need for change is more likely when a long-time CEO retires and a new CEO is brought in, especially if the new CEO is an outsider charged with a mandate for change by the board of directors. A steady trend of mediocre performance in an organization that aspires to be a leader in its industry sector may signal the need for a change in leadership, employee ranks, or strategies. In January 2007, Michael Dell took back the leadership of Dell Inc. from Kevin Rollins after more than a year of mounting problems.[106] Even a one-time strategic blunder that results in a significant decline in key performance metrics (profitability, stock price, and so on) may trigger the calls for a change in leadership. Such was the case with Citigroup and American Express, whose high-performing CEOs were fired due to huge losses resulting from bad investments in the subprime housing market. When an organization is in crisis (financial or nonfinancial), the need for change increases.[107]

Evidence seems to be tilting more toward the view that real change does not start to happen until the organization is experiencing some external threat or imminent danger of significant loss due to an internal weakness. There is a need to establish a sense of urgency. People need to know that change is needed—now—and why. This is what Edgar Schein—Sloan Fellows Professor of Management Emeritus and senior lecturer at MIT's Sloan School of Management—refers to as "survival anxiety." **Survival anxiety** *is the feeling that unless an organization makes a change, it is going to be out of business or fail to achieve some important goals.* According to Schein, survival anxiety is a necessary but not sufficient stimulus to change. He argues that the reason survival anxiety is not sufficient to stimulate change is because the prospect of learning something new itself produces anxiety, what he calls "learning anxiety"; and this can create resistance to change even with a high survival anxiety.[108] It is for this reason that many experts point out that a "buy in" by followers is crucial for change to succeed.[109] This topic will be further discussed in the later section on why people resist change. Awareness of the need for change, and a leader's ability to inspire followers to transcend their own immediate interests for the sake of the organization's mission, underscores the importance of effective leadership in implementing change.

Opening Case APP[illegible]ATION

7. Does a successful company like Google s[illegible] change?

In one word, yes. As mentioned earlier, Google's [illegible] environment keeps changing and with it comes opportunities and threats. Goog[illegible]tinue to anticipate changes and adapt its strategies, systems, culture, and [illegible]ign with such changes. Some of the changes that Google has undertaken [illegible] the decision by Larry Page to step down into a VP role and let Eric Schmidt [illegible] front man, as well as the decision to make many acquisitions of companie[illegible]ages of development. So far Google has acquired more than 50 companie[illegible]tion brings in a company that may be different in its way of doing things [illegible] Being able to merge these companies under the Google culture and achie[illegible] of results that the company is getting so far is a mark of effective change implementation.

The Role of Leadership in Implementing Change

Despite the growing consensus that change is imperative if organizations are to grow and thrive in the current and future environment, effecting change, especially major change, is still not an easy undertaking. Many change efforts don't meet the expectations of the organization.[110,111] The following three statistics tell the story: (1) approximately 75 percent of mergers and acquisitions among European and Americans companies fail to reach their financial targets or expected synergies; (2) fewer than 50 percent of companies undergoing restructuring (such as downsizing or re-engineering) realize the anticipated lower costs or higher productivity gains envisioned by the organization; and (3) approximately 30 percent of all mergers and acquisitions fail outright.

A central strategic challenge for many leaders is managing people during the change process and dealing with resistance. Resistance to change and the absence of effective leadership are major reasons for why most transformation efforts fail.[112,113] Focusing on the role of effective leadership, one study revealed that the likelihood of employee resistance reflects the type of influence a leader uses and the strength of the leader–member exchange (discussed in Chapter 7).[114]

There is growing interest in understanding how to increase the success rate of change initiatives.[115] Experts stress the importance of leadership involvement throughout the process.[116,117,118] There has been much focus on strategies that leaders can use to effectively manage change rather than simply reacting to it.[119] These strategies include articulating a compelling reason for change; having open and regular communications, a road map for implementation, and training programs for required skills/competencies; forming a coalition of supporters and experts in the field during the early stages of the change process; staying the course in spite of perceived difficulties; recognizing and rewarding the contributions of others to the process; carefully managing resources and priorities; keeping the process transparent; and last but not least, having a plan for dealing with resistance.[120,121,122]

Leadership must make every effort to eliminate policies, procedures, and behaviors that undermine the change efforts. Followers who are charged with implementing change must see in the behavior of their leaders an honest effort to share in the challenges of the change.[123,124,125] The leader must be willing to alter his or her own behavior if it will minimize resistance. A leader must embody the change that he or she wants to see in followers. Ghandhi put it best when he said, "We must become the change we want to see." Finally, effective change agents must be good listeners. Effective listening helps a leader to have a better understanding of the root causes of resistance. A better understanding of the reasons followers are resisting a particular change initiative can help the leader to come up with better solutions for resolving the issues.

Ultimately, the role of the leader is to implement change that results in better organizational performance; however, the question has always been how to do it effectively and successfully, given the stress, discomfort, and dislocation associated with it. For example, a change in leadership may affect members' initial trust in the new leader, communications with the new leader, motivation to perform, job satisfaction, and even turnover.[126] The change management process described below enhances the chances of successful change implementation and the likelihood that more people will support and commit to the change effort rather than resist it. It is a tool, or the means to get to the end result.

The Change Management Process

Many experts and scholars recommend viewing change as a process, not a product. The change process is the means for a leader to transform the organization, a way to realize a new vision for the organization.[127] It requires moving through several stages and executing different tasks, including performing an organizational audit, planning, formulating the change strategy, communicating, persuading others, and consolidating the change.[128,129] It takes effective transformational leadership (at the individual, group, and organizational levels) to accomplish all these activities.[130]

One of the earliest and most widely used change process theories is the *force-field model*. This model proposes that the change process is divided into three phases: unfreezing, changing, and refreezing (see Exhibit 11.2 on the next page). A more recent theory is the *eight-stage model* of planned organizational change.[131] The two models complement each other; however, the difference between the two models is in the implementation phase.

The eight-stage model of planned organizational change provides considerably more detail in the implementation phase than does the force-field model. It stipulates eight sequential steps compared to one step (the changing phase) for the force-field model. The steps in the eight-stage model are as follows:

1. Establish a sense of urgency.
2. Form a support platform (pro-change coalition).
3. Develop a compelling vision.
4. Diffuse the vision throughout the organization.
5. Train and empower followers to act on the vision.
6. Allow for short-term accomplishments, and reward performance.
7. Consolidate gains by changing the culture, systems, policies, and structures to align with the new vision.
8. Institutionalize the change in the organizational culture.

We will focus on the three basic phases of the force-field model and incorporate some of the elements of the eight-stage model into the discussion.

Learning Outcome 6 *Describe the three phases of the change process.*

Unfreezing Phase

Instigated by the actions of a charismatic, strategic, or transformational leader, people in an organization may become aware of the need for change. In other words, a leader may inspire people with a vision of a better future that is sufficiently

EXHIBIT 11.2 Stages in the Change Process: A Comparison of the Force-Field Model and Eight-Stage Model

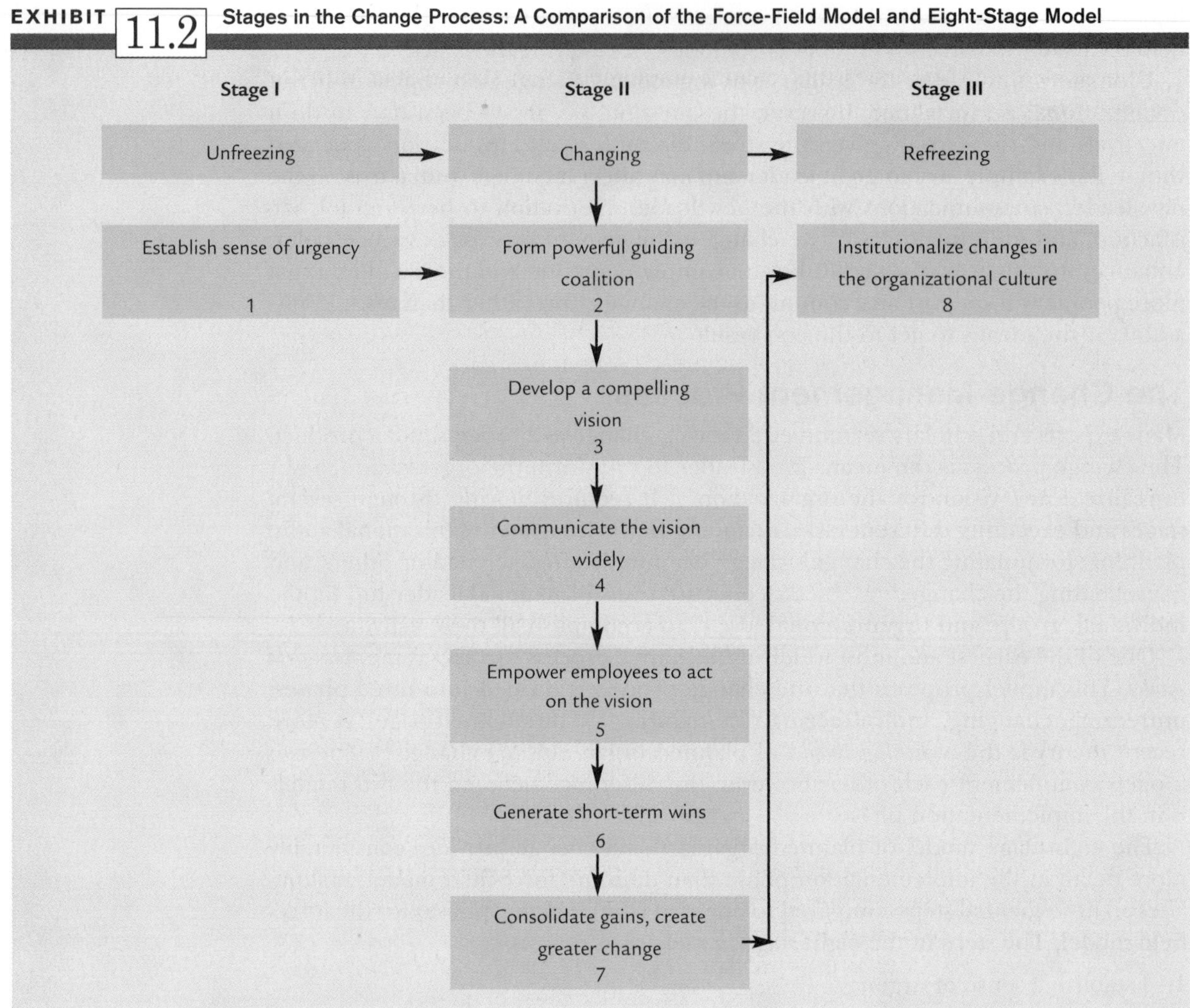

attractive to convince them that the old ways of doing business are no longer adequate. This recognition may occur as a result of an immediate crisis, or it may result from the efforts of a transformational leader who is able to describe threats and opportunities not yet evident to most people in the organization.

The key is to identify the problems or threats facing the organization that make for an urgent need to change. It is important to invest the time at this early stage to uncover not just the threat, but its root cause(s) because the rest of the steps will focus on the specific threat. People have to be convinced of the need for change, and a focus on the wrong threat and/or root causes can complicate later stages of the change process. When followers are not convinced of the need for change or don't understand it, there is a greater likelihood of resistance. The next phase of the force-field model of change management is the changing phase.

Changing Phase

This is the phase where the actual change takes place. It is the implementation phase. Here, people look for leadership in finding new ways of doing things. Lack of a carefully designed plan of action at this stage will result in an uninspiring outcome. As mentioned above, the difference between the force-field model and the eight-stage model occurs during this stage. The eight-stage model prescribes six steps that, in essence, are part of the changing phase in the force-field model. As shown in Exhibit 11.2, these are steps two through seven.

The second step stipulates that change implementation should start with the leader forming a powerful guiding coalition that supports the change initiative. One way to do this is by establishing a cross-functional team with the necessary expertise and power to guide the change process. Scholars and practitioners generally agree that a support platform of personalities who can rally followers to "buy into" the change effort should be the number one consideration. Examples of such personalities include people who are well respected, seen as credible, and well liked. Another recommendation is that such a pro-change coalition should consist of people who are effective communicators and who understand the roadblocks, inertia, fears, and political issues that would impede adoption of change initiatives.

With a pro-change coalition in place, the third step in the eight-stage model is for the leader to develop and articulate a compelling vision that will guide the change effort and formulate the strategies for achieving that vision. To be committed to the change process, people need to believe in the leader's vision of a promising future that is significantly better than the present to justify the costs and hardships that the transformation will bring. Researchers caution that the context for change needs to be established by the CEO or the top leadership of the organization. Also, a shared vision with the top leadership team must be debated and a consensus hammered out before any attempt is undertaken to communicate the vision more broadly to the entire organization.

The fourth step is active communication of the new vision and strategies for effecting the change. The leader's excellent communication skills and ability to mobilize widespread participation in the change process are critical for success. Effective communication of the new vision and change initiative requires that senior leadership stay in constant contact with members of the organization, in a consistent manner and from a unified front. It is generally believed that the most effective leaders have strong interpersonal skills that blend the instrumental and charismatic qualities of change leadership.

The fifth step describes the importance of empowering employees throughout the organization to act on the vision. The leader must empower people with resources, information, and discretion to make decisions. Successful implementation is increasingly dependent on winning employee support and enthusiasm for proposed changes, rather than merely overcoming resistance. Empowerment must also include removing obstacles to change, which may include adapting the infrastructure (systems, structure, policies, procedures, and rules) to match the requirements of the change effort.

The sixth and seventh steps require the leader to organize the change activities in ways that highlight and celebrate short-term accomplishments. Major change takes time to complete, and without some visible signs of progress, the transformation effort may lose momentum. Charismatic and transformational leaders understand that actions speak louder than words in creating and sustaining internal momentum for change, even if such actions are merely symbolic. Confidence, enthusiasm, and pride gained via short-term wins will create the drive and motivation to tackle bigger challenges and bring about a faster completion of the change. This leads us to the last phase of the force-field model of change—the refreezing phase.

Refreezing Phase

In the refreezing phase, old habits, values, traditions, attitudes, and mindsets are permanently replaced. New behaviors, values, and attitudes are instilled or "refreezed" in the culture in order to avoid a reversion to the old ways after implementation. Complete transformation can only occur when the desired change in behavior becomes habitual. This phase involves institutionalizing the new changes so they become part and parcel of the organizational culture. This is step eight of the eight-stage model. This last phase is critical because, as the saying goes, "old habits die hard." Resistance that seemed to have been resolved may resurface as resentment for those who supported and committed to the change. As one study points out, in the long run, resistance to change can create *ex post* or after-the-fact effects in that change agents (leaders/managers) may face reprisals for their role in the change process.[132]

Work Application 5

Think of a time when a major change initiative at an organization you were or are affiliated with succeeded or failed. Identify possible reasons for the success or failure, and tie them to the three phases of the force-field model—unfreezing, changing, and refreezing.

Though stages in the change process generally overlap, each phase is critical for success. An attempt to start implementing change without first unfreezing old attitudes is likely to meet with strong resistance. Not refreezing new attitudes and behaviors may result in the change being reversed soon after implementation. Understanding these phases is important for change-oriented leaders, who must exercise good judgment throughout the process.

It should be noted that following these steps does not guarantee success, it only enhances the chances of success. It increases the likelihood that the majority of organizational members will commit to, rather than resist, the change. Even with the best change implementation efforts, a few people will always resist the change. However, it is generally the case that these holdouts tend to come around when confronted by fellow group members whose majority membership is committed to the change.[133]

Learning Outcome 7 *Identify the major reasons for resisting change.*

Why People Resist Change

Change implies learning new ways to do things. Change can disrupt the status quo and lead to stress, discomfort, and for some even dislocation. These conditions motivate people to resist change.[134] Resistance is a natural response by employees who want to protect their self-interest in the organization. For leaders and their followers, change is often perceived as a win-lose proposition where some leaders see it as a positive way to strengthen the organization while some followers view it as a threat to their status and livelihood. Change has to be perceived as a win-win proposition by all leaders and followers.

People realize that trying to learn something new may make them temporarily incompetent, may expose them to rejection by valued groups, and, in the extreme, may cause them to lose their jobs or positions. This can lead to learning anxiety. **Learning anxiety** *is the prospect of learning something new in itself.* As mentioned above, survival anxiety is a necessary but not a sufficient stimulus for change because the prospect of learning something new itself produces anxiety, which then makes us react defensively by denying the reality or validity of the information that triggered the survival anxiety.[135] This then allows us to rationalize that we do not really need the change after all.

Effective change agents/leaders create psychological safety for followers by recognizing the existence of learning anxiety and reducing it by providing ample opportunities for training and education. Focused education and training can be the difference between success and failure in implementing change. To manage change is to manage the learning process.

Effective leaders do not downplay resistance or perceive it as a discipline problem to be dealt with through punishment or coercion.[136,137] Rather, leaders view resistance as energy that can be redirected to support change.[138] As one expert puts it, "shifting the weight of the resistance and turning it into positive momentum will focus the energy where it will do the most good."[139] Exhibit 11.3 summarizes some of the most common reasons found in the literature on why people resist change.[140]

EXHIBIT 11.3 Reasons for Resisting Change

a. Threat to one's self-interest
b. Uncertainty
c. Lack of confidence that change will succeed
d. Lack of conviction that change is necessary
e. Distrust of leadership
f. Threat to personal values
g. Fear of being manipulated

Threat to One's Self-Interest

An employee's self-interest in protecting his or her power, position, prestige, pay, and company benefits is a major reason for opposing change. When an organization embarks on a major change, such as pursuing a new strategy, it often results in a shift in the relative power structure and the status of individuals and units within the organization. For example, changes in job design or technology may require knowledge and skills not currently possessed by employees. For these employees, the fear of losing their jobs or status is a major impetus for resisting change, regardless of the benefits to the organization. This is what was referred to as learning anxiety.

Uncertainty

Uncertainty represents a fear of the unknown. Lack of information about a change initiative creates a sense of uncertainty. When employees don't have full knowledge of how a proposed change will affect them, they may worry that replacing skills they have mastered over the years with new ones may prove too difficult to achieve. Therefore, a proposed change may have a better chance of acceptance if it includes a generous provision for helping employees learn new skills required by the change. This is the psychological safety net that was discussed above. The key to creating psychological safety is to try to make the learning process as painless as possible.

Lack of Confidence That Change Will Succeed

A proposed change may require such a radical transformation from the old ways of doing business that employees will question its likelihood of succeeding. In this case, even though there may be a general acknowledgment of problems and the need for change, the lack of confidence that the change will succeed creates resistance. Also, if there have been instances of past failures, this may create cynicism and doubt of future change proposals.

Lack of Conviction That Change Is Necessary

People may resist change if the leader has failed to articulate a real need and urgency for change. This is especially true in cases in which employees believe that the current strategy has been successful and there is no clear evidence of impending problems in the near future. In other words, survival anxiety is absent or very low; there is no sense that the organization is facing a real threat that could impact its survival or future well-being.

Distrust of Leadership

Trust between parties is the basic requirement for sustaining any relationship. The absence of trust will cause people to resist change, even if there are no obvious threats. Change is resisted if people suspect that there are hidden consequences or motives that management is not revealing. Trust is a valuable currency for leaders to have, because it is the basis upon which the benefits of a proposed change can be sold to employees who may suffer personal losses from such action.

Threat to Personal Values

When a proposed change threatens a person's values, it ignites powerful feelings that fuel resistance to change. Any proposed change must take into account its impact on the values of those who are affected by the change, especially values that are closely aligned with an entrenched organizational culture. If threatened, values that are aligned with an entrenched organizational culture will ignite resistance that is organization-wide rather than isolated.

Fear of Being Manipulated

When people perceive change as an attempt by others to control them, they will resist. However, when people understand and accept the need for change and believe that they have a voice in determining how to implement the change, resistance is lessened.

In the end, leaders who regard resistance as a distraction rather than a real and legitimate concern will find it hard to move beyond the first stage of the change model (see Exhibit 11.2 on page 436). Effective leaders will not only follow the steps in the model but also employ the best implementation techniques or strategies to minimize employee resistance.

Work Application **6**

Give an example of when you were resistant to change. Be sure to identify your resistance by one of the seven reasons in Exhibit 11.3 on page 439.

Opening Case APPLICATION

8. Why have Schmidt, Page, and Brin encountered less resistance in bringing about changes at Google than most companies experience?

Google's leadership style and its culture have largely contributed to the lack of resistance. At Google, there is a sense of "we are in this together." There is little in the way of corporate hierarchy, and everyone wears several hats. Everyone realizes that they are an important part of Google's success. Though growing rapidly, Google still maintains a small-company feel. At its headquarters, almost everyone eats in the Google café (known as "Charlie's Place"), sitting at whatever table has an opening and enjoying conversations with Googlers from different departments. Google's culture of transparency and open communication minimizes the chances that the reasons given in Exhibit 11.3 on page 439 for resisting change will develop among employees.

Applying the **Concept 3**

Resistance to Change

Using the letters a through g that accompany the reasons listed in Exhibit 11.3 on page 439, identify which reason for resisting change explains each employee statement.

____ 16. I'm not too sure about this new program. Is it going to be another fad?

____ 17. If we get these new machines, we will need fewer operators.

____ 18. How can management ask us to take a pay cut when they are the ones who are making all the money? We shouldn't let them take advantage of us.

____ 19. Why should our company get bought out? What do we know about that foreign company anyway?

____ 20. Why do we have to put in a new system when the current one is only a year old and is working fine?

Learning Outcome 8 *Discuss people- and task-centered recommendations for minimizing resistance to change.*

Strategies for Minimizing Resistance to Change

A few basic guidelines, if followed, can significantly reduce the level of resistance encountered during the change implementation process.[141] These guidelines or actions can be grouped into two separate but overlapping categories—people-centered and task-centered recommendations.[142] People-centered recommendations acknowledge the human element of change.[143,144] The human element views resistance to change as having cognitive, emotional, and behavioral states that mutually reinforce each other.

Resistance as a cognitive state is a rational calculation that change cannot occur unless the forces driving the need for change are stronger than the forces resisting it. Resistance to change as an emotional state focuses on the frustration of those affected by the change because of the fear of loss (status, position, job, pay, and so forth) and a fear of the unknown. Resistance to change as a behavior focuses on the actions of members opposed to the change.[145] People-centered recommendations discuss ways to overcome resistance to change by addressing the cognitive, emotional, and behavioral states of organizational members.

People-Centered Recommendations for Minimizing Resistance

Leaders can use certain guidelines to keep employees informed, supportive, and motivated about a change. Effective communication before, during, and after the change implementation process will prevent misunderstandings, false rumors, and conflict. It is important that those responsible for implementing change not learn about it from secondhand sources. It is important for followers to be informed of *what* is changing, *why* it is changing, *who* is affected, *how* the change will affect each person individually, and *when* the change will start and end.[146] One study referred to these elements of change as the "5-Ps"—*purpose, priorities, people, process, and proof.* According to the 5-P model, a stated purpose describes what is changing with specific targets identified and prioritized, people potentially affected by the change, a process that employs appropriate levels of participation and consultation, and proof revealing what the change accomplished.[147,148] Also, because major change involves adjustments, disruptions, and even dislocation, training and guidance are needed to help employees acquire skills and capabilities for their role in the implementation process or for their new responsibilities.[149]

Through research and case studies, several strategies for minimizing resistance to change have been identified. Software is even available to facilitate change management and reduce resistance. Web-based Change Management (CM) Pilot Professional is a software that allows business leaders to use various tools and best-practice techniques for managing people during change. It comes with downloadable templates that include communication plans, training plans, coaching plans, and resistance management plans.[150] Exhibit 11.4 on the next page lists people-centered recommendations for minimizing resistance.

Task-Centered Recommendations for Minimizing Resistance

These are task-centered activities dealing with power and structural issues of implementing major change. Focusing on key tasks needed to implement change enables leaders to design appropriate structures, procedures, and processes that can simplify and facilitate successful completion of each task. Effective strategic leaders are adopting flatter, more agile structures and more empowering team-oriented cultures.[151,152] Although it is time-consuming, getting employees involved

EXHIBIT 11.4 People-Centered Recommendations for Minimizing Resistance

To reduce or eliminate resistance to change, effective leaders:

- Show relentless support and unquestionable commitment to the change process.
- Communicate the need and the urgency for change to everyone.
- Maintain ongoing communication about the progress of change.
- Avoid micromanaging and empower people to implement the change.
- Ensure that change efforts are adequately staffed and funded.
- Anticipate and prepare people for the necessary adjustments that change will trigger, such as career counseling and/or retraining.

in designing change activities pays off in that it gives people a sense of control.[153] Specific recommendations for designing appropriate structures, procedures, processes, and controls that enhance change acceptance and minimize resistance are summarized in Exhibit 11.5.[154] Now that you have learned about strategic leadership and change leadership, complete Self-Assessment 1 to determine how your personality affects your strategic planning and ability to change.

EXHIBIT 11.5 Task-Centered Recommendations for Minimizing Resistance

To reduce or eliminate resistance to change, effective leaders:

- Assemble a coalition of supporters inside and outside the organization.
- Align organizational structure with a new strategy, for consistency.
- Transfer the implementation process to a working team.
- Recruit and fill key positions with competent and committed supporters.
- Know when and how to use ad hoc committees or task forces to shape implementation activities.
- Recognize and reward the contributions of others to the change process.

SELF-ASSESSMENT 1

Personality, Leadership, and Change

Strategic leadership is less based on personality than charismatic and transformational leadership. Management level also has a lot to do with strategic planning and leadership, as it is primarily a function of top-level managers. Are you a strategic thinker with a focus on long-term planning? Do you have any business or personal plans for three to five years from now, or do you take things as they come without planning for the future?

____

____

____

Change leadership is based on the Big Five personality type openness to experience. Charismatic, transformational, and strategic leadership all require being receptive to change and influencing others to change. Are you open to trying new things and to change, or do you tend to like the status quo and resist change? Do you attempt to influence others to try new things?

____

____

____

Go to the Internet (www.cengage.com/management/lussier)
where you will find a broad array of resources to help maximize your learning.

- **Review the vocabulary**
- **Try a quiz**
- **Find related links**

Chapter Summary

The chapter summary is organized to answer the nine learning outcomes for Chapter 11.

1. **Discuss the role of strategic leadership in the strategic management process.**

   Strategic leaders establish organizational direction through vision and strategy. They are responsible for analyzing the organization's environment, considering how it may be different in the future, and setting a direction everyone can believe in and work toward. Strategic leaders must then craft the organization's mission, which includes its core values and purpose for existence. Strategy formulation is the leader's responsibility: He or she must guide the selection among alternative plans and choose the best option for translating goals and objectives into action. The final step is strategy implementation and evaluation. Successful completion of the strategic management process and the attainment of superior organizational performance is not a chance occurrence. It is determined by the decisions and actions that strategic leaders take during the process.

2. **Describe the relevance of analyzing the internal and external environment to the strategic management process.**

   The underlying tenet of strategic management is that organizations need to formulate strategies to take advantage of external opportunities and to avoid or reduce the negative impact of external threats. This takes place by monitoring customer behavior, supplier and vendor activities, actions of competitors, market trends, economic conditions, government policies, and technological advances. Analyzing the internal environment focuses on assessing the organization's position in the market, financial position, capabilities, core competencies, culture, and structure. This process reveals the organization's strengths and weaknesses. The combined analysis of the external environment (i.e., to identify opportunities and threats) and internal environment (i.e., to identify strengths and weaknesses) is commonly referred to as SWOT or situation analysis.

3. **Explain the importance of a vision and a mission statement.**

   Many organizations develop both a vision and a mission statement. Whereas the vision statement answers the question, "What do we want to become?" the mission statement answers the question, "What is our business?" Both the vision and mission statements ensure unanimity of purpose within the organization and make important statements about "who the firm is" and "what it wants to become" to outside stakeholders. In other words, reaching agreement on formal mission and vision statements can greatly facilitate the process of reaching agreement on an organization's strategies, objectives, and policies. Organizational success depends on reasonable agreement on these issues.

4. **Explain the relationship between corporate goals and strategies.**

   Goals are the desired outcomes that an organization seeks to achieve for its various stakeholders. Strategies are the means by which goals will be realized. It is for this reason that the mission and goals of an organization are established before the strategy formulation phase in the strategic management model.

5. **Explain the importance of strategy evaluation in the strategic management model.**

   Note in the strategic management model that feedback is critically important. Changes can occur that impact all strategic management activities. The strategy evaluation stage allows these changes to be identified and adjustments to be made. The feedback that results from the strategy evaluation process promotes the creation of a climate for two-way communication throughout the organization. Strategy evaluation involves three fundamental activities: (1) reviewing internal and external factors that are the bases for the current strategies; (2) measuring performance against stated objectives; and (3) taking corrective action. Corrective action utilizes the feedback that results from the strategy evaluation process.

6. **Describe the three phases of the change process.**

   The force-field model proposes that the change process can be divided into three phases: unfreezing, changing, and refreezing. During the unfreezing phase, the leader establishes the need for change by establishing the problems associated with the current situation and presenting a vision of a better future. Awareness of the need for change and acceptance of a new vision sets the stage for the changing phase. It is during the second phase that the proposed vision is implemented. It is action oriented. The leader must actively and effectively communicate the vision with a tone of urgency. He or she must empower followers to act on the vision by giving them resources, information, and discretion to make decisions. Empowerment must also include removing obstacles to change, which may include adapting the infrastructure to the new strategy or strategies of the organization. Other motivational strategies for achieving success at this stage are described in the text. The third phase, refreezing, involves cementing the new vision in the organizational culture so that the change is not reversed soon after it is implemented. The change must be institutionalized so that old habits, values, traditions, and attitudes are permanently replaced.

7. **Identify the major reasons for resisting change.**

Change is not a risk-free proposition. Change often brings with it pain and stress. Some people get demoted, reassigned, relocated, or even fired from their jobs. With all of these negative possibilities, the first reaction of most people is to resist any attempts at making a change. Some of the major reasons why people resist change are the threat to one's self-interest, lack of conviction that change is necessary, fear of being manipulated, threat to personal values, lack of confidence that change will succeed, distrust of leadership, and uncertainty. These reasons are further elaborated on in the text.

8. **Discuss people- and task-centered recommendations for minimizing resistance to change.**

To overcome resistance to change, effective managers must think in terms of people actions and task actions. People actions involve undertaking the following: anticipate change and prepare people for the necessary adjustments that change will trigger, avoid micromanaging and empower people to implement the change, ensure that change efforts are adequately staffed and funded, communicate a strong message about the urgency for change, celebrate and maintain ongoing communication about the progress of change, and show a strong commitment to the change process. Task-based actions include assembling a coalition of supporters inside and outside the organization, recruiting and filling key positions with competent and committed supporters, aligning the organizational structure and other infrastructure with the new strategy, using qualified task forces to shape and support implementation activities, and recognizing and rewarding others' contributions to the change process.

9. **Define the following key terms (in order of appearance in the chapter).**

Select one or more methods: (1) fill in the missing key terms from memory; (2) match the key terms from the following list with their definitions below; and (3) copy the key terms in order from the list at the beginning of the chapter.

__________ is a person's ability to anticipate, envision, maintain flexibility, think strategically, and work with others to initiate changes that will create a viable future for the organization.

__________ is the set of decisions and actions used to formulate and implement specific strategies that will achieve a competitively superior fit between the organization and its environment, so as to achieve organizational goals.

__________ is an ambitious view of the future that everyone in the organization can believe in and that is not readily attainable, yet offers a future that is better in important ways than what now exists.

__________ is an enduring statement of purpose that distinguishes one organization from other similar enterprises.

__________ is an integrated, overarching plan of how an organization will achieve its objectives.

__________ is the ratio of benefits received to the cost incurred by the customer.

__________ is a capability that allows an organization to perform extremely well in comparison to competitors.

__________ an alteration in an organization's alignment with its external environment.

__________ is the feeling that unless an organization makes a change, it is going to be out of business or fail to achieve some important goals.

__________ is the prospect of learning something new in itself.

Key Terms

core competence, 427
learning anxiety, 438
mission statement, 425
organizational change, 432
strategic leadership, 418
strategic management, 420
strategic vision, 424
strategy, 427
survival anxiety, 433
value, 427

Review Questions

1. Discuss how an organization's objectives may affect its search for opportunities.
2. What are the key elements of the strategic management process?
3. What is the difference between a strategic vision and a mission statement?
4. The essence of the strategic management process is adapting to change. Discuss.
5. Describe the role of leadership in successful change implementation.
6. What are the phases of the eight-stage model of planned change?
7. Why is change often perceived as a win–lose proposition between leaders and followers?
8. What is the difference between people- and task-centered strategies for minimizing resistance to change?

Communication Skills

The following critical-thinking questions can be used for class discussion and/or as written assignments to develop communication skills. Be sure to give complete explanations for all questions.

1. What, in your opinion, are the risks and benefits of the leadership arrangement at Google, where the two founders (Larry Page and Sergey Brin) elected to bring in Eric Schmidt to be the CEO while they function as presidents under him?
2. Comment on this statement: "Google is so successful it does not need to change anything in its strategic framework."
3. As leaders make strategic decisions, they must balance the interests of various stakeholders—employees, customers, shareholders, suppliers, unions/activists, and the community. Describe the best approach for doing this.
4. Many decisions made by strategic leaders benefit some people at the expense of others, thus raising ethical issues. Give specific examples for each of the following categories of unethical behavior:
   - breaking laws or evading regulations
   - legal but unethical behavior
   - acts of omission rather than commission
5. For CEOs and many other senior executives, strategic leadership is an important role they must perform well. Briefly describe some of the specific actions or responsibilities of the CEO that strategic leadership entails.
6. Resistance to change is more likely to succeed if the forces resisting the change are stronger than the forces driving the need for change. Describe some of the specific tactics that resisters would employ to thwart change efforts.

CASE

Mark Parker: A Seasoned Veteran Takes the Helm at Nike

In January 2006, Phil Knight replaced CEO William Perez, his hand-picked successor, after only 13 months on the job and replaced him with Mark Parker. Reflecting on his resignation, Perez said, "Nike is an incredible organization with tremendous growth opportunities. However, Phil and I weren't entirely aligned on some aspects of how to best lead the company's long-term growth." In naming Parker as CEO and a director, the board turned to a seasoned Nike veteran with 27 years of experience at the company who has been involved in many of Nike's most significant product innovations and integrated brand companies. He also has been one of the key executives leading the company's long-term strategic planning. Mark Parker is described as someone who has a proven track record in driving creativity, innovation, and growth. "He's an experienced, talented executive and has played an instrumental role in building our business and making the Nike brand as strong as it is today," said Knight.[155]

Parker, 51, joined Nike in 1979 and has served in various management capacities in product design, development, marketing, and brand management. He is widely recognized as the product visionary for the Nike

Air franchise and many other industry-leading product design and performance innovations. Prior to heading the Nike brand, Parker ran the company's multibillion-dollar footwear and apparel businesses. "I've spent my life building the Nike brand, and I'm excited to lead one of the world's most dynamic organizations," Parker said. Since assuming the role of CEO of Nike, Parker's team has overhauled the way Nike runs, shifting the brand away from the previous sub-brand and product-based structure to a customer-driven structure. He has structured Nike into six "customer focused" categories, such as running, basketball, and women's fitness. Parker has personally shaped Nike's innovation processes. For example, he estabished a group for pursuing long-range innovation, called *Explore.* He describes *Explore* as a multidisciplinary group pursuing "deep space" innovation possibilities with academics, inventors, and other companies. *Explore,* he points out, was chiefly responsible for the cooperation with Steve Jobs and Apple that led to the launch of the Nike Plus program in 2006. The Nike + iPod is a wireless system that allows Nike + footwear to talk with your iPod nano to connect you to the ultimate personal running and workout experience.[156]

According to most analysts, Parker's biggest strength is his ability to key into consumer trends. In addition to being a product guru, he fits the Phil Knight mold and therefore will have a better working relationship with Knight than did Perez, who was an outsider to the athletic industry.

Mark Parker has taken the helm of Nike at the time when the stakes in the U.S. market are particularly high, especially as Adidas has become more powerful with the acquisition of Reebok. However, Parker believes he is the right person to lead Nike through the challenges of the future. As he sees it, Nike's success depends upon its continuous focus on the customer. "At Nike we all work for one boss—the consumer," he said. As long as Nike stays connected to the consumer, it will be able to keep its products innovative and relevant.[157]

Parker believes his job is to help carry the torch to make sure Nike's passion for real innovation continues to thrive. Nike is still the world's largest sportswear company with over $18 billion in annual sales, employing more than 32,000 employees, and operating in more than 200 countries. How long this leadership position will last depends on the leadership effectiveness of Mark Parker and his team.

GO TO THE INTERNET: To learn more about Mark Parker and Nike, visit their Web site **(http://www.nike.com)**.

Support your answers to the following questions with specific information from the case and text or with other information you get from the Web or other sources.

1. What external and internal pressures did Mark Parker face when he assumed the leadership of Nike, and how did he respond to these challenges?
2. Strategic management is about formulating strategies that align an organization's internal capabilities with external opportunities while avoiding or minimizing threats. How effective has Mark Parker been as a strategist so far?
3. Part of strategic management is accomplished via SWOT analysis. What is the evidence that the leadership at Nike is making use of this tool?
4. As revealed in the text, an effective strategist develops strategies that (1) enhance value to its customers, (2) create synergistic opportunities, and (3) build on the company's core competencies. What evidence shows that Mark Parker is pursuing this course or shares this viewpoint?

CUMULATIVE CASE QUESTIONS

5. According to the Big Five Model of Personality, what traits would Mark Parker consider critical for his managers to possess (Chapter 2)?
6. The interactions among power, politics, networking, and negotiation are a common occurrence in organizational life (Chapter 4). CEOs have to deal with various stakeholders (shareholders, employees, board of directors, customers, suppliers, unions, government and state regulators, and so on). Describe how a CEO like Mark Parker would employ power, politics, networking, and negotiation as effective tools of leadership.
7. Communication, coaching, and conflict management are said to be skills that have a direct and significant impact on a leader's career success (Chapter 6). Given the weak market and financial position that Nike was in prior to Mark Parker's appointment, how critical are these skills in his efforts to reposition the company and address its weaknesses?

CASE EXERCISE AND ROLE-PLAY

Preparation: Assume you are part of the leadership of an organization or organizational unit that is in need of training the management team of its foreign subsidiary to embrace and practice diversity at the highest levels. Under Mark Parker, Nike is leading the way in diversity.

Nike's vision is *for every team to be high performing, diverse, and inclusive.* To achieve this vision, Nike strategy is to

- cultivate diversity and inclusion to develop world-class, high-performing teams;
- ignite change and inspire critical conversations around diversity, inclusion, and innovation;
- create venues and environments for open dialogue, diverse opinions, and a multitude of perspectives.

A multinational corporation like Nike wants to ensure that all its subsidiaries around the world have high diversity standards (visit Nike's Web site at **www.nike.com** for more information). Your task is to help your foreign subsidiary develop diversity standards for its respective units that are in congruence with the overall diversity standards of the parent corporation.

Role-Play: The instructor forms students into small groups (representing top leadership of the foreign subsidiary or partner) to develop a diversity statement of no more than 100 words. Here are some guidelines:

1. Make a case for diversity by identifying key benefits of a diversified workforce.
2. Create a list of core values that your organization now holds or you would want it to have, and incorporate them into your diversity statement.
3. Share your diversity statement with other members of the class, and vote on who has the best diversity statement.

VIDEO CASE

Original Penguin Spreads Its Wings

Chris Kolbe is a master of change. Now president of Original Penguin, Kolbe essentially runs the division for its parent company, Perry Ellis International. Original Penguin was a 1950s icon—the penguin logo appeared on Munsingwear Penguin knit sport shirts for men. Eventually, its popularity faded, and Perry Ellis International later acquired the brand. Chris Kolbe was working in merchandising at retailer Urban Outfitters when he conceived the idea of rejuvenating the penguin—but with a new twist and for a new market. Starting with a few new shirts, which sold out almost immediately, the "new" Original Penguin began to grow, and Perry Ellis tapped Kolbe to complete the transformation as head of a new venture team. Kolbe recognizes that the fashion industry is a hotbed of change—and any clothing company that wants to survive must embrace innovation. He also understands that change takes time and patience.

1. Why has it been important for Perry Ellis International to give freedom to a new venture team in order to relaunch Original Penguin?
2. In what respects does Original Penguin represent a cultural change for Perry Ellis?

Skill-Development Exercise 1

Strategic Planning

Preparing for Skill-Development Exercise 1

Think of a business that you would like to start someday. Develop a simple strategic plan for your proposed business by following steps 1 through 4 below. If you cannot think of a business you would like to start, select an existing business. Do not select a company if you are familiar with their strategic plan. What is the name and location of the business?

1. What would be some of your strengths and weaknesses, opportunities and threats, compared to your competitors? It may be helpful to think about your answer to step 4 below before doing your SWOT analysis.

2. Develop a vision statement for your business.

3. Develop a mission statement for your business.

4. As part of the strategy formulation, identify your core competencies. Be sure they answer the questions, "What will your business do better or different than your competitors? Why should someone do business with you rather than your competitors?" This stage is related to the SWOT analysis in step 1 above.

Doing Skill-Development Exercise 1 in Class

Objective

To develop a simple strategic plan for a business you would like to start someday.

The primary AACSB learning standard skill developed through this exercise is strategic management.

Procedure *(10–30 minutes)*

Option A: Break into groups of 3 to 6 and share your strategic plans. Offer each other suggestions for improvements.

Option B: Same as A, but select the best strategy from the group to be presented to the entire class. Each group's selected strategy is presented to the class.

Conclusion

The instructor may make concluding remarks.

Apply It *(2–4 minutes)* What did I learn from this exercise? How will I use this knowledge in the future?

Sharing

In the group, or to the entire class, volunteers may give their answers to the "Apply It" questions.

Skill-Development Exercise 2

Planning a Change Using the Force-Field Model

Preparing for Skill-Development Exercise 2

Select a change at work or in your personal life that you would like to make, and develop a plan as follows.

1. *Unfreezing.* Briefly describe the change and why it is needed.

2. *Changing.* State the beginning-of-change date ________ and end-of-change date ________. Develop a plan for making the change.

3. *Refreezing.* Identify plans for maintaining the new change.

Doing Skill-Development Exercise 2 in Class

Objective

To develop a personal plan for change.

The primary AACSB learning standard skill developed through this exercise is analytic skills.

Procedure *(10–30 minutes)*

Option A: Break into groups of 3 to 6 and share your change plans. Offer each other suggestions for improvements.

Option B: Same as A, but select the best plan from the group to be presented to the entire class. Each group's selected plan is presented to the class.

Conclusion

The instructor may make concluding remarks.

Apply It *(2–4 minutes)* What did I learn from this experience? How will I use this knowledge in the future? Relist your beginning and ending target dates for the change.

Sharing

In the group, or to the entire class, volunteers may give their answers to the "Apply It" questions.

Skill-Development Exercise 3

Managing Change at Your College

Objective

To develop a large-scale plan for change.

The primary AACSB learning standard skills developed through this exercise are analytic skills and strategic management.

Procedures *(10–30 minutes)*

As an individual, group, or class, select a change you would like to see implemented at your college. Answer the following questions and conduct the force-field analysis.

1. State the change you want.

2. State which of the four types of change it is.

3. Identify possible resistance to the change.

4. Select strategies for overcoming the resistance.

5. Conduct a force-field analysis for the change. Below, write the present situation in the center and the forces that hinder the change and the forces that can help get the change implemented.

Hindering Forces ⟶ Present Situation ⟵ Driving Forces

Conclusion

The instructor may make concluding remarks.

Apply It *(2–4 minutes)* What did I learn from this experience? How will I use this knowledge in the future?

Sharing

In the group, or to the entire class, volunteers may give their answers to the "Apply It" questions.

12
Crisis Leadership and the Learning Organization

Chapter Outline

Crisis Leadership
The Impact of Environmental Factors
Crisis Management Plan
Effective Crisis Communication

The Learning Organization and Knowledge Management
What Is a Learning Organization?
The Traditional versus the Learning Organization Culture
The Role of Leaders in Creating a Learning Organization

Learning Outcomes

After studying this chapter, you should be able to:

1. Explain why crisis leadership competence is an important consideration when hiring new leaders. p. 452
2. Identify the benefits of pre-crisis planning. p. 454
3. Identify three key components of the pre-crisis planning phase. p. 455
4. Describe the five-step process for crisis risk assessment. p. 456
5. Describe the role of the CEO and communication in managing a crisis. p. 459
6. List five or more attributes that can be used to describe the learning organization. p. 464
7. Distinguish between the traditional organization and the learning organization. p. 466
8. Describe the role of leadership in creating a learning organization. p. 469
9. Define the following **key terms** (in order of appearance in the chapter):

    crisis
    press release
    press kit
    learning organization
    organizational knowledge
    discontinuous change

Opening Case APPLICATION

According to Rick Wagoner (GM's CEO), the company is in a crucial period in its 100-year history.[1] In a CBS *60 Minutes* interview in 2006, Steve Kroft described GM as a company "limping" along in the breakdown lane in need of a lot more than a minor tuneup. David Cole, an automotive expert, describes the situation facing GM as a real crisis, "not a phantom or fake crisis." GM's problems are compounded by competition from Japanese and Korean brands, higher gasoline prices, the bankruptcy of its largest parts supplier (Delphi), and perhaps, most critically, an overstock of SUVs and sedans. GM has a cost disadvantage when it comes to its health and labor costs. GM provides pension and health insurance to its 1.1 million employees and their dependents at a cost of $6 billion a year. It's a cost that most of GM's foreign competitors don't have because their workers are usually covered by some form of government health insurance in their own countries.[2]

Another area where GM is losing ground is with its product mix. GM is playing catch-up in the hot market for hybrids because it has been losing sales to Toyota and Honda. The Japanese companies began developing hybrids in the 1990s while U.S. manufacturers scoffed at the technology as not being economically viable. With SUVs and trucks bringing in good profits, GM and its leaders saw no need to change—buying into the cliché, "If it's not broken, why fix it." Today, both GM and Ford are coming to the market with their first hybrid models, while Toyota and Honda are already selling second generations.[3,4]

Today, GM's shares are trading at historic lows. In 2006 and 2007, GM posted $10 billion and $39 billion losses, respectively. GM is on the verge of losing its number one status to Toyota. As a sign of the urgency of the crisis, Rick Wagoner offered to cut his base salary by 50 percent in 2006 and 25 percent in 2007. Many of Rick Wagoner's critics accuse him of being clueless and lacking the urgency that GM's crisis dema[illegible]. The flood of bad news has brought increa[illegible] that Rick Wagoner will lose his [illegible]

[illegible] facing GM as a [illegible]

2. [illegible] factors to GM's [illegible] have revealed?
3. [illegible] een under Rick W[illegible] pany's crisis?
4. S[illegible] that GM is on the ve[illegible] ptcy. How can GM's leadership add[illegible] these rumors to avoid further panic among shareholders and employees?
5. Describe the threats facing GM in its external environment.
6. In your opinion, does GM represent the traditional organization or the learning organization?
7. What actions can GM's leadership take to make it more of a learning organization?

Can you answer any of these questions? You'll find answers to these questions and learn more about GM and its leadership throughout the chapter.

To learn more about GM and Rick Wagoner, visit GM's Web site at **http://www.gm.com**.

A key aspect of a strategic leader's responsibility is dealing with crisis. A crisis can strike any organization without warning. A crisis by its very nature is an event that could not be predicted or anticipated prior to its occurrence. Therefore, avoidance is rarely possible. Crises are indeed damaging to an organization if not properly managed. In a crisis, stock prices plummet and operating costs escalate, causing both short- and long-term financial losses. A crisis that is mismanaged can also damage an organization's reputation and diminish consumer confidence in the organization's mission, or in some cases lead to its demise altogether. Also, an organization in crisis tends to be defensive and vulnerable to attacks from its competitors. An effective strategist must have the skills necessary to manage a crisis successfully.

The first half of this chapter discusses crisis leadership in depth. The last half of the chapter focuses on the important topic of organizational learning and knowledge management. The learning organization is one that emphasizes creativity, innovation, and knowledge creation.

Learning Outcome 1 *Explain why crisis leadership competence is an important consideration when hiring new leaders.*

Crisis Leadership

A **crisis** *is a low-probability, high-impact event that threatens the viability of the organization and is characterized by ambiguity of cause, effect, and means of resolution, as well as by a belief that decisions must be made swiftly.*[5] Today, more than ever, there is a great need for leaders from all walks of life to show that they possess the skills and competence to lead during times of crisis.[6,7] As one author bluntly puts it, "Mismanage a crisis today and your career may end up in the dumps."[8] The importance of crisis management in every organization's strategic plan is critical.[9] We are all aware of the headlines involving corporate scandals, accounting fraud, ethical lapses in judgment, and allegations of workplace discrimination. In fact, according to one study, discrimination lawsuits now rank among the leading types of crises faced by business leaders in the United States today, with a 100 percent increase in the number of class action discrimination lawsuits in 2003.[10]

In today's volatile global marketplace, many experts believe that organizations (whether for-profit or not-for-profit) should recognize the inevitable—that crises can and will emerge. Unfortunately, crisis response plans are not as widespread as one would expect.[11] The results of a recent survey revealed that about 53 percent of marketing executives said they have experienced a business crisis resulting in negative news coverage, declining sales, or reduced profitability. Surprisingly, about the same number (57 percent) said their company does not have a crisis response plan currently in place.[12] Many experts and scholars agree that while a pre-crisis response plan will not prevent a crisis, it can minimize financial loss and long-term damage to a firm's reputation.

Some proactive corporations are now putting in place strategic planning and crisis readiness plans. These organizations are taking appropriate steps to design systems and tools to respond effectively to a crisis before it happens.[13] Strategic crisis leadership requires three things:

1. Using environmental monitoring techniques to identify events that could trigger crises in the future.
2. Integrating crisis management into the strategic management process so it remains a regular part of the overall strategy-evaluation process.
3. Establishing a culture that embraces crisis awareness and preparation as a way of life.[14,15,16,17]

Crises come in many forms—natural disasters (hurricanes and tsunamis), terrorist attacks (9/11 and the 2005 London bombings), product failures (Firestone and Ford tire problems), human error disasters (Bhopal and *Exxon Valdez* oil spill incidents), unexpected death of the CEO (McDonald's CEO and Chairman, Jim Catalupo), and system failures (*Challenger* accident and Chernobyl nuclear plant explosion). Also, many crises don't always make the front pages of newspapers or aren't featured in the TV news, such as sexual harassment, executive misconduct, product recalls, and computer hackings.[18] Regardless of the nature of the crises, what they all have in common is the stress and pressure they place on key organizational resources and systems. Any weaknesses that may have been present in the system prior to a crisis are exposed and further compound the negative consequences of the crisis.[19] Any crisis has the potential for damaging a firm's reputation, credibility, integrity, and financial position.

The Impact of Environmental Factors

Factors and trends are emerging in the current business environment that underscore the importance of crisis leadership. As the economy limps on and speculation of it sliding into a recession builds, the real prospect looms that many corporations are going to face a crisis of survival. Rising oil prices, the housing downturn, the subprime crisis, the credit crunch, and talk of possible inflation and recession are all ingredients that could stymie even the best-prepared CEOs. More than ever, people are looking for leaders who can provide stability, reassurance, confidence, and a sense of control during and after a crisis.

Technological advances involving the Internet and communication networks allow millions to analyze and critique virtually every aspect of an organization's response to a crisis—such as a violent act on the job, a major accident, or a product recall.[20] Technologies such as e-mail, Web pages, and social networking sites are weapons for affected organizations and the outside world to use during a crisis. A crisis is instantly visible and viral with the potential to inflict terminal damage on the affected organization. These technologies have diminished an organization's attempts to control crisis communications by opening channels that others can use to explain their positions and build support. As a result, leaders must learn to improvise.[21]

A company today may have only minutes, not hours, to contain a crisis. In many cases, there is a minute-by-minute real-time analysis of the financial implications of the crisis by investors, customers, and analysts, as Internet and cable television are linked with investment portfolios. Stakeholders may have more information at their fingertips about an ongoing crisis than the company itself. To stay ahead, effective leaders are incorporating crisis management into their strategic management models.

Anticipating the kinds of crises that an organization can encounter is not an easy task for any leader. Literally thousands of incidents can turn into crises and handicap an organization's attempts to successfully achieve its strategic goals. The problem is detecting the signals that warn of a crisis. Many organizations are presented with early warning signals of an impending crisis but fail to recognize and heed them. A crisis can present the opportunity for an organization to learn and adapt when the next crisis hits. Therefore, the same degree of care invested in putting together a strategic plan for growth, stability, or renewal must be devoted to crisis planning.

A study of the perceived importance of crisis planning for small businesses found that interest in crisis planning is motivated more by experiencing crisis events than by management's proactive behavior. In other words, a small business's commitment to crisis planning is not due to its leader's proactive mindset on crisis management, but rather to the past crisis history of the organization.[22] This approach is dangerous because there may not always be a second chance to learn from your mistakes.

Crisis Management Plan

Though suffering some loss is almost unavoidable, proper management can reduce the duration of a crisis, enhance or retain a socially responsible corporate image, and secure future profitability. Effective crisis management depends on planning and people.[23] According to experts in the field, an effective crisis management plan is one that is (1) comprehensive, with clear leadership, team, and individual assignments in the form of roles and responsibilities; (2) upgraded frequently and supported by training and periodic drill sessions; and (3) coordinated and controlled across levels and units of the organization.[24] Collectively, all three requirements seem to be pointing to the important role that human resource development plays in crisis management.[25,26,27]

Readiness to respond appropriately to a crisis is a function of

1. knowing and accepting one's assigned role in the crisis management plan;
2. sufficient training specific to the assigned role to enable one to perform his or her responsibilities competently;
3. complementary and integrated roles and responsibilities at all levels of the organization, so the crisis management response is controlled and coordinated.[28]

A crisis management plan should address what happens before, during, and after a crisis. A pre-crisis plan is the first step of any crisis management program. It allows an organization to establish procedures and practices for risk analysis, early signal detection, and preventative measures. During a crisis, successful execution of a prepared plan improves damage control and recovery; and after the crisis, organizational learning and change are vital for future survival.[29,30]

In the next section, we propose a model of crisis leadership that includes the following components: pre-crisis planning, a crisis response team during a crisis, and post-crisis management.

Opening Case APPLICATION

1. Would you describe the situation facing GM as a crisis?

By the definition offered above, GM is definitely facing a crisis. As described in the case, the financial impact on GM has been severe and is getting worse. In July 2008, it was reported that GM was laying off 30,000 employees and closing down more plants in order to cut costs. One analyst predicted that GM does not have the cash to continue operations beyond 2009. Rick Wagoner's position on the cause, effect, and means of resolution of the crisis is not shared by many analysts and experts. Some say he should be fired because he does not fully understand the urgency of the crisis and his strategies for resolving it are outdated.

Learning Outcome 2 *Identify the benefits of pre-crisis planning.*

Work Application 1

Find out if your college or university has a pre-crisis plan. If you find one, read and critique it for its effectiveness and present your findings to your classmates. If there is none, present an argument for having one.

Pre-Crisis Planning

Although no one can develop a pre-crisis plan that would accurately anticipate and address every possibility in the future, it is still the best way to mitigate the negative consequences of any crisis. A pre-crisis plan enables leaders and their followers to make good decisions under severe pressure in the most difficult and unpleasant circumstances.[31] Many people seldom contemplate the chances that a fire, coworker violence, robbery, or natural disaster could occur where they work. The tendency is to develop a mental detachment from the issue—it happens to other people, not to me or our organization. Some leaders rationalize that the present systems are adequate to deal with such crises should they arise, while others find solace in the "positive thinking" (nothing bad will happen) approach. Denial of the occurrence of these low-probability events makes thinking the unthinkable a major leadership challenge.[32] Leaders who are able to overcome these psychological roadblocks and perceive risks realistically can approach pre-crisis management in a logical and systematic way.[33] One study investigating the relationship between crisis preparedness and firm performance found that high-performing organizations reported higher levels of crisis preparedness. The same study also reported that learning from failures is an important facilitator of preparedness for future crises.[34]

Opening Case APPLICATION

2. What are some of the contributing factors to GM's crisis that pre-crisis planning would have revealed?

Pre-crisis planning would have set in place systems and personnel to identify weak signals that had the potential to affect the economy, such as rising oil prices and the effect on gas prices; the housing meltdown; inflation, the credit crunch, and their effects on consumer spending; and even the possibility of a recession. Even GM's health care cost problem should have been anticipated. The problem is that GM became complacent. Things were going well—the economy was strong, GM sales and profits were strong, consumers had a love affair with big SUVs, and the threat from foreign competitors was low. There was no need to worry.

Learning Outcome 3

Identify three key components of the pre-crisis planning phase.

Pre-crisis planning entails three components that every organization (large, small, for-profit, or non-profit) should address when putting together a comprehensive crisis response plan: (1) *appointing a crisis leader,* (2) *creating a crisis response team,* and (3) *assessing risk.*[35] We will briefly describe each one of these separately.

Crisis Leader Given the dynamic environment of business, proactive organizations have found it prudent to designate one or more senior executives with the task of scanning and monitoring the internal and external environments for potential threats or warning signs of a crisis. In the event of a crisis, the leader must be visible, in control, and overseeing all aspects of the plan's execution. The crisis leader may report directly to the CEO or to the head of communications or public relations. The primary duties of the crisis leader may include activities such as the following:

- requiring individuals or departments to keep logs of complaints or incidents
- monitoring customer and employee complaints and behavior
- identifying emerging patterns or trends in the regulatory environment, competitive landscape, and social environment
- coordinating the activities of the crisis management team to ensure that the members work well together

The ability of crisis leaders to grasp the impact of events in the early stages of development has helped some organizations avert a crisis and has even helped others turn would-be crises into opportunities. The attributes or qualities of an effective crisis leader include expertise coupled with real experience dealing with crises, insight, influence, selflessness, and pragmatism.[36]

To be effective, a crisis leader must have the power, resources, position, and stature to influence events when a crisis erupts. For example, an organization must empower the crisis leader to make a critical decision such as shutting down a product line if a defect is suspected, or halting operations on an assembly line if multiple injuries or malfunctions have occurred.

Crisis Response Team Having a standing crisis response team increases an organization's ability to respond to a crisis immediately and effectively.[37,38] A crisis response team should involve a good mix of representatives from all sectors of the organization. It should draw on critical internal resources (e.g., human resources) and external resources (e.g., trauma counselors). In most medium- to large-sized organizations, the crisis management team is led by a senior-level executive and composed of representatives from the Production/Operations, HR, Legal, Security and Maintenance, Marketing, R&D, and Finance/Accounting departments. Diversity in the makeup of the crisis management team is emphasized because crises can affect any number of areas or the entire organization.

In the pre-crisis planning phase, a leader wants a team that is representative of the different functions or divisions within the organization—hardworking, creative, organized, and motivated. Therefore, the personality of the crisis team is as important as the crisis plan itself. During an actual crisis, the team whose members are calm, self-confident, assertive, and dependable is more likely to succeed than a team whose members have the opposite personality traits.[39]

It is often the case that during a crisis, people who must work together have no history of doing so because they have never practiced or rehearsed the plan; thus, they have no understanding of each other's roles and responsibilities. It is also sometimes the case during a crisis that resources brought to bear may have never been exercised to see how well they function together.[40] Some blame these limitations on the fact that often crisis personnel receive little individual, team, and media training for effective crisis response.[41] Leaders must develop comprehensive training programs for crisis response team personnel and engage them in frequent drills that simulate an actual crisis situation.[42]

This team approach contrasts with what many organizations practice, which is to divide the duties of crisis management throughout the organization without a central command. Experience reveals that this divided approach often results in conflict—sometimes motivated by varying ideologies, resource allocation, or office politics—over just who will be singularly responsible for managing a crisis. In this situation, it is not uncommon to have the directors of various company departments argue that they and their staff are best equipped to manage a crisis, often to the disapproval of other directors.

Work Application 2

Identify someone who has been or is part of a crisis prevention and management team, preferably someone on your campus's crisis prevention and management team. Ask him or her to describe the makeup and function of the team.

An effective team functions as one unit with one voice under a single unit command. Such a team is made up of members who can challenge one another's ideas without resorting to personal attacks, engage in debates without coercion or blame, and unite behind decisions once they are made. Members don't circumvent or undermine each other; instead they work cooperatively, sharing information and encouraging teamwork. This unity and spirit prevent the team from becoming dysfunctional. In the words of one expert, "If a team is dysfunctional before a crisis, that team will have a dysfunctional response during an incident."

Because the warning signals of an impending crisis may be too weak to identify or accurately interpret, they are often missed or ignored. For this reason, an increasing number of organizations are employing risk assessment techniques to monitor and assess the risks of potential crises before they happen.

Learning Outcome 4 *Describe the five-step process for crisis risk assessment.*

Crisis Risk Assessment Risk assessment is a common tool used in crisis planning. Borrowing from the field of risk management, crisis teams set out to identify potential incidents that could hit the organization and then determine the degree of preparedness necessary.[43,44] A crisis will negatively impact an organization's people, its financial condition, or its image. The crisis leader and crisis team members begin the risk assessment process by engaging in "what-if" scenario analysis that focuses on creating realistic incidents under each crisis category.[45] Scenario analysis and planning is a tool that helps leaders prevent or respond to crises through decision-making skills based on possible outcomes of crises.[46] Members may entertain questions such as, "What could happen? Where are we vulnerable? What is the worst-case scenario? What is the short- and long-term outlook?" This series of "what-if" scenarios set the stage for a five-step risk assessment plan. See Exhibit 12.1 for the model depicting these steps.

EXHIBIT 12.1 Risk Assessment Model

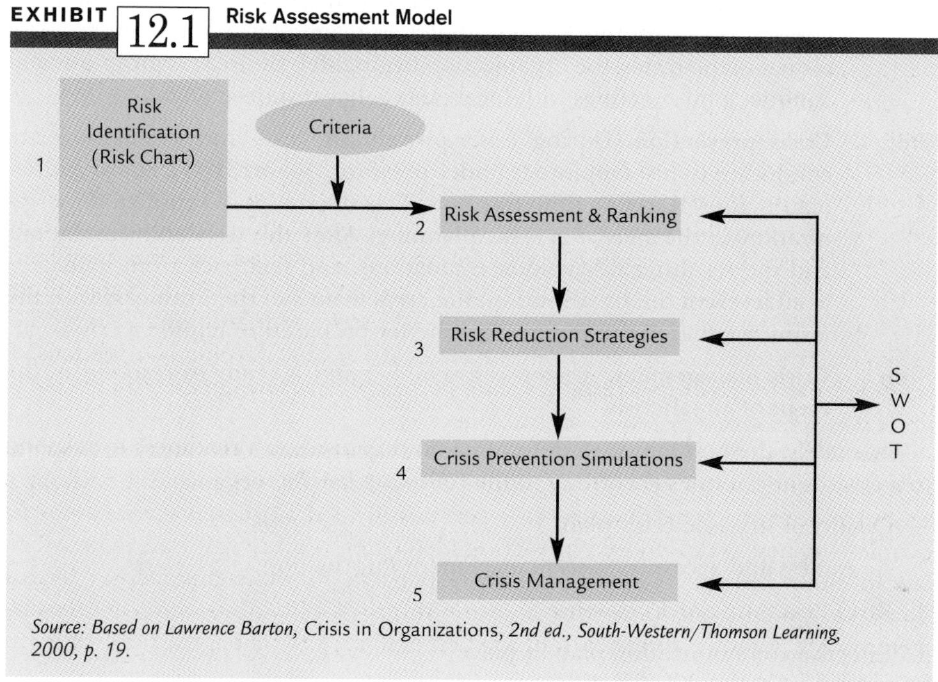

Source: Based on Lawrence Barton, Crisis in Organizations, *2nd ed., South-Western/Thomson Learning, 2000, p. 19.*

The five-step process for risk assessment consists of (1) risk identification, (2) risk assessment and ranking, (3) risk reduction, (4) crisis prevention, and (5) crisis management.[47,48]

Step 1. **Risk identification.** Crisis team members will begin by first identifying the worst-case incidents that could have severe consequences on people, the organization's financial position, or its image. This process is described as risk identification and results in the creation of a risk chart.

Step 2. **Risk assessment and ranking.** Next, these incidents are analyzed and ranked using criteria such as loss of life, injuries, emotional trauma, or minimal inconvenience for each incident's human impact. On the financial and image side, ranking criteria such as extraordinary impact (i.e., it will bankrupt the organization), serious but insured (i.e., we are covered), or small impact (i.e., nothing to worry about) may be employed. This information is then used as the basis for launching the third step, which is risk reduction.[49]

Step 3. **Risk reduction.** During the risk reduction step, the crisis leader shares the risk chart created during risk assessment and ranking with team members or larger audiences, and they begin debating and formulating strategies for countering each crisis or threat. SWOT analysis comes into play as a tool in determining what resources and capabilities are available or needed to better manage each crisis. For instance, say the organization is a chemical plant. An item on the risk chart may indicate the risk of a "poisonous gas leak" as a likely event. A SWOT analysis of this particular risk may progress as follows: the crisis team identifies capabilities the organization has if such an incident should occur (such as poison gas scientists and materials), weaknesses (such as the present lack of a poisonous gas leak response plan), opportunities (such as community support for the plant because of its economic impact on the area), and threats (such as environmentalists who are likely to protest and demand that the plant be closed). Based on this analysis, the crisis team may recommend as a risk reduction plan that the organization begin safety awareness programs and conduct joint meetings with local emergency response teams.

Step 4. **Crisis prevention.** During crisis prevention, tests and simulations are conducted to test employees under pressure. Again, SWOT analysis information is used to fine-tune this step. This step helps to sensitize the organization to the need for crisis planning. After the tests and simulations and the resulting discussions, evaluations, and feedback from managers at all levels of the organization, the crisis team can then rest easy with the assurance that the organization is better prepared to handle a crisis.

Step 5. **Crisis management.** A team is assembled and is ready to respond in the event of a real crisis.

Ultimately, the best gauge to determine an organization's readiness to respond to a crisis is how it rates according to the following five factors:

1. Quality of strategic crisis plan
2. Awareness and access to crisis management information
3. Readiness for a quick response
4. Effective communication plan in place
5. Effective crisis leadership

A comprehensive crisis response plan based on risk analysis indicates who is in charge of making key decisions, who is on the team and what their roles and responsibilities are, who is to respond to media inquiries, how the plan will be executed, and what other employees are required or not required to do or say. This plan can mean the difference between survival and the total demise of an organization. The benefits of a pre-crisis response plan are obvious—faster response time, better judgments, ready and available resources, fewer costly mistakes, less panic, and quicker resolution of the crisis.

As mentioned earlier, unless the crisis response plan is rehearsed and practiced regularly, it becomes just another document collecting dust on the bookshelf. Some call this practice *pre-crisis drills.* Effective crisis leadership requires that employees be oriented and trained on the plan's execution and that resources be made available and ready to be deployed in the event of a crisis.

It is a fact of life that in spite of all the crisis prevention planning that organizations undergo, sooner or later a crisis will emerge and an organization will have to deal with it. The next section focuses on crisis management during an actual crisis.

Work Application **3**

Using your college or university as a reference, identify five risk areas that could result in crisis if nothing is done now. Recommend a risk reduction plan or strategy that can help your school avert or deal with a crisis for one of these risk areas.

Learning Outcome 5 *Describe the role of the CEO and communication in managing a crisis.*

Managing During a Crisis

When a crisis erupts, a rapid response is vital. An effective response in the event of a crisis is critical to an organization's survival. An organization should make itself accessible as quickly and as openly as possible. It is generally believed that within an hour of becoming aware that a crisis situation may exist, company officials must be prepared to issue an initial statement to the media and other key stakeholder groups—providing facts as they are known and an indication of when additional details will be made available.[50] The purpose of an immediate response on the part of the affected organization is to fill an information vacuum with facts and perspectives. Such quick action can help to preserve the credibility and reputation of the organization and its leaders during the crisis.[51] Experience has shown that the longer companies wait, the more likely the vacuum will be filled with inaccurate statements and outright misinformation that becomes accepted as truth.

The Role of Senior Leaders An organization's degree of preparedness for a potential crisis depends upon senior leaders and other responsible personnel. When there is a crisis, employees will seek guidance from company senior leaders as to how business operations will continue and ways to cope with the situation. Unfortunately, some senior leaders have been known to retreat behind closed doors when a crisis hits. They delegate to lower managers the task of facing the media and other stakeholder groups. Three key tenets of crisis leadership, according to some experts, are (1) stay engaged and lead from the front, (2) focus on the big picture and communicate the vision, and (3) work with your crisis management team. Organizations with established crisis management teams are able to communicate and effectively respond during a crisis.[52,53]

An example of how not to lead during a crisis is the leader who digs deeper into his or her foxhole after a crisis hits. Leaders who develop this type of bunker mentality start playing not to lose instead of playing to win.

In times of crisis, effective leaders try not to lose sight of the big picture. They remain focused on the vision and mission of the organization despite dealing with the reality of the present. Effective leaders rely on the values and principles found in their mission statements to guide company decision making during a crisis. There is an unwavering faith that they and their followers will prevail.

Effective leaders view crisis management as a team effort. They understand clearly that it is precisely at this time that a good leader needs a team who can offer wise counsel, debate opposing points of view without coercion, and challenge one another without blame, thereby arriving at a consensus in a timely manner. In a time of crisis, a team with a balance of complementary skills and talents can move quickly and effectively. This is where having gone through pre-crisis planning and risk assessment pays big dividends and often means the difference between survival and extinction. Not only should a leader seek wise counsel from his or her team, he or she should also instill a greater feeling of camaraderie among all employees by allowing them to share their emotions and feelings with each other in group settings.

Work Application **4**

Think of a leader whom you have observed in a crisis situation, either in person or on TV. Critique the leader's handling of the crisis using the text discussion as your guide.

How a company deals with a crisis from a communications standpoint can make or break it. The next section focuses on the importance of effective communication during a crisis.

Opening Case APPLICATION

3. How effective has GM's leadership been under Rick Wagoner so far in addressing the company's crisis?

In 2005, Rick Wagoner laid out a turnaround plan that emphasized the following: product excellence, revitalized sales and marketing strategy, acceleration in cost reductions and quality improvements, and a solution for the company's health care/legacy cost problems. Since this plan went into effect, Wagoner has managed $9 billion in annual cost reductions and negotiated a landmark money-saving labor deal with the United Auto Workers union. He is bringing in executives from outside, a break from GM's tradition of promoting from within. In response to rising oil prices and intense competition from Toyota and other Japanese auto manufacturers, Wagoner nows says GM is working on hybrids and hydrogen fuel cell-powered vehicles. Many experts think Rick Wagoner is a little late in entering this market because the Japanese had long ago seen these technologies as the future of the next generation of vehicles. Some will argue that Rick Wagoner has kept to the three tenets of crisis leadership: (1) stay engaged and lead from the front, (2) focus on the big picture and communicate the vision, and (3) work with your crisis management team. However, GM's continuing financial difficulties are an indication that Wagoner's handling of the crisis is not yielding results, which is why some analysts and investors are calling for the firing of Wagoner and his team. These opponents believe that Wagoner is failing with tenet number 2. They don't agree with his big picture and vision for GM.

Effective Crisis Communication

Effective crisis communication is important because it can make or break a company's reputation.[54] Over the past few years, it has become increasingly clear that maintaining an effective crisis communication system with primary stakeholders—employees, customers, board members, the news media, and regulatory bodies—is critical for survival when a crisis hits.[55] Effective pre-crisis planning should designate who will speak for the organization in the event of a crisis. Public relations staff may field questions from the media while legal staff may respond to legal inquiries. It is generally believed that it does makes a difference whether the company representative or spokesperson is a senior-level manager or someone at a lower level of responsibility.[56] The level of seniority demonstrates to the public the seriousness with which the incident is viewed.

Four questions that often emerge after a crisis are: What happened? How did it happen? What are you doing to address this crisis? and What are you going to do to ensure it never happens again? Providing honest and accurate answers to these questions is the essence of effective crisis communication.[57]

A well-designed crisis communication system should inform employees at all levels who to call, what procedures to follow, and what they should and should not say to a variety of individuals and agencies. Such procedures should also inform appropriate managers what role(s) they would play in the event of a crisis, and how communication will be handled within and between offices. Getting the message right is critical, and so is choosing the right communications medium.[58]

Investing time and other resources in developing an effective crisis communication system with employees has significant short- and long-term benefits. In the short term, well-informed employees will assist the organization in presenting the facts to the outside world. Invariably, someone from outside is going to ask an employee what happened, or how it happened, or what the organization is doing to remedy the situation. Also, employees, even those at the lower levels of the organization, may have excellent insight on the incident and valuable suggestions on solution alternatives. Their immediate input may provide the pathway to a quick recovery.

In the long term, the organization will have won over the confidence, loyalty, and commitment of the employees, who appreciate being involved and listened to during the crisis. Employees' sense of belonging and self-worth is enhanced, and a culture of teamwork and cohesion is created. The post-crisis feeling of "we did it together" can carry over into other areas as the organization moves forward.

The literature is rich with several "dos" and "don'ts" when it comes to responding to questions such as those posed above. Whether the audience is internal or external stakeholders, these guidelines will apply.

Guidelines for Effective Crisis Communication

It is generally believed that the first 24 hours of a crisis are crucial because of the media's need to know what happened so they can tell their audiences. There is an information vacuum that, if left unfilled by the organization(s) involved, will be filled for them by others. The longer companies wait, the more likely falsehoods will become accepted as truths. It is for this reason that most consultants in the field recommend telling the truth and telling it quickly. Telling the truth up front is the simplest and most effective way of defusing public hostility, no matter how bad the incident is. Rather than being preoccupied with protecting itself from liability, a company must demonstrate a strong sense of integrity, responsibility, and commitment.[59]

An organization can use a number of avenues to disseminate its information or tell its side of the story to weather the storm brought on by a crisis. These include press releases, press kits, news conferences, and one-on-one interviews with the various media. *A* **press release** *is a printed statement that describes how an organization is responding to a crisis and who is in charge. A* **press kit** *is a package of information about a company, including names and pictures of its executives, a fact sheet, and key milestones in the company's history.* In the event of a crisis, the last item included in the press kit is a specific press release related to the current incident. This package is ready for distribution to the media when a crisis breaks.

Telling what your organization is doing to address a crisis is especially important to family or close relatives of victims. These family members must be handled with utmost sensitivity. The absence of concern and empathy can lead to a perception of arrogance. It is also important to add to the discussion of what is being done, a plan showing how a similar crisis will be avoided in the future. This is when input from the crisis management team and other technical experts becomes very valuable to the spokesperson. In addition to providing an overview of the progress being made to address the crisis, the spokesperson should involve technical specialists to provide more expert and detailed background information. This is especially critical during a press conference. Also, enlisting the support of objective third parties to speak on the organization's behalf can lessen the damage.[60] Exhibit 12.2 on the next page presents ten simple communication rules to remember during a crisis.

Ethical **Dilemma 1**

HP Corporate Spy Pretexting Scandal

Hewlett-Packard (HP) was facing a problem of a board member spilling private corporate information to the press. To stop the leak, HP investigated the matter. HP used pretexting to find out which board member(s) was leaking information. The pretexting included obtaining private confidential phone records under false pretenses

continued

(Ethical Dilemma 1 continued)

of company directors, employees, and journalists. The abuse of privacy rights hit the press, and the government came after HP. The chairman of the board, Patricia Dunn, resigned, and HP settled the civil lawsuit, paying $14.5 billion and avoiding criminal charges.[61]

1. Was this bad press of civil and criminal charges a crisis situation for HP?
2. If you were asked to, would you lie by giving false information to obtain phone records?
3. Using the guidelines for effective communications, what would you say to the press and Congress at the government investigation? Would you come out with the entire truth right away or try to cover it up?
4. Should the chairman of HP's board have been fired? Why or why not?

EXHIBIT 12.2 Guidelines to Effective Crisis Communications and Management

a. Be present.
b. Don't "spin."
c. Communicate plan of action.
d. Be sensitive with affected parties.
e. Avoid conflicting messages.
f. Show a plan for how you will avoid a repeat in the future.
g. Don't make excuses for the leader.
h. Go the extra mile. Go beyond the requirements of the situation.
i. When things are going good, take credit for it without being self-absorbed.
j. The media is your friend and link to the public. Be honest and straightforward with them.

Applying the **Concept 1**

Guidelines to Effective Crisis Communications

Using the letters a through j that accompany the guidelines in Exhibit 12.2, identify which guideline is explained by the statement below.

____ 1. The CEO of a company is on vacation when a crisis breaks out, but refuses to cancel his vacation and return home to deal with the crisis.

____ 2. Information is held back or filtered to say only what the leaders or those in charge want you to know about a crisis.

____ 3. Family or close ones of victims, or those affected, are brought to a central location and provided with services such as counseling, support, and other facilities that might be needed to help them cope.

____ 4. Expect and treat victims and/or family members' emotional outbursts with empathy.

____ 5. After the Concorde crashed, the French authorities along with British Airways immediately grounded all Concorde flights until the designers came up with a fuel tank protection solution.

Managing After a Crisis

It is quite possible for an organization to experience growth and prosperity after a crisis. Effective leaders know how to turn a negative event such as a crisis into a growth and learning experience. It is about looking beyond the present crisis and into the future. Most forward-looking organizations now do what the experts have long recommended; that is, in the aftermath of a crisis, top management should launch an evaluation (preferably conducted by an objective third party) of the organization's effectiveness in managing the crisis. Such an evaluation should include effectiveness in communicating with key stakeholder groups and effectiveness in addressing the root cause(s) of the crisis.[62] The analysis should focus on questions pertaining to how effectively the crisis team and the crisis management plan performed, how effectively the organization handled victims and family members, and what worked the least in mitigating the problem. These questions are relevant for many reasons, the most important of which are the lessons learned that can help prevent future crises.[63,64]

It is evident from the discussion so far that effective crisis communication rests on the following principles: prepare for crises, respond quickly, act with integrity, and disclose fully. The bottom line, according to one researcher, is to be mindful of the "three As": *acknowledge* or admit to the situation, specify what *action* you are taking to contain or repair the damage, and tell the public what you are going to do to *avoid* a repeat in the future.

If there is one certainty in organizational life today, it is that change will happen. More and more organizations are discovering that they operate in highly turbulent environments where the level of change is discontinuous, rendering past models of successful leadership obsolete. Therefore, future success will depend on an organization's ability to learn and adapt. In the second half of this chapter, we describe and explore the emerging concept of the learning organization and knowledge management.

Opening Case APPLICATION

4. Several rumors are circulating that GM is on the verge of bankruptcy. How can GM's leadership address these rumors to avoid further panic among shareholders and employees?

Effective communication is the key. An effective internal crisis communication system that informs the employees early of pertinent facts of an incident equips them to respond to questions from outsiders. Also, employees, even those at the lower levels of the organization, may have excellent insight on the crisis and provide valuable suggestions on solution alternatives. Their immediate input may provide the pathway to a quick recovery. The CEO should be out there communicating the what, how, and when. People need to know the facts and what leadership is doing to address the crisis.

The Learning Organization and Knowledge Management

It is an established fact that most of the world is transitioning from a production-based to a knowledge-based economy. As a result, organizations are increasingly dependent on innovative knowledge to create value for their customers. The question for many leaders is how to organize people, systems, and processes within the organization to generate and exploit new forms of knowledge.[65] In his book,

The Fifth Discipline, Peter Senge makes a compelling case that an organization's survival is linked to its ability to learn and adapt. He described a true learning organization as one that can develop not only new capabilities but also a fundamental mindset transformation.[66] To stay competitive, organizations must continuously innovate.

The responsibility of any organization desirous of change and innovation in a rapidly changing environment must be for its leaders to make it a priority to build and maintain a learning culture that supports and allows risk taking.[67] Organizational learning is seen as a fundamental component of the knowledge creation process.

In this section, we examine what a learning organization represents, how a learning organization differs from a traditional organization, and the role of leadership in creating a learning organization.

Learning Outcome 6 *List five or more attributes that can be used to describe the learning organization.*

What Is a Learning Organization?

In a stable environment, change is slow and incremental, and organizations have time to react and still retain their competitive positions. However, in rapidly changing environments, change is frequent and discontinuous; and reacting is not the best approach to staying competitive. The challenge is for affected organizations to overcome obstacles and exploit opportunities that are the products of accelerating industry dynamics.[68] To succeed, organizations must display continuous learning and adaptive characteristics.[69]

A **learning organization** *is one that is skilled at creating, acquiring, and transferring knowledge, and at modifying behavior to reflect new knowledge and insights.*[70] It is through learning that knowledge is created. Examples of effective organizational learning methods include the implementation of reverse innovation, the stage-gate innovation process, and team-to-team and person-to-person baton-passing.[71] Researchers generally agree that managing knowledge effectively can provide an organization with sustainable competitive advantages. Leaders, especially those in top positions, must create avenues that support and nurture collective learning (also known as organizational learning), for it is through this process that members acquire new knowledge and develop innovative capabilities to create value.[72,73]

Organizational knowledge *is the tacit and explicit knowledge that individuals possess about products, services, systems, and processes.*[74] Explicit or formal knowledge is expressed in a system of rules and is easily communicated and shared. It is often codified in manuals, databases, and information systems. Tacit or informal knowledge is highly personal, difficult to communicate, strongly rooted in action, and highly contextual in nature. Unlike explicit knowledge, such as the design of a product or the description of a business process, tacit knowledge is the instinct and intuition that an experienced practitioner possesses.[75]

Organizational learning involves external and internal sources. Externally, an organization can learn from its customers, suppliers, competitors, industry and academic publications, business partners, and consultants.[76] Internally, organizations can learn from their employees. Every employee, especially those who work directly with customers, is a great source of new ideas.

Opening Case APPLICATION

5. Describe the threats facing GM in its external environment.

GM is an organization facing major threats from the technological, economic, political/legal, sociocultural, competitive, and demographic environments. Technological innovations in hybrid and hydrogen fuel cell-powered vehicles are moving at a fast pace and causing GM to play catch-up or react to competitor moves in this area. The economy is going through some uncertain times, and some think it is sliding into a recession due to high oil and gas prices, the housing and subprime mortgage crisis, and decreased consumer spending. Politically, there is increased talk of regulating the auto industry in a variety of areas including emissions, mileage, and safety standards. From a competitive standpoint, there is intense competition from foreign competitors like Toyota, Honda, and Kia. Demographically, the consumer market is global and undergoing some significant transformations. The Baby Boomers are getting older and changing their tastes and desires to align with their needs. The younger generations (GenX, GenY, and the Milleniums) are savvy consumers who are not easily swayed by promotions and rely on their own judgments for brand choice. They are the Internet, iPod, and cell phone generation that has information available at their fingertips. This type of environment requires an organization like GM to make learning and knowledge management a priority.

Before we get into the details of the learning organization and knowledge management, complete Self-Assessment 1.

SELF-ASSESSMENT 1

Learning Organizations

Select an organization you work or have worked for and rate it for each question on a scale of 1–5. If you are not sure, rate it as 3.

5—4—3—2—1

Describes organization *Does NOT describe organization*

_____ 1. The organization has a flat structure, few layers of management, and makes decisions quickly.

_____ 2. Decision making is decentralized; lower-level managers make important decisions.

_____ 3. There are no job descriptions, or they are very general and focused on getting the job done.

_____ 4. There is a focus on continuous improvement and change.

_____ 5. Everyone has easy access to communicate with anyone.

_____ 6. Managers encourage creative thinking.

_____ 7. Managers listen to and implement employee ideas for improvement.

_____ 8. The climate encourages experimentation of new ideas.

_____ 9. There are incentives for learning new things.

_____ 10. There are incentives for contributing new ideas and innovations.

_____ 11. Employees are encouraged to identify and solve problems.

_____ 12. There are no departmental boundaries; people don't focus on developing departmental power.

_____ 13. When new methods are developed, they are shared for everyone throughout the organization to use.

_____ 14. The focus is on teamwork, not individual accomplishments.

_____ 15. When employees implement new ideas that fail, they are encouraged to keep trying rather than being punished.

Add up your score. Place the score here _____ and on the continuum below.

75—70—65—60—55—50—45—40—35—30—25—20—15

Learning organization *NOT a learning organization*

The higher the score, the more characteristic the firm is of a learning organization. Most organizations group around the middle.

Learning Outcome 7 *Distinguish between the traditional organization and the learning organization.*

The Traditional versus the Learning Organization Culture

By all accounts, most organizations today operate in environments characterized by continuous change, and for some—like the high-tech companies—the level of change is discontinuous.[77] **Discontinuous change** *occurs when anticipated or expected changes bear no resemblance to the present or the past.* The emergence of better and cheaper technologies, rivals' introduction of new or better products and services, competition from low-cost foreign competitors, and demographic shifts represent major threats to the profitability and even survival of many organizations. In stable, less turbulent environments, organizations focus on being efficient and on achieving stated objectives through highly structured command systems with strong vertical hierarchies and specialized jobs. However, given the realities of the current environment, this traditional organizational form is being replaced by the learning organizational form. A simple distinction between the traditional organization and the learning organization is one word—culture. See Exhibit 12.3 for a comparison of the two organization types.

EXHIBIT 12.3 The Traditional Organization versus the Learning Organization

Traditional (efficiency driven)	Learning (learning driven)
• Stable environment	• Changing environment
• Vertical structure	• Flat horizontal structure
• Strategy is formulated from the top and passed down	• Strategy is a collaborative effort within the organization and with other companies
• Centralized decision making	• Decentralized decision making
• Rigidly defined and specialized tasks	• Loose, flexible, and adaptive roles
• Rigid culture that is not responsive to change	• Adaptive culture that encourages continuous improvement and change
• Formal systems of communication tied to the vertical hierarchy with lots of filters	• Personal and group networks of free, open exchanges with no filters

The Traditional Organization Culture

The traditional organization has the following characteristics:

- The traditional organization is based on the bureaucratic model that emphasizes a command-and-control structure, centralized decision making, highly formalized systems, specialized tasks, and a rigid, closed culture. These vertical structures are effective under stable environmental conditions where the pace of change is slow or incremental at best.
- The culture of the traditional organization is oriented toward the individual, and rewards are individualized. This fosters competition among individuals.
- There is a mindset that there is a "right way" to do things, and only when that way is followed will the organization be successful. An elaborate formal system of reporting allows leaders to closely monitor work operations. This formal system is a powerful tool for controlling information and often acts as a filter

in determining what information leaders decide to pass down to lower-level employees.[78]

- Because the traditional organization is efficiency-driven, deviating from standard operating procedures is frowned upon and mistakes are viewed as a symptom of poor performance. Therefore, employees don't take chances, and mistakes and problems are hidden.[79]

The Learning Organization Culture

In contrast, the learning organization culture is characterized by the following attributes:

- In learning organizations, the vertical structure is abandoned for a flat, horizontal structure. The horizontal structure is constituted around work flows or processes rather than functional specialties. The learning organization recognizes that work processes and procedures are the means to satisfying customer needs rather than ends in themselves. Flexible structures are appropriate in today's rapidly changing business environment, in which competitive pressures, technological innovations, global market changes, and evolving customer needs require constant adjustments and adaptation.
- Teamwork is highly valued, and network systems facilitate open communication and exchange throughout the organization and with other external sources. Researchers interested in network relationships have recognized the knowledge dimension of networks and its link with competitive success. They propose that networks provide firms with access to knowledge, resources, markets, and technologies.[80]
- To encourage innovation and creativity in meeting current challenges, learning organizations are designing tasks that are much looser, free flowing, and adaptive. Few strict rules and procedures prescribe how things should be done. The term *organic* has been used to describe this type of organization. Responsibility and authority are decentralized to lower-level workers, empowering them to think, experiment, create, learn, and solve problems at their level.
- Organizational learning is a multilevel process, bringing together individual, group, and organizational levels of analysis.[81] It is dynamic, bridging the levels with specific mechanisms. It involves multiple learning processes (intuition, integrating, interpreting, and institutionalization) that allow learning to feed forward to the organizational level and feed back to the individual. The most successful learning organizations compound their advantage by encouraging employees at all levels to collect and share information across boundaries rather than hoarding it.[82] This is facilitated through communication and information hubs that make knowledge sharing a way of life.[83] In the end, one of the most important qualities for a learning organization to have is a strong culture that supports not just knowledge creation but its transfer across functional or divisional boundaries.[84] In a study examining the use of knowledge for technological innovation within diversified firms, the findings revealed that the use of interdivisional knowledge on the impact of an invention is stronger than the effect of using knowledge from within divisional boundaries alone.[85]
- The learning organization embraces the idea that people will learn if encouraged to face challenges, experiment, fail, and reflect on their experiences.[86,87,88]

Work Application 5

Using Exhibit 12.3, explain whether where you work or have worked is more a traditional organization or a learning organization.

Examples of learning organizations today include Microsoft, Toyota, W. L. Gore & Associates, Xerox, 3M, Johnson & Johnson, Procter & Gamble, and Internet-based companies such as Google and eBay. These companies are finding that success is more about nurturing the imagination, creativity, and passion of employees to solve customer problems than focusing on costs and profits.

6. In your opinion, does GM represent the traditional organization or the learning organization?

Organizations that operate in highly turbulent environments need to adopt a learning organization culture. Unfortunately, GM cannot be described as a learning organization despite its highly turbulent business enviroment. In a *60 Minutes* interview on CBS in 2006, GM is described as a corporation that has "become too big, too bloated, and too slow to compete with more nimble foreign competitors." The fact that GM's product mix is still heavily weighted toward trucks, pickups, and SUVs at a time when gas prices are skyrocketing is an indication that GM is not a learning organization. GM has been extremely slow to adapt to new trends relative to its competitors. The best that can be said about GM is that it is an organization that is attempting to make the transition from a traditional to a learning, knowledge-driven organization. However, many analysts don't see it happening given GM's huge bureaucratic structure.

Applying the **Concept 2**

Traditional or Learning Organization

Identify each statement by its type of organization. Write the appropriate letter in the blank before each item.

a. traditional

b. learning

____ 6. Top-level managers make all the important decisions around here.

____ 7. There aren't many levels of management in our company.

____ 8. With a union, we have clearly defined jobs and are not allowed to do other work.

____ 9. Our organization's structure can be described as flat or horizontal with much decision-making responsibility delegated downward.

____ 10. In our organization, employees are encouraged to experiment and take risk without fear of punishment when they fail.

Learning and Knowledge Acquisition versus Firm Performance

Increasingly, researchers are finding that the higher the level of learning and knowledge acquisition, the greater the level of firm performance.[89,90,91,92] From a micro-level standpoint, different studies have focused on the relationship between knowledge acquisition and specific performance indicators:

- Studies investigating the relationship between knowledge creation and value creation found that a firm's ability to create and share knowledge is positively related to new product development success.[93,94]
- The findings of several studies support the proposition that organizational learning and knowledge creation have a direct positive influence on the level of innovation.[95,96,97,98,99,100]

- The learning organizational culture has a positive direct impact on employee, customer, and supplier satisfaction levels.[101,102]
- External knowledge acquisition has a positive impact on the processes of creativity and learning in problem solving.[103]

Learning Outcome 8 *Describe the role of leadership in creating a learning organization.*

The Role of Leaders in Creating a Learning Organization

Leaders play a key role in fostering a learning culture. Many studies and experts agree that knowledge management is a key leader function.[104] Knowledge has been identified as one of the most important resources that contribute to the competitive advantage of an organization.[105] Superior performance is achieved when newly acquired knowledge is interpreted and integrated with existing knowledge and applied to problem solving.

Problems associated with failed efforts to create a learning culture are often attributed to poor leadership.[106] To succeed in the knowledge-based economy, leaders are challenged to transform their organizations into flexible systems capable of continuous learning and greater adaptation.[107] Removing obstacles to information sharing, such as the unwillingness of some members to share information, increases not only the learning process but also knowledge creation and exchange.[108] Leaders in learning organizations face a dual challenge to maintain efficient operations and create an adaptive organization at the same time.[109] Here, we identify important leadership initiatives that enhance learning and lead to new knowledge. The following guidelines (summarized in Exhibit 12.4) are ways in which leaders can create conditions conducive to learning and knowledge creation.[110,111,112]

EXHIBIT 12.4 Guidelines for Enhancing Organizational Learning

- Encourage creative thinking.
- Create a climate in which experimentation is encouraged.
- Provide incentives for learning and innovation.
- Build confidence in followers' capacity to learn and adapt.
- Encourage systems thinking.
- Create a culture conducive to individual and team learning.
- Institute mechanisms for channeling and nurturing creative ideas for innovation.
- Create a shared vision for learning.
- Broaden employees' frame of reference.
- Create an environment in which people can learn from their mistakes.

Encourage Creative Thinking

Although an organization's capacity to become more creative must begin at the individual level, creativity at the organizational level is also essential. At the organizational level, creativity is affected by the type of leadership style, culture, climate, structure, and systems that the organization has in place. Also, the resources and skills that the organization has in place will play a role. These organizational factors are further examined as part of the discussion on guidelines for enhancing organizational learning.

At the individual level, leaders can enhance learning by encouraging members to "think outside the box"—in other words, consider possibilities that do not already exist. Rather than responding to known challenges, employees are encouraged to create the future. This is a culture that encourages innovation. People with maverick ideas or out-of-the-ordinary proposals have to be welcomed and given room to operate in a learning organization. People who advocate radical or different ideas must not be looked on as disruptive or troublesome.

Another approach to enhance creative thinking is to encourage employees to research and learn from some of the best competitors in the industry. This process, known as *benchmarking*, allows a company to imitate the best practices of others. However, mere imitation does not yield a competitive advantage; it is a follower strategy. An organization must improve upon the best practices of competitors and launch innovations ahead of competitors.

Create a Climate in Which Experimentation Is Encouraged

Learning is more likely to take place in an organization in which experimentation on a small scale is encouraged and permitted. The purpose of an experiment is to learn by trial in a controlled environment. The costs of failure are not as significant as in a real attempt. People who are afraid of failing and risking their reputations or careers may be more likely to try something new or creative on a small scale. Also, the leader must create a culture that nurtures and even celebrates experimentation and innovation.[113] Everybody must be expected to contribute ideas, show initiative, and pursue continuous improvement. One way to do this is to create a sense of urgency in the organization, so that people see change and innovation as a necessity. Another way is to sometimes reward those who fail, because it symbolizes the importance of taking risks.

Provide Incentives for Learning and Innovation

The use of incentives and rewards is a powerful tool that leaders can apply to encourage learning and innovation. Organizations are often criticized for proclaiming themselves as champions of learning but not being able to provide workers with the kind of tangible support needed to motivate them. Rewards for successful ideas and innovations must be large and visible for others to notice. Rewards and incentives reinforce positive learning and innovation in the organization. CEOs must take steps to encourage and support learning and innovation in the workplace.

Build Confidence in Followers' Capacity to Learn and Adapt

The environment of the learning organization is one of rapid change, wherein survival depends on a timely response to threats and opportunities. Providing opportunities for employees to solve problems within the group or unit will increase their confidence and pride in the process. With each celebrated success comes greater confidence in dealing with change. Over time, familiarity with the change process will create an appreciation for flexibility and learning.

Encourage Systems Thinking

To enhance learning, the leader should help members regard the organization as a system in which everybody's work affects the work of everybody else. Therefore, everyone in the organization considers how their actions affect other elements of the organization. The emphasis on the whole system reduces boundaries both within the organization and with other companies, which allows for collaboration and continuous learning. Members begin to see how relationships with other companies can lower costs, increase sales, or bring in new competencies.

Ethical **Dilemma 2**

Departmentalization

Colleges and universities are known to have rigid departments, such as economics, management, marketing, accounting, and finance. At some schools, these departments are more concerned about themselves (related to budgets and number of faculty and courses) than serving students and cooperating with other departments. For example, some economics faculty have stated that they are concerned with theory and don't need to teach anything practical. There is also overlap in some courses offered by different departments, such as strategy being taught in management and marketing courses. In the business world, there is a trend to break down the barriers between departments and to be much more cooperative. However, academia doesn't seem to be following this trend.

1. Should the faculty's top priority be students, their department, or cooperating with other departments?
2. Should faculty move away from a focus on theory to more practical applications to business?
3. Should colleges follow the business trend of breaking away from departments and cooperate more? Or are they different from businesses, thus needing clear departments differentiated by discipline?

Create a Culture Conducive to Individual and Team Learning

Personal development and a lifetime of learning must be strong cultural values in learning organizations. Leaders must create a culture in which each person is valued, and the organization promotes and supports people to develop to their full potential. This type of learning culture encourages self-initiated activity, serendipity, and intracompany communications. In this type of learning culture, top leadership offers total support, employees take ownership of their work, and managers function more like facilitators than taskmasters.[114,115] Another aspect of creating a culture conducive to learning is the concept of team diversity (discussed in Chapter 10). Leaders must ensure that diversity is present in their teams. Studies have found that diverse teams enhance learning because members from different areas of expertise combine to generate novel insights or knowledge.[116,117]

Institute Mechanisms for Channeling and Nurturing Creative Ideas for Innovation

The birth of a new idea or knowledge begins with the individual. Making personal knowledge available to others is the central activity of the knowledge-creating organization. Knowledge that is shared can help an employee with a difficult problem or provide an opportunity for employees from different parts of the organization to interact with each other, getting advice and providing support about common problems. Ideas generated within or outside an organization may become the source of new products or innovations. Venture teams, task forces, information systems networks, seminars, and workshops can be used to diffuse knowledge and to channel creative ideas to appropriate locations for evaluation and application. Once this process is institutionalized, knowledge creation and exchange become part of the culture.[118]

Create a Shared Vision for Learning

Creating a shared vision enhances learning as organization members develop a common purpose and commitment to make learning an ongoing part of the organization. If employees all believe that the organization is headed toward greatness, they will be motivated to be part of it by learning and contributing their best ideas and solutions.

Broaden Employees' Frame of Reference

People's frame of reference determines how they see the world. The ways we gather, analyze, and interpret information—and how we make decisions based on such information—are affected by our personal frames of reference. A frame of reference determines what implicit assumptions people hold, and those assumptions, consciously or unconsciously, affect how they interpret events. To enhance employees' ability to learn, it is helpful for leaders to broaden the frames employees use to see the organization and its external environment. Learning is constrained when leaders and their followers fail to see the world from a different perspective and therefore are unable to help the organization adapt to a changing environment. Broadening employees' frames of reference or perspective provides for a greater variety of approaches to solving problems and thus facilitates learning and continuous improvement.

Create an Environment in Which People Can Learn from Their Mistakes

Some of the most important inventions or scientific breakthroughs resulted from investigating failed outcomes. Unfortunately, in many organizations, when experiments or full-scale ventures fail, the tendency is to immediately abandon the activity to save face or avoid negative consequences. This is often the wrong approach, because more learning takes place from things that go wrong than from things that go right. After all, when things turn out as expected, it just confirms existing theories or assumptions. New insights are more likely when there is an investigation into why expected outcomes were not realized. Therefore, to encourage learning, leaders must communicate the view that failure is tolerated. Then, they must provide opportunities for people to engage in post-activity reviews regardless of outcome.

Creating a culture that rewards those who succeed, as well as occasionally rewarding those who fail, sends a message that the organization encourages risk-taking. Creating a strong risk culture and environment is a leadership responsibility that cannot be taken for granted. Organizations with risk-sensitive cultures are noted for high levels of accountability, reinforcement, and communication, with the appropriate risk management and infrastructure resources in place.[119]

Learning is a never-ending exercise. Leaders must communicate the message that learning and continuous improvements are imperative in today's highly dynamic business environment. Leaders must take the lead in challenging the status quo and creating organizational conditions that are conducive to learning and continuous innovation.[120]

Opening Case APPLICATION

7. What actions can GM's leadership take to make it more of a learning organization?

Rick Wagoner can employ many of the guidelines for enhancing organizational learning listed in Exhibit 12.4 on page 469 and described in this section. Action on all or any number of these guidelines will increase GM's efforts to become a learning organization.

Now that you have learned about crisis leadership and the learning organization, you may find it interesting to see how your own personality traits match up. Complete Self-Assessment 2.

SELF-ASSESSMENT 2

Personality and Crisis and the Learning Organization

Crisis

When facing a crisis, surgency personalities tend to take the leadership position to solve the crisis, and agreeableness personalities are glad to follow. Those with adjustment problems tend to get emotional under the pressure of a crisis and often get defensive and deny there is a problem, whereas conscientious personalities with a openness to experience tend to want to resolve the crisis. How do you handle crisis situations? How can you improve?

____

____

Learning Organization

The key personality trait that differs between the traditional organization and the learning organization is openness to new experience. If you are closed to new experience, you will tend to like a traditional organization in which change is slow and top management makes the decisions. If you are open to new experience, you will tend to enjoy a learning organization in which you are encouraged and valued for implementing change and making many of your own decisions. Would you be more comfortable in a traditional or learning organization? Why?

____

____

Go to the Internet (www.cengage.com/management/lussier)
where you will find a broad array of resources to help maximize your learning.

- Review the vocabulary
- Try a quiz
- Find related links

Chapter Summary

The chapter summary is organized to answer the nine learning outcomes for Chapter 12.

1. **Explain why crisis leadership competence is an important consideration when hiring new leaders.**

   Crises are inevitable. It is not a question of "if" a crisis will happen, but "when." A crisis can inflict severe damage to an organization if not properly managed. In a crisis, stock prices plummet and operating costs escalate, causing both short- and long-term financial losses. A crisis that is mismanaged can also damage an organization's reputation and diminish consumer confidence in the organization's mission, or in some cases can lead to its demise altogether. As the economy limps on and speculation of it sliding into a recession builds, the real prospect exists that many corporations are going to face a crisis of survival. Rising oil prices, the housing downturn, the subprime crisis, the credit crunch, and talk of possible inflation and recession are all ingredients that could stymie even the best-prepared CEOs.

2. **Identify the benefits of pre-crisis planning.**

   Pre-crisis planning buys you time. You are ready when a crisis strikes. Many organizations are presented with early warning signals of an impending crisis but fail to recognize and heed them. The problem is detecting the signals that warn of a crisis. It is for this reason that experts recommend pre-crisis planning for any size of business. Pre-crisis planning allows you to create systems and procedures for detecting signals that warn of an impending crisis before it happens. Effective pre-crisis planning leads to effective crisis management during and after a crisis.

3. **Identify three key components of the pre-crisis planning phase.**

Three components to pre-crisis planning that every organization (large, small, for-profit, or non-profit) should address are: (1) appointing a crisis leader, (2) creating a crisis response team, and (3) assessing risk.

4. **Describe the five-step process for crisis risk assessment.**

The five-step process for risk assessment consists of: (1) risk identification, (2) risk assessment and ranking, (3) risk reduction strategies, (4) crisis prevention simulations, and (5) crisis management. In step one, crisis team members begin by first identifying the worst-case incidents that could have severe consequences on people, the organization's financial position, or its image. This process is described as risk identification and results in the creation of a risk chart. Next, these incidents are analyzed and ranked. During the risk reduction step, the crisis leader shares the risk chart created during risk assessment and ranking with team members or larger audiences, and they begin debating and formulating strategies for countering each crisis or threat. The fourth step in the risk assessment process is crisis prevention. Here, tests and simulations are conducted to test employees under pressure. The fifth step of risk assessment is crisis management. A team is assembled and readied to respond in the event of a real crisis.

5. **Describe the role of the CEO and communication in managing a crisis.**

The CEO must be out leading the charge before, during, and after a crisis. The CEO's involvement demonstrates to the public the seriousness with which the incident is viewed. Before a crisis, the CEO should be actively involved in pre-crisis planning. During a crisis, he or she cannot develop a bunker mentality. As mentioned in the chapter, the three key tenets of crisis leadership are (1) stay engaged and lead from the front, (2) focus on the big picture and communicate the vision, and (3) work with your crisis management team. During a crisis, the CEO must have answers to the following questions: What happened? How did it happen? What are you doing to address the crisis? And after the crisis, what you going to do to ensure that it never happens again? For all of these things to happen, the organization must have in place a well-designed communication system and the leader must be an effective communicator.

6. **List five or more attributes that can be used to describe the learning organization.**

- Learning from mistakes and past experience
- Learning from others
- Systematic problem solving
- Experimentation
- Sharing knowledge
- Strong leadership support

7. **Distinguish between the traditional organization and the learning organization.**

The traditional, efficiency-driven organization has a bureaucratic structure (a tall pyramid), starting with the CEO at the top and everyone else functionally organized in layers below. Decision making is centralized at the top of the hierarchy, which controls and coordinates all functional units throughout the organization. To ensure reliable and predictable results, tasks are rigidly defined and broken down into specialized jobs. Strict formal rules and procedures for performing each task are enforced. Though repetitive, boring, and unchallenging, it is an efficient way of keeping the production line running smoothly. An elaborate formal system of reporting allows leaders to closely monitor work operations and maintain efficient, steady performance. This formal system is a powerful tool for controlling information and often acts as a filter in determining what information leaders decide to pass down to lower-level employees.

By contrast, in learning organizations the vertical structure is abandoned for a flat, horizontal structure. The horizontal structure is constituted around work flows or processes rather than functional specialties. To encourage innovation and creativity in meeting current challenges, learning organizations are designing tasks that are much looser, free flowing, and adaptive. Few strict rules and procedures prescribe how things should be done. The term *organic* has been used to describe this type of organization. Responsibility and authority are decentralized to lower-level workers, empowering them to think, experiment, create, learn, and solve problems at their level.

8. **Describe the role of leadership in creating a learning organization.**

The learning organization represents a paradigmic shift in the approach organizations take to managing their internal and external relationships. In today's rapidly changing business environment, organizations must transform into active learning organisms or risk becoming extinct. To succeed, organizations must be proactive and anticipatory, which requires continuous improvement. Thus, the traditional organization model that emphasized efficiency and stability is being replaced by a model that is learning-driven and adaptable.

Leaders play a critical role in effecting this transformation. Without effective leadership from the top and throughout the organizational structure, it is hard to imagine how the learning organization can succeed. A shared vision and mission are the basis for the emergence of strategy in a learning organization, and this is the responsibility of leadership. Leaders can play a key role in enhancing organizational learning by encouraging creative thinking, creating a climate in which experimentation and risk taking are encouraged, providing incentives for learning and innovation, building confidence in followers' capacity to learn and adapt, encouraging systems thinking, and creating a culture conducive to individual and team learning.

9. **Define the following key terms (in order of appearance in the chapter).**

Select one or more methods: (1) fill in the missing key terms from memory; (2) match the key terms from the following list with their definitions below; and (3) copy the key terms in order from the list at the beginning of the chapter.

__________ is a low-probability, high-impact event that threatens the viability of the organization and is characterized by ambiguity of cause, effect, and means of resolution, as well as by a belief that decisions must be made swiftly.

__________ is a printed statement that describes how an organization is responding to a crisis and who is in charge.

__________ is a package of information about a company, including names and pictures of its executives, a fact sheet, and key milestones in the company's history.

__________ is one that is skilled at creating, acquiring, and transferring knowledge, and at modifying behavior to reflect new knowledge and insights.

__________ is the tacit and explicit knowledge that individuals possess about products, services, systems, and processes.

__________ occurs when anticipated or expected changes bear no resemblance to the present or the past.

Key Terms

crisis, 452
discontinuous change, 466
learning organization, 464
organizational knowledge, 464
press kit, 461
press release, 461

Review Questions

1. Strategic crisis leadership is about a leader taking action in three key areas. What are these areas?
2. How has the Internet affected the way crises are perceived in our society today?
3. What are the main components of a pre-crisis plan?
4. The pre-crisis response plan requires the appointment of a crisis leader. Describe the responsibilities of this person.
5. The best indicator of an organization's readiness to respond to a crisis is how it rates on five factors. What are these five factors?
6. What is the appropriate role of an organization's top leadership during a crisis?
7. What does it mean to say that organizational learning is a multi-level sharing process?
8. What factors account for the fact that the learning organization is described as more creative and innovative than the traditional organization form?

Communication Skills

The following critical-thinking questions can be used for class discussion and/or as written assignments to develop communication skills. Be sure to give complete explanations for all questions.

1. Describe why a senior leader's physical presence is critical during a crisis.
2. What are the purpose and benefits of creating a comprehensive crisis response plan before a crisis happens?
3. What advice would you give to a leader who wants to improve his or her organization's communications function so that it is more effective during a crisis?
4. How important to an organization is internal (employee) communication during a crisis?
5. What message does it send when the organizational culture encourages employees to view mistakes/problems as opportunities for improvement rather than reasons to blame or punish those involved?

CASE

CEO A. G. Lafley's Transformation of P&G

In 2000, A. G. Lafley was appointed CEO and Chairman of Procter & Gamble at a time when the company was undergoing some serious crises. Under the leadership of the previous CEO (Durk Jager), whose tenure lasted for only 17 months (the shortest in P&G's 171-year history), the company lost $50 billion in market capitalization, its stock price declined 50 percent, half of its brands were losing market share, and the firm was struggling with morale problems. Since 2000, Lafley has led P&G to an impressive turnaround. The company has delivered consistent double-digit earnings-per-share growth, grown its market capitalization to over $200 billion, and diversified into beauty and personal care with the mega-acquisitions of Wella and Gillette.[121]

Lafley's leadership style is a marked contrast to Jager's. While Jager had questioned the competence of many P&G employees, Lafley assured them that he knew they were capable of restoring the marketing powerhouse to its former greatness. Whereas Jager has been described as gruff and confrontational, Lafley is relentlessly inquisitive in a calm, respectful manner that builds trust with employees. The most striking aspect of Lafley's leadership approach has been his decision to turn P&G into a learning organization. To accomplish this, he instituted a number of things:[122]

- He set a goal to improve the flow of knowledge throughout P&G.
- He emphasized listening more than lecturing. Listening is what facilitates knowledge flow in an organization, and knowledge flow is one of the elements in an engaging work environment that unlocks organizational productivity and innovation.
- Lafley requires regular interactions between managers and non-managers. In his opinion, getting employees to learn from each other helps them concentrate on the human dimension of understanding consumers.
- At P&G's corporate headquarters, Lafley transformed the 11th floor where senior executives maintained plush offices. Art was donated to a museum, oak walls were torn down, and 11 of the executives were moved to be closer to the people they lead.
- Lafley believes that P&G's employees are at the core of the company's success. To make his point, he has instituted a variety of programs to recognize and tangibly reward P&G's frontline employees.

Lafley's order to "tear down the walls" on P&G's executive floor was both pragmatic and symbolic. These actions signaled his intention to tear down "the walls" that prevented knowledge, the lifeblood of every organization, from flowing throughout P&G. A part of that symbolism was the transformation of P&G into a team culture.

Lafley has had a long-standing reputation for delegating responsibility. He is known as a consensus builder. His personality is that of a soft-spoken, easygoing, and down-to-earth individual. He is described as calm and quiet, direct, decisive, and tough.

It is because of Lafley's deep commitment to serving customers that he was named *Chief Executive Magazine*'s CEO of the Year in 2006. In accepting the honor, Lafley joined a list of notable CEOs such as Jack Welch of GE, Andy Grove of Intel, Herb Kelleher of Southwest Airlines, and Bill Gates of Microsoft.[123]

In P&G's 2007 annual report, Lafley reminded shareholders that over the past six years, annual sales more than doubled from $30 billion to $76 billion; the number of brands with more that $1 billion in annual sales more than doubled to a total of 23 brands; the number of brands with annual sales between $500 million and $1 billion more than quadrupled to a total of 18 brands; the number of retail customers that do $1 billion or more in annual sales more than with P&G jumped from two to seven; $43 billion in net earnings and $50 billion in free cash flow were generated; and P&G's market capitalization increased to more than $200 billion, making it the seventh most valuable company in the United States and the thirteenth most valuable in the world. Asked what has contributed to P&G's remarkable turnaround and sustainable growth, Lafley highlighted P&G's focus on eight key factors: purpose and values, goals, strategies, strengths, organizational structure, innovation, leadership and people, and culture.

GO TO THE INTERNET: To learn more about A. G. Lafley and Procter & Gamble, visit their Web site **(http://www.pg.com)**.

Support your answers to the following questions with specific information from the case and text or with other information you get from the Web or other sources.

1. Under Durk Jager, would you describe P&G as being more of a traditional organization or a learning organization?
2. In what ways has A. G. Lafley demonstrated his effectiveness as a crisis leader?
3. What actions and decisions did Lafley take in his efforts to transform P&G into a learning and knowledge-driven organization?
4. Find specific evidence from P&G's Web site that Lafley's emphasis on knowledge creation and innovation is working or not working. Report your findings.
5. The text discusses that, in the learning organization, there are external and internal sources of learning. What type of learning source prevailed at P&G prior to A. G. Lafley's appointment, and what type of learning source did he prefer when he became CEO?
6. Describe Lafley's personality and leadership style. How did it foster or hinder his efforts to transform P&G into a learning organization?

CUMULATIVE CASE QUESTIONS

7. What is CEO Lafley's source of power? Also, what type of power and influencing tactics has he used, and is it the appropriate power type? If not, which power type should he be using (Chapter 4)?
8. Based on the description of A. G. Lafley's personality and leadership style, in your opinion, is he more of a charismatic leader, a transformational leader, or both (Chapter 9)? Support your answer.
9. A. G. Lafley seemed to have encountered little or no resistance in his efforts to change P&G into a learning organization. Review the guidelines for minimizing resistance to change and describe the extent to which Lafley employed all or some of the guidelines (Chapter 11).

CASE EXERCISE AND ROLE-PLAY

Preparation: Put yourself in the role of the head of the crisis management team. There has been an accident at one of P&G's manufacturing plants resulting in a number of fatalities and injured personnel. You and Mr. Lafley are getting ready for a news conference with the media on the crisis. Prepare a list of questions you anticipate the media will be asking and what you or CEO Lafley's response should be. Decide who will speak first and why. Who else from the crisis management team will you bring along to the news conference, and what role will they be playing?

In-Class Groups: Break into groups of 4 to 6 members, and discuss the preparation questions.

Role-Play: Taking turns, one group will represent the crisis management team, led by Mr. Lafley or the crisis leader. Each team will have to decide what role Mr. Lafley will play during the news conference. Let another group play the role of the media. They should select no more than three questions from their prepared list to ask. The rest of the class should listen and judge the performance of the P&G crisis management team in addressing the media. Each group should take turns role-playing the media, the P&G crisis management team, or the judges. Each team playing the role of the media should ask a different set of three questions, so the same questions are not repeated during each round.

Observer Role: As the rest of the class members watch the role-play, they should judge (1) the opening remarks of the crisis management team—their demeanor, body language, tone, style, and substance; (2) the quality of questions that the media team asked; and (3) the quality of responses given by the P&G team—how honest and truthful they are with their answers. Use the guidelines for effective crisis communication as the tool to judge P&G's crisis management team performance during the news conference. Look for things that the person playing Mr. Lafley did well or did not do well during the news conference.

Discussion: After the role-plays, the class votes for the crisis management team that did the best job addressing the news media with its opening remarks and responding to questions. The instructor should weigh in with his or her opinion on which team did the best job in the questioning and which team did the best job in responding to the questions. Which team member playing Mr. Lafley did the best job and why? Where did the others fall short?

VIDEO CASE

Managing in Turbulent Times at Second City Theater

Managers today are expected to deal with uncertainty, unexpected events, diversity, and change. They must demonstrate flexibility, foster trust, and engage the hearts and minds of employees. The managers at Second City Theater have a leg up in developing these skills and dealing with these situations because Second City has been doing it for years—on stage. In 1975, owner and executive producer, Andrew Alexander, started the Second City television series (*SCTV*) in response to the new trend of television sketch comedy. Later, the company opened the Second City Training Center, an educational center offering classes in improvisation, acting, writing, and other skills. Most recently, Second City opened a corporate communications division, which provides training in the areas of internal communications, external marketing and branding, and learning development. With its focus on human skills, Second City demonstrates all of the qualities of a learning organization. The managers at Second City foster a climate where experimentation and learning are encouraged.

1. Many students of the Second City Training Center are businesspeople looking to gain skills for the corporate context. What skills from the world of improvisational comedy would be valuable to a business manager?
2. What do you think would be the challenges of a manager in a learning organization? Why?

Skill-Development Exercise 1

Handling a Crisis

Preparation for Skill-Development Exercise 1

Research the business news and find an organization that has just had a crisis. Below, identify the firm and the crisis. Also, read Procedure 2 below and think of your "Three As" response to the crisis.

Acknowledge:

Action:

Avoid:

Doing Skill-Development Exercise 1 in Class

Objective

To develop your ability to handle a crisis.

The primary AACSB learning standard skill developed through this exercise is strategic management.

Preparation

You should have selected a business in crisis.

Procedure 1 *(3–5 minutes)* Break into crisis teams of 4 to 6 and select one business crisis that the group will work on resolving.

Procedure 2 *(10–15 minutes)* Develop a crisis communication plan, identifying your "Three As".

Procedure 3 *(10–20 minutes)* Each crisis team selects a spokesperson who tells the class the organization chosen and its crisis followed by the team's "Three As" plan.

Conclusion

The instructor may lead a class discussion and/or make concluding remarks.

Apply It *(2–4 minutes)* What did I learn from this experience? How will I use this knowledge in the future?

Sharing
In the group, or to the entire class, volunteers may give their answers to the "Apply It" questions.

Skill-Development Exercise 2

The Learning Organization

Preparation for Skill-Development Exercise 2

Return to Self-Assessment 1, Learning Organizations, on page 465. Below, identify the firm you assessed and its score.

Select any three of the 15 characteristics of learning organization questions that can be improved. Below, list the numbers and develop a plan on how the organization can improve on each of the three characteristics.

Doing Skill-Development Exercise 2 in Class

Objective

To develop your skill to improve a firm's ability to learn.

The primary AACSB learning standard skill developed through this exercise is strategic management.

Preparation

You should have developed plans to improve learning on three characteristics of learning organizations.

Procedure 1 *(10–15 minutes)* Break into teams of 4 to 6 and share your preparation plans. Help each other improve the plans.

Procedure 2 *(10–20 minutes)* Each team selects a spokesperson who tells the class the organization chosen and the plans to improve learning.

Conclusion

The instructor may lead a class discussion and/or make concluding remarks.

Apply It *(2–4 minutes)* What did I learn from this experience? How will I use this knowledge in the future?

Sharing

In the group, or to the entire class, volunteers may give their answers to the "Apply It" questions.

Leadership and Spirituality in the Workplace

Judith A. Neal, PhD*

Appendix Outline

Spirituality in the Workplace
Defining Spirituality in the Workplace
Levels of Spirituality Development
Guidelines for Leading from a Spiritual Perspective
Know Thyself
Act with Authenticity and Congruency
Respect and Honor the Beliefs of Others
Be as Trusting as You Can Be
Maintain a Spiritual Practice
Spirit at Work Web Site

The purpose of this appendix is twofold: (1) It provides an overview of the concept of spirituality in the workplace. (2) It provides spiritual principles that have been useful to many leaders in their personal and professional development.

Spirituality in the Workplace

Tom Aageson, former Director of Aid to Artisans—a nonprofit organization that helps artists in third-world countries—takes an annual retreat in which he contemplates questions about the purpose of his life, and evaluates how well he is living in alignment with his values. Angel Martinez, former CEO of Rockport Shoes, invited all his top executives to a retreat that included exploring the integration of each person's spiritual journey with his or her work journey. At Integrated Project Systems (IPS) in San Francisco, former CEO Bill Kern created a document called "The Corporate Stand" that is very explicit about "The Integrity of the Human Spirit." These are key principles that employees live by at IPS. Rodale Press, publisher of such well-known magazines as *Prevention, Men's Health, Runner's World,* and *Organic Gardening,* has a "kiva room" at corporate headquarters where employees may go to meditate, pray, or just spend quiet time when things get too stressful. ANZ Bank in Australia and New Zealand sends all its employees through personal transformation programs, conducts an audit based on levels of corporate consciousness, and allows each bank branch to design its own meditation/quiet room.

Stories like these are becoming more and more common in all kinds of workplaces. Academic and professional conferences are offering an increasing number of sessions that have words such as *Spirituality, Consciousness,* or *Soul* in the title. There is a new openness in management education to recognition of our spiritual nature. This recognition can be on a personal level, such as when a person explores his or her own spiritual journey and struggles with what this means for their work. It is also on a conceptual level, as both academics and practitioners explore the role that spirituality might have in bringing meaning, purpose, and increased performance to organizational life. A major change is going on in the personal and professional lives of leaders, as many of them more deeply integrate their spirituality and their work. And most would agree that this integration is leading to positive changes in their relationships and their effectiveness.

*Appendix written by Judith A. Neal, Ph.D., Executive Director, International Center for Spirit at Work, http://www.spiritatwork.org.

Defining Spirituality in the Workplace

Spirituality is difficult to define. The Latin origin of the word "spirit" is *spirare*, meaning, "to breathe." At its most basic, then, spirit is what inhabits us when we are alive and breathing; it is the life force. Spirituality has been defined as "that which is traditionally believed to be the vital principle or animating force within living beings; that which constitutes one's unseen intangible being; the real sense or significance of something."[1] A fairly comprehensive definition, part of which is provided here, is as follows:

> *One's spirituality is the essence of who he or she is. It defines the inner self, separate from the body, but including the physical and intellectual self.... Spirituality also is the quality of being spiritual, of recognizing the intangible, life-affirming force in self and all human beings. It is a state of intimate relationship with the inner self of higher values and morality. It is a recognition of the truth of the inner nature of people.... Spirituality does not apply to particular religions, although the values of some religions may be a part of a person's spiritual focus. Said another way, spirituality is the song we all sing. Each religion has its own singer.*[2]

Perhaps the difficulty people have had in defining spirituality is that they are trying to objectify and categorize an experience and way of being that is at its core very subjective and beyond categorizing. For this reason, some have resorted to poetry as a way of trying to capture the essence of the experience of spirituality. Lee Bolman did this very effectively in his keynote presentation on spirituality in the workplace to the Eastern Academy of Management in May 1995. He quoted the Persian poet Rumi:[3]

> *All day I think about it, then at night I say it*
> *Where did I come from and what am I supposed to be doing?*
> *I have no idea*
> *My soul is elsewhere, I'm sure of that*
> *And I intend to end up there.*

James Autry, a successful *Fortune 500* executive, wrote a poem called "Threads." Here is an excerpt from that poem:[4]

> *Listen.*
> *In every office*
> *You hear the threads*
> *of love and joy and fear and guilt,*
> *the cries for celebration and reassurance,*
> *and somehow you know that connecting those threads*
> *is what you are supposed to do*
> *and business takes care of itself.*

Spirituality in the workplace is about people seeing their work as a spiritual path, as an opportunity to grow personally and to contribute to society in a meaningful way. It is about learning to be more caring and compassionate with fellow employees, with bosses, with subordinates and customers. It is about integrity, being true to oneself, and telling the truth to others. Spirituality in the workplace can refer to an individual's attempts to live his or her values more fully in the workplace. Or it can refer to the ways in which organizations structure themselves to support the spiritual growth of employees.

In the final analysis, the understanding of spirit and of spirituality in the workplace is a very individual and personal matter. There are as many expressions of these concepts as there are people who talk or write about them.

Levels of Spirituality Development

In practice, organizations are implementing spirituality in the workplace approaches at one or more of the following four levels:[5]

Level 1: Individual Development

At this level, programs focus on helping the individual employee understand more about his or her values, spiritual principles, and sense of purpose. The organization is committed to helping individuals live in alignment with their spiritual path, and may offer meditation rooms or courses on spiritual practices and/or teachings, and may bring in speakers who talk about spiritual development. There is an understanding that if people can discover and respond to their own "calling" or sense of purpose, they will be more creative, committed, and service-oriented.

Level 2: Leadership and Team Development

Organizations are offering courses to leaders with titles like "Authentic Leadership," "Leading with Soul," and "Spiritual Leadership." Leaders are encouraged to apply spiritual values such as humility, trust, courage, integrity, and faith to their work with teams. They may offer courses such as "Team Spirit" and "Noble Purpose" developed by Barry Heerman.[6] Some organizations are offering lunchtime Spirit at Work discussion groups. Others are offering team-building courses that incorporate spiritual values or practices.

Level 3: Total System Development

A growing number of CEOs and organizational leaders have become personally committed to creating organizations that nurture the human spirit of the company's employees, customers, and other stakeholders. Several systemic approaches have been developed to help organizations evolve to a higher level of congruence with spiritual values. These include "Corporate Tools" by Richard Barrett,[7] "Spiral Dynamics" by Don Beck and Chris Cowan,[8] "Appreciative Inquiry" by David Cooperrider and colleagues,[9] "Positive Organizational Scholarship" and "The Abundance Framework" by Kim Cameron,[10] and "Open Space Technology" by Harrison Owen.[11] The key aim in each of these organizational development processes is to help an organization move beyond just a focus on profits and the bottom line to a commitment to human development and a positive contribution to society.

Level 4: Redefining the Role of Business

A new paradigm is emerging among business leaders that redefines the purpose of business as the solution to solving problems in society and around the globe, rather than being a contributor to them. The focus is on using the creative energy and talent of their employees, along with their vast capital resources and international reach, to truly make a positive difference in the world. Willis Harman, cofounder of the Institute of Noetic Sciences and of the World Business Academy, was probably the first person to speak about the important role of business in increasing consciousness in the world.[12] More recently, Case Western Reserve's Wetherhead School of Management has created a Center of Excellence called the *Center of Business as an Agent of World Benefit (BAWB)*, which has sponsored an ongoing inquiry research project into the ways business is making a positive difference in the world. People can get involved by going to its Web site at **http://worldbenefit.case.edu**.

Each organization is unique in terms of its values, vision, and readiness for spirituality in the workplace, so there is no one formula that leaders can use to implement spiritual values and practices in their organizations. The best thing to do is to learn as much as possible from organizations that have been successful in this integration. A great place to start is to study the organizations that have received the International Spirit at Work Award for their explicit spiritual practices and commitment to nurturing the human spirit of their employees; for more information, go to **http://www.spiritatwork.org/**.

Guidelines for Leading from a Spiritual Perspective

Following are five spiritual principles that have been useful to many leaders in their personal and professional development.

Know Thyself

All spiritual growth processes incorporate the principle of self-awareness. Leading provides a great opportunity to become more self-aware. Examine why you respond to situations the way you do. Take a moment in the morning to reflect on the kind of leader you would like to be today. At the end of the day, take quiet time to assess how well you did, and to what extent you were able to live in alignment with your most deeply held core values. It is also helpful to take personal and leadership assessment tools, such as the Myers-Briggs Type Indicator. You might also consider taking the *Spiritual Intelligence Assessment* (see **http://www.spiritatwork.org/library/SpiritualIntelligenceAssessment.pdf**).

Act with Authenticity and Congruency

Followers learn a lot more from who we are and how we behave than from what we say. Authenticity means being oneself, being fully congruent, and not playing a role. Many managers really get into the role of "leader," and they see managing as a place to assert their superiority and control. They would never want employees to see the more human, softer parts of them. Yet we are finding that managers who are more authentic, humble, and congruent tend to be more effective.[13]

It is a real challenge to be authentic and congruent in the workplace. Most people feel that if they are truly themselves and if they say what they are really thinking, it will be the end of their careers. But I believe that if we don't do this, we sell a little bit of our souls every time we are inauthentic, and that saps our creative energy and our emotional intelligence. It also reduces our sense of commitment to the work we do, and we cannot perform at our highest level. Experiment with greater authenticity and with showing more of your humanness. You will be surprised at how positively people will respond.

It is also important to create a climate in which employees are encouraged to behave authentically and congruently. This means that they should be comfortable expressing feelings as well as thoughts and ideas. Contrary to popular opinion, humility accompanied by a strong will does create an enduring organization, and is a much more powerful tool for success than a strong ego.

Respect and Honor the Beliefs of Others

It can be very risky and maybe even inappropriate to talk about your own spirituality in the workplace. Yet if spirituality is a guiding force in your life and your leading, and if you follow the guideline of authenticity and congruency, you cannot hide that part of yourself. It is a fine line to walk.

What seems to work best is to build a climate of trust and openness first, and to model an acceptance of opinions and ideas that are different from yours. Then, if an appropriate opportunity comes up in which you can mention something about your spiritual beliefs, you should emphasize that they are yours alone. Explain that people have different beliefs and that you respect those differences. It is extremely important that employees do not feel that you are imposing your belief system (spiritual, religious, or otherwise) on them. At the same time, it is worthwhile to do anything that you can do to nurture spiritual and ethical development in your employees in a way that allows them to explore their own deepest values and beliefs.

Be as Trusting as You Can Be

This guideline operates on many levels. On the personal level, this guideline of "being as trusting as you can be" applies to trusting oneself, one's inner voice, or one's source of spiritual guidance. This means trusting that there is a Higher Power in your life and that if you ask you will receive guidance on important issues. It also operates on the interpersonal, team, and organizational level. If you truly learn to see yourself as trustworthy, and believe that it is our essential nature as humans to be trustworthy, then you will naturally feel trusting of colleagues and subordinates. And you will also feel more trusting that the processes and events that are happening have a higher purpose to them if you look for it and amplify it.

Maintain a Spiritual Practice

In a research study on people who integrate their spirituality and their work, the most frequently mentioned spiritual practice is spending time in nature. Examples of other practices are meditation, prayer, reading inspirational literature, hatha yoga, shamanistic practices, writing in a journal, and walking a labyrinth. People reported that it is very important for them to consistently commit to whatever individual spiritual practice they have chosen. The regular involvement in a chosen practice appears to be the best way to deepen one's spirituality.[14]

When leaders faithfully commit to a particular spiritual practice they are calmer, more creative, more in tune with employees and customers, and more compassionate.[15]

Work Application

A-1. Give an example of spirituality in the workplace where you work or have worked.

A-2. Have you or anyone you know struggled with spiritual journey and what this means for work? Explain.

Spirit at Work Web Site

The International Center for Spirit at Work Web site, **http://www.spiritatwork.org**, is the most comprehensive site devoted to spirituality in the workplace. It is designed to be a resource to people interested in integrating their deepest values and their work. It consists of information about the International Center for Spirit at Work; A Community section that has case studies, research, presentations, and exercises; and other change management tools for members of our organization. In addition, there is an entire section devoted to the International Spirit at Work Award. For more information, visit the Web site.

Appendix Summary

There is a growing trend to talk more openly about spirituality and to want to integrate spiritual principles into all aspects of life—relationships, community, and work. This appendix has presented some resources for leaders who are interested in more fully integrating their spirituality and their leadership. A newly emerging field expands beyond just the focus on spirituality in the workplace. It goes by such names as Spiritual Capitalism, Compassionate Capitalism, and Conscious Capitalism. Leading-edge thinkers are now exploring ideas about spiritual and humanistic values applied to economic and political systems.

Living more congruently with deeply held spiritual principles is never easy, but it is extremely rewarding and meaningful. I hope that some of the resources provided here will help to make the journey a little easier.

Review Questions

1. Spirituality is about learning to be more caring and compassionate in the workplace. Should we be more caring and compassionate with others at work? Why or why not?
2. Spirituality is about integrity, being true to oneself, and telling the truth to others in the workplace. Should we be honest with others at work? Why or why not?
3. Is knowing oneself important to leading from a spiritual perspective? Why or why not?
4. Should leaders let followers see the more human, softer parts of them (truly be themselves)? What effect would this have on productivity?

Communication Skills

The following critical-thinking questions can be used for class discussion and/or as written assignments to develop communication skills. Be sure to give complete explanations for all questions.

1. There is no single accepted definition of spirituality in the workplace. What is your definition?
2. Are managers who have a spiritual practice more effective leaders than those who do not?
3. Do you have a spiritual practice? If yes, what is it?
4. If our capitalistic system were based on spiritual principles, what would it look like? How would business and government be different?

A

Achievement Motivation Theory attempts to explain and predict behavior and performance based on a person's need for achievement, power, and affiliation

acquired needs theory proposes that people are motivated by their need for achievement, power, and affiliation

adaptive culture represents a leadership belief in active monitoring of the external environment for emerging opportunities and threats

adjustment personality dimension traits related to emotional stability

advantageous comparison the process of comparing oneself to others who are worse

agreeableness personality dimension traits related to getting along with people

alienated follower someone who is low on involvement yet is high on critical thinking

arbitrator a neutral third party who makes a binding decision to resolve a conflict

attitudes positive or negative feelings about people, things, and issues

attribution of blame the process of claiming the unethical behavior was caused by someone else's behavior

attribution theory used to explain the process managers go through in determining the reasons for effective or ineffective performance and deciding what to do about it

B

BCF model describes a conflict in terms of behavior, consequences, and feelings

behavioral leadership theories attempt to explain distinctive styles used by effective leaders, or to define the nature of their work

Big Five Model of Personality categorizes traits into dimensions of surgency, agreeableness, adjustment, conscientiousness, and openness to experience

bureaucratic culture represents a leadership that values order, stability, status, and efficiency

C

charisma a distinct social relationship between the leader and follower, in which the leader presents a revolutionary idea, a transcendent image or ideal which goes beyond the immediate ... or the reasonable; while the follower accepts this course of action not because of its rational likelihood of success ... but because of an effective belief in the extraordinary qualities of the leader

coaching the process of giving motivational feedback to maintain and improve performance

coaching feedback based on a good, supportive relationship; it is specific and descriptive; and it is not judgmental criticism

coercive power involves punishment and withholding of rewards to influence compliance

collectivism the state of mind wherein the values and goals of the group—whether extended family, ethnic group, or company—are primary

communication the process of conveying information and meaning

competitive culture represents a leadership that encourages and values a highly competitive work environment

conflict exists whenever people are in disagreement and opposition

conformist follower someone who is high on involvement but low on critical thinking

connection power based on the user's relationships with influential people

conscientiousness personality dimension traits related to achievement

content motivation theories focus on explaining and predicting behavior based on people's needs

contingency leadership model determines if a person's leadership style is task- or relationship-oriented, and if the situation (leader–member relationship, task structure, and position power) matches the leader's style to maximize performance

contingency leadership theories attempt to explain the appropriate leadership style based on the leader, followers, and situation

cooperative culture represents a leadership belief in strong, mutually reinforcing exchanges and linkages between employees and departments

core competence a capability that allows an organization to perform extremely well in comparison to competitors

crisis a low-probability, high-impact event that threatens the viability of the organization and is characterized by ambiguity of cause, effect, and means of resolution, as well as by a belief that decisions must be made swiftly

cross-functional team is made up of members from different functional departments of an organization who are brought together to perform unique tasks to create new and nonroutine products or services

culture the aggregate of beliefs, norms, attitudes, values, assumptions, and ways of doing things that is shared by members of an organization and taught to new members

D

decisional leadership roles entrepreneur, disturbance-handler, resource-allocator and negotiator

delegation the process of assigning responsibility and authority for accomplishing objectives

delegation model (1) explain the need for delegating and the reasons for selecting the employee; (2) set objectives that define responsibility, level of authority, and deadline; (3) develop a plan; and (4) establish control checkpoints and hold employees accountable

demographic diversity any characteristic that serves as a basis for social categorization and self-identification

descriptive leadership models identify contingency variables and leadership styles without specifying which style to use in a given situation

diffusion of responsibility the process of the group using the unethical behavior with no one person being held responsible

discontinuous change occurs when anticipated or expected changes bear no resemblance to the present or the past

displacement of responsibility the process of blaming one's unethical behavior on others

disregard or distortion of consequences the process of minimizing the harm caused by the unethical behavior

distributed leadership multiple leaders take complementary leadership roles in rotation within the same self-managed team, according to their area of expertise or interest

diversity the inclusion of all groups at all levels in an organization

dyadic refers to the individualized relationship between a leader and each follower in a work unit

dyadic theory an approach to leadership that attempts to explain why leaders vary their behavior with different followers

E

effective follower someone who is high on critical thinking and involvement

equity theory proposes that people are motivated when their perceived inputs equal outputs

ethics the standards of right and wrong that influence behavior

ethnocentrism the belief that one's own group or subculture is naturally superior to other groups and cultures

euphemistic labeling the process of using "cosmetic" words to make the behavior sound acceptable

evidence-based management (EBM) means that decisions and organizational practices are based on the best available scientific evidence

expectancy theory proposes that people are motivated when they believe they can accomplish the task, they will get the reward, and the rewards for doing the task are worth the effort

expert power based on the user's skill and knowledge

F

feedback the process of verifying messages and determining if objectives are being met

femininity describes a culture that emphasizes developing and nurturing personal relationships and a high quality of life

follower a person who is being influenced by a leader

followership the behavior of followers that results from the leader–follower influence relationship

functional team a group of employees belonging to the same functional department, such as marketing, R&D, production, human resources, or information systems, who have a common objective

G

giving praise model (1) Tell the employee exactly what was done correctly. (2) Tell the employee why the behavior is important. (3) Stop for a moment of silence. (4) Encourage repeat performance

glass ceiling an invisible barrier that separates women and minorities from top leadership positions

goal-setting theory proposes that specific, difficult goals motivate people

groupthink when members of a cohesive group tend to agree on a decision not on the basis of its merit but because they are less willing to risk rejection for questioning a majority viewpoint or presenting a dissenting opinion

H

hierarchy of needs theory proposes that people are motivated through five levels of needs—physiological, safety, belongingness, esteem, and self-actualization

high power-distance culture leaders and followers rarely interact as equals

high uncertainty avoidance not tolerating risk, avoiding the unknown, and being comfortable when the future is relatively predictable and certain

I

impressions management a follower's effort to project a favorable image in order to gain an immediate benefit or improve long-term relationship with the leader

individualism a psychological state in which people see themselves first as individuals and believe their own interest and values are primary

influencing the process of a leader communicating ideas, gaining acceptance of them, and motivating followers to support and implement the ideas through change

information power based on the user's data desired by others

informational leadership roles monitor, disseminator, and spokesperson

ingratiation the effort to appear supportive, appreciative, and respectful

in-group includes followers with strong social ties to their leader in a supportive relationship characterized by high mutual trust, respect, loyalty, and influence

initiating conflict resolution model (1) plan a BCF statement that maintains ownership of the problem; (2) present your BCF statement and agree on the conflict; (3) ask for, and/or give, alternative conflict resolutions; and (4) make an agreement for change

integrative leadership theories attempt to combine the trait, behavioral, and contingency theories to explain successful, influencing leader–follower relationships

interpersonal leadership roles figurehead, leader, and liaison

J

job instructional training (1) trainee receives preparation; (2) trainer presents the task; (3) trainee performs the task; and (4) trainer follows up

L

Leader Motive Profile (LMP) includes a high need for power, which is socialized; that is, greater than the need for affiliation and with a moderate need for achievement

Leader Motive Profile Theory attempts to explain and predict leadership success based on a person's need for achievement, power, and affiliation

leader–member exchange (LMX) the quality of the exchange relationship between an employee and his or her superior

leadership the influencing process of leaders and followers to achieve organizational objectives through change

leadership continuum model determines which one of seven styles to select, based on the use of boss-centered versus subordinate-centered leadership, to meet the situation (boss, subordinates, situation/time) in order to maximize performance

Leadership Grid identifies five leadership styles: 1,1 impoverished; 9,1 authority compliance; 1,9 country club; 5,5 middle of the road; and 9,9 team leader

leadership model an example for emulation or use in a given situation

leadership paradigm a shared mindset that represents a fundamental way of thinking about, perceiving, studying, researching, and understanding leadership

leadership style the combination of traits, skills, and behaviors leaders use as they interact with followers

leadership theory an explanation of some aspect of leadership; theories have practical value because they are used to better understand, predict, and control successful leadership

leadership theory classifications trait, behavioral, contingency, and integrative

leadership trait theories attempt to explain distinctive characteristics accounting for leadership effectiveness

learning anxiety the prospect of learning something new in itself

learning organization one that is skilled at creating, acquiring, and transferring knowledge, and at modifying behavior to reflect new knowledge and insights

legacy that which allows an individual's accomplishments to "live on" in the ideals, actions, and creations of one's followers, long after his or her death

legitimate power based on the user's position power, given by the organization

levels of analysis of leadership theory individual, group, and organizational

locus of control is on a continuum between an external and internal belief over who has control of a person's destiny

low power-distance culture leaders and their members interact on several levels as equals

low uncertainty avoidance being comfortable with and accepting of the unknown, and tolerating risk and unpredictability

M

management to the leadership theory paradigm a shift from the older autocratic management style to the newer participative leadership style of management

managerial role categories interpersonal, informational, and decisional

masculinity describes a culture that emphasizes assertiveness and a competitive drive for money and material objects

mediator a neutral third party who helps resolve a conflict

mentoring a form of coaching in which a more-experienced manager helps a less-experienced protégé

message-receiving process listening, analyzing, and checking understanding

mission statement an enduring statement of purpose that distinguishes one organization from other similar enterprises

moral justification the process of reinterpreting immoral behavior in terms of a higher purpose

motivation anything that affects behavior in pursuing a certain outcome

motivation process people go from need to motive to behavior to consequence to satisfaction or dissatisfaction

N

negotiating a process in which two or more parties are in conflict and attempt to come to an agreement

networking the process of developing relationships for the purpose of socializing and politicking

normative leadership model a time-driven and developmental-driven decision tree that enables the user to select one of five leadership styles (decide, consult individually, consult group, facilitate, and delegate) appropriate for the situation (seven questions/variables) to maximize decisions

O

Ohio State University Leadership Model identifies four leadership styles: low structure and high consideration, high structure and high consideration, low structure and low consideration, and high structure and low consideration

ombudsperson a single person entrusted with the responsibility of acting as the organization's conscience

one-minute self-sell an opening statement used in networking that quickly summarizes your history and career plan and asks a question

openness-to-experience personality dimension traits related to being willing to change and try new things

oral message-sending process (1) develop rapport; (2) state your communication objective; (3) transmit your message; (4) check the receiver's understanding; and (5) get a commitment and follow up

organizational change an alteration in an organization's alignment with its external environment

organizational knowledge the tacit and explicit knowledge that individuals possess about products, services, systems, and processes

out-group includes followers with few or no social ties to their leader, in a strictly task-centered relationship characterized by low exchange and top-down influence

P

paraphrasing the process of having the receiver restate the message in his or her own words

passive follower someone who is neither high on critical thinking nor involvement

path-goal leadership model selects the leadership style (directive, supportive, participative, or achievement-oriented) appropriate to the situation (subordinate and environment) to maximize both performance and job satisfaction

performance formula explains performance as a function of ability, motivation, and resources

personal meaning the degree to which people's lives make emotional sense and to which the demands confronted by them are perceived as being worthy of energy and commitment

personality a combination of traits that classifies an individual's behavior

personality profiles identify individual stronger and weaker traits

personalized charismatic leader (PCL) one who possesses a dominant, Machiavellian, and narcissistic personality

politics the process of gaining and using power

power the leader's potential influence over followers

pragmatic follower exhibits a little of all four styles—depending on which style fits the prevailing situation

prejudice the tendency to form an adverse opinion without just cause about people who are different from the mainstream in terms of their gender, race, ethnicity, or any other definable characteristic

prescriptive leadership models tell the user exactly which style to use in a given situation

press kit a package of information about a company, including names and pictures of its executives, a fact sheet, and key milestones in the company's history

press release a printed statement that describes how an organization is responding to a crisis and who is in charge

process motivation theories focus on understanding how people choose behavior to fulfill their needs

Pygmalion effect proposes that leaders' attitudes toward and expectations of followers, and their treatment of them, explain and predict followers' behavior and performance

R

reciprocity involves creating obligations and developing alliances, and using them to accomplish objectives

referent power based on the user's personal relationship with others

reinforcement theory proposes that through the consequences for behavior, people will be motivated to behave in predetermined ways

relationship management relates to the ability to work well with others

reward power based on the user's ability to influence others with something of value to them

S

self-awareness relates to being conscious of your emotions and how they affect your personal and professional life

self-belief knowing who you are based on your lifespan of experiences, motivation states, and action orientation

self-concept the positive or negative attitudes people have about themselves

selflessness an unselfish regard for or devotion to the welfare of others

self-managed team champion an advocate of the self-managed team concept whose responsibility is to help the team obtain necessary resources, gain political support from top management and other stakeholders of the organization, and defend it from enemy attacks

self-managed team facilitator the external leader of a self-managed team, whose job is to create optimal working conditions so team members take on responsibilities to work productively and solve complex problems on their own

self-managed teams (SMTs) relatively autonomous teams whose members share or rotate leadership responsibilities and hold themselves mutually responsible for a set of performance goals assigned by higher management

self-management relates to the ability to control disruptive emotions

self-promotion the effort to appear competent and dependable

servant leadership leadership that transcends self-interest to serve the needs of others, by helping them grow professionally and personally

social awareness relates to the ability to understand others

social loafing the conscious or unconscious tendency by some team members to shirk responsibilities by withholding effort toward group goals when they are not individually accountable for their work

socialized charismatic leader (SCL) one who possesses an egalitarian, self-transcendent, and empowering personality

spirituality concerns an individual's awareness of connections between human and supernatural phenomena, which provide faith explanations of past and present experiences and, for some, predict future experiences

stakeholder approach to ethics creates a win-win situation for relevant parties affected by the decision

stewardship an employee-focused form of leadership that empowers followers to make decisions and have control over their jobs

strategic leadership a person's ability to anticipate, envision, maintain flexibility, think strategically, and work with others to initiate changes that will create a viable future for the organization

strategic management the set of decisions and actions used to formulate and implement specific strategies that will achieve a competitively superior fit between the organization and its environment, so as to achieve organizational goals

strategic vision an ambitious view of the future that everyone in the organization can believe in and that is not readily attainable, yet offers a future that is better in important ways than what now exists

strategy an integrated, overarching plan of how an organization will achieve its objectives

substitutes for leadership include characteristics of the subordinate, task, and organization that replace the need for a leader or neutralize the leader's behavior

surgency personality dimension leadership and extraversion traits

survival anxiety the feeling that unless an organization makes a change, it is going to be out of business or fail to achieve some important goals

T

360-degree feedback a formal evaluation process based on receiving performance evaluations from many people

team a unit of interdependent individuals with complementary skills who are committed to a common purpose and set of performance goals and to common expectations, for which they hold themselves accountable

team cohesion the extent to which team members band together and remain committed to achieving team goals

team creativity the creation of a valuable, useful, and novel product, service, idea, procedure, or process carried out via discovery rather than a predetermined step-by-step procedure, by individuals working together in a complex social system

team effectiveness has three components: (1) task performance—the degree to which the team's output (product or service) meets the needs and expectations of those who use it; (2) group process—the degree to which members interact or relate in ways that allow the team to work increasingly well together over time; and (3) individual satisfaction—the degree to which the group experience, on balance, is more satisfying than frustrating to team members

team learning the collective acquisition, combination, creation, and sharing of knowledge

team norms acceptable standards of behavior that are shared by team members

teamwork an understanding and commitment to group goals on the part of all team members

Theory X and Theory Y attempt to explain and predict leadership behavior and performance based on the leader's attitude about followers

traits distinguishing personal characteristics

transactional leadership seeks to maintain stability within an organization through regular economic and social exchanges that achieve specific goals for both the leaders and their followers

transformational leadership serves to change the status quo by articulating to followers the problems in the current system and a compelling vision of what a new organization could be

two-factory theory proposes that people are motivated by motivators rather than maintenance factors

U

University of Michigan Leadership Model identifies two leadership styles: job-centered and employee-centered

V

value the ratio of benefits received to the cost incurred by the customer

values generalized beliefs or behaviors that are considered by an individual or a group to be important

vertical dyadic linkage (VDL) theory examines how leaders form one-on-one relationships with followers, and how these often create in-groups and out-groups within the leader's work unit

virtual team one whose members are geographically distributed, requiring them to work together through electronic means with minimal face-to-face interaction

vision the ability to imagine different and better conditions and the ways to achieve them

W

whistle blowing employee disclosure of illegal or unethical practices on the part of the organization

writing objectives model (1) To + (2) action verb + (3) singular, specific, and measurable result to be achieved + (4) target date

ENDNOTES

Preface

[1] J. Pfeffer and R. I. Sutton, *The Knowing-Doing Gap* (Boston: Harvard Business School Press, 2000).

Chapter 1

[1] G. Colvin, "Leader Machines," *Fortune*, (October 1, 2007): 98–106.

[2] Information taken from the GE Web site: http://www.ge.com: accessed March 28, 2008.

[3] Ibid.

[4] R. B. Kaiser and R. B. Kaplan, "The Deeper Work of Executive Development: Outgrowing Sensitivities," *Academy of Management Learning & Education* 5(4) (2006): 463–483.

[5] J. B. Carson, P. E. Tesluck, and J. A. Marrone, "Shared Leadership in Teams: An Investigation of Antecedent Conditions and Performance," *Academy of Management Journal* 50(5) (2007): 1217–1234.

[6] E. White, "To Keep Employees, Domino's Decides It's Not All About Pay," *The Wall Street Journal* (February 17, 2005): A1.

[7] J. Kelly and S. Nadler, "Leading From Below," *The Wall Street Journal* (March 3–4, 2007): R4.

[8] C. Hajim, "The Top Companies for Leaders," *Fortune* (October 1, 2007): 109–116.

[9] J. S. Lublin, "For Boards, Firing or Keeping a CEO Can be Tough Call," *The Wall Street Journal* (October 22, 2007): B1.

[10] "Citigroup Names New Chairman," *The Wall Street Journal* (November 5, 2007): A1.

[11] "Merrill's O'Neal Had It Coming, Enemies Say," *The Wall Street Journal* (October 29, 2007): A1.

[12] J. Raelin, "Does Action Learning Promote Collaborative Leadership?" *Academy of Management Learning & Education* 5(2) (2006): 152–168.

[13] See note 4.

[14] G. J. Jolley, "Leadership Can Be Taught: A Bold Approach for a Complex World," *Academy of Management Learning & Education* 6(1) (2007): 149–150.

[15] A. Murray and K. A. Strassel, "Ahead of the Pack," *The Wall Street Journal* (March 24, 2008): R3.

[16] G. Williams, "Comic Belief: Is Leadership Really a Crock?" *Entrepreneur* (April 2003): 28.

[17] See note 5.

[18] W. K. Clark, "The Potency of Persuasion," *Fortune* (November 12, 2007): 48.

[19] D. C. Hambrick, "Upper Echelons Theory: An Update," *Academy of Management Review* 32(2) (2007): 334–343.

[20] See note 7.

[21] See note 5.

[22] J. Immelt, GE Annual Shareowners Meeting, April 26, 2006, http://www.ge.com/pdf/investors/events/068/ge_annualshareownersmeeting_042606_en.pdf.

[23] See note 18.

[24] S. Maitlis and T. B. Lawrence, "Triggers and Enablers of Sensegiving in Organizations," *Academy of Management Journal* 50(1) (2007): 57–84.

[25] M. Williams, "Building Genuine Trust Through Interpersonal Emotion Management: A Threat Regulation Model of Trust and Collaboration Across Boundaries," *Academy of Management Review* 32(2) (2007): 595–621.

[26] See note 5.

[27] See note 19.

[28] See note 12.

[29] See note 18.

[30] See note 5.

[31] See note 25.

[32] See note 24.

[33] S. P. Forrest and T. O. Peterson, "It's Called Andragogy," *Academy of Management Learning & Education* 5(1) (2006): 113–122.

[34] See note 18.

[35] M. R. Blood, "Only You Can Create Actionable Knowledge," *Academy of Management Learning & Education* 5(2) (2006): 209–212.

[36] See note 7.

[37] See note 12.

[38] G. Toczdlowski, COO Travelers, presentation April 24, 2007.

[39] See note 1.

[40] See note 12.

[41] A. J. Wefald and J. P. Katz, "Leaders: The Strategies for Taking Charge," *Academy of Management Perspective* 21(3) (2007): 105–106.

[42] See note 14.

[43] See note 8.

[44] N. F. Krueger, "What Lies Beneath? The Experiential Essence of Entrepreneurial Thinking," *Entrepreneurship Theory and Practice* (January 2007), 123–136.

[45] See note 41.

[46] See note 8.

[47] R. Simpson, "Masculinity and Management Education: Feminizing the MBA," *Academy of Management Learning & Education* 5(2) (2006): 182–193.

[48] H. Mintzberg, *The Nature of Managerial Work* (New York: Harper & Row, 1973).

[49] See note 19.

[50] See note 24.

[51] See note 47.

[52] D. M. Rousseau and S. McCarthy, "Educating Managers From an Evidence-Based Perspective," *Academy of Management Learning & Education* 6(1) (2007): 84–101; and see note 47, Simpson (2006).

[53] A. H. Van De Ven and P. E. Johnson, "Knowledge for Theory and Practice," *Academy of Management Review* 31(4) (2006): 802–821.

[54] See note 44.

[55] See note 52.

[56] See note 19.

[57] D. M. Rousseau, V. T. Ho, and J. Greenberg, "I-Deals: Idiosyncratic Terms in Employment Relations," *Academy of Management Review* 31(4) (2006): 977–994.

[58] S. L. Rynes, T. L. Giluk, and K. G. Brown, "The Very Separate Worlds of Academic and Practitioner Periodicals in Human Resource Management: Implications for Evidence-Based Management," *Academy of Management Journal* 50(5) (2007): 987–1008.

[59] D. J. Brass, J. Galaskiewicz, H. R. Greve, and W. Tsai, "Taking Stock of Networks and Organizations: A Multilevel Perspective," *Academy of Management Journal* 47(6) (2004): 795–817.

[60] See note 25.

[61] See note 24.

[62] See note 5.

[63] D. A. Wren, J. R. B. Halbesleben, and M. R. Buckley, "The Theory-Application Balance in Management Pedagogy: A Longitudinal Update," *Academy of Management Learning & Education* 6(4) (2007): 484–492.

[64] F. K. Pil and S. K. Cohen, "Modularity: Implications for Imitation, Innovation, and Sustained Advantage," *Academy of Management Review* 31(4) (2006): 995–1011.

[65] M. J. Canyan, "Executive Compensation and Incentives," *Academy of Management Perspectives* 20(1) (2006): 25–44.

[66] B. R. Agle, N. J. Nagarajan, J. A. Sonnenfeld, and D. Srinivasan, "Does CEO Charisma Matter? An Empirical Analysis of the Relationship Among Organizational Performance, Environmental Uncertainty, and Top Management Team Perceptions of CEO Charisma," *Academy of Management Journal* 49(1) (2006): 161–174.

[67] C. Hymowitz, "Sky-High Payouts to Top Executives Prove Hard to Curb," *The Wall Street Journal* (June 26, 2006): B1.

[68] J. A. Raelin, "Toward and Epistemology of Practice," *Academy of Management Learning & Education* 6(4) (2007): 495–519.

[69] M. L. Tushman, C. A. O'Reilly, A. Fenollosa, A. M. Kleinbaum, and D. McGrath, "Relevance

and Rigor: Executive Education as a Lever in Shaping Practice and Research," *Academy of Management Learning & Education* 6(3) (2007): 345–362.

70 R. J. House and R. N. Aditya, "The Social Scientific Study of Leadership: Quo Vadis?" *Journal of Management* 23(3) (1997): 409–474.

71 L. Kurke and H. Aldrich, "Mintzberg Was Right! A Replication and Extension of the Nature of Managerial Work," *Management Science* 29(8) (1983): 975–984; C. Pavett and A. Lau, "Managerial Work: The Influence of Hierarchical Level and Functional Specialty," *Academy of Management Journal* 26(1) (1983): 170–177; and C. Hales, "What Do Managers Do? A Critical Review of the Evidence," *Journal of Management Studies* 23 (1986): 88–115.

72 See note 70.

73 J. Samuelson, "The Right Rigor: Beyond the Right Answer," *Academy of Management Learning & Education* 5(3) (2006): 356–365.

74 S. L. D. Restubog, "Running Hot and Cold: Can Weather and Wealth Make Bosses Self-Centered?" *Academy of Management Perspectives* 20(3) (2006): 113–115.

75 See note 70.

76 See note 41.

77 See note 5.

78 See note 1.

79 See note 8.

80 See note 5.

81 H. Mintzberg, "Leadership and Management Development: An Afterword," *Academy of Management Executive* 18(3) (2004): 140–142.

82 T. G. Cummings, "Quest for an Engaged Academy," *Academy of Management Review* 32(2) (2007): 355–360.

83 See note 58.

84 D. M. Rousseau and S. McCarthy, ""Educating Managers From an Evidence-Based Perspective," *Academy of Management Learning & Education* 5(3) (2006): 356–365.

85 R. T. Harrison, C. M. Leitch, and R. Chia, "Developing Paradigmatic Awareness in University Business Schools: The Challenge for Executive Education," *Academy of Management Learning & Education* 6(3) (2007): 332–343.

86 D. J. Cohen, "The Very Separate Worlds of Academic and Practitioner Publications in Human Resource Management: Reasons for the Divide and Concrete Solutions for Bridging the Gap," *Academy of Management Journal* 50(5) (2007): 1013–1019.

87 G. P. Latham, "A Speculative Perspective on the Transfer of Behavioral Science Findings to the Workplace: 'The Times They Are A-Changin'," *Academy of Management Journal* 50(5) (2007): 1027–1032.

88 E. E. Lawler, "Why HR Practices are not Evidence-Based," *Academy of Management Journal* 50(5) (2007): 1033–1036.

89 D. M. Rousseau, "Is There Such a Thing as "Evidence-Based Management?" *Academy of Management Review* 31(2) (2006): 256–263.

90 See note 4.

91 P. Navarro, "The Hidden Potential of Managerial Macroeconomics for CEO Decision Making in MBA Programs," *Academy of Management Learning & Education* 5(2) (2006): 463–483.

92 Information taken from the AACSB Web site: http://www.aacsb.edu, accessed April 9, 2008.

93 C. Tice, "Building the 21st Century Leader," *Entrepreneur* (February 2007): 64–69.

94 See note 68.

95 See note 86.

96 See note 88.

97 D. L. Shapiro, B. L. Kirkman, and H. G. Courtney, "Perceived Causes and Solutions of the Translation Problem in Management Research," *Academy of Management Journal* 50(2) (2007): 249–266.

98 See note 69.

99 See note 82.

100 See note 87.

101 See note 86.

102 See note 53.

103 See note 4.

104 M. N. Ashkanasy, "Introduction: Arguments for a More Grounded Approach in Management Education," *Academy of Management Learning & Education* 5(2) (2006): 207–208.

105 See note 63.

106 See note 91.

107 See note 12.

108 See note 14.

109 M. Sorcher and A. P. Goldstein, "A Behavior Modeling Approach in Training," *Personnel Administration* 35 (1972): 35–41.

110 A. Gupta, "Leadership in a Fast-Paced World: An Interview with Ken Blanchard," *Mid-American Journal of Business* 20(1) (2005): 7–10.

111 See note 104.

112 See note 68.

113 See note 35.

114 See note 110.

115 B. Morris, "What Makes Apple Golden," *Fortune* (March 17, 2008): 68–74.

116 "America's Most Admired Companies," *Fortune* (March 17, 2008): 116–133.

117 Ibid.

118 B. Schlender, "Apple's Surprise Weapon: Computers," *Fortune* (September 3, 2007).

119 P. Elkind, "The Trouble With Steve Jobs," *Fortune* (March 17, 2008): 68–74.

120 Ibid.

121 "Two of the Luckiest Guys on the Planet," *The Wall Street Journal* (June 1, 2007): B1, B5.

122 See note 115.

123 See note 119.

Chapter 2

1 Information taken from the Lorraine Monroe Leadership Institute Web site: http://www.lorrainemonroe.com, April 18, 2008.

2 A. J. Wefald and J. P. Katz, "Leaders: The Strategies for Taking Charge," *Academy of Management Perspectives* 21(3) (2007): 105–106.

3 T. A. Judge, R. Ilies, J. E. Bono, and M. W. Gerhardt, "Personality and Leadership: A Qualitative and Quantitative Review," *Journal of Applied Psychology* 87(4) (2002): 765–768.

4 D. C. Hambrick, "Upper Echelons Theory: An Update," *Academy of Management Review* 32(2) (2007): 334–343.

5 R. Ilies, B. A. Scott, and T. A. Judge, "The Interactive Effects of Personal Traits and Experienced States on Intraindividual Patterns of Citizenship Behavior," *Academy of Management Journal* 49(3) (2006): 561–575.

6 S. L. Rynes, T. L. Giluk, and K. G. Brown, "The Very Separate Worlds of Academic and Practitioner Periodicals in Human Resource Management: Implications for Evidence-Based Management," *Academy of Management Journal* 50(5) (2007): 987–1008.

7 J. W. Westerman and S. Vanka, "A Cross-Cultural Empirical Analysis of Person–Organization Fit Measures as Predictors of Student Performance in Business Education: Comparing Students in the United States and India," *Academy of Management Learning & Education* 4(4) (2005): 409–420.

8 See note 2.

9 H. Le, I. S. Oh, J. Shaffer, and F. Schmidt, "Implications of Methodological Advances for the Practice of Personnel Selection: How Practitioners Benefit from Meta-analysis," *Academy of Management Perspectives* 21(3) (2007): 6–15.

10 S. G. Barsade and D. E. Gibson, "Why Does Affect Matter in Organizations?" *Academy of Management Perspectives* 21(1) (2007): 36–59.

11 M. F. R. Kets De Vries and K. Korotov, "Creating Transformational Executive Education Programs," *Academy of Management Learning & Education* 6(3) (2007): 375–387.

12 J. C. Santora, "Managing Open Employees: Do Resources and Leadership Style Matter?" *Academy of Management Perspectives* 21(3) (2007): 83–84.

13 See note 3.

14 M. W. Morgan and M. M. Lombardo, *Off the Track: Why and How Successful Executives Get Derailed* (Greensboro, NC: Center for Creative Leadership, January 1988), Technical Report nos 21 & 34.

15 R. B. Kaiser and R. B. Kaplan, "The Deeper Work of Executive Development: Outgrowing

Sensitivities," *Academy of Management Learning & Education* 5(4) (2006): 463–483.

16 See note 10.

17 See note 11.

18 See note 3.

19 S. Fineman, "On Being Positive: Concerns and Counterpoints," *Academy of Management Review* 31(2) (2006): 270–291.

20 E. Bernstein, "Therapy That Keeps on the Sunny Side of Life," *The Wall Street Journal* (September 26, 2006): D1.

21 R. L. Hotz, "Except in One Career, Our Brains Seem Built for Optimism," *The Wall Street Journal* (November 9, 2007): B1.

22 P. Dvorak, "A Different Animal Seeks the No. 1 Post: Often, It's Not No. 2," *The Wall Street Journal* (October 22, 2007): B1.

23 R. Wolter, "Yes, You Can!" *Entrepreneur* (July 2007): 120.

24 B. M. Wiesenfeld, W. B. Swann, J. Brockner, and C. A. Bartel, "Is More Fairness Always Preferred? Self-Esteem Moderates Reactions to Procedural Justice," *Academy of Management Journal* 50(5) (2007): 1235–1253.

25 See note 23.

26 Ibid.

27 See note 19.

28 See note 23.

29 See note 10.

30 Ibid.

31 J. Sandberg, "Avoiding Conflicts, The Too-Nice Boss Make Matters Worse," *The Wall Street Journal* (February 26, 2008): B1.

32 See note 15.

33 D. Geddes and R. R. Callister, "Crossing the Lines(s): A Dual Threshold Model of Anger in Organizations," *Academy of Management Review* 32(3) (2007): 721–746.

34 J. Clements, "How to Stop Your Emotions From Wrecking Your Returns," *The Wall Street Journal* (December 12, 2007): D1.

35 E. A. Locke, "Business Ethics: A Way Out of the Morass," *Academy of Management Learning & Education* 5(3) (2006): 324–332.

36 C. A. Henle, "Bad Apples or Bad Barrels? A Former CEO Discusses the Interplay of Person and Situation With Implications for Business Education," *Academy of Management Learning & Education* 5(3) (2006): 346–355.

37 S. Waddock, "Leadership Integrity in a Fractured Knowledge World," *Academy of Management Learning & Education* 6(4) (2007): 543–557.

38 E. M. Hartman, "Can We Teach Character? An Aristotelian Answer," *Academy of Management Learning & Education* 5(1) (2006): 68–81.

39 S. Puffer, "CompUSA's CEO James Halpin on Technology, Rewards, and Commitment," *Academy of Management Executive* 13(3) (1999): 29–36.

40 See note 6.

41 See note 9.

42 See note 22.

43 See note 6.

44 P. Dvorak and J. Badal, "This Is Your Brain on the Job," *The Wall Street Journal* (September 20, 2007): B1.

45 See note 19.

46 See note 10.

47 M. Henricks, "Like A Book," *Entrepreneur* (October 2006): 28.

48 See note 15.

49 D. Burke, C. Hajim, J. Elliott, J. Mero, and C. Tkaczyk, "Top 10 Companies for Leaders," *Fortune* (October 1, 2007): 109–116.

50 R. E. Boytzis and D. Goleman, *The Emotional Competence Inventory* (Boston: Hay Group, 2001).

51 See note 15.

52 R. L. Hotz, "How Your Brain Allows You to Walk In Another's Shoes," *The Wall Street Journal* (August 17, 2007): B1.

53 See note 23.

54 See note 19.

55 See note 23.

56 J. Houde, "Analogically Situated Experiences: Creating Insight Through Novel Contexts," *Academy of Management Learning & Education* 6(3) (2007): 321–331.

57 D. McClelland, *The Achieving Society* (New York: Van Nostrand Reinhold, 1961); and D. McClelland and D. H. Burnham, "Power Is the Great Motivator," *Harvard Business Review* (March/April 1978): 103.

58 See note 3.

59 D. C. McClelland and R. E. Boyatzis, "Leadership Motive Pattern and Long-Term Success in Management," *Journal of Applied Psychology* 6 (1982): 737–743.

60 D. C. McClelland, *Human Motivation* (Glenview, IL: Scott Foresman, 1985).

61 D. A. Harrison, D. A. Newman, and P. L. Roth, "How Important Are Job Attitudes? Meta-analytic Comparisons of Integrative Behavioral Outcomes and Time Sequences," *Academy of Management Journal* 49(2) (2006): 305–325.

62 See note 5.

63 See note 10.

64 D. McGregor, *Leadership and Motivation* (Cambridge, MA: MIT Press, 1966).

65 M. Williams, "Building Genuine Trust Through Interpersonal Emotion Management: A Threat Regulation Model of Trust and Collaboration Across Boundaries," *Academy of Management Review* 32(2) (2007): 595–621.

66 J. Hall and S. M. Donnell, "Managerial Achievement: The Personal Side of Behavioral Theory," *Human Relations 32* (1979): 77–101.

67 J. S. Livingston, "Pygmalion in Management," in Harvard Business Review, *Harvard Business Review on Human Relations* (New York: Harper & Row, 1979).

68 P. Osterman, "Comment on Le, Oh, Shaffer, and Schmidt," *Academy of Management Perspectives* 21(3) (2007): 16–18.

69 D. Reynolds, "Restraining Golem and Harnessing Pygmalion in the Classroom: A Laboratory Study of Managerial Expectations and Task Design," *Academy of Management Learning & Education* 6(4) (2007): 475–483.

70 S. P. Forrest and T. O. Peterson, "It's Called Andragogy," *Academy of Management Learning & Education* 5(1) (2006): 113–122.

71 See note 23.

72 T. A. Judge and R. Ilies, "Is Possessiveness in Organizations Always Desirable?" *Academy of Management Executive* 18(4) (2004): 151–155.

73 C. Reeve, "Peter Lowe's Success Yearbook: A Message from Christopher Reeve," *Success 1998 Yearbook* (1998): 77.

74 D. Seidman, "The Case for Ethical Leadership," *Academy of Management Executive* 18(2) (2004): 134–138.

75 J. Van Oosterhout, P. M. Heugens, and M. Kaptein, "The Internal Morality of Contracting: Advancing the Contractualist Endeavor in Business Ethics," *Academy of Management Review* 31(3) (2006): 521–539.

76 J. F. Veiga, "'Special Topic' Ethical Behavior in Management, Bringing Ethics into the Mainstream: An Introduction to the Special Topic," *Academy of Management Executive* 18(2) (2004): 37–38.

77 See note 35.

78 R. A. Giacalone, "Taking a Red Pill to Disempower Unethical Students: Creating Ethical Sentinels in Business Schools," *Academy of Management Learning & Education* 6(4) (2007): 534–542.

79 B. E. Litzky, K. A. Eddleston, and D. L. Kidder, "The Good, the Bad, and the Misguided: How Managers Inadvertently Encourage Deviant Behaviors," *Academy of Management Perspectives* 20(1) (2006): 91–103.

80 K. Whitehouse, "Why CEOs Need to be Honest With Their Boards," *The Wall Street Journal* (January 14, 2008): R1.

81 See note 36.

82 See note 78.

83 See note 38.

84 See note 79.

85 See note 75.

86 S. Sonenshein, "The Role of Construction, Intuition, and Justification in Responding to Ethical Issues at Work: The Sensemaking Intuition Model," *Academy of Management Review* 32(4) (2007): 1022–1028.

87 K. Cameron, "Good or Not Bad: Standards and Ethics in Managing Change," *Academy of Management Learning & Education* 5(3) (2006): 317–323.

88 Margin Note, *Entrepreneur* (June 2007): 34.

89 Margin Note, *Entrepreneur* (October 2006): 78.

90 See note 36.

91 J. F. Veiga, T. D. Golden, and K. Dechant, "Why Managers Bend Company Rules," *Academy of Management Executive* 18(2) (2004): 84–90.

92 Ibid.

93 See note 79.

94 See note 75.

95 See note 76.

96 S. Shellenberger, "How and Why We Lie at the Office: From Pilfered Pens to Padded Accounts," *The Wall Street Journal* (March 24, 2005): B1.

97 See note 116.

98 M. Chase, "The 50 Women to Watch," *The Wall Street Journal* (November 20, 2006): R3.

99 P. Sellers, "Melinda Gates Goes Public," *Fortune* (January 21, 2008): 44–56.

100 Ibid.

101 Information taken from the Bill & Melinda Gates Foundation Web site: http://www.gatesfoundation.org, accessed May 5, 2008.

102 See note 99.

Chapter 3

1 Opening case and answers to questions throughout the chapter are taken from the Market America Web site: http://www.marketamerica.com, accessed May 20, 2008.

2 R. B. Kaiser and R. B. Kaplan, "The Deeper Work of Executive Development: Outgrowing Sensitivities," *Academy of Management Learning & Education* 5(4) (2006): 463–483.

3 M. A. Griffin, A. Neal, and S. K. Parker, "A New Model of Work Role Performance: Positive Behavior in Uncertain and Interdependent Contexts," *Academy of Management Journal* 50(2) (2007): 327–347.

4 J. C. Santora, "Managing Open Employees: Do Resources and Leadership Style Matter?" *Academy of Management Perspectives* 21(3) (2007): 83–84.

5 J. L. Yang, "Reviving John Deere," *Fortune* (October 15, 2007): 50.

6 J. R. Harrison, G. R. Carroll, and K. M. Carley, "Simulation Modeling in Organizational and Management Research," *Academy of Management Review* 32(4) (2007): 1229–1245.

7 See note 4.

8 J. B. Miner, "The Rated Importance, Scientific Validity, and Practical Usefulness of Organizational Behavior Theories," *Academy of Management Learning and Education* 2(3) (2003): 250–268.

9 See note 3.

10 See note 6.

11 A. J. Wefald and J. P. Katz, "Leaders: The Strategies for Taking Charge," *Academy of Management Perspectives* 21(3) (2007): 105–106.

12 D. M. Sluss and B. E. Ashforth, "Relational Identity and Identification: Defining Ourselves Through Work Relationships," *Academy of Management Review* 32 (2007): 9–32.

13 K. Lewin, R. Lippitt, and R. K. White, "Patterns of Aggressive Behavior in Experimentally Created 'Social Climates,'" *Journal of Social Psychology* 10 (1939): 271–301.

14 R. Likert, *New Patterns of Management* (New York: McGraw-Hill, 1961).

15 R. M. Stogdill and A. E. Coons, eds., *Leader Behavior: Its Description and Measurement* (Columbus: Ohio State University Bureau of Business Research, 1957).

16 B. M. Bass, *Bass and Stogdill's Handbook of Leadership: A Survey of Theory and Research* (New York: Free Press, 1990).

17 D. B. McFarlin, "Hard Day's Work: A Boon for Performance by a Bane for Satisfaction?" *Academy of Management Perspectives* 20(4) (2006): 115–116.

18 R. Likert, *The Human Organization: Its Management and Value* (New York: McGraw-Hill, 1967).

19 R. Blake and J. Mouton, *The Managerial Grid* (Houston, TX: Gulf Publishing, 1964); R. Blake and J. Mouton, *The New Managerial Grid* (Houston, TX: Gulf Publishing, 1978); R. Blake and J. Mouton, *The Managerial Grid III: The Key to Leadership Excellence* (Houston, TX: Gulf Publishing, 1985); and R. Blake and A. A. McCanse, *Leadership Dilemmas—Grid Solutions* (Houston, TX: Gulf Publishing, 1991).

20 "R. Blake and J. Mouton: The Managerial Grid," *Thinkers* (March 2002).

21 D. J. Jung and B. J. Avolio, "Effects of Leadership Style and Followers' Cultural Orientation on Performance in Group and Individual Task Conditions," *Academy of Management Journal* 42 (April 1999): 208–218; and L. Pheng and B. Lee, "'Managerial Grid' and Zhuge Liang's 'Art of Management': Integration for Effective Project Management," *Management Decision* 35 (May–June 1997): 382–392.

22 See Blake and Mouton (1964) in note 19.

23 See Blake and Mouton (1978) in note 19.

24 P. Nystrom, "Managers and the Hi-Hi Leader Myth," *Academy of Management Journal* 21 (June 1978): 325–331.

25 B. M. Fisher and J. E. Edwards, "Consideration and Initiating Structure and Their Relationship with Leader Effectiveness: A Meta-Analysis," *Proceeding of the Academy of Management* (August 1988): 201–205.

26 See note 25.

27 R. Cropanzano, D. E. Bowen, and S. W. Gilliland, "The Management of Organizational Justice," *Academy of Management Perspectives* 21(4) (2007): 34–48.

28 See note 12.

29 T. A. Wright, "To Be Or Not To Be [Happy]: The Role of Employee Well-Being," *Academy of Management Perspectives* 20 (2006): 118–120.

30 A. M. Grant, M. K. Christanson, and R. H. Price, "Happiness, Health, or Relationships? Managerial Practices and Employee Well-Being Tradeoffs," *Academy of Management Perspectives* 21(3) (2007): 51–63.

31 D. M. Bergeron, "The Potential Paradox of Organizational Citizendship Behavior: Good Citizens at What Costs?" *Academy of Management Review* 32(4) (2007): 1078–1095.

32 R. M. J. Wells, "Outstanding Customer Satisfaction: The Key to a Talented Workforce?" *Academy of Management Perspectives* 21(3) (2007): 87–89.

33 D. M. Rousseau, V. T. Ho, and J. Greenberg, "I-Deals: Idiosyncratic Terms in Employment Relations," *Academy of Management Review* 31(4) (2006): 977–994.

34 P. Dvorak, "Hotelier Finds Happiness Keeps Staff Checked In," *The Wall Street Journal* (December 17, 2007): B3.

35 A. M. Grant, "Relational Job Design and the Motivation to Make a Prosocial Difference," *Academy of Management Review* 32(2) (2007): 393–417.

36 R. Kiyosaki, "Hear This," *Entrepreneur* (September 2008): 164.

37 O. Gottschalg and M. Zollo, "Interest Alignment and Competitive Advantage," *Academy of Management Review* 32(2) (2007): 418–437.

38 Y. Zhu, "What Drives Differences in Reward Allocation Principles Across Countries and Organizations?" *Academy of Management Perspectives* 21(3) (2007): 90–92.

39 Ibid.

40 See note 31.

41 E. A. Locke, "Business Ethics: A Way Out of the Morass," *Academy of Management Learning & Education* 5(3) (2006): 324–332.

42 P. Steel and C. J. Konig, "Integrating Theories of Motivation," *Academy of Management Review* 31(4) (2007): 889–913.

43 See note 29.

44 See note 37.

45 A. Maslow, "A Theory of Human Motivation," *Psychological Review* 50 (1943): 370–396.

46 See note 11.

47 See note 37.

48 See note 12.

49 F. Herzberg, "The Motivation-Hygiene Concept and Problems of Manpower," *Personnel Administrator* (1964): 3–7; and F. Herzberg, "One More Time: How Do You Motivate Employees?" *Harvard Business Review* (January–February 1968): 53–62.

50 N. Wasserman, "Stewards, Agents, and the Founder Discount: Executive Compensation in New Ventures," *Academy of Management Journal* 49(5) (2006): 960–976.

51 J. Clements, "Money and Happiness: Here's Why You Won't Laugh All the Way to the Bank," *The Wall Street Journal* (August 29, 2006): D1.

52 J. Clements, "No Satisfaction: Why What You Have Is Never Enough," *The Wall Street Journal* (May 2, 2007): D1.

53 J. Clements, "The Pursuit of Happiness: Six Experts Tell What They've Done to Achieve It," *The Wall Street Journal* (December 6, 2006): D1.

54 S. L. Rynes, T. L. Giluk, and K. G. Brown, "The Very Separate Worlds of Academic and Practitioner Periodicals in Human Resource Management: Implications for Evidence-Based Management," *Academy of Management Journal* 50(5) (2007): 987–1008.

55 See note 17.

56 See note 3.

57 See note 35.

58 H. Murray, *Explorations in Personality* (New York: Oxford University Press, 1938).

59 J. Atkinson, *An Introduction to Motivation* (New York: Van Nostrand Reinhold, 1964).

60 D. McClelland, *The Achieving Society* (New York: Van Nostrand Reinhold, 1961); and D. McClelland and D. H. Burnham, "Power Is the Great Motivator," *Harvard Business Review* (March/April 1978): 103.

61 Y. Baruch, "The Opt-out Revolt: Why People are Leaving Companies to Create Kaleidoscope Careers," *Academy of Management Perspectives* 21(1) (2007): 80–83.

62 Ibid.

63 See note 30.

64 J. R. Edwards and N. P. Rothbard, "Mechanisms Linking Work and Family: Clarifying the Relationship between Work and Family Constructs," *Academy of Management Review* 25 (2000): 178–199.

65 See note 37.

66 B. M. Wiesenfeld, W. B. Swann, J. Brockner, and C. A. Bartel, "Is More Fairness Always Preferred? Self-Esteem Moderates Reactions to Procedural Justice," *Academy of Management Journal* 50(5) (2007): 1235–1253.

67 See note 30.

68 See note 27.

69 J. S. Adams, "Toward an Understanding of Inequity," *Journal of Abnormal and Social Psychology* 67 (1963): 422–436.

70 See note 38.

71 O. Janssen, "Fairness Perceptions as a Moderator in the Curvilinear Relationships between Job Demands, and Job Performance and Job Satisfaction," *Academy of Management Journal* 44 (2001): 1039–1050.

72 V. Vroom, *Work and Motivation* (New York: John Wiley & Sons, 1964).

73 C. B. Gibson and P. C. Earley, "Collective Cognition in Action: Accoumulation, Interaction, Examination, and Accommodation in the Development and Operation of Group Efficacy Beliefs in the Workplace," *Academy of Management Review* 32(2) (2007): 438–458.

74 See note 30.

75 P. Steel and C. J. Konig, "Integrating Theories of Motivation," *Academy of Management Review* 32(2) (2007): 438–458.

76 D. Ilgen, D. Nebeker, and R. Pritchard, "Expectancy Theory Measures: An Empirical Comparison in an Experimental Simulation," *Organizational Behavior and Human Performance* 28 (1981): 189–223; W. Van Eerde and H. Thierry, "Vroom's Expectancy Models and Work-Related Criteria: A Meta-Analysis," *Journal of Applied Psychology* 81 (October 1996): 548–556; and R. Fudge and J. Schlacter, "Motivating Employees to Act Ethically: An Expectancy Theory Approach," *Journal of Business Ethics* 18 (February 1999): 295–296.

77 See note 54.

78 A. Gupta, "Leadership in a Fast-Paced World: An Interview with Ken Blanchard," *Mid-American Journal of Business* 20(1) (2005): 7–10.

79 M. Diener, "Take a Look Inside," *Entrepreneur* (February 2007): 78.

80 B. Tracy, "7 Secrets to Success," *Entrepreneur* (February 2007): 96–100.

81 See note 75.

82 J. Adamy, "Will a Twist on an Old Vow Deliver for Domino's Pizza," *The Wall Street Journal* (December 17, 2007): A1.

83 See note 11.

84 See note 80.

85 E. A. Locke, "Guest Editor's Introduction: Goal-Setting Theory and Its Applications to the World of Business," *Academy of Management Executive* 18(4) (2004): 124–125.

86 B. F. Skinner, *Beyond Freedom and Dignity* (New York: Alfred A. Knopf, 1971).

87 A. D. Stajkovic and F. Luthans, "Differential Effects of Incentive Motivators on Work Performance," *Academy of Management Journal* 44(4) (2001): 580–590.

88 See note 31.

89 See note 17.

90 See note 34.

91 P. B. Barger and A. A. Grandey, "Service With a Smile and Encounter Satisfaction: Emotional Contagion and Apprisal Mechanisms," *Academy of Management Journal* 49(6) (2006): 1229–1238.

92 S. Kerr, "On the Folly of Rewarding A, While Hoping for B," *Academy of Management Executive* 9 (February 1995): 32–40.

93 See note 80.

94 See note 17.

95 J. Zaslow, "In Praise of Less Praise," *The Wall Street Journal* (May 3, 2007): D1.

96 See note 34.

97 See note 54.

98 P. Dvorak and J. Badal, "This Is Your Brain on the Job," *The Wall Street Journal* (September 20, 2007): B1.

99 J. Zaslow, "The Most-Praised Generation Goes to Work," *The Wall Street Journal* (April 20, 2007): W1.

100 See note 95.

101 K. Blanchard and S. Johnson, *The One-Minute Manager* (New York: Wm. Morrow & Co., 1982).

102 Based on the consulting work of Robert N. Lussier.

103 D. Leonard, "How Bob Iger Works," *Fortune* (December 10, 2007): 38.

104 See note 41.

105 See note 75.

106 Information taken from the Friedmans Appliance Web site: http://www.friedmansappliance.com, accessed May 27, 2008.

107 See note 82.

108 A. Chozick, "Toyota's Goal: First to Sell 10 Million," *The Wall Street Journal* (September 1, 2007): A3.

109 "Nissan CEO Talks of Optimism for Electric Cars," *The Wall Street Journal* (May 2, 2008): A1.

110 "BMW Shuffles Management, Plans New Models to Increase Margins," *The Wall Street Journal* (Septemeber 28, 2007): A1.

Chapter 4

1 Case information taken from Wikipedia's entry on Mark Cuban: http://en.wikipedia.org/wiki/Mark_Cuban, accessed May 28, 2008; and D. Leonard, "Mark Cuban Wants a Little R-E-S-P-E-C-T," *Fortune* (October 15, 2007): 172–182.

2 J. B. Carson, P. E. Tesluck, and J. A. Marrone, "Shared Leadership in Teams: An Investigation of Antecedent Conditions and Performance," *Academy of Management Journal* 50(5) (2007): 1217–1234.

3 P. J. Frederickson, "Political Skill at Work," *Academy of Management Perspectives* 20(2) (2006): 95–96.

4 D. C. Hambrick, "Upper Echelons Theory: An Update," *Academy of Management Review* 32(2) (2007): 334–343.

5 W. K. Clark, "The Potency of Persuasion," *Fortune* (November 12, 2007): 48.

6 M. J. Gelfand, V. A. Major, J. L. Raver, L. H. Nishii, and K. O'Brien, "Negotiating Relationally: The Dynamics of the Relational Self in Negotiations," *Academy of Management Review* 31(2) (2007): 427–451.

7 See note 5.

8 L. A. Bebchuck and J. M. Fried, "Pay without Performance: Overview of the Issues," *Academy of Management Perspectives* 20(1) (2006): 5–24.

9 See note 5.

10 J. M. Evans, L. K. Trevino, and G. R. Weaver, "Who's in the Ethics Driver's Seat? Factors Influencing Ethics in the

MBA Curriculum," *Academy of Management Learning & Education* 5(3) (2006): 278–293.

11 G. Colvin, "Power: A Cooling Trend," *Fortune* (December 10, 2007): 113–114.

12 See note 4.

13 See note 11.

14 J. D. Westphal and I. Stern, "Flattery Will Get You Everywhere (Especially if You are a Male Caucasian): How Ingratiation, Boardroom Behavior, and Demographic Minority Status Affect Additional Board Appointments at U.S. Companies," *Academy of Management Journal* 50(2) (2007): 267–286.

15 J. R. P. French and B. H. Raven, "The Bases of Social Power," in D. Cartwright, ed., *Studies of Social Power* (Ann Arbor, MI: Institute for Social Research, 1959): 150–167.

16 S. Maitlis and T. B. Lawrence, "Triggers and Enablers of Sensegiving in Organizations," *Academy of Management Journal* 50(1) (2007): 57–84.

17 B. A. Hudson, "Against All Odds: A Consideration of Core-Stigmatized Organizations," *Academy of Management Review* 33(1) (2008): 252–266.

18 See note 16.

19 See note 11.

20 See note 14.

21 G. J. Jolley, "Leadership Can Be Taught: A Bold Approach for a Complex World," *Academy of Management Learning & Education* 6(1) (2007): 149–150.

22 N. L. Torres, "Making it Big," *Entrepreneur* (July 2007): 118–119.

23 See note 11.

24 See note 14.

25 See note 11.

26 G. Colvin "Spitzer's Bully Pulpit," *Fortune* (March 31, 2008): 18.

27 See note 11.

28 M. Miller, "What Makes History Happen?" *Fortune* (October 1, 2007): 78.

29 See note 22.

30 See note 8.

31 D. M. Rousseau, V. T. Ho, and J. Greenberg, "I-Deals: Idiosyncratic Terms in Employment Relations," *Academy of Management Review* 31(4) (2006): 977–994.

32 See note 16.

33 M. Diener, "Fight or Flight?" *Entrepreneur* (November 2006): 108.

34 See note 10.

35 B. P. Matherne, "Does Whom You Know Matter in Venture Capital Networks?" *Academy of Management Perspectives* 21(4) (2007): 85–86.

36 See note 11.

37 M. Learmonth, "Critical Management Education in Action: Personal Tales of Management Unlearning," *Academy of Management Learning & Education* 6(1) (2007): 109–113.

38 See note 10.

39 S. G. Barsade and D. E. Gibson, "Why Does Affect Matter in Organizations?" *Academy of Management Perspectives* 21(1) (2007): 36–59.

40 J. Sandberg, "Avoiding Conflicts, The Too-Nice Boss Makes Matters Worse," *The Wall Street Journal* (February 26, 2008): B1.

41 J. Sandberg, "People Can't Resist Doing a Big Favor—Or Asking for One," *The Wall Street Journal* (December 18, 2007): B1.

42 See note 3.

43 E. A. Locke, "Business Ethics: A Way Out of the Morass," *Academy of Management Learning & Education* 5(3) (2006): 324–332.

44 See note 3.

45 Ibid.

46 S. Robbins and D. De Cenzo, *Fundamentals of Management* (Englewood Cliffs, NJ: Prentice-Hall, 2007).

47 See note 2.

48 F. D. Schoorman, R. C. Mayer, and J. H. Davis, "An Integrative Model of Organizational Trust: Past, Present, and Future," *Academy of Management Review* 32(2) (2007): 344–354.

49 See note 41.

50 See note 10.

51 G. Ip, K. Kelly, S. Craig, and I. J. Dugan, "How Grasso's Rule Kept NYSE On Top but Hid Deep Troubles," *The Wall Street Journal* (December 30, 2003): A1, A6; and K. Kelly, "Grasso, Spitzer Keep Door Open for a Deal Despite Tough Talk," *The Wall Street Journal* (April 27, 2004): B1.

52 See note 3.

53 M. Boyle, "Carly Fiorina Talks Tough," *Fortune* (October 29, 2007): 68.

54 See note 39.

55 J. Sandberg, "How Office Tyrants in Critical Positions Get Others to Grovel," *The Wall Street Journal* (August 23, 2007): B1.

56 See note 3.

57 A. Gupta, "Leadership in a Fast-Paced World: An Interview with Ken Blanchard," *Mid-American Journal of Business* 20(1) (2005): 7–10.

58 J. Sandberg, "Your Boss's Obsession Too Often Becomes Your Job Obligation," *The Wall Street Journal* (December 11, 2007): B1.

59 See note 41.

60 See note 43.

61 See note 48.

62 See note 2.

63 M. Kilduff, W. Tsai, and R. Hanke, "A Paradigm Too Far? A Dynamic Stability Reconsideration of the Social Network Research Program," *Academy of Management Review* 31(4) (2006): 1031–1048.

64 See note 35.

65 P. Capell, "How to Find a Search Executive Who Can Help You Advance," *The Wall Street Journal* (September 4, 2007): B8.

66 N. L. Torres, "Good Connections," *Entrepreneur* (December 2006): 112.

67 G. Labianca and D. J. Brass, "Exploring the Social Ledger: Negative Relationships and Negative Asymmetry in Social Networks in Organizations," *Academy of Management Review* 31(3) (2006): 596–614.

68 C. Hymowitz, "Women Get Better at Forming Networks to Help Their Climb," *The Wall Street Journal* (November 19, 2007): B1.

69 J. Nebus, "Building Collegial Information Networks: A Theory of Advice Network Generation," *Academy of Management Review* 31(3) (2006): 615–637.

70 See note 3. See note 57.

71 This section is adapted from A. Gumbus and R. N. Lussier, "Career Development: Enhancing Your Networking Skill," *Clinical Leadership & Management Review* 17(1) (January–February 2003). Adapted with permission. Also see A. Gumbus, "Networking: A Long-Term Management Strategy," *Clinical Leadership & Management Review* 17(3) (May–June 2003).

72 B. Farber, "Have No Fear," *Entrepreneur* (April 2007): 80.

73 M. Diener, "Talk the Talk," *Entrepreneur* (August 2007): 68.

74 See note 69.

75 C. Bialik, "Sorry, You May Have Gone Over Your Limit of Network Friends," *The Wall Street Journal* (November 16, 2007): B1.

76 See note 73.

77 C. Seda, "Squeeze Play," *Entrepreneur* (April 2007): 83.

78 V. Vara, "Just How Much Do We Want to Share on Social Networks?" *The Wall Street Journal* (November 28, 2007): B1.

79 S. E. Needleman, "How Faith-Based Networking Can Aid Job Searches," *The Wall Street Journal* (October 2, 2007): B4.

80 See note 73.

81 See note 66.

82 See note 74.

83 See note 33.

84 See note 66.

85 See note 68.

86 E. White, "Art of Persuasion Becomes Key," *The Wall Street Journal* (May 19, 2008): 1.

87 See note 39.

88 See note 6.

89 Ibid.

90 See note 31.

91 See note 22.

92 R. N. Lussier, "The Negotiation Process," *Clinical Leadership & Management Review* 14(2) (2000): 55–59.

93 See note 22.

[94] See note 73.

[95] See note 74.

[96] M. Diener, "Take A Look Inside," *Entrepreneur* (February 2007): 78.

[97] See note 33.

[98] See note 87.

[99] Ibid.

[100] M. Diener, "Break It Up," *Entrepreneur* (October 2006): 116.

[101] See note 8.

[102] See note 3.

[103] See note 33.

[104] See note 66.

[105] See note 22.

[106] B. Farber, "Listen and Learn," *Entrepreneur* (February 2007): 76.

[107] See note 73.

[108] See note 101.

[109] B. Farber, "The Trust Factor," *Entrepreneur* (March 2007): 84.

[110] Ibid.

[111] See note 97.

[112] R. Trudel and J. Cotte, "Does Being Ethical Pay?" *The Wall Street Journal* (May 12, 2008): R4.

[113] See note 43.

[114] See note 37.

[115] See note 110.

[116] R. Kiyosaki, "In Control," *Entrepreneur* (October 2006): 188.

[117] This is an actual case, but the names have been changed to protect identities.

Chapter 5

[1] "The Fortune 500," *Fortune* (May 5, 2008): F1–F60.

[2] C. C. Berk, "PepsiCo's CEO Sees No Need to Change Strategy," *The Wall Street Journal* (October 24, 2006): B4.

[3] B. Morris, "The Pepsi Challenge," *Fortune* (March 3, 2008): 55–66.

[4] See note 1.

[5] K. Benner, E. Levenson, and R. Arora, "The Power 50," *Fortune* (October 15, 2007): 107–116.

[6] B. Morris, "Power 25," *Fortune* (December 10, 2007): 116–133.

[7] See note 3.

[8] See note 2.

[9] See note 3.

[10] C. A. Henle, "Bad Apples or Bad Barrels? A Former CEO Discusses the Interplay of Person and Situation With Implications for Business Education," *Academy of Management Learning & Education* 5(3) (2006): 346–355.

[11] A. Gupta, "Leadership in a Fast-Paced World: An Interview with Ken Blanchard," *Mid-American Journal of Business* 20(1) (2005): 7–10.

[12] D. Jacobs, "Critical Biography and Management Education," *Academy of Management Learning & Education* 6(1) (2007): 104–108.

[13] E. M. Hartman, "Can We Teach Character? An Aristotelian Answer," *Academy of Management Learning & Education* 5(1) (2006): 68–81.

[14] J. Houde, "Analogically Situated Experiences: Creating Insight Through Novel Contexts," *Academy of Management Learning & Education* 6(3) (2007): 321–331.

[15] P. Dvorak, "A Different Animal Seeks the No. 1 Post: Often, It's Not No. 2," *The Wall Street Journal* (October 22, 2007): B1.

[16] J. C. Santora, "Managing Open Employees: Do Resources and Leadership Style Matter?" *Academy of Management Perspectives* 21(3) (2007): 83–84.

[17] D. M. Rousseau and S. McCarthy, "Educating Managers From an Evidence-Based Perspective," *Academy of Management Learning & Education* 5(3) (2006): 356–365.

[18] E. White, "Advice for Women on Developing a Leadership Style," *The Wall Street Journal* (August 28, 2007): B5.

[19] M. C. Sonfield and R. N. Lussier, "Family Business Ownership and Management: A Gender Comparison," *Journal of Small Business Strategy* 15(2) (2005): 59–75.

[20] J. Samuelson, "The Right Rigor: Beyond the Right Answer," *Academy of Management Learning & Education* 5(3) (2006): 356–365.

[21] N. Wasserman, "Stewards, Agents, and the Founder Discount: Executive Compensation in New Ventures," *Academy of Management Journal* 49(5) (2006): 960–976.

[22] S. L. D. Restubog, "Running Hot and Cold: Can Weather and Wealth Make Bosses Self-Centered?" *Academy of Management Perspectives* 20(3) (2006): 113–115.

[23] D. C. Hambrick, "Upper Echelons Theory: An Update," *Academy of Management Review* 32(2) (2007): 334–343.

[24] W. Ouchi, *Theory Z: How American Business Can Meet the Japanese Challenge* (Reading, MA: Addison-Wesley, 1981).

[25] F. E. Fiedler, *A Theory of Leadership Effectiveness* (New York: McGraw-Hill, 1967).

[26] J. C. Santora, "Assertiveness and Effective Leadership: Is There a Tipping Point?" *Academy of Management Perspectives* 21(3) (2007): 84–86.

[27] F. E. Fiedler and M. M. Chemers, *Improving Leadership Effectiveness: The Leader Match Concept,* 2nd ed. (New York: Wiley, 1982).

[28] J. Raelin, "Does Action Learning Promote Collaborative Leadership?" *Academy of Management Learning & Education* 5(2) (2006): 152–168.

[29] F. E. Fiedler, "The Contingency Model and the Dynamics of the Leadership Process," in L. Berkowitz, ed., *Advances in Experimental Social Psychology* (New York: Academic Press, 1978).

[30] C. Schriesheim and S. Kerr, "Theories and Measures of Leadership: A Critical Appraisal of Present and Future Directions," in J. G. Hunt and L. L. Larson, eds., *Leadership: The Cutting Edge* (Carbondale, IL: Southern Illinois University Press, 1977): 9–44; and A. S. Ashour, "Further Discussion of Fiedler's Contingency Model of Leadership Effectiveness: An Evaluation," *Organizational Behavior and Human Performance* 9 (1973): 339–355.

[31] F. E. Fiedler, "A Rejoinder to Schriesheim and Kerr's Premature Obituary of the Contingency Model," in J. G. Hunt and L. L. Larson, eds., *Leadership: The Cutting Edge* (Carbondale, IL: Southern Illinois University Press, 1977): 45–50; and F. E. Fiedler, "The Contingency Model: A Reply to Ashour," *Organizational Performance and Human Behavior* 9 (1973): 356–368.

[32] M. J. Strube and J. E. Garcia, "A Meta-Analytical Investigation of Fiedler's Contingency Model of Leadership Effectiveness," *Psychology Bulletin* 90 (1981): 307–321; and L. H. Peters, D. D. Hartke, and J. T. Pohlmann, "Fiedler's Contingency Theory of Leadership: An Application of the Meta-Analysis Procedure of Schmidt and Hunter," *Psychological Bulletin* 97 (1985): 274–285.

[33] F. E. Fiedler and J. E. Garcia, *New Approaches to Effective Leadership: Cognitive Resources and Organizational Performance* (New York: Wiley, 1987).

[34] F. E. Fiedler, "Research on Leadership Selection and Training: One View of the Future," *Administrative Science Quarterly* 41 (1996): 241–250; and F. E. Fiedler, "Cognitive Resources and Leadership Performance," *Applied Psychology—An International Review 44* (1995): 5–28.

[35] R. P. Vecchio, "A Theoretical and Empirical Examination of Cognitive Resource Theory," *Journal of Applied Psychology 75* (1990): 141–147; and P. J. Bettin and J. K. Kennedy, "Leadership Experience and Leader Performance: Some Empirical Support at Last," *Leadership Quarterly* 1 (1990): 219–228.

[36] R. L. Hughes, R. C. Ginnett, and G. J. Curphy, *Leadership: Enhancing the Lessons of Experience*, 4th ed. (Burr Ridge, IL: Irwin/McGraw-Hill, 2008).

[37] R. Tannenbaum and W. H. Schmidt, "How to Choose a Leadership Pattern," *Harvard Business Review* (March–April 1958): 95–101.

[38] R. Tannenbaum and W. H. Schmidt, "How to Choose a Leadership Pattern," *Harvard Business Review* (May–June 1973): 166.

[39] R. Tannenbaum and W. H. Schmidt, excerpts from "How to Choose a Leadership Pattern," *Harvard Business Review* (July–August 1986): 129.

[40] R. J. House, "A Path-Goal Theory of Leader Effectiveness," *Administrative Science Quarterly* 16(2) (1971): 321–329; and M. G. Evans, "The Effects of Supervisory Behavior on the Path-Goal Relationship," *Organizational Behavior and Human Performance* 5 (1970): 277–298.

41 R. N. House and R. J. Aditya, "The Social Scientific Study of Leadership: Quo Vadis?" *Journal of Management* 23 (May–June 1997): 409–474.

42 R. J. House and T. R. Mitchell, "Path-Goal Theory of Leadership," *Contemporary Business* (Fall 1974): 81–98.

43 J. C. Wofford and L. Z. Liska, "Path-Goal Theories of Leadership: A Meta-Analysis," *Journal of Management* 19 (1993): 858–876; and P. M. Podsakoff, S. B. MacKenzie, M. Ahearne, and W. H. Bommer, "Searching for a Needle in a Haystack: Trying to Identify the Illusive Moderators of Leadership Behavior," *Journal of Management* 21 (1995): 423–470.

44 C. Schriesheim and L. L. Nieder, "Path-Goal Leadership Theory: The Long and Winding Road," *Leadership Quarterly* 7(3) (1996): 317–321; see note 41, House and Aditya (1997); and J. Beeler, "A Survey Report of Job Satisfaction and Job Involvement among Governmental and Public Auditors," *Government Accountants Journal* 45 (Winter 1997): 26–32.

45 See note 41, House and Aditya (1997); and see note 40, House (1971) for a discussion of how the original path-goal theory led to the development of the 1976 charismatic theory and a description of the 1996 version of path-goal theory.

46 V. H. Vroom and P. W. Yetton, *Leadership and Decision Making* (Pittsburgh: University of Pittsburgh Press, 1973).

47 V. H. Vroom and A. G. Jago, *The New Leadership: Managing Participation in Organizations* (Englewood Cliffs, NJ: Prentice-Hall, 1988).

48 V. H. Vroom, "Leadership and the Decision-Making Process," *Organizational Dynamics* 28 (Spring 2000): 82–94.

49 R. H. G. Field, P. C. Read, and J. J. Louviere, "The Effect of Situation Attributes on Decision Method Choice in the Vroom-Jago Model of Participation in Decision Making," *Leadership Quarterly* 1 (1990): 165–176; and see note 47, Vroom and Jago (1988).

50 See note 47.

51 R. H. G. Field, "A Test of the Vroom-Yetton Normative Model of Leadership," *Journal of Applied Psychology* (October 1982): 523–532; R. H. G. Field, "A Critique of the Vroom-Yetton Contingency Model of Leadership Behavior," *Academy of Management Review* 4 (1979): 249–257; and J. B. Miner, "The Uncertain Future of the Leadership Concept: An Overview," in J. G. Hunt and L. L. Larson, eds., *Leadership Frontiers* (Kent, OH: Kent State University, 1975).

52 See note 48.

53 Ibid.

54 "Executive Perspectives: John Sinnot, Chairman & CEO, Marsh Inc.," *Risk Management* 49 (September 2002): 20–25.

55 "Effective Leaders . . . Made or Born?" *Leadership for the Front Lines* (June 15, 2002): 3–5.

56 R. L. Ackoff, *Re-Creating the Corporation: A Design of Organizations for the 21st Century* (Oxford: Oxford University Press, 1999).

57 C. Markides and C. D. Charitou, "Competing with Dual Business Models: A Contingency Approach," *Academy of Management Executive* 18(3) (2004): 22–36.

58 J. Pfeiffer, "The Ambiguity of Leadership," *Academy of Management Review* (April 1977): 104–112; and J. Howell, D. E. Bowen, P. W. Dorfman, S. Kerr, and P. Podsakoff, "Substitutes for Leadership: Effective Alternatives to Ineffective Leadership," *Organizational Dynamics* (Summer 1990): 23.

59 S. Kerr and J. Jermier, "Substitutes for Leadership: Their Meaning and Measurement," *Organizational Behavior and Human Performance* 22 (1978): 375–403.

60 P. M. Podsakoff, S. B. MacKenzie, and W. H. Bommer, "Transformational Leader Behaviors and Substitutes for Leadership as Determinants of Employee Satisfaction, Commitment, Trust, and Organizational Citizenship Behaviors," *Journal of Management* 22(2) (1996): 259–298; and see note 58, Howell et al (1990).

61 J. E. Sheridan, D. J. Vredenburgh, and M. A. Abelson, "Contextual Model of Leadership Influence in Hospital Units," *Academy of Management Journal* 27(1) (1984): 57–78; see note 60, Podsakoff et al. (1996); and R. E. de Vries, R. A. Roe, and T. C. B. Taillieu, "Need for Supervision: Its Impact on Leadership Effectiveness," *Journal of Applied Behavioral Science* 34 (December 1998): 486–487.

62 P. M. Podsakoff, S. B. MacKenzie, and W. H. Bommer, "Meta-Analysis of the Relationships between Kerr and Jermier's Substitutes for Leadership and Employee Job Attitudes, Role Perceptions, and Performance," *Journal of Applied Psychology* 81 (August 1996): 380–400.

63 See note 1.

64 S. Kilman and J. S. Lublin, "ADM Chooses an Energy-Savvy Outsider as Its New CEO," *The Wall Street Journal* (April 28, 2006): B1, B5.

65 "The Global Power 50," *Fortune* (October 15, 2007): 121.

66 See note 5.

67 ADM is an existing company. However, Rick Parr, Ed Carlton, and Jose Goizueta are not the names of actual managers at ADM; they are used to illustrate contingency leadership.

Chapter 6

1 Information taken from personal interviews with the Clarks and The Ranch Web site: http: //www.theranchgolfclub.com, accessed June 12, 2008.

2 T. Aeppel, "Tire Recalls Show Flaws in the System," *The Wall Street Journal* (November 2007): D1.

3 G. Williams, "Let's Talk Shop," *Entrepreneur* (March 2007): 40.

4 E. White, "Art of Persuasion Becomes Key," *The Wall Street Journal* (May 19, 2008): 1.

5 R. Simpson, "Masculinity and Management Education: Feminizing the MBA," *Academy of Management Learning & Education* 5(2) (2006): 182–193.

6 M. J. Gelfand, V. A. Major, J. L. Raver, L. H. Nishii, and K. O'Brien, "Negotiating Relationally: The Dynamics of the Relational Self in Negotiations," *Academy of Management Review* 31(2) (2007): 427–451.

7 P. J. Frederickson, "Political Skill at Work," *Academy of Management Perspectives* 20(2) (2006): 95–96.

8 See note 4.

9 S. Maitlis and T. B. Lawrence, "Triggers and Enablers of Sensegiving in Organizations," *Academy of Management Journal* 50(1) (2007): 57–84.

10 Y. Zhu, "What Drives Differences in Reward Allocation Principles Across Countries and Organizations?" *Academy of Management Perspectives* 21(3) (2007): 90–92.

11 See note 3.

12 G. Toczydlowski, Travelers Chief Operating Officer—Personal Insurance, Talk given at Springfield College, April 24, 2007.

13 See note 7.

14 See note 3.

15 Ibid.

16 S. Bernhut, "Managing the Dream: Warren Bennis on Leadership," *Ivey Business Journal* 65 (May 2001): 36.

17 R. Kiyosaki, "Hear This," *Entrepreneur* (September 2006): 164.

18 D. M. Rousseau, "Is There Such a Thing as "Evidence-Based Management?"" *Academy of Management Review* 31(2) (2006): 256–263.

19 J. M. Brett, M. Olekalns, R. Friedman, N. Goates, C. Anderson, and C. C. Lisco, "Sticks and Stones: Language, Face, and Online Dispute Resolution," *Academy of Management Journal* 50(1) (2007): 85–99.

20 See note 12.

21 B. Tracy, "7 Secrets to Success," *Entrepreneur* (February 2007): 96–100.

22 B. Zhao, "Error Reporting in Organizations," *Academy of Management Review* 31(4) (2006): 1012–1030.

23 See note 17.

24 See note 20.

25 R. Kiyosaki, "Leading Edge," *Entrepreneur* (February 2007): 148.

26 A. Gupta, "Leadership in a Fast-Paced World: An Interview with Ken Blanchard," *Mid-American Journal of Business* 20(1) (2005): 7–10.

27 See note 21.

28 D. Burke, C. Hajim, J. Elliott, J. Mero, and C. Tkacyzk, "Top 10 Companies for Leaders," *Fortune* (October 1, 2007): 109–116.

29 E. Holmes, "Career Mentors Today Seem Short on Advice But Give a Mean Tour," *The Wall Street Journal* (August 28, 2007): B1.

30 See note 26.

31 See note 17.

32 See note 22.

33 See note 20.

34 See note 26.

35 J. Falvey, "To Raise Productivity, Try Saying Thank You," *The Wall Street Journal* (December 6, 1982): B1.

36 See note 29.

37 See note 28.

38 See note 29.

39 J. B. O. Buchanan, "An Integrative Model of Experiencing and Responding to Mistreatment at Work," *Academy of Management Review* 33(1) (2008): 76–96.

40 R. Cropanzano, D. E. Bowen, and S. W. Gilliland, "The Management of Organizational Justice," *Academy of Management Perspectives* 21(4) (2007): 34–48.

41 D. M. Rousseau, V. T. Ho, and J. Greenberg, "I-Deals: Idiosyncratic Terms in Employment Relations," *Academy of Management Review* 31(4) (2006): 977–994.

42 S. G. Barsade and D. E. Gibson, "Why Does Affect Matter in Organizations?" *Academy of Management Perspectives* 21(1) (2007): 36–59.

43 Ibid.

44 Margin Note, *Entrepreneur* (February 2007): 26.

45 See note 40.

46 See note 42.

47 See note 10.

48 See note 19.

49 See note 39.

50 See note 40.

51 See note 42.

52 See note 19.

53 See note 18.

54 See note 39.

55 See note 40.

56 See note 19.

57 See note 42.

58 See note 57.

59 L. DiCarlo, "Unisys Has Steak, But No Sizzle," *Forbes* (February 8, 2002), http://www.forbes.com/2002/02/08/0208weinstrike.html.

60 Information taken from the Unisys Web site: http://www.unisys.com, accessed June 17, 2008.

61 "Fortune 500," *Fortune* (May 5, 2008): F1–F60.

Chapter 7

1 W. C. Symonds, B. Grow, and J. Cady, "Earthly Empires—How Evangelical Churches are Borrowing from the Business Playbook," *Business Week* (May 23, 2005).

2 Ibid.

3 L. Romano, "'The Smiling Preacher' Builds on Large Following," *The Washington Post* (Sunday, January 30, 2005): A01.

4 G. Graen, "Letter to the Editor," *Academy of Management Perspectives* 21(1) (2007): 5.

5 F. J. Yammarino and F. Dansereau, "Individualized Leadership: A New Multiple-Level Approach," *Journal of Leadership & Organizational Studies* 9 (Summer 2002): 90–100.

6 Ibid.

7 R. Kark and D. Dijk, "Motivation to Lead, Motivation to Follow: The Role of the Self-Regulatory Focus in Leadership Processes," *Academy of Management Review* 32(2) (2007): 500–528.

8 A. Joshi, H. Liao, and S. Jackson, "Cross-Level Effects of Workplace Diversity on Sales Performance and Pay," *Academy of Management Journal* 49(3) (2006): 459–481.

9 R. Liden, B. Erdogan, S. Wayne, and R. Sparrowe, "Leader–Member Exchange, Differentiation, and Task Interdependence: Implications for Individual and Group Performance," *Journal of Organizational Behavior* 27 (2006): 723–746.

10 R. Sparrowe, B. Soetjipto, and M. Kraimer, "Do Leaders' Influence Tactics Relate to Members' Helping Behavior? It Depends on the Quality of the Relationship," *Academy of Management Journal* 49(6) (2006): 1194–1208.

11 W. Lam, X. Huang, and E. Snape, "Feedback Seeking Behavior and Leader–Member Exchange: Do Supervisor Attributed Motives Matter?" *Academy of Management Journal* 50 (2007): 348–363.

12 B. Erdogan, R. Liden, and L. Kraimer, "Justice and Leader–Member Exchange: The Moderating Role of Organizational Culture," *Academy of Management Journal* 49 (2006): 395–406.

13 P. Balkundi and D. Harrison, "Ties, Leaders, and Time in Teams: Strong Inference about Network Structures Effects on Team Viability and Performance," *Academy of Management Journal* 49(1) (2006): 49–68.

14 M. Zellmer-Bruhn and C. Gibson, "Multinational Organization Context: Implications for Team Learning and Performance," *Academy of Management Journal* 49(3) (2006): 501–518.

15 H. Guttman, "Leading High-Performance Teams: Horizontal, High-Performance Teams with Real Decision-Making Clout and Accountability for Results Can Transform a Company," *Chief Executive (U.S.)* (January–February 2008): 33–35.

16 R. Rico, M. Manzanares, F. Gil, and C. Gibson, "Team Implicit Coordination Processes: A Team Knowledge-Based Approach," *Academy of Management Review* 33 (2008): 163–184.

17 H. Oh, G. Labianca, and M. Chung, "A Multilevel Model of Group Social Capital," *Academy of Management Review* 31 (2006): 569–582.

18 A. Srivastava, K. Bartol, and E. Locke, "Empowering Leadership in Management Teams: Effects on Knowledge Sharing, Efficacy, and Performance," *Academy of Management Journal* 49(6) (2006): 1239–1254.

19 D. J. Brass, J. Galaskiewicz, H. R. Greve, and W. Tsai, "Taking Stock of Networks and Organizations: A Multilevel Perspective," *Academy of Management Review* 47 (2004): 795–817.

20 B. H. Mueller and J. Lee, "Leader–Member Exchange and Organizational Communication Satisfaction in Multiple Contexts," *Journal of Business Communication* 39 (April 2002): 220–245.

21 K. S. Campbell, C. D. White, and D. E. Johnson, "Leader–Member Relations as a Function of Rapport Management," *Journal of Business Communication* 40 (July 2003): 170–195.

22 See note 19.

23 J. Gimeno, "Competition within and between Networks: The Contingent Effect of Competitive Embeddedness on Alliance Formation," *Academy of Management Review* 47 (2004): 820–842.

24 See note 19.

25 A. C. Inkpen and E. W. K. Tsang, "Social Capital, Networks, and Knowledge Transfer" *Academy of Management Review* 30 (2005): 146–165.

26 An Economist Intelligence Unit White Paper (sponsored by CISCO Systems), "Collaboration: Transforming the way business works," *The Economist* (April 2007).

27 See note 12.

28 See note 4.

29 See note 10.

30 See note 9.

31 M. Brewer, "The Importance of Being We: Human Nature And Intergroup Relations," *The American Psychologist* 62 (2007): 728–38.

32 H. Oh, M.-H. Chung, and G. Labianca, "Group Social Capital and Group Effectiveness: The Role of Informal Socializing Ties," *Academy of Management Review* 47 (2004): 860–875.

33 See note 25.

34 See note 12.

35 K. Bhal and M. Ansari, "Leader–Member Exchange–Subordinate Outcomes Relationship: Role of Voice and Justice," *Leadership & Organization Development Journal* 28 (2007): 20–35.

36 J. Felfe and B. Schyns, "Is Similarity in Leadership Related to Organizational Outcomes? The Case of Transformational Leadership," *Journal of Leadership & Organizational Studies* 10 (Spring 2004): 92–103.

37 M. A. Gagnon and J. H. Michael, "Outcomes of Perceived Supervisor Support for Wood Production Employees," *Forest Products Journal* 54 (December 2004): 172–178.

38 See note 20.

39 See note 37.

40 See note 20.

41 B. Erdogan, M. L. Kraimer, and R. C. Liden, "Work Value Congruence and Intrinsic Career Success: The Compensatory Roles of Leader–Member Exchange and Perceived Organizational Support," *Personnel Psychology* 57 (Summer 2004): 305–333.

42 B. Erdogan and J. Enders, "Support from the Top: Supervisors' Perceived Organizational Support as a Moderator of Leader–Member Exchange to Satisfaction and Performance Relationships," *Journal of Applied Psychology* 92 (2007) i2: 321–330.

43 L. Lapierre and R. Hackett, "Trait Conscientiousness, Leader–Member Exchange, Job Satisfaction and Organizational Citizenship Behavior: A Test of an Integrative Model," *Journal of Occupational and Organizational Psychology* 80 (2007): 539–554.

44 See note 11.

45 Ibid.

46 See note 12.

47 See note 31.

48 D. J. Campbell, "The Proactive Employee: Managing Workplace Initiative," *Academy of Management Executive* 14(3) (2000): 52–66.

49 R. Sparrowe, B. Soetjipto, and M. Kraimer, "Do Leaders' Influence Tactics Relate to Members' Helping Behavior? It Depends on the Quality of the Relationship," *Academy of Management Journal* 49(15) (2006): 1194–1208.

50 See note 12.

51 R. Piccolo and J. Colquitt, "The Transformational Leadership and Job Behaviors: The Mediating Role of Core Job Characteristics," *Academy of Management Journal* 49(2) (2006): 327–340.

52 R. K. House and R. N. Aditya, "The Social Scientific Study of Leadership: Quo Vadis?" *Journal of Management* 23 (May–June 1997): 409–474; and V. Singh and S. Vinnicombe, "Impression Management, Commitment and Gender: Managing Others' Good Opinions," *European Management Journal* 19(2) (April 2001): 183–194.

53 See note 49.

54 Ibid.

55 See note 11.

56 See note 21.

57 See note 4.

58 J. Bernerth, A. Armenakis, H. Field, W. Giles, and J. Walker, "Leader–Member Social Exchange: Development and Validation of a Scale," *Journal of Organizational Behavior"* 28 (2007): 979–1003.

59 See note 4.

60 R. J. Deluga and T. J. Perry, "The Role of Subordinate Performance and Ingratiation in Leader–Member Exchanges," *Group and Organization Management* 19 (1994): 67–86; R. C. Liden, S. J. Wayne, and D. Stilwell, "A Longitudinal Study on the Early Development of Leader–Member Exchanges," *Journal of Applied Psychology* 78 (1993): 662–674; A. S. Philips and A. G. Bedeian, "Leader-Follower Exchange Quality: The Role of Personal and Interpersonal Attributes," *Academy of Management Journal* 37 (1994): 990–1001; and R. A. Scandura and C. A. Schriesheim, "Leader–Member Exchange and Supervisor Career Mentoring as Complementary Constructs in Leadership Research," *Academy of Management Journal* 37 (1995): 1588–1602.

61 See note 4.

62 S. Baker, "Followership: The Theoretical Foundation of a Contemporary Construct," *Journal of Leadership & Organizational Studies* 14 (2007): 50–60.

63 See note 62.

64 M. Vugt, R. Hogan, and R. Kaiser, "Leadership, Followership, and Evolution: Some Lessons from the Past," *The American Psychologist* 63 (2008): 182–196.

65 B. Avolio, "Promoting More Integrative Strategies for Leadership Theory-Building," *The American Psychologist* 62 (January 2007): 25–33.

66 R. G. Lord and D. J. Brown, "Leadership Processes and Follower Self-Identity," *Personnel Psychology* 57 (Summer 2004): 517–521.

67 See note 62.

68 Ibid.

69 S. Yun, J. Cox, and H. Sims Jr. "The Forgotten Follower: A Contingency Model of Leadership and Follower Self-Leadership," *Journal of Managerial Psychology* 21 (April 2006): 374–388.

70 G. Chen, R. Kanfer, B. Kirkman, D. Allen, and B. Rosen, "A Multilevel Study of Leadership, Empowerment, and Performance in Terms," *Journal of Applied Psychology* 92 (2007): 331–346.

71 See note 62.

72 B. Kellerman, "What Every Leader Needs to Know about Followers," *Harvard Business Review* 85 (December 2007): 84–91.

73 R. E. Kelley, "In Praise of Followers," *Harvard Business Review*, (1988): 142–148.

74 See note 74.

75 A. J. DeLellis. "Clarifying the Concept of Respect: Implications for Leadership," *Journal of Leadership Studies* 7 (Spring 2000): 2–37.

76 See note 64.

77 D. Cavell, "Leadership or Followership: One or Both? All Successful Leaders Need Good Followers." *Healthcare Financial Management* 61 (November 2007): 142–143.

78 S. Tangirals, S. Green, and R. Ramanjuam, "In The Shadow of the Boss's Boss: Effects of Supervisors' Upward Exchange Relationships on Employees," *Journal of Applied Psychology* 92 (2007): 309–310.

79 B. Gunn, "Letting Go to Get Ahead," *Strategic Finance* 2 (February 2004): 8.

80 P. M. Buhler, "Managing in the New Millennium: The Top Ten Managerial Mistakes," *Supervision* 65 (August 2004): 15–18.

81 R. Wolter, "Trust Your Team," *Entrepreneur* (November 2006).

82 D. Orme, "A Corporate Cultivator's Guide to Growing Leaders," *New Zealand Management* 51 (September 2004): 41–44.

83 See note 81.

84 See note 79.

85 A. P. Grimshaw, "Time Management for Busy Managers," *Asia Africa Intelligence Wire* (March 16, 2004).

86 K. Niratpattanasai, "The Art of Time Management by Effective Delegation," *Asia Africa Intelligence Wire* (December 20, 2004).

87 C. Hymowitz, "A Vacationing Boss Should Take a Break; Let Staffers Step Up," *The Wall Street Journal* (August 20, 2007): B1.

88 See note 80.

89 M. Ogwo, "Delegation: An Abused Management Tool," *Fire* 97 (June 2004): 24–27.

90 See note 81.

91 Ibid.

92 T. A. Sykes, "Get Time on Your Side: Accomplish More Using Less Energy," *Black Enterprise* 34 (June 2004): 312–313.

93 F. Dalton, "Improving Delegation: When 'Just Do It' Just Won't Do It," *Contract Management* 44 (November 2004): 4–7.

94 Information taken from the W. L. Gore & Associates Web site: http://www.gore.com, accessed July 8, 2008.

Chapter 8

1 K. Maney, "Chambers, Cisco born again," *USA TODAY*, January 21, 2004.

2 http://www.cisco.com

3 "Collaboration: Transforming the way business works," Economist Intelligence Unit White paper, Sponsored by Cisco Systems, April 2007.

4 See note 1.

5 A. Ellis, "System Breakdown: The Role of Mental Models and Transactive Memory in the Relationship Between Acute Stress and Team Performance," *Academy of Management Review* 49(3) (2006): 576–589.

6 G. B. Graen, C. Hui, and E. A. Taylor, "Experience-Based Learning About LMX Leadership and Fairness in Project Teams: A Dyadic Directional Approach," *Academy of Management Learning & Education* 5(4) (2006): 448–460.

7 P. Balkundi and D. Harrison, "Ties, Leaders, and Time in Teams: Strong Inference About Network Structures Effects on Team Viability and Performance," *Academy of Management Journal* 49(1) (2006): 49–68.

8 M. D. Johnson, J. R. Hollenbeck, S. E. Humphrey, D. R. Ilgen, D. Jundt, and C. Meyer, "Cutthroat Cooperation: Asymmetrical Adaptation to Changes in Team Reward Structures," *Academy of Management Journal* 49(1) (2006): 103–119.

9 J. Gordon, "Work Teams: How Far Have They Come?" *Training* 29 (1992): 59–65; E. E. Lawler, III, S. A. Mohrman, and G. E. Ledford, Jr., *Creating High Performance Organizations: Practices and Results of Employee Involvement and Total Quality Management in Fortune 1000 Companies* (San Francisco, CA: Jossey-Bass Publishers, 1995); and T. L. Baker and T. G. Hunt, "An Exploratory Investigation Into the Effects of Team Composition on Moral Orientation," *Journal of Managerial Issues* 15 (Spring 2003): 106–120.

10 A. Vengel, "Lead Your Team to Victory: The Do's & Don'ts of Effective Group Leadership," *Supervision* 67 (September 2006): 8–10.

11 H. Oh, M.-H. Chung, and G. Labianca, "Group Social Capital and Group Effectiveness: The Role of Informal Socializing Ties," *Academy of Management Review* 47 (2004): 860–875.

12 Ibid.

13 See note 6.

14 M. Butler, "Our HR columnist." *People Management* 13 (November 2007): 43.

15 R. J. Trent, "Becoming an Effective Teaming Organization," *Business Horizons* 47 (March–April 2004): 33–41.

16 See note 5.

17 See note 6.

18 S. Sidle, "Do Teams Who Agree to Disagree Make Better Decisions?" *Academy of Management Perspectives* 21(2) (May 2007): 74–75.

19 See note 15.

20 L. Hsieh and S. Chen, "A Study of Cross-Functional Collaboration in New Produce Development: A Social Capital Perspective," *International Journal of Productivity and Quality Management* 2 (November 2006): 23.

21 B. Dineen, R. Noe, J. Shaw, M. Duffy, and C. Wiethoff, "Level and Dispersion of Satisfaction in Teams: Using Foci and Social Context to Explain the Satisfaction–Absenteeism Relationship," *Academy of Management Journal* 50 (2007): 623–643.

22 R. Batt, "Who Benefits from Teams? Comparing Workers, Supervisors, and Managers," *Industrial Relations* 43 (January 2004): 183–212.

23 See note 21.

24 K. L. Towry, "Control in a Teamwork Environment—The Impact of Social Ties on the Effectiveness of Mutual Monitoring Contracts," *Accounting Review* 78 (2003): 1069–1096.

25 K. Price, D. Harrison, and J. Gavin, "Withholding Inputs in Team Contexts: Member Composition, Interaction Processes, Evaluation Structure, and Social Loafing," *Journal of Applied Psychology* 91 (November 2006): 1375–1384.

26 E. Stark, J. Shaw, and M. Duffy, "Preference for Group Work, Winning Orientation, and Social Loafing Behavior Groups," *Group & Organization Management* 32 (December 2007): 699–723.

27 See note 24.

28 K. McFarland, "Where Group-Think Is Good; Groups Often Provide the Best Answers to Business Problems—Provided You Know How to Structure the Team," *Business Week Online* (April 2007).

29 See note 18.

30 W. Schiano and J. Weiss, "Y2K All Over Again: How Groupthink Permeates IS and Compromises Security," *Business Horizons* 49 (March–April 2006): 115–123.

31 See note 28.

32 See note 5.

33 P. Lencioni, "The Five Dysfunctions of a Team: A Leadership Fable," Reviewed by J. R. Hackman and E. Pierce *Academy of Management Perspectives* 20 (2006): 122–125.

34 J. Wilson, P. Goodman, and M. Cronin, "Group Learning," *Academy of Management Review* 32 (2007): 1041–1059.

35 J. E. Mathieu and W. Schulze, "The Influence of Team Knowledge and Formal Plans on Episodic Team Process–Performance Relationships," *Academy of Management Review* 49(3) (2006): 605–619.

36 M. Zellmer-Bruhn and C. Gibson, "Multinational Organization Context: Implications for Team Learning and Performance," *Academy of Management Journal* 49(3) (2006): 501–518.

37 J. R. Hackman, *Leading Teams: Setting the Stage for Great Performances.* (Boston, MA: Harvard Business School Press, 2002).

38 D. E. Warren, "Constructive and Destructive Deviance in Organizations," *Academy of Management Review* 28(4) (2003): 622–632.

39 See note 36.

40 See note 24.

41 See note 7.

42 P. M. Lencioni, "The Five Dysfunctions of a Team," *HR Magazine 49* (July 2004): S41; G. B. Brumback, review of "*Teams that Lead: A Matter of Market Strategy, Leadership Skills, and Executive Strength,*" by T. J. B. Kline, *Personnel Psychology* 57 (Summer 2004): 544–549.

43 See note 8.

44 See note 10.

45 S. Yun, J. Cox, and H. Sims, Jr., "The Forgotten Follower: A Contingency Model of Leadership and Follower Self-Leadership," *Journal of Managerial Psychology* 21 (April 2006): 374–388.

46 A. P. Kakabadse, "A Process Perspective on Leadership and Team Development," *Journal of Management Development* 23(1) (January 2004): 7–106.

47 R. Hackett, "Bring Out the Best," *Canadian Business* 79 (June 2006): 73(2).

48 B. V. Knippenberg and D. V. Knippenberg, "Leader Self-Sacrifice and Leadership Effectiveness: The Moderating Role of Leader Self-Confidence," *Journal of Applied Psychology* 90 (January 2005): 25–38; and D. D. Cremer and D. V. Knippenberg, "Leader Self-Sacrifice and Leadership Effectiveness: The Moderating Role of Leader Self-Confidence," *Organizational Behavior & Human Decision Processes* 95 (November 2004): 140–156.

49 See note 47.

50 L. Hughes, "Do's and Don'ts of Effective Team Leadership," *Women in Business* 56 (January–February 2004): 10.

51 R. Sparrowe, B. Soetjipto, and M. Kraimer, "Do Leaders' Influence Tactics Relate to Members' Helping Behavior? It Depends on the Quality of the Relationship," *Academy of Management Journal* 49 (2006): 1194–1208.

52 C. Crother-Laurin, "Effective Teams: A Symptom of Healthy Leadership," *The Journal of Quality and Participation* 29 (Fall 2006): 4–8.

53 J. Z. King, "There's No Substitute for Effective Leadership Training Skills," *Hotel & Motel Management* 219 (November 15, 2004): 20–28; N. Gorla and Y. W. Lam, "Who Should Work with Whom? Building Effective Software Project Teams," *Communications of the ACM* 47 (August 2004): 79–83; and J. A. Raelin, "Growing Group Leadership Skills: Managers Will Get the Most from Workers When They Teach Them to Work in Self-Directed Teams," *Security Management* 48 (June 2004): 34–38.

54 See note 52.

55 See note 10.

56 K. T. Jones, "I'm In Charge Now? Understanding Your Role as a Leader Will Benefit Both You and Your Employees," *Journal of Property Management* 69 (July–August 2004): 72; and S. Sarin and C. McDermott, "The Effect of Team-Leader Characteristics on Learning, Knowledge Applications, and Performance of Cross-Functional New Product Development Teams," *Decision Sciences* 34 (Fall 2003): 707–740.

57 See note 45.

58 S. Faraj and V. Sambamurthy, "Leadership of Information Systems Development Projects," *IEEE Transactions on Engineering Management* 53 (May 2006): 238–249.

59 A. Srivastava, K. M. Bartol, and E. Locke, "Empowering Leadership in Management Teams: Effects on Knowledge Sharing, Efficacy, and Performance," *Academy of Management Journal* 49(6) (2006): 1239–1254.

60 G. Chen, R. Kanfer, B. Kirkman, D. Allen, and B. Rosen, "A Multilevel Study of Leadership, Empowerment, and Performance in Terms," *Journal of Applied Psychology* 92 (2007): 331–346.

61 See note 47.

62 J. Birkinshaw, C. Bouquet, and T. Ambos, "Leaders Relate," *Business Strategy Review* 17 (2006): 19–23.

63 See note 7.

64 T. Butler and J. Waldroop, "Understanding 'People' People," *Harvard Business Review* 82 (2004): 78–87.

65 J. E. Perry-Smith, "Social Yet Creative: The Roles of Social Relationships in Facilitating Individual Creativity," *Academy of Management Journal* 49(1) (2006): 85–101.

66 H. Oh, G. Labianca, and M. Chung, "A Multilevel Model of Group Social Capital," *Academy of Management Review* 31 (2006): 569–582.

67 See note 53, King (2004).

68 M. Barrick, B. Bradley, A. Brown, and A. Colbert, "The Moderating Role of Top Management Team Interdependence: Implications For Real Teams and Working

Groups," *Academy of Management Journal* 50 (2007): 544–557.

69 See note 7.

70 D. Sluss and B. Ashforth, "Relational Identity and Identification: Defining Ourselves Through Work Relationships," *Academy of Management Review* 32(1) (2007): 9–32.

71 R. Rico, M. Sanchez-Manzanares, F. Gil, and C. Gibson, "Team Implicit Coordination Processes: A Team Knowledge-Based Approach," *Academy of Management Review* 33 (2008): 163–184.

72 F. Perretti and G. Negro, "Filling Empty Seats: How Status and Organizational Hierarchies Affect Exploration Versus Exploitation in Team Design," *Academy of Management Journal* 49(7) (2006): 759–777.

73 J. Polzer, C. Crisp, S. Jarvenpaa, and J. Kim, "Extending the Faultline Model to Geographically Dispersed Teams: How Colocated Subgroups Can Impair Group Functioning," *Academy of Management Journal* 49(4) (2006): 679–692.

74 A. Taylor and H. Greve, "Superman or the Fantastic Four? Knowledge Combination and Experience in Innovative Teams," *Academy of Management Journal* 49(4) (2006): 723–740.

75 G. Bushe and G. Coetzer, "Group Development and Team Effectiveness Using Cognitive Representations to Measure Group Development and Predict Task Performance and Group Viability," *Journal of Applied Behavioral Science* 43 (June 2007): 184–212.

76 See note 53, Gorla and Lam (2004).

77 S. J. Chen and L. Lin, "Modeling Team Member Characteristics for the Formation of a Multifunctional Team in Concurrent Engineering," *IEEE Transactions on Engineering Management* 51 (May 2004): 111–125.

78 See note 74.

79 R. Hirschfeld, M. Jordan, H. Field, W. Giles, and A. Armenakis, "Becoming Team Players: Team Members' Mastery of Teamwork Knowledge as a Predictor of Team Task Proficiency and Observed Teamwork Effectiveness," *Journal of Applied Psychology* 91 (March 2006): 467–474.

80 G. Van Der Vegt, J. Bunderson, and A. Oosterhof, "Expertness Diversity and Interpersonal Helping in Teams: Why Those Who Need the Most Help End up Getting the Least," *Academy of Management Journal* 49(5) (2006): 877–893.

81 A. Joshi, "The Influence of Organizational Demography on the External Networking Behavior of Teams," *Academy of Management Review* 31(3) (2006): 583–595.

82 See note 73.

83 B. L. Kirkman, P. E. Tesluk, and B. Rosen, "The Impact of Demographic Heterogeneity and Team Leader–Team Member Demographic Fit on Team Empowerment and Effectiveness," *Group & Organization Management* 29 (June 2004): 334–368.

84 See note 80.

85 M. Cronin and L. Weingart, "Representational Gaps, Information Processing, and Conflict in Functionally Diverse Teams," *Academy of Management Review* 32 (2007): 761–773.

86 K. Behfar, R. Peterson, E. Mannix, and W. Trochim, "The Critical Role of Conflict Resolution in Teams: A Close Look at the Links Between Conflict Type, Conflict Management Strategies, and Team Outcomes," *Journal of Applied Psychology* 93 (January 2008): 170–188.

87 See note 66.

88 See note 64.

89 H. M. Guttman, "Leading High-Performance Teams: Horizontal, High-Performance Teams with Real Decision-Making Clout and Accountability for Results Can Transform a Company," *Chief Executive (U.S.)* (January–February 2008): 33–35.

90 G. Hirst and L. Mann, "A Model of R&D Leadership and Team Communication: The Relationship with Project Performance," *R&D Management* 34 (March 2004): 147–161.

91 M. L. Kraimer and S. J. Wayne, "An Examination of Perceived Organizational Support as a Multidimensional Construct in the Context of an Expatriate Assignment," *Journal of Management* 30 (March–April 2004): 209–238.

92 See note 91.

93 T. Doolen, M. E. Hacker, and E. M. Van Aken, "The Impact of Organizational Context on Work Team Effectiveness: A Study of Production Teams," *IEEE Transactions on Engineering Management* 50 (August 2003): 285–297.

94 See note 74.

95 See note 65.

96 See note 74.

97 See note 65.

98 R. Leenders, J. Kratzer, and J. Engelen, "Innovation Team Networks: The Centrality of Innovativeness and Efficiency," *International Journal of Networking and Virtual Organization* 4 (November 2007): 459.

99 J. George and J. Zhou, "Dual Tuning in a Supportive Context: Joint Contributions of Positive Mood, Negative Mood, and Supervisory Behaviors to Employee Creativity," *Academy of Management Journal* 50 (2007): 605–622.

100 See note 65.

101 See note 99.

102 See note 60.

103 T. M. Amabile, "How to Kill Creativity," *Harvard Business Review* 76(5) (September/October 1998): 76–87.

104 A. Carr, H. Kaynak, and S. Muthusamy, "The Cross-Functional Coordination Between Operations, Marketing, Purchasing, and Engineering and the Impact on Performance," *International Journal of Manufacturing Technology and Management* 13 (December 2007): 55.

105 T. Galpin, R. Hilpirt, and B. Evans, "The Connected Enterprise: Beyond Division of Labor," *Journal of Business Strategy* 28 (March 2007): 38–47.

106 D. Antonucci and K. Kono, "High Energy," *Marketing Management* 15 (April 2006): 14–16.

107 See note 104.

108 B. Ebrahimi, R. McGowan, and T. Chung, "Key Success Factors in New Product Development," *International Journal of Management and Decision Making* 7(2–3) (March 6, 2006): 313.

109 K. E. Soderquist, "Organising Knowledge Management and Dissemination in New Product Development: Lessons from 12 Global Corporations," *Long Range Planning* 39(5) (October 2006): 497–523.

110 See note 20.

111 See note 85.

112 T. L. Legare, "How Hewlett-Packard Used Cross-Functional Teams to Deliver Healthcare Industry Solutions," *Journal of Organizational Excellence* 20(4) (Autumn 2001): 29–38.

113 C. O. Longenecker, and M. Neubert, "Barriers and Gateways to Management Cooperation and Teamwork," *Business Horizons* 43(5) (September/October 2000): 37–44.

114 H. Peelle, "Appreciative Inquiry and Creative Problem Solving in Cross-Functional Teams," *Journal of Applied Behavioral Science* 42 (December 2007): 447–467.

115 A. Malhotra, A. Majchzak, and B. Rosen, "Leading Virtual Teams," *Academy of Management Perspectives* 21(1) (February 2007): 60–70.

116 P. Dvorak, "How Teams Can Work Well Together From Far Apart," *The Wall Street Journal* (September 17, 2007).

117 See note 115.

118 B. S. Caldwell, R. C. Palmer III, and H. M. Cuevas, "Information Alignment and Task Coordination in Organizations: An 'Information Clutch' Metaphor," *Information Systems Management* 25 (2008): 33–44.

119 N. W. Coppola, S. R. Hiltz, and N. G. Rotter, "Building Trust in Virtual Teams," *IEEE Transactions on Professional Communication* 47 (June 2004): 95–105.

120 See note 115.

121 D. M. DeRosa, D. A. Hantula, J. D'Arcy, and N. Kock, "Trust and Leadership in Virtual Teamwork: A Media Naturalness Perspective," *Human Resource Management* 43 (Summer–Fall 2004); Y. Y. Shin, "A Person–Environment Fit Model for Virtual Organizations," *Journal of Management* 30 (September–October 2004): 725–744; and S. L. Jarvenpaa, T. R Shaw, and D. S. Staples, "Toward Contextualized Theories of Trust: The Role of Trust in Global Virtual Teams," *Information Systems Research* 15 (September 2004): 250–268.

122 D. Thomas and R. Bostrom, "Building Trust and Cooperation Through Technology Adaptation in Virtual Teams: Empirical Field

Evidence," *Information Systems Management* 25 (2008): 45–56.

123 L. F. Mesquita, "Starting Over When the Bickering Never Ends: Rebuilding Aggregate Trust Among Clustered Firms Through Trust Facilitators," *Academy of Management Review* 32(1) (2007): 72–91.

124 See note 116.

125 K. Siakas and E. Siakas, "The Need for Trust Relationships to Enable Successful Virtual Team Collaboration in Software Outsourcing," *International Journal of Technology, Policy, and Management* 8 (December 2007): 593.

126 T. Clemmensen, M. Khryashcheva, and O. Podshibikhina, "Combining Bases of Trust Development in Virtual Teams," *International Journal of Networking and Virtual Organisations* 5 (December 2007): 17.

127 C. Langfred, "The Downside of Self-Management: A Longitudinal Study of the Effects of Conflict on Trust, Autonomy, and Task Interdependence in Self-Managing Teams," *Academy of Management Journal* 50 (2007): 885–900.

128 J. Tata and S. Prasad, "Team Self-Management, Organizational Structure, and Judgments of Team Effectiveness," *Journal of Managerial Issues* 16 (Summer 2004): 248–268.

129 Ibid.

130 F. Brodbeck, R. Kerschreiter, A. Mojzisch, and S. Hardt, "Group Decision Making Under Conditions of Distributed Knowledge: The Information Asymmetries Model," *Academy of Management Review* 32 (2007): 459–479.

131 K. J. Valadares, "The Practicality of Employee Empowerment: Supporting a Psychologically Safe Culture," *The Health Care Manager* 23 (July–September 2004): 220–225.

132 See note 89.

133 M. Seo and L. Barrett, "Being Emotional During Decision Making—Good or Bad? An Empirical Investigation," *Academy of Management Journal* 50 (2007): 923–940.

134 See note 89.

135 Ibid.

136 See note 133.

137 I. Bens, "Facilitating With Ease! Core Skills for Facilitators, Team Leaders and Members, Managers, Consultants, and Trainers," Reviewed by J. K. Williams, *Academy of Management Learning & Education* 6(2) (June 2007): 294.

138 J. E. Ruin, "Conducting Effective Meetings," *Asia Africa Intelligence Wire* (March 27, 2004).

139 Ibid.

140 See note 137.

141 R. Donkin, "Lessons from History: Life to Become a Work of Art," *Financial Times* (September 27, 2004): 2.

142 A. D. Jong and J. C. Ruyter, "Adaptive versus Proactive Behavior in Service Recovery: The Role of Self-Managing Teams," *Decision Sciences* 35 (Summer 2004): 457–492.

143 See note 127.

144 E. L. Trist, G. Higgins, H. Murray, and A. Pollock, *Organizational Choice* (London: Tavistock, 1963).

145 S. Humphrey, C. Meyer, J. Hollenbeck, and D. Ilgen, "Trait Configurations in Self-Managed Teams: A Conceptual Examination of the Use of Seeding for Maximizing and Minimizing Trait Variance in Teams," *Journal of Applied Psychology* 93 (May 2007): 885–892.

146 S. B. Yang and M. E. Guy, "Self-Managed Work Teams: Who Uses Them? What Makes Them Successful?" *Public Performance and Management Review* 27 (2004): 60–80.

147 L. I. Glassop, "The Organizational Benefits of Teams," *Human Relations* 55 (February 2002): 225–250.

148 See note 22.

149 S. C. Kundu and J. A. Vora, "Creating a Talented Workforce for Delivering Service Quality," *Human Resource Planning* 27 (June 2004): 40–52.

150 L. D. Fredendall and C. R. Emery, "Productivity Increases Due to the Use of Teams in Service Garages," *Journal of Managerial Issues* 15 (Summer 2003): 221–255.

151 S. Kalliola, "Self-Designed Teams in Improving Public Sector Performance and Quality of Working Life," *Public Performance and Management Review* 27 (2003): 110–123.

152 D. Oliver and J. Roos, "Dealing with the Unexpected: Critical Incidents in the LEGO Mindstorms Team," *Human Relations* 56 (September 2003): 1057–1083.

153 See note 127.

154 M. Moravec, O. J. Johannessen, and T. A. Hjelmas, "The Well-Managed SMT," *Management Review* 87 (June 1998): 56–58.

155 See note 58.

156 See note 154.

157 V. U. Druskat and J. V. Wheeler, "Managing from the Boundary: The Effective Leadership of Self-Managing Work Teams," *Academy of Management Journal* 46 (August 2003): 435–456.

158 J. Carson, P. Tesluk, and J. Marrone, "Shared Leadership in Teams: An Investigation of Antecedent Conditions and Performance," *Academy of Management Journal* 50 (October 2007): 1214–1231.

159 J. A. Raelin, "Growing Group Leadership Skills: Managers Will Get the Most from Workers When They Teach Them to Work in Self-Directed Teams," *Security Management* 48 (June 2004): 34–38.

160 See note 158.

161 S. Miles and M. Watkins, "The Leadership Team: Complementary Strengths or Conflicting Agendas?" *Harvard Business Review* 85 (April 2007): 90–98.

162 See note 157.

163 See note 157.

164 See note 22.

165 See note 127.

Chapter 9

1 S. Schechner, "Can't Get Enough Oprah? Wait a Few Years," *The Wall Street Journal* (January 16, 2008): B1.

2 C. Hoppe, "Caucus to Test Whether Oprah Winfrey Can Help Barack Obama," *Dallas Morning News* (December 8, 2007).

3 C. Hall, "The Philanthropists; the Celebrities Who Are Most Influential in Creating Awareness about Their Causes," *WWD*, (September 6, 2007): 18.

4 D. Jung and J. Sosik, "Who Are the Spellbinders? Identifying Personal Attributes of Charismatic Leaders," *Journal of Leadership & Organizational Studies* 12 (2006): 12–26.

5 Ibid.

6 M. Glynn and T. Dowd, "Charisma (Un) Bound: Emotive Leadership in Martha Stewart Living Magazine," *Journal of Applied Behavioral Science* 44 (March 2008): 71–92.

7 J. Welch and S. Welch, "It's Not About Empty Suits," *Business Week* (October 2007): 132.

8 T. Mannarelli, "Accounting for Leadership: Charismatic, Transformational Leadership through Reflection and Self-awareness," *Accountancy Ireland* (2006): 46–49.

9 M. Nowicki and J. Summers, "Changing Leadership Styles: The New Leadership Philosophy Emphasizes Purpose, Process, and People," *Healthcare Financial Management* 61 (2007): 118–119.

10 J. A. Conger, *The Charismatic Leadership: Behind the Mystique of Exceptional Leadership* (San Francisco: Jossey-Bass, 1989).

11 S. A. Flaum, "The 10th 'P' to Succeed as a Leader, You Need Purpose, Performance, Persistence, Passion, and Much More. But Some of the Top Figures in Industry Give Credit to Another Factor: Providence," *Pharmaceutical Executive* 27 (March 2007): 46.

12 See note 4.

13 J. J. Sosik, "The Role of Personal Meaning in Charismatic Leadership," *The Journal of Leadership Studies* 7(2) (Spring 2000): 60–75.

14 See note 4.

15 J. Choi, "A Motivational Theory of Charismatic Leadership: Envisioning, Empathy, and Empowerment," *Journal of Leadership & Organizational Studies* 13 (2006): 24–43.

16 See note 10.

17 P. Rieff, "Charisma," *International Herald Tribune* (2007): 10.

18 D. McKie, "Comment & Debate: The Magic Ingredient: Charisma is a Quality to be Treated with a Proper Degree of Skepticism, Rather than Bathed in," *The Guardian* (2006): 32.

19 J. C. Pastor, M. Mayo, and B. Shamir, "Adding Fuel to Fire: The Impact of Followers' Arousal on Ratings of Charisma," *Journal of Applied Psychology* 92 (November 2007): 1584–1596.

20 See note 15.

21 T. E. Dow, Jr., "The Theory of Charisma," *Sociological Quarterly* 10 (1969): 306–318.

22 H. R. Bromley and V. A. Kirschner-Bromley, "Are You a Transformational Leader?" *Physician Executive* 33 (2007): 54–58.

23 See note 15.

24 See note 4.

25 See note 15.

26 J. M. Howell and B. Shamir, "The Role of Followers in the Charismatic Leadership Process: Relationships and Their Consequences," *Academy of Management Review* 30(1) (January 2005): 96–112.

27 See note 15.

28 K. S. Jaussi and S. D. Dionne, "Unconventional Leader Behavior, Subordinate Satisfaction, Effort and Perception of Leader Effectiveness," *Journal of Leadership & Organizational Studies* 10(3) (Winter 2004): 15–27

29 See note 22.

30 See note 15.

31 Ibid.

32 See note 4.

33 See note 15.

34 M. Javidan and D. E. Carl, "East Meets West: A Cross-Cultural Comparison of Charismatic Leadership Among Canadian and Iranian Executives," *Journal of Management Studies* 41(4) (June 2004): 665.

35 D. N. Den Hartog, A. Hoogh, and A. Keegan, "The Interactive Effects of Belongingness and Charisma on Helping and Compliance," *Journal of Applied Psychology* 92 (July 2007): 1131–1139.

36 See note 15.

37 See note 4.

38 See note 19.

39 T. A. Judge and R. Ilies, "Is Positiveness in Organizations Always Desirable?" *Academy of Management Executive* 18(4) (2004): 151–156.

40 See note 7.

41 See note 4.

42 S. Johnson and R. Dipboye, "Effects of Charismatic Content and Delivery on Follower Task Performance," *Group & Organizational Management* 33 (February 2008): 77–106.

43 T. Macalister, "Financial: Leadership Style: Fallen Titans Show Charisma is the Most Volatile Stock of All," *The Guardian* (October 2007): 29.

44 See note 42.

45 K. Higginbottom, "It's About Influence, Not Just Charisma," *The Guardian* (April 2008).

46 B. R. Agle, N. Nagarajan, J. Sonnenfeld, and D. Srinivasan, "Does CEO Charisma Matter? An Empirical Analysis of the Relationships among Organizational Performance, Environmental Uncertainty, and Top Management Team Perceptions of CEO Charisma," *Academy of Management Journal* 49 (2006): 161–174.

47 "Despite Compensation Levels That Suggest Otherwise, a CEO's Charisma Has Little Lasting Effect on a Company's Financial Performance," *Risk Management* 53(9) (September 2006): 8.

48 A. Fanelli and V. Misangyi, "Bringing Out Charisma: CEO Charisma and External Stakeholders," *Academy of Management Review* 31(4) (2006): 1049–1061.

49 Ibid.

50 See note 4.

51 See note 22.

52 See note 4.

53 See note 15.

54 Ibid.

55 C. Gallo, "The Governator's Charisma: You Can Borrow a Page from California Governor Arnold Schwarzenegger's Playbook to Improve Your Business Communication Skills," *Business Week Online* (2006).

56 Ibid.

57 G. P. Hollenbeck and D. T. Hall, "Self-Confidence and Leader Performance," *Organizational Dynamics* 33(3) (August 2004): 254–270.

58 See note 55.

59 See note 45.

60 "Oprah Winfrey Biography," *Shwing.com*, February 9, 2004, http://www.shwing.com/.

61 See note 7.

62 P. Kampert, "Charisma: It's All in the Ears," *Chicago Tribune* (2007).

63 See note 22.

64 See note 62.

65 M. Frese, S. Biemel, and S. Schoenborn, "Action Training for Charismatic Leadership: Two Evaluations of Studies of a Commercial Training Module on Inspirational Communication of a Vision," *Personnel Psychology* 56(3) (Fall 2003): 671–699.

66 See note 42.

67 See note 43.

68 See note 45.

69 See note 15.

70 See note 7.

71 See note 4.

72 See note 15.

73 M. E. Brown and L. Trevino, "Socialized Charismatic Leadership, Values Congruence, and Deviance in Work Groups," *Journal of Applied Psychology* 91 (2006): 954–962.

74 S. Spreir, M. Fontaine, and R. Malloy, "Leadership Run Amok: The Destructive Potential of Overachievers," *Harvard Business Review* 84 (June 2006): 72–82.

75 See note 15.

76 See note 73.

77 See note 43.

78 See note 45.

79 B. McKay and S. Vranica, "Government Ads Urge Americans to Shed Pounds," *The Wall Street Journal* (March 10, 2004): B1.

80 S. Ellison, "Divided, Companies Fight for Right to Plug Kids' Food," *The Wall Street Journal* (January 26, 2005): A1.

81 See note 79.

82 See note 26.

83 J. M. Burns. *Leadership.* (New York: Harper & Row, 1978).

84 See note 22.

85 A. G. Tekleab, H. Sims Jr., S. Yun, P. Tesluk and J. Cox, "Are We on the Same Page? Effects of Self-awareness of Empowering and Transformational Leadership," *Journal of Leadership & Organizational Studies* 14(2008): 185–201.

86 C. D. Beugre, W. Acar, and W. Brawn, "Transformational Leadership in Organizations: An Environment-induced Model," *International Journal of Manpower* 27 (2006): 52–62.

87 A. Xenikou, M. Simosi, "Organizational Culture and Transformational Leadership as Predictors of Business Unit Performance," *Journal of Managerial Psychology* 6 (2006): 566–579.

88 F. W. Brown, S. Bryant, and M. Reilly, "Does Emotional Intelligence—as Measured by EQI—Influence Transformational Leadership and/or Desirable Outcomes?" *Leadership & Organization Development Journal* 27 (2006): 330–351.

89 See note 87.

90 B. A. Tucker and R. Russell, "The Influence of the Transformational Leader," *Journal of Leadership & Organizational Studies* 10(4) (Spring 2004): 103–112.

91 H. Liao and A. Chuang, "Transforming Service Employees and Climate: A Multilevel, Multisource Examination of Transformational Leadership in Building Long-Term Service Relations," *Journal of Applied Psychology* 92 (2007): 1006–1019.

92 F. O. Walumbwa, P. Wang, J. J. Lawler, and K. Shi, "The Role of Collective Efficacy in the Relations between Transformational Leadership and Work Outcomes," *Journal of Occupational & Organizational Psychology* 77(4) (December 2004): 515–531.

93 D. Herold, D. Fedor, S. Caldwell, and Y. Liu, "The Effects of Transformational and Change Leadership on Employees' Commitment to Change: A Multilevel Study," *Journal of Applied Psychology* 93 (March 2008): 346–357.

94 J. E. Bono, H. J. Foldes, G. Vinson, and J. P. Muros, "Workplace Emotions: The Role of Supervision and Leadership," *Journal of Applied Psychology* 92 (2007): 1354–1364.

95 R. F. Piccolo and J. A. Colquitt, "Transformational Leadership and Job Behaviors: The Mediating Role of Core Job Characteristics," *Academy of Management Journal* 49 (2006): 324–337.

96 N. Ozaralli, "Effects of Transformational Leadership on Empowerment and Team Effectiveness," *Leadership and Organizational Development Journal* 24(5–6) (May 2003): 335–345.

97 See note 85.

98 J. Schaubroeck, S. E. Cha, and S. S. K. Lam, "Embracing Transformational Leadership: Team Values and the Impact of Leader Behavior on Team Performance," *Journal of Applied Psychology* 92 (2007): 1020–1030.

99 C. V. Chen and H. Lee, "Effects of Transformational Team Leadership on Collective Efficacy and Team Performance," *International Journal of Management and Enterprise Development* 4 (2006): 202.

100 G. Becker, "Organizational Climate and Culture: Competing Dynamics for Transformational Leadership," *Review of Business Research* 7 (2007): 116–123.

101 J. A. Aragon-Correa, V. J. Garcia-Morales and E. Cordon-Pozo, "Leadership and Organizational Learning's Role on Innovation and Performance: Lessons from Spain," *Industrial Marketing Management* 36 (2007): 349–359.

102 K. Trautmann, J. K. Maher, and D. G. Motley, "Learning Strategies as Predictors of Transformational Leadership: The Case of Nonprofit Managers." *Leadership & Organizational Development Journal* 28 (2007): 269–287.

103 S. P. Lopez, J. M. M. Peon, and C. J. K. Ordas, "The Organizational Context of Learning: An Empirical Analysis," *International Journal of Technology Management* 35 (2006): 193.

104 B. Muniapan, "Transformational Leadership Style Demonstrated by Sri Rama in Valmiki Ramayana," *International Journal of Indian Culture and Business Management* 1 (2007): 104.

105 See note 8.

106 B. M Bass and B. J. Avilio, *Improving Organizational Effectiveness Through Transformational Leadership* (Thousand Oaks, CA: Sage, 1994).

107 See note 22.

108 See note 104.

109 J. E. Bono and T. A. Judge, "Personality and Transformational and Transactional Leadership: A Meta-Analysis," *Journal of Applied Psychology* 89(5) (October 2004): 901–911.

110 J. Detert and E. Burris, "Leadership Behavior and Employee Voice: Is the Door Really Open?" *Academy of Management Journal* 50 (2007): 869–884.

111 See note 90.

112 D. McGuire and K. Hutchings, "Portrait of a Transformational Leader: The Legacy of Dr. Martin Luther King Jr.," *Leadership & Organization Development Journal* 28 (2007): 154–166.

113 See note 83.

114 See note 8.

115 See note 83.

116 See note 106.

117 A. Zaleznik, "Managers and Leaders: Are They Different?" in W. W. Rosenbach & R. L. Taylor (eds.), *Contemporary Issues in Leadership* (Oxford: Westview Press, 1993): 36–56.

118 R. Moore, "Lead Your Organization with a Higher Purpose," *Planet Engineering* 6 (2007): 23.

119 See note 94.

120 See note 118.

121 See note 22.

122 S. E. Bryant, "The Role of Transformational and Transactional Leadership in Creating, Sharing, and Exploiting Organizational Knowledge," *Journal of Leadership & Organizational Studies* 9(4) (Spring 2003): 23–36.

123 Y. Zhu, "Do Cultural Values Shape Employee Receptivity to Leadership Styles?" *Research Briefs* 21(3) (2007): 89–90.

124 See note 118.

125 B. M. Bass, B. J. Avolio, D. I. Jung, and Y. Berson, "Predicting Unit Performance by Assessing Transformational and Transactional Leadership," *Journal of Applied Psychology* 88(2) (April 2003): 207–219.

126 T. Judge and R. Piccolo, "Transformational and Transactional Leadership: A Meta-Analytic Test of Their Relative Validity," *Journal of Applied Psychology* 89(5) (October 2004): 755–768.

127 See note 22.

128 N. Wingfield and S. McBride, "Green Light for Grokster," *The Wall Street Journal* (August 20, 2004): B1.

129 B. N. Smith. R. V. Montagno, and T. N. Kuzmenko, "Transformational and Servant Leadership: Content and Contextual Comparisons," *Journal of Leadership & Organizational Studies* 10(4) (Spring 2004): 80–92.

130 P. C. Vargas, J. Hanlon, "Celebrating a Profession: The Servant Leadership Perspective," *Journal of Research Administration* 38 (2007): 45–50.

131 R. R. Washington, C. Sutton, and H. Field, "Individual Differences in Servant Leadership: the Roles of Values and Personality," *Leadership & Organization Development Journal* 27 (2006): 700–716.

132 J. K. Dittmar, "An Interview with Larry Spears: President & CEO for the Greenleaf Center for Servant Leadership," *Journal of Leadership & Organizational Studies* 13 (2006): 108–118.

133 R. F. Russell and A. G. Stone, "A Review of Servant Leadership Attributes: Developing a Practical Model," *Leadership & Organization Development Journal* (March–April 2002): 145–158.

134 See note 131.

135 See note 129.

136 See note 130.

137 S. Sendjaya, J. C. Sarros, and J. C. Santora, "Defining and Measuring Servant Leadership Behaviour in Organizations," *Journal of Management Studies* 45 (2008): 402–424.

138 See note 130.

139 See note 129.

140 See note 136.

141 See note 131.

142 See note 130.

Chapter 10

1 E. A. Platonova, S. R. Hernandez, R. M. Shewchuk, and K. M. Leddy, "Study of the Relationship Between Organizational Culture and Organizational Outcomes Using Hierarchical Linear Modeling Methodology," *Quality Management in Health Care* 15 (2006): 200–210.

2 C. Proval, "Meeting Radiology's Greatest Challenges: Culture and Leadership: What Makes Good Organizations Great? Business Expert Jim Collins Reveals What Separates the Best From the Rest—and What That Means for Your Practice," *Imaging Economics* 20 (2007): 24–29.

3 M. Skerlavaj, M. I. Stemberger, R. Skrinjar, and V. Dimovski, "Organizational Learning Culture—The Missing Link Between Business Process Change and Organizational Performance," *International Journal of Production Economics* 106 (2007): 346–367.

4 T. M. Jones, W. Felps, and G. A. Bigley, "Ethical Theory and Stakeholder Related Decisions: The Role of Stakeholder Culture," *Academy of Management Review* 32(1) (2007): 137–155.

5 P. A. Balthazard, R. A. Cooke, and R. E. Potter, "Dysfunctional Culture, Dysfunctional Organization: Capturing the Behavioral Norms That Form Organizational Culture and Drive Performance," *Journal of Managerial Psychology* 21 (2006): 709–732.

6 Ibid.

7 F. Moran, D. W. Palmer, and P. C. Borstorff, "An Exploratory Analysis of the Relationship Between Organizational Culture, Regional Culture, Casual Ambiguity and Competitive Advantage in an International Setting," *Journal of International Business Research* 6 (2007): 61–75.

8 A. Xenikou and M. Simosi, "Organizational Culture and Transformational Leadership as Predictors of Business Unit Performance," *Journal of Managerial Psychology* 21 (2006): 566–579.

9 G. N. Stock, K. L. McFadden, and C. R. Gowen III, "Organizational Culture, Critical Success Factors, and the Reduction of Hospital Errors," *International Journal of Production Economics* 106 (2007): 358–382.

10 See note 1.

11 See note 3.

12 W. Belossi, A. Z. Kondra, and O. I. Tukel, "New Product Development Projects: The Effects on Organizational Culture," *Project Management Journal* 38 (2007): 12–24.

13 M. M. Ajmal and K. U. Koskinen, "Knowledge Transfer in Project-Based

Organizations: An Organizational Culture Perspective," *Project Management Journal* 39 (2008): 7–15.

14 E. Schien, *Organizational Culture and Leadership*, 2nd ed. (San Francisco, CA: Jossey-Bass, 1992).

15 See note 2.

16 R. F. Korte and T. J. Chermack, "Changing Organizational Culture with Scenario Planning," *Futures* 39 (2007): 645–656.

17 P. M. Buhler, "Managing in the New Millennium: Building an Organizational Culture of Respect & Trust," *Supervision* 68 (2007): 16–20.

18 D. Ravasi and M. Schultz, "Responding to Organizational Identify Threats: Exploring the Role of Organizational Culture," *Academy of Management Journal* 49 (2006): 433–458.

19 See note 16.

20 C. Jarnagin and J. W. Slocum, Jr., "Creating Corporate Cultures Through Mythopoetic Leadership," *Organizational Dynamics* 36(3) (August 2007): 288–302.

21 M. Henderson, D. Thompson, and S. Henderson, "Implementing Values-Based Leadership," *NZ Business* 20(3) (April 2006): 12.

22 See note 14.

23 See note 18.

24 Ibid.

25 See note 2.

26 See note 18.

27 See note 2.

28 See note 1.

29 H. Kabasakal, G. Asugman, and K. Develioglu, "The Role of Employee Preferences and Organizational Culture in Explaining E-Commerce Orientations," *International Journal of Human Resource Management* 17 (2006): 464–483.

30 See note 18.

31 See note 7.

32 See note 29.

33 C. Free, N. Macintosh, and M. Stein, "Management Controls: The Organizational Fraud Triangle of Leadership, Culture and Control in Enron," *Ivey Business Journal Online* (2007).

34 D. Sams, "Grady's Culture, Leadership Criticized," *Atlanta Business Chronicle* 28 (2007): 2.

35 See note 29.

36 See note 1.

37 See note 2.

38 L. A. Runy, "Attributes of a High-Performing Culture," *H&HN Hospitals & Health Networks* 81 (2007): 60–62.

39 See note 7.

40 L. Sabyanji, "Designing Effective Change Interventions: The 4C Model of Organizational Culture," *Organisations & People* 13 (2006): 9–16.

41 Y. S. Choi and D. K. Scott, "Assessing Organizational Culture Using the Competing Values Framework Within American Triple-A Baseball," *International Journal of Sports Management and Marketing* 4 (March 2008): 33.

42 P. Aitken, "Walking the Talk: The Nature and Role of Leadership Culture Within Organization Culture," *Journal of General Management* 32 (2007): 17–38.

43 J. Connolly, "High Performance Cultures," *Business Strategy Review* 17 (2006): 19–23.

44 See note 4.

45 See note 2.

46 See note 17.

47 See note 7.

48 See note 38.

49 S. E. Fawcett, J. C. Brau, G. K. Rhoads, D. Whitlark, and A. M. Fawcett, "Spirituality and Organizational Culture: Cultivating the ABCs of an Inspiring Workplace," *International Journal of Public Administration* 31 (2008): 420–438.

50 R. Miick, "Lead by Aloha: Language Is a Powerful Tool in Culture and Leadership. As a Restaurant Leader, 'Restoring' Your Staff and Guests' Attitudes and Energy Should Be Among Your Main Objectives," *Food and Drink* 6 (2007): 14–16.

51 See note 17.

52 See note 49.

53 See note 17.

54 See note 49.

55 A. Oshiotse and R. Leary, "Corning Creates an Inclusive Culture to Drive Technology Innovation and Performance," *Global Business and Organizational Excellence* 26 (2007): 7.

56 See note 5.

57 D. Van Fleet and R. W. Griffin, "Dysfunctional Organization Culture: The Role of Leadership in Motivating Dysfunctional Work Behaviors," *Journal of Managerial Psychology* 21 (2006): 698–708.

58 N. O'Regan, A. Ghobadian, and M. Sims, "Fast Tracking Innovation in Manufacturing SMEs," *Technovation* 26 (2006): 251–261.

59 See note 33.

60 See note 17.

61 Ibid.

62 See note 49.

63 See note 16.

64 See note 43.

65 See note 58.

66 B. Altim-Metclafe and M. Bradley, "Cast in a New Light," *People Management* 14 (2008): 38–42.

67 See note 14.

68 See note 17.

69 See note 29.

70 See note 17.

71 See note 33.

72 See note 17.

73 See note 18.

74 See note 58.

75 M. H. Kavanagh and N. M. Ashkanasy, "The Impact of Leadership and Change Management Strategy on Organizational Culture and Individual Acceptance of Change during a Merger," *British Journal of Management* 17 (2006): 581–604.

76 See note 17.

77 See note 41.

78 See note 18.

79 J. Kotter and J. Heskett, *Corporate Culture and Performance.* (New York: The Free Press, 1992).

80 See note 40.

81 See note 3.

82 See note 40.

83 Ibid.

84 See note 16.

85 See note 20.

86 See note 21.

87 A. Buchko, "The Effect of Leadership on Values-Based Management," *Leadership & Organizational Development Journal* 28 (2007): 36–50.

88 A. Lewis, "Values-Centered Leadership—Practical Tools for SMEs (small to medium enterprises)," *Organizations & People* 14(3) (August 2007): 10–16.

89 F. E. Six, "Judging a Corporate Leader's Integrity," *European Management Journal* 25(3) (June 2007): 185–194.

90 R. Gulati and M. Sytch, "The Dynamics of Trust," *Academy of Management Review* 33(1) (2007): 276–278.

91 N. M. Tichy and W. G. Bennis, "Making The Tough Call," *Inc.* 29(11) (November 2007): 36–37.

92 J. Ferguson and J. Milliman, "Creating Effective Core Organizational Values: A Spiritual Leadership Approach," *International Journal of Public Administration*, 31(4) (March 2008): 439–459.

93 See note 21.

94 See note 42.

95 See note 87.

96 R. Barrett, "Value-Based Leadership," *The Times of India*, (Nov. 15, 2007), http://timesofindia.indiatimes.com/articleshow/2541691.cms

97 D. McGuire and K. Hutchings, "Portrait of a Transformational Leader: The Legacy of Dr. Martin Luther King, Jr.," *Leadership & Organization Development Journal* 28 (2007): 154–166.

98 M. J. Lankau, A. Ward, A. Amason, T. Ng, J. S. Sonnenfeld, and B. R. Agle, "Examining the Impact of Organizational Value Dissimilarity in Top Management Teams," *Journal of Managerial Issues* 19(1) (Spring 2007): 11–35.

99 See note 92.

100 R. Kashyap, R. Mir, and E. Iyer, "Toward a Responsive Pedagogy: Linking Social Responsibility to Firm Performance Issues in the Classroom," *Academy of Management Learning & Education* 5(3) (2006): 366–376.

101 N. Bontis and A. Mould-Mograbi, "Ethnical Values and Leadership: A Study of Business School Deans in Canada," *International Journal of Business Governance Ethics* 2 (2006): 217.

102 See note 92.

103 D. J. Moberg, "Best Intentions, Worst Results: Grounding Ethics Students in the Realities of Organizational Context," *Academy of Management Learning & Education* 5(3) (2006): 307–316.

104 D. L. McCabe, K. D. Butterfield, and L. K. Trevino, "Academic Dishonesty in Graduate Business Programs: Prevalence, Causes, and Proposed Action," *Academy of Management Learning & Education* 5(3) (2006): 294–305.

105 See note 100.

106 R. A. Giacalone and K. R. Thompson, "Business Ethics and Social Responsibility Education: Shifting the Worldview," *Academy of Management Learning & Education* 5(2) (2006): 266–277.

107 A. Pomeroy (reviewer) and R. Johnson, "Whistleblowing: When It Works—and Why," *Academy of Management Perspectives* 20 (2006): 128–129.

108 Ibid.

109 G. Graen, "In the Eye of the Beholder: Cross-Cultural Lesson in Leadership from Project GLOBE: A Response Viewed from the Third Culture Bonding (TCB) Model of Cross-Cultural Leadership," *Academy of Management Perspective* 20(4) (2006): 95–101.

110 G. Hofstede, "Cultural Constraints in Management Theories," *Academy of Management Executive* 7(1) (February 1993): 81–94.

111 Y. Zhu, "Do Cultural Values Shape Employee Receptivity to Leadership Styles?" *Research Briefs* 21(3) (2007): 89–90.

112 G. S. Van Der Vegt, E. Van De Viliert, and X. Huang, "Location-Level Links Between Diversity and Innovative Climate Depend on National Power Distance," *Academy of Management Journal* 48(6) (2005): 1171–1182.

113 J-L. Farh, R. D. Hackett, and J. Liang, "Individual Level Cultural Values as Moderators of Perceived Organizational Support Employee Outcome Relationships in China: Comparing the Effects of Power Distance and Traditionality," *Academy of Management Journal* 50 (2007): 715–729.

114 See note 110.

115 C. Robert and S. A. Wasti, "Organizational Individualism and Collectivism: Theoretical Development and an Empirical Test of a Measure," *Journal of Management* 28(4) (August 2002): 544.

116 D. R. Avery and K. M. Thomas, "Blending Content and Contact: The Roles of Diversity Curriculum and Campus Heterogeneity in Fostering Diversity Management Competency," *Academy of Management Learning & Education 3*(4) (2004): 380–396.

117 E. H. Buttner, K. B. Lowe, and L. Billings-Harris, "The Influence of Organizational Diversity Orientation and Leader Attitude on Diversity Activities," *Journal of Managerial Issues* 18 (2006): 356–371.

118 See note 112.

119 L. Roberson and C. Kulik, "Stereotype Threat at Work," *Academy of Management Perspectives* 21(2) (May 2007): 24–40.

120 A. Joshi, "The Influence of Organizational Demography on the External Networking Behavior of Teams," *Academy of Management Review* 31(3) (2006): 583–595.

121 K. Lofton, "Diversity Needed in C-Suit: Healthcare Leadership Does Not Look Like America, and That Must Change," *Modern Healthcare* 37 (2007): 26.

122 Ibid.

123 S. E. Black-Beth, "Understanding Generational Diversity in the Workplace: 2007 Leadership Conference, an Annual Convention Highlight," *Franchising World* 38 (2006): 73.

124 See note 121.

125 N. T. Dickerson, "We Are a Force to be Reckoned With, Black and Lataina Women's Leadership in the Contemporary U.S. Labor Movement," *WorkingUSA* 9 (2006): 293–313.

126 See note 119.

127 M. Javidan, P. Dorfman, M. Sully de Luque, and R. House, "In the Eye of the Beholder: Cross Cultural Lessons in Leadership from Project GLOBE," *Javidan, Dorfman, Sully de Luque, and House* 21(1) (2006): 67–90.

128 R. Ely and I. Padavic, "A Feminist Analysis of Organizational Research on Sex Differences," *Academy of Management Review* 32 (2007): 1121–1143.

129 See note 112.

130 M. Weil, "Diversity Management Is Out: Diversity Leadership Is In," *Richard Ivey School of Business Media Release* (April 29, 2008).

131 See note 127.

132 S. Page, "Making the Difference: Applying a Logic of Diversity," *Academy of Management Perspectives* 21(4) (2007): 6–20.

133 M. E. Mor Barak (Reviewed by C. Barzantny), "Managing Diversity: Toward a Globally Inclusive Workplace," *Book & Resource Reviews* 6(2) (2007): 285.

134 R. Dossani and M. Kenny, "Reflections upon Sizing the Emerging Global Labor Market," *Dossani and Kenny* 20(4) (2006): 35–41.

135 See note 132.

136 See note 133.

137 See note 127.

138 See note 111.

139 Ibid.

140 See note 132.

141 See note 117.

142 See note 120.

143 O. M. Robertson and H. J. Park, "Examining the Link Between Diversity and Firm Performance: The Effects of Diversity Reputation and Leader Racial Diversity," *Group & Organization Management* 32 (2007): 548–568.

144 D. Worman, "Teetering on the Brink. Research on Diversity and the Glass Cliff Phenomenon," *People Management* 13 (2007): 63.

145 See note 121.

146 See note 132.

147 See note 121.

148 M. Cronin and L. Weingart, "Representational Gaps, Information Processing, and Conflict in Functionally Diverse Teams," *Academy of Management Review* 32 (2007): 761–773.

149 See note 112.

150 See note 120.

151 See note 112.

152 See note 132.

153 See note 148.

154 See note 119.

155 G. Van Der Vegt, J. Bunderson, and A. Oosterhof, "Expertness Diversity and Interpersonal Helping in Teams: Why Those Who Need the Most Help End up Getting the Least," *Academy of Management Journal* 49(5) (2006): 877–893.

156 See note 148.

157 See note 143.

158 See note 119.

159 See note 133.

160 See note 119.

161 E. E. Duehr and J. E. Bono, "Men, Women and Managers: Are Stereotypes Finally Changing?" *Personnel Psychology* 59 (2006): 815–846.

162 B. Ragins, "Disclosure Disconnects: Antecedents and Consequences of Disclosing Invisible Stigmas Across Life Domains," *Academy of Management Review* 33 (2008): 194–215.

163 E. H. James and L. P. Wooten, "Diversity Crises: How Firms Manage Discrimination Lawsuits," *Academy of Management Journal* 49(6) (2006): 1103–1118.

164 L. M. Roth, "Women on Wall Street: Despite Diversity Measures, Wall Street Remains Vulnerable to Sex Discrimination Charges," *Academy of Management Perspectives* 21(1) (2007): 24–35.

165 C. T. Kulik, H. T. J. Bainbridge, and C. Cregan, "Known by the Company We Keep: Stigma-By-Association Effects in the Workplace." *Academy of Management Review* 33 (2008): 216–230.

166 J. L. Berdahl, "Harassment Based on Sex: Protecting Social Studies in the Context of Gender Hierarchy," *Academy of Management Review* 32(1) (2007): 641–658.

167 J. Dreachslin and F. Hobby, "Racial and Ethnic Disparities: Why Diversity Leadership Matters," *Journal of Healthcare Management* 53 (2008): 8(6).

168 A. Joshi, H. Liao, and S. Jackson, "Cross-Level Effects of Workplace Diversity on Sales Performance and Pay," *Academy of Management Journal* 49(3) (2006): 459–481.

169 F. D. Blau and L. M. Kahn, "The Gender Pay Gap: Have Women Gone as Far as They Can?" *Academy of Management Perspective* 21(1) (2007): 7–23.

170 D. Stafford, "Women Still Hitting Glass Ceiling in Business," *The Houston Chronicle* (April 10, 2006).

171 Ibid.

172 Ibid.

173 See note 144.

174 C. Helfat, D. Harris, and P. Wolfson, "The Pipeline to the Top," *Academy of Management Perspective* 20(4) (November 2006): 42–64.

175 R. Cohen and L. Kornfeld, "Women Leaders Boost Profit," *Barron's* 86 (2006): 37.

176 See note 125.

177 See note 164.

178 See note 165.

179 J. L. Dreachslin, "The Role of Leadership in Creating a Diversity-Sensitive Organization," *Journal of Healthcare Management* 52 (2007): 151–156.

180 See note 121.

181 See note 130.

182 See note 117.

183 See note 133.

184 See note 179.

185 Ibid.

186 See note 167.

187 See note 179.

188 See note 117.

189 See note 167.

190 See note 164.

191 See note 167.

192 See note 179.

193 See note 167.

194 F. Shipper, R. Hoffman, and D. Rotondo, "Does the 360 Feedback Process Create Actionable Knowledge Equally Across Cultures?" *Academy of Management Learning & Education* 6(1) (2007): 33–50.

195 See note 179.

196 See note 117.

197 Ibid.

198 See note 119.

199 See note 121.

200 Ibid.

201 See note 174.

202 See note 164.

203 See note 163.

204 See note 121.

Chapter 11

1 Google Investor Relations, "Letter from the Founders" (from the December 31, 2007 annual report), http://investor.google.com/2007_founders_letter.html.

2 R. Levering and M. Moskowitz, "Top 50 Employers," *Fortune* (February 4, 2008).

3 See note 1.

4 Ziff Davis Media Inc., "Brin Page Show No Signs of Slowing Down," *CioInsight* (March 15, 2007).

5 S. Aravamudhan and T. J. Kamalanabhan, "Identifying Balance in a Balanced Scorecard System," *International Journal of Learning and Change* 2(4) (April 18, 2008): 386.

6 R. Becherer, J. Finch, and M. Helms, "The Influences of Entrepreneurial Motivation and New Business Acquisition on Strategic Decision Making," *Journal of Small Business Strategy* 16(2) (2005/2006): 1–13.

7 D. Pollard and S. Hotho, "Crises, Scenarios and the Strategic Management Process," *Management Decision* 44(6) (June 2006) 721–736.

8 E. Dane and M. Pratt, "Exploring Intuition and Its Role in Managerial Decision Making," *Academy of Management Review* 32(1) (2007): 33–54.

9 See note 6.

10 C. Proval, "Meeting Radiology's Greatest Challenges: Culture and Leadership: What Makes Good Organizations Great? Business Expert Jim Collins Reveals What Separates the Best from the Rest—And What That Means for Your Practice," *Imaging Economics* 20 (2007): 24–29.

11 J. Kirby and T. A. Stewart, "The Institutional Yes: How Amazon's CEO Leads Strategic Change in a Culture Obsessed with Today's Customer," *Harvard Business Review* 85(10) (Oct 2007): 74–82.

12 B. M. Bass, "Executive and Strategic Leadership," *International Journal of Business* 12(1) (Winter 2007): 33–52.

13 Ibid.

14 See note 6.

15 S. Stern, "Eight Skills That Make You a Good Leader," *The Financial Times* (November 29, 2006): 14.

16 J. Gandz, "Great Leadership Is Good Leadership," *Ivey Business Journal Online* (2007).

17 A. Carmeli and A. Tishler, "The Relative Importance of the Top Management Team's Managerial Skills," *International Journal of Manpower* 27 (1) (January 2006): 9–36.

18 See note 12.

19 H. M. Guttman, "Leading High-Performance Teams: Horizontal, High-Performance Teams with Real Decision-Making Clout and Accountability for Results Can Transform a Company," *Chief Executive (U.S.)* (January–February 2008): 33–35.

20 H. Greve and H. Mitsuhashi, "Power and Glory: Concentrated Power in Top Management Teams," *Organization Studies* 28 (August 2007): 1197–1221.

21 B. Wiesenfeld, K. Wurthmann, and D. Hambrick, "The Stigmatization and Devaluation of Elites Associated with Corporate Failures: A Process Model," *Academy of Management Review* 33 (2008): 231–251.

22 See note 12.

23 See note 11.

24 R. More, "How to Create Market-Focused Product Winners." *Ivey Business Journal Online* (March–April 2008), http://www.iveybusinessjournal.com/article.asp?intArticle_ID=749.

25 See note 12.

26 E. S. Smith and E. Shefy, "The Intuitive Executive: Understanding and Applying 'Gut Feel' in Decision-Making," *Academy of Management Executive* 18 (2004): 76–91.

27 See note 16.

28 T. Thomas, J. R. Schermerhorn, and J. W. Dienhart, "Strategic Leadership of Ethical Behavior in Business," *The Academy of Management Executive* 18(2) (May 2004): 56–66.

29 See note 15.

30 See note 12.

31 See note 11.

32 D. Hambrick and M. Chen, "New Academic Fields as Admittance Seeking Social Movements: The Case of Strategic Management," *Academy of Management Review* 33 (2008): 32–54.

33 See note 12.

34 L. Markoczy, "The Competent Organization: A Psychological Analysis of the Strategic Management Process," *Organization Studies* 27(1) (Jan 2006): 150–153.

35 P. R. Willging, "You Can't Get There Without a Road Map," *Nursing Homes* 55(11) (Nov 2006): 14–16.

36 M. S. Lane and K. Klenke, "The Ambiguity Tolerance Interface: A Modified Social Cognitive Model for Leading under Uncertainty," *Journal of Leadership & Organizational Studies* 10 (Winter 2004): 69–81.

37 See note 10.

38 K. Shimizu and M. A. Hitt, "Strategic Flexibility: Organizational Preparedness to Reverse Ineffective Strategic Decisions," *Academy of Management Executive* 18 (2004): 44–59.

39 D. J. Ketchen Jr., C. C. Snow, and V. L. Street, "Improving Firm Performance by Matching Strategic Decision-Making Processes to Competitive Dynamics," *Academy of Management Executive* 18 (2004): 29–43.

40 See note 12.

41 S. M. B. Thatcher and X. Zhu, "Changing Identities in a Changing Workplace: Identification, Identity Enactment, Self-Verification, and Telecommuting," *Academy of Management Review* 41(4) (2006): 1076–1088.

42 C. Zatzick and R. Iverson, "High-Involvement Management and Workforce Reduction: Competitive Advantage or Disadvantage?" *Academy of Management Journal* 49(5) (2006): 999–1015.

43 D. Forbes, "Reconsidering the Strategic Implications of Decision Comprehensiveness," *Academy of Management Review* 32(2) (2007): 361–376.

44 See note 12.

45 See note 8.

46 See note 12.

47 W. Bennis, *On Becoming a Leader,* 2nd ed. (New York: Perseus Publishing; Upper Saddle River, New Jersey: HarperCollins Publishing, 2003).

48 See note 19.

49 K. Groves, "Leader Emotional Expressivity, Visionary Leadership, and Organizational Change," *Leadership & Organization Development Journal* 27 (2006): 566–583.

50 M. Akdere and R. Foster, "Effective Organizational Vision: Implications for Human Resource Development," *Journal of European Industrial Training* 31 (2007): 100–111).

51 Ibid.

52 B. Orwig and R. Z. Finney, "Analysis of the Mission Statements of AACSB-Accredited Schools," *Competitiveness Review* 17(4) (Fall 2007): 261–273.

53 Ibid.

54 Ibid.

55 S. M. J. Bonini, L. T. Mendonca, and J. M. Oppenheim, "When Social Issues Become Strategic," *The McKinsey Quarterly* 2 (Spring 2006): 20–32.

56 G. P. Latham, "The Motivational Benefits of Goal-Setting," *Academy of Management Executive* 18 (2004): 126–129.

57 S. Kerr and S. Landauer, "Using Stretch Goals to Promote Organizational Effectiveness and Personal Growth: General Electric and Goldman Sachs," *Academy of Management Executive* 18 (2004): 134–138.

58 See note 56.

59 D. J. Collis and M. G. Rukstad, "Can You Say What Your Strategy Is?" *Harvard Business Review* 86(4) (April 2008): 82–90.

60 P. Puranam, H. Singh, and M. Insead, "Organizing For Innovation: Managing the Coordination–Autonomy Dilemma in Technology," *Academy of Management Journal* 49(2) (2006): 263–280.

61 G. Trauffler, C. Herstatt, and H. Tschirky, "How to Transfer Discontinuous Technology into Radical Innovation: Some Evidence from Three Nanotech Cases," *International Journal of Technology Intelligence and Planning* 1(4) (Jan 4, 2006): 357.

62 See note 12.

63 N. Acur and L. Englyst, "Assessment of Strategy Formulation: How to Ensure Quality in Process and Outcome," *International Journal of Operations & Production Management* 26(1) (Jan 2006): 69–91.

64 N. O'Regan, A. Ghobadian, and M. Sims, "Fast Tracking Innovation in Manufacturing SMEs," *Technovation* 26 (2006): 251–261.

65 A. Larsson and Y. Sugasawa, "A Unified Methodology for Innovation Strategy Formulation: Product and Resource Perspectives on the Firm Combined," *International Journal of Process Management and Benchmarking* 2(2) (Sept 18, 2007): 118.

66 See note 61.

67 "How Whirlpool Defines Innovation; Nancy Snyder, Vice-President of Leadership and Strategic Competency Development, Discusses the Appliance Maker's Criteria—and Its Incentives," (INNOVATION Q & A) (Interview) *Business Week Online* (March 6, 2006), http://www.businessweek.com/innovate/content/mar2006/id20060306_287425.htm.

68 D. Depperu and L. Gnan, "The Role of the Competitive Context in the Business Strategy-Formulation Process," *International Studies of Management & Organization* 36(3) (Fall 2006): 110–130.

69 See note 35.

70 D. G. Sirmon, M. A. Hitt, and R. D. Ireland, "Managing Firm Resources in Dynamic Environments to Create Value: Looking Inside the Black Box," *Academy of Management Review* 32(1) (2007): 273–292.

71 R. L. Priem, "A Consumer Perspective on Value Creation," *Academy of Management Review* 32(1) (2007): 219–235.

72 See note 63.

73 Ibid.

74 See note 42.

75 S.-C. Kang, S. S. Morris, and S. A. Snell, "Relational Archetypes, Organizational Learning, and Value Creation: Extending the Human Resource Architecture," *Academy of Management Review* 32(1) (2007): 236–256.

76 R. I. Ricciardi, A. C. O. Barroso, and J.-L. Ermine, "Knowledge Evaluation for Knowledge Management Implementation: A Case Study of the Radiopharmaceutical Centre of IPEN," *International Journal of Nuclear Knowledge Management* 2(1) (May 2, 2006): 64.

77 C. Collins and K. Smith, "Knowledge Exchange and Combination: The Role of Human Resource Practices in the Performance of High-Technology Firms," *Academy of Management Journal* 49(3) (2006): 544–560.

78 See note 70.

79 A. W. King, "Disentangling Interfirm and Intrafirm Causal Ambiguity: A Conceptual Model of Casual Ambiguity and Sustainable Competitive Advantage," *Academy of Management Review* 32(1) (2007): 156–178.

80 See note 35.

81 See note 71.

82 J.-H. Thun, "Empirical Analysis of Manufacturing Strategy Implementation," *International Journal of Production Economics* 113(1) (May 2008): 370–382.

83 H. Atkinson, "Strategy Implementation: A Role for the Balanced Scorecard?" *Management Decision* 44(10) (October 2006): 1441–1460.

84 M. Benz and B. Frey, "Corporate Governance: What Can We Learn from Public Governance?" *Academy of Management Review* 32(1) (2007): 92–104.

85 See note 12.

86 See note 17.

87 A. Payne and P. Frow, "Customer Relationship Management: From Strategy to Implementation," *Journal of Marketing Management* 22(1–2) (February 2006): 135–168.

88 L. G. Hrebiniak, "Obstacles to Effective Strategy Implementation." *Organizational Dynamics* 35(1) (February 2006): 12–31.

89 M. Hitt, L. Bierman, K. Uhlenbruck, and K. Shimizu, "The Importance of Resources in the Internationalization of Professional Service Firms: The Good, The Bad, and The Ugly," *Academy of Management Journal* 49(6) (2006): 1137–1157.

90 E. R. Thorpe and R. E. Morgan, "In Pursuit of the 'Ideal Approach' to Successful Marketing Strategy Implementation," *European Journal of Marketing* 41(5–6) (May–June 2007): 659–677.

91 K. Behfar, R. Peterson, E. Mannix, and W. Trochim, "The Critical Role of Conflict Resolution in Teams: A Close Look at the Links Between Conflict Type, Conflict Management Strategies, and Team Outcomes," *Journal of Applied Psychology* 93 (January 2008): 170–188.

92 See note 90.

93 C. A. O'Reilly, "Corporations, Culture, and Commitment: Motivation and Social Control in Organizations," *California Management Review* 50(2) (Winter 2008): 85–101.

94 See note 19.

95 See note 5.

96 See note 83.

97 A. Fox, "Refreshing a Beverage Company's Culture: The Coca-Cola Co. Turned from Flat to Fizz by Engaging Leaders and Employee,." *HR Magazine* 52(11) (November 2007): 58–60.

98 P. Fiss and E. Zajac, "The Symbolic Management of Strategic Change: Sensegiving Via Framing and Decoupling," *Academy of Management Journal* 49(6) (2006): 1173–1193.

99 See note 12.

100 D. A. Plowman, L. T. Baker, T. E. Beck, M. Kulkarni, S. T. Solansky, and D. V. Travis, "Radical Change Accidentally: The

Emergence and Amplification of Small Change," *Academy of Management Journal* 50 (2007): 515–543.

101 R. Greenwood and R. Suddaby, "Institutional Entrepreneurship in Mature Fields: The Big Five Accounting Firms," *Academy of Management Journal* 49(1) (2006): 24–48.

102 See note 12.

103 See note 98.

104 See note 12.

105 M. G. Mupepi, S. C. Mupepi, R. V. Tenkasi, and G. Jewell, "Precision in Managing Organizational Change: Identifying and Analyzing Needs Using Social Constructs," *International Journal of Management Practice* 3(2) (May 18, 2008): 150.

106 D. Darlin, "Dell's Founder Returns as Chief Executive; Problems Grow at Computer Giant, Leading to Change at the Top," *The Houston Chronicle* (Houston, TX) (February 1, 2007): 1.

107 See note 7.

108 J. C. Quick and J. H. Gavin, "The Next Frontier: Edgar Schein on Organizational Therapy," *Academy of Management Executive* 14(1) (2000).

109 See note 98.

110 M. F. Thompson, "Diagnosing and Changing Organizational Culture," *Training* 43 (2006): 51.

111 D. Dixon, "Lean in the Job Shop; Managing the Lean Transition: Overcoming Resistance to Change," *Fabricating & Metalworking* 6(4) (April 2007): 16–18.

112 J. P. Kotter, "Leading Change: Why Transformation Efforts Fail," *Harvard Business Review* 85(1) (January 2007): 96–103.

113 See note 111.

114 S. A. Furst and D. M. Cable, "Employee Resistance to Organizational Change: Managerial Influence Tactics and Leader–Member Exchange," *Journal of Applied Psychology* 93(2) (March 2008): 453–462.

115 M. H. Kavanagh and N. M. Ashkanasy, "The Impact of Leadership and Change Management Strategy on Organizational Culture and Individual Acceptance of Change During a Merger." *British Journal of Management* 17 (2006): 581–604.

116 R. Ford, W. Heisler, and William McCreary, "Leading Change with the 5-P Model: 'Complexing' the Swan and Dolphin Hotels at Walt Disney World," *Cornell Hospitality Quarterly* 49(2) (May 2008): 191–205.

117 T. A. Stewart and D. Champion, "Leading Change from the Top Line," *Harvard Business Review* 84(7–8) (July–August 2006): 90–97.

118 See note 111.

119 F. B. Barnes and D. F. Karney, "Setting the Stage for Effective Execution of Change: Practical Advice for Leading Change Efforts," *International Journal of Business Research* 7(6) (November 2007): 45–56.

120 N. H. Woodward, "To Make Changes, Manage Them: As Change Accelerates, It Becomes Increasingly Important to Include Employees in the Overall Change Management Process," *HR Magazine* 52(5) (May 2007): 62–67.

121 See note 112.

122 W. S. Sherman and G. E. Garland, "Where to Bury the Survivors? Exploring Possible Ex Post Effects of Resistance to Change," *SAM Advanced Management Journal* 72(1) (Winter 2007): 52–63.

123 "On Leading Change," *Training* 43(10) (October 2006): 2.

124 See note 117.

125 J. D. Ford, L. W. Ford, and A. D'Amelio, "Resistance to Change: The Rest of the Story," *Academy of Management Review* 33(2) (April 2008): 362–377.

126 G. Ballinger and F. Schoorman, "Individual Reactions to Leadership Succession in Workgroups," *Academy of Management Review* 32(1) (2007): 118–136.

127 G. Ghislanzoni, "Leading Change: An Interview with the CEO of ENI," *The McKinsey Quarterly* (3) (Summer 2006): 55–63.

128 See note 115.

129 See note 112.

130 See note 123.

131 J. P. Kotter, *The New Rules: How to Succeed in Today's Post-Corporate World.* Adapted with permission from *U.S. News & World Report* 118(12) (March 27, 1995): 62.

132 See note 122.

133 See note 111.

134 Ibid.

135 See note 108.

136 See note 114.

137 E. J. O'Connor and C. M. Fiol, "Moving from Resistance to Support," *Physician Executive* 32(5) (September–October 2006): 68–69.

138 See note 125.

139 "Overcoming Resistance to Change Via Designs That Drive ROI," *Packaging Strategies* 25(3) (February 15, 2007): 4–5.

140 R. E. Landaeta, J. H. Mun, G. Rabadi, and D. Levin, "Identifying Sources of Resistance to Change in Healthcare," *International Journal of Healthcare Technology and Management* 9(1) (January, 25, 2008): 74.

141 A. Murray, "Overcoming Resistance to Change." *KMWorld* 16(19) (Oct. 2007): 24.

142 See note 125.

143 See note 119.

144 See note 137.

145 See note 122.

146 See note 120.

147 See note 116.

148 J. Brownell, a commentary on "Leading Change with the 5-P Model: 'Complexing' the Swan and Dolphin Hotels at Walt Disney World." *Cornell Hospitality Quarterly* 49(2) (May 2008): 206–210.

149 See note 120.

150 "Software Facilitates Change Management Planning/Process," *Product New Network* (March 3, 2006), http://news.thomasnet.com/fullstory/476296.

151 See note 19.

152 D. Dobosz-Bourne and A. D. Jankowicz, "Reframing Resistance to Change: Experience from General Motors Poland," *The International Journal of Human Resource Management* 17(12) (Dec 2006): 2021–2034.

153 See note 120.

154 See note 125.

155 http://www.nikebiz.com.

156 J. Birchall, "The Man Who Made a Career Out of Cool," *The Financial Times* (March 19, 2007): 12.

157 J. Carofano, "Insiders Applaud Inside Pick at Nike," *Footwear News* (January 30, 2004): 14.

Chapter 12

1 Information taken from the General Motors Web site: http://www.gm.com, accessed July 30, 2008.

2 S. Kroft, "GM's Difficult Road Ahead," *CBS News* (April 2, 2006).

3 C. Loomis, "The Tragedy of General Motors," *Fortune* (February 20, 2006).

4 D. Fonda, "How GM Can Fix Itself," *TIME Magazine* (November 27, 2005).

5 A. Carmeli and J. Schaubroeck, "Organizational Crisis-Preparedness: The Importance of Learning from Failures," *Long Range Planning* 41(2) (Apr 2008): 177–196.

6 A. Nancherla, "Crisis Leadership Now: A Real-World Guide to Preparing for Threats, Disaster, Sabotage, and Scandal," *T+D* 62(6) (Jun 2008): 83.

7 L. P. Wooten and E. H. James, "Linking Crisis Management and Leadership Competencies: The Role of Human Resource Development" *Advances in Developing Human Resources* 10(3) (June 2008): 352–379.

8 R. Dezenhall and J. Weber, "Corporate Crisis? Go on the Attack!," *Brandweek* 48(18) (April 30, 2007): 27.

9 D. Pollard and S. Hotho, "Crises, Scenarios and the Strategic Management Process," *Management Decision* 44(6) (June 2006): 721–736.

10 E. H. James and L. P. Wooten, "Diversity Crises: How Firms Manage Discrimination Lawsuits," *Academy of Management Journal* 49(6) (2006): 1103–1118.

11 R. J. Holland and K. Gill, "Ready for Disaster?" *Communication World* 23(2) (March/April 2006): 20–24.

12 M. Schwartz, "Survey: Majority of B-to-B Marketers Lack Crisis Plan," *B to B* 29(13) (October 8, 2007): 1–44.

13 C. Sapriel, "Talking the Long View," *Communication World* 24(5) (September/October 2007): 24–27.

14 See note 7.

15 T. Jaques, "Issue Management and Crisis Management: An Integrated, Non-Linear, Relational Construct," *Public Relations Review* 33(2) (June 2007): 147–157.

16 See note 13.

17 O. Cordonnier, "Toward Risk Governance," *Communication World* 23(2) (March/April 2006): 25–27.

18 D. E. Jones, "Corporate Crisis: The Readiness Is All," *Directors & Boards* 31(3) (2007 2nd Quarter): 61–63.

19 B. Walle and M. Turoff, "Decision Support for Emergency Situations," *Information Systems & e-Business Management* 6(3) (July 2008): 295–316.

20 M. E. Vielhaber and J. L. Waltman, "Changing Uses of Technology," *Journal of Business Communication* 45(3) (July 2008): 308–330.

21 D. J. Mendonca and W. A. Wallace, "A Cognitive Model of Improvisation in Emergency Management," *IEE Transactions on Systems, Man & Cybernetics: Part A.*" 37(4) (July 2007): 547–561.

22 See note 5.

23 H. M. Hutchins and J. Wang, "Organizational Crisis Management and Human Resource Development: A Review of the Literature and Implications to HRD Research and Practice," *Advances in Developing Human Resources* 10(3) (June 2008): 310–330.

24 A. Pang, F. Cropp, and G. Cameron, "Corporate Crisis Planning: Tensions, Issues and Contradictions," *Journal of Communication Management* 10(4) (2006): 371–389.

25 D. H. Midanek, "The Protocol of a Turnaround Manager," *Directors & Boards* 32(3) (2008 2nd Quarter): 38–41.

26 A. C. Rusaw and M. F. Rusaw, "The Role of HRD in Integrated Crisis Management: A Public Sector Approach," *Advances in Developing Human Resources* 10(3) (June 2008): 380–396.

27 H. M. Hutchins, "What Does HRD Know About Organizational Crisis Management?" *Advances in Developing Human Resources* 10(3) (June 2008): 299–309.

28 C. McCarthy, "Don't Let Disasters Proliferate," *Business Insurance* 42(24) (June 16, 2008): 9–10.

29 B. Beaman and B. Albin, "Steps to Disaster-Recovery Planning," *Network World* 25(26) (June 30, 2008): 25.

30 G. Boatwright, "Crisis Management: The Need for a Comprehensive Approach," *Pipeline & Gas Journal* 234(5) (May 2007): 34–36.

31 See note 12.

32 See note 17.

33 See note 28.

34 See note 5.

35 See note 30.

36 J. E. Lukaszewski, "Becoming a Crisis Guru," *Public Relations Strategist* 13(3) (Summer 2007): 44–45.

37 J. Lumb, "Former SEC Chairman Gives Advice on Handling Corporate Crises," *Federal Ethics Report* 14(8) (August 2007): 5–6.

38 J. Lee, J. H. Woeste, and R. L. Heath, "Getting Ready for Crisis: Strategic Excellence," *Public Relations Review* 33(3) (September 2007): 334–336.

39 A. Sommer and C. Pearson, "Antecedents Of Creativity Decision Making in Organizational Crisis: A Team-Based Simulation," *Technological Forecasting & Social Change* 74 (October 2007): 1234–1251.

40 See note 19.

41 See note 38.

42 J. Jarrett, "Maintaining Credibility During a Crisis: Challenges for the Manager," *Public Management* 89(3) (April 2007): 14–16.

43 C. Dautun, J. Tixier, J. Chapelain, F. Fontaine, and G. Dusserre, "Crisis Management: Improvement of Knowledge and Development of a Decision Aid Process," *Loss Prevention Bulletin* 201(1) (June 2008): 16–21.

44 See note 28.

45 See note 12.

46 J. B. Moats, T. J. Chermack, and L. M. Dooley, "Using Scenarios to Develop Crisis Managers: Applications of Scenario Planning and Scenario-Based Training," *Advances in Developing Human Resources* 10(3) (June 2008): 397–424.

47 See note 46.

48 L. Barton, *Crisis in Organizations*, 2nd ed. (Cincinnati, OH: South-Western Thomson Learning, 2001).

49 See note 29.

50 M. K. Pratt, "Crisis Over: Now What?" *Computerworld* 41(19) (May 7, 2007): 25–29.

51 See note 42.

52 See note 36.

53 See note 27.

54 K. C. Brown, "Betting the Business," *Public Relations Strategist* 13(3) (Summer 2007): 48–49.

55 A. Acquier, S. Gand, and M. Szpirglas, "From Stakeholder to StakeSholder Management in Crisis Episodes: A Case Study in a Public Transportation Company," *Journal of Contingencies & Crisis Management* 16(2) (June 2008): 101–114.

56 M. Orey, "Would I Lie To You?" *Business Week* 4088 (June 16, 2008): 20.

57 A. H. Reilly, "The Role of Human Resource Development Competencies in Facilitating Effective Crisis Communication," *Advances in Developing Human Resources* 10(3) (June 2008): 331–351.

58 R. C. Hyde, "In Crisis Management, Getting the Message Right Is Critical," *Public Relations Strategist* 13(3) (Summer 2007): 32–35.

59 P. McLagan, "Breaking the Sound Barrier," *Government Executive* 39(3) (March 2007): 70–71.

60 R. Levick and G. A. Pudles, "When Bad Things Happen to Good Companies," *Risk Management* 54(2) (February 2007): 6.

61 C. Lawton, "H-P Settles Civil Charges in Pretexting Scandal, *The Wall Street Journal* (December 8, 2006): A3.

62 T. J. Cousins, "Devising Post-Disaster Continuity Plans that Meet Actual Recovery Needs," *IEEE Technology & Society Magazine* 26(3) (Fall 2007): 13–23.

63 J. A. Clair and R. L. Dufresne, "Changing Poison into Medicine: How Companies can Experience Positive Transformation from a Crisis," *Organizational Dynamics* 36(1) (2007): 63–77.

64 See note 27.

65 N. Anand, H. Gardner, and T. Morris, "Knowledge-Based Innovation: Emergence and Embedding of New Practice Areas in Management Consulting Firms," *Academy of Management Journal* 50 (2007): 406–428.

66 D. A. Bonebright, "Built to Learn: The Inside Story of How Rockwell Collins Became a True Learning Organization," *T&D 57*(8) (August 2003): 67.

67 K. Korth, "Re-establishing the Importance of the Learning Organization," *Automotive Design UY Production* 119(11) (November 2007): 12.

68 M. Kodama, "Innovation and Knowledge Creation Through Leadership-Based Strategic Community: Case Study on High-Tech Company in Japan," *Technovation* 27(3) (March 2007): 115–132.

69 R. Kramer, "Leading Change Through Action Learning: Agency Managers Can Change Organizational Culture and Build a Learning Environment, as Demonstrated by APHIS," *The Public Manager* 36(3) (Fall 2007): 38–44.

70 D. A. Garvin, A. C. Edmondson, and F. Gina, "Is Yours a Learning Organization?" *Harvard Business Review* 86(3) (March 2008): 109–116.

71 V. Newman, "Integrating Learning into Your Processes," *KM Review* 10(2) (June 2007): 14–19.

72 T. J. Chermack, S. A. Lynham, and L. van der Merwe, "Exploring the Relationship Between Scenario Planning and Perceptions of Learning Organization Characteristics," *Futures* 38(7) (Sept 2006): 767–777.

73 R. K. Yeo, "Learning Institution to Learning Organization: Kudos to Reflective Practitioners," *Journal of European Industrial Training* 30(5) (May 2006): 396–419.

74 See note 67.

75 K. Miller, M. Zhao, and R. Calantone, "Adding Interpersonal Learning and Tacit Knowledge to March's Exploration–Exploitation Model," *Academy of Management Journal* 49(4) (2006): 709–722.

76 P. E. Bierly III and P. S. Daly, "Sources of External Organizational Learning in Small Manufacturing Firms," *International Journal of Technology Management* 38(1/2) (2007): 45–68.

77 See note 25.

78 See note 69.

79 C. Musselwhite, "The Culture of Discovery: What Does a Learning Organization Look Like, Why Is It Better, and How Can You Get There Sooner Rather Than Later? Organizational Development Expert Chris Musselwhite Has the Answers," *American Executive* 4(4) (April 2006): 38–40.

80 See note 79.

81 See note 34.

82 S. Trautman, "Teach What You Know: A Practical Leader's Guide to Knowledge Transfer Using Peer Mentoring," Reviewed by D. DeLong, MIT, AgeLab, *Book & Resource Review* 6(3) (2007): 425–428.

83 D. Schachter, "The Learning Organization," (business management) (organizational learning) 10(12) (December 2006): 8–9.

84 See note 13.

85 D. Miller, M. Fern, and L. Cardinal, "The Use of Knowledge for Technological Innovation Within Diversified Firms," *Academy of Management Journal* 50 (2007): 308–326.

86 See note 83.

87 See note 72.

88 See note 73.

89 J. G. Cegarra-Navarro and F. Dewhurst, "Linking Organizational Learning and Customer Capital Through an Ambidexterity Context: An Empirical Investigation in SMEs," *International Journal of Human Resource Management* 18(10) (October 2007): 1720–1735.

90 S. Pool and B. Pool, "A Management Development Model: Measuring Organizational Commitment and Its Impact on Job Satisfaction Among Executives in a Learning Organization," *Journal of Management Development* 26(4) (April 2007): 353–369.

91 H-H. Teo, X. Wang, K-K Wei, C-L. Sia, and M. K. O. Lee, "Organizational Learning Capacity and Attitude Toward Complex Technological Innovations: An Empirical Study," *Journal of the American Society for Information Science and Technology* 57(2) (January 15, 2006): 265–314.

92 R. C. Rose and N. Kumar, "Facilitating Learning and Change for Performance Improvement," *International Journal of Learning and Change* 1(3) (September 24, 2006): 317.

93 K. E. Soderquist, "Organising Knowledge Management and Dissemination in New Product Development: Lessons from 12 Global Corporations," *Long Range Planning* 39(5) (October 2006): 497–523.

94 B. Ebrahimi, R. McGowan, and T. Chung, "Key Success Factors in New Product Development," *International Journal of Management and Decision Making,* 7(2–3) (March 6, 2006): 313.

95 C. Collins and K. Smith, "Knowledge Exchange and Combination: The Role of Human Resource Practices in the Performance of High-Technology Firms," *Academy of Management Journal* 49(3) (2006): 544–560.

96 S-C. Kang, S. S. Morris, and S. A. Snell, "Relational Archetypes, Organizational Learning, and Value Creation: Extending the Human Resource Architecture," *Academy of Management Review* 32(1) (2007): 236–256.

97 D. Couillard, "Why Creating a Learning Organization Leads the High Tech Form to Succeed," *Ivey Business Journal Online* (July–August 2007), http://www.iveybusinessjournal.com/article.asp?intArticle_ID=700.

98 J. A. Aragon-Correa, V. J. Garcia-Morales, and E. Cordon-Pozo, "Leadership and Organizational Learning's Role on Innovation and Performance: Lessons from Spain," *Industrial Marketing Management* 36 (2007): 349–359.

99 R. Leenders, J. Kratzer, and J. Engelen, "Innovation Team Networks: The Centrality of Innovativeness and Efficiency," *International Journal of Networking and Virtual Organization* 4 (November 2007): 459.

100 T. Hoc-Hai, W. Xinwei, W. Kwok-Kee, S. Chong-Ling, and M. K. O. Lee, "Organizational Learning Capacity and Attitude Toward Complex Technological Innovations: An Empirical Study," *Journal of the American Society for Information Science & Technology* 57(2) (January 2006): 264–279.

101 M. Skerlavaj, M. Stemberger, R. Skrinjar, and V. Dimovski, "Organizational Learning Culture—The Missing Link Between Business Process Change and Organizational Performance," *International Journal of Production Economics* 106 (2007): 346–367.

102 J. Arthur and C. Huntley, "Ramping Up the Organizational Learning Curve: Assessing the Impact of Deliberate Learning on Organizational Performance Under Gainsharing," *Academy of Management Journal* 49(6) (2005): 1159–1170.

103 C. W. Soo, R. M. Devinney, and D. F. Midgley, "External Knowledge Acquisition, Creativity and Learning in Organizational Problem Solving," *International Journal of Technology Management* 38(1/2) (2007): 137–159.

104 C. Lakshman, "Organizational Knowledge Leadership: A Grounded Theory Approach," *Leadership & Organizational Development Journal* 28, (January 2007): 51–75.

105 K. L. Turner and M. V. Makhija, "The Role of Organizational Controls in Managing Knowledge," *Academy of Management Review* 31(1) (2006): 197–217.

106 See note 70.

107 See note 69.

108 M. Cronin and L. Weingart, "Representational Gaps, Information Processing, and Conflict in Functionally Diverse Teams," *Academy of Management Review* 32 (2007): 761–773.

109 See note 99.

110 See note 70.

111 See note 69.

112 See note 97.

113 See note 70.

114 Ibid.

115 See note 84.

116 G. Van Der Vegt, J. Bunderson, and A. Oosterhof, "Expertness Diversity and Interpersonal Helping in Teams: Why Those Who Need the Most Help End Up Getting the Least," *Academy of Management Journal* 49(5) (2006): 877–893.

117 M. Zellmer-Bruhn and C. Gibson, "Multinational Organization Context: Implications for Team Learning and Performance," *Academy of Management Journal* 49(3) (2006): 501–518.

118 See note 67.

119 See note 70.

120 J. Frahm and K. Brown, "Developing Communicative Competencies for a Learning Organization," *Journal of Management Development* 25(3) (March 2006): 201–212.

121 W. Holstein, "Man with a Mission," *Chief Executive* 217 (April/May 2006): 30.

122 G. So, "Marketing Club Kicks off Distinguished Speakers Series with P&G CEO," *The Harbus* (October 3, 2006), http://media.www.harbus.org/media/storage/paper343/news/2006/10/03/News/Marketing.Club.Kicks.Off.Distinguished.Speakers.Series.With.Pg.Ceo-2328567.shtml.

123 "P&G's A. G. Lafley Honored," *Chief Executive* (September 2006): 54(3).

Appendix

1 K. T. Scott, "Leadership and spirituality: A quest for reconciliation," in J. Conger (ed.), *Discovering the Spirituality in Leadership* (San Francisco: Jossey-Bass, 1994), 63–99.

2 G. Fairholm, *Capturing the heart of leadership: Spirituality and community in the new American workplace.* (Westport, CT: Praeger), 1997.

3 C. Barks, *The Essential Rumi* (San Francisco: Harper, 1996).

4 J. Autry, *Love and profit: The art of caring leadership* (New York: Avon Books, 1991).

5 For details on the four levels of spirituality in the workplace implementation, with case studies, worksheets, and assessments, the *Creating Enlightened Organizations Manual* by J. Neal can be ordered from the Association for Spirit at Work, http://www.spiritatwork.org.

6 B. Heermann, *Building team spirit: Activities for inspiring and energizing teams* (New York: McGraw-Hill, 1997). *Noble purpose: Igniting* *extraordinary passion for life and work* (Fairfax, VA: QSU Publishing, 2004).

7 R. Barrett, *Liberating the corporate soul: Building the visionary organization* (Cambridge, MA: Butterworth-Heinemann, 1998); http://www.corptools.com.

8 D. Beck and C. Cowen, *Spiral dynamics: Mastering values, leadership, and change* (Malden, MA: Blackwell Publishing, 1996); http://www.spiraldynamics.com.

9 David Cooperrider and Suresh Srivastva first developed the concept of Appreciative Inquiry in 1987, in D. Cooperrider and S. Srivastva, "Appreciative inquiry in organizational life," in R. W. Woodman & W. A. Pasmore (eds.), *Research in organizational change and development.* (Greenwich, CT: JAI Press, 1987). The most recent book in this field is D. Whitney, A. Trosten-Bloom, and D. Cooperrider, *The power of appreciative inquiry: A practical guide to positive change* (San Francisco: Berrett-Koehler, 2003); http://appreciativeinquiry. cwru.edu/.

10 Kim Cameron coedited, with Jane Dutton and Robert Quinn, *Positive Organization Scholarship* (San Francisco: Berrett-Koehler, 2003). This book was widely acclaimed by the academic community; however the business community responded that it was too "ivory tower." Cameron has recently written a book for the business community called *The abundance framework* (in press); http://www.bus.umich.edu/Positive/.

11 H. Owen, *Open space technology: A user's guide,* 2nd ed. (San Francisco: Berrett-Koehler, 1997); http://www.openspaceworld.org/.

12 W. Harman and J. Hormann, *Creative work: The constructive role of business in transforming society* (Indianapolis: Knowledge Systems, 1990).

13 J. Collins, *Good to great: Why some companies make the leap . . . and others don't* (NY: HarperBusiness, 2001). See Chapter 2 on "Level 5 Leadership," which documents the success of leaders who demonstrate the virtue of humility.

14 J. Neal, B. Lichtenstein, and D. Banner, "Spiritual perspectives on individual, organizational, and societal transformation," *Journal of Organizational Change Management,* 12(3), 175–185.

15 C. Schaefer and J. Darling, "Does spirit matter? A look at contemplative practice in the workplace," Spirit at Work newsletter, July 1997.

A

Aageson, Tom, 481
Ability, 162
Academic grades, 198
Academic standards, 91–92
Accommodating conflict style, 212
Accomplishments, 42, 129
Accountability, 268, 307
Achievement, 35, 377
  acquired needs theory and, 85–86
  congratulating, 132–133
  need for (n Ach), 42, 51
Achievement Motivation Theory, 42–43, 47
Achievement-oriented style, 164
Ackoff, Russell, 171
Acquired needs theory, 85–86
Action orientation, 343
Activist mind-set, 332
Acton, Lord, 110
Adams, J. Stacy, 87
Adams, Scott, 4
Adaptation, 470
Adaptive culture, 384–385
Adjustment personality dimension, 30, 35, 60
Adjustment traits, 35
Advanced Micro Devices, 40
Advantageous comparison, 57
Advertising, 193, 395
Affection, 249
Affiliation, need for (n Aff), 43, 45, 86
African-Americans, 394, 398
Agreeableness personality dimension, 34
Airlines
  culture of, 380–381
  ethics and, 95
  team players in, 343
Alienated follower, 256
Allen, Paul, 62
America Online (AOL), 40, 127
American Express, 425, 433
Americans with Disabilities Act (ADA), 395
Analysis levels, 13–15
Analyzing, 196
Angel Network, 329
Anne Mulcahy and Ursula Burns: Xerox's Dynamic Duo, 364–365
Apple, 24
Arbitrator, 218
Archer Daniels Midland (ADM) Company, 178–179
Armed forces, power and, 114
Arrogance, 374
Art Friedman—Friedmans Appliance, 24–25, 102–103
Arthur Andersen, 54, 266–267
Asea Brown Boveri, 311
Asian Americans, 411
Attitudes, 47–52, 54–56
  and ethical behavior, 54–55
  leadership styles and, 52–54
  Pygmalion effect, 31, 49
  self-concept, 50–51
  Theory X and Theory Y, 48–49
Attribution of blame, 57
Attribution theory, 207
Authenticity, 484
Authoritarianism, 162
Authority-compliance leader, 76
Autocratic communication style, 70–71, 229
Autocratic leadership style, 159
Autry, James, 482
Average leadership style (ALS) approach, 242
Avoidance reinforcement, 93
Avoiding conflict style, 211
Avon Company, 369, 371–372, 378, 386, 390, 405

B

Barnevik, Percy, 311
Barrett, Richard, 483
Bass, Bernard, 347
Bates, Rowland, 189
BCF model, 216
Beck, Don, 483
Behavior, 7
Behavior skills model training, 320
Behavioral leadership theories, 18
Behavioral models, 21
Belongingness needs, 81
Benchmarking, 470
Bennis, Warren, 193
Bezos, Jeff, 347
Bias, 254
Big Five Model of Personality, 33–34
Bill & Melinda Gates Foundation, 62–63
Blake, Robert, 75–76
Blame, 202–203
Blanchard, Ken, 97–98
Blue Man Group, 40
Bolman, Lee, 482
Boundary-spanning relationships, 246
Brandon, David, 4
Branson, Richard, 339, 344
Brin, Sergey, 417
Buffett, Warren, 59
Bureaucratic culture, 385–386
Burns, Ursula, 364–365
"Buy American," 393

C

Calloway, Wayne, 385
Cameron, Kim, 483
Career development, 128
Carroll, Chuck, 271
Case, Steve, 40, 127
Case studies
  Anne Mulcahy and Ursula Burns: Xerox's Dynamic Duo, 364–365
  Art Friedman—Friedmans Appliance, 24–25, 102–103
  Avon Company, 369
  Bill & Melinda Gates Foundation, 62–63
  CEO A. G. Lafley's Transformation of P&G, 476–477
  Cisco Systems, 279
  Cuban, Mark, 109
  Frederick W. Smith—FedEx, 318–319
  General Electric (GE), 3
  General Motors (GM), 451
  Google, 417
  Lakewood Church, 239
  Lawrence Weinbach—from Unisys Corporation to Yankee Hill Capital Management, 222–223
  Mark Parker: A Seasoned Veteran Takes the Helm at Nike, 445–447
  Market America, 69
  Monroe, Lorraine, 31
  PepsiCo, 151
  Ranch Golf Club, 189
  Rick Parr—Archer Daniels Midland (ADM) Company, 178–179
  Robert Stevens Continues Lockheed Martin's Diversity Initiatives, 410–412
  Ron Johnson—Department of Accounting, 143–144

- Steve Jobs—Apple, 24–25
- Winfrey, Oprah, 329
- W. L. Gore & Associates, 271–273

Case Western Reserve's Wetherhead School of Management, 483
Censorship, 57
Center for Educational Innovation, 31
Center of Business as Agent of World Benefit (BAWB), 483
CEO A. G. Lafley's Transformation of P&G, 476–477
Cereal Partners Worldwide, 395
Ceremonial events, 380
Chambers, John, 279
Change, 8–9, 33, 484–493
- activism and, 332
- change process theories, 435
- crisis management, 431–432
- culture of learning organization, 467–468
- discontinuous, 466
- flexibility and, 40
- need for, 432–433
- organizational change, 432–433
- process, 435–438
- resistance to, 36, 438–439, 441. *See also* Resistance to change, reasons
- upgrading as, 432

Changing phase, 436–437
Charismatic leadership, 165, 337–360
- behavioral components, 351
- change and, 436–437
- charisma defined, 337
- developing charismatic qualities, 344–345
- dissatisfaction with status quo, 335–336
- effects of, 338–340
- locus of, 337–338
- negative aspect of, 345–346
- personal meaning, 330–331
- qualities of, 341
- resource needs assessment, 336
- and transformational leadership compared, 349–350
- unconventional behavior and, 336
- vision formulation and articulation, 336
- Weber's conceptualization of charisma, 334–335

Chiu, Bernard, 189
Churchill, Winston, 345
Cisco Systems, 279
Citibank, 424
Civil Rights Acts, 394
Clark, Korby, 189, 201
Clark, Peter, 189, 201, 209, 215, 218
Class-action lawsuits, 475
Clinton, Bill, 123, 332
Coaching, 201–209
- attribution theory, 207
- avoiding blame/embarrassment, 202–203
- developing a supportive working relationship, 202
- feedback, 204–206
- focus on behavior, 203
- improving performance with, 208
- and leadership, 201
- mentoring, 209
- model for employees performing below standard, 207
- performance formula, 207
- praise/recognition and, 202
- specific/descriptive feedback, 203–204
- timely/flexible feedback, 205

Coalition influencing tactic, 117
Coalitions, 117
Coca-Cola, 395, 424, 431
Code of ethics, 388–389
Coercive power, 113–114
Cognitive resources theory, 158
Cole, David, 451
Coleadership, 78
Collaborating conflict style, 213–217
Collectivism, 391–392
Commitment
- decision implementation and, 168
- to objectives, 91

Communication, 189–197
- advertising, 193
- analyzing, 196
- charismatic leaders' skill in, 342
- checking understanding, 194
- determining preferred style of, 193–194
- on diversity, 402
- effective crisis communication, 460–461
- listening skills, 193–194
- at Navistar International, 224
- of new vision/strategies, 436–437
- nonverbal, 194–195
- oral message-sending process, 190–191
- planning the message, 190
- press release/press kit, 461
- receiving messages, 193–194
- selecting styles of, 193
- sending messages/giving instructions, 190
- situational communications model, 229–232
- teams and, 294–295
- written, 192

Community service, 131
Compensation of executives, 14
Competition, change and, 432–433
Competitive culture, 385
Compliments, 51
CompUSA, 39
Concern for production/concern for people, 76
Confidence, lack of, 439
Conflict management, 210–222
- arbitrator, 218
- collaborating conflict management style models, 215–222
- dysfunctional/functional conflict, 210
- initiating conflict resolution, 215–216
- leadership and, 210
- mediating conflict resolution, 217–218
- psychological contract, 210
- relationship-oriented, 210
- responding to conflict resolution, 217–218
- styles, 210–214

Conflict resolution, 215–219
Conformist follower, 256
Congruency, 484
Connection power, 117
Conscientiousness personality dimension, 35, 60–61
Consequences, disregard or distortion of, 57
Consideration style, 77
Consult group style, 166
Consult individually style, 166
Consultation influencing tactic, 111
Consultative communication style, 230
Content motivation theories, 80–86
- acquired needs theory, 85–86
- comparison of, 86
- hierarchy of needs, 81–83
- maintenance (extrinsic factors), 82
- two-factor, 82

Contingency leadership theories, 17, 22, 75, 78, 150–177
- changing the situation, 156, 174
- charismatic leadership, 165
- determining appropriate leadership style, 156
- framework for variables, 153
- global contingency leadership, 153–154
- leadership continuum theory and model, 159–161
- *vs.* leadership models, 152
- leadership style and the LPC, 155
- leadership substitutes theory, 173–174
- and model variables, 152–153
- normative theory/models, 165–166
- path-goal leadership theory and model, 161–162
- prescriptive/descriptive models, 173

putting behavioral/contingency theories together, 171–172
research, 158
situational favorableness, 156
value-based leadership, 165
Continuous reinforcement, 94
Conventional level of moral development, 56–57
Conviction, lack of, 439
Cooperative culture, 384
Cooperrider, David, 483
Co-optation, 122–123
Core competence, 427–428
Country-club leader, 76
Courage, 59
Cowan, Chris, 483
Creativity, 291
diversity and, 397, 469–470
recognition/rewarding of, 291
teams and, 291
Credibility, 35
Crisis, defined, 452
Crisis leadership, 452–462
crisis communication, 460–461
crisis leader, 455
organizational preparedness, 459
postcrisis evaluation plan, 454
precrisis planning, 454–455
risk assessment, 457–459
team, 456–458
Crisis prevention, 457–458
Criticism, 204–206
Cross-cultural differences, 395–396
Cross-functional team, 294–295, 437
Cuban, Mark, 109
Cultural differences
communication problems and, 198–199
conflict management and, 210
negotiation and, 139
Cultural heritage and traditions, 332
Culture
defined, 370
of organization. *See* Organizational culture
reinforcement tools, 376

D

Day care centers, on-site, 87
Death, unexpected, 452
Decide style, 182
Decision making
decentralized, 358
delegation and, 265–266
failure of strategic decisions, 419
teams and, 297
Decision significance, 168
Decisional leadership roles, 11
Delegate style, 182
Delegation, 264–269
benefits of, 264
at Boyne USA Resorts, 274
control checkpoints, 268
of decisions, 265
observer form, 234–235
obstacles to, 264–265
with use of a model, 267–268
Delegation model, 267–268
Democratic leadership, 17, 70
Demographic diversity, 394
Demotivating, 206
Descriptive feedback, 203–204
Descriptive models, 173
Diana, Princess of Wales, 332
Diffusion of responsibility, 57
Directive style, 262
Disabled workers, 395
Discontinuous change, 466
Discrimination, 394, 405–406
Displacement of responsibility, 57
Disseminator role, 11
Distributed leadership, 312
Distrust, 439–440
Disturbance-handler role, 12–13
Diversity, in workforce, 394–407
corporate philosophy, 402
creating a supportive culture for, 371–372
current state of, 394–395
demographic diversity, 394
diversity defined, 394
globalization and, 396
leadership initiatives for achieving, 401–402
management support/commitment, 404
obstacles. *See* Obstacles to achieving diversity
at PepsiCo, 412
reasons for embracing, 396–397
Dominance, 34
Domino's Pizza, 4
Douglass, Frederick, 332
Downsizing, 39, 434
Drucker, Peter, 82
Drug research, 163
Dunlap, Al, 347
Dunn, Patricia, 462
Dyadic process, 13–14
Dyadic theory, 240–247
systems and networks, 245–247
team building, 244–245
vertical dyadic linkage (VDL) theory, 241–243
Dysfunctional conflict, 210

E

Edison, Thomas, 59
Education and diversity, 403–405
Effective follower, 255–268
Einstein, Albert, 70
Embarrassment, 202–203
Emery Air Freight, 96
Emotional instability, 55
Emotional intelligence, 40
Emotional stability, 35, 331
Empathy, 40
Employee-centered leadership style, 72–73, 75, 171
Employee(s)
broadening frame of reference of, 472
classification of, 7
cognitive structures of, 246
delegating to, 264–268
distress, and leader–member interaction, 244
downsizing to part-time, 39
effect of leadership on, 4
empowerment of, 110, 298, 437
meeting personal needs of, 87
motivating with equity theory, 88
motivating with goal setting, 90
motivating with hierarchy of needs theory, 81–82
motivating with reinforcement, 92–93
motivating with two-factor theory, 82–83
Networks at Whirlpool Corporation, 145
rewarding with equity theory, 87–88
self-assessment, 203
turnover, 78
Empowerment, 110, 298, 321–322, 437
communication style, 230
Energy, high level of, 38, 42
Enron Corporation, 4, 54, 57, 266, 286, 374–375, 390
Entrepreneur role, 11
Environmental situational factors, 159
Equality assumption, 358
Equity theory, 87
Esteem needs, 82
Ethical behavior
advocating, 388
code of ethics, 388–389
disclosure mechanism, 389–390
ethics committees, 389
ethics ombudsperson, 389
presidential call for, 419–420

simple guides to, 58
strategists and, 420
training programs, 389
Ethical leadership, 52–60
ethical behavior assessment, 52–53
finding courage for, 59
moral development and, 55–56
personality traits/attitudes and, 54–55
positive result of, 54
situations affecting, 56
Ethics, 39
airlines and, 95
defined, 54
delegation, 264
influencing process and, 109
justifying unethical behavior, 56–57
stakeholder approach to, 58–59
Ethnicity. *See* Diversity, in workforce
Ethnocentrism, 399
Euphemistic labeling, 57
Evans, M. G., 161
EXCEL Award, 222
Excellence, 377
Exchange influencing tactic, 113, 122
Exclusionary practices, 398
Expectancy theory, 88–89
motivating with, 89
three variables, 89
Expectations, 49
Experience, openness to, 35
Experimentation, 470
External locus of control, 262
Externalizers, 38
Extinction, 94
Extraversion traits, 34
Extrinsic motivators, 82
Exxon Valdez, 452
Eye contact, 98

F

Facilitate style, 182
Facilitative skills, 286–287
Facilities design, 382
Faith, 332–333
Falvey, Jack, 205
Federal Communications Commission (FCC), and censorship, 58
FedEx, 318
Feedback, 97, 197–201
coaching feedback, 201–202
criticism and coaching feedback compared, 204
effective leader feedback, 252
employee assessment of performance, 203
flexibility, 205
importance of, 197
meeting objectives and, 197
on messages, 197
negative, 205, 259
openness to criticism, 198
seeking/encouraging honest, 259–260
360-degree multirater, 200
timely and flexible, 202
Femininity, 392
Fiedler, Fred E., 154, 157
Fifth Discipline, The (Senge), 464
Figurehead role, 10
Financial objectives, 426
Fiorina, Carleton (Carly), 124
Fixed interval schedule, 95
Flexibility, 40, 296
of feedback, 205
strategic, 422
Flextime, 87
Fluor Corporation, 432
Followers/followership, 254–269
appreciation shown to leaders, 260
clarifying role/expectations of, 260
delegation, 264–267
determinants of influence of, 261
education/experience and, 262–263
effective leader feedback, 263–264
follower defined, 256–257
follower power position, 261–262
follower types, 256–257
guidelines for effective, 258–261
influence of, 261–263
informing leaders, 260
inspiring, 115
vs. leaders, 6–7
locus of control, 262
loyalty and, 254
power position, 261–262
Pygmalion effect and, 49
raising issues/concerns, 259
resisting inappropriate leader influence, 260
Food and Drug Administration, 163, 193
Force-field model, 435
Forcing conflict style, 212–213
Ford Motor Company, 300, 418, 425, 451
Formal authority, 162
Four-way test, 58
Frederick Douglass Academy, 31, 36, 49, 56
Frederick W. Smith—FedEx, 318–319
French, J. R. P., 111
Friedman, Art, 102–103
Friedmans Appliance, 24–25, 102–103
Friendship, and power, 115
Frito-Lay, 151
Functional conflict, 210
Functional team, 293–294
Future vision, 336, 339

G

Gandhi, Mohandas, 5, 126, 332–333, 338–339, 342, 345, 350, 357, 359, 361
Garcia, J. E., 158
Gates, Bill, 62–63
Gates, Melinda, 62–63
Gender issues, 403
General Electric (GE), 3, 7–8, 14, 279, 339, 395, 427, 476
General Mills, 395
General Motors (GM), 374, 385, 451
Gherty, Jack, 132
Giving praise model, 97–98
Glass ceiling, 399–400
Glaxo-SmithKline, 163
Global business, and cultural differences, 153–154
framework of value dimensions, 391
high to low power-distance cultures, 392
high to low uncertainty avoidance cultures, 392
individualistic to collectivistic cultures, 391–392
leadership implications, 392–393
long-term to short-term oriented cultures, 392
masculinity–femininity, 392
Global contingency leadership, 153–154
Global Crossing, 266–267
Global Leadership and Organizational Behavior Effectiveness (GLOBE), 391
Global virtual teams, 296
Globalization, 395–396
creating culture that supports diversity, 400–403
corporate philosophy, 402
diversity as criterion for measuring success, 402–403
organizational communications on diversity, 402
pro-diversity human resource practices, 402
top leadership support and commitment, 401–402
diversity awareness training and leadership education, 403–405
diversity training, 403–404
education, 404–405

obstacles to achieving diversity, 398–400
ethnocentrism, 399
glass ceiling, 399–400
policies and practices, 399
stereotypes and prejudice, 398–399
unfriendly work environment, 400
reasons for embracing diversity, 396–398
Goal-setting theory, 90–92
Goals
charismatic leaders and, 338–340
corporate-level, 426
networking, 128–129
setting and achieving, 129
shared (goal congruence), 125
team cohesiveness and, 288
Goizueta, Jose, 178–179
Golden rule, 58
Goldman, Matt, 40
Goodrich, B. F., 96
Google, 417
Gore, Bill and Vieve, 271
Graham, Rev. Billy, 332–333
Grasso, Dick, 124
Greed, 36
Grid Theory, 75–76
Group-centered team approach, 319
Group level of analysis, 14
Group process, 14, 285
Groups and coercive power, 113
Groupthink, 283–284, 314
Grove, Andy, 476

H

Harman, Willis, 483
Harpo Productions, Inc., 329, 352
Hayek, Salma, 369
Heerman, Barry, 483
Heroic characteristics, 336
Herzberg, Frederick, 82, 84
Hewlett-Packard, 40, 209, 289
Hierarchy of needs theory, 81–82
High energy, 38, 41, 343
High-high leader, 77–78
High power-distance culture, 392
High structure and high consideration style, 77
High structure and low consideration style, 74
High uncertainty avoidance, 392
Hispanics, in U.S., 401–402, 404
Hitler, Adolf, 342, 345
Hofstede, Geert, 391–392, 408
Holtz, Lou, 47, 49, 91, 198
Honesty, 39, 138–139
Honoring beliefs of others, 484–485
House, Robert, 161, 163, 165
Human error disasters, 452
Human relations skills, 36, 111
Human resources
crisis management and, 456
diversity and, 402
Hygiene needs, 82

I

IBM Corp., 24, 85, 209, 222–223
Immelt, Jeffery (Jeff), 3–4, 7–8, 12
Impoverished leader, 76
Impressions management, 249
Incentives, 422
Inclusionary practices, 398
Individual development, 483
Individual level of analysis, 13–14
Individualism, 391–392
Influencing process, 7
ethics and, 140
negotiation, 133–138
networking, 130–133
organizational politics, 120–126
power, 111–126
Information gathering, 11
Information power, 116–117
Informational interview, 131
Informational leadership role, 11
Ingratiation influencing tactics, 112, 115, 249
In-groups, 241–243, 246, 269–270
Initiating conflict resolution, 215–217
Initiating structure style, 73–74
Initiative, 258–259
Inner spirit, 359
Innovation, 470
Inspirational appeals influencing tactic, 115, 119
Instrumentality, 89
Insular thinking, 374
Integrated Project Systems, 481
Integrative leadership theories, 17, 22
Integrity, 39, 55, 240, 257, 342
Intel, 476
Intelligence, 39–40
Intermittent reinforcement, 94–95
Internal conflict, 343
Internal locus of control, 262, 307
Internalizers, 38–39
International Center for Spirit at Work, 481
International joint venture studies, 393
International Spirit at Work Award, 484–485
Interpersonal leadership roles, 10
Intrinsic motivators, 82–84
Intuition, 419, 467
Izen, Ronald, 189

J

Jago, Arthur, 165, 170
Japanese productivity, 153–154, 460
Jermier, John, 173
JetBlue Airways, 80, 285
Jiffy Lube, 189
Job-centered leadership style, 72–73, 78, 155
Job enrichment, 85, 174
Job instructional training, 204
Job interviews
one-minute self-sell, 129–130
tie your accomplishments to, 129
Job satisfaction, 115, 164, 210
Jobs, Steve, 24–25
Johnson, Spencer, 97
Jones, Reverend Jim, 345
Jung, Andrea, 369, 372, 386, 390

K

Kay, Mary, 202
Kelleher, Herb, 80, 343
Kelley, R. E., 255
Kennedy, John F., 345, 350, 424
Kentucky Fried Chicken (KFC), 113
Kern, Bill, 481
Kerr, Steven, 96, 173
Key power players, 135
King, Martin Luther Jr., 332–333, 338, 342–343, 350, 359, 361
Kmart, 374
Knight, Philip H., 446
Komatsu, 424
Koresh, David, 345

L

LaBranch, Michael, 124
Lafley, A. G., 476–477
Land O'Lakes, 132
Lakewood Church, 239
Latham, Gary, 99
Lawrence Weinbach—from Unisys Corporation to Yankee Hill Capital Management, 222–223
Leader Behavior Description Questionnaire, 74–75

Leader-centered team approach, 298–299
Leader/follower relations
  dual leader/follower role, 257
  dyadic theory, 239–240
  followership, 254–268
  gender differences, 266
  leader–member exchange theory, 240, 247–254
  life-cycle model, 249
  personality differences, 266
  social skills and, 287
Leader–member exchange (LMX) theory, 243–245, 247–254
  bias in, 254
  factors determining quality of, 250–251
  influence of, on follower behavior, 247–248
  limitation of, 252–254
  strategies for positive relations, 249–250
  team building, 244–245
Leader–member relations, 156
Leader Motive Profile Theory, 44–46
Leader role, 10
Leaders
  appropriate counseling/coaching of, 259
  as culture creators, 370–371
  development of leadership ability, 9
  ethical and moral conduct of, 388
  vs. followers, 6–7
  influencing process and, 7
  multicultural, 394–395
  role in creating a learning organization, 463–465
  as role models, 342–343
  self-sacrificing, 357
  special appearances by, 380
Leadership. *See also* Leadership styles; Leadership theory; Values-based leadership
  attitudes, 47–52
  behavior, 70
  decision-making model, 298–300
  defined, 5–8, 46–47
  development, 426
  distrust of, 439–440
  diversity education and, 403
  failure of, 36, 50–51
  Grid Theory, 75–76
  importance of, 4–5
  in culture creation and sustainability, role of, 378–379
    aligning reward/incentive system with culture, 382
    celebrating achievements, 380
    creating a strategy–culture fit, 381–382
    developing a written values statement, 382
    face-to-face interactions with rank-and-file, 380
    leaders serving as role models, 380
    matching HR practices, 380–381
    matching operating policies and practices, 381
    matching organizational structure, 380
    matching work environment design, 382
  key elements of, 46
  managerial roles, 9–12
  at McDonald's, 179
  at P.F. Chang's, 26
  skill development, 21
Leadership continuum model, 159
Leadership gender, 153
Leadership Grid®, 77–78
Leadership model, defined, 152
Leadership styles
  consideration, 73–75
  employee-centered, 73–75
  initiating structure, 74
  job-centered, 72–73
  Ohio State University model, 75
  relationship-oriented, 154, 156–157
  task-oriented, 155, 174, 429
  University of Iowa research, 70–71
  University of Michigan, 71–72
Leadership theory, 15–20
  application of, 20
  classifications, 15–18
  levels of analysis of, 13–15
  from management to leadership paradigm, 17–18
  paradigms, 15–18
Learning anxiety, 433, 438
Learning organization, 450–468
  defined, 452
  role of leaders in creating, 469
  vs. traditional organization, 466–467
Least preferred coworker scales, 155
Lee, Vernita, 338
Legacy, 331–332
Legitimate power, 111–114
Legitimization influencing tactic, 111
Lewin, Kurt, 70
Liaison leadership role, 10
Likert, Rensis, 72, 75, 82
Listening skills, 193–194, 196
Livingston, J. Sterling, 49
LMX-7 scale, 252–253
Locke, Edwin, 99
Lockheed Martin, 410–412
Locus of control, 38, 42, 55, 162, 261–262, 331
Lombardi, Vince, 9, 21, 115
Long-term orientation, 392
Low-and high-performance cultures, 373
Low power-distance culture, 392
Low structure and high consideration style, 74
Low structure and low consideration style, 74
Low uncertainty avoidance, 392
Loyalty, 254
  organizational politics and, 123
  power and, 115
Lutz, Robert, 385

M

Maintenance needs, 82, 85
Malcolm Baldrige National Quality Award, 318
Malcolm X, 350
Managerial Grid®, 75
Managers/management
  common reward follies, 96
  developing working relationship with, 125–126
  functions of, 7
  managerial roles, 10–14
Managing in Turbulent Times at Second City Theater, 478
Mandela, Nelson, 349, 350–351, 359
Manipulation, 440
Manson, Charles, 345
March of Dimes, 425
Mark Parker: A Seasoned Veteran Takes the Helm at Nike, 445–447
Market America, 69, 77
  acquired needs theory and, 85–86
  equity theory and, 87
  expectancy theory and, 89
  goal-setting theory, 90
  hierarchy of needs and, 81–82
  positive reinforcement and, 93
  two-factor theory and, 84
Marriott Corporation, 47
Marriott, W. Jr., 47
Martinez, Angel, 481
Mary Kay Cosmetics, 380, 429
Masculinity, 392
Maslow, Abraham, 81–82, 86
McCanse, Anne Adams, 75–76
McClelland, David, 42–44, 85–86
McGregor, Douglas, 49–50, 82
McNerney, James Jr., 384
Media portrayal of sex and violence, 57–58

Mediating conflict resolution, 217–218
Mediators, 217
Meeting(s), 300–305
  agenda, 301–303
  conducting, 302–303
  date/time/place, 302
  leadership style, 302
  objectives, 301, 303
  participants and assignments, 301, 333
  parts of effective, 303
  technology and, 302
Mentality of detachment, 454
Mentors/mentoring, 132, 209
Merck, 163, 425
Mergers and acquisitions, 381–382, 427–428, 434
Merrill Lynch, 418
Michigan Bell, 96
Microsoft, 62–63, 91, 427, 467
Middle-of-the-road leader, 76
Minority groups, 394
Mintzberg, Henry, 9, 16
Mission conceptualization, 420
Mission statement, 422, 424–426, 443
  crisis management and, 453–454
  strategy formation and, 427–428
Mistakes, learning from, 472
Mitchell, T. R., 163
Money, as motivator, 85
Monitor role, 11
Monroe, Lorraine, 31, 36, 41, 46, 50, 56
Monster.com, 40
Moral conviction, 341–342
Moral development, 55–56
Moral justification, for immoral behavior, 56–57
Moral leadership, 419–420
Mother Teresa, 332, 359
Motivation, 84–86
  content motivation theories, 80–93
  feedback and, 197–200
  money as, 85
  process, 79–80
  process motivation theories, 87–92
  reinforcement theory, 92–97
  theory classification, 80
  tying theories within process, 99–100
  at Washburn Guitars, 104
Motivators (two-factor theory), 82, 85
Motive profile, 42–44
Motive profile with socialized power, 45
Motorola, 425, 428
Mouton, Jane, 77–78
Mulcahy, Anne, 364–365
Multiculturalism, 404
Multifunctional teams, 294
Multiple intelligence, 40
Murphy, Robert, 124
Murray, Henry, 85–86

N

Name(s)
  recognition, 126
  remembering, 26–27, 131
Narcissism, 345
National Child Protection Act, 332
National culture identities–Hofstede's value dimensions
  high to low power-distance cultures, 392
  high to low uncertainty avoidance cultures, 392
  individualistic to collectivistic cultures, 391–392
  long-term to short-term oriented cultures, 392
  masculinity–femininity, 392
Natural disasters, 452
NEADS Team: People and Dogs, 320
Needs (Achievement Motivation Theory), 42
Needs, balancing professional/personal, 87–88
Neeleman, David, 80
Negative attitude, 47, 50–51, 60
Negative reinforcement, 93
Negotiating conflict style, 213–214
Negotiation, 137–143
  agreement, 139
  cultural differences, 139
  honesty/integrity and, 138–139
  no agreement, 139
  plan, 135–136
  postponement of, 134–135
  process, 135–137
  rapport and, 137
  skill development, 134–135
  steps, 135–137
  tradeoffs, 133
  win for each party, 134, 136
Negotiator role, 12, 41
Neo-charismatic theory, 17
Nestlé, 395
Network(ing), 10, 117, 120, 122, 125, 127–133
  developing your network, 130–131
  goals, setting, 11, 29
  interviews, conducting, 131–132
  maintaining, 132–133
  one-minute self-sell, 130
  online, 130
Neutralizers, 173
Nike, Inc., 395, 425, 427, 445–447
Nonverbal communication, 115, 193–194, 303
Nooyi, Indra K., 151
Nordstrom, 380–381
Normative leadership theory and models, 165–166, 177
  computerized normative model, 170
  determining appropriate style, 170–173
  development-driven model, 169–170
  leadership participation styles, 166
  research, 170
  time-driven model, 211, 214
Norms, 286–287
Nurse performance, 174

Obesity, 347
Objectives, 49, 90–92
  communication, 189
  criteria for, 90–92
  of delegation, 264
  financial, 426
  group support for, 169
  for negotiation process, 135–137
  SMART, 426
  strategy formation and, 429
  writing, 90
Obstacles to achieving diversity, 398
  ethnocentrism, 399
  glass ceiling, 399–400
  policies and practices, 399
  stereotypes and prejudice, 398–399
  unfriendly work environment, 430
Ohio State University leadership model, 72–78, 102
Oil Spill Response Preparedness Plan, 452
Okuda, Hiroshi, 114
Ombudsperson, 389
O'Neal, Stanley, 4
One-Minute Manager, The (Blanchard and Johnson), 97
One-minute self-sell, 129–130
Online networking, 130
Openness to experience, 30–36, 38, 362
Openness to new ideas/viewpoints, 333
"Oprah Bill," 332
Oprah Winfrey Show. See Winfrey, Oprah
Optimism, 38, 342
Oral communication, 191–192
Organic organization, 461, 481
Organizational citizenship, 79–80

Organizational culture, 124–125, 370–383. See also Values-based leadership
characteristics of high-performance, 375–377
characteristics of low-performance, 373–375
cultural value types, 382–386
culture defined, 370
culture reinforcement tools, 376
diversity and, 400–401
external adaptation, 372
insular thinking, 374
internal unity, 371–372
organizational structure and, 380
politicized internal environment, 374–375
power of culture, 371–372
resistance to change, 374
strong culture, 375, 377
unhealthy promotion practices, 375
weak culture, 373
weak *vs.* strong, 373
Organizational knowledge, 464
Organizational level of analysis, 14
Organizational objectives, 7–8
Organizational politics, 10, 120–126
coalitions, 122–123
connection power and, 117
culture and power players, 124–125
ethics and, 140–141
gaining recognition, 123
guidelines for developing skills in, 112
as medium of exchange, 122
nature of, 121
networking, 122, 127
politics defined, 121
reciprocity, 122
working well with others, 125–126
Organizational process, 14
Original Penguin Spreads Its Wings, 447
Osteen, Joel, 239
Ouchi, William, 153–154
Out-groups, 242–243, 246–247
Overtime work, 85
Owen, Harrison, 483

P

Page, Larry, 417
Paraphrasing, 196–197, 199
Parker, Mark, 445–447
Parr, Rick, 178–179
Participative communication style, 230
Participative leadership styles, 75, 153
Participative management, 111
Passive-aggressive behavior, 212
Passive follower, 256
Passive job hunt, 130
Path clarification, 161
Path-goal leadership theory/model, 161–165
leadership styles, 163–164
research, 164–165
situational factors, 162–163
Pay-for-performance compensation, 402
People, 8
People-oriented cultures, 374–375
People-oriented functions, 78
Pepsi-Cola, 385, 395
PepsiCo, 151
Perceived organizational support, 248
Perez, William, 445–446
Performance evaluations, 113
Performance formula, 207–208
Personal appeals influencing tactic, 115
Personal interests, 333
Personal meaning, 330–363
Personal power, 110
Personality traits, 31–36
benefits of classifying, 34
Big Five Model of Personality, 33
of effective leaders, 35–41
and ethical behavior, 52–54
personality dimensions, 33
personality profiles, 32, 35
profile of effective leaders, 37
Personalized charismatic leader, 345–346
Personalized power, 45, 119, 140
Pessimism, 49, 51
P.F. Chang's Serves Its Workers Well, 64
Physical traits, 16
Physiological needs, 81, 83, 86
Policies and practices, 399
Politics. *See* Organizational politics
Position power, 110, 154
Positive affirmations, 65
Positive attitude, 47, 50–51
Positive LMX relations, three-stage process for developing, 249–250
Positive reinforcement, 93–94
Postconventional level of moral development, 56–57
Power, 108–121
acquiring and losing, 119–120
coercive power, 114, 120
connection power, 117
defined, 110
increasing, 111–112
information power, 116–117
legitimate, 111–114
need for (n Pow), 42–43
personal power, 110
position power, 110
referent power, 115
relational power base, 343
reward power, 113
sources and types of, 111
Power players, 124–126
Pragmatic follower, 256
Praise, 97–98
Preconventional level of moral development, 55
Precrisis planning, 454–455
Prejudice, 398, 402
Prescriptive models, 21, 173
Press release/press kit, 461
Pressure influencing tactic, 113
Principle, 257
Priorities, shared, 125
Problem-solving skills, 307
style, 213
Process motivation theories, 87–99
equity theory, 87–88
expectancy theory, 88–89
goal-setting theory, 90–98
Procter & Gamble (P&G), 476–477
Product failures, 452
Production-oriented functions, 78
Productivity, 49, 75, 419
Professional associations, 116
Promotion practices, 375
Psychological contract, 210
Psychological traits, 16
Publicity, 117
Punishment, 94
Purpose in life (PIL), 330–331
Pygmalion effect, 49, 60, 70, 97, 254

Q

Questioning, 283, 340

R

Railroad industry, 425
Ranch Golf Club (Southwick, Mass), 189
Rapport, 131, 137, 191
Ratio schedule, 95
Rational analysis, 423
Rational persuasion influencing tactic, 111, 116
Raven, B. H., 111
Reciprocity, 122–123
Recognition, 123, 202

Reeve, Christopher, 51
Referent power, 115, 120
Refreezing change phase, 437–438
Reinforcement theory, 92–99
  actions based on reinforcement, 98
  components of, 93
  consequences of behavior, 93
  giving praise, 97–98
  motivating with reinforcement, 96–97
  schedules of reinforcement, 94–95
  types of reinforcement, 93–94
Relational power base, 343
Relationship management, 40
Relationship-oriented leadership style, 154, 156–157
Relationships, negotiation and, 133–134
Religious diversity, 388
Resistance to change, reasons
  distrust of leadership, 439–440
  fear of being manipulated, 440
  lack of confidence that change will succeed, 439
  lack of conviction that change is necessary, 439
  threat to one's self-interest, 439
  threat to personal values, 440
  uncertainty, 439
Resource allocation, 456
Resource allocator role, 12
Respect, 484–485
Results-oriented culture, 377
Resumes, 128–131
Rewards, 426
  assumption, 358
  expectancy theory and, 88–89
  management reward follies, 96
  power, 113
Rick Parr—Archer Daniels Midland (ADM) Company, 178–179
Ridinger, J. R., 69
Risk
  assessment, 456–458
  high risk orientation, 343
  without fear of failure, 59
Robert Stevens Continues Lockheed Martin's Diversity Initiatives, 410–412
Robert's Rules of Order, 302
Rockport Shoes, 481
Rodale Press, 481
Role episodes, 251
Role model(s), 51, 329, 379, 420
Role playing, 404
Ron Johnson—Department of Accounting, 143–144
Rotary International, 58
Rowley, Colleen, 59
Rudenstine, Neil, 265
Rumi, 482

S

Safety needs, 81, 83
Salomon Brothers, 59
SAP, 432
Sarbanes-Oxley Act of 2002, 54
Schein, Edgar, 433
Schmidt, Warren, 159–160, 193
School Leadership Academy, 31
Self-actualization needs, 82–83
Self-assessment, 128–129
Self-awareness, 40, 404, 484
Self-belief, 331
Self-concept, 50–52, 56
Self-confidence, 38, 40, 336, 338
Self-efficacy, 50
Self-fulfilling prophecy, 97
Self-image, 50
Self-interest, threat to, 439
Selflessness, 332
Self-managed team champion, 310
Self-managed teams (SMTs), 305–314, 357–358
  accountability of, 307
  benefits of, 308–309
  changing role of leadership in, 312–313
  creating successful program of, 309
  effectiveness of, 306–307, 309–311
  facilitator of, 313
  implementation challenges, 311
  member characteristics, 306–307
  nature of, 306
  organizational support of, 314
  and traditional compared, 305–306
Self-management, 40
Self-promotion, 249, 344
Self-sacrifice, 287
Senge, Peter, 464
Sensitivity to others, 41, 45, 65
September 11 attacks, 59
Servant leadership. *See* Stewardship and servant leadership
Service, over self-interest, 357
Sex discrimination, 405–406
Sexual harassment, 398
Sexual orientation diversity, 394–395
Short-term orientation, 392
Situation analysis, 423
Situational communications model, 229–233
Situational favorableness, 156
Situational leadership models, 78
Situational leadership theory, 154
Skilling, Jeffrey K., 374
Skinner, B. F., 92
SMART
  goals, 91
  objectives, 426
Smith, Frederick W., 318–319
Sociability, 34
Social awareness, 40
Social exchange theory, 119–120
Social loafing, 283
Social needs, 81, 83
Social reinforcers (praise), 97
Social responsibility, 96
Social skills, 249, 287, 289
Socialized charismatic leader, 346
Socialized power, 45–46, 58
Sociotechnical systems theory, 305–306
Southwest Airlines, 80, 343, 380–381
Specific feedback, 203–204
Spirit at Work Web site, 485
Spirituality
  defining, 481
  guidelines, 484
  in the workplace, 481
  individual, 483
  integrating spiritual practice, 481
  leadership and team development, 483
  levels of development, 483–484
  redefining role of business, 483–484
  systemic approaches, 483
  total system development, 483
Spokesperson role, 11
Sponsor program (W. L. Gore & Associates), 272
Stability, 35–37
Stakeholder approach to ethics, 58–59
Stamina, 38
Standards, 54, 91
Starbucks Corporation, 383, 389
Status quo, 335–336
Stereotypes, 398–399
Steve Jobs—Apple, 24–25
Stevens, Robert, 410–412
Stewardship and servant leadership, 356–357
  nature of, 357
  roots of, 332
  servant leadership defined, 356
  servant leadership framework, 358–359
  stewardship defined, 356
  stewardship framework, 357–358

Stogdill, Ralph, 73–74
Strategic leadership, 418–431
  corporate-level goals, 426
  defined, 418
  environment analysis, 422–423
  framework, 421
  mission statement, 425
  strategic management defined, 418–419
  strategic vision, 424–425
  strategy evaluation, 471–473
  strategy formulation, 427–429
  strategy implementation, 429–430
Strategy, defined, 427
Strategy-culture gap, 381
Stress
  delegation and, 264–265
  tolerance for, 38
Stretch goals, 90, 426
Subordinate situational characteristics, 162
Substitutes theory, 173–174
Succession planning, 452
Supermarket chains, 39
Support for self-worth, 240–141
Supportive style, 164–165
Surgency personality dimension, 34, 60
Survival anxiety, 416–490
SWOT analysis, 423, 446–458
Synergy, 451
System failures, 451
Systems theory, 304–305
Systems thinking, 470

T

Tannenbaum, Robert, 159–160, 166
Task-oriented leadership style, 155, 174, 429
Task structure, 156, 162
Taylor, Frederick, 293
Taylor, Jeff, 40
Team cohesion, 288
Team leader, 76
Team learning, 285
Team potency, 348–349
Teams. *See also* Self-managed teams (SMTs)
  advantages of teamwork, 282–283
  cohesiveness/interdependence of, 288
  competence, 166
  composition of, 288–289
  creativity and, 291
  crisis management, 453–454
  decision making in, 298–300
  defined, 280
  disadvantages of teamwork, 283–284
  diversity and, 296
  groups *vs.*, 281
  leader- *vs.* group-centered, 319
  leadership of, 278–305
  normative leadership model, 300
  organizational support/use of, 290–292
  problem members, 303–305
  self-managed, 296–308
  size of, 289
  structure of, 293
  team defined, 280
  team effectiveness, 285–286
  team norms, 286
  teamwork defined, 280
  types of, 293–295
Technology, 159, 293
Telephone conferences, 302
Television, 344
Thank-you follow-ups, 132
Theory X and Theory Y, 52
Theory Z, 154
360-degree multirater feedback, 200
3M, 96, 376, 380, 385, 425, 427, 467
Timbuk2: Former CEO Sets a Course, 366
Time Warner, 127
Timing, 216
Top-down directive approach, 263
Total quality management (TQM), 306
Touching, 98
Toyota, 91, 114, 154
Training, diversity, 397–398
Trait theories of leadership, 32
Trait theory paradigm, 16
Transactional leadership, 352–354
Transformational leadership, 328–360
  behaviors and attributes, 350–352
  change and, 352–355
  and charismatic leadership compared, 337–340
  defined, 347–348
  vs. transactional leadership, 352–354
  transformation process, 354–355
Trauma, 456
Trist, Eric, 305
Trust, 39, 126
  ability to inspire, 342–343
  earning and keeping, 359
Trustworthiness, 39
Tupperware, 113
Tutu, Desmond, 332
"Twelve Non-Negotiable Rules," 31
Two-factor theory, 82–85, 100

U

Uncertainty, 439
Unconventionalism, 336, 361
Understanding, checking, 190–191
Unfreezing change phase, 436–437
Unions, 110, 393
Unisys Corporation, 222–223
United Parcel Service (UPS), 318
Universal theories, 17
University of Iowa leadership styles, 70–71
University of Michigan Leadership Model, 72–73, 75, 78, 102, 155, 160
Upgrading, 432
U.S. Army mission statement, 425

V

Values, 333
  cultural value types, 382–384
  differences, in global cultures, 395–396
  shared, of organizational culture, 124–125
  statement, 379, 382
  threat to personal, 439–440
  value defined, 427
Values-based leadership, 165, 387
  advocating ethical behavior, 388–390
  cultural differences and, 391–392
  values defined, 387
Variable interval schedule, 95
Variable ratio schedule, 95, 98
Vertical dyadic linkage (VDL) theory, 240–242
Video cases
  Communication at Navistar International, 224
  Delegation at Boyne USA Resorts, 274
  Diversity at PepsiCo, 412
  Employee Networks at Whirlpool Corporation, 145
  Leadership at McDonald's, 179
  Leadership at P.F. Chang's, 26
  Managing in Turbulent Times at Second City Theater, 478
  Motivation at Washburn Guitars, 104
  NEADS Team: People and Dogs, 320
  Original Penguin Spreads Its Wings, 447
  P.F. Chang's Serves Its Workers Well, 64
  Timbuk2: Former CEO Sets a Course, 366
Videoconferences, 302
Virtual team, 296
Vision
  articulation of, 336
  change and, 436–437

communication of, 437
conceptualization of, 420
for learning, 472
status quo/future vision discrepancy, 336
strategic vision, 424
Vision statement, 424–425
Volunteering, 51, 305
Vroom, Victor, 88, 165–168

Wagoner, Rick, 451
Wal-Mart, 39, 381, 405–406
culture, Sam Walton's conception, 370–371
Walton, Sam, 370, 381
Watkins, Sherron, 390
Weber, Max, 334, 360
Weinbach, Lawrence, 222–223
Welch, Jack, 85, 87, 90, 297, 339, 476
Whistle blower/whistle blowing, 52, 54, 56, 59, 389–390
Winfrey, Oprah, 329–330, 333, 340, 344, 346, 352
Winfrey, Vernon, 338
W. L. Gore & Associates, 271–273
Work environment
minorities and, 400
as reflection of corporate values, 382
supportive of creativity, 291
Work group, 163
Work–life balance, 330
WorldCom, 4, 54
Writing objectives model, 90
Writing tips, 192

X

Xerox Corporation, 364–365, 399

Y

Yetton, Philip, 165, 170

Z

Zenith, 425
Ziglar, Zig, 65